DICTIONARY OF
BUSINESS

third edition

Titles in the series

English Dictionary for Students	1-901659-06-2
English Study Dictionary	1-901659-63-1
Dictionary of Accounting	0-948549-27-0
Dictionary of Aeronautical English	1-901659-10-0
Dictionary of Agriculture, 2nd ed	0-948549-78-5
Dictionary of American Business, 2nd ed	1-901659-22-4
Dictionary of Astronomy	0-948549-43-2
Dictionary of Automobile Engineering	0-948549-66-1
Dictionary of Banking & Finance, 2nd ed	1-901659-30-5
Dictionary of Business, 3rd ed	1-901659-50-X
Dictionary of Computing, 4th ed	1-901659-46-1
Dictionary of Ecology & Environment, 3rd ed	0-948549-74-2
Dictionary of Government & Politics, 2nd ed	0-948549-89-0
Dictionary of Hotels, Tourism, Catering Management	0-948549-40-8
Dictionary of Human Resources & Personnel, 2nd ed	0-948549-79-3
Dictionary of Information Technology, 2nd ed	0-948549-88-2
Dictionary of Law, 3rd ed	1-901659-43-7
Dictionary of Library & Information Management	0-948549-68-8
Dictionary of Marketing	0-948549-73-4
Dictionary of Medicine, 3rd ed	1-901659-45-3
Dictionary of Military Terms	1-901659-24-0
Dictionary of Multimedia, 3rd ed	1-901659-51-8
Dictionary of PC & the Internet, 3rd ed	1-901659-52-6
Dictionary of Printing & Publishing, 2nd ed	0-948549-99-8
Dictionary of Science & Technology	0-948549-67-X

Workbooks

Check your:

Vocabulary for Banking & Finance	0-948549-96-3
Vocabulary for Business, 2nd ed	1-901659-27-5
Vocabulary for Colloquial English	0-948549-97-1
Vocabulary for Computing, 2nd ed	1-901659-28-3
Vocabulary for English	1-901659-11-9
Vocabulary for Hotels, Tourism, Catering	0-948549-75-0
Vocabulary for the IELTS examination	1-901659-60-7
Vocabulary for Law, 2nd ed	1-901659-21-6
Vocabulary for Marketing	1-901659-48-8
Vocabulary for Medicine, 2nd ed	1-901659-47-X
Vocabulary for the TOEFL examination	1-901659-68-2

Visit our web site for full details of all our books

www.petercollin.com

DICTIONARY OF
BUSINESS

third edition

P.H. Collin

PETER COLLIN PUBLISHING

Third edition published 2001

Second edition published 1994
reprinted 1995, 1997, 1999

First published in Great Britain 1985
as *English Business Dictionary*

Published by Peter Collin Publishing Ltd
32-34 Great Peter Street, London, SW1P 2DB

British Library Cataloguing-in-Publication Data

A catalogue record for this book is available from the British Library

ISBN 1-901659-50-X

Text computer typeset by PCP
Printed and bound in Finland by WS Bookwell
Cover artwork by Gary Weston

Preface to the first edition

This dictionary gives the user the basic business vocabulary used in both British and American English. The dictionary contains 4,500 words and phrases which cover all aspects of business life from the office to the Stock Exchange and the international trade fair. Each word is clearly defined in very simple English (only 470 words are used in the definitions which do not appear in the dictionary as main words); many examples are given to show how the words are used in normal contexts, and the examples themselves are 'translated' into simple English. Some entries have simple grammar notes to remind the user of irregular word forms, constructions used with particular words, differences between American and British usage and other useful points. Because English is a world language of business, we have included short quotations to show how it is used in various countries round the world. These quotations are from newspapers and magazines published in England, the United States, Canada, Australia, Hong Kong and Nigeria.

At the back of the book, the user will find a supplement giving useful information about numbers (how to speak and write them), telephoning, writing business letters, understanding financial documents, together with a list of important world currencies.

Preface to the second edition

The rapid development of English as the international business language has meant that a new edition of the dictionary has become necessary: many new words have been added, together with new examples and new quotations. In some cases, encyclopaedic comments have also been added to expand on the definitions. The supplement at the back of the book has also been enlarged and updated.

Because the pronunciation of some specialized words can pose problems, we have added the IPA phonetic transcription for all the main words.

Preface to the third edition

New developments in business, especially business over the Internet, have produced a mass of new terms which have been added to this third edition of the dictionary. We have also expanded the coverage of American usage, and added new quotations from various sources.

Phonetics

The following symbols have been used to show the pronunciation of the main words in the dictionary.

Stress has been indicated by a main stress mark ('), but these are only guides as the stress of the word may change according to its position in the sentence.

Vowels		*Consonants*	
æ	back	b	buck
ɑː	harm	d	dead
ɒ	stop	ð	other
aɪ	type	dʒ	jump
aʊ	how	f	fare
aɪə	hire	g	gold
aʊə	hour	h	head
ɔː	course	j	yellow
ɔɪ	loyalty	k	cab
e	head	l	leave
eə	fair	m	mix
eɪ	make	n	nil
ə	abroad	ŋ	bring
əʊ	float	p	post
əʊə	lower	r	rule
ɜː	word	s	save
iː	keep	ʃ	shop
ɪ	fit	t	take
ɪə	near	tʃ	change
u	supreme	χ	loch
uː	pool	θ	theft
ʊ	book	v	value
ʌ	shut	w	work
		z	zone
		ʒ	measure

Aa

A, AA, AAA ['sɪŋgl'eɪ or 'dʌbəl'eɪ or 'trɪpl'eɪ] letters indicating that a share, bond or company has a certain rating for reliability; *these bonds have a AAA rating*

> COMMENT: the AAA rating is given by Standard & Poor's or by Moody's, and indicates a very high level of reliability for a corporate or municipal bond in the US

the rating concern lowered its rating to single-A from double-A, and its senior debt rating to triple-B from single-A

Wall Street Journal

'A' shares ['eɪ 'ʃeəz] *plural noun* ordinary shares with limited voting rights or no voting rights at all

> COMMENT: a company may be set up with two classes of share: 'A' shares, which are available to the general investor, and 'B' shares which are only bought by certain individuals, such as the founder and his family. Such division of shares is becoming less usual nowadays

A1 ['eɪ 'wʊn] *adjective* **(a)** in very good condition; *we sell only goods in A1 condition* **(b)** ship which is A1 at Lloyd's = ship which is in best condition according to Lloyd's Register

A1, A2, A3, A4, A5 ['eɪ 'wʊn or 'eɪ 'tuː or 'eɪ 'θriː or 'eɪ 'fɔː or 'eɪ 'faɪv] *noun* standard international sizes of paper; *you must photocopy the spreadsheet on A3 paper*; *we must order some more A4 headed notepaper*

> COMMENT: A sizes of paper are based on the largest size (A0), which

is 1189 x 841mm; folded once, this gives A1 (841 x 594mm), which if folded once gives A2 (594 x 420mm), and so on

abandon [ə'bændən] *verb* **(a)** to give up, not to continue (doing something); *we abandoned the idea of setting up a New York office*; *the development programme had to be abandoned when the company ran out of cash*; **to abandon an action** = to give up a court case **(b)** to leave (something); *the crew abandoned the sinking ship*

abandonment [ə'bændənmənt] *noun* act of giving something up; **abandonment of a ship** = giving up a ship and cargo to the underwriters against payment for total loss

abatement [ə'beɪtmənt] *noun* act of reducing; **tax abatement** = reduction of tax

above par [ə'bʌv 'pɑː] *adjective* **shares above par** = shares with a market price which is higher than their par value

above the line [ə'bʌv ðə 'laɪn] *adjective & adverb* **(a)** *(companies)* referring to normal income and expenditure before tax; *exceptional items are noted above the line in company accounts* **(b)** *(advertising)* advertising for which payment is made (such as an ad in a magazine or a stand at a trade fair) and for which a commission is paid to an advertising agency; *compare* BELOW THE LINE

abroad [ə'brɔːd] *adverb* to or in another country; *the consignment of cars was shipped abroad last week*; *the chairman is abroad on business*; *half of our profit comes from sales abroad*

absence ['æbsəns] *noun* not being at work or at a meeting; **in the absence of** = when someone is not there; *in the absence of the chairman, his deputy took the chair*; **leave of absence** = being allowed to be absent from work; *he asked for leave of absence to visit his mother in hospital*

absent ['æbsənt] *adjective* not at work, not at a meeting; *ten of the workers are absent with flu*; *the chairman is absent in Holland on business*

absentee [æbsən'tiː] *noun* worker who stays away from work for no good reason

absenteeism [æbsən'tiːɪzm] *noun* staying away from work for no good reason; *absenteeism is high in the week before Christmas*; *the rate of absenteeism or the absenteeism rate always increases in fine weather*

> but the reforms still hadn't fundamentally changed conditions on the shop floor: absenteeism was as high as 20% on some days
>
> *Business Week*

absolute ['æbsəluːt] *adjective* complete or total; **absolute monopoly** = situation where only one producer or supplier produces or supplies something; *the company has an absolute monopoly of imports of French wine*

absolutely [æbsə'luːtli] *adverb* completely; *we are absolutely tied to our suppliers' schedules*

absorb [əb'zɔːb] *verb* (a) to take in a small item so as to form part of a larger one; **to absorb overheads** = to include a proportion of overhead costs into a production cost (this is done at a certain rate, called the 'absorption rate'); **overheads have absorbed all our profits** = all our profits have gone in paying overhead expenses; **to absorb a loss by a subsidiary** = to write a subsidiary company's loss into the group accounts (b) business which has been absorbed by a competitor = a small business which has been made part of a larger one

absorption [əb'zɔːpʃən] *noun* (a) making a smaller business part of a larger one, so that the smaller company in effect no longer exists (b) **absorption costing** =

costing a product to include both the direct costs of production and the indirect overhead costs as well; **absorption rate** = rate at which overhead costs are absorbed into each unit of production

abstract ['æbstrækt] *noun* short form of a report or document; *to make an abstract of the company accounts*; **abstract of title** = summary of the details of the ownership of a property which has not been registered

a/c *or* **acc** = ACCOUNT; **a/c payee** = words written between the two lines on a crossed cheque, to show that it can only be paid into the account of the person whose name is written on the cheque (all cheques have this printed on them)

ACAS ['eɪkæs] = ADVISORY, CONCILIATION AND ARBITRATION SERVICE

accelerated depreciation [ək'seləreɪtɪd dɪpriːʃɪ'eɪʃən] *noun* system of depreciation which reduces the value of assets at a high rate in the early years to encourage companies, because of tax advantages, to invest in new equipment

> COMMENT: this applied in the UK until 1984; then companies could depreciate new equipment at 100% in the first year of purchase

acceleration clause [əksələ'reɪʃən 'klɔːz] *noun US* clause in a contract providing for immediate payment of the total balance if there is a breach of contract

accept [ək'sept] *verb* (a) to take something which is being offered; **to accept a bill of exchange** = to sign a bill of exchange to indicate that you promise to pay it; **to accept delivery of a shipment** = to take goods into the warehouse officially when they are delivered (b) to say 'yes' or to agree to something; *she accepted the offer of a job in Australia*; *he accepted £200 for the car*

acceptable [ək'septəbl] *adjective* which can be accepted; *the offer is not acceptable to both parties*

acceptance [ək'septəns] *noun* (a) signing a bill of exchange to show that you agree to pay it; **to present a bill for acceptance** = to ask for payment by the person who has accepted it; **acceptance**

house _US_ acceptance bank = ACCEPTING HOUSE **(b) acceptance of an offer** = agreeing to an offer; **to give an offer a conditional acceptance** = to accept provided that certain things happen or that certain terms apply; **we have his letter of acceptance** = we have received a letter from him accepting the offer; **acceptance sampling** = testing a small part of a batch to see if the whole batch is good enough

accepting house _or_ **acceptance house** [ək'septɪŋ 'haʊs _or_ ək'septəns 'haʊs] _noun_ firm (usually a merchant bank) which accepts bills of exchange (i.e. promises to pay them) at a discount, in return for immediate payment to the issuer, in this case the Bank of England; **Accepting Houses Committee** = the main London merchant banks, which act as accepting houses; they receive slightly better discount rates from the Bank of England

access ['ækses] **1** _noun_ **to have access to something** = to be able to obtain or reach something; _he has access to large amounts of venture capital_; **access time** = time taken by a computer to find data stored in it **2** _verb_ to call up (data) which is stored in a computer; _she accessed the address file on the computer_

accident ['æksɪdənt] _noun_ something unpleasant which happens by chance (such as the crash of a plane); **industrial accident** = accident which takes place at work; **accident insurance** = insurance which will pay when an accident takes place

accommodation [əkɒmə'deɪʃən] _noun_ **(a)** money lent for a short time **(b) to reach an accommodation with creditors** = to agree terms for settlement with your creditors **(c) accommodation bill** = bill of exchange where the person signing (the 'drawee') is helping another company (the 'drawer') to raise a loan **(d)** place to live; _visitors have difficulty in finding hotel accommodation during the summer_; _they are living in furnished accommodation_; **accommodation address** = address used for receiving messages but which is not the real address of the company (NOTE: no plural in British English, but American English can have **accommodations** for this meaning)

> an airline ruling requires airlines to provide a free night's hotel accommodation for full fare passengers in transit
> _Business Traveller_

> any non-resident private landlord can let furnished or unfurnished accommodation to a tenant
> _Times_

> the airline providing roomy accommodations at below-average fares
> _Dun's Business Month_

accompany [ə'kʌmpni] _verb_ to go with; _the chairman came to the meeting accompanied by the finance director; they sent a formal letter of complaint, accompanied by an invoice for damage_ (NOTE: accompanied **by** something)

accordance [ə'kɔːdəns] _noun_ **in accordance with** = in agreement with, according to; _in accordance with your instructions we have deposited the money in your current account; I am submitting the claim for damages in accordance with the advice of our legal advisers_

according to [ə'kɔːdɪŋ tʊ] _preposition_ as someone says or writes; _the computer was installed according to the manufacturer's instructions_

> the budget targets for employment and growth are within reach according to the latest figures
> _Australian Financial Review_

accordingly [ə'kɔːdɪŋli] _adverb_ in agreement with what has been decided; _we have received your letter and have altered the contract accordingly_

account [ə'kaʊnt] **1** _noun_ **(a)** record of financial transactions over a period of time, such as money paid, received, borrowed or owed; _please send me your account or a detailed or an itemized account_; **expense account** = money which a businessman is allowed by his company to spend on travelling and entertaining clients in connection with his business; _he charged his hotel bill to his expense account_ **(b)** _(in a shop)_ arrangement which a customer has to buy goods and pay for them at a later date (usually the end of the month); *to have an account or a charge account or a credit account with Harrods*; *put it on my account or charge it to my account*; *(of a customer)* **to open an account** = to ask a shop to supply goods which you will pay for at a later date; *(of a shop)* **to open an account or to close an account** = to start or to stop supplying a customer on credit; **to settle an account** = to pay all the money owed on an account; **to stop an account** = to stop supplying a customer until he has paid what he owes **(c) on account** = as part of a total bill; **to pay money on account** = to pay to settle part of a bill; **advance on account** = money paid as a part payment **(d)** customer who does a large amount of business with a firm and has an account; *Smith Brothers is one of our largest accounts*; *our salesmen call on their best accounts twice a month*; **account executive** = employee who is the only person to deal with a certain customer, who is the link between a certain customer and his company **(e) the accounts of a business or a company's accounts** = detailed records of a company's financial affairs; **to keep the accounts** = to write each sum of money in the account book; *the bookkeeper's job is to enter all the money received in the accounts*; **account book** = book with printed columns ready for accounts to be entered; **annual accounts** = accounts prepared at the end of a financial year; **management accounts** = financial information (sales, expenditure, credit, and profitability) prepared for a manager so that he or she can take decisions; **profit and loss account (P&L account)** = statement of company expenditure and income over a period of time, almost always one calendar year, showing whether the company has made a profit or loss (the balance sheet shows the state of a company's finances at a certain date; the profit and loss account shows the movements which have taken place since the last balance sheet) (NOTE: the US equivalent is the **profit and loss statement** or **income statement**); **accounts department** = department in a company which deals with money paid, received, borrowed or owed; **accounts manager** = manager of an

accounts department; **accounts payable** = money owed by a company; **accounts receivable** = money owed to a company **(f)** **bank account** *US* **banking account** = arrangement to keep money in a bank; *she has two building society accounts*; *he has an account with Lloyds Bank*; *I have an account with the Royal Bank of Scotland*; *to put money in(to) your account*; *to take money out of your account or to withdraw money from your account*; **budget account** = bank account where you plan income and expenditure to allow for periods when expenditure is high, by paying a set amount each month; **current account or cheque account** *US* **checking account** = account which pays little or no interest but from which the customer can withdraw money when he wants by writing cheques; **deposit account** = account which pays interest but on which notice usually has to be given to withdraw money; **external account** = account in a British bank of someone who is living in another country; **frozen account** = account where the money cannot by used or moved because of a court order; **joint account** = account for two people; *most married people have joint accounts so that they can each take money out when they want it*; **overdrawn account** = account where you have taken out more money than you have put in (i.e. where the bank is lending you money); **savings account** = account where you put money in regularly and which pays interest, often at a higher rate than a deposit account; **to open an account** = to start an account by putting money in; *she opened an account with the Bradford & Bingley Building Society*; **to close an account** = to take all money out of a bank account and stop the account; *he closed his account with Lloyds* **(g)** *(Stock Exchange)* period during which shares are traded for credit, and at the end of which the shares bought must be paid for (on the London Stock Exchange, there are twenty-four accounts during the year, each running usually for ten working days); **rolling account** = system of paying for shares bought on the stock exchange, were the buyer pays at the end of a certain number of days after the purchase is made; **account day** = day on which shares which have been bought must be paid for **(h)** notice; **to take account of inflation** *or* **to take inflation into account** = to assume that there will be a certain percentage inflation when making calculations **2** *verb* **to account for** = to explain and record a money transaction; *to account for a loss or a discrepancy*; *the reps have to account for all their expenses to the sales manager*

accountability [əkaʊntə'bɪləti] *noun* being responsible to someone for something (such as the accountability of directors to the shareholders)

accountable [ə'kaʊntəbl] *adjective* (person) who is responsible for something (such as to record and then explain a money transaction) (NOTE: you are accountable to someone for something)

accountancy [ə'kaʊntənsi] *noun* work of an accountant; *he is studying accountancy or he is an accountancy student* (NOTE: American English uses only accounting in this meaning)

accountant [ə'kaʊntənt] *noun* (i) person who keeps a company's accounts; (ii) person who advises a company on its finances; (iii) person who examines accounts; *the chief accountant of a manufacturing group*; *I send all my income tax queries to my accountant*; **certified accountant** = accountant who has passed the professional examinations and is a member of the Association of Certified Accountants; *US* **certified public accountant** = accountant who has passed professional examinations; **chartered accountant** = accountant who has passed the professional examinations and is a member of the Institute of Chartered Accountants; **cost accountant** = accountant who gives managers information about their business costs; **management accountant** = accountant who prepares financial information for managers so that they can take decisions

accounting [ə'kaʊntɪŋ] *noun* **(a)** work of recording money paid, received, borrowed or owed; *the company has introduced a new accounting system*; **accounting period** = period usually covered by a company's accounts (the balance sheet shows the state of the company's affairs at the end of the accounting period, while the profit-and-loss account shows the changes which have taken place since the end of the previous period); **cost accounting** = preparing special accounts of manufacturing and sales costs; **current cost accounting** = method of accounting which notes the cost of replacing assets at current prices, rather than valuing assets at their original cost **(b)** accountancy, the work of an accountant as a course of study

applicants will be professionally qualified and have a degree in Commerce or Accounting

Australian Financial Review

accredited [ə'kredɪtɪd] *adjective* (agent) who is appointed by a company to act on its behalf

accrual [ə'kruːəl] *noun* **(a)** noting financial transactions when they take place, and not when payment is made **(b)** **accruals** = ACCRUED LIABILITIES **(c)** gradual increase by addition; **accrual of interest** = automatic addition of interest to capital

accrue [ə'kruː] *verb* **(a)** to record a financial transaction in accounts when it takes place, and not when payment is made or received; **accrued liabilities** *or* **accruals** = liabilities which are recorded in an accounting period, although payment has not yet been made (this refers to liabilities such as rent, electricity, etc.) **(b)** to increase and be due for payment at a later date; *interest accrues from the beginning of the month*; **accrued dividend** = dividend earned since the last dividend was paid; **accrued interest** = interest which has been earned by an interest-bearing investment; *accrued interest is added quarterly*

acct = ACCOUNT

accumulate [ə'kjuːmjʊleɪt] *verb* to grow larger by adding; *we allow dividends to accumulate in the fund*; **accumulated profit** = profit which is not paid as dividend but is taken over into the accounts of the following year

accumulation units [əkjuːmjʊ'leɪʃn 'juːnɪts] *noun* type of units in a unit trust, where dividends accumulate and form more units (as opposed to income units, where the investor receives the dividends as income)

accurate ['ækjurət] *adjective* correct; *the sales department made an accurate forecast of sales*; *the designers produced an accurate copy of the plan*

accurately ['ækjurətli] *adverb* correctly; *the second quarter's drop in sales was accurately forecast by the computer*

accuse [ə'kju:z] *verb* to say that someone has committed a crime; *she was accused of stealing from the petty cash box*; *he was accused of industrial espionage* (NOTE: you accuse someone of a crime or of doing something)

achieve [ə'tʃi:v] *verb* to succeed in doing something, to do something successfully; *the company has achieved great success in the Far East*; *we achieved all our objectives last year*

> the company expects to move to
> profits of FFr 2m next year
> and achieve equally rapid
> growth in following years
> *Financial Times*

acid test ratio ['æsɪd 'test 'reɪʃɪəu] *noun* ratio of liquid assets (that is, current assets less stocks, but including debtors) to current liabilities, giving an indication of a company's solvency

acknowledge [ək'nɒlɪdʒ] *verb* to tell a sender that a letter, package or shipment has arrived; *he has still not acknowledged my letter of the 24th*; *we acknowledge receipt of your letter of June 14th*

acknowledgement [ək'nɒlɪdʒmənt] *noun* act of acknowledging; *she sent an acknowledgement of receipt*; *the company sent a letter of acknowledgement after I sent in my job application*

acoustic hood [ə'ku:stɪk 'hud] *noun* cover which is put over a printer to reduce the noise level

acquire [ə'kwaɪə] *verb* to buy; *to acquire a company*; *we have acquired a new office building in the centre of town*

acquirer [ə'kwaɪərə] *noun* person or company which buys something

acquisition [ækwɪ'zɪʃən] *noun* **(a)** thing bought; *the chocolate factory is our latest*

acquisition **(b)** act of getting or buying something; **data acquisition** *or* **acquisition of data** = obtaining and classifying data

acre ['eɪkə] *noun* measure of the area of land (= 0.45 hectares) (NOTE: the plural is used with figures, except before a noun: **he has bought a farm of 250 acres, he has bought a 250 acre farm**)

across-the-board [ə'krɒs ðə 'bɔːd] *adjective* applying to everything or everyone; *an across-the-board price increase*

ACT = ADVANCE CORPORATION TAX

act [ækt] **1** *noun* **(a)** law passed by parliament which must be obeyed by the people; *GB* **Companies Act** = Act which rules how companies should do their business; **Finance Act** = annual Act of Parliament which gives the government power to raise taxes as proposed in the budget; **Financial Services Act** = Act of the British Parliament which regulates the offering of financial services (such as hire-purchase, mortgages, loans, etc.) to the public; **Health and Safety at Work Act** = Act which rules how the health of workers should be protected by the companies they work for **(b)** act of God = something you do not expect to happen, and which cannot be avoided (such as a storm or flood) **2** *verb* **(a)** to work; *he has agreed to act as an agent for an American company*; *the solicitor is acting for us or on our behalf* **(b)** to do something; *the board will have to act quickly if the company's losses are going to be reduced*; *the lawyers are acting on our instructions*; **to act on a letter** = to do what a letter asks to be done

acting ['æktɪŋ] *adjective* working in place of someone for a short time; *acting manager*; *the Acting Chairman*

action ['ækʃən] *noun* **(a)** thing which has been done; **to take action** = to do something; *you must take action if you want to stop people cheating you* **(b)** **direct action** = strike or go-slow by the workforce; **to take industrial action** = to do something (usually to go on strike) to show that you are not happy with conditions at work **(c)** case in a law court where a person or company sues another person or company; **to take legal action** = to sue someone; **action for libel** *or* **libel action**; *she brought an action for wrongful dismissal against her former employer*; **civil action** = case brought by a person or company against someone who has done them wrong; **criminal action** = case brought by the state against someone who is charged with a crime

active ['æktɪv] *adjective* busy; *an active demand for oil shares*; *computer shares are very active*; *an active day on the Stock Exchange*; **active partner** = partner who works in the company

actively ['æktɪvli] *adverb* in a busy way; *the company is actively recruiting new personnel*

activity [æk'tɪvəti] *noun* being active or busy; *a low level of business activity*; *there was a lot of activity on the Stock Exchange*; **activity chart** = plan showing work which has been done so that it can be compared to the plan of work to be done; **monthly activity report** = report by a department on what has been done during the past month

> preliminary indications of the level of business investment and activity during the March quarter will provide a good picture of economic activity in the year
> *Australian Financial Review*

actual ['æktʃʊəl] **1** *adjective* real, correct; *what is the actual cost of one unit?*; *the actual figures for directors' expenses are not shown to the shareholders* **2** *plural noun* **actuals** = real figures; *these figures are the actuals for last year*

actuarial [æktjʊ'eərɪəl] *adjective* calculated by an actuary; *the premiums are worked out according to actuarial calculations*; **actuarial tables** = lists showing how long people of certain ages are likely to live, used to calculate life assurance premiums and annuities

actuary ['æktjʊəri] *noun* person employed by an insurance company or other organization to calculate the risk involved in an insurance, and therefore the premiums payable by persons taking out insurance

ad [æd] *noun* (*informal*) = ADVERTISEMENT; *we put an ad in the paper*; *she answered an ad in the paper*; *he found his job through an ad in the paper*; **classified ads** *or* **small ads** *or* **want ads** = advertisements listed in a newspaper under special headings (like 'property for sale', 'jobs wanted'); *look in the small ads to see if anyone has a filing cabinet for sale*; **coupon ad** = advertisement with a form attached, which you cut out and return to the advertiser with your name and address for further information; **display ad** = advertisement which is well designed or printed in bold letters to attract attention

add [æd] *verb* **(a)** to put figures together to make a total; *if you add the interest to the capital you will get quite a large sum*; *interest is added monthly*; **added value** = amount added to the value of a product or service, being the difference between its cost and the amount received when it is sold (wages, taxes, etc., are deducted from the added value to give the retained profit); *see also* VALUE ADDED **(b)** to put things together to make a large group; *we are adding to the sales force*; *they have added two new products to their range*; **this all adds to the company's costs** = this makes the company's costs higher

adding ['ædɪŋ] *adjective* which adds, which makes additions; *an adding machine*

addition [ə'dɪʃən] *noun* **(a)** thing or person added; *the management has stopped all additions to the staff*; *we are exhibiting several additions to our product line*; *the marketing director is the latest addition to the board* **(b)** **in addition to** = added to, as well as; *there are twelve registered letters to be sent in addition to this packet* **(c)** putting numbers together; *you don't need a calculator to do simple addition*

additional [ə'dɪʃənl] *adjective* extra which is added; *they sent us a list of additional charges*; *some additional clauses were added to the contract*; *additional duty will have to be paid*

address [ə'dres] **1** *noun* details of number, street and town where an office is or a person lives; *my business address and phone number are printed on the card*; **accommodation address** = address used for receiving messages but which is not the real address of the company; **cable address** = short address for sending cables; **email address** = series of letters and full stops which make up an address for email; *my email address is: peter@pcp.co.uk*; **forwarding address** = address to which a person's mail can be sent on; **home address** = address of a house or flat where someone lives; *please send the documents to my home address*; **address book** = special notebook, with columns printed in such a way that names, addresses and phone numbers can be entered; **address label** = label on which an address can be written; **address list** = list of addresses; *we keep an address list of two thousand addresses in Europe* **2** *verb* **(a)** to write the details of an address on an envelope, etc.; *to address a letter or a parcel*; *please address your enquiries to the manager*; *a letter addressed to the managing director*; *an incorrectly addressed package* **(b)** to speak; *the chairman addressed the meeting*

addressee [ædre'si:] *noun* person to whom a letter or package is addressed

addressing machine [ə'dresɪŋ mə'ʃi:n] *noun* machine which puts addresses on envelopes automatically

add up ['æd 'ʌp] *verb* to put several figures together to make a total; *he made a mistake in adding up the column of figures*; **the figures do not add up** = the total given is not correct

add up to ['æd 'ʌp tʊ] *verb* to make a total of; *the total expenditure adds up to more than £1,000*

adequate ['ædɪkwət] *adjective* **(a)** large enough; **to operate without adequate cover** = to act without being completely protected by insurance **(b)** more or less satisfactory; *the results of the tests on the product were adequate*

adhesive [əd'hi:zɪv] **1** *adjective* which sticks; *he sealed the parcel with adhesive*

tape **2** *noun* glue; *she has a tube of adhesive in the drawer of her desk*

adjourn [ə'dʒɜ:n] *verb* to stop a meeting for a period; *to adjourn a meeting*; *the chairman adjourned the meeting until three o'clock*; *the meeting adjourned at midday*

adjournment [ə'dʒɜ:nmənt] *noun* act of adjourning; *he proposed the adjournment of the meeting*

adjudicate [ə'dʒu:dɪkeɪt] *verb* to give a judgement between two parties in law; *to decide a legal problem*; *to adjudicate a claim*; *to adjudicate in a dispute*; **he was adjudicated bankrupt** = he was declared legally bankrupt

adjudication [ədʒu:dɪ'keɪʃən] *noun* act of giving a judgement or of deciding a legal problem; **adjudication order** *or* **adjudication of bankruptcy** = order by a court making someone bankrupt; **adjudication tribunal** = group which adjudicates in industrial disputes

adjudicator [ə'dʒu:dɪkeɪtə] *noun* person who gives a decision on a problem; *an adjudicator in an industrial dispute*

adjust [ə'dʒʌst] *verb* to change something to fit new conditions; *to adjust prices to take account of inflation*; *prices are adjusted for inflation*

inflation-adjusted GNP moved
up at a 1.3% annual rate
Fortune

Saudi Arabia will no longer
adjust its production to
match short-term supply with
demand
Economist

on a seasonally-adjusted
basis, output of trucks,
electric power, steel and
paper decreased
Business Week

adjuster [ə'dʒʌstə] *noun* person who calculates losses for an insurance company; **average adjuster** = person who calculates how much of a maritime insurance is to be paid by the insurer against a claim; **loss adjuster** = person who calculates how much insurance should be paid on a claim

adjustment [ə'dʒʌstmənt] *noun* act of adjusting; slight change; *details of tax adjustments are set out in the enclosed document*; *to make an adjustment to salaries*; *adjustment of prices to take account of rising costs*; **average adjustment** = calculation of the share of cost of damage or loss of a ship

adjustor [ə'dʒʌstə] = ADJUSTER

adman ['ædmæn] *noun (informal)* man who works in advertising; *our admen are using balloons as promotional material*

admin ['ædmɪn] *noun (informal)* **(a)** work of administration, especially paperwork; *all this admin work takes a lot of my time*; *there is too much admin in this job*; *admin costs seem to be rising each quarter*; *the admin people have sent the report back* **(b)** administration staff or the administration department; *admin say they need the report immediately*; *she did not answer my note but sent it on to admin* (NOTE: no plural; as a group of people it can have a plural verb)

administer [əd'mɪnɪstə] *verb* to organize or to manage; *he administers a large pension fund; US* **administered price** = price fixed by a manufacturer which cannot be varied by a retailer (NOTE: in the UK this is called **resale price maintenance**)

administration [ədmɪnɪ'streɪʃən] *noun* **(a)** organization, control or management of a company; **administration costs** *or* **the expenses of the administration** *or* **administration expenses** = costs of management, not including production, marketing or distribution costs **(b) letters of administration** = letter given by a court to allow someone to deal with the estate of a person who has died

administrative [əd'mɪnɪstrətɪv] *adjective* referring to administration; *all these administrative details take time to get right*

administrator [əd'mɪnɪstreɪtə] *noun* **(a)** person who directs the work of other employees in a business **(b)** person appointed by a court to manage the affairs of someone who dies without leaving a will **(c)** person appointed by a court to administer a company which is insolvent

admission [əd'mɪʃən] *noun* **(a)** allowing someone to go in; *there is a £1 admission charge*; *admission is free on presentation of this card*; *free admission on Sundays* **(b)** saying that something really happened; *he had to resign after his admission that he had passed information to the rival company*

admit [əd'mɪt] *verb* **(a)** to allow someone to go in; *children are not admitted to the bank*; *old age pensioners are admitted at half price* **(b)** to say that something is correct, to say that something really happened; *the chairman admitted he had taken the cash from the company's safe* (NOTE: **admitting - admitted**)

admittance [əd'mɪtəns] *noun* allowing someone to go in; *no admittance except on business*

adopt [ə'dɒpt] *verb* to agree to (something), to accept (something); *they asked the AGM to adopt the resolution*; *the proposals were adopted unanimously*

ADR = AMERICAN DEPOSITARY RECEIPT

ad valorem ['æd və'lɔːrəm] *Latin phrase* meaning 'according to value', showing that a tax is calculated according to the value of the goods taxed; *ad valorem duty*; *ad valorem tax*

> COMMENT: most taxes are 'ad valorem'; VAT is calculated as a percentage of the charge made, income tax is a percentage of income earned, etc.

advance [əd'vɑːns] **1** *noun* **(a)** money paid as a loan or as a part of a payment to be made later; *she asked if she could have a cash advance*; *to receive an advance from the bank*; *we paid her an advance on account*; *to make an advance of £100 to someone*; *to pay someone an advance against a security*; *can I have an advance of £100 against next month's salary?* **(b)** increase; *an advance in trade with Eastern European countries* **(c) in advance** = early, before something happens; *to pay in advance*; *freight payable in advance*; *price fixed in advance* **2** *adjective* early; *advance holiday bookings are up on last year*; *you must give seven days' advance notice of withdrawals from the account*;

Advance Corporation Tax (ACT) = tax paid by a company in advance of its main corporation tax payments; it is paid when dividends are paid to shareholders and is deducted from the main tax payment when that falls due; it appears on the tax voucher attached to a dividend warrant **3** *verb* **(a)** to lend; *the bank advanced him £100,000 against the security of his house* **(b)** to increase; *prices generally advanced on the stock market* **(c)** to make something happen earlier; *the date of the AGM has been advanced to May 10th*; *the meeting with the German distributors has been advanced from 11.00 to 09.30*

advantage [əd'vɑːntɪdʒ] *noun* something useful which may help you to be successful; *keyboarding skills are an advantage in a secretary*; *knowledge of two foreign languages is an advantage*; *there is no advantage in arriving at the exhibition before it opens*; **to take advantage of something** = to use something which helps you

adverse ['ædvɜːs] *adjective* bad, not helpful; **adverse balance of trade** = situation when a country imports more than it exports; **adverse trading conditions** = bad conditions for trade

advert ['ædvɜːt] *noun GB (informal)* = ADVERTISEMENT; *to put an advert in the paper*; *to answer an advert in the paper*; *classified adverts*; *display adverts*

advertise ['ædvətaɪz] *verb* to announce that something is for sale, that a job is vacant or that a service is offered; *to advertise a vacancy*; *to advertise for a secretary*; *to advertise a new product*

advertisement [əd'vɜːtɪsmənt] *noun* notice which shows that something is for sale, that a service is offered, that someone wants something or that a job is vacant, etc.; *to put an advertisement in the paper*; *to answer an advertisement in the paper*; **classified advertisements** = advertisements listed in a newspaper under special headings (such as 'property for sale' or 'jobs wanted'); **display advertisement** = advertisement which is well designed or printed in bold type to attract attention; **advertisement manager** = manager in charge of the advertisement section of a newspaper

advertiser ['ædvətaɪzə] *noun* person or company which advertises; *the catalogue gives a list of advertisers*

advertising ['ædvətaɪzɪŋ] *noun* business of announcing that something is for sale or of trying to persuade customers to buy a product or service; *she works in advertising or she has a job in advertising*; *our advertising budget has been increased*; *their new advertising campaign is being launched next week*; **advertising agency** = office which plans, designs and manages advertising for other companies; **advertising manager** = manager in charge of advertising a company's products; **advertising rates** = amount of money charged for advertising space in a newspaper or advertising time on TV; **advertising space** = space in a newspaper set aside for advertisements; **to take advertising space in a paper** = to book space for an advertisement in a newspaper

advertorial [ædvə'tɔːrɪəl] *noun* text in a magazine, which is not written by the editorial staff but by an advertiser

advice [əd'vaɪs] *noun* **(a)** **advice note** = written notice to a customer giving details of goods ordered and shipped but not yet delivered; **as per advice** = according to what is written on the advice note **(b)** opinion as to what action to take; **to take legal advice** = to ask a lawyer to say what should be done; *the accountant's advice was to send the documents to the police*; *we sent the documents to the police on the advice of the accountant or we took the accountant's advice and sent the documents to the police*

advise [əd'vaɪz] *verb* **(a)** to tell someone what has happened; *we have been advised that the shipment will arrive next week* **(b)** to suggest to someone what should be done; *we are advised to take the shipping company to court*; *the accountant advised us to send the documents to the police*

advise against [əd'vaɪz ə'genst] *verb* to suggest that something should not be done; *the bank manager advised against closing* *the account; my stockbroker has advised against buying those shares*

adviser *or* **advisor** [əd'vaɪzə] *noun* person who suggests what should be done; *he is consulting the company's legal adviser;* **financial adviser** = person or company which gives advice on financial problems for a fee

advisory [əd'vaɪzəri] *adjective* as an adviser; *he is acting in an advisory capacity;* **an advisory board** = a group of advisers; **Advisory, Conciliation and Arbitration Service (ACAS)** = British government service which arbitrates in disputes between management and employees

aerogramme ['eərəgræm] *noun US* sheet of thin blue paper which when folded can be sent as an airmail letter without an envelope (NOTE: British English for this is an **air letter**)

affair [ə'feə] *noun* business or dealings; *are you involved in the copyright affair?; his affairs were so difficult to understand that the lawyers had to ask accountants for advice*

affect [ə'fekt] *verb* to change, to have a bad effect on (something); *the new government regulations do not affect us; the company's sales in the Far East were seriously affected by the embargo*

> the dollar depreciation has yet to affect the underlying inflation rate
> *Australian Financial Review*

affidavit [æfɪ'deɪvɪt] *noun* written statement which is signed and sworn before a solicitor, judge, JP, etc., and which can then be used as evidence in court

affiliated [ə'fɪlɪeɪtɪd] *adjective* connected with or owned by another company; *Smiths Ltd is one of our affiliated companies*

affinity card [ə'fɪnɪti 'kɑːd] *noun* credit card where a percentage of each purchase made is given by the credit card company to a stated charity

affirmative [ə'fɜːmətɪv] *adjective* meaning 'yes'; **the answer was in the affirmative** = the answer was yes; *US* **affirmative action program** = programme

to avoid discrimination in employment (NOTE: the British equivalent is 'equal opportunities')

affluent ['æfluənt] *adjective* very rich; *we live in an affluent society*

afford [ə'fɔːd] *verb* to be able to pay or to buy; *we could not afford the cost of two telephones; the company cannot afford the time to train new staff* (NOTE: only used after can, cannot, could, could not, able to)

AFL-CIO ['eɪef'el'siːaɪ'əʊ] = AMERICAN FEDERATION OF LABOR - CONGRESS OF INDUSTRIAL ORGANIZATIONS an organization linking US trade unions

afraid [ə'freɪd] *adjective* sorry, because something has happened; *I am afraid there are no seats left on the flight to Amsterdam; we are afraid your order has been lost in the post* (NOTE: only used after the verb **to be**)

after-hours ['ɑːftə'aʊəz] *adjective* **after-hours buying** *or* **selling** *or* **dealing** *or* **trading** = buying, selling or dealing in shares after the Stock Exchange has officially closed for the day, such deals being subject to normal Stock Exchange rules (in this way, dealers can take advantage of the fact that because of time differences, the various stock exchanges round the world are open almost all twenty-four hours of the day)

after-sales service ['ɑːftəseɪlz 'sɜːvɪs] *noun* service of a machine carried out by the seller for some time after the machine has been bought

after-tax profit ['ɑːftətæks 'prɒfɪt] *noun* profit after tax has been deducted

against [ə'genst] *preposition* relating to, part of; *to pay an advance against a security; can I have an advance against next month's salary?; the bank advanced him £100,000 against the security of his house*

> investment can be written off against the marginal rate of tax
> *Investors Chronicle*

aged debtors analysis *or* **ageing schedule** ['eɪdʒd 'detəz ə'næləsɪs or 'eɪdʒɪŋ 'ʃedjuːl] *noun* list which analyses a company's debtors, showing the number of days their payments are outstanding (NOTE: American spelling is **aging**)

COMMENT: an ageing schedule shows all the debtors of a company and lists (usually in descending order of age) all the debts that are outstanding; the debtors will be shown as: £X at 30 days, £Y at 60 days, £Z at 90 days, etc.

agency ['eɪdʒənsi] *noun* **(a)** office or job of representing another company in an area; *they signed an agency agreement or an agency contract*; **sole agency =** agreement to be the only person to represent a company or to sell a product in a certain area; *he has the sole agency for Ford cars* **(b)** office or business which arranges things for other companies; **advertising agency =** office which plans, designs and manages advertising for companies; **employment agency =** office which finds jobs for staff; **estate agency =** office which arranges for the sale of properties; **news agency =** office which distributes news to newspapers and television stations; **travel agency =** office which arranges travel for customers (NOTE: plural is **agencies;** the person running an agency is an **agent**)

agenda [ə'dʒendə] *noun* list of things to be discussed at a meeting; *after two hours we were still discussing the first item on the agenda*; *the secretary put finance at the top of the agenda*; *the chairman wants two items removed from or taken off the agenda*; *the conference agenda or the agenda of the conference is in the information pack given to delegates*

agent ['eɪdʒənt] *noun* **(a)** person who represents a company or another person in an area; *to be the agent for BMW cars*; **agent's commission =** money (often a percentage of sales) paid to an agent; **sole agent =** person who has the sole agency for a company in an area; *he is the sole agent for Ford cars* **(b)** person in charge of an agency; *the estate agent sent me a list of properties for sale*; *our trip was organized through out local travel agent*; **commission agent =** agent who is paid by commission, not by fee; **forwarding agent** = person or company which arranges shipping and customs documents; **insurance agent =** person who arranges insurance for clients; **land agent =** person who runs a farm or a large area of land for the owner **(c)** *US* **(business) agent =** chief local official of a trade union

aggregate ['ægrɪgət] *adjective* total, with everything added together; *aggregate output*

agio ['ædʒɪəʊ] *noun* charge made for changing money of one currency into another

AGM ['eɪdʒiː'em] = ANNUAL GENERAL MEETING

agree [ə'griː] *verb* **(a)** to approve; *the auditors have agreed the accounts*; *the figures were agreed between the two parties*; *we have agreed the budgets for next year*; *terms of the contract are still to be agreed*; *the boss has agreed your prices* **(b)** to say yes, to accept; *it has been agreed that the lease will run for 25 years*; *after some discussion he agreed to our plan*; *the bank will never agree to lend the company £250,000*; *we all agreed on the plan* (NOTE: to agree **to** or **on** a plan) **(c)** to agree **to do something =** to say that you will do something; *she agreed to be chairman*; *will the finance director agree to resign?* **(d)** to be the same as; *the two sets of calculations do not agree*

agreed [ə'griːd] *adjective* which has been accepted by everyone; *we pay an agreed amount each month*; *the shop is leased on agreed terms*

agreement [ə'griːmənt] *noun* contract between two parties which explains how they will act; *written agreement*; *unwritten or verbal agreement*; *to draw up or to draft an agreement*; *to break an agreement*; *to sign an agreement*; *to witness an agreement*; *an agreement has been reached or concluded or come to*; *to reach an agreement or to come to an agreement on prices or salaries*; *an international agreement on trade*; *a collective wage agreement*; *an agency agreement*; *a marketing agreement*; **blanket agreement =** agreement which covers many different items; **exclusive agreement =** agreement where a company is appointed sole agent for a product in a market; **gentleman's agreement** *US* **gentlemen's agreement** = verbal agreement between two parties who trust each other

---

after three days of tough negotiations the company has reached agreement with its 1,200 unionized workers

Toronto Star

---

agree with [ə'griː wɪð] *verb* **(a)** to say that your opinions are the same as someone else's; *I agree with the chairman that the figures are lower than normal* **(b)** to be the same as; *the auditors' figures do not agree with those of the accounts department*

agribusiness ['ægrɪbɪznəs] *noun* farming, and making products used by farmers (considered as a business)

agricultural [ægrɪ'kʌltʃərəl] *adjective* referring to agriculture, referring to farms; **agricultural co-operative** = farm run by groups of workers who are the owners and share the profits; **agricultural economist** = person who specializes in the study of finance and investment in agriculture; **Common Agricultural Policy (CAP)** = agreement between members of the EU to protect farmers by paying subsidies to fix prices of farm produce

agriculture ['ægrɪkʌltʃə] *noun* use of land for growing crops or raising animals, etc.; *agriculture is still an important part of the nation's economy*

ahead [ə'hed] *adverb* in front of, better than; *we are already ahead of our sales forecast*; *the company has a lot of work ahead of it if it wants to increase its market share*

aim [eɪm] **1** *noun* something which you try to do; *one of our aims is to increase the quality of our products*; *the company has achieved all its aims* = the company has done all the things it had hoped to do **2** *verb* to try to do something; *we aim to be No. 1 in the market in two years' time*; *each salesman must aim to double his previous year's sales*

air [eə] **1** *noun* method of travelling or sending goods using aircraft; *to send a letter or a shipment by air*; **air carrier** =

company which sends cargo or passengers by air; **air forwarding** = arranging for goods to be shipped by air; **air letter** = special sheet of thin blue paper which when folded can be sent by air mail without an envelope (NOTE: American English for this is **aerogramme**) **2** *verb* **to air a grievance** = to talk about, to discuss a grievance; *the management committee is useful because it allows the workers' representatives to air their grievances*

air cargo ['eə 'kɑːgəʊ] *noun* goods sent by air

aircraft ['eəkrɑːft] *noun* machine which flies in the air, carrying passengers or cargo; *the airline has a fleet of ten commercial aircraft*; *the company is one of the most important American aircraft manufacturers*; **to charter an aircraft** = to hire an aircraft for a special purpose (NOTE: no plural: **one aircraft, two aircraft**)

air freight ['eə 'freɪt] *noun* method of shipping goods in an aircraft; *to send a shipment by air freight*; *air freight tariffs are rising*

airfreight ['eəfreɪt] *verb* to send goods by air; *to airfreight a consignment to Mexico*; *we airfreighted the shipment because our agent ran out of stock*

airline ['eəlaɪn] *noun* company which carries passengers or cargo by air

airmail ['eəmeɪl] **1** *noun* way of sending letters or parcels by air; *to send a package by airmail*; *airmail charges have risen by 15%*; **airmail envelope** = very light envelope for sending airmail letters; **airmail sticker** = blue sticker with the words 'by air mail' which can be stuck to an envelope or packet to show it is being sent by air **2** *verb* to send letters or parcels by air; *we airmailed the document to New York*

airport ['eəpɔːt] *noun* place where planes land and take off; *we leave from London Airport at 10.00*; *O'Hare Airport is the main airport for Chicago*; **airport bus** = bus which takes passengers to and from an airport; **airport tax** = tax added to the price of the air ticket to cover the cost of running an airport; **airport terminal** = main building at an airport where passengers arrive and depart

air terminal ['eə 'tɜːmɪnl] *noun* building in a town where passengers meet to be taken by bus to an airport outside the town

airtight ['eətaɪt] *adjective* which does not allow air to get in; *the goods are packed in airtight containers*

airworthiness ['eəwɜːðɪnəs] *noun* being able and safe to fly; **certificate of airworthiness** = certificate to show that an aircraft is safe to fly

all [ɔːl] *adjective & pronoun* everything or everyone; *all (of) the managers attended the meeting; a salesman should know the prices of all the products he is selling*

all-in ['ɔːl 'ɪn] *adjective* including everything; **all-in price** *or* **rate** = price which covers all items in a purchase (goods, delivery, tax, insurance)

allocate ['æləkeɪt] *verb* to divide (a sum of money) in various ways and share it out; *we allocate 10% of revenue to publicity; $2,500 was allocated to office furniture*

allocation [ælə'keɪʃən] *noun* **(a)** dividing a sum of money in various ways; *the allocation of funds to a project* **(b)** **share allocation** *or* **allocation of shares** = spreading a small number of shares among a large number of people who have applied for them

allot [ə'lɒt] *verb* to share out; **to allot shares** = to give a certain number of shares to people who have applied for them (NOTE: **allotting - allotted**)

allotment [ə'lɒtmənt] *noun* **(a)** sharing out funds by giving money to various departments; *the allotment of funds to each project is the responsibility of the finance director* **(b)** **share allotment** = giving some shares in a new company to people who have applied for them; *payment must be made in full on allotment;* **letter of allotment** *or* **allotment letter** = letter which tells someone who has applied for shares in a new company how many shares he or she has been allotted

all-out ['ɔːl'aʊt] *adjective* complete, very serious; *the union called for an all-out strike; the personnel manager has launched an all-out campaign to get the staff to work on Friday afternoons*

allow [ə'laʊ] *verb* **(a)** to say that someone can do something; *junior members of staff are not allowed to use the chairman's lift; the company allows all members of staff to take six days' holiday at Christmas* **(b)** to give; *we allow her a discount because she's the manager's sister;* **to allow 5% discount to members of staff;** *the best customers are allowed 90 days' credit* **(c)** to agree, to accept legally; *to allow a claim or an appeal*

allowable [ə'laʊəbl] *adjective* legally accepted; **allowable expenses** = expenses which can be claimed against tax

allowance [ə'laʊəns] *noun* **(a)** money which is given for a special reason; *travel allowance or travelling allowance;* **cost-of-living allowance** = addition to normal salary to cover increases in the cost of living; **entertainment allowance** = money which a manager is allowed to spend each month on meals with visitors **(b)** part of an income which is not taxed; **capital allowances** = allowances which may be deducted from profits following the purchase of capital assets; **tax allowances** *or* **allowances against tax** *or* **personal allowances** = part of someone's personal income which is not taxed **(c)** money removed in the form of a discount; *allowance for depreciation; allowance for exchange loss*

most airlines give business class the same baggage allowance as first class
Business Traveller

the compensation plan includes base, incentive and car allowance totalling $50,000+
Globe and Mail (Toronto)

allowed time [ə'laʊd 'taɪm] *noun* paid time which the management agrees a worker can spend on rest, cleaning or meals, not working

allow for [ə'laʊ fɔː] *verb* to give a discount for, to add an extra sum to cover something; *to allow for money paid in advance; allow an extra 10% for postage and packing;* **delivery is not allowed for** = delivery charges are not included; **allow 28**

days for delivery = calculate that delivery will take at least 28 days

all-risks policy ['ɔːl'rɪsks 'pɒlɪsi] *noun* insurance policy which covers risks of any kind, with no exclusions

all-time ['ɔːl'taɪm] *adjective* **all-time high** *or* **all-time low** = highest or lowest point ever reached; *sales have fallen from their all-time high of last year*

> shares closed at an all-time high yesterday as expectations grew of lower interest rates
>
> *Times*

alphabet ['ælfəbet] *noun* the 26 letters used to make words

alphabetical order [ælfə'betɪkəl 'ɔːdə] *noun* arrangement of records (such as files, index cards) in the order of the letters of the alphabet (A,B,C,D, etc.)

alter ['ɒltə] *verb* to change; *to alter the terms of a contract*

alteration [ɒltə'reɪʃən] *noun* change which has been made; *he made some alterations to the terms of a contract*; *the agreement was signed without any alterations*

alternate director [ɒl'tɜːnɪt daɪ'rektə] *noun* person nominated by a director to attend meetings in his place

alternative [ɒl'tɜːnətɪv] **1** *noun* thing which can be done instead of another; *what is the alternative to firing half the staff?*; **we have no alternative** = there is nothing else we can do **2** *adjective* other, which can take the place of something; **to find someone alternative employment** = to find someone another job

altogether [ɔːltə'geðə] *adverb* putting everything together; *the staff of the three companies in the group come to 2,500 altogether*; *the company lost £2m last year and £4m this year, making £6m altogether for the two years*

a.m. *US* **A.M.** ['eɪ'em] *adverb* in the morning, before 12 midday; *the flight leaves at 9.20 a.m.*; *telephone calls before 6 a.m. are charged at the cheap rate*

amend [ə'mend] *verb* to change and make more correct or acceptable; *please*

amend your copy of the contract accordingly

amendment [ə'mendmənt] *noun* change to a document; *to propose an amendment to the constitution*; *to make amendments to a contract*

American Depositary Receipt (ADR) [ə'merɪkən dɪ'pɒzɪtri rɪ'siːt] *noun* document issued by an American bank to US citizens, making them unregistered shareholders of companies in foreign countries; the document allows them to receive dividends from their investments, and ADRs can themselves be bought or sold

> COMMENT: buying and selling ADRs is easier for American investors than buying or selling the actual shares themselves, as it avoids stamp duty and can be carried out in dollars without incurring exchange costs

Amex ['æmeks] *noun (informal)* = AMERICAN STOCK EXCHANGE; AMERICAN EXPRESS

amortizable [æmɔː'taɪzəbl] *adjective* which can be amortized; *the capital cost is amortizable over a period of ten years*

amortization [əmɔːtaɪ'zeɪʃn] *noun* act of amortizing; *amortization of a debt*

amortize ['æmɔːtaɪz] *verb* to pay off (a debt) by putting money aside regularly over a period of time; *the capital cost is amortized over five years*

amount [ə'maʊnt] **1** *noun* quantity of money; *a small amount has been deducted to cover our costs*; *a large amount is still owing*; *what is the amount to be written off?*; *what is the amount outstanding?*; *a small amount invested in gilt-edged stock* **2** *verb* **to amount to** = to make a total of; *their debts amount to over £1m*

analyse *or* **analyze** ['ænəlaɪz] *verb* to examine in detail; *to analyse a statement of account*; *to analyse the market potential*

analysis [ə'næləsɪs] *noun* detailed examination and report; *his job is to produce a regular sales analysis or to carry out an analysis of the market potential or to write an analysis of the sales position*; **cost analysis** = examination in advance of the costs of a new product; **systems analysis** = using a computer to suggest how a company can work more efficiently by analysing the way in which it works at present (NOTE: plural is **analyses** ə'næləsi:z]

analyst ['ænəlɪst] *noun* person who analyses; *market analyst*; *systems analyst*

announce [ə'naʊns] *verb* to tell something to the public; *to announce the first year's trading results*; *the director has announced a programme of investment*

announcement [ə'naʊnsmənt] *noun* telling something in public; *announcement of a cutback in expenditure*; *announcement of the appointment of a new managing director*; *the managing director made an announcement to the staff*

annual ['ænjʊəl] *adjective* for one year; *annual statement of income*; *he has six weeks' annual leave*; *the annual accounts have been sent to the shareholders*; *the company has an annual growth of 5%*; **annual report** = report of a company's financial situation at the end of a year, sent to all the shareholders; **annual return** = official report which a registered company has to make each year to the Registrar of Companies; **on an annual basis** = each year; *the figures are revised on an annual basis*

real wages have risen at an annual rate of only 1% in the last two years
Sunday Times

the remuneration package will include an attractive salary, profit sharing and a company car together with four weeks annual holiday
Times

annual general meeting (AGM) ['ænjʊəl 'dʒenrəl 'mi:tɪŋ] *noun* annual meeting of all the members (that is, the shareholders) of a company, when the company's financial situation is presented by and discussed with the directors, when the accounts for the past year are approved, when dividends are declared and auditors are appointed, etc. (NOTE: the American term

is **annual meeting** or **annual stockholders' meeting**)

annualized ['ænjʊəlaɪzd] *adjective* shown on an annual basis; **annualized percentage rate** = yearly percentage rate, calculated by multiplying the monthly rate by twelve (not as accurate as the APR, which includes fees and other charges)

he believes this may have caused the economy to grow at an annualized rate of almost 5 per cent in the final quarter of last year
Investors Chronicle

annually ['ænjʊəli] *adverb* each year; *the figures are updated annually*

Annual Percentage Rate (APR) ['ænjʊəl pə'sentɪdʒ 'reɪt] *noun* rate of interest (such as on a hire-purchase agreement) shown on an annual compound basis, including fees and charges

annuitant [ə'nju:ɪtənt] *noun* person who receives an annuity

annuity [ə'nju:əti] *noun* money paid each year to a retired person, usually in return for a lump-sum payment; *to buy or to take out an annuity*; **annuity for life** *or* **life annuity** = annual payments made to someone as long as he is alive; **reversionary annuity** = annuity paid to someone on the death of another person (NOTE: plural is **annuities**)

annul [ə'nʌl] *verb* to cancel, to stop something being legal; *the contract was annulled by the court* (NOTE: **annulling - annulled**)

annullable [ə'nʌləbl] *adjective* which can be cancelled

annulling [ə'nʌlɪŋ] **1** *adjective* which cancels; *annulling clause* **2** *noun* act of cancelling; *the annulling of a contract*

annulment [ə'nʌlmənt] *noun* act of cancelling; *annulment of a contract*

answer ['ɑːnsə] **1** *noun* reply, a letter or conversation coming after someone has written or spoken; *I am writing in answer to your letter of October 6th*; *my letter got no answer or there was no answer to my letter*; *I tried to phone his office but there was no answer* **2** *verb* to speak or write after someone has spoken or written to you;

to answer a letter = to write a letter in reply to a letter which you have received; **to answer the telephone** = to lift the telephone when it rings and listen to what the caller is saying

answering ['ɑːnsrɪŋ] *noun* **answering machine** = *ANSWERPHONE*; **answering service** = office which answers the telephone and takes messages for someone or for a company

answerphone ['ɑːnsə'fəʊn] *noun* machine which answers the telephone automatically when a person is not in the office and allows messages to be recorded; *he wasn't in when I called so I left a message on his answerphone*

antedate ['æntɪdeɪt] *verb* to put an earlier date on a document; *the invoice was antedated to January 1st*

anti- ['ænti] *prefix* against

anti-dumping ['ænti'dʌmpɪŋ] *adjective* which protects a country against dumping; *anti-dumping legislation*

anti-inflationary ['æntiɪn'fleɪʃnəri] *adjective* which tries to restrict inflation; *anti-inflationary measures*

anti-trust ['ænti'trʌst] *adjective* which attacks monopolies and encourages competition; *anti-trust laws or legislation*

any other business (AOB) ['eni 'ʌðə 'bɪznəs] *noun* item at the end of an agenda, where any matter can be raised

AOB ['eɪəʊ'biː] = ANY OTHER BUSINESS

aperture ['æpətjʊə] *noun* hole; **aperture envelope** = envelope with a hole in it so that the address on the letter inside can be seen

apologize [ə'pɒlədʒaɪz] *verb* to say you are sorry; *to apologize for the delay in answering*; *she apologized for being late*

apology [ə'pɒlədʒi] *noun* saying you are sorry; *to write a letter of apology*; *I enclose a cheque for £10 with apologies for the delay in answering your letter*

appeal [ə'piːl] **1** *noun* **(a)** being attractive; **customer appeal** = being attractive to customers; **sales appeal** = quality in a product which makes customers want to buy it **(b)** asking a court or a government department to change its decision; *the appeal against the planning decision will be heard next month*; *he lost his appeal for damages against the company*; *she won her case on appeal* = her case was lost in the first court, but the appeal court said that she was right **2** *verb* **(a)** to attract; *this disk appeals to the under-25 market*; *the idea of working in Australia for six months appealed to her* **(b)** to ask a government department or a law court to alter its decision; *the company appealed against the decision of the planning officers* (NOTE: you appeal **to** a court or a person **against** a decision)

appear [ə'pɪə] *verb* to seem; *the company appeared to be doing well*; *the managing director appears to be in control*

appendix [ə'pendɪks] *noun* additional sheets at the back of a contract; additional pages at the back of a book

applicant ['æplɪkənt] *noun* person who applies for something; **applicant for a job** *or* **job applicant**; *there were thousands of applicants for shares in the new company*

application [æplɪ'keɪʃən] *noun* asking for something, usually in writing; *shares payable on application*; *she sent off six applications for job or six job applications*; **application form** = form to be filled in when applying; *to fill in an application (form) for a job or a job application (form)*; *attach the cheque to the share application form*; **letter of application** = letter in which someone applies for a job

apply [ə'plaɪ] *verb* **(a)** to ask for something, usually in writing; *to apply for a job*; *to apply for shares*; *to apply in writing*; *to apply in person* **(b)** to affect or to relate to; *this clause applies only to deals outside the EU*

appoint [ə'pɔɪnt] *verb* to choose someone for a job; *to appoint James Smith (to the post of) manager*; *we have appointed a new distribution manager* (NOTE: you appoint a person **to** a job)

appointee [əpɔɪn'tiː] *noun* person who is appointed to a job

appointment [ə'pɔɪntmənt] *noun* **(a)** arrangement to meet; *to make or to fix an appointment for two o'clock*; *to make an appointment with someone for two* o'clock; *he was late for his appointment*; *she had to cancel her appointment*; **appointments book** = desk diary in which appointments are noted **(b)** being appointed to a job; **on his appointment as manager** = when he was made manager; **letter of appointment** = letter in which someone is appointed to a job **(c)** job; **staff appointment** = job on the staff; **appointments vacant** = list (in a newspaper) of jobs which are available

apportion [ə'pɔːʃən] *verb* to share out (costs); *costs are apportioned according to projected revenue*

apportionment [ə'pɔːʃənmənt] *noun* sharing out of (costs)

appraisal [ə'preɪzəl] *noun* calculation of the value of someone or something; **staff appraisals** = reports on how well each member of staff is working

we are now reaching a stage in industry and commerce where appraisals are becoming part of the management culture. Most managers now take it for granted that they will appraise and be appraised
Personnel Management

appraise [ə'preɪz] *verb* to assess or to calculate the value of something or someone

appreciate [ə'priːʃieɪt] *verb* **(a)** to notice how good something is; *the customer always appreciates efficient service*; *tourists do not appreciate long delays at banks* **(b)** *(of currency, shares, etc.)* to increase in value; *the dollar has appreciated in terms of the yen*; *these shares have appreciated by 5%*

appreciation [əpriːʃi'eɪʃən] *noun* **(a)** increase in value; *these shares show an appreciation of 10%*; *the appreciation of the dollar against the peseta* **(b)** valuing something highly; *he was given a rise in appreciation of his excellent work*

faced with further appreciation of the yen, Japanese executives are accelerating their efforts to increase efficiency
Nikkei Weekly

on top of an 11% appreciation of the yen to ¥116.43 for the half-year period, robust trade led to an 8.8% increase in the trade surplus
Nikkei Weekly

apprentice [ə'prentɪs] **1** *noun* young person who works under contract with a skilled workman to learn from him **2** *verb* **to be apprenticed to someone** = to work with a skilled workman to learn from him

apprenticeship [ə'prentɪsʃɪp] *noun* time spent learning a skilled trade; *he served a six-year apprenticeship in the steel works*

appro ['æprəu] *noun* = APPROVAL; **to buy something on appro** = to buy something which you will only pay for if it is satisfactory

approach [ə'prəutʃ] **1** *noun* getting in touch with someone with a proposal; *the company made an approach to the supermarket chain*; *the board turned down all approaches on the subject of mergers*; *we have had an approach from a Japanese company to buy our car division* **2** *verb* to get in touch with someone with a proposal; *he approached the bank with a request for a loan*; *the company was approached by an American publisher with the suggestion of a merger*; *we have been approached several times but have turned down all offers*

appropriate 1 *adjective* [ə'prəupriət] suitable; *I leave it to you to take appropriate action* **2** *verb* [ə'prəuprieɪt] to put a sum of money aside for a special purpose; *to appropriate a sum of money for a capital project*

appropriation [əprəupri'eɪʃən] *noun* act of putting money aside for a special purpose; *appropriation of funds to the reserve*; **appropriation account** = part of a profit and loss account which shows how the profit has been dealt with (i.e. how much has been given to the shareholders as dividends, how much is being put into the reserves, etc.)

approval [ə'pruːvəl] *noun* **(a)** agreement; *to submit a budget for approval*; **certificate of approval** = document showing that an item has been approved officially **(b) on approval** = sale where the buyer only pays for goods if they are satisfactory; *to buy a photocopier on approval*

approve [əˈpruːv] *verb* **(a) to approve of** = to think something is good; *the chairman approves of the new company letter heading*; *the sales staff do not approve of interference from the accounts division* **(b)** to agree to something officially; *to approve the terms of a contract*; *the proposal was approved by the board*

approximate [əˈprɒksɪmət] *adjective* not exact, but almost correct; *the sales division has made an approximate forecast of expenditure*

approximately [əˈprɒksɪmətli] *adverb* almost correctly; *expenditure on marketing is approximately 10% down on the previous quarter*

approximation [əprɒksɪˈmeɪʃən] *noun* rough calculation; *each department has been asked to provide an approximation of expenditure for next year*; *the final figure is only an approximation*

APR = ANNUAL PERCENTAGE RATE

aptitude [ˈæptɪtjuːd] *noun* ability to do something; **aptitude test** = test to see if a candidate is suitable for a certain type of work

arbitrage [ˈɑːbɪtreɪdʒ] *noun* **(a)** selling foreign currency on one market and buying on another at almost the same time to profit from different exchange rates **(b) risk arbitrage** = buying shares in companies which are likely to be taken over and so rise in price; **arbitrage syndicate** = group of people formed to raise the capital to invest in arbitrage deals

arbitrager *or* **arbitrageur** [ˈɑːbɪtreɪdʒə or ɑːbɪtrɑːˈʒɜː] *noun* person whose business is arbitrage

COMMENT: arbitrageurs buy shares in companies which are potential takeover targets, either to force up the price of the shares before the takeover bid, or simply as a position while waiting for the takeover bid to take place. They also sell shares in the company which is expected to make the takeover bid, since one of the consequences of a takeover bid is usually that the price of the target company rises while that of the bidding company falls. Arbitrageurs may then sell the shares in the target company at a profit, either to one of the parties making the takeover bid, or back to the company itself

arbitrate [ˈɑːbɪtreɪt] *verb (of an outside party)* to be chosen by both sides to try to settle an industrial dispute; *she has been asked to arbitrate in the dispute*

arbitration [ɑːbɪˈtreɪʃən] *noun* settling of a dispute by an outside person, chosen by both sides; *the two sides decided to submit the dispute to arbitration or to refer the question to arbitration*; *to take a dispute to arbitration or to go to arbitration*; **arbitration board** *or* **arbitration tribunal** = group which arbitrates; **industrial arbitration tribunal** = court which decides in industrial disputes; *to accept the ruling of the arbitration board*

arbitrator [ˈɑːbɪtreɪtə] *noun* person not concerned with a dispute who is chosen by both sides to try to settle it; *they refused to accept or they rejected the arbitrator's ruling*

arcade [ɑːˈkeɪd] *noun* covered passageway; **shopping arcade** = covered passageway with small shops on either side

archives [ˈɑːkaɪvz] *noun* old documents which are kept safely; *the company's archives go back to its foundation in 1892*; **archive box** = cardboard box in which old documents can be kept

area [ˈeərɪə] *noun* **(a)** measurement of the space taken up by something (calculated by multiplying the length by the width); *the area of this office is 3,400 square feet*; *we are looking for a shop with a sales area of about 100 square metres* **(b)** region of the world; **free trade area** = group of countries practising free trade; **dollar area** = area of the world where the dollar is the main trading currency **(c)** subject; *a problem area or an area for concern* **(d)** district or part of a town; *the office is in the commercial area of the town*; *their factory is in a very good area for getting to the* *motorways and airports* (**e**) part of a country, a division for commercial purposes; *her sales area is the North-West*; *he finds it difficult to cover all his area in a week*

area code ['eərɪə 'kəʊd] *noun* special telephone number which is given to a particular area; *the area code for central London is 0207*

area manager ['eərɪə 'mænɪdʒə] *noun* manager who is responsible for a company's work in a part of the country

argue ['ɑːgjuː] *verb* to discuss something about which you do not agree; *they argued over or about the price*; *we spent hours arguing with the managing director about the site for the new factory*; *the union officials argued among themselves over the best way to deal with the ultimatum from the management* (NOTE: you argue **with** someone **about** *or* **over** something)

argument ['ɑːgjʊmənt] *noun* discussing something without agreeing; *they got into an argument with the customs officials over the documents*; *he was sacked after an argument with the managing director*

around [ə'raʊnd] *preposition* approximately; *the office costs around £2,000 a year to heat*; *his salary is around $85,000*

arrange [ə'reɪndʒ] *verb* (**a**) to put in order; *the office is arranged as an open-plan area with small separate rooms for meetings*; *the files are arranged in alphabetical order*; *can you arrange the invoices in order of their dates?* (**b**) to organize; *we arranged to have the meeting in their offices*; *she arranged for a car to meet him at the airport* (NOTE: you arrange **for** someone to do something; you arrange **for** something to be done; or you arrange **to** do something)

arrangement [ə'reɪndʒmənt] *noun* (**a**) way in which something is organized; *the company secretary is making all the arrangements for the AGM*; **arrangement fee** = charge made by a bank to a client for arranging credit facilities (**b**) settling of a financial dispute; *he came to an arrangement with his creditors*; **scheme of arrangement** = scheme drawn up by an individual or company to offer ways of paying debts, so as to avoid bankruptcy proceedings

on the upside scenario the outlook is reasonably optimistic, bankers say, the worst scenario being that a scheme of arrangement cannot be achieved, resulting in liquidation

Irish Times

arrears [ə'rɪəz] *plural noun* (**a**) money which is owed, but which has not been paid at the right time; *we are pressing the company to pay arrears of interest*; *you must not allow the mortgage payments to fall into arrears*; *salary with arrears effective from January 1st* (**b**) **in arrears** = owing money which should have been paid earlier; *the payments are six months in arrears*; *he is six weeks in arrears with his rent*

arrival [ə'raɪvəl] *noun* reaching a place; *we are waiting for the arrival of a consignment of spare parts*; '**to await arrival**' = note written on an envelope to ask for it to be kept safe until the person it is addressed to arrives; **arrivals** = part of an airport dealing with passengers who are arriving

arrive [ə'raɪv] *noun* (**a**) to reach a place; *the consignment has still not arrived*; *the shipment arrived without any documentation*; *the plane arrives in Sydney at 04.00*; *the train leaves Paris at 09.20 and arrives at Bordeaux two hours later* (NOTE: you arrive **at** or **in** a place or town, but only **in** a country) (**b**) **to arrive at** = to calculate and agree; *they very quickly arrived at an acceptable price*; *after some discussion we arrived at a compromise*

article ['ɑːtɪkl] *noun* (**a**) product or thing for sale; *to launch a new article on the market*; *a black market in luxury articles* (**b**) section of a legal agreement; *see article 8 of the contract* (**c**) **articles of association** = document which lays down the rules for a company regarding the issue of shares, the conduct of meetings, the appointment of directors, etc. (NOTE: in the USA, called **bylaws**); *a director appointed under the articles of the company*; *this procedure is not allowed under the articles of association of the company* US

articles of incorporation = document which sets up a company and lays down the relationship between the shareholders and the company (NOTE: in the UK called **Memorandum of Association**) **(d) articles** = time when a clerk is working in a solicitor's office learning the law (NOTE: officially this is now called a **training contract**, though the old term is still used)

articled clerk ['ɑːtɪkld 'klɑːk] *noun* clerk who is bound by contract to work in a solicitor's office for some years to learn the law (NOTE: officially now called a **trainee solicitor**, though the old term is still used)

articulated lorry *or* **articulated vehicle** [ɑː'tɪkjʊleɪtɪd 'lɒri or ɑː'tɪkjʊleɪtɪd 'viːɪkl] *noun* large lorry formed of two parts, the second pulled by the first

asap ['eɪes'eɪ'piː or 'æsæp] = AS SOON AS POSSIBLE

aside [ə'saɪd] *adverb* to one side, out of the way; **to put aside** *or* **to set aside** = to save (money); *he is putting £50 aside each week to pay for his car*

ask [ɑːsk] *verb* **(a)** to put a question to someone; *he asked the information office for details of companies exhibiting at the motor show*; *ask the salesgirl if the bill includes VAT* **(b)** to tell someone to do something; *he asked the switchboard operator to get him a number in Germany*; *she asked her secretary to fetch a file from the managing director's office*; *customs officials asked him to open his case*

ask for ['ɑːsk 'fɔː] *verb* **(a)** to say that you want or need something; *he asked for the file on 1998 debtors*; *they asked for more time to repay the loan*; *there is a man in reception asking for Mr Smith* **(b)** to put a price on something for sale; *they are asking £24,000 for the car*

asking price ['ɑːskɪŋ 'praɪs] *noun* price which the seller asks for the goods being sold; *the asking price is £24,000*

as per *see* PER

assay mark [ə'seɪ 'mɑːk] *noun* mark put on gold or silver items to show that the metal is of the correct quality

assemble [ə'sembl] *verb* to put a product together from various parts; *the engines are made in Japan and the bodies in Scotland, and the cars are assembled in France*

assembly [ə'sembli] *noun* **(a)** putting an item together from various parts; *there are no assembly instructions to show you how to put the computer together*; **car assembly plant** = factory where cars are put together from parts made in other factories **(b)** official meeting

assembly line [ə'sembli 'laɪn] *noun* production system where the product (such as a car) moves slowly through the factory with new sections added to it as it goes along; *he works on an assembly line or he is an assembly line worker*

assess [ə'ses] *verb* to calculate the value of something; *to assess damages at £1,000*; *to assess a property for the purposes of insurance*

assessment [ə'sesmənt] *noun* calculation of value; *assessment of damages*; *property assessment*; **staff assessments** = reports on how well members of staff are working

asset ['æset] *noun* thing which belongs to a company or person, and which has a value; *he has an excess of assets over liabilities*; *her assets are only £640 as against liabilities of £24,000*; **capital assets** *or* **fixed assets** = property or machinery which a company owns and uses in its business, but which the company does not buy or sell as part of its regular trade; **current assets** = assets used by a company in its ordinary work (such as materials, finished goods, cash, monies due) and which are held for a short time only; **frozen assets** = assets of a company which cannot be sold because someone has a claim against them; **intangible assets** = assets which have a value, but which cannot be seen (such as goodwill, or a patent, or a trademark); **liquid assets** = cash, or investments which can be quickly converted into cash; **personal assets** = moveable assets which belong to a person; **tangible assets** = assets which are visible (such as furniture, jewels or cash); **tangible (fixed) assets** = assets which have a value and actually exist (such as buildings, machines, fittings, etc.); **asset stripper** = person who buys a company to sell its assets; **asset stripping** = buying a company in order to sell its assets; **asset value** = value of a company calculated by adding together all its assets

```
many      companies      are
discovering      that      a
well-recognised  brand  name
can be a priceless asset that
lessens    the    risk    of
introducing a new product
                Duns Business Month
```

assign [əˈsaɪn] *verb* **(a)** to give legally; *to assign a right to someone*; *to assign shares to someone* **(b)** to give someone a job of work; *he was assigned the job of checking the sales figures*

assignation [æsɪgˈneɪʃən] *noun* legal transfer; *the assignation of shares to someone*; *the assignation of a patent*

assignee [æsaɪˈniː] *noun* person who receives something which has been assigned

assignment [əˈsaɪnmənt] *noun* **(a)** legal transfer of a property or of a right; *the assignment of a patent or of a copyright*; *to sign a deed of assignment* **(b)** particular job of work; *he was appointed managing director with the assignment to improve the company's profits*; *the oil exploration team is on an assignment in the North Sea*

assignor [æsaɪˈnɔː] *noun* person who assigns something to someone

assist [əˈsɪst] *verb* to help; *can you assist the stock controller in counting the stock?*; *he assists me with my income tax returns* (NOTE: you assist someone **in** doing something or **with** something)

assistance [əˈsɪstəns] *noun* help; **clerical assistance** = help with office work; **financial assistance** = help in the form of money

assistant [əˈsɪstənt] *noun* person who helps, a clerical employee; **personal assistant** *US* **administrative assistant** = secretary who also helps the boss in various ways; **shop assistant** = person who serves the customers in a shop; **assistant manager** = person who helps a manager

associate [əˈsəʊsɪət] **1** *adjective* linked; **associate company** = ASSOCIATED COMPANY; **associate director** = director

who attends board meetings, but has not been elected by the shareholders **2** *noun* person who works in the same business as someone; *she is a business associate of mine*

associated [əˈsəʊsɪeɪtɪd] *adjective* linked; **associated company** = company which is partly owned by another (though less than 50%), and where the share-owning company exerts some management control or has a close trading relationship with the associate; *Smith Ltd and its associated company, Jones Brothers*

association [əsəʊsɪˈeɪʃən] *noun* **(a)** group of people or of companies with the same interest; *our company has applied to join the trade association*; *the manufacturers' association has sent a letter to the minister* **(b)** **articles of association** = document which lays down the rules for a company regarding the issue of shares, the conduct of meetings, the appointment of directors, etc.; **Memorandum of Association** = document drawn up at the same time as the articles of association of a company, in which the company's objects are defined, the details of the share capital, directors, registered office, etc., are set out (NOTE: in the USA, called **articles of incorporation**)

asst = ASSISTANT

assume [əˈsjuːm] *verb* **(a)** to suppose, to believe something to be true; *I assume you have enough money to pay these expenses?*; *we assume the shipment has arrived on time* **(b)** to take on; *to assume all risks*; *he has assumed responsibility for marketing*

assumption [əˈsʌmpʃən] *noun* **(a)** general belief; *we are working on the assumption that the exchange rate will stay the same* **(b)** taking on; *assumption of risks*

assurance [əˈʃʊərəns] *noun* insurance, an agreement that in return for regular payments, a company will pay compensation for loss of life; *assurance company*; *assurance policy*; **life assurance** = insurance which pays a sum of money when someone dies

assure [ə'ʃuə] *verb* to insure, to have a contract with a company where if regular payments are made, the company will pay compensation if you die; *to assure someone's life*; *he has paid the premiums to have his wife's life assured*; **the life assured** = the person whose life has been covered by the life assurance

assurer *or* **assuror** [ə'ʃuərə] *noun* insurer or company which insures (NOTE: **assure, assurer,** and **assurance** are used in Britain for insurance policies relating to something which will certainly happen (such as death); for other types of policy (i.e., those against something which may or may not happen, such as an accident) use the terms **insure, insurer,** and **insurance**)

at best ['æt 'best] *phrase* **sell at best** = instruction to a stockbroker to sell shares at the best price possible

ATM ['eɪtiː'em] *noun* = AUTOMATED TELLER MACHINE

> Swiss banks are issuing new cards which will allow cash withdrawals from ATMs in Belgium, Denmark, Spain, France, the Netherlands, Portugal and Germany
> *Banking Technology*

> the major supermarket operator is planning a new type of bank that would earn 90% of its revenue from fees on automated teller machine transactions. With the bank setting up ATMs at 7,000 group outlets nationwide, it would have a branch network at least 20 times larger than any of the major banks
> *Nikkei Weekly*

at par ['æt 'pɑː] *phrase* **share at par** = share whose value on the stock market is the same as its face value

at sight ['æt 'saɪt] *phrase* (financial instrument) which is payable when it is presented

attach [ə'tætʃ] *verb* to fasten or to link; *I am attaching a copy of my previous letter*; *please find attached a copy of my letter of June 24th*; *the machine is attached to the*

floor so it cannot be moved; *the bank attaches great importance to the deal*

attaché [ə'tæʃeɪ] *noun* junior diplomat who does special work; **commercial attaché** = diplomat whose job is to promote the commercial interests of his country; **attaché case** = small case for carrying papers and documents

attachment [ə'tætʃmənt] *noun* holding a debtor's property to prevent it being sold until debts are paid; **attachment of earnings** = legal power to take money from a person's salary to pay money, which is owed, to the court

attempt [ə'tempt] **1** *noun* trying to do something; *the company made an attempt to break into the American market*; *the takeover attempt was turned down by the board*; *all his attempts to get a job have failed* **2** *verb* to try; *the company is attempting to get into the tourist market*; *we are attempting the takeover of a manufacturing company*; *he attempted to have the sales director sacked*

attend [ə'tend] *verb* to be present at; *the chairman has asked all managers to attend the meeting*; *none of the shareholders attended the AGM*

attend to [ə'tend tu] *verb* to give careful thought to (something) and deal with it; *the managing director will attend to your complaint personally*; *we have brought in experts to attend to the problem of installing the new computer*

attention [ə'tenʃən] *noun* giving careful thought; *your orders will have our best attention*; **for the attention of (attn** *or* **fao)** = words written on a letter to show that a certain person must see it and deal with it; *mark your letter 'for the attention of the Managing Director'*

attn = FOR THE ATTENTION OF

attorney [ə'tɜːni] *noun* **(a)** person who is legally allowed to act on behalf of someone else; **power of attorney** = legal document giving someone the right to act on someone's behalf in legal matters; *his solicitor was granted power of attorney* **(b)** *US* **attorney-at-law** = lawyer who has a state licence to practise in a court

attract [ə'trækt] *verb* **(a)** to make something or someone join or come in; *the company is offering free holidays in Spain to attract buyers*; *we have difficulty in attracting skilled staff to this part of the country* **(b)** to bring something or someone to something; *the deposits attract interest at 15%*

> airlines offer special stopover rates and hotel packages to attract customers and to encourage customer loyalty
>
> *Business Traveller*

attractive [ə'træktɪv] *adjective* which attracts; **attractive prices** = prices which are cheap enough to make buyers want to buy; **attractive salary** = good salary to make high-quality applicants apply for the job

attributable profit [ə'trɪbjutəbl 'prɒfɪt] *noun* profit which can be shown to come from a particular area of the company's operations

auction ['ɔːkʃən] **1** *noun* selling of goods where people make bids, and the item is sold to the person who makes the highest offer; *their furniture will be sold in the auction rooms next week*; *they announced a sale by auction of the fire-damaged stock*; *the equipment was sold goods by auction or at auction*; **to put something up for auction** = to offer an item for sale at an auction; **Dutch auction** = auction where the auctioneer offers an item for sale at a high price and gradually reduces the price until someone makes a bid **2** *verb* to sell at an auction; *the factory was closed and the machinery was auctioned off*

auctioneer [ɔːkʃə'nɪə] *noun* person who conducts an auction

audio-typing ['ɔːdɪəʊ'taɪpɪŋ] *noun* typing to dictation from a recording

audio-typist ['ɔːdɪəʊ'taɪpɪst] *noun* typist who types to dictation from a recording on a dictating machine

audit ['ɔːdɪt] **1** *noun* examination of the books and accounts of a company; *to carry out the annual audit*; **external audit** *or* **independent audit** = audit carried out by an independent auditor (who is not employed by the company); **internal audit** = audit carried out by a department inside the company; *he is the manager of the internal audit department* **2** *verb* to examine the books and accounts of a company; *Messrs Smith have been asked to audit the accounts*; *the books have not yet been audited*

auditing ['ɔːdɪtɪŋ] *noun* action of examining the books and accounts

auditor ['ɔːdɪtə] *noun* person who audits; *the AGM appoints the company's auditors*; **external auditor** = independent person who audits the company's accounts; **internal auditor** = member of staff who audits a company's accounts; **auditors' report** = report written by a company's auditors after they have examined the accounts of the company (if they are satisfied, the report certifies that, in the opinion of the auditors, the accounts give a 'true and fair' view of the company's financial position)

COMMENT: auditors are appointed by the company's directors and voted by the AGM. In the USA, audited accounts are only required by corporations which are registered with the SEC, but in the UK all limited companies with a turnover over a certain limit must provide audited annual accounts

authenticate [ɔː'θentɪkeɪt] *verb* to say that something is true

authority [ɔː'θɒrəti] *noun* **(a)** power to do something; *he has no authority to act on our behalf* **(b) local authority** = elected section of government which runs a small area of a country; **the authorities** = the government, the people in control

authorization [ɔːθəraɪ'zeɪʃən] *noun* permission or power to do something; *do you have authorization for this expenditure?*; *he has no authorization to act on our behalf*

authorize ['ɔːθəraɪz] *verb* **(a)** to give permission for something to be done; *to authorize payment of £10,000* **(b)** to give someone the authority to do something; *to authorize someone to act on the company's behalf*

> in 1934 Congress authorized President Franklin D.

Roosevelt to seek lower
tariffs with any country
willing to reciprocate
Duns Business Month

authorized [ˈɔːθəraɪzd] *adjective*
permitted; **authorized capital** = amount of
capital which a company is allowed to
have, as stated in the memorandum of
association; **authorized dealer** = person or
company (such as a bank) which is allowed
to buy and sell foreign currency

automated [ˈɔːtəmeɪtɪd] *adjective*
worked automatically by machines; *a fully
automated car assembly plant*;
Automated Teller Machine (ATM) =
machine which gives out cash when a
special card is inserted and special
instructions given; *see also* PIN

automatic [ɔːtəˈmætɪk] *adjective* which
works or takes place without any person
making it happen; *there is an automatic
increase in salaries on January 1st*;
automatic data processing = data
processing done by a computer; **automatic
telling machine** *or* **Automated Teller
Machine (ATM)** = machine which gives
out money when a special card is inserted
and special instructions given; **automatic
vending machine** = machine which
provides drinks, cigarettes, etc., when
coins are put in

automatically [ɔːtəˈmætɪkəli] *adverb*
working without a person giving
instructions; *the invoices are sent out
automatically*; *addresses are typed in
automatically*; *a demand note is sent
automatically when the invoice is overdue*

automation [ɔːtəˈmeɪʃən] *noun* use of
machines to do work with very little
supervision by people

availability [əveɪləˈbɪləti] *noun* being
easily obtained; **offer subject to
availability** = the offer is valid only if the
goods are available

available [əˈveɪləbl] *adjective* which can
be obtained or bought; *this item is
available in all branches*; *an item which is
no longer available*; *these articles are
available to order only*; *funds which are
made available for investment in small
businesses*; **available capital** = capital
which is ready to be used

average [ˈævərɪdʒ] **1** *noun* **(a)** number
calculated by adding together several
figures and dividing by the number of
figures added; *the average for the last
three months or the last three months'
average*; **moving average** = average of
share prices on a stock market, where the
calculation is made over a period which
moves forward regularly (the commonest
are 100-day or 200-day averages, or 10- or
40-week moving averages, where the
average is calculated for the whole period,
and moves forward one day or week at a
time); **weighted average** = average which
is calculated taking several factors into
account, giving some more value than
others **(b) on average** = in general; *on
average, £15 worth of goods are stolen
every day* **(c)** sharing of the cost of damage
or loss of a ship between the insurers and
the owners; **average adjuster** = person
who calculates how much of a maritime
insurance is to be paid by the insurer
against a claim; **general average** = sharing
of the cost of the lost goods by all parties to
an insurance; **particular average** =
situation where part of a shipment is lost or
damaged and the insurance costs are borne
by the owner of the lost goods and not
shared among all the owners of the
shipment **2** *adjective* **(a)** middle (figure);
the average cost per unit is too high; *the
average sales per representative are
rising*; *the average figures for the last
three months*; *the average increase in
prices* **(b)** not very good; *the company's
performance has been only average*; *he is
an average worker* **3** *verb* to produce as an
average figure; *price increases have
averaged 10% per annum*; *days lost
through sickness have averaged
twenty-two over the last four years*

a share with an average rating
might yield 5 per cent and
have a PER of about 10
Investors Chronicle

the average price per
kilogram for this season to
the end of April has been 300
cents
Australian Financial Review

averaged over the three
months ended February, the

merchandise goods deficit was over 5% worse than for the preceding three months

Forbes Magazine

average due date [ˈævərɪdʒ ˈdjuː ˈdeɪt] *noun* the average date when several different payments fall due

average out [ˈævərɪdʒ ˈaʊt] *verb* to come to a figure as an average; *it averages out at 10% per annum*; *sales increases have averaged out at 15%*

averager [ˈævərɪdʒə] *noun* person who buys the same share at various times and at various prices to get an average value

average-sized [ˈævərɪdʒˈsaɪzd] *adjective* not large or small; *they are an average-sized company*; *he has an average-sized office*

averaging [ˈævərɪdʒɪŋ] *noun* buying shares at different times and at different prices to produce an average value

avoid [əˈvɔɪd] *verb* to try not to do something; *the company is trying to avoid bankruptcy*; *my aim is to avoid paying too much tax*; *we want to avoid direct competition with Smith Ltd* (NOTE: you avoid something or avoid **doing** something)

avoidance [əˈvɔɪdəns] *noun* trying not to do something; *avoidance of an agreement or of a contract*; **tax avoidance** = trying (legally) to pay as little tax as possible

avoirdupois [ævədəˈpɔɪz] *noun* non-metric system of weights used in the UK, the USA and other countries (the basic units are the ounce, the pound, the hundredweight and the ton) (NOTE: the system is now no longer officially used in the UK)

COMMENT: avoirdupois weight is divided into drams (16 drams = 1 ounce); ounces (14 ounces = one pound); pounds (100 pounds = 1 hundredweight); hundredweight (20 hundredweight = 1 ton). Avoirdupois weights are slightly heavier than troy weights with the same names: the avoirdupois pound equals 0.45kg, whereas the troy pound equals 0.37kg. See also TROY

await [əˈweɪt] *verb* to wait for; *we are awaiting the decision of the planning department*; *they are awaiting a decision of the court*; *the agent is awaiting our instructions*

award [əˈwɔːd] **1** *noun* decision which settles a dispute or claim; *an award by an industrial tribunal*; *the arbitrator's award was set aside on appeal*; *the latest pay award has been announced* **2** *verb* to decide the amount of money to be given to someone; *to award someone a salary increase*; *he was awarded £10,000 damages in the libel case*; *the judge awarded costs to the defendant*; **to award a contract to someone** = to decide that someone will have the contract to do work

away [əˈweɪ] *adverb* not here, somewhere else; *the managing director is away on business*; *my secretary is away sick*; *the company is moving away from its down-market image*

awkward [ˈɔːkwəd] *adjective* difficult to deal with; *the board is trying to solve the awkward problem of the managing director's son*; *when he asked for the loan the bank started to ask some very awkward questions*; *the suppliers are being very awkward about giving us further credit*

axe *US* **ax** [æks] **1** *noun* **the project got the axe** = the project was stopped **2** *verb* to cut or to stop; *to axe expenditure*; *several thousand jobs are to be axed*

Bb

'B' shares ['biː 'ʃeəz] *plural noun* ordinary shares with special voting rights (often owned by the founder of a company and his family); *see the COMMENT at* '**A**' **SHARES**

baby bonds ['beɪbi 'bɒndz] *plural noun US* bonds in small denominations (i.e. $100) which the small investor can afford to buy

back [bæk] **1** *noun* opposite side to the front; *write your address on the back of the envelope*; *the conditions of sale are printed on the back of the invoice*; *please endorse the cheque on the back* **2** *adjective* referring to the past; **back interest** = interest not yet paid; **back orders** = orders received in the past and not fulfilled (usually because the item is out of stock); *after the strike it took the factory six weeks to clear all the accumulated back orders*; **back pay** = salary which has not been paid; *I am owed £500 in back pay*; **back payment** = paying money which is owed; *the salesmen are claiming for back payment of unpaid commission*; **back payments** = payments which are due; **back rent** = rent due but not paid; *the company owes £100,000 in back rent* **3** *adverb* as things were before; *he will pay back the money in monthly instalments*; *the store sent back the cheque because the date was wrong*; *the company went back on its agreement to supply at £1.50 a unit* **4** *verb* **(a)** **to back someone** = to help someone financially; *the bank is backing him to the tune of £10,000*; *he is looking for someone to back his project* **(b)** **to back a bill** = to sign a bill promising to pay it if the person it is addressed to is not able to do so

the businesses we back range from start-up ventures to established companies in need of further capital for expansion

Times

back burner ['bæk 'bɜːnə] *noun* **to put something on the back burner** = to file a plan or document as the best way of forgetting about it; *the whole project has been put on the back burner*

backdate ['bækdeɪt] *verb* to put an earlier date on a document such as a cheque or an invoice; *backdate your invoice to April 1st*; *the pay increase is backdated to January 1st*

backer ['bækə] *noun* **(a)** person or company that backs someone; *he has an Australian backer*; *one of the company's backers has withdrawn* **(b)** **backer of a bill** = person who backs a bill

background ['bækgraʊnd] *noun* **(a)** past work or experience; *his background is in the steel industry*; *the company is looking for someone with a background of success in the electronics industry*; *she has a publishing background*; *what is his background? or do you know anything about his background?* **(b)** past details; *he explained the background of the claim*; *I know the contractual situation as it stands now, but can you fill in the background details?*

backhander [bæk'hændə] *noun (informal)* bribe, money given to someone to get him to help you; *he was accused of taking backhanders from the company's suppliers*

backing ['bækɪŋ] *noun* **(a)** financial support; *he has the backing of an Australian bank*; *the company will succeed only if it has sufficient backing*;

who is providing the backing for the project? or where does the backing for the project come from? **(b) currency backing** = gold or government securities which maintain the strength of a currency

> the company has received the backing of a number of oil companies who are willing to pay for the results of the survey
>
> *Lloyd's List*

backlog ['bæklɒg] *noun* work (such as orders or letters) which has piled up waiting to be done; *the warehouse is trying to cope with a backlog of orders*; *my secretary can't cope with the backlog of paperwork*

back office ['bæk 'ɒfɪs] *noun* (i) the part of a broking firm where the paperwork involved in buying and selling shares is processed; (ii) *US* part of a bank where cheques are processed, statements of account drawn up, etc.

back out ['bæk 'aʊt] *verb* to stop being part of a deal or an agreement; *the bank backed out of the contract*; *we had to cancel the project when our German partners backed out*

back-to-back loan ['bæktə'bæk 'ləʊn] *noun* loan from one company to another in one currency arranged against a loan from the second company to the first in another currency (used by international companies to get round exchange controls)

back up ['bæk 'ʌp] *verb* **(a)** to support, to help; *he brought along a file of documents to back up his claim*; *the finance director said the managing director had refused to back him up in his argument with the VAT office* **(b)** *(computers)* to copy a file or disk onto another file or disk; *he forgot to back up his files*

backup ['bækʌp] *adjective* supporting or helping; *we offer a free backup service to customers*; *after a series of sales tours by representatives, the sales director sends backup letters to all the contacts*; **backup copy** = copy of a computer disk to be kept in case the original disk is damaged

backwardation [bækwə'deɪʃən] *noun* penalty paid by the seller when postponing delivery of shares to the buyer

bad [bæd] *adjective* not good; **bad bargain** = item which is not worth the price asked; **bad buy** = thing bought which was not worth the money paid for it; **bad cheque** = cheque which is returned to the drawer for any reason; **bad debt** = debt which will not be paid (usually because the debtor has gone out of business) and which has to be written off in the accounts; *the company has written off £30,000 in bad debts*

badge [bædʒ] *noun* piece of plastic or card, which can be clipped to a person's shirt or coat, and on which a name can be written; *all the staff at the exhibition must wear badges*; *visitors have to sign in at reception, and will be given visitors' badges*

bag [bæg] *noun* thing made of paper, cloth, or plastic for carrying items; *he brought his files in a Harrods bag*; *we gave away 5,000 plastic bags at the exhibition*; **shopping bag** = bag used for carrying shopping

baggage ['bægɪdʒ] *noun* suitcases or bags for carrying clothes when travelling; **free baggage allowance** = amount of baggage which a passenger can take with him free on a plane; *US* **baggage cart** = metal holder on wheels, on which baggage can be placed to be moved easily in an airport, train station, etc. (NOTE: British English is **luggage trolley**); **baggage room** = room where cases can be left while passengers are waiting for a plane or train (NOTE: no plural; to show one suitcase, etc., you can say **a piece of baggage**. British English also uses **luggage**)

bail [beɪl] *noun* payment made to a court as guarantee that a prisoner will return after being released; *he was released on bail of $3,000 or he was released on payment of $3,000 bail*; **to stand bail of £3,000 for someone** = to pay £3,000 to a court, as a guarantee that someone will come to face trial (the money will be kept by the court and is refunded if the person comes to face trial); **to jump bail** = not to appear in court after having been released on bail

bail out ['beɪl 'aʊt] *verb* **(a)** to rescue a company which is in financial difficulties **(b) to bail someone out** = to pay money to a court as a guarantee that someone will return to face charges; *she paid $3,000 to bail him out*

the government has decided to bail out the bank which has suffered losses to the extent that its capital has been wiped out

bail-out ['beɪlaʊt] *noun* rescue of a company in financial difficulties

balance ['bæləns] **1** *noun* **(a)** amount to be put in one of the columns of an account to make the total debits and credits equal; **balance in hand** = cash held to pay small debts; **balance brought down** *or* **forward** = the closing balance of the previous period used as the opening balance of the current period; **balance carried down** *or* **forward** = the closing balance of the current period **(b)** rest of an amount owed; *you can pay £100 deposit and the balance within 60 days*; **balance due to us** = amount owed to us which is due to be paid **(c)** **balance of payments** = comparison between total receipts and payments arising from a country's international trade in goods, services and financial transactions; **balance of trade** *or* **trade balance** = international trading position of a country, excluding invisible trade; **adverse** *or* **unfavourable balance of trade** = situation where a country imports more than it exports; **favourable trade balance** = situation where a country exports more than it imports; *the country has had an adverse balance of trade for the second month running* **(d)** **bank balance** = state of an account at a bank at a particular time; **credit balance** = balance in an account showing that more money has been received than is owed; **debit balance** = balance in an account showing that more money is owed than has been received; *the account has a credit balance of £100*; *because of large payments to suppliers, the account has a debit balance of £1,000* **2** *verb* **(a)** *(of two sides in a balance sheet)* to be equal (i.e., the assets owned must always equal the total liabilities plus capital); **the February accounts do not balance** = the two sides are not equal **(b)** to calculate the amount needed to make the

two sides of an account equal; *I have finished balancing the accounts for March* **(c)** to plan a budget so that expenditure and income are equal; *the president is planning for a balanced budget*

balance sheet ['bæləns 'ʃiːt] *noun* statement of the financial position of a company at a particular time, such as the end of the financial year or the end of a quarter, showing the company's assets and liabilities; *the company balance sheet for last year shows a worse position than for the previous year*; *the accountant has prepared the balance sheet for the first half-year*

COMMENT: the balance sheet shows the state of a company's finances at a certain date; the profit and loss account shows the movements which have taken place since the end of the previous accounting period. A balance sheet must balance, with the basic equation that assets (i.e., what the company owns, including money owed to the company) must equal liabilities (i.e., what the company owes to its creditors) plus capital (i.e., what it owes to its shareholders). A balance sheet can be drawn up either in the horizontal form, with (in the UK) liabilities and capital on the left-hand side of the page (in the USA, it is the reverse) or in the vertical form, with assets at the top of the page, followed by liabilities, and capital at the bottom. Most are usually drawn up in the vertical format, as opposed to the more old-fashioned horizontal style

bale [beɪl] **1** *noun* large pack of wool, paper, cotton, etc.; *a bale of cotton*; *2,520 bales of wool were destroyed in the fire* **2** *verb* to tie wool, paper or cotton to make a bale

ballast ['bæləst] *noun* material carried in a ship to give it extra weight, so that it will keep steady even if it is not carrying any cargo

balloon [bə'luːn] *noun* (i) loan where the last repayment is larger than the others; (ii) large final payment on a loan, after a number of periodic smaller loans; *US* **balloon mortgage** = mortgage where the final payment (called a 'balloon payment') is larger than the others

ballot ['bælət] **1** *noun* **(a)** election where people vote for someone by marking a cross on a paper with a list of names; **ballot box** = sealed box into which ballot papers are put; **ballot paper** = paper on which the voter marks a cross to show who he wants to vote for; **postal ballot** = election where the voters send their ballot papers by post; **secret ballot** = election where the voters vote in secret **(b)** selecting by taking papers at random out of a box; *the share issue was oversubscribed, so there was a ballot for the shares* **2** *verb* to take a vote by ballot; *the union is balloting for the post of president*

ballot-rigging ['bælət'rɪgɪŋ] *noun* illegal arranging of the votes in a ballot, so that a particular candidate or party wins

ballpark figure ['bɔːlpɑːk 'fɪgə] *noun* general figure which can be used as the basis for discussion

ban [bæn] **1** *noun* order which forbids someone from doing something; *a government ban on the import of weapons*; *a ban on the export of farm animals*; **overtime ban** = order by a trade union which forbids overtime work by its members; **to impose a ban on smoking** = to make an order which forbids smoking; **to lift the ban on smoking** = to allow people to smoke; **to beat the ban on something** = to do something which is banned - usually by doing it rapidly before a ban is imposed, or by finding a legal way to avoid a ban **2** *verb* to forbid something, to make something illegal; *the council has banned the sale of alcohol at the sports ground* (NOTE: **banning - banned**)

band [bænd] *noun* **(a)** **rubber band** = thin ring of rubber for attaching things together; *put a band round the filing cards to stop them falling on the floor* **(b)** range of figures between low and high, within which a figure can move (used for the range of movement which a currency is allowed to make against other currencies)

bank [bæŋk] **1** *noun* **(a)** business which holds money for its clients, which lends money at interest, and trades generally in money; *Lloyds Bank*; *The First National*

Bank; *The Royal Bank of Scotland*; *he put all his earnings into my bank*; *I have had a letter from my bank telling me my account is overdrawn*; **bank loan** *or* **bank advance** = loan from a bank; *he asked for a bank loan to start his business*; **bank borrowing** = money borrowed from a bank; *the new factory was financed by bank borrowing*; **bank borrowings have increased** = loans given by banks have increased; **bank deposits** = all money placed in banks by customers **(b)** **central bank** = main government-controlled bank in a country, which controls the financial affairs of the country by fixing main interest rates, issuing currency and trying to control the foreign exchange rate; **the Federal Reserve Banks** = central banks in the USA which are owned by the state, and directed by the Federal Reserve Board; **the World Bank** = central bank, controlled by the United Nations, whose funds come from the member states of the UN and which lends money to member states **(c)** **savings bank** = bank where you can deposit money and receive interest on it; **merchant bank** = bank which lends money to companies and deals in international finance; **the High Street banks** = main British banks which accept deposits from and allow withdrawals by individuals **(d)** **data bank** = store of information in a computer **2** *verb* to deposit money into a bank or to have an account with a bank; *he banked the cheque as soon as he received it*; **where do you bank?** = where do you have a bank account?; *I bank at or with Barclays*

bankable ['bæŋkəbl] *adjective* which a bank will accept as security for a loan; *a bankable paper*

bank account ['bæŋk ə'kaunt] *noun* account which a customer has with a bank, where the customer can deposit and withdraw money; *to open a bank account*; *to close a bank account*; *how much money do you have in your bank account?*; *she has £100 in her savings bank account*; *if you let the balance in your bank account fall below £100, you have to pay bank charges*

bank balance ['bæŋk 'bæləns] *noun* state of a bank account at any particular time; *our bank balance went into the red last month*

bank bill ['bæŋk 'bɪl] *noun* **(a)** *GB* bill of exchange by one bank telling another bank (usually in another country) to pay money to someone **(b)** *US* piece of printed paper money

bank book ['bæŋk 'bʊk] *noun* book, given by a bank, which shows money which you deposit or withdraw from your savings account (also called a 'passbook')

bank charges ['bæŋk 'tʃɑːdʒɪz] *plural noun* charges which a bank makes for carrying out work for a customer (NOTE: in American English this is **a service charge**)

bank clerk ['bæŋk 'klɑːk] *noun* person who works in a bank, but not a manager

bank draft ['bæŋk 'drɑːft] *noun* order by one bank telling another bank (usually in another country) to pay money to someone

banker ['bæŋkə] *noun* **(a)** person who is in an important position in a bank; **merchant banker** = person who has a high position in a merchant bank **(b)** generally, a bank; *the company's banker is Barclays*; **banker's bill** = order by one bank telling another bank (usually in another country) to pay money to someone; **banker's order** = order written by a customer asking a bank to make a regular payment; *he pays his subscription by banker's order*

Bank for International Settlements (BIS) *noun* bank (based in Basle) which acts as a clearing bank for the central banks of various countries, through which they settle their currency transactions

bank giro ['bæŋk 'dʒaɪrəʊ] *noun GB* method used by clearing banks to transfer money rapidly from one account to another

bank holiday ['bæŋk 'hɒlədi] *noun* a weekday which is a public holiday when the banks are closed; *New Year's Day is a bank holiday*

banking ['bæŋkɪŋ] *noun* the business of banks; *he is studying banking*; *she has gone into banking*; *US* **banking account** = account which a customer has with a bank; **a banking crisis** = crisis affecting the banks; **banking hours** = hours when a bank is open for its customers; *you cannot*

get money out of the bank after banking hours

bank manager ['bæŋk 'mænɪdʒə] *noun* person in charge of a branch of a bank; *he asked his bank manager for a loan*

bank note *or* **banknote** ['bæŋknəʊt] *noun* piece of printed paper money; *he pulled out a pile of used bank notes* (NOTE: American English is **bill**)

Bank of England ['bæŋk əv 'ɪŋlənd] central British bank, owned by the state, which, together with the Treasury, regulates the nation's finances

> COMMENT: the Bank of England issues banknotes which carry the signatures of its officials. It is the lender of last resort to commercial banks and supervises banking institutions in the UK. Its Monetary Policy Committee is independent of the government, and sets interest rates. The Governor of the Bank of England is appointed by the government

bank on ['bæŋk 'ɒn] *verb* to do something because you are sure something will happen; *he is banking on getting a loan from his father to set up in business*; *do not bank on the sale of your house*

bank rate ['bæŋk 'reɪt] *noun* discount rate of a central bank; formerly, the rate at which the Bank of England lent to other banks (now called the 'base rate')

bankroll ['bæŋkrəʊl] *verb (informal)* to pay for or to finance (a project); *how long can he go on bankrolling his daughter's art gallery?*

bankrupt ['bæŋkrʌpt] **1** *adjective & noun* (person) who has been declared by a court not to be capable of paying his debts and whose affairs are put into the hands of a receiver; *he was adjudicated or declared bankrupt*; *a bankrupt property developer*; *he went bankrupt after two years in business*; **certificated bankrupt** = bankrupt who has been discharged from bankruptcy with a certificate to show he was not at fault; **discharged bankrupt** = person who has been released from being bankrupt because he has paid his debts; **undischarged bankrupt** = person who has been declared bankrupt and has not been released from that state **2** *verb* to make someone become bankrupt; *the recession bankrupted my father*

bankruptcy ['bæŋkrəpsi] *noun* state of being bankrupt; *the recession has caused thousands of bankruptcies*; **adjudication of bankruptcy** *or* **declaration of bankruptcy** = legal order making someone bankrupt; **discharge in bankruptcy** = being released from bankruptcy after paying debts; **to file a petition in bankruptcy** = to apply officially to be made bankrupt, to ask officially for someone else to be made bankrupt

COMMENT: in the UK, 'bankruptcy' is applied only to individual persons, but in the USA the term is also applied to corporations. In the UK, a bankrupt cannot hold public office (for example, he cannot be elected an MP) and cannot be the director of a company. He also cannot borrow money. In the USA, there are two types of bankruptcy: 'involuntary', where the creditors ask for a person or corporation to be made bankrupt; and 'voluntary', where a person or corporation applies to be made bankrupt (in the UK, this is called 'voluntary liquidation')

bank statement ['bæŋk 'steɪtmənt] *noun* written statement from a bank showing the balance of an account at a certain date

bar [bɑː] *noun* **(a)** place where you can buy and drink alcohol; *the sales reps met in the bar of the hotel* **(b)** small shop; **sandwich bar** = small shop where you can buy sandwiches to take away; **snack bar** = small restaurant where you can get simple meals **(c)** thing which stops you doing something; *government legislation is a bar to foreign trade* **(d)** *GB* the profession of barrister; **to be called to the bar** = to become a barrister

bar chart ['bɑː 'tʃɑːt] *noun* chart where values or quantities are shown as columns of different heights

bar code ['bɑː 'kəʊd] *noun* system of lines printed on a product which when read by a computer give a reference number or price

bareboat charter ['beəbəʊt 'tʃɑːtə] *noun* system of chartering a ship where the owner provides only the ship, but not the crew, fuel or insurance

barely ['beəli] *adverb* almost not; *there is barely enough money left to pay the staff*; *she barely had time to call her lawyer before the police arrived*

bargain ['bɑːgɪn] **1** *noun* **(a)** agreement on the price of something; **to strike a bargain** *or* **to make a bargain**; **to drive a hard bargain** = to be a difficult negotiator; **it is a bad bargain** = it is not worth the price **(b)** thing which is cheaper than usual; *that car is a (real) bargain at £500*; **bargain hunter** = person who looks for cheap deals **(c)** sale and purchase of one lot of shares on the Stock Exchange; **bargains done** = number of deals made on the Stock Exchange during a day **2** *verb* to discuss a price for something; *you will have to bargain with the dealer if you want a discount*; *they spent two hours bargaining about* *or* *over the price* (NOTE: you bargain **with** someone **over** *or* **about** *or* **for** something)

bargain basement ['bɑːgɪn 'beɪsmənt] *noun* basement floor in a shop where goods are sold cheaply; **I'm selling this at a bargain basement price** = I'm selling this very cheaply

bargain counter ['bɑːgɪn 'kaʊntə] *noun* counter in a shop where goods are sold cheaply

bargaining ['bɑːgɪnɪŋ] *noun* act of discussing a price, wage increases for workers, etc.; **(free) collective bargaining** = negotiations between employers and workers' representatives over wage increases and conditions; **bargaining power** = strength of one person or group when discussing prices or wage settlements; **bargaining position** = statement of position by one group during negotiations

bargain offer ['bɑːgɪn 'ɒfə] *noun* sale of a particular type of goods at a cheap price; *this week's bargain offer - 30% off all carpet prices*

bargain price ['bɑːgɪn 'praɪs] *noun* cheap price; *these carpets are for sale at a bargain price*

bargain sale ['bɑːgɪn 'seɪl] *noun* sale of all goods in a store at cheap prices

barrel ['bærəl] *noun* **(a)** large round container for liquids; *he bought twenty-five barrels of wine*; *to sell wine by the barrel* **(b)** amount of liquid contained in a barrel; *the price of oil has reached $30 a barrel*

> if signed, the deals would give effective discounts of up to $3 a barrel on Saudi oil
> *Economist*

> US crude oil stocks fell last week by nearly 2.6m barrels
> *Financial Times*

> the average spot price of Nigerian light crude oil for the month of July was 27.21 dollars a barrel
> *Business Times (Lagos)*

barrier ['bærɪə] *noun* thing which stops someone doing something, especially sending goods from one place to another; **customs barriers** *or* **tariff barriers** = customs duty intended to make trade more difficult; **to impose trade barriers on certain goods** = to restrict the import of certain goods by charging high duty; *the unions have asked the government to impose trade barriers on foreign cars*; **to lift trade barriers from imports** = to remove restrictions on imports; *the government has lifted trade barriers on foreign cars*

> a senior European Community official has denounced Japanese trade barriers, saying they cost European producers $3 billion a year
> *Times*

> to create a single market out of the EC member states, physical, technical and tax barriers to free movement of trade between member states had to be removed. Imposing VAT on importation of goods from other member states was seen as one such tax barrier
> *Accountancy*

barrister ['bærɪstə] *noun GB (especially in England)* lawyer who can speak or argue a case in one of the higher courts

barter ['bɑːtə] **1** *noun* system where goods are exchanged for other goods and not sold for money; **barter agreement** *or* **barter arrangement** *or* **barter deal** = agreement to exchange goods by barter; *the company has agreed a barter deal with Bulgaria* **2** *verb* to exchange goods for other goods, but not buy them for money; *they agreed a deal to barter tractors for barrels of wine*

> under the barter agreements, Nigeria will export 175,000 barrels a day of crude oil in exchange for trucks, food, planes and chemicals
> *Wall Street Journal*

bartering ['bɑːtərɪŋ] *noun* act of exchanging goods for other goods and not for money

base [beɪs] **1** *noun* **(a)** lowest or first position; *turnover increased by 200%, but starting from a low base*; **(bank) base rate** = basic rate of interest on which the actual rate a bank charges on loans to its customers is calculated; *US* **base pay** = pay for a job which does not include extras such as overtime pay or bonuses; **base year** = first year of an index, against which later years' changes are measured; *see also* DATABASE **(b)** place where a company has its main office or factory, place where a businessman has his office; *the company has its base in London and branches in all European countries*; *he has an office in Madrid which he uses as a base while he is travelling in Southern Europe* **2** *verb* **(a)** to start to calculate or to negotiate from a position; *we based our calculations on the forecast turnover*; **based on** = calculating from; *based on last year's figures*; *based on population forecasts* **(b)** to set up a company or a person in a place; *the European manager is based in our London office*; *our overseas branch is based in the Bahamas*; *a London-based sales executive*

> the base lending rate, or prime rate, is the rate at

which banks lend to their top
corporate borrowers

Wall Street Journal

other investments include a
large stake in the
Chicago-based insurance
company

Lloyd's List

basement ['beɪsmənt] *noun* section of a shop which is underground; **bargain basement** = basement floor in a shop where goods are sold cheaply; *I am selling this at a bargain basement price*

basic ['beɪsɪk] **1** *adjective* **(a)** normal; **basic pay** *or* **basic salary** *or* **basic wage** *US* **base pay** = normal salary without extra payments; **basic discount** = normal discount without extra percentages; *our basic discount is 20%, but we offer 5% extra for rapid settlement* **(b)** most important; **basic commodities** = ordinary farm produce, produced in large quantities (such as corn, rice, sugar, etc.) **(c)** simple, from which everything starts; *he has a basic knowledge of the market*; *to work at the cash desk, you need a basic qualification in maths*

basically ['beɪsɪkli] *adverb* seen from the point from which everything starts

basics ['beɪsɪks] *plural noun* simple and important facts; *he has studied the basics of foreign exchange dealing*; **to get back to basics** = to consider the main facts again

basis ['beɪsɪs] *noun* **(a)** point or number from which calculations are made; *we forecast the turnover on the basis of a 6% price increase* **(b)** general terms of agreement; **on a short-term** *or* **long-term basis** = for a short or long period; *he has been appointed on a short-term basis*; *we have three people working on a freelance basis* (NOTE: the plural is **bases**)

basket ['bɑːskɪt] *noun* **(a)** container made of thin pieces of wood, metal, plastic, etc.; *a basket of apples*; **filing basket** = container kept on a desk for documents which have to be filed; **shopping basket** = basket used for carrying shopping; **waste paper basket** *US* **wastebasket** = container into which paper or pieces of rubbish can be thrown **(b)** group of prices or currencies taken as a standard; *the pound has fallen against a basket of European currencies*; *the price of the average shopping basket US the market basket has risen by 6%* **(c)** *(informal)* **basket case** = company which is in financial difficulties and is not likely to recover

the weekly adjusted average
total basket price of £37.89
was just 3p more than the week
before Christmas

The Grocer

batch [bætʃ] **1** *noun* **(a)** group of items which are made at one time; *this batch of shoes has the serial number 25-02* **(b)** group of documents which are processed at the same time; *today's batch of invoices is ready to be mailed*; *the factory is working on yesterday's batch of orders*; *the accountant signed a batch of cheques*; *we deal with the orders in batches of fifty at a time*; **batch processing** = system of data processing where information is collected into batches before being loaded into the computer **2** *verb* to put items together in groups; *to batch invoices or cheques*

batch number ['bætʃ 'nʌmbə] *noun* number attached to a batch; *when making a complaint always quote the batch number on the packet*

battery ['bætəri] *noun* small object for storing electric power; *the calculator needs a new battery*; *a battery-powered calculator*

battle ['bætl] *noun* fight; **boardroom battles** = arguments between directors; **circulation battle** = fight between two newspapers to sell more copies in the same section of the market

bay [beɪ] *noun* **loading bay** = section of road in a warehouse, where lorries can drive in to load or unload

b/d = BARRELS PER DAY, BROUGHT DOWN

bear [beə] **1** *noun (Stock Exchange)* person who sells shares because he thinks the price will fall and he will be able to buy them again more cheaply later; **bear market** = period when Stock Exchange prices fall because shareholders are selling since they believe the market will fall further (NOTE: the opposite is **bull**) **2** *verb* **(a)** to give interest; *government bonds which* bear 5% interest **(b)** to have (a name), to have something written on it; *the cheque bears the signature of the company secretary*; *an envelope which bears a London postmark*; *a letter bearing yesterday's date*; *the share certificate bears his name* **(c)** to pay costs; *the costs of the exhibition will be borne by the company*; *the company bore the legal costs of both parties* (NOTE: **bearing - bore - has borne**)

bearer ['beərə] *noun* person who holds a cheque or certificate; **the cheque is payable to bearer** = is paid to the person who holds it, not to any particular name written on it

bearer bond ['beərə 'bɒnd] *noun* bond which is payable to the bearer and does not have a name written on it

bearing ['beərɪŋ] *adjective* which bears, which produces; *certificates bearing interest at 5%*; *interest-bearing deposits*

beat [biːt] *verb* **(a)** to win in a fight against someone; *they have beaten their rivals into second place in the computer market* **(b)** to beat a ban = to do something which is forbidden by doing it rapidly before the ban is enforced (NOTE: **beating - beat - has beaten**)

become [bɪ'kʌm] *verb* to change into something different; *the export market has become very difficult since the rise in the dollar*; *the company became very profitable in a short time* (NOTE: **becoming - became - has become**)

bed-and-breakfast deal
['bedənd'brekfəst 'diːl] *noun* formerly, an arrangement where shares were sold one day and bought back the following day, in order to establish a profit or loss for tax declaration (doing such deals was called 'bed-and-breakfasting')

> COMMENT: this is no longer possible, since a period of thirty days has to elapse between the sale and repurchase of the same shares to allow a new price to be established

begin [bɪ'gɪn] *verb* to start; *the company began to lose its market share*; *he began to write the report which the shareholders had asked for*; *the auditors' report began*

with a description of the general principles adopted (NOTE: you begin something *or* begin **to do** something *or* begin **with** something. Note also: **beginning - began - has begun**)

beginning [bɪ'gɪnɪŋ] *noun* first part; *the beginning of the report gives a list of the directors and their shareholdings*

behalf [bɪ'hɑːf] *noun* **on behalf of** = acting for (someone or a company); *I am writing on behalf of the minority shareholders*; *she is acting on my behalf*; *solicitors acting on behalf of the American company*

behind [bɪ'haɪnd] **1** *preposition* at the back, after; *the company is No. 2 in the market, about £4m behind their rivals* **2** *adverb* **we have fallen behind our rivals** = we have fewer sales or make less profit than our rivals; **the company has fallen behind with its deliveries** = it is late with its deliveries

believe [bɪ'liːv] *verb* to think that something is true; *we believe he has offered to buy 25% of the shares*; *the chairman is believed to be in South America on business*

belong [bɪ'lɒŋ] *verb* **(a)** to belong to = to be the property of; *the company belongs to an old American banking family*; *the patent belongs to the inventor's son* **(b)** to **belong with** = to be in the correct place with; *those documents belong with the sales reports*

below [bɪ'ləʊ] *preposition* lower down than or less than; *we sold the property at below the market price*; *you can get a ticket for New York at below £150 on the Internet*

below-the-line [bɪ'ləʊðə'laɪn] *adjective & adverb* **below-the-line expenditure** = (i) payments which do not arise from a company's normal activities (such as redundancy payments); (ii) extraordinary items which are shown in the profit and loss account below net profit after taxation (as opposed to exceptional items which are included in the figure for profit before taxation); **below-the-line advertising** = advertising which is not paid for (such as work by staff manning an exhibition) and for which no commission is paid to the advertising agency; *compare* ABOVE THE LINE

benchmark ['bentʃmɑːk] *noun* figure which is important, and can be used to compare with other figures

> the US bank announced a cut in its prime, the benchmark corporate lending rate, from 10½% to 10%
> *Financial Times*

> the dollar dropped below three German marks - a benchmark with more psychological than economic significance - for the first time since October
> *Fortune*

> the benchmark 11¾% due 2003/2007 was quoted at 107 11/32, down 13/32 from Monday
> *Wall Street Journal*

beneficial [benɪ'fiʃəl] *adjective* **beneficial occupier** = person who occupies a property but does not own it fully; **beneficial interest** = interest which allows someone to occupy or receive rent from a property, but not to own it

beneficiary [benɪ'fiʃəri] *noun* person who gains money from something; *the beneficiaries of a will*

> the pound sterling was the main beneficiary of the dollar's weakness
> *Business Times (Lagos)*

benefit ['benɪfit] **1** *noun* **(a)** payments which are made to someone under a national or private insurance scheme; *she receives £75 a week as unemployment benefit*; *the sickness benefit is paid monthly*; *the insurance office sends out benefit cheques each week*; **death benefit** = money paid to the family of someone who dies in an accident at work **(b) fringe benefits** = extra items given by a company to workers in addition to their salaries (such as company cars, private health insurance) **2** *verb* **(a)** to make better or to improve; *a fall in inflation benefits the exchange rate* **(b) to benefit from** *or* **by something** = to be improved by something, to gain more money because of something; *exports have benefited from the fall in the*

exchange rate; *the employees have benefited from the profit-sharing scheme*

> the retail sector will also benefit from the expected influx of tourists
> *Australian Financial Review*

> what benefits does the executive derive from his directorship? Compensation has increased sharply in recent years and fringe benefits for directors have proliferated
> *Duns Business Month*

> salary is negotiable to £30,000, plus car and a benefits package appropriate to this senior post
> *Financial Times*

> California is the latest state to enact a program forcing welfare recipients to work for their benefits
> *Fortune*

> salary range is $54,957 - $81,189, with a competitive benefits package
> *Washington Post*

bequeath [bɪ'kwiːð] *verb* to leave property, money, etc. (but not freehold land) to someone in a will

bequest [bɪ'kwest] *noun* giving of property, money, etc. (but not freehold land), to someone in a will; *he made several bequests to his staff*

berth [bɜːθ] **1** *noun* place in a harbour where a ship can tie up **2** *verb* to tie up at a berth; *the ship will berth at Rotterdam on Wednesday*

best [best] **1** *adjective* very good, better than all others; *his best price is still higher than all the other suppliers*; *last year was the company's best year ever* **2** *noun* very good effort; *the salesmen are doing their best, but the stock simply will not sell at that price*

best-seller ['best'selə] *noun* item (especially a book) which sells very well

best-selling ['best'selɪŋ] *adjective* which sells very well; *these computer disks are our best-selling line*

bet [bet] **1** *noun* amount deposited when you risk money on the result of a race or of a game **2** *verb* to risk money on the result of something; *he bet £100 on the result of the election*; *I bet you £25 the dollar will rise against the pound*; **betting tax** = tax levied on betting on horses, dogs, etc. (NOTE: **betting - bet - has bet**)

better ['betə] *adjective* very good compared with something else; *this year's results are better than last year's*; *we will shop around to see if we can get a better price*

Better Business Bureau ['betə 'bɪznəs 'bjuərəu] *US* organization of local business executives that promotes better business practices in their town

beware [bɪ'weə] *verb* to be careful; **beware of imitations** = be careful not to buy cheap low-quality items which are made to look like more expensive items

b/f = BROUGHT FORWARD

bi- [baɪ] *prefix* twice; **bi-monthly** = twice a month; **bi-annually** = twice a year

bid [bɪd] **1** *noun* **(a)** offer to buy something at a certain price; **to make a bid for something** = to offer to buy something; *he made a bid for the house*; *the company made a bid for its rival*; **to make a cash bid** = to offer to pay cash for something; **to put in a bid for something** *or* **to enter a bid for something** = to offer (usually in writing) to buy something; **bid price** = price at which investors sell shares or units in a unit trust (the opposite, i.e., the buying price, is called the 'offer price'; the difference between the two is the 'spread') **(b)** *(at an auction)* **opening bid** = first bid; **closing bid** = last bid at an auction, the bid which is successful **(c)** offer to do some work at a certain price; *he made the lowest bid for the job* **(d)** *US* offer to sell something at a certain price; *they asked for bids for the supply of spare parts* **(e)** **takeover bid** = offer to buy all or a majority of shares in a company so as to control it; *they made make a takeover bid for the company*; *he had to withdraw his takeover bid when he failed to find any backers*; **the company rejected the takeover bid** = the directors recommended that the shareholders should not accept it **2**

verb (at an auction) **to bid for something** = to offer to buy something; **he bid £1,000 for the jewels** = he offered to pay £1,000 for the jewels (NOTE: **bidding - bid - has bid**)

bidder ['bɪdə] *noun* person who makes a bid (usually at an auction); *several bidders made offers for the house*; **the property was sold to the highest bidder** = to the person who had made the highest bid or who offered the most money; **the tender will go to the lowest bidder** = to the person who offers the best terms or the lowest price for services

bidding ['bɪdɪŋ] *noun* action of making offers to buy (usually at an auction); **the bidding started at £1,000** = the first and lowest bid was £1,000; **the bidding stopped at £250,000** = the last bid (and the successful bid) was for £250,000; **the auctioneer started the bidding at £100** = he suggested that the first bid should be £100

Big Bang ['bɪg 'bæŋ] *noun* the change in practices on the London Stock Exchange, with the introduction of electronic trading on October 27th 1986

> COMMENT: the changes included the abolition of stock jobbers and the removal of the system of fixed commissions; the Stock Exchange trading floor closed and deals are now done by phone or computer or on the Internet

Big Board ['bɪg 'bɔːd] *noun* *US (informal)* = NEW YORK STOCK EXCHANGE

> at the close, the Dow Jones Industrial Average was up 24.25 at 2,559.65, while New York S.E. volume totalled 180m shares. Away from the Big Board, the American S.E. Composite climbed 2.31 to 297.87
>
> *Financial Times*

bilateral [baɪ'lætərəl] *adjective* between two parties or countries; *the minister signed a bilateral trade agreement*

> trade between Japan and China will probably exceed $30 billion this year to mark a record high. Ministry of

Finance trade statistics show that bilateral trade in the first half of the year totalled $16.60 billion, up 29.7% from a year earlier

Nikkei Weekly

bill [bɪl] **1** *noun* **(a)** written list of charges to be paid; *the salesman wrote out the bill*; *does the bill include VAT?*; *the bill is made out to Smith Ltd*; *the builder sent in his bill*; *he left the country without paying his bills*; **to foot the bill** = to pay the costs **(b)** list of charges in a restaurant; *can I have the bill please?*; *the bill comes to £20 including service*; *does the bill include service?*; *the waiter has added 10% to the bill for service* **(c)** written paper promising to pay money; **bills payable (B/P)** = bills (especially bills of exchange) which a company will have to pay (to its creditors); **bills receivable (B/R)** = bills (especially bills of exchange) which are due to be paid by a company's debtors; **due bills** = bills which are owed but not yet paid; *see also* BILL OF EXCHANGE **(d) bill of lading** = list of goods being shipped, which the transporter gives to the person sending the goods to show that the goods have been loaded **(e)** *US* piece of paper money; *a $5 bill* (British English for this is **note** *or* **banknote**) **(f) bill of sale** = document which the seller gives to the buyer to show that the sale has taken place **(g)** draft of a new law which will be discussed in Parliament **2** *verb* to present a bill to someone so that it can be paid; *the builders billed him for the repairs to his neighbour's house*

billing ['bɪlɪŋ] *noun US* writing of invoices or bills

bill of exchange ['bɪl əv ɪks'tʃeɪnʒ] *noun* document signed by the person authorizing it, which tells another to pay money unconditionally to a named person on a certain date (usually used in payments in foreign currency); **accommodation bill** = bill of exchange where the person signing is helping someone else to raise a loan; **bank bill** = bill of exchange endorsed by a bank; **bill broker** = discount house, a firm which buys and sells bills of exchange for a fee; **demand bill** = bill of exchange which must be paid when payment is asked for; **trade bill** = bill of exchange between

two companies who are trading partners; **to accept a bill** = to sign a bill of exchange to show that you promise to pay it; **to discount a bill** = to sell a bill of exchange at a lower price than that written on it in order to cash it before its maturity date

COMMENT: a bill of exchange is a document raised by a seller and signed by a purchaser, stating that the purchaser accepts that he owes the seller money, and promises to pay it at a later date. The person raising the bill is the 'drawer', the person who accepts it is the 'drawee'. The seller can then sell the bill at a discount to raise cash. This is called a 'trade bill'. A bill can also be accepted (i.e. guaranteed) by a bank, and in this case it is called a 'bank bill'

billion ['bɪljən] one thousand million (NOTE: in the USA it has always meant one thousand million, but in British English it formerly meant one million million, and it is still sometimes used with this meaning. With figures it is usually written **bn**: **$5bn** say 'five billion dollars')

gross wool receipts for the selling season to end June 30 appear likely to top $2 billion

Australian Financial Review

at its last traded price the bank was capitalized at around $1.05 billion

South China Morning Post

bin [bɪn] *noun* **(a)** large container; **dump bin** = display container like a large round box, filled with cheap goods for sale **(b)** separate section of shelves in a warehouse; **bin card** = stock record card in a warehouse

bind [baɪnd] *verb* to tie or to attach; *the company is bound by its articles of association*; *he does not consider himself bound by the agreement which was signed by his predecessor* (NOTE: **binding - bound**)

binder ['baɪndə] *noun* **(a)** stiff cardboard cover for papers; **ring binder** = cover with rings in it which fit into special holes made in sheets of paper **(b)** *US* temporary agreement for insurance sent before the insurance policy is issued (NOTE: the British

English for this is **cover note**) **(c)** *US* money paid as part of the initial agreement to purchase property (NOTE: the British English for this is **deposit**)

binding ['baɪndɪŋ] *adjective* which legally forces someone to do something; *a binding contract*; *this document is not legally binding*; *the agreement is binding on all parties* = all parties signing it must do what is agreed

BIS = BANK FOR INTERNATIONAL SETTLEMENTS

bit [bɪt] *noun* smallest unit of information on a computer

black [blæk] **1** *adjective* **(a) black market** = buying and selling goods or currency in a way which is not allowed by law (as in a time of rationing); *there is a flourishing black market in spare parts for cars*; *you can buy gold coins on the black market*; **to pay black market prices** = to pay high prices to get items which are not easily available **(b) black economy** = goods and services which are paid for in cash, and therefore not declared for tax **(c) in the black** = in credit; *the company has moved into the black*; *my bank account is still in the black* **2** *verb* to forbid trading in certain goods or with certain suppliers; *three firms were blacked by the government*; *the union has blacked a trucking firm*

Black Friday ['blæk 'fraɪdeɪ] *noun* any sudden collapse on a stock market (called after the first major collapse of the US stock market on 24th September, 1869)

blackleg ['blækleg] *noun* worker who goes on working when there is a strike

black list ['blæk 'lɪst] *noun* list of goods, people or companies which have been blacked

blacklist ['blæklɪst] *verb* to put goods, people or a company on a black list; *his firm was blacklisted by the government*

Black Monday ['blæk 'mʌndi] Monday, 19th October, 1987, when world stock markets crashed

Black Tuesday ['blæk 'tjuːzdi] Tuesday, 29th October, 1929, when the US stock market crashed

Black Wednesday ['blæk 'wenzdi] Wednesday, 16th September, 1992, when the pound sterling left the European Exchange Rate Mechanism and was devalued against other currencies

COMMENT: not always seen as 'black', since some people believe it was a good thing that the pound left the ERM

blame [bleɪm] **1** *noun* saying that someone has done something wrong, that someone is responsible; *the sales staff got the blame for the poor sales figures* **2** *verb* to say that someone has done something wrong or is responsible for a mistake; *the managing director blamed the chief accountant for not warning him of the loss*; *the union is blaming the management for poor industrial relations*

blank [blæŋk] **1** *adjective* with nothing written; **a blank cheque** = a cheque with no amount of money or name written on it, but signed by the drawer **2** *noun* space on a form which has to be completed; *fill in the blanks and return the form to your local office*

blanket ['blæŋkɪt] *noun* **blanket agreement** = agreement which covers many items; **blanket insurance (cover)** = insurance which covers various items (such as a house and its contents); **blanket refusal** = refusal to accept many different items

blind testing ['blaɪnd 'testɪŋ] *noun* testing a product on consumers without telling them what brand it is

blip [blɪp] *noun* short period when movement forwards or upwards is stopped; *this month's bad trade figures are only a blip*

whether these pressures are just a cyclical blip in a low inflation era, or whether the UK is drifting back to the bad old days will be one of the crucial questions for the stock market this year
Financial Times

blister pack ['blɪstə 'pæk] *noun* type of packing where the item for sale is covered with a stiff plastic sheet sealed to a card backing

block [blɒk] **1** *noun* **(a)** series of items grouped together; *he bought a block of 6,000 shares*; **block booking** = booking of several seats or rooms at the same time; *the company has a block booking for twenty seats on the plane or for ten rooms at the hotel*; **block vote** = voting of a large number of votes at the same time (such as those of a delegation at a conference) **(b)** series of buildings forming a square with streets on all sides; *they want to redevelop a block in the centre of the town*; a **block of offices** *or* an **office block** = a large building which only contains offices **(c)** **block capitals** *or* **block letters** = capital letters (as A,B,C); *write your name and address in block letters* **2** *verb* to stop something taking place; *he used his casting vote to block the motion*; *the planning committee blocked the redevelopment plan*; **blocked currency** = currency which cannot be taken out of a country because of exchange controls; *the company has a large account in blocked roubles*

blue [bluː] *adjective* **blue-chip investments** *or* **blue-chip shares** *or* **blue chips** = low risk shares in good companies; **blue-collar worker** = manual worker in a factory; **blue-collar union** = trade union formed mainly of blue-collar workers; *US* **Blue Laws** = regulations governing business activities on Sundays

> soaring blue-chips and offshore buying helped Australian shares to a new high yesterday. The market opened higher as hopes of an interest rate cut buoyed sentiment
>
> *West Australian*

blurb [blɜːb] *noun* piece of advertising, especially an advertisement written by a publisher for a book

bn [ˈbɪljən] = BILLION

board [bɔːd] **1** *noun* **(a)** *see* BOARD OF DIRECTORS **(b)** group of people who run an organization, trust or society; **advisory board** = group of advisors; **editorial board** = group of editors;

training board = government organization set up by each industry to provide and coordinate training for that industry **(c)** **on board** = on a ship, plane or train; **free on board** (f.o.b.) = price includes all the seller's costs until the goods are on the ship for transportation **(d)** large flat piece of wood or card; **clipboard** = stiff board with a clip at the top so that a piece of paper can be clipped to the board to allow you to write on it easily; **noticeboard** = board fixed to a wall where notices can be put up **2** *verb* to go on to a ship, plane or train; *customs officials boarded the ship in the harbour*

boarding card *or* **boarding pass** [ˈbɔːdɪŋ ˈkɑːd or ˈbɔːdɪŋ ˈpɑːs] *noun* card given to passengers who have checked in for a flight or for a sailing to allow them to board the plane or ship

board of directors [ˈbɔːd əv daɪˈrektəz] *noun* **(a)** *GB* group of directors elected by the shareholders to run a company; *the bank has two representatives on the board*; *he sits on the board as a representative of the bank*; *two directors were removed from the board at the AGM*; *she was asked to join the board* = she was asked to become a director; **board meeting** = meeting of the directors of a company **(b)** *US* group of people elected by the shareholders to draw up company policy and to appoint the president and other executive officers who are responsible for managing the company; *see also the comment at* DIRECTOR

> a proxy is the written authorization an investor sends to a stockholder meeting conveying his vote on a corporate resolution or the election of a company's board of directors
>
> *Barrons*

> CEOs, with their wealth of practical experience, are in great demand and can pick and choose the boards they want to serve on
>
> *Duns Business Month*

boardroom [ˈbɔːdrʊm] *noun* room where the directors of a company meet;

boardroom battles = arguments between directors

boat [bəut] *noun* ship; *he travelled to South America, working on a cargo boat*; *we took the night boat to Belgium*; *boats for Greece leave every morning*

bona fide ['bəunə 'faɪdi] *adjective* trustworthy, which can be trusted; **a bona fide offer** = an offer which is made honestly

bonanza [bə'nænzə] *noun* great wealth; very profitable business; *the oil well was a bonanza for the company*; *last year was a bonanza year for the electronics industry*

bond [bɒnd] *noun* (a) contract document promising to repay money borrowed by a company or by the government at a certain date, and paying interest at regular intervals; **government bonds** *or* **treasury bonds** = bonds issued by the central government; **municipal bond** *or* **local authority bond** = bond issued by a town or district; **bearer bond** = bond which is payable to the bearer and does not have a name written on it; **debenture bond** = certificate showing that a debenture has been issued; **mortgage bond** = certificate showing that a mortgage exists and that property is security for it; *GB* **premium bond** = government bond, part of the National Savings scheme, which pays no interest, but gives the owner the chance to win a weekly or monthly prize (b) **goods (held) in bond** = goods held by customs until duty has been paid; **entry of goods under bond** = bringing goods into a country in bond; **to take goods out of bond** = to pay duty on goods so that they can be released by customs

COMMENT: bonds are in effect another form of long-term borrowing by a company or government. They can carry a fixed interest or a floating interest, but the yield varies according to the price at which they are bought; bond prices go up and down in the same way as share prices

bonded ['bɒndɪd] *adjective* held in bond; **bonded warehouse** = warehouse where goods are stored in bond until duty is paid

bondholder ['bɒndhəuldə] *noun* person who holds government bonds

bond-washing ['bɒndwɒʃɪŋ] *noun* selling American Treasury bonds with the interest coupon, and buying them back ex coupon, so as to reduce tax

bonus ['bəunəs] *noun* (a) extra payment (in addition to a normal payment); **capital bonus** = extra payment by an insurance company which is produced by capital gain; **cost-of-living bonus** = money paid to meet the increase in the cost of living; **Christmas bonus** = extra payment made to staff at Christmas; **incentive bonus** = extra pay offered to a worker to encourage him to work harder; **productivity bonus** = extra payment made because of increased productivity (b) **bonus issue** = scrip issue or capitalization issue, where a company transfers money from reserves to share capital and issues free extra shares to the shareholders (the value of the company remains the same, and the total market value of shareholders' shares remains the same, the market price of each share falls to account for the new shares); **bonus share** = extra share given to an existing shareholder (c) **no-claims bonus** = reduction of premiums on an insurance because no claims have been made (NOTE: plural is **bonuses**)

book [buk] **1** *noun* (a) set of sheets of paper attached together; **a company's books** = the financial records of a company; **account book** = book which records sales and purchases; **cash book** = ledger which records cash received and paid out; **order book** = book which records orders received; **the company has a full order book** = it has sufficient orders to keep the workforce occupied; **purchase book** = records of purchases; **sales book** = records of sales; **book sales** = sales as recorded in the sales book; **book value** = value as recorded in the company's books (b) **bank book** = book which shows money which you have deposited or withdrawn from a bank account; **cheque book** = book of new cheques; **phone book** *or* **telephone book** = book which lists names of people or companies with their addresses and telephone numbers **2** *verb* to order or to reserve something; *to book a room in a hotel or a table at a restaurant or a ticket on a plane*; *I booked a table for*

7.45; *he booked a ticket through to Cairo*; **to book someone into a hotel** *or* **onto a flight** = to order a room *or* a plane ticket for someone else; *he was booked on the 09.00 flight to Zurich*; **the hotel** *or* **the flight is fully booked** *or* **is booked up** = all the rooms or seats are reserved; *the restaurant is booked up over the Christmas period*

booking ['bʊkɪŋ] *noun* act of ordering a room or a seat; *hotel bookings have fallen since the end of the tourist season*; **booking clerk** = person who sells tickets in a booking office; **booking office** = office where you can book seats at a theatre or tickets for the railway; **block booking** = booking of several seats or rooms at the same time; **to confirm a booking** = to say that a booking is certain; **double booking** = booking by mistake of two people into the same hotel room or the same seat on a plane

bookkeeper ['bʊkkiːpə] *noun* person who keeps the financial records of a company

bookkeeping ['bʊkkiːpɪŋ] *noun* keeping of the financial records of a company or an organization; **single-entry bookkeeping** = recording only one entry per transaction (usually in the cash book); **double-entry bookkeeping** = system of bookkeeping where both debit and credit entries are recorded in the accounts at the same time (e.g., when a sale is credited to the sales account the purchaser's debt is debited to the debtors account)

booklet ['bʊklət] *noun* small book with a paper cover

bookseller ['bʊkselə] *noun* person who sells books

bookshop ['bʊkʃɒp] *noun* shop which sells books

bookstall ['bʊkstɔːl] *noun* small open bookshop (as in a railway station)

bookstore ['bʊkstɔː] *noun US* bookshop

bookwork ['bʊkwɜːk] *noun* keeping of financial records

boom [buːm] **1** *noun* time when sales, production or business activity are increasing; *a period of economic boom*; *the boom of the 1970s*; **boom industry** = industry which is expanding rapidly; **a**

boom share = share in a company which is expanding; **the boom years** = years when there is an economic boom **2** *verb* to expand, to become prosperous; *business is booming*; *sales are booming*

booming ['buːmɪŋ] *adjective* which is expanding or becoming prosperous; *a booming industry* *or* *company*; *technology is a booming sector of the economy*

boost [buːst] **1** *noun* help to increase; *this publicity will give sales a boost*; *the government hopes to give a boost to industrial development* **2** *verb* to make something increase; *we expect our publicity campaign to boost sales by 25%*; *the company hopes to boost its market share*; *incentive schemes are boosting production*

> the company expects to boost turnover this year to FFr 16bn from FFr 13.6bn last year
> *Financial Times*

booth [buːð] *noun* **(a)** small place for one person to stand or sit; **telephone booth** = public box with a telephone; **ticket booth** = small wooden building where a person sells tickets **(b)** *US* section of a commercial fair where a company exhibits its products or services (NOTE: the British English for this is a **stand**)

borrow ['bɒrəʊ] *verb* to take money from someone for a time, possibly paying interest for it, and repaying it at the end of the period; *he borrowed £1,000 from the bank*; *the company had to borrow heavily to repay its debts*; *they borrowed £25,000 against the security of the factory*; **to borrow short** *or* **long** = to borrow for a short or long period

borrower ['bɒrəʊə] *noun* person who borrows; *borrowers from the bank pay 12% interest*

borrowing ['bɒrəʊɪŋ] *noun* **(a)** action of borrowing money; *the new factory was financed by bank borrowing*; **borrowing power** = amount of money which a company can borrow **(b) borrowings** = money borrowed; *the company's borrowings have doubled*; **bank borrowings** = loans made by banks

> we tend to think of building societies as having the best

borrowing rates and indeed many do offer excellent terms
Financial Times

> COMMENT: borrowings are sometimes shown as a percentage of shareholders' funds (i.e. capital and money in reserves); this gives a percentage which is the 'gearing' of the company

boss [bɒs] *noun (informal)* employer, person in charge of a company or an office; *if you want a pay rise, go and talk to your boss*; *he became a director when he married the boss's daughter*

bottleneck ['bɒtlnek] *noun* position when business activity is slowed down because one section of the operation cannot cope with the amount of work; *a bottleneck in the supply system*; *there are serious bottlenecks in the production line*

bottom ['bɒtəm] **1** *noun* lowest part or point; **sales have reached rock bottom** = the very lowest point of all; **the bottom has fallen out of the market** = sales have fallen below what previously seemed to be the lowest point; **bottom price** = lowest price; **rock-bottom price** = lowest price of all; **bottom line** = last line on a profit-and-loss account indicating the total profit or loss; **the boss is interested only in the bottom line** = he is only interested in the final profit **2** *verb* **to bottom (out)** = to reach the lowest point; **the market has bottomed out** = has reached the lowest point and does not seem likely to fall further

bottomry ['bɒtəmri] *noun* mortgage of a ship to pay for repairs

bought [bɔːt] *see* BUY; **bought ledger** = set of accounts recording money owed to each supplier (i.e., the creditors of the company); **bought ledger clerk** = office worker who deals with the bought ledger

bounce [baʊns] *verb (of a cheque)* to be returned by the bank to the person who has tried to cash it, because there is not enough money in the payer's account to pay it; *he paid for the car with a cheque that bounced*

bounty ['baʊnti] *noun* government subsidy made to help an industry

boutique [buːˈtiːk] *noun* small specialized shop, especially for up-to-date clothes; section of a department store selling up-to-date clothes; *a jeans boutique*; *a ski boutique*

box [bɒks] *noun* **(a)** cardboard, wood or plastic container; *the goods were sent in thin cardboard boxes*; *the watches are prepacked in plastic display boxes*; **paperclips come in boxes of two hundred** = packed two hundred to a box; **box file** = file (for papers) made like a box **(b)** **box number** = reference number used in a post office or an advertisement to avoid giving an address; *please reply to Box No. 209*; *our address is: P.O. Box 74209, Edinburgh* **(c)** **cash box** = metal box for keeping cash; **letter box** *or* **mail box** = place where incoming mail is put; **call box** = outdoor telephone kiosk

boxed [bɒkst] *adjective* put in a box, sold in a box; **boxed set** = set of items sold together in a box

boycott ['bɔɪkɒt] **1** *noun* refusal to buy or to deal in certain products; *the union organized a boycott against or of imported cars* **2** *verb* to refuse to buy or to deal in a certain product; *we are boycotting all imports from that country*; *the management has boycotted the meeting* = has refused to attend the meeting

B/P = BILLS PAYABLE

B/R = BILLS RECEIVABLE

bracket ['brækɪt] **1** *noun* group of items or people taken together; **people in the middle-income bracket** = people with average incomes, not high or low; **he is in the top tax bracket** = he pays the highest level of tax **2** *verb* **to bracket together** = to treat several items together in the same way; *in the sales reports, all the European countries are bracketed together*

brainstorming ['breɪnstɔːmɪŋ] *noun* intensive discussion by a small group of people as a method of producing new ideas or solving problems

branch [brɑːntʃ] **1** *noun* local office of a bank or large business; local shop of a large chain of shops; *we are out of stock of that item - try our Oxford Street branch*; *the bank or the store has branches in most towns in the south of the country*; *the* *insurance company has closed its branches in South America*; *he is the manager of our local branch of Lloyds bank*; *we have decided to open a branch office in Chicago*; *the manager of our branch in Lagos or of our Lagos branch*; **branch manager** = manager of a branch **2** *verb* **to branch out** = to start a new (but usually related) type of business; *from car retailing, the company branched out into car leasing*

```
a  leading  manufacturer  of
business,  industrial  and
commercial products requires
a branch manager to head up
its   mid-western   Canada
operations based in Winnipeg
                Globe and Mail (Toronto)
```

brand [brænd] *noun* make of product, which can be recognized by its name or by its design which gives the company making it an advantage over its competitors; *the top-selling brands of toothpaste*; *the company is launching a new brand of soap*; **brand leader** = the brand with the largest market share; **brand name** = name of a brand; **brand image** = idea of a product which is associated with the brand name; **brand loyalty** = loyalty by the customer who always buys the same brand; **brand recognition** = being able to recognise a brand on sight; **Brand X** = the anonymous brand used in TV commercials to compare with the brand being advertised; **own brand** = name of a store which is used on products which are specially packed for that store

```
the  multiple  brought  the
price down to £2.49 in some
stores. We had not agreed to
this deal and they sold out
very  rapidly.  When  they
reordered we would not give it
to them. This kind of activity
is bad for the brand and we
cannot afford it
                         The Grocer
```

branded ['brændɪd] *adjective* **branded goods** = goods sold under brand names

brand new ['bræn 'njuː] *adjective* quite new, very new

breach [briːtʃ] *noun* failure to carry out the terms of an agreement; **breach of**

contract = failing to do something which is in a contract; **the company is in breach of contract** = it has failed to carry out the duties of the contract; **breach of warranty** = supplying goods which do not meet the standards of the warranty applied to them

break [breɪk] **1** *noun* short space of time, when you can rest; *she keyboarded for two hours without a break*; **coffee break** *or* **tea break** = rest time during work when the workers can drink coffee or tea **2** *verb* **(a)** to fail to carry out the duties of a contract; *the company has broken the contract or the agreement by selling at a lower price*; **to break an engagement to do something** = not to do what has been agreed **(b)** to cancel (a contract); *the company is hoping to be able to break the contract* (NOTE: **breaking - broke - has broken**)

breakages ['breɪkɪdʒɪz] *plural noun* breaking of items; *customers are expected to pay for breakages*

break down ['breɪk 'daʊn] *verb* **(a)** to stop working because of mechanical failure; *the fax machine has broken down*; *what do you do when your photocopier breaks down?* **(b)** to stop; *negotiations broke down after six hours* **(c)** to show all the items in a total list of costs or expenditure; *we broke the expenditure down into fixed and variable costs*; *can you break down this invoice into spare parts and labour?*

breakdown ['breɪkdaʊn] *noun* **(a)** stopping work because of mechanical failure; *we cannot communicate with our Nigerian office because of the breakdown of the telephone lines* **(b)** stopping talking; *a breakdown in wage negotiations* **(c)** showing details item by item; *give me a breakdown of investment costs*

break even ['breɪk 'iːvən] *verb* to balance costs and receipts, but not make a profit; *last year the company only just broke even*; *we broke even in our first two months of trading*

breakeven point [breɪk'iːvn 'pɔɪnt] *noun* point at which sales cover costs, but do not show a profit

break off ['breɪk 'ɒf] *verb* to stop; *we broke off the discussion at midnight*;

management broke off negotiations with the union

break up ['breɪk 'ʌp] *verb* **(a)** to split something large into small sections; *the company was broken up and separate divisions sold off* **(b)** to come to an end; *the meeting broke up at 12.30*

bribe [braɪb] **1** *noun* money given to someone in authority to get him or her to help; *the minister was dismissed for taking bribes* **2** *verb* to pay someone money to get him or her to do something for you; *we had to bribe the minister's secretary before she would let us see her boss*

bridging loan ['brɪdʒɪŋ 'ləʊn] *US* **bridge loan** ['brɪdʒ 'ləʊn] *noun* short-term loan to help someone buy a new house when his old one has not yet been sold

brief [briːf] **1** *noun* instructions given to someone; *he went into the negotiations with the brief to get a deal at any price* **2** *verb* to explain to someone in detail; *the salesmen were briefed on the new product*; *the managing director briefed the board on the progress of the negotiations*

briefcase ['briːfkeɪs] *noun* case with a handle for carrying papers and documents; *he put all the files into his briefcase*

briefing ['briːfɪŋ] *noun* telling someone details; *all salesmen have to attend a sales briefing on the new product*

bring [brɪŋ] *verb* to come to a place with someone or something; *he brought his documents with him*; *the finance director brought his secretary to take notes of the meeting*; **to bring a lawsuit against someone** = to tell someone to appear in court to settle an argument (NOTE: **bringing - brought**)

bring down ['brɪŋ 'daʊn] *verb* **(a)** to reduce; *petrol companies have brought down the price of oil* **(b)** = BRING FORWARD (b)

bring forward ['brɪŋ 'fɔːwəd] *verb* **(a)** to make earlier; *to bring forward the date of repayment*; *the date of the next meeting has been brought forward to March* **(b)** to take an account balance from the end of the previous period as the starting point for the current period; *balance brought down or forward: £365.15*

bring in ['brɪŋ 'ɪn] *verb* to earn (an interest); *the shares bring in a small amount*

bring out ['brɪŋ 'aʊt] *verb* to produce something new; *they are bringing out a new model of the car for the Motor Show*

bring up ['brɪŋ 'ʌp] *verb* to refer to something for the first time; *the chairman brought up the question of redundancy payments*

brisk [brɪsk] *adjective* selling actively; *sales are brisk*; *the market in oil shares is particularly brisk*; *a brisk market in technology shares*

broadside ['brɔːdsaɪd] *noun* *US* publicity leaflet

brochure ['brəʊʃə] *noun* publicity booklet; *we sent off for a brochure about holidays in Greece or about postal services*

broke [brəʊk] *adjective* (*informal*) having no money; *the company is broke*; *he cannot pay for the new car because he is broke*; **to go broke** = to become bankrupt

broker ['brəʊkə] *noun* **(a)** dealer who acts as a middleman between a buyer and a seller; **foreign exchange broker** = person who buys and sells foreign currency on behalf of other people; **insurance broker** = person who sells insurance to clients; **ship broker** = person who sells shipping or transport of goods to clients; *see also* HONEST **(b)** **(stock)broker** = person or firm that buys or sells shares for clients

brokerage *or* **broker's commission** ['brəʊkərɪdʒ *or* 'brəʊkəz kə'mɪʃən] *noun* payment to a broker for a deal carried out

broking ['brəʊkɪŋ] *noun* dealing in stocks and shares

brought down (b/d) *or* **brought forward (b/f)** ['brɔːt 'daʊn *or* 'brɔːt 'fɔːwəd] *phrase* balance in an account from the previous period taken as the starting point for the current period; *balance brought down or forward: £365.15*

brownfield site ['braʊnfiːld 'saɪt] *noun* site for a new housing development which was originally the site of a factory; *compare* GREENFIELD

B2B ['biːtuːˈbi] = BUSINESS-TO-BUSINESS two businesses doing business on the Internet; **B2B web site** = web site that is designed to help businesses trade with each other on the Internet

buck ['biːtuːˈsi] = BUSINESS-TO-CONSUMER a business that trades with consumers and the general public (not with other businesses); **B2C web site** = an online shop that sells products to consumers via its web site

bubble ['bʌbl] *noun* **bubble envelope** = envelope lined with a sheet of plastic with bubbles in it, which protects the contents of the envelope; **bubble pack** = *see* BLISTER PACK; **bubble wrap** = sheet of clear plastic with bubbles of air in it, used as a protective wrapping material

buck [bʌk] **1** *noun US (informal)* dollar; **to make a quick buck** = to make a profit very quickly **2** *verb* **to buck the trend** = to go against the trend

bucket shop ['bʌkɪt 'ʃɒp] *noun (informal)* **(a)** travel agent selling airline tickets at a discount **(b)** *US* dishonest stockbroking firm where customers' orders to buy and sell stock are treated as bets on the rise and fall of prices

> at last something is being done about the thousands of bucket shops across the nation that sell investment scams by phone
>
> *Forbes Magazine*

budget ['bʌdʒɪt] **1** *noun* **(a)** plan of expected spending and income (usually for one year); *to draw up a budget*; *we have agreed the budgets for next year*; **advertising budget** = money planned for spending on advertising; **cash budget** = plan of cash income and expenditure; **overhead budget** = plan of probable overhead costs; **publicity budget** = money allowed for expected expenditure on publicity; **sales budget** = plan of probable sales **(b) the Budget** = the annual plan of taxes and government spending proposed by a finance minister (in the UK, the Chancellor of the Exchequer); *the minister put forward a budget aimed at boosting*

the economy; **to balance the budget** = to plan income and expenditure so that they balance; *the president is planning for a balanced budget* **(c)** *(in a bank)* **budget account** = bank account where you plan income and expenditure to allow for periods when expenditure is high, by paying a set amount each month **(d)** *(in shops)* cheap; **budget department** = cheaper department; **budget prices** = low prices **2** *verb* to plan probable income and expenditure; *we are budgeting for £10,000 of sales next year*

> he budgeted for further growth of 150,000 jobs (or 2.5 per cent) in the current financial year
>
> *Sydney Morning Herald*

> the minister is persuading the oil, gas, electricity and coal industries to target their advertising budgets towards energy efficiency
>
> *Times*

> the Federal government's budget targets for employment and growth are within reach according to the latest figures
>
> *Australian Financial Review*

> an increasing number of business travellers from the US or Europe are becoming budget conscious and are spending less on hotel accommodation
>
> *South China Morning Post*

budgetary ['bʌdʒɪtəri] *adjective* referring to a budget; **budgetary control** = keeping check on spending; **budgetary policy** = policy of planning income and expenditure; **budgetary requirements** = spending or income required to meet the budget forecasts

budgeting ['bʌdʒɪtɪŋ] *noun* preparing of budgets to help plan expenditure and income

buffer stocks ['bʌfə 'stɒks] *noun* stocks of a commodity bought by an international body when prices are low and held to resell at a time when prices have risen (the intention is to prevent sharp movements in world prices of the commodity)

build [bɪld] *verb* to make by putting pieces together; *the new director's job is to build a sales structure*; *he want to demolish the old factory and build an office block on the site*; **to build on past experience** = to use experience as a base on which to act in the future (NOTE: **building - built**)

building ['bɪldɪŋ] *noun* house, factory, office block, etc.; *they have redeveloped the site of the old office building*; **the Shell Building** = the office block where the head office of Shell is

building and loan association ['bɪldɪŋ ənd 'ləʊn əsəʊsɪ'eɪʃən] *noun US* = SAVINGS AND LOAN ASSOCIATION

building society ['bɪldɪŋ sə'saɪəti] *noun GB* financial institution which accepts and pays interest on deposits, and lends money to people who are buying property against the security of the property which is being bought; *he put his savings into a building society or into a building society account*; *I have an account with the Chelsea Building Society*; *I saw the building society manager to ask for a mortgage*

COMMENT: building societies mainly invest the money deposited with them as mortgages on properties, but a percentage is invested in government securities. Societies can now offer a range of banking services, such as cheque books, standing orders, overdrafts, etc., and now operate in much the same way as banks. Indeed, many building societies have changed from 'mutual status' where the owners of the society are its investors and borrowers, to become publicly-owned banks whose shares are bought and sold on the stock exchange. The comparable US institutions are the Savings & Loan Associations, or 'thrifts'

build into ['bɪld 'ɪntʊ] *verb* to add something to something being set up; *you must build all the forecasts into the budget*; **we have built 10% for contingencies into our cost forecast** = we have added 10% to our basic forecast to allow for items which may appear suddenly

build up ['bɪld 'ʌp] *verb* **(a)** to create something by adding pieces together; *he bought several shoe shops and gradually built up a chain* **(b)** to expand something gradually; *to build up a profitable business*; *to build up a team of salesmen*

buildup ['bɪldʌp] *noun* gradual increase; *a buildup in sales or a sales buildup*; *there will be a big publicity buildup before the launch of the new model*

built-in ['bɪlt'ɪn] *adjective* forming part of the system or of a machine; *the PC has a built-in modem*; *the accounting system has a series of built-in checks*

bulk [bʌlk] *noun* large quantity of goods; **in bulk** = in large quantities; *to buy rice in bulk*; **bulk buying** *or* **bulk purchase** = buying large quantities of goods at a lower price; **bulk carrier** = ship which carries large quantities of loose goods (such as coal); **bulk discount** = discount given to a purchaser who buys in bulk; **bulk shipments** = shipments of large quantities of goods

bulky ['bʌlki] *adjective* large and awkward; *the Post Office does not accept bulky packages*

bull [bʊl] *noun (Stock Exchange)* dealer who believes the market will rise, and therefore buys shares to sell at a higher price later; **bull market** = period when share prices rise because people are optimistic and buy shares (NOTE: the opposite is **bear**)

> lower interest rates are always a bull factor for the stock market
>
> *Financial Times*

bullion ['bʊljən] *noun* gold or silver bars; *a shipment of gold bullion was stolen from the security van*; *the price of bullion is fixed daily*

bullish ['bʊlɪʃ] *adjective* optimistic, felling that prices of shares will rise

> another factor behind the currency market's bullish mood may be the growing realisation that Japan stands to benefit from the current

combination of high domestic interest rates and a steadily rising exchange rate

Far Eastern Economic Review

currency traders chose to ignore better unemployment statistics from France, preferring to focus on the bullish outlook for the dollar

Times

bumper ['bʌmpə] *noun* very large crop; *a bumper crop of corn*; **1999 was a bumper year for computer sales** = 1999 was an excellent year for sales

bumping ['bʌmpɪŋ] *noun US* situation where a senior employee takes the place of a junior (in a restaurant or in a job)

bureau ['bjuərəu] *noun* office which specializes in a certain service; **computer bureau** = office which offers to do work on its computers for companies which do not own their own computers; **employment bureau** = office which finds jobs for people; **information bureau** = office which gives information; **trade bureau** = office which specializes in commercial enquiries; **visitors' bureau** = office which deals with visitors' questions; **word-processing bureau** = office which specializes in word-processing; *we farm out the office typing to a local bureau* (NOTE: the plural is **bureaux**)

bureau de change ['bjuərəu də 'ʃɑːnʒ] *noun* office where you can change foreign currency

burn [bɜːn] *verb* to destroy by fire; *the chief accountant burnt the documents before the police arrived* (NOTE: **burning - burnt**)

burn down ['bɜːn 'daun] *verb* to destroy (a building) completely in a fire; *the warehouse burnt down and all the stock was destroyed*; *the company records were all lost when the offices were burnt down*

bus [bʌs] *noun* motor vehicle for carrying passengers; *he goes to work by bus*; *she took the bus to go to her office*; **bus company** = company which runs the buses in a town

bushel ['buʃl] *noun* measure of dry goods, such as corn (= 56 pounds)

business ['bɪznəs] *noun* **(a)** occupation or trade; *business is expanding*; *business is slow*; *he does a thriving business in repairing cars*; *what's your line of business?*; **business call** = visit to talk to someone on business; **business centre** = part of a town where the main banks, shops and offices are located; **business class** = type of airline travel which is less expensive than first class and more comfortable than tourist class; **business college** *or* **business school** = place where commercial studies are taught; **business correspondent** = journalist who writes articles on business news for newspapers; **business cycle** = period during which trade expands, then slows down and then expands again; **business efficiency exhibition** = exhibition which shows products (computers, word-processors) which help businesses to be efficient; **business hours** = time (usually 9.30 a.m. to 5.30 p.m.) when a business is open; **business letter** = letter about commercial matters; **business lunch** = lunch to discuss business matters; **business plan** = document drawn up to show how a business is planned to work, with cash flow forecasts, sales forecasts, etc. (often used when trying to raise a loan, or when setting up a new business); **business trip** = trip to discuss business matters with clients; **to be in business** = to be in a commercial firm; **to go into business** = to start a commercial firm; *he went into business as a car dealer*; **to go out of business** = to stop trading; *the firm went out of business during the recession*; **the chairman is in Holland on business** (b) commercial company; *he owns a small car repair business*; *she runs a business from her home*; *he set up in business as an insurance broker*; **business address** = details of number, street and town where a company is located; **business card** = card showing a businessman's name and the name and address of the company he works for; **business correspondence** = letters concerned with a business; **business equipment** = machines used in an office; **business expenses** = money spent on running a business, not on stock or assets; **big business** = very large commercial firms; **small businesses** = small commercial concerns **(c)** affairs discussed; *the main business of the meeting was finished by 3 p.m.*; **any other business (AOB)** = item at the end of an agenda, where any matter can be raised

business agent ['bɪznəs 'eɪdʒənt] *noun US* chief local official of a trade union

businessman *or* **businesswoman** ['bɪznɪsmæn *or* 'bɪznɪswʊmən] *noun* man or woman engaged in business; **she's a good businesswoman** = she is good at commercial deals; **a small businessman** = man who owns a small business

bust [bʌst] *adjective (informal)* **to go bust** = to become bankrupt; *the company went bust last month*

busy ['bɪzi] *adjective* occupied in doing something or in working; *he is busy preparing the annual accounts*; *the manager is busy at the moment, but he will be free in about fifteen minutes*; *the busiest time of year for stores is the week before Christmas*; *summer is the busy season for hotels*; **the line is busy** = the telephone line is being used

buy [baɪ] **1** *verb* to get something by paying money; *he bought 10,000 shares*; *the company has been bought by its leading supplier*; *to buy wholesale and sell retail*; **to buy forward** = to buy foreign currency before you need it, in order to be sure of the exchange rate (NOTE: **buying - bought**) **2** *noun* **(a) good buy** *or* **bad buy** = thing bought which is or is not worth the money paid for it; *that watch was a good buy*; *this car was a bad buy* **(b)** thing which should be bought; *those shares are a definite buy*

buy back ['baɪ 'bæk] *verb* to buy something which you sold earlier; *he sold the shop last year and is now trying to buy it back*

buyback ['baɪbæk] *noun* **share buyback** *US* **stock buyback** = arrangement where a company buys its own shares on the stock market

the corporate sector also continued to return cash to shareholders in the form of buy-backs, while raising

little money in the form of new or rights issues

buyer ['baɪə] *noun* **(a)** person who buys; **there were no buyers** = no one wanted to buy; **a buyer's market** = market where products are sold cheaply because there are few people who want to buy them (NOTE: the opposite is a **seller's market**); **buyer's risk** = risk taken by a buyer when accepting goods or services without a guarantee; **impulse buyer** = person who buys something when he sees it, not because he was planning to buy it **(b)** person who buys stock on behalf of a trading organization for resale or for use in production; **head buyer** = most important buyer in a store; *she is the shoe buyer for a London department store*; *he is the paper buyer for a large magazine chain*

buy in ['baɪ 'ɪn] *verb (of a seller at an auction)* to buy the thing which you are trying to sell because no one will pay the price you want

buyin ['baɪɪn] *noun* **management buyin** = purchase of a company by a group of outside directors

buying ['baɪɪŋ] *noun* getting something for money; **bulk buying** = getting large quantities of goods at low prices; **forward buying** *or* **buying forward** = buying shares, commodities or currency for delivery at a later date; **impulse buying** = buying items which you have just seen, not because you had planned to buy them; **panic buying** = rush to buy something at any price because stocks may run out; **buying department** = department in a company which buys raw materials or goods for use in the company; **buying power** = ability to buy; *the buying power of the pound has fallen over the last five years*

buyout ['baɪaʊt] *noun* **management buyout (MBO)** = takeover of a company by a group of employees (usually managers and directors); **leveraged buyout (LBO)** = buying all the shares in a company by borrowing money against the security of the shares to be bought

we also invest in companies whose growth and

```
profitability   could   be
improved   by   a   management
buyout
```
Times

```
in a normal leveraged buyout,
the acquirer raises money by
borrowing against the assets
or cash flow of the target
company
```
Fortune

bylaws ['baɪlɔːz] *noun* **(a)** rule made by a local authority or organization, and not by central government **(b)** *US* rules governing the internal running of a corporation (the number of meetings, the appointment of officers, etc.) (NOTE: in the UK, called **Articles of Association**)

by-product ['baɪprɒdʌkt] *noun* product made as a result of manufacturing a main product

byte [baɪt] *noun* storage unit in a computer, equal to one character

Cc

cab [kæb] *noun* taxi, a car which takes people from one place to another for money; *he took a cab to the airport*; *the office is only a short cab ride from the railway station*; *cab fares are very high in New York*

cab driver *(Informal)* **cabbie** ['kæbi] *noun* driver of a cab

cabinet ['kæbɪnət] *noun* piece of furniture for storing records or display; **filing cabinet** = piece of furniture, made of metal, with wide deep drawers so that files (called 'suspension files') can be hooked inside them; *we need two more four-drawer filing cabinets*; *last year's correspondence is in the bottom drawer of the filing cabinet*; **display cabinet** = piece of furniture with a glass top or glass doors for showing goods for sale

cable ['keɪbl] **1** *noun* telegram, message sent by telegraph; *he sent a cable to his office asking for more money*; **cable address** = specially short address for sending cables **2** *verb* to send a message or money by telegraph; *he cabled his office to ask them to send more money*; *the office cabled him £1,000 to cover his expenses*

calculate ['kælkjʊleɪt] *verb* **(a)** to find the answer to a problem using numbers; *the bank clerk calculated the rate of exchange for the dollar* **(b)** to estimate; *I calculate that we have six months' stock left*

calculating machine ['kælkjʊleɪtɪŋ məˈʃiːn] *noun* machine which calculates; *she added up the sales figures on the calculating machine next to the typewriter*

calculation [kælkjʊˈleɪʃən] *noun* answer to a problem in mathematics; *according to my calculations, we have six months'*

stock left; **rough calculation** = approximate answer; *I made some rough calculations on the back of an envelope*; **we are £20,000 out in our calculations** = we have £20,000 too much or too little

calculator ['kælkjʊleɪtə] *noun* electronic machine which works out the answers to problems in mathematics; *my pocket calculator needs a new battery*; *he worked out the discount on his calculator*

calendar ['kæləndə] *noun* book, set of sheets of paper showing the days and months in a year, often attached to pictures; *for the New Year the garage sent me a calendar with photographs of old cars*; **calendar month** = a whole month as on a calendar, from the 1st to the 30th or 31st; *ninety days' credit is almost three calendar months*; **calendar year** = year from the 1st January to 31st December

call [kɔːl] **1** *noun* **(a)** conversation on the telephone; **local call** = call to a number on the same exchange as your own; **national call** = call to any part of the country more than 56km from your own exchange; **regional call** = call to a number within 56km of your own exchange; **trunk call** *or* **long-distance call** = call to a number in a different zone or area; **overseas call** *or* **international call** = call to another country; **person-to-person call** = call where you ask the operator to connect you with a named person; **collect call** *or* **reverse charge call** *or* **transferred charge call** = call where the person receiving the call agrees to pay for it; **to make a call** = to dial and speak to someone on the telephone; **to take a call** = to answer the telephone; **to log calls** = to note all details of telephone calls made **(b)** demand for repayment of a loan by a lender; **money at**

call *or* **money on call** *or* **call money** = money loaned for which repayment can be demanded without notice **(c)** *(Stock Exchange)* demand to pay for new shares which then become paid up; **call option** = option to buy shares at a future date and at a certain price (NOTE: the opposite, an option to sell, is a **put option**) **(d)** visit; *the salesmen make six calls a day*; **business call** = visit to talk to someone on business; **cold call** = telephone call or sales visit where the salesman has no appointment and the client is not an established customer; **call rate** = number of calls (per day or per week) made by a salesman **2** *verb* **(a)** to telephone to someone; *I'll call you at your office tomorrow* **(b) to call on someone** = to visit someone; *our salesmen call on their best accounts twice a month* **(c)** to ask someone to do something; **the union called a strike** = the union told its members to go on strike

callable bond ['kɔːləbl 'bɒnd] *noun* bond which can be redeemed before it matures

call-back pay ['kɔːlbæk 'peɪ] *noun* pay given to a worker who has been called back to work after his normal working hours

call box ['kɔːl 'bɒks] *noun* outdoor telephone kiosk; *he phoned the office from a call box near the railway station*

call centre ['kɔːl 'sentə] *noun* central office, where telephone calls are received, as in a mail-order operation or telephone banking system; *all complaints are dealt with by the call centre*

called up capital ['kɔːld ʌp 'kæpɪtl] *noun* share capital in a company which has been called up but not yet paid for

```
a circular to shareholders
highlights that the company's
net assets as at August 1,
amounted to £47.9 million -
less than half the company's
called-up share capital of
£96.8 million. Accordingly,
an EGM has been called for
October 7
                           Times
```

caller ['kɔːlə] *noun* **(a)** person who telephones **(b)** person who visits

call in ['kɔːl 'ɪn] *verb* **(a)** to visit; *their sales representative called in twice last week* **(b)** to telephone to make contact; *we ask the reps to call in every Friday to report the weeks' sales* **(c)** to ask for a debt to be paid

call off ['kɔːl 'ɒf] *verb* to ask for something not to take place; *the union has called off the strike*; *the deal was called off at the last moment*

call up ['kɔːl 'ʌp] *verb* to ask for share capital to be paid

calm [kɑːm] *adjective* quiet, not excited; *the markets were calmer after the government statement on the exchange rate*

campaign [kæm'peɪn] **1** *noun* planned method of working; **sales campaign** = planned work to achieve higher sales; **publicity campaign** *or* **advertising campaign** = planned period when publicity takes place; *they are working on a campaign to launch a new brand of soap* **2** *verb* to work in an organized way to get something; *they are campaigning for better pay for low-paid workers*

cancel ['kænsəl] *verb* **(a)** to stop something which has been agreed or planned; *to cancel an appointment or a meeting*; *the government has cancelled the order for a fleet of buses* **(b) to cancel a cheque** = to stop payment of a cheque which has been signed (NOTE: British English is **cancelling - cancelled** but American English spelling is **canceling - canceled**)

cancellation [kænsə'leɪʃən] *noun* stopping something which has been agreed or planned; *cancellation of an appointment*; *cancellation of an agreement*; **cancellation clause** = clause in a contract which states the terms on which the contract may be cancelled

cancel out ['kænsəl 'aʊt] *verb (of two things)* to balance and so make each other invalid; *the two clauses cancel each other out*; *higher costs have cancelled out the increased sales revenue*

candidate ['kændɪdət] *noun* person who applies for a job; *there are six candidates for the post of assistant manager*; *we have called three candidates for interview*

canteen [kæn'tiːn] *noun* restaurant which belongs to a factory or office, where the staff can eat

canvass ['kænvəs] *verb* to visit people to ask them to buy goods, to vote or to say what they think; *he's canvassing for customers for his hairdresser's shop*; *we have canvassed the staff about raising the prices in the staff restaurant*

canvasser ['kænvəsə] *noun* person who canvasses

canvassing ['kænvəsɪŋ] *noun* action of asking people to buy, to vote or to say what they think; *she trains canvassers in canvassing techniques*; *door-to-door canvassing is usually done at election time*

CAP = COMMON AGRICULTURAL POLICY

cap [kæp] **1** *noun* upper level for something (such as a maximum rate of interest) **2** *verb* to place an upper limit on something; *to cap a local authority's budget* (NOTE: **capping - capped**)

capable ['keɪpəbl] *adjective* **(a) capable of** = able or clever enough to do something; *she is capable of very fast keyboarding speeds*; *the sales force should be capable of selling all the stock in the warehouse* **(b)** efficient; *she is a very capable departmental manager* (NOTE: you are capable **of** something or **of doing** something)

capacity [kə'pæsəti] *noun* **(a)** amount which can be produced, amount of work which can be done; *industrial or manufacturing or production capacity*; **to work at full capacity** = to do as much work as possible **(b)** amount of space; **to use up spare** *or* **excess capacity** = to make use of time or space which is not fully used; **storage capacity** = space available for storage; **warehouse capacity** = space available in a warehouse **(c)** ability; *he has a particular capacity for detailed business deals with overseas companies*; **earning capacity** = amount of money someone is able to earn **(d) in a capacity** = acting as; *in his capacity as chairman*; **speaking in an official capacity** = speaking officially

> analysts are increasingly convinced that the industry simply has too much capacity
>
> *Fortune*

capita ['kæpɪtə] *see* PER CAPITA

capital ['kæpɪtl] *noun* **(a)** money, property and assets used in a business; *company with £10,000 capital or with a capital of £10,000*; **authorized capital** *or* **registered capital** *or* **nominal capital** = maximum capital which is permitted by a company's memorandum of association; **circulating capital** = capital in the form of raw materials, finished products and work in progress needed for a company to carry on its business; **equity capital** = a company's capital which is owned by its ordinary shareholders (note that preference shares are not equity capital; if the company were wound up, none of the equity capital would be distributed to preference shareholders); **fixed capital** = capital in the form of fixed assets; **issued capital** = amount of capital issued as shares to the shareholders; **paid-up capital** = amount of money paid for the issued share capital; **risk capital** *or* **venture capital** = capital for investment in the early stages of projects which may easily be lost; **working capital** = capital in the form of cash, stocks and debtors (less creditors) used by a company in its day-to-day operations; **capital account** = account of dealings (money invested in the company, or taken out of the company) by the owners of a company; **capital assets** = property, machines, etc., which a company owns and uses but which the company does not buy and sell as part of its regular trade; **capital equipment** = equipment which a factory or office uses to work; **capital expenditure** *or* **investment** *or* **outlay** = money spent on fixed assets (property, machines, furniture); **capital goods** = goods used to manufacture other goods (i.e. machinery); **capital reserves** = part of share capital which can be distributed to the shareholders only when a company is wound up; **capital structure of a company** = way in which a company's capital is made up from various sources **(b)** money owned by individuals or companies, used for investment; **capital**

bonus = bonus payment by an insurance company which is produced by capital gain; **capital levy** = tax on the value of a person's property and possessions; **capital loss** = loss made by selling assets (the opposite of a capital gain); *(on the Stock Exchange)* **capital shares** = shares in investment trusts which increase in value as the value of the investments rises, but do not receive any income; **capital transfer tax** = formerly, a tax on gifts or bequests of money or property; **movements of capital** = changes of investments from one country to another; **flight of capital** = rapid movement of capital out of one country because of lack of confidence in that country's economic future; **capital market** = places where companies can look for investment capital **(c) capital letters** or **block capitals** = letters written as A, B, C, D, etc., and not a, b, c, d; *write your name in block capitals at the top of the form*

---

issued and fully paid capital is $100 million, comprising 2340 shares of $100 each and 997,660 ordinary shares of $100 each

Hongkong Standard

---

capital allowances ['kæpɪtl ə'lauənsɪz] *noun* allowances based on the value of fixed assets which may be deducted from a company's profits and so reduce its tax liability

COMMENT: under current UK law, depreciation is not allowable for tax on profits, whereas capital allowances, based on the value of fixed assets owned by the company, are tax-allowable

capital gain ['kæpɪtl 'geɪn] *noun* money made by selling fixed assets, shares or certain other types of property (such as works of art, leases, etc.; if the asset is sold for less than its purchase price, the result is a capital loss); **capital gains tax (CGT)** = tax paid on capital gains

---

Canadians' principal residences have always been exempt from capital gains tax

Toronto Star

COMMENT: in the UK, capital gains tax is payable on capital gains from the sale of assets, in particular shares and properties, above a certain minimum level

capitalism ['kæpɪtəlɪzəm] *noun* economic system where each person has the right to invest money, to work in business, to buy and sell, with no restriction from the state

capitalist ['kæpɪtəlɪst] **1** *noun* person who invests money in businesses **2** *adjective* working according to the principles of capitalism; *a capitalist economy*; *the capitalist system*; *the capitalist countries or world*

capitalization [kæpɪtəlaɪ'zeɪʃən] *noun* **market capitalization** = value of a company calculated by multiplying the price of its shares on the stock exchange by the number of shares issued; *company with a £1m capitalization*; **capitalization of reserves** = issuing free bonus shares to shareholders

---

she aimed to double the company's market capitalization

Fortune

---

capitalize ['kæpɪtəlaɪz] *verb* to invest money in a working company; **company capitalized at £10,000** = company with a working capital of £10,000

---

at its last traded price the bank was capitalized at around $1.05 billion with 60 per cent in the hands of the family

South China Morning Post

---

capitalize on ['kæpɪtəlaɪz ɒn] *verb* to make a profit from; *we are seeking to capitalize on our market position*

captive market ['kæptɪv 'maːkɪt] *noun* market where one supplier has a monopoly and the buyer has no choice over the product which he must purchase

capture ['kæptʃə] *verb* to take or to get control of something; **to capture 10% of the market** = to sell hard, and so take a 10% market share; **to capture 20% of a company's shares** = to buy shares in a company rapidly and so own 20% of it

car [kɑː] *noun* **company car** = car owned by a company and lent to a member of staff to use for business or other purposes; **car boot sale** = type of jumble sale, organised in a large car park or sports field, where people sell unwanted items which they bring to the sale in their cars

carat [ˈkærət] *noun* **(a)** measure of the quality of gold (pure gold being 24 carat); *a 22-carat gold ring* **(b)** measure of the weight of precious stones; *a 5-carat diamond*

COMMENT: pure gold is 24 carats and is too soft to make jewellery; most jewellery and other items made from gold are not pure, but between 19 and 22 carats. 22 carat gold has 22 parts of gold to two parts of alloy

carbon [ˈkɑːbən] *noun* **(a)** carbon paper; *you forgot to put a carbon in the typewriter* **(b)** carbon copy; *make a top copy and two carbons*

carbon copy [ˈkɑːbən ˈkɒpi] *noun* copy made with carbon paper; *give me the original, and file the carbon copy*

carbonless [ˈkɑːbənləs] *adjective* which makes a copy without using carbon paper; *our reps use carbonless order pads*

carbon paper [ˈkɑːbən ˈpeɪpə] *noun* sheet of paper with a black material on one side, used in a typewriter to make a copy; *you put the carbon paper in the typewriter the wrong way round*

card [kɑːd] *noun* **(a)** stiff paper; *we have printed the instructions on thick white card* **(b)** small piece of stiff paper or plastic; **business card** = card showing a businessman's name and the address of the company he works for; **cash card** = plastic card used to obtain money from a cash dispenser; **charge card** = credit card (like an American Express card) for which a fee is payable, but which does not allow the user to take out a loan (he has to pay off the total sum charged at the end of each month); **cheque (guarantee) card** = plastic card from a bank which guarantees payment of a cheque up to a certain amount, even if the user has no money in his account; **credit card** = plastic card which allows you to borrow money or to buy goods without paying for them

immediately; **debit card** = plastic card, similar to a credit card, but which debits the holder's account immediately through an EPOS system; **filing card** = card with information written on it, used to classify information in correct order; **index card** = card used to make a card index; **smart card** = credit card with a microchip, used for withdrawing money from ATMs, or for purchases at EFTPOS terminals; **store card** = credit card issued by a department store and which can only be used for purchases within that store; *see also* PHONECARD **(c)** postcard; **reply paid card** = card to be sent back to the sender with a reply on it, the sender having already paid the postage **(d) to get your cards** = to be dismissed

ever since October, when the banks' base rate climbed to 15 per cent, the main credit card issuers have faced the prospect of having to push interest rates above 30 per cent APR. Though store cards have charged interest at much higher rates than this for some years, 30 per cent APR is something the banks fight shy of

Financial Times Review

cardboard [ˈkɑːdbɔːd] *noun* thick stiff brown paper; **cardboard box** = box made of cardboard

cardholder [ˈkɑːdhəʊldə] *noun* person who holds a credit card or bank cash card

card index [ˈkɑːd ˈɪndeks] *noun* series of cards with information written on them, kept in special order so that the information can be found easily; **card-index file** = information kept on filing cards

card-index [ˈkɑːdˈɪndeks] *verb* to put information onto a card index

card-indexing [ˈkɑːdˈɪndeksɪŋ] *noun* putting information onto a card index; *no one can understand her card-indexing system*

card phone [ˈkɑːd ˈfəʊn] *noun* public telephone which works when you insert a phonecard

career [kəˈrɪə] *noun* job which you are trained for, and which you expect to do all your life; *he made his career in electronics*; **career woman** *or* **girl** = woman who is working in business and does not plan to stop working to look after the house or children

care of [ˈkeər ɒv] *phrase; (in an address)* words to show that the person is living at the address, but only as a visitor; *Herr Schmidt, care of Mr W. Brown*

caretaker [ˈkeərteɪkə] *noun* person who looks after a building, making sure it is clean and that the rubbish is cleared away (a caretaker often lives on the premises); *go and ask the caretaker to replace the light bulb* (NOTE: American English is **janitor**)

cargo [ˈkɑːgəʊ] *noun* load of goods which are sent in a ship, plane, etc.; **the ship was taking on cargo** = it was being loaded with goods; **to load cargo** = to put cargo on a ship; **air cargo** = goods sent by air; **cargo ship** *or* **cargo plane** = ship or plane which carries only cargo and no passengers (NOTE: plural is **cargoes**)

car-hire [ˈkɑːˈhaɪə] *noun* business of lending cars to people for money; *he runs a car-hire business*

carnet [ˈkɑːneɪ] *noun* international document which allows dutiable goods to cross several European countries by road without paying duty until the goods reach their final destination

carriage [ˈkærɪdʒ] *noun* (i) transporting goods from one place to another; (ii) cost of transport of goods; *to pay for carriage*; *to allow 10% for carriage*; *carriage is 15% of the total cost*; **carriage forward** = deal where the customer will pay for the shipping when the goods arrive; **carriage free** = deal where the customer does not pay for the shipping; **carriage paid** = deal where the seller has paid for the shipping

carrier [ˈkærɪə] *noun* **(a)** company which transports goods; *we only use reputable carriers*; **air carrier** = company which sends cargo or passengers by air; **carrier's risk** = responsibility of a carrier to pay for damage or loss of goods being shipped **(b)** vehicle or ship which transports goods; **bulk carrier** = ship which carries large quantities of loose goods (such as corn or coal)

carry [ˈkæri] *verb* **(a)** to take from one place to another; *the truck was carrying goods to the supermarket*; *a tanker carrying oil from the Gulf*; *the train was carrying a consignment of cars for export* **(b)** to vote to approve; **the motion was carried** = the motion was accepted after a vote **(c)** to produce; *the bonds carry interest at 10%* **(d)** to keep in stock; *to carry a line of goods*; *we do not carry pens*

carry down *or* **carry forward** [ˈkæri ˈdaʊn or ˈkæri ˈfɔːwəd] *verb* to take an account balance at the end of the current period as the starting point for the next period; **balance carried forward** *or* **balance c/f** = amount entered in an account at the end of a period or page of an account book to balance the debit and credit entries; it is then taken forward to start the next period or page

carrying [ˈkæriɪŋ] *noun* transporting from one place to another; *carrying charges have increased because of the increased duty on petrol*

carry on [ˈkæri ˈɒn] *verb* to continue or to go on doing something; *the staff carried on working in spite of the fire*; **to carry on a business** = to be active in running a business

carry over [ˈkæri ˈəʊvə] *verb* **(a)** to **carry over a balance** = to take a balance from the end of one page or period to the beginning of the next **(b)** **to carry over stock** = to hold stock from the end of one stocktaking period to the beginning of the next

cart [kɑːt] *noun US* **baggage cart** = metal holder on wheels, on which baggage can be placed to be moved easily in an airport, train station, etc.; **shopping cart** = metal basket on wheels, used by shoppers to put their purchases in as they go round a supermarket (NOTE: British English for these are **luggage trolley** and **shopping trolley** *or* **supermarket trolley**)

cartage [ˈkɑːtɪdʒ] *noun* carrying goods by road

cartel [kɑːˈtel] *noun* group of companies which try to fix the price or to regulate the supply of a product because they can then profit from this situation

carter ['kɑːtə] *noun* person who transports goods by road

carton ['kɑːtən] *noun* (**a**) thick cardboard; *a folder made of carton* (**b**) box made of cardboard; *a carton of cigarettes*

cartridge ['kɑːtrɪdʒ] *noun* sealed box with film, tape or printer toner in it; *the instructions for inserting the toner cartridge are printed on the box*; **data cartridge** = stiff box with magnetic tape inside, used for recording data from a computer; *copy the information from the computer onto a cartridge*; **laser cartridge** = cartridge of toner for a laser printer

case [keɪs] **1** *noun* (**a**) suitcase, box with a handle for carrying clothes and personal belongings when travelling; *customs officials made him open his case*; *she had a small case which she carried onto the plane* (**b**) cardboard or wooden box for packing and carrying goods; **six cases of wine** = six boxes, each containing twelve bottles; **a packing case** = large wooden box for carrying items which can be easily broken (**c**) **display case** = table or counter with a glass top, used for displaying items for sale (**d**) **court case** = legal action or trial; **the case is being heard next week** = the case is coming to court next week **2** *verb* to pack (items) in a case

cash [kæʃ] **1** *noun* (**a**) money in coins or notes; **cash in hand** *US* **cash on hand** = money and notes, kept to pay small amounts but not deposited in the bank; **hard cash** = money in notes and coins, as opposed to cheques or credit cards; **petty cash** = small amounts of money; **ready cash** = money which is immediately available for payment; **cash account** = account which records the money which is received and spent; **cash advance** = loan in cash against a future payment; **cash balance** = balance in cash, as opposed to amounts owed; **cash book (CB)** = book in which cash transactions are entered; **cash box** = metal box for keeping cash; **cash budget** = plan of cash income and expenditure; **cash card** = card used to obtain money from a cash dispenser; **cash cow** = product or subsidiary company that consistently generates good profits but does not provide growth; **cash desk** =

place in a store where you pay for the goods bought; **cash dispenser** = machine which gives out money when a special card is inserted and instructions given; **cash economy** = black economy, where goods and services are paid for in cash, and therefore not declared for tax; **cash float** = cash put into the cash box at the beginning of the day or week to allow change to be given to customers; **cash limit** = fixed amount of money which can be spent during a certain period; **cash offer** = offer to pay in cash; **cash payment** = payment in cash; **cash purchases** = purchases made in cash; **cash register** *or* **cash till** = machine which shows and adds the prices of items bought, with a drawer for keeping the cash received; **cash reserves** = a company's reserves in cash, deposits or bills, kept in case of urgent need (**b**) using money in coins or notes; **to pay cash down** = to pay in cash immediately; **cash price** *or* **cash terms** = lower price or better terms which apply if the customer pays cash; **settlement in cash** *or* **cash settlement** = paying a bill in cash; **cash sale** *or* **cash transaction** = transaction paid for in cash; **terms: cash with order (CWO)** = terms of sale showing the payment has to be made in cash when the order is placed; **cash on delivery (COD)** = payment in cash when goods are delivered; **cash discount** *or* **discount for cash** = discount given for payment in cash **2** *verb* **to cash a cheque** = to exchange a cheque for cash

cashable ['kæʃəbl] *adjective* which can be cashed; *a crossed cheque is not cashable at any bank*

cash and carry ['kæʃ ənd 'kæri] *noun* large store selling goods at low prices, where the customer pays cash and has to take the goods away himself; *he gets his supplies every morning from a cash and carry warehouse*

the small independent retailer who stocks up using cash and carries could be hit hard by the loss of footfall associated with any increase in smuggled goods

The Grocer

cash flow ['kæʃ 'fləʊ] *noun* cash which comes into a company from sales (cash inflow) or the money which goes out in purchases or overhead expenditure (cash outflow); **cash flow forecast** = forecast of when cash will be received or paid out; **cash flow statement** = report which shows cash sales and purchases; **net cash flow** = difference between the money coming in and the money going out; **negative cash flow** = situation where more money is going out of a company than is coming in; **positive cash flow** = situation where more money is coming into a company than is going out; **the company is suffering from cash flow problems** = cash income is not coming in fast enough to pay the expenditure going out

cashier [kæˈʃɪə] *noun* **(a)** person who takes money from customers in a shop **(b)** person who deals with customers' money in a bank; *US* **cashier's check** = a bank's own cheque, drawn on itself and signed by a cashier or other bank official

cash in [ˈkæʃ ˈɪn] *verb* to sell (shares) for cash

cash in on [ˈkæʃ ˈɪn ɒn] *verb* to profit from; *the company is cashing in on the interest in computer games*

cashless society [ˈkæʃləs səˈsaɪəti] *noun* society where no one uses cash, all purchases being made by credit cards, charge cards, cheques or direct transfer from one account to another

cashpoint [ˈkæʃpɔɪnt] *noun* place where there are cash dispensers where a card holder can get cash by using his cash card

cash up [ˈkæʃ ˈʌp] *verb* to add up the cash in a shop at the end of the day

casting vote [ˈkɑːstɪŋ ˈvəʊt] *noun* vote used by the chairman in the case where the votes for and against a proposal are equal; *the chairman has the casting vote*; *he used his casting vote to block the motion*

casual [ˈkæʒjʊəl] *adjective* not permanent, not regular; **casual labour** = workers who are hired for a short period; **casual work** = work where the workers are hired for a short period; **casual labourer** *or* **casual worker** = worker who can be hired for a short period

catalogue *US* **catalog** [ˈkætəlɒg] **1** *noun* list of items for sale, usually with prices; *an office equipment catalogue*; *they sent us a catalogue of their new range of products*; **mail order catalogue** = catalogue from which a customer orders items to be sent by mail; **catalogue price** = price as marked in a catalogue **2** *verb* to put an item into a catalogue

category [ˈkætəgəri] *noun* type or sort of item; *we deal only in the most expensive categories of watches*

caterer [ˈkeɪtərə] *noun* person who supplies food and drink, especially for parties

cater for [ˈkeɪtə ˈfɔː] *verb* to deal with or to provide for; *the store caters mainly for overseas customers*

catering [ˈkeɪtərɪŋ] **1** *noun* supply of food and drink for a party, etc.; **the catering trade** = food trade, especially supplying food ready to eat **2** *adjective* **catering for** = which provides for; *a store catering for overseas visitors*

cause [kɔːz] **1** *noun* thing which makes something happen; *what was the cause of the bank's collapse?*; *the police tried to find the cause of the fire* **2** *verb* to make something happen; *the recession caused hundreds of bankruptcies*

caveat [ˈkævɪæt] *noun* warning; **to enter a caveat** = to warn legally that you have an interest in a case, and that no steps can be taken without your permission

caveat emptor [ˈkævɪæt ˈemptɔː] = LET THE BUYER BEWARE *phrase* meaning that the buyer is himself responsible for checking that what he buys is in good order

> the idea that buyers at a car boot sale should have any rights at all is laughable. Even those who do not understand Latin know that caveat emptor is the rule
>
> *Times*

CB = CASH BOOK

CBI [ˈsiːbiːˈaɪ] = CONFEDERATION OF BRITISH INDUSTRY

cc [ˈkɒpɪz] = COPIES (NOTE: **cc** is put at the bottom of a letter, under the signature, to show who has been sent a copy of it)

CCA = CURRENT COST ACCOUNTING

CD [siːˈdiː] = CERTIFICATE OF DEPOSIT

c/d = CARRIED DOWN

cede [ɒiːd] *verb* to give up property to someone else

ceiling [ˈsiːlɪŋ] *noun* highest point, such as the highest interest rate, the highest amount of money which a depositor may deposit, etc.; *output has reached its ceiling*; *there is a ceiling of $100,000 on deposits*; *to fix a ceiling to a budget*; **ceiling price** *or* **price ceiling** = highest price that can be reached

cellular telephone *or* **cell telephone** [ˈseljʊlə ˈtelɪfəʊn or ˈsel ˈtelɪfəʊn] *noun* telephone which can be carried around; *if I'm not in the office for some reason you can always reach me on my cellular telephone* (NOTE: British English uses **mobile phone**)

cent [sent] *noun* (a) small coin, one hundredth of a dollar; *the stores are only a 25-cent bus ride away*; *they sell oranges at 99 cents each* (NOTE: cent is usually written ¢ in prices: **25¢** but not when a dollar price is mentioned: **$1.25**) (b) *see also* PER CENT

centimetre *US* **centimeter** [ˈsentɪmiːtə] *noun* measurement of length (one hundredth of a metre); *the paper is fifteen centimetres wide* (NOTE: **centimetre** is usually written **cm** after figures: **260cm**)

central [ˈsentrəl] *adjective* organized by one main point; **central bank** = main government-controlled bank in a country, which controls the financial affairs of the country by fixing main interest rates, issuing currency, supervising the commercial banks and trying to control the foreign exchange rate; **central office** = main office which controls all smaller offices; **central purchasing** = purchasing organized by a central office for all branches of a company

central bankers in Europe and Japan are reassessing their intervention policy
Duns Business Month

centralization [sentrəlaɪˈzeɪʃən] *noun* organization of everything from a central point

centralize [ˈsentrəlaɪz] *verb* to organize from a central point; *all purchasing has been centralized in our main office*; *the group benefits from a highly centralized organizational structure*

centre *US* **center** [ˈsentə] *noun* (a) **business centre** = part of a town where the main banks, shops and offices are situated (b) important town; *Sheffield is a major industrial centre*; *Nottingham is the centre for the shoe industry* (c) *GB* **job centre** = government office which lists jobs which are vacant; **shopping centre** = group of shops linked together with car parks and restaurants (d) group of items in an account; **cost centre** = person or group whose costs can be itemized in accounts; **profit centre** = person or department which is considered separately for the purposes of calculating a profit

CEO [siːiːˈəʊ] = CHIEF EXECUTIVE OFFICER

certain [ˈsɜːtn] *adjective* (a) sure; *the chairman is certain we will pass last year's total sales* (b) a certain = one particular; **a certain number** *or* **a certain quantity** = some; *a certain number of lines are being discontinued*

certificate [səˈtɪfɪkət] *noun* official document which shows that something is true; **clearance certificate** = document showing that goods have been passed by customs; **insurance certificate** = document from an insurance company showing that an insurance policy has been issued; **savings certificate** = document showing you have invested money in a government savings scheme; **share certificate** = document proving that you own shares; **certificate of airworthiness** = document to show that an aircraft is safe to fly; **certificate of approval** = document showing that an item has been officially approved; **certificate of incorporation** = document showing that a company has been legally set up and officially registered; **certificate of origin** = document showing where goods were made; **certificate of registration** =

document showing that an item has been registered

certificated [səˈtɪfɪkeɪtɪd] *adjective* **certificated bankrupt** = bankrupt who has been discharged from bankruptcy with a certificate to show that he or she was not at fault

certificate of deposit (CD) [səˈtɪfɪkət əv dɪˈpɒzɪt] *noun* document from a bank showing that money has been deposited at a certain guaranteed interest rate for a certain period of time

> COMMENT: a CD is a bearer instrument, which can be sold by the bearer. It can be sold at a discount to the value, so that the yield on CDs varies

```
interest      rates      on
certificates of deposit may
have little room to decline in
August  as  demand  for  funds
from  major  city  banks  is
likely  to  remain  strong.
After  delaying  for  months,
banks  are  now  expected  to
issue a large volume of CDs.
If banks issue more CDs on the
assumption  that  the official
discount  rate  reduction  will
be delayed, it is very likely
that CD rates will be pegged
for  a  longer  period  than
expected
```
Nikkei Weekly

certify [ˈsɜːtɪfaɪ] *verb* to make an official declaration in writing; *I certify that this is a true copy*; *the document is certified as a true copy*; **certified accountant** = accountant who has passed the professional examinations and is a member of the Chartered Association of Certified Accountants; **certified cheque** *US* **certified check** = cheque which a bank says is good and will be paid out of money put aside from the bank account

cession [ˈseʃən] *noun* giving up property to someone (especially a creditor)

c/f = CARRIED FORWARD

CFO [ˈsiːefˈəu] = CHIEF FINANCIAL OFFICER

CGT = CAPITAL GAINS TAX

chain [tʃeɪn] *noun* series of stores or other businesses belonging to the same company; *a chain of hotels or a hotel chain*; *the chairman of a large do-it-yourself chain*; *he runs a chain of shoe shops*; *she bought several garden centres and gradually built up a chain*

```
the giant US group is better
known for its chain of cinemas
and  hotels  rather  than  its
involvement in shipping
```
Lloyd's List

chain store [ˈtʃeɪn ˈstɔː] *noun* one store in a chain

chair [tʃeə] **1** *noun* position of the chairman, presiding over a meeting; *Mr Smith was in the chair*; *Mrs Brown was voted into the chair*; **Mr Jones took the chair** = Mr Jones presided over the meeting; *(in a meeting)* **to address the chair** = to speak to the chairman and not to the rest of the people at the meeting; *please address your remarks to the chair* **2** *verb* to preside over a meeting; *the meeting was chaired by Mrs Smith*

chairman [ˈtʃeəmən] *noun* **(a)** person who is in charge of a meeting; *Mr Howard was chairman or acted as chairman*; **Mr Chairman** *or* **Madam Chairman** = way of speaking to the chairman **(b)** person who presides over the board meetings of a company; *the chairman of the board or the company chairman*; **the chairman's report** = annual report from the chairman of a company to the shareholders (NOTE: the plural is **chairmen**. Note also that in a British company, the chairman is less important than the managing director, although one person can combine both posts. In the USA, a company president is less important than the chairman of the board)

```
the          corporation's
entrepreneurial   chairman
seeks     a    dedicated    but
part-time president. The new
president   will   work   a
three-day week
```
Globe and Mail (Toronto)

chairmanship [ˈtʃeəmənʃɪp] *noun* being a chairman; *the committee met under the chairmanship of Mr Jones*

chairperson ['tʃeəpɜːsn] *noun* person who is in charge of a meeting (NOTE: the plural is **chairpersons**)

chairwoman ['tʃeəwʊmən] *noun* woman who is in charge of a meeting (NOTE: the plural is **chairwomen**)

Chamber of Commerce ['tʃeɪmbər əv 'kɒməs] *noun* group of local business people who meet to discuss problems which they have in common and to promote commerce in their town

chambers ['tʃeɪmbəz] *plural noun* office of a lawyer or judge; **the judge heard the case in chambers** = he heard the case in his private office, and not in court

chance [tʃɑːns] *noun* **(a)** being possible; *the company has a good chance of winning the contract*; *his promotion chances are small* **(b)** opportunity to do something; *she is waiting for a chance to see the managing director*; *he had his chance of promotion when the finance director's assistant resigned* (NOTE: you have a chance **of doing** something or **to do** something)

Chancellor of the Exchequer ['tʃɑːnsələr əv ði: ɪks'tʃekə] *noun GB* chief finance minister in the government (NOTE: the American equivalent is the **Secretary of the Treasury**)

chandler ['tʃɑːndlə] *noun* person who deals in goods, especially supplies to ships; *there is a ship chandler's near the yacht club*

chandlery ['tʃɑːndləri] *noun* chandler's shop

change [tʃeɪndʒ] **1** *noun* **(a)** money in coins or small notes; **small change** = coins; **to give someone change for £10** = to give someone coins or notes in exchange for a ten pound note; **change machine** = machine which gives small change for a note or larger coin **(b)** money given back by the seller, when the buyer can pay only with a larger note or coin than the amount asked; *he gave me the wrong change*; *you paid the £5.75 bill with a £10 note, so you should have £4.25 change*; **keep the change** = keep it as a tip (said to waiters, etc.) **(c)** *(of a business)* **change of ownership** = being sold to a new owner; *the change of ownership has had an effect*

on staff morale **2** *verb* **(a) to change a £20 note** = to give change in smaller notes or coins for a £20 note **(b)** to give one type of currency for another; *to change £1,000 into dollars*; *we want to change some traveller's cheques* **(c)** *(of a business, property, etc.)* **to change hands** = to be sold to a new owner; *the shop changed hands for £100,000*

changer ['tʃeɪndʒə] *noun* person who changes money

channel ['tʃænl] **1** *noun* way in which information or goods are passed from one place to another; **to go through the official channels** = to deal with government officials (especially when making a request); **to open up new channels of communication** = to find new ways of communicating with someone; **distribution channels** *or* **channels of distribution** = ways of sending goods from the manufacturer for sale by retailers **2** *verb* to send in a certain direction; *they are channelling their research funds into developing European communication systems*

chapter ['tʃæptə] *noun US* section of an Act of Congress; **Chapter 7** = section of the Bankruptcy Reform Act 1978, which sets out the rules for the liquidation of an incorporated company; **Chapter 11** = section of the Bankruptcy Reform Act 1978, which allows a corporation to be protected from demands made by its creditors for a period of time, while it is reorganized with a view to paying its debts; the officers of the corporation will negotiate with its creditors as to the best way of reorganizing the business; **Chapter 13** = section of the Bankruptcy Reform Act 1978, which allows a business to continue trading and to pay off its creditors by regular monthly payments over a period of time

---

the company filed under Chapter 11 of the federal bankruptcy code, the largest failure ever in the steel industry

Fortune

---

the firm, whose trademark dates back to 1871, has been desperately trying to cut costs to compete with manufacturers in cheaper countries, but has also been hit by management problems. It said the filing for Chapter 11 protection should have little impact on customers and employees and would allow it to restructure

Times

charge [tʃɑːdʒ] **1** *noun* **(a)** money which must be paid, price of a service; *to make no charge for delivery*; *to make a small charge for rental*; *there is no charge for this service*; *or no charge is made for this service*; **admission charge** *or* **entry charge** = price to be paid before going into an exhibition, etc.; **bank charges** *US* **service charge** = charges made by a bank for carrying out work for a customer; **handling charge** = money to be paid for packing, invoicing and dealing with goods which are being shipped; **inclusive charge** = charge which includes all items; **interest charges** = money paid as interest on a loan; **scale of charges** = list showing various prices; **service charge** = charge added to a bill in a restaurant to pay for service; *a 10% service charge is added*; *does the bill include a service charge?*; **charge account** = arrangement which a customer has with a store to buy goods and to pay for them at a later date, usually when the invoice is sent at the end of the month; **charges forward** = charges which will be paid by the customer; **a token charge is made for heating** = a small charge is made which does not cover the real costs at all; **free of charge** = free, with no payment to be made **(b)** debit on an account; *it appears as a charge on the accounts*; **floating charge** = charge linked to any of the company's assets of a certain type, but not to any specific item; **charge by way of legal mortgage** = way of borrowing money on the security of a property, where the mortgagor signs a deed which gives the mortgagee an interest in the property **(c)** being formally accused in a court; *he appeared in court on a charge of embezzling or on an embezzlement charge* **2** *verb* **(a)** to ask someone to pay for services later; **to charge the packing to the customer** *or* **to charge the customer**

with the packing = the customer has to pay for packing **(b)** to ask for money to be paid; *to charge £5 for delivery*; *how much does he charge?*; **he charges £16 an hour** = he asks to be paid £16 for an hour's work **(c)** to pay for something by putting it on a charge account; *can you charge the meal to my room?*; *I want to charge these purchases to the company account* **(d)** *(in a court)* to accuse someone formally of having committed a crime; *he was charged with embezzling his clients' money*

traveller's cheques cost 1% of their face value - some banks charge more for small amounts

Sunday Times

chargeable [ˈtʃɑːdʒəbl] *adjective* which can be charged; *repairs chargeable to the occupier*; **sums chargeable to the reserve** = sums which can be debited to a company's reserves

charge card [ˈtʃɑːdʒ ˈkɑːd] *noun* type of credit card (such as American Express) for which a fee is payable, but which does not allow the user to take out a loan (he has to pay off the total sum charged at the end of each month)

chargee [tʃɑːˈdʒiː] *noun* person who has the right to force a debtor to pay

chargehand [ˈtʃɑːdʒhænd] *noun* chief of a group of workers under a foreman

chart [tʃɑːt] *noun* diagram showing information as a series of lines, blocks, etc.; **bar chart** = diagram where quantities and values are shown as thick columns of different heights or lengths; **flow chart** = diagram showing the arrangement of various work processes in a series; **organization chart** = diagram showing how a company or an office is organized; **pie chart** = diagram where information is shown as a circle cut up into sections of different sizes; **sales chart** = diagram showing how sales vary from month to month

charter [ˈtʃɑːtə] **1** *noun* **(a) bank charter** = official government document allowing the establishment of a bank **(b)** hiring transport for a special purpose; **charter flight** = flight in an aircraft which has been hired for that purpose; **charter plane** =

plane which has been chartered; **boat on charter to Mr Smith** = boat which Mr Smith has hired for a voyage **2** *verb* to hire for a special purpose; *to charter a plane* or *a boat* or *a bus*

chartered ['tʃɑːtəd] *adjective* **(a) chartered accountant** = accountant who has passed the professional examinations and is a member of the Institute of Chartered Accountants **(b)** (company) which has been set up by charter, and not registered under the Companies Act; *a chartered bank* **(c) chartered ship** or **bus** or **plane** = ship, bus or plane which has been hired for a special purpose

charterer ['tʃɑːtərə] *noun* person who hires a ship, etc., for a special purpose

chartering ['tʃɑːtərɪŋ] *noun* act of hiring for a special purpose

chartist ['tʃɑːtɪst] *noun* person who studies stock market trends and forecasts future rises or falls

chase [tʃeɪs] *verb* **(a)** to run after someone or something to try to catch them **(b)** to try to speed up work by asking how it is progressing; *we are trying to chase up the accounts department for the cheque*; *I will chase your order with the production department*

chaser ['tʃeɪsə] *noun* **(a) progress chaser** = person whose job is to check that work is being carried out on schedule or that orders are fulfilled on time **(b)** letter to remind someone of something (especially to remind a customer that an invoice has not been paid); *the computer automatically sends chasers after sixty days to customers who have not paid*

chattels ['tʃætlz] *plural noun* **goods and chattels** = moveable property (but not freehold real estate)

cheap [tʃiːp] *adjective* & *adverb* not costing a lot of money, not expensive; **cheap labour** = workforce which does not earn much money; *we have opened a factory in the Far East because of the cheap labour* or *because labour is cheap there*; **cheap money** = money which can be borrowed at low interest; **cheap rate** = rate which is not expensive; *cheap rate phone calls start at 8 p.m.*; **to buy something cheap** = at a low price; *he*

bought two companies cheap and sold them again at a profit; *they work out cheaper by the box* = these items are cheaper per unit if you buy a box of them

cheaply ['tʃiːpli] *adverb* without paying much money; *the salesman was living cheaply at home and claiming a large hotel bill on his expenses*

cheapness ['tʃiːpnəs] *noun* being cheap; *the cheapness of the currency means that many more tourists will go to Europe*

cheat [tʃiːt] *verb* to trick someone so that he loses money; *he cheated the Income Tax out of thousands of pounds*; *she was accused of cheating clients who came to ask her for advice*

check [tʃek] **1** *noun* **(a)** sudden stop; **to put a check on imports** = to stop some imports **(b)** investigation or examination; *the auditors carried out checks on the petty cash book*; *a routine check of the fire equipment*; **baggage check** = examination of passengers' baggage to see if it contains bombs **(c) check sample** = sample to be used to see if a consignment is acceptable **(d)** *US* (in restaurant) bill **(e)** *US* = CHEQUE **(f)** *US* mark on paper to show that something is correct; *make a check in the box marked 'R'* (NOTE: British English is **tick**) **2** *verb* **(a)** to stop, to delay; *to check the entry of contraband into the country*; *to check the flow of money out of a country* **(b)** to examine or to investigate; *to check that an invoice is correct*; *to check and sign for goods*; *he checked the computer printout against the invoices* = he examined the printout and the invoices to see if the figures were the same **(c)** *US* to mark with a sign to show that something is correct; *check the box marked 'R'* (NOTE: British English is to **tick**)

checkbook *noun US* = CHEQUE BOOK

check in ['tʃek 'ɪn] *verb* **(a)** (at a hotel) to arrive at a hotel and sign for a room; *he checked in at 12.15* **(b)** (at an airport) to give in your ticket to show you are ready to take the flight **(c) to check baggage in** = to pass your baggage to the airline to put it on the plane for you

check-in ['tʃekɪn] *noun* place where passengers give in their tickets for a flight;

the check-in is on the first floor; **check-in counter** = counter where passengers check in; **check-in time** = time at which passengers should check in

checking ['tʃekɪŋ] *noun* **(a)** examination or investigation; *the inspectors found some defects during their checking of the building* **(b)** *US* **checking account** = bank account on which you can write cheques

checklist ['tʃeklɪst] *noun* list of points which have to be checked before something can be done

checkoff ['tʃekɒf] *noun US* system where union dues are automatically deducted by the employer from a worker's paycheck

check out ['tʃek 'aʊt] *verb (at a hotel)* to leave and pay for a room; *we will check out before breakfast*

checkout ['tʃekaʊt] *noun* **(a)** *(in a supermarket)* place where you pay for the goods you have bought; *we have opened two more checkouts to cope with the Saturday rush* **(b)** *(in a hotel)* **checkout time is 12.00** = time by which you have to leave your room

checkroom ['tʃekrʊm] *noun US* place where you leave your coat, luggage, etc.

cheque *US* **check** [tʃek] *noun* note to a bank asking them to pay money from your account to the account of the person whose name is written on the note; *a cheque for £10 or a £10 cheque*; **cheque account** = bank account which allows the customer to write cheques; **cheque to bearer** = cheque with no name written on it, so that the person who holds it can cash it; **crossed cheque** = cheque with two lines across it showing that it can only be deposited at a bank and not exchanged for cash; **open** *or* **uncrossed cheque** = cheque which can be cashed anywhere (these cheques no longer exist in Britain); **blank cheque** = cheque with the amount of money and the payee left blank, but signed by the drawer; **pay cheque** *or* **salary cheque** = monthly cheque by which an employee is paid; **traveller's cheques** = cheques taken by a traveller, which can be cashed in a foreign country; **dud cheque** *or* **bouncing cheque** *or* **cheque which bounces** *US* **rubber check** = cheque which cannot be cashed

because the person writing it has not enough money in the account to pay it **(b)** **to cash a cheque** = to exchange a cheque for cash; **to endorse a cheque** = to sign a cheque on the back to show that you accept it; **to make out a cheque to someone** = to write someone's name on a cheque; *who shall I make the cheque out to?*; **to pay by cheque** = to pay by writing a cheque, and not using cash or a credit card; **to pay a cheque into your account** = to deposit a cheque; **the bank referred the cheque to drawer** = it returned the cheque to the person who wrote it because there was not enough money in the account to pay it; **to sign a cheque** = to sign on the front of a cheque to show that you authorize the bank to pay the money from your account; **to stop a cheque** = to ask a bank not to pay a cheque which has been signed and sent

cheque book *US* **checkbook** ['tʃekbʊk] *noun* booklet with new blank cheques

cheque (guarantee) card ['tʃek gærənti: 'kɑːd] *noun* plastic card from a bank which guarantees payment of a cheque up to a certain amount, even if there is no money in the account

chief [tʃiːf] *adjective* most important; *he is the chief accountant of an industrial group*; *she is the chief buyer for a department store*; **chief executive** *or* **chief executive officer (CEO)** = executive in charge of a company; **chief financial officer (CFO)** = executive in charge of a company's financial operations, reporting to the CEO

Chinese walls ['tʃaɪniːz 'wɔːlz] *noun* imaginary barriers between departments in the same organization, set up to avoid insider dealing or conflict of interest (as when a merchant bank is advising on a planned takeover bid, its investment department should not know that the bid is taking place, or they would advise their clients to invest in the company being taken over)

chip [tʃɪp] *noun* **(a) a computer chip** = a small piece of silicon able to store data, used in a computer **(b) blue chip** = very safe investment, risk-free share in a good company

chit [tʃɪt] *noun* bill (for food or drink in a club)

choice [tʃɔɪs] **1** *noun* **(a)** thing which is chosen; *you must give the customer time to make his choice* **(b)** range of items to choose from; *we have only a limited choice of suppliers*; **the shop carries a good choice of paper** = the shop carries many types of paper to choose from **2** *adjective* specially selected (food); *choice meat*; *choice wines*; *choice foodstuffs*

choose [tʃuːz] *verb* to decide to do a particular thing or to buy a particular item (as opposed to something else); *there were several good candidates to choose from*; *they chose the only woman applicant as sales director*; *you must give the customers plenty of time to choose* (NOTE: **choosing - chose - chosen**)

chop [tʃɒp] *noun* (*in the Far East*) stamp, a mark made on a document to show that it has been agreed, acknowledged, paid, or that payment has been received

chronic ['krɒnɪk] *adjective* permanently bad; *the company has chronic cash flow problems*; *we have a chronic shortage of skilled staff*; **chronic unemployment** = being unemployed for more than six months

chronological order [krɒnə'lɒdʒɪkəl 'ɔːdə] *noun* arrangement of records (files, invoices, etc.) in order of their dates

churning ['tʃɜːnɪŋ] *noun* **(a)** practice employed by stockbrokers, where they buy and sell on a client's discretionary account in order to earn their commission (the deals are frequently of no advantage to the client) **(b)** practice employed by insurance salesmen where the salesman suggests that a client should change his insurance policy solely in order to earn the salesman a commission

> more small investors lose money through churning than almost any other abuse, yet most people have never heard of it. Churning involves brokers generating income simply by buying and selling investments on behalf of their clients. Constant and needless churning earns them

hefty commissions which bites into the investment portfolio
> *Guardian*

c.i.f. *or* **CIF** ['siː'aɪ'ef] = COST, INSURANCE AND FREIGHT

circular ['sɜːkjʊlə] **1** *adjective* sent to many people; **circular letter of credit** = letter of credit sent to all branches of the bank which issues it **2** *noun* leaflet or letter sent to many people; *they sent out a circular offering a 10% discount*

circularize ['sɜːkjʊləraɪz] *verb* to send a circular to; *the committee has agreed to circularize the members of the society*; *they circularized all their customers with a new list of prices*

circulate ['sɜːkjʊleɪt] *verb* **(a)** (*of money*) **to circulate freely** = to move about without restriction by the government **(b)** to send or to give out without restrictions; **to circulate money** = to issue money, to make money available to the public and industry **(c)** to send information to; *they circulated a new list of prices to all their customers*

circulating capital ['sɜːkjʊleɪtɪŋ 'kæpɪtəl] *noun* capital in the form of cash or debtors, raw materials, finished products and work in progress required for a company to carry on its business

circulation [sɜːkjʊ'leɪʃən] *noun* **(a)** movement; *the company is trying to improve the circulation of information between departments*; **circulation of capital** = movement of capital from one investment to another **(b) to put money into circulation** = to issue new notes to business and the public; *the amount of money in circulation increased more than was expected* **(c)** (*of newspapers*) number of copies sold; *the audited circulation of a newspaper*; *the new editor hopes to improve the circulation*; **a circulation battle** = competition between two papers to try to sell more copies in the same market

> the level of currency in circulation increased to N4.9 billion in the month of August
> *Business Times (Lagos)*

city ['sɪti] *noun* **(a)** large town; *the largest cities in Europe are linked by hourly* *flights*; **capital city** = main town in a country, where the government is located; **inter-city** = between cities; *inter-city train services are often quicker than going by air* (b) **the City (of London)** = the old centre of London, where banks and large companies have their main offices; the British financial centre; *he works in the City* or *he is in the City*; **City desk** = section of a newspaper office which deals with financial and business news; **City editor** = business or finance editor of a British paper; **they say in the City that the company has been sold** = the business world is saying that the company has been sold

civil ['sɪvl] *adjective* referring to ordinary people; **civil action** = court case brought by a person or a company against someone who has done them wrong; **civil law** = laws relating to people's rights and agreements between individuals

civil servant ['sɪvl 'sɜːvənt] *noun* person who works in the civil service

civil service ['sɪvl 'sɜːvɪs] *noun* organization and personnel which administer a country; *you have to pass an examination to get a job in the civil service* or *to get a civil service job*

claim [kleɪm] **1** *noun* (a) asking for money; **wage claim** = asking for an increase in wages; **the union put in a 6% wage claim** = the union asked for a 6% increase in wages for its members (b) **legal claim** = statement that you think you own something legally; *he has no legal claim to the property* (c) **insurance claim** = asking an insurance company to pay for damages or for loss; **claims department** = department of an insurance company which deals with claims; **claim form** = form to be filled in when making an insurance claim; **claims manager** = manager of a claims department; **no claims bonus** = lower premium paid because no claims have been made against the insurance policy; **to put in a claim** = to ask the insurance company officially to pay damages; *to put in a claim for repairs to the car*; *she put in a claim for £250,000 damages against the driver of the other car*; **to settle a claim** = to agree to pay what is asked for; *the insurance company*

refused to settle his claim for storm damage (d) **small claim** = claim for less than £5000 in the County Court; **small claims court** = court which deals with claims for small amounts of money **2** *verb* (a) to ask for money; *he claimed £100,000 damages against the cleaning firm*; *she claimed for repairs to the car against her insurance* (b) to say that something is your property; *he is claiming possession of the house*; *no one claimed the umbrella found in my office* (c) to state that something is a fact; *he claims he never received the goods*; *she claims that the shares are her property*

claimant ['kleɪmənt] *noun* person who makes a claim against someone in the civil courts; **rightful claimant** = person who has a legal claim to something (NOTE: this term has now replaced **plaintiff**. The other side in a case is the **defendant**)

claim back ['kleɪm 'bæk] *verb* to ask for money to be paid back

claimer ['kleɪmə] *noun* = CLAIMANT

claiming ['kleɪmɪŋ] *noun* act of making a claim

class [klɑːs] *noun* category or group into which things are classified according to quality or price; **first-class** = top quality, most expensive; *he is a first-class accountant*; **economy class** or **tourist class** = lower quality, less expensive way of travelling; *I travel economy class because it is cheaper*; *tourist class travel is less comfortable than first class*; *he always travels first class because tourist class is too uncomfortable*; *GB* **first-class mail** = more expensive mail service, designed to be faster; *a first-class letter should get to Scotland in a day*; **second-class mail** = less expensive, slower mail service; *the letter took three days to arrive because he sent it second-class*

classify ['klæsɪfaɪ] *verb* to put into classes or categories; **classified advertisements** = advertisements listed in a newspaper under special headings (such as 'property for sale' or 'jobs wanted'); **classified directory** = book which lists businesses grouped under various headings (such as computer shops or newsagents)

classification [klæsɪfɪ'keɪʃən] *noun* way of putting into classes; **job classification** = describing jobs listed in various groups

clause [klɔːz] *noun* section of a contract; *there are ten clauses in the contract*; *according to clause six, payments will not be due until next year*; **exclusion clause** = clause in an insurance policy or warranty which says which items are not covered by the policy; **penalty clause** = clause which lists the penalties which will happen if the contract is not fulfilled; **termination clause** = clause which explains how and when a contract can be terminated

claw back ['klɔː 'bæk] *verb* to take back money which has been allocated; *income tax claws back 25% of pensions paid out by the government*; *of the £1m allocated to the project, the government clawed back £100,000 in taxes*

clawback ['klɔːbæk] *noun* money taken back

clean bill of lading ['kliːn 'bɪl əv 'leɪdɪŋ] *noun* bill of lading with no note to say the shipment is faulty or damaged

clear [klɪə] **1** *adjective* **(a)** easily understood; *when the cheque bounced, it was a clear sign that the company was in trouble*; *he made it clear that he wanted the manager to resign*; *you will have to make it clear to the staff that productivity is falling* **(b) clear profit** = profit after all expenses have been paid; *we made $6,000 clear profit on the sale* **(c)** free, total period of time; **three clear days** = three whole working days; *allow three clear days for the cheque to be paid into your account* **2** *verb* **(a)** to sell cheaply in order to get rid of stock; *'demonstration models to clear'* **(b) to clear goods through customs** = to have all documentation passed by customs so that goods can leave the country **(c) to clear 10%** *or* **$5,000 on the deal** = to make 10% or $5,000 clear profit; **we cleared only our expenses** = the sales revenue only paid for the costs and expenses without making any profit **(d) to clear a cheque** = to pass a cheque through the banking system, so that the money is transferred from the payer's account to another; *the cheque took ten days to clear*

or the bank took ten days to clear the cheque

clearance ['klɪərəns] *noun* **(a) customs clearance** = passing goods through customs so that they can enter or leave the country; **to effect customs clearance** = to clear goods through customs; **clearance certificate** = certificate showing that goods have been passed by customs **(b) clearance sale** = sale of items at low prices to get rid of stock **(c) clearance of a cheque** = passing of a cheque through the banking system, transferring money from one account to another; *you should allow six days for cheque clearance*

clearing ['klɪərɪŋ] *noun* **(a) clearing of goods through customs** = passing of goods through customs **(b) clearing of a debt** = paying all of a debt **(c)** passing of a cheque through the banking system, transferring money from one account to another; **clearing bank** = bank which clears cheques, one of the major British High Street banks, specializing in normal banking business for ordinary customers (loans, cheques, overdrafts, interest-bearing deposits, etc.); **clearing house** = central office where clearing banks exchange cheques

clear off ['klɪər 'ɒf] *verb* **to clear off a debt** = to pay all of a debt

clerical ['klerɪkəl] *adjective* (work) done in an office or done by a clerk; **clerical error** = mistake made in an office; **clerical staff** = staff of an office; **clerical work** = paperwork done in an office; **clerical worker** = person who works in an office

clerk [klɑːk *US* klɜrk] **1** *noun* **(a)** person who works in an office; **articled clerk** = clerk who is bound by a contract to work in a lawyer's office for some years to learn the trade; **chief clerk** *or* **head clerk** = most important clerk; **filing clerk** = clerk who files documents; **invoice clerk** = clerk who deals with invoices; **shipping clerk** = clerk who deals with shipping documents **(b) bank clerk** = person who works in a bank; **booking clerk** = person who works in a booking office; *US* **sales clerk** = person who sells in a store **2** *verb US* to work as a clerk

clerkess [klɑːˈkes] *noun (in Scotland)* woman clerk

clever [ˈklevə] *adjective* intelligent, able to learn quickly; *he is very clever at spotting a bargain*; *clever investors have made a lot of money on the share deal*

clicks and mortar [ˈklɪks ən ˈmɔːtə] *noun* a combination of computers and shop premises, as in a group which sells over the Internet but also maintains a chain of normal shops

> there may be a silver lining for 'clicks-and-mortar' stores that have both an online and a high street presence. Many of these are accepting returns of goods purchased online at their traditional stores. This is a service that may make them more popular as consumers become more experienced online shoppers
>
> *Financial Times*

client [ˈklaɪənt] *noun* person with whom business is done, person who pays for a service; *one of our major clients has defaulted on his payments*

clientele [kliːənˈtel] *noun* all the clients of a business; all the customers of a shop

climb [klaɪm] *verb* to go up; *the company has climbed to No. 1 position in the market*; *profits climbed rapidly as the new management cut costs*

clinch [klɪntʃ] *verb* to settle (a business deal), to come to an agreement; *he offered an extra 5% to clinch the deal*; *they need approval from the board before they can clinch the deal*

clip [klɪp] *noun* thing with a spring which holds pieces of paper together; **paperclip =** piece of bent wire, used to hold pieces of paper together

clipboard [ˈklɪpbɔːd] *noun* stiff board with a clip at the top so that a piece of paper can be clipped to the board to allow you to write on it easily

clipping service [ˈklɪpɪŋ ˈsɜːvɪs] *noun* service of cutting out references to a client in newspapers or magazines and sending them to him

clock [klɒk] *noun* machine which shows the time; *the office clock is fast*; *all computer have built-in clocks*; **digital clock =** clock which shows the time using numbers (as 12:05)

clock card [ˈklɒk ˈkɑːd] *noun* special card which a worker puts into the time clock when clocking on or off

clock in *or* **clock on** [ˈklɒk ˈɪn *or* ˈklɒk ˈɒn] *verb (of worker)* to record the time of arriving for work by putting a card into a special timing machine

clock out *or* **clock off** [ˈklɒk ˈaʊt *or* ˈklɒk ˈɒf] *verb (of worker)* to record the time of leaving work by putting a card into a special timing machine

clocking in *or* **clocking on** [ˈklɒkɪŋ ˈɪn *or* ˈklɒkɪŋ ˈɒn] *noun* arriving for work and recording the time on a time-card

clocking out *or* **clocking off** [ˈklɒkɪŋ ˈaʊt *or* ˈklɒkɪŋ ˈɒf] *noun* leaving work and recording the time on a time-card

close 1 [kləʊz] *noun* end of a day's trading on the Stock Exchange; *at the close of the day's trading the shares had fallen 20%* **2** [kləʊs] *adjective* **close to =** very near, almost; *the company was close to bankruptcy*; *we are close to meeting our sales targets* **3** [kləʊz] *verb* to end **(a)** to stop doing business for the day; *the office closes at 5.30*; *we close early on Saturdays* **(b) to close (off) the accounts =** to come to the end of an accounting period and take the closing balances on the ledger accounts to the profit and loss account **(c) to close an account =** (i) to stop supplying a customer on credit; (ii) to take all the money out of a bank account and stop the account; *he closed his building society account =* he took all the money out and stopped using the account **(d) the shares closed at $15 =** at the end of the day's trading the price of the shares was $15

> Toronto stocks closed at an all-time high, posting their fifth straight day of advances in heavy trading
>
> *Financial Times*

close company *US* **close(d) corporation** [ˈkləʊs ˈkʌmpənɪ *or* ˈkləʊs kɔːpəˈreɪʃən *or* ˈkləʊzd kɔːpəˈreɪʃən] *noun* privately owned company where the public may own only a small number of shares

closed [kləuzd] *adjective* (a) shut, not open, not doing business; *the office is closed on Mondays*; *all the banks are closed on the National Day* (b) restricted; **closed shop** = system where a company agrees to employ only union members in certain jobs; *the union is asking the management to apply a closed shop agreement*; **closed market** = market where a supplier deals only with one agent or distributor and does not supply any others direct; *they signed a closed market agreement with an Egyptian company*

close down [ˈkləuz ˈdaun] *verb* to shut a shop or factory or service for a long period or for ever; *the company is closing down its London office*; *the strike closed down the railway system*

> the best thing would be to have a few more plants close down and bring supply more in line with current demand
>
> *Fortune*

closing [ˈkləuzɪŋ] **1** *adjective* (a) final, coming at the end; **closing bid** = last bid at an auction, the bid which is successful; **closing date** = last date; *the closing date for tenders to be received is May 1st*; **closing price** = price of a share at the end of a day's trading (b) at the end of an accounting period; *at the end of the quarter the bookkeeper has to calculate the closing balance*; *at the end of the month the closing stock was 10% higher than at the end of the previous month* **2** *noun* (a) shutting of a shop; being shut; **Sunday closing** = not opening a shop on Sundays; **closing time** = time when a shop or office stops work; **early closing day** = weekday (usually Wednesday or Thursday) when some shops close in the afternoon (b) **closing of an account** = act of stopping supply to a customer on credit

closing down sale [ˈkləuzɪŋ ˈdaun ˈseɪl] *noun* sale of goods when a shop is closing for ever

closure [ˈkləuʒə] *noun* act of closing

club [klʌb] *noun* group of people who have the same interest; place where these people meet; *if you want the managing*

director, you can phone him at his club; *he has applied to join the sports club*; **club membership** = all the members of a club; **club subscription** = money paid to belong to a club; **staff club** = club for the staff of a company, which organizes staff parties, sports and meetings

cm = CENTIMETRE

C/N = CREDIT NOTE

c/o [ˈsiːˈəu] = CARE OF

Co. [kəu] = COMPANY; *J. Smith & Co.*

co- [kəu] *prefix* working or acting together

co-creditor [ˈkəuˈkredɪtə] *noun* person who is a creditor of the same company as you are

COD *or* **c.o.d.** [ˈsiːəuˈdiː] = CASH ON DELIVERY

code [kəud] *noun* (a) system of signs, numbers or letters which mean something; **area code** = part of a telephone number which indicates a certain area of the country; *what is the area code for Edinburgh?*; *the area code for Chicago is 312*; **bar code** = system of lines printed on a product which can be read by a computer to give a reference number or price; **international (dialling) code** = part of a telephone number used for dialling to another country; **machine-readable codes** = sets of signs or letters (such as bar codes or post codes) which can be read by computers; **post code** *US* **ZIP code** = letters and numbers used to indicate a town or street in an address on an envelope; **stock code** = numbers and letters which refer to an item of stock (b) set of rules; **code of practice** *US* **code of ethics** = rules drawn up by an association which the members must follow when doing business

coding [ˈkəudɪŋ] *noun* act of putting a code on something; *the coding of invoices*

co-director [kəudɪˈrektə] *noun* person who is a director of the same company as you

coin [kɔɪn] *noun* piece of metal money; *he gave me two 10-franc coins in my change*; *I need some 10p coins for the telephone*

coinage [ˈkɔɪnɪdʒ] *noun* system of metal money used in a country

co-insurance [kəʊɪn'ʃʊərəns] *noun* insurance policy where the risk is shared among several insurers

cold [kəʊld] *adjective* **(a)** not hot; *the machines work badly in cold weather; the office was so cold that the staff started complaining; the coffee machine also sells cold drinks* **(b)** without being prepared; **cold call** = telephone call or sales visit where the salesman has no appointment and the client is not an established customer; **cold start** = starting a new business, opening a new shop where there was none before

> the board is considering the introduction of a set of common provisions on unsolicited calls to investors. The board is aiming to permit the cold calling of customer agreements for the provision of services relating to listed securities. Cold calling would be allowed when the investor is not a private investor
>
> *Accountancy*

collaborate [kə'læbəreɪt] *verb* to work together; *to collaborate with a French firm on a building project; they collaborated on the new aircraft* (NOTE: you collaborate **with** someone **on** something)

collaboration [kəlæbə'reɪʃən] *noun* working together; *their collaboration on the project was very profitable*

collapse [kə'læps] **1** *noun* **(a)** sudden fall in price; *the collapse of the market in silver; the collapse of the dollar on the foreign exchange markets* **(b)** sudden failure of a company; *investors lost thousands of pounds in the collapse of the company* **2** *verb* **(a)** to fall suddenly; *the market collapsed; the yen collapsed on the foreign exchange markets* **(b)** to fail suddenly; *the company collapsed with £250,000 in debts*

collar ['kɒlə] *noun* part of a coat or shirt which goes round the neck; **blue-collar worker** = manual worker in a factory; **white-collar crime** = crimes committed by business people or office workers (such as embezzlement, computer fraud, insider dealings); **white-collar worker** = office worker; **he has a white-collar job** = he works in an office

collateral [kɒ'lætərəl] *adjective & noun* (security) used to provide a guarantee for a loan

> examiners have come to inspect the collateral that thrifts may use in borrowing from the Fed
>
> *Wall Street Journal*

colleague ['kɒliːg] *noun* person who works with you; *his colleagues gave him a present when he got married; I know Jane Gray - she was a colleague of mine at my last job*

collect [kə'lekt] **1** *verb* **(a)** to make someone pay money which is owed; **to collect a debt** = to go and make someone pay a debt **(b)** to take things away from a place; *we have to collect the stock from the warehouse; can you collect my letters from the typing pool?;* **letters are collected twice a day** = the post office workers take them from the letter box to the post office for dispatch **2** *adverb & adjective* **collect call** = phone call where the person receiving the call agrees to pay for it; *to make a collect call; he called his office collect*

collecting agency [kə'lektɪŋ 'eɪdʒənsi] *noun* agency which collects money owed to other companies for a commission

collection [kə'lekʃən] *noun* **(a)** getting money together, making someone pay money which is owed; *tax collection or collection of tax;* **debt collection** = collecting money which is owed; **debt collection agency** = company which collects debts for other companies for a commission; **bills for collection** = bills where payment is due **(b)** fetching of goods; *the stock is in the warehouse awaiting collection;* **collection charges or collection rates** = charge for collecting something; **to hand something in for collection** = to leave something for someone to come and collect **(c)** **collections** = money which has been collected **(d)** taking of letters from a letter box or mail room to the post office for dispatch; *there are four collections a day* *from the letter box at the corner of the street*

collective [kə'lektɪv] *adjective* working together; **free collective bargaining** = negotiations between management and trade unions about wage increases and working conditions; **collective ownership** = ownership of a business by the workers who work in it; **they signed a collective wage agreement** = an agreement was signed between management and the trade union about wages

collector [kə'lektə] *noun* person who makes people pay money which is owed; *he works as a debt collector*

college ['kɒlɪdʒ] *noun* place where people can study after they have left full-time school; **business college** *or* **commercial college** = college which teaches general business methods; **secretarial college** = college which teaches skills which a secretary needs, such as shorthand, typing and word-processing

colour *US* **color** ['kʌlə] *noun* shade which an object has in light (red, blue, yellow, etc.); **colour printer** = printer which prints material in colour; *all our publicity leaflets are printed on the colour printer here in the office*

column ['kɒləm] *noun* (a) series of numbers, one under the other; *to add up a column of figures*; *put the total at the bottom of the column*; **credit column** = right-hand side in accounts showing money received; **debit column** = left-hand side in accounts showing money paid or owed (b) section of printed words in a newspaper or magazine; **column-centimetre** = space in centimetres in a newspaper column, used for calculating charges for advertising

.com ['dɒt'kɒm] a company that primarily does business via the Internet; *the first .com launches targetted the B2C market, the latest group are targetting B2B*

combine 1 ['kɒmbaɪn] *noun* large financial or commercial group; *a German industrial combine* **2** [kəm'baɪn] *verb* to join together; *the workforce and management combined to fight the takeover bid*

combination [kɒmbɪ'neɪʃən] *noun* (a) several things which are joined together; *a* combination of cash flow problems and difficult trading conditions caused the company's collapse* (b) series of numbers which open a special lock; *I have forgotten the combination of the lock on my briefcase*; *the office safe has a combination lock*

comfort ['kʌmfət] *noun* **letter of comfort** *or* **comfort letter** = letter supporting someone who is trying to get a loan

```
comfort  letters  in  the
context  of  a  group  of
companies can take the form of
(a)  an  undertaking  by  a
holding  company  to  provide
finance  to  a  subsidiary;  (b)
an  undertaking  to  meet  the
debts  and  liabilities  of  a
subsidiary  as  they  fall  due.
Comfort   letters   are
encountered  in  numerous  other
situations:  where  a  bank  is  to
grant  finance  to  a  subsidiary
company,  it  may  seek  a  comfort
letter  from  the  parent  to  the
effect  that  the  parent  will
not dispose of its interest in
the subsidiary
```
Accountancy

commerce ['kɒmɜːs] *noun* business, the buying and selling of goods and services; **Chamber of Commerce** = group of local businessmen who meet to discuss problems which they have in common and to promote business in their town

commercial [kə'mɜːʃəl] **1** *adjective* (a) referring to business; **commercial aircraft** = aircraft used to carry cargo or passengers for payment; **commercial artist** = artist who designs advertisements, posters, etc., for payment; **commercial attaché** = diplomat who represents and tries to promote his country's business interests; **commercial bank** = bank which offers banking services to the public, as opposed to a merchant bank; **commercial college** = college which teaches business studies; **commercial course** = course where business skills are studied; *he took a commercial course by correspondence*; **commercial directory** = book which lists all the businesses and business people in a town; **commercial district** = part of a town where offices and shops are; **commercial law** = laws regarding business; **commercial load** = amount of goods or number of passengers which a bus, train or plane has to carry to make a profit; **commercial port** = port which has only goods traffic and no passengers; **commercial traveller** = salesman who travels round an area visiting customers on behalf of his company; **commercial vehicle** = van, truck, etc., used for business purposes; **sample only - of no commercial value** = not worth anything if sold (b) profitable; **not a commercial proposition** = not likely to make a profit **2** *noun* advertisement on television; **commercial break** = time set aside for commercials on television

commercialization [kəmɜːʃəlaɪˈzeɪʃn] *noun* making something into a business proposition; *the commercialization of museums*

commercialize [kəˈmɜːʃəlaɪz] *verb* to make something into a business; *the holiday town has become so commercialized that it is unpleasant*

commercially [kəˈmɜːʃəli] *adverb* in a business way; **not commercially viable** = not likely to make a profit

commission [kəˈmɪʃən] *noun* **(a)** money paid to a salesman or agent, usually a percentage of the sales made; *she gets 10% commission on everything she sells*; **he charges 10% commission** = he asks for 10% of sales as his payment; **commission agent** = agent who is paid a percentage of sales; **commission rep** = representative who is not paid a salary, but receives a commission on sales; **commission sale** *or* **sale on commission** = sale where the salesman is paid a commission **(b)** group of people officially appointed to examine some problem; *the government has appointed a commission of inquiry to look into the problems of small exporters*; *he is the chairman of the government commission on export subsidies*

commit [kəˈmɪt] *verb* **(a)** to carry out (a crime); *she was accused of committing several thefts from the storeroom* **(b)** to **commit funds to a project** = to agree to

spend money on a project (NOTE: **committing - committed**)

commitments [kəˈmɪtmənts] *plural noun* things which you have agreed to do, especially money which you have agreed to spend; **to meet your commitments** = to pay money which you had agreed to pay

committee [kəˈmɪti] *noun* official group of people who organize or plan for a larger group; *to be a member of a committee or to sit on a committee*; *he was elected to the committee of the staff club*; *the new plans have to be approved by the committee members*; **to chair a committee** = to be the chairman of a committee; *he is the chairman of the planning committee*; *she is the secretary of the finance committee*; **management committee** = committee which manages a club, a pension fund, etc.

commodity [kəˈmɒdəti] *noun* thing sold in very large quantities, especially raw materials or food, such as metals or corn; **primary** *or* **basic commodities** = farm produce grown in large quantities, such as corn, rice, cotton; **staple commodity** = basic food or raw material which is most important in a country's economy; **commodity market** *or* **commodity exchange** = place where people buy and sell commodities; **commodity futures** = trading in commodities for delivery at a later date; *silver rose 5% on the commodity futures market yesterday*; **commodity trader** = person whose business is buying and selling commodities

COMMENT: commodities are either traded for immediate delivery (as 'actuals' or 'physicals'), or for delivery in the future (as 'futures'). Commodity markets deal either in metals (aluminium, copper, lead, nickel, silver, zinc) or in 'soft' items, such as cocoa, coffee, sugar and oil

common [ˈkɒmən] *adjective* **(a)** which happens very often; *putting the carbon paper in the wrong way round is a common mistake*; *being caught by customs is very common these days* **(b)** belonging to several different people or to everyone; **common carrier** = firm which carries goods or passengers, and which anyone can use; **common ownership** =

ownership of a company or a property by a group of people; **common pricing** = illegal fixing of prices by several businesses so that they all charge the same price; *US* **common stock** = ordinary shares in a company, giving shareholders a right to vote at meetings and to receive dividends; *(in the EU)* **Common Agricultural Policy (CAP)** = agreement between members of the EU to protect farmers by paying subsidies to fix prices of farm produce

common law ['kɒmən 'lɔ:] *noun* **(a)** law as laid down in decisions of courts, rather than by statute **(b)** general system of laws which formerly were the only laws existing in England, and which in some cases have been superseded by statute (NOTE: you say **at common law** when referring to something happening according to the principles of common law)

Common Market ['kɒmən 'mɑ:kɪt] *noun* **the European Common Market** = formerly the name for the European Community, an organization which links several European countries for the purposes of trade

communautaire [kəmju:nəʊ'teə] *adjective* sympathetic to the European Union; (person) who works happily with EU officials

communicate [kə'mju:nɪkeɪt] *verb* to pass information to someone; *he finds it impossible to communicate with his staff; communicating with head office has been quicker since we installed the fax*

communication [kəmju:nɪ'keɪʃən] *noun* **(a)** passing of information; *communication with the head office has been made easier by the fax machine*; **to enter into communication with someone** = to start discussing something with someone, usually in writing; *we have entered into communication with the relevant government department* **(b)** official message; *we have had a communication from the local tax inspector* **(c)** **communications** = being able to contact people or to pass messages; *after the flood all communications with the outside world were broken*

community [kə'mju:nəti] *noun* **(a)** group of people living or working in the same place; **the local business community** = the business people living and working in the area **(b)** **the European Community** = formerly the name of the European Union

commute [kə'mju:t] *verb* **(a)** to travel to work from home each day; *he commutes from the country to his office in the centre of town* **(b)** to change a right into cash; *he decided to commute part of his pension rights into a lump sum payment*

> Commuting is never business use. A trip to work is personal and not deductible. And making a business phone call or holding a business meeting in your car while you drive will not change that fact
>
> *Nation's Business*

commuter [kə'mju:tə] *noun* person who commutes to work; **he lives in the commuter belt** = area of country where the commuters live round a town; **commuter train** = train which commuters take in the morning and evening; *the rail strike caused disruption to the commuter services*

company ['kʌmpəni] *noun* business, a group of people organized to buy, sell or provide a service **(a)** **to put a company into liquidation** = to close a company by selling its assets for cash; **to set up a company** = to start a company legally; **associate company** = company which is partly owned by another company; **family company** = company where most of the shares are owned by members of a family; **holding company** = company which exists only to own shares in subsidiary companies; **joint-stock company** = company whose shares are held by many people; **limited (liability) company** = company where each shareholder is responsible for repaying the company's debts only to the face value of the shares he or she owns; **listed company** = company whose shares can be bought or sold on the Stock Exchange; **parent company** = company which owns more than half of another company's shares; **private (limited) company** = (i) company with a small number of shareholders whose shares are not traded on the Stock Exchange; (ii) subsidiary company whose shares are not listed on the Stock Exchange, while those of its parent company are; **public limited company (Plc)** = company whose shares can be bought on the Stock Exchange; **subsidiary company** = company which is owned by a parent company **(b) finance company** = company which provides money for hire-purchase; **insurance company** = company whose business is insurance; **shipping company** = company whose business is in transporting goods; **a tractor** *or* **aircraft** *or* **chocolate company** = company which makes tractors, aircraft or chocolate **(c) company car** = car which belongs to a company and is lent to an employee to use for business or other purposes; **company doctor** = (i) doctor who works for a company and looks after sick workers; (ii) specialist businessman who rescues companies which are in difficulties; **company director** = person appointed by the shareholders to help run a company; **company law** = laws which refer to the way companies may work; **company secretary** = person responsible for the company's legal and financial affairs; **company town** = town in which most of the property and shops are owned by a large company which employs most of the population; *GB* **the Companies Acts** = Acts of Parliament which regulate the workings of companies, stating the legal limits within which companies may do their business; **Companies Registration Office (CRO)** *or* **Companies House** = official organization where the records of companies must be deposited, so that they can be inspected by the public

COMMENT: a company can be incorporated (with memorandum and articles of association) as a private limited company, and adds the initials 'Ltd' after its name, or as a public limited company, when its name must end in 'Plc'. Unincorporated companies are partnerships such as firms of solicitors, architects, accountants, etc., and they add the initials 'Co.' after their name

comparable [ˈkɒmpərəbl] *adjective* which can be compared; *the two sets of figures are not comparable*; **which is the**

nearest company comparable to this one in size? = which company is of a similar size and can be compared with this one?

comparability [kəmpærəˈbɪləti] *noun* being able to be compared; **pay comparability** = similar pay system in two different companies

compare [kəmˈpeə] *verb* to look at several things to see how they differ; *the finance director compared the figures for the first and second quarters*

compare with [kəmˈpeə ˈwɪð] *verb* to put two things together to see how they differ; *how do the sales this year compare with last year's?*; *compared with the previous month, last month was terrific*

comparison [kəmˈpærɪsn] *noun* way of comparing; *sales are down in comparison with last year*; *there is no comparison between overseas and home sales* = overseas and home sales are so different they cannot be compared

compassionate leave [kəmˈpæʃənət ˈliːv] *noun* time off work granted to an employee to deal with personal or with family problems; *the staff have been told that compassionate leave will only be granted in extreme cases, such as a death in the family*

compensate [ˈkɒmpenseɪt] *verb* to pay for damage done; *to compensate a manager for loss of commission* (NOTE: you compensate someone **for** something)

it was rumoured that the government was prepared to compensate small depositors
South China Morning Post

compensation [kɒmpenˈseɪʃən] *noun* **(a) compensation for damage** = payment for damage done; **compensation for loss of office** = payment to a director who is asked to leave a company before his contract ends; **compensation for loss of earnings** = payment to someone who has stopped earning money or who is not able to earn money **(b)** *US* salary; **compensation package** = salary, pension and other benefits offered with a job

golden parachutes are liberal compensation packages given

to executives leaving a company

Publishers Weekly

compete [kəmˈpiːt] *verb* **to compete with someone** or **with a company** = to try to do better than another person or another company; *we have to compete with cheap imports from the Far East*; *they were competing unsuccessfully with local companies on their home territory*; *the two companies are competing for a market share* or *for a contract* = each company is trying to win a larger part of the market, trying to win the contract

competence or **competency** [ˈkɒmpətəns or ˈkɒmpətənsi] *noun* **the case falls within the competence of the court** = the court is legally able to deal with the case

competent [ˈkɒmpətənt] *adjective* **(a)** able to do something, efficient; *she is a competent secretary* or *a competent manager* **(b)** **the court is not competent to deal with this case** = the court is not legally able to deal with the case

competing [kəmˈpiːtɪŋ] *adjective* which competes; **competing firms** = firms which compete with each other; **competing products** = products from different companies which have the same use and are sold in the same markets at similar prices

competition [kɒmpəˈtɪʃən] *noun* **(a)** trying to do better than another supplier; **free competition** = being free to compete without government interference; **keen competition** = strong competition; *we are facing keen competition from European manufacturers* **(b)** **the competition** = companies which are trying to compete with your product; *we have lowered our prices to beat the competition*; *the competition have brought out a new range of products* (NOTE: singular, but can take a plural verb in this sense)

profit margins in the industries most exposed to foreign competition are worse than usual

Sunday Times

competition is steadily increasing and could affect

profit margins as the company tries to retain its market share

Citizen (Ottawa)

competitive [kəmˈpetɪtɪv] *adjective* which competes fairly; **competitive price** = low price aimed to compete with a rival product; **competitive pricing** = putting low prices on goods so as to compete with other products; **competitive products** = products made to compete with existing products

the company blamed fiercely competitive market conditions in Europe for a £14m operating loss last year

Financial Times

competitively [kəmˈpetɪtɪvli] *adverb* **competitively priced** = sold at a low price which competes with the price of similar products from other companies

competitiveness [kəmˈpetɪtɪvnəs] *noun* being competitive

farmers are increasingly worried by the growing lack of competitiveness for their products on world markets

Australian Financial Review

competitor [kəmˈpetɪtə] *noun* person or company which competes; *two German firms are our main competitors*

sterling labour costs continue to rise between 3% and 5% a year faster than in most of our competitor countries

Sunday Times

complain [kəmˈpleɪn] *verb* to say that something is no good or does not work properly; *the office is so cold the staff have started complaining*; *she complained about the service*; *they are complaining that our prices are too high*; *if you want to complain, write to the manager*

complaint [kəmˈpleɪnt] *noun* statement that you feel something is wrong; *when making a complaint, always quote the reference number*; *she sent her letter of complaint to the managing director*; **to make** or **lodge a complaint against someone** = to write and send an official complaint to someone's superior;

complaints department = department which deals with complaints from customers; **complaints procedure** = agreed way for workers to make complaints to the management about working conditions

complete [kəm'pliːt] **1** *adjective* whole, with nothing missing; *the order is complete and ready for sending*; *the shipment will be delivered only if it is complete* **2** *verb* to finish; *the factory completed the order in two weeks*; *how long will it take you to complete the job?*

completely [kəm'pliːtli] *adverb* all or totally; *the cargo was completely ruined by water*; *the warehouse was completely destroyed by fire*

completion [kəm'pliːʃən] *noun* act of finishing something; **completion date** = date when something will be finished; **completion of a contract** = signing of a contract for the sale of a property when the buyer pays and the seller passes ownership to the buyer

complex ['kɒmpleks] **1** *noun* series of large buildings; *a large industrial complex* (NOTE: plural is **complexes**) **2** *adjective* with many different parts; *a complex system of import controls*; *the specifications for the machine are very complex*

compliance [kəm'plaɪəns] *noun* agreement to do what is ordered; **compliance department** = department in a stockbroking firm which makes sure that the Stock Exchange rules are followed and that confidentiality is maintained in cases where the same firm represents rival clients

complimentary [kɒmplɪ'mentəri] *adjective* **complimentary ticket** = free ticket, given as a present

compliments slip ['kɒmplɪmənts 'slɪp] *noun* piece of paper with the name of the company printed on it, sent with documents, gifts, etc., instead of a letter

comply [kəm'plaɪ] *verb* **to comply with a court order** = to obey an order given by a court

component [kəm'pəʊnənt] *noun* piece of machinery or part which will be put into a final product; *the assembly line stopped because supply of a component was*

delayed; **components factory** = factory which makes parts which are used in other factories to make finished products

composition [kɒmpə'zɪʃən] *noun* agreement between a debtor and creditors, where the debtor settles a debt by repaying only part of it

compound 1 ['kɒmpaʊnd] *adjective* **compound interest** = interest which is added to the capital and then earns interest itself **2** [kəm'paʊnd] *verb* to agree with creditors to settle a debt by paying part of what is owed

comprehensive [kɒmprɪ'hensɪv] *adjective* which includes everything; **comprehensive insurance** = insurance policy which covers you against all risks which are likely to happen

compromise ['kɒmprəmaɪz] **1** *noun* agreement between two sides, where each side gives way a little; *management offered £5 an hour, the union asked for £9, and a compromise of £7.50 was reached* **2** *verb* to reach an agreement by giving way a little; *he asked £15 for it, I offered £7 and we compromised on £10*

comptometer [kɒmp'tɒmɪtə] *noun* machine which counts automatically

comptroller [kən'trəʊlə] *noun* financial controller

compulsory [kəm'pʌlsəri] *adjective* which is forced or ordered; **compulsory liquidation** *or* **compulsory winding up** = liquidation which is ordered by a court; **compulsory winding up order** = order from a court saying that a company must be wound up; **compulsory purchase order** = order from a local authority by which property is purchased whether the owner wants to sell or not (as when buying properties to widen a road)

computable [kəm'pjuːtəbl] *adjective* which can be calculated

computation [kɒmpjʊ'teɪʃən] *noun* calculation

computational [kɒmpjʊ'teɪʃənl] *adjective* **computational error** = mistake made in calculating

compute [kəm'pjuːt] *verb* to calculate, to do calculations

computer [kəm'pju:tə] *noun* electronic machine which calculates, stores information and processes it automatically; **computer bureau** = office which offers to do work on its computers for companies which do not have their own computers; **computer department** = department in a company which manages the company's computers; **computer error** = mistake made by a computer; **computer file** = section of information on a computer (such as the payroll, list of addresses, customer accounts); **computer language** = system of signs, letters and words used to instruct a computer; **computer listing** = printout of a list of items taken from data stored in a computer; **computer manager** = person in charge of a computer department; **computer program** = instructions to a computer, telling it to do a particular piece of work; **computer programmer** = person who writes computer programs; **computer services** = work using a computer, done by a computer bureau; **computer time** = time when a computer is being used (paid for at an hourly rate); *running all those sales reports costs a lot in computer time*; **business computer** = powerful small computer which is used in a business; **personal computer (PC)** *or* **home computer** = small computer which can be used in the home

computerize [kəm'pju:təraɪz] *verb* to change from a manual system to one using computers; *our stock control has been completely computerized*

computerized [kəm'pju:təraɪzd] *adjective* worked by computers; *a computerized invoicing system*

computer-readable
[kəm'pju:tə'ri:dəbl] *adjective* which can be read and understood by a computer; *computer-readable codes*

computing [kəm'pju:tɪŋ] *noun* referring to computers; **computing speed** = speed at which a computer calculates

con [kɒn] **1** *noun (informal)* trick done to try to get money from someone; *trying to get us to pay him for ten hours' overtime was just a con* **2** *verb (informal)* to trick someone to try to get money; *they conned the bank into lending them £25,000 with*

no security; *he conned the finance company out of £100,000* (NOTE: **con - conning - conned**)

concealment [kən'si:lmənt] *noun* hiding for criminal purposes; **concealment of assets** = hiding assets so that creditors do not know they exist

concern [kən'sɜ:n] **1** *noun* **(a)** business or company; **his business is a going concern** = the company is working (and making a profit); **sold as a going concern** = sold as an actively trading company **(b)** being worried about a problem; *the management showed no concern at all for the workers' safety* **2** *verb* to deal with, to be connected with; *the sales staff are not concerned with the cleaning of the store*; *he filled in a questionnaire concerning computer utilization*

concert ['kɒnsət] *noun (of several people)* **to act in concert** = to work together to achieve an aim (this is illegal if the aim is to influence a share price by all selling or buying together); **concert party** = arrangement where several people or companies work together in secret (usually to acquire another company through a takeover bid)

concession [kən'seʃn] *noun* **(a)** right to use someone else's property for business purposes; **mining concession** = right to dig a mine on a piece of land **(b)** right to be the only seller of a product in a place; *she runs a jewellery concession in a department store* **(c)** allowance such as a reduction of tax or price; **tax concession** = allowing less tax to be paid

concessionaire [kənseʃə'neə] *noun* person who has the right to be the only seller of a product in a place

concessionary [kən'seʃnəri] *adjective* which is allowed as a concession; **concessionary fare** = reduced fare for certain types of passenger (such as pensioners, students, employees of a transport company, etc.); **concessionary ticket** = cheaper entrance ticket to an exhibition for pensioners, students, etc.

conciliation [kənsɪlɪ'eɪʃən] *noun* bringing together the parties in a dispute so that the dispute can be settled; *see also* ACAS

conclude [kənˈkluːd] *verb* **(a)** to complete successfully; *to conclude an agreement with someone* **(b)** to believe from evidence; *the police concluded that the thief had got into the building through the main entrance*

condition [kənˈdɪʃən] *noun* **(a)** something imposed by a contract, duties which have to be carried out as part of a contract, something which has to be agreed before a contract becomes valid; **conditions of employment** *or* **conditions of service** = terms of a contract of employment; **conditions of sale** = agreed ways in which a sale takes place (such as discounts or credit terms); **on condition that** = provided that; *they were granted the lease on condition that they paid the legal costs* **(b)** general state; *the union has complained of the bad working conditions in the factory*; *item sold in good condition*; *what was the condition of the car when it was sold?*; *adverse trading conditions affected our profits*

conditional [kənˈdɪʃənl] *adjective* **(a)** provided that certain things take place; **to give a conditional acceptance** = to accept, provided that certain things happen or certain terms apply; **he made a conditional offer** = he offered to buy, provided that certain terms applied; **conditional sale** = sale which is subject to certain conditions, such as a hire-purchase agreement **(b) conditional on** = subject to (certain conditions); **the offer is conditional on the board's acceptance** = the offer is only valid provided the board accepts

condominium [kɒndəˈmɪnɪəm] *noun* US system of ownership, where a person owns an apartment in a building, together with a share of the land, stairs, roof, etc.

conduct [kənˈdʌkt] *verb* to carry on; *to conduct negotiations*; *the chairman conducted the negotiations very efficiently*

Confederation of British Industry (CBI) [kɒnfedəˈreɪʃn əv ˈbrɪtɪʃ ˈɪndəstri] organization which represents British employers in commerce and industry

conference [ˈkɒnfərəns] *noun* **(a)** meeting of people to discuss problems; **to be in conference** = to be in a meeting;

conference phone = telephone so arranged that several people can speak into it from around a table; **conference room** = room where small meetings can take place; **press conference** = meeting where newspaper and TV reporters are invited to hear news of a new product, a takeover bid, etc.; **sales conference** = meeting of sales managers, representatives, publicity staff, etc., to discuss future sales plans **(b)** meeting of an association, a society, a union, etc.; *the annual conference of the Electricians' Union*; *the conference of the Booksellers' Association*; *the conference agenda* *or the agenda of the conference was drawn up by the secretary*; **Trades Union Conference (TUC)** = association of British trade unions

confidence [ˈkɒnfɪdəns] *noun* **(a)** feeling sure or being certain; *the sales teams do not have much confidence in their manager*; *the board has total confidence in the managing director* **(b) in confidence** = in secret; *I will show you the report in confidence*

confidence trick *US* **confidence game** [ˈkɒnfɪdəns ˈtrɪk] *noun* business deal where someone gains another person's confidence and then tricks him

confidence trickster *US* **confidence man** [ˈkɒnfɪdəns ˈtrɪkstə] *noun* person who carries out a confidence trick on someone

confident [ˈkɒnfɪdənt] *adjective* certain or sure; *I am confident the turnover will increase rapidly*; *are you confident the sales team is capable of handling this product?*

confidential [kɒnfɪˈdenʃəl] *adjective* secret, not to be told or shown to other people; *he sent a confidential report to the chairman*; *please mark the letter 'Private and Confidential'*

confidentiality [kɒnfɪdenʃɪˈælətɪ] *noun* being secret; **he broke the confidentiality of the discussions** = he told someone about the secret discussions

confirm [kənˈfɜːm] *verb* to say that something is certain; *to confirm a hotel reservation or a ticket or an agreement or a booking*; **to confirm someone in a job** = to say that someone is now permanently in the job

confirmation [kɒnfə'meɪʃən] *noun* **(a)** being certain; **confirmation of a booking** = checking that a booking is certain **(b)** document which confirms something; *he received confirmation from the bank that the deeds had been deposited*

conflict of interest ['kɒnflɪkt əv 'ɪntrest] *noun* (i) situation where a person may profit personally from decisions which he takes in his official capacity and may not be able to act properly because of some other person or matter with which he is connected; (ii) situation where a firm may be recommending a course of action to clients which is not in their best interest, but may well profit the firm, or where different departments of the same firm are acting for rival clients

confuse [kən'fjuːz] *verb* to make it difficult for someone to understand something, to make something difficult to understand; *the chairman was confused by all the journalists' questions*; *to introduce the problem of VAT will only confuse the issue*

conglomerate [kən'glɒmərət] *noun* group of subsidiary companies linked together and forming a group, each making very different types of products

congratulate [kən'grætjʊleɪt] *verb* to give someone your good wishes for having done something well; *the sales director congratulated the salesmen on doubling sales*; *I want to congratulate you on your promotion*

congratulations [kəngrætjʊ'leɪʃənz] *plural noun* good wishes; *the staff sent him their congratulations on his promotion*

conman ['kɒnmæn] *noun (informal)* = CONFIDENCE TRICKSTER (NOTE: plural is **conmen**)

connect [kə'nekt] *verb* **(a)** to link or to join; *the company is connected to the government because the chairman's father is a minister* **(b)** the flight from New York connects with a flight to Athens = the plane from New York arrives in time for passengers to catch the plane to Athens

connecting flight [kə'nektɪŋ 'flaɪt] *noun* plane which a passenger will be on time to catch and which will take him to his final destination; *check at the helicopter desk for connecting flights to the city centre*

connection [kə'nekʃən] *noun* **(a)** link, something which joins; *is there a connection between his argument with the director and his sudden move to become warehouse manager?*; **in connection with** = referring to; *I want to speak to the managing director in connection with the sales forecasts* **(b) connections** = people you know, customers or contacts; *he has useful connections in industry*

conservative [kən'sɜːvətɪv] *adjective* careful, not overestimating; *his forecast of expenditure was very conservative or he made a conservative forecast of expenditure*; **at a conservative estimate** = calculation which probably underestimates the final figure; *their turnover has risen by at least 20% in the last year, and that is probably a conservative estimate*

```
we are calculating our next
budget income at an oil price
of $15 per barrel. We know it
is a conservative projection,
but we do not want to come in
for a shock should prices dive
at any time during the year
```
Lloyd's List

---

conservatively [kən'sɜːvətɪvli] *adverb* not overestimating; *the total sales are conservatively estimated at £2.3m*

consider [kən'sɪdə] *verb* to think seriously about something; **to consider the terms of a contract** = to examine and discuss if the terms are acceptable

consideration [kənsɪdə'reɪʃən] *noun* **(a)** serious thought; *we are giving consideration to moving the head office to Scotland* **(b)** something valuable exchanged as part of a contract; **for a small consideration** = for a small fee or payment

considerable [kən'sɪdərəbl] *adjective* quite large; *we sell considerable quantities of our products to Africa*; *they lost a considerable amount of money on the commodity market*

considerably [kən'sɪdərəbli] *adverb* quite a lot; *sales are considerably higher than they were last year*

consign [kən'saɪn] *verb* **to consign goods to someone** = to send goods to someone for him to use or to sell for you

consignation [kɒnsaɪ'neɪʃən] *noun* act of consigning

consignee [kɒnsaɪ'niː] *noun* person who receives goods from someone for his own use or to sell for the sender

consignment [kən'saɪnmənt] *noun* **(a)** sending of goods to someone who will sell them for you; **consignment note** = note saying that goods have been sent; **goods on consignment** = goods kept for another company to be sold on their behalf for a commission **(b)** group of goods sent for sale; *a consignment of goods has arrived*; *we are expecting a consignment of cars from Japan*

> some of the most prominent stores are gradually moving away from the traditional consignment system, under which manufacturers agree to repurchase any unsold goods, and in return dictate prices and sales strategies and even dispatch staff to sell the products
>
> *Nikkei Weekly*

consignor [kən'saɪnə] *noun* person who consigns goods to someone

> COMMENT: the goods remain the property of the consignor until the consignee sells or pays for them

consist of [kən'sɪst əv] *verb* to be formed of; *the trade mission consists of the sales directors of ten major companies*; *the package tour consists of air travel, six nights in a luxury hotel, all meals and visits to places of interest*

consolidate [kən'sɒlɪdeɪt] *verb* **(a)** to include the accounts of several subsidiary companies as well as the holding company in a single set of accounts **(b)** to group goods together for shipping

consolidated [kən'sɒlɪdeɪtɪd] *adjective* **(a) consolidated accounts** = accounts where the financial position of several different companies (i.e., a holding company and its subsidiaries) are recorded together **(b) consolidated shipment** = goods from different companies grouped together into a single shipment

consolidation [kənsɒlɪ'deɪʃən] *noun* grouping together of goods for shipping

consolidator [kən'sɒlɪdeɪtə] *noun* **(a)** firm which groups together orders from different companies into one shipment **(b)** firm which groups together bookings made by various travel agents so as to get cheaper group fares on normal scheduled flights

consols ['kɒnsɒlz] *plural noun GB* government bonds which pay an interest but do not have a maturity date

consortium [kən'sɔːtjəm] *noun* group of companies which work together on a particular project; *a consortium of Canadian companies* or *a Canadian consortium has tendered for the job*; *a consortium of French and British companies is planning to construct the new aircraft* (NOTE: plural is **consortia**)

> the consortium was one of only four bidders for the £2 billion contract to run the lines, seen as potentially the most difficult contract because of the need for huge investment
>
> *Times*

constant ['kɒnstənt] *adjective* which does not change; *the calculations are in constant dollars*

constitution [kɒnstɪ'tjuːʃən] *noun* written rules or regulations of a society, association, club or state; *under the society's constitution, the chairman is elected for a two-year period*; *payments to officers of the association are not allowed by the constitution*

constitutional [kɒnstɪ'tjuːʃənl] *adjective* according to a constitution; *the reelection of the chairman is not constitutional*

construct [kən'strʌkt] *verb* to build; *the company has tendered for the contract to construct the new airport*

construction [kənˈstrʌkʃən] *noun* building; **construction company** = company which specializes in building; **construction industry** = all companies specializing in building; **under construction** = being built; *the airport is under construction*

constructive [kənˈstrʌktɪv] *adjective* which helps in the making of something; *she made some constructive suggestions for improving management-worker relations*; *we had a constructive proposal from a distribution company in Italy*; **constructive dismissal** = situation when a worker does not leave his job voluntarily but because of pressure from the management

constructor [kənˈstrʌktə] *noun* person or company which constructs

consult [kənˈsʌlt] *verb* to ask an expert for advice; *he consulted his accountant about his tax*

consultancy [kənˈsʌltənsi] *noun* act of giving specialist advice; *a consultancy firm*; *he offers a consultancy service*

consultant [kənˈsʌltənt] *noun* specialist who gives advice; *engineering consultant*; *management consultant*; *tax consultant*

consulting [kənˈsʌltɪŋ] *adjective* person who gives specialist advice; *consulting engineer*

consumable goods *or* **consumables** [kənˈsjuːməbl ˈɡʊdz *or* kənˈsjuːməblz] *noun* goods which are bought by members of the public and not by companies

consumer [kənˈsjuːmə] *noun* person or company which buys and uses goods and services; *gas consumers are protesting at the increase in prices*; *the factory is a heavy consumer of water*; **consumer council** = group representing the interests of consumers; **consumer credit** = credit given by shops, banks and other financial institutions to consumers so that they can buy goods; **Consumer Credit Act, 1974** = Act of Parliament which licenses lenders, and requires them to state clearly the full terms of loans which they make (including the APR); **consumer durables** = items such as washing machines, refrigerators or cookers which are bought and used by the

public; **consumer goods** = goods bought by consumers, that is by ordinary members of the public; **consumer panel** = group of consumers who report on products they have used so that the manufacturers can improve them or use what the panel says about them in advertising; **Consumer Price Index** = American index showing how prices of consumer goods have risen over a period of time, used as a way of measuring inflation and the cost of living (the British equivalent is the Retail Prices Index or RPI); **consumer protection** = protecting consumers against unfair or illegal traders; **consumer research** = research into why consumers buy goods and what goods they really want to buy; **consumer resistance** = lack of interest by consumers in buying a product; *the latest price increases have produced considerable consumer resistance*; **consumer society** = type of society where consumers are encouraged to buy goods; **consumer spending** = spending by consumers

```
analysis of the consumer
price index for the first half
of the year shows that the
rate of inflation went down by
about 12.9 per cent
                  Business Times (Lagos)
```

consumption [kənˈsʌmʃən] *noun* buying or using goods or services; *a car with low petrol consumption*; *the factory has a heavy consumption of coal*; **home consumption** *or* **domestic consumption** = use of something in the home; **industrial consumption** = consumption of something by an industry

contact 1 [ˈkɒntækt] *noun* **(a)** person you know, person you can ask for help or advice; *he has many contacts in the city*; *who is your contact in the ministry?* **(b)** act of getting in touch with someone; **I have lost contact with them** = I do not communicate with them any longer; **he put me in contact with a good lawyer** = he told me how to get in touch with a good lawyer **2** [ˈkɒntækt *or* kənˈtækt] *verb* to get in touch with someone, to communicate with someone; *he tried to contact his office by phone*; *can you contact the managing director at his club?*

contain [kən'teɪn] *verb* to hold something inside; *each crate contains two computers and their peripherals*; *a barrel contains 250 litres*; *we have lost a file containing important documents*

container [kən'teɪnə] *noun* **(a)** box, bottle, can, etc., which can hold goods; *the gas is shipped in strong metal containers*; *the container burst during shipping* **(b)** very large metal case of a standard size for loading and transporting goods on trucks, trains and ships; *container ship*; *container berth*; *container port*; *container terminal*; *to ship goods in containers*; *a* **container-load of spare parts** = a shipment of spare parts sent in a container

containerization [kənteɪnəraɪ'zeɪʃən] *noun* putting into containers; shipping in containers

containerize [kən'teɪnəraɪz] *verb* to put goods into containers; to ship goods in containers

contango [kən'tæŋgəu] *noun* payment of interest by a stockbroker for permission to carry payment for shares from one account to the next (no longer applied on the London Stock Exchange because of the rolling account system, but still applied on some other exchanges); **contango day** = day when the rate of contango payments is fixed

contempt of court [kən'temt əv 'kɔːt] *noun* being rude to a court, as by bad behaviour in court or by refusing to carry out a court order

content ['kɒntent] *noun* the ideas inside a letter, etc.; **the content of the letter** = the real meaning of the letter

contents ['kɒntents] *plural noun* things contained by something, what is inside something; *the contents of the bottle poured out onto the floor*; *customs officials inspected the contents of the crate*; **the contents of the letter** = the words written in the letter

contested takeover [kən'testɪd 'teɪkəuvə] *noun* takeover bid where the board of the target company does not recommend it to the shareholders and tries to fight it (NOTE: also called a **hostile bid**)

contingency [kən'tɪndʒənsi] *noun* possible state of emergency when decisions will have to be taken quickly; **contingency fund** *or* **contingency reserve** = money set aside in case it is needed urgently; **contingency plans** = plans which will be put into action if something happens which no one expects; **to add on 10% to provide for contingencies** = to provide for further expenditure which may be incurred; *we have built 10% for contingencies into our cost forecast*

contingent [kən'tɪndʒənt] *adjective* **(a)** **contingent expenses** = expenses which will be incurred only if something happens; **contingent liability** = liability which may or may not occur, but for which provision is made in a company's accounts (as opposed to 'provisions', where money is set aside for an anticipated expenditure) **(b)** **contingent policy** = policy which pays out only if something happens (as if the person named in the policy dies before the person due to benefit)

continual [kən'tɪnjuəl] *adjective* which happens again and again; *production was slow because of continual breakdowns*

continually [kən'tɪnjuəli] *adverb* again and again; *the photocopier is continually breaking down*

continuation [kəntɪnju'eɪʃən] *noun* act of continuing; **continuation sheet** = second (or third) page of a document

continue [kən'tɪnjuː] *verb* to go on doing something; to do something which you were doing earlier; *the chairman continued speaking in spite of the noise from the shareholders*; *the meeting started at 10 a.m. and continued until six p.m.*; *negotiations will continue next Monday*

continuous [kən'tɪnjuəs] *adjective* with no end, with no breaks; *continuous production line*; **continuous feed** = device which feeds continuous stationery into a printer; **continuous stationery** = paper made as one long sheet, used in the computer printers

contra ['kɒntrə] **1** *noun* **contra account** = account which offsets another account (where a company's supplier is not only a creditor in that company's books but also a debtor because it has purchased goods on credit); **contra entry** = entry made in the opposite side of an account to offset an earlier entry; **per contra** *or* **as per contra** = words showing that a contra entry has been made **2** *verb* **to contra an entry** = to enter a similar amount in the opposite side of an account

contraband ['kɒntrəbænd] *noun* **contraband (goods)** = goods brought into a country illegally, without paying customs duty

contract 1 ['kɒntrækt] *noun* **(a)** legal agreement between two parties; *to draw up a contract*; *to draft a contract*; *to sign a contract*; **the contract is binding on both parties** = both parties signing the contract must do what is agreed; **under contract** = bound by the terms of a contract; *the firm is under contract to deliver the goods by November*; **to void a contract** = to make a contract invalid; **contract of employment** = contract between management and employee showing all conditions of work; **service contract** = contract between a company and a director showing all conditions of work; **exchange of contracts** = point in the sale of a property when the buyer and seller both sign the contract of sale which then becomes binding **(b)** **contract law** *or* **law of contract** = laws relating to agreements; **by private contract** = by private legal agreement; **contract note** = note showing that shares have been bought or sold but not yet paid for **(c)** agreement for supply of a service or goods; *contract for the supply of spare parts*; *to enter into a contract to supply spare parts*; *to sign a contract for £10,000 worth of spare parts*; **to put work out to contract** = to decide that work should be done by another company on a contract, rather than employing members of staff to do it; **to award a contract to a company** *or* **to place a contract with a company** = to decide that a company shall have the contract to do work for you; **to tender for a contract** = to put forward an estimate of cost for work under contract; **breach of contract** = breaking the terms of a contract; **the company is in breach of contract** = the company has failed to do what was agreed in the contract;

conditions of contract *or* **contract conditions** = conditions which are listed in a contract and which are legally binding; **contract work** = work done according to a written agreement **2** ['kɒntrækt or kən'trækt] *verb* to agree to do some work by a legally binding contract; *to contract to supply spare parts* *or* *to contract for the supply of spare parts*; **the supply of spare parts was contracted out to Smith Ltd** = Smith Ltd was given the contract for supplying spare parts; **to contract out of an agreement** = to withdraw from an agreement with written permission of the other party

COMMENT: a contract is an agreement between two or more parties to create legal obligations between them. Some contracts are made 'under seal', i.e. they are signed and sealed by the parties; most contracts are made orally or in writing. The essential elements of a contract are: (a) that an offer made by one party should be accepted by the other; (b) consideration (i.e. payment of money); (c) the intention to create legal relations. The terms of a contract may be express or implied. A breach of contract by one party entitles the other party to sue for damages or to ask for something to be done

contracting [kən'træktɪŋ] *adjective* **contracting party** = person or company which signs a contract

contractor [kən'træktə] *noun* person or company which does work according to a written agreement; **haulage contractor** = company which transports goods by contract; **government contractor** = company which supplies the government with goods by contract

contractual [kən'træktjuəl] *adjective* according to a contract; **contractual liability** = legal responsibility for something as stated in a contract; **to fulfil your contractual obligations** = to do what you have agreed to do in a contract; **he is under no contractual obligation to buy** = he has signed no agreement to buy

contractually [kən'træktjuəli] *adverb* according to a contract; *the company is contractually bound to pay his expenses*

contrary ['kɒntrəri] *noun* opposite; **failing instructions to the contrary** = unless different instructions are given; **on the contrary** = quite the opposite; *the chairman was not annoyed with his assistant - on the contrary, he promoted him*

contribute [kən'trɪbjuːt] *verb* to give money; to add to money; *to contribute 10% of the profits*; *he contributed to the pension fund for 10 years*

contribution [kɒntrɪ'bjuːʃən] *noun* money paid to add to a sum; **contribution of capital** = money paid to a company as additional capital; **employer's contribution** = money paid by an employer towards a worker's pension; **National Insurance contributions (NIC)** = money paid each month by a worker and the company to the National Insurance; **pension contributions** = money paid by a company or worker into a pension fund

contributor [kən'trɪbjutə] *noun* **contributor of capital** = person who contributes capital

contributory [kən'trɪbjutəri] *adjective* **(a) contributory pension plan** *or* **scheme** = pension plan where the employee has to contribute a percentage of salary **(b)** which helps to cause; *falling exchange rates have been a contributory factor in or to the company's loss of profits*

con trick ['kɒn 'trɪk] *noun (informal)* = CONFIDENCE TRICK

control [kən'trəʊl] **1** *noun* **(a)** power, being able to direct something; *the company is under the control of three shareholders*; **to gain control of a business** = to buy more than 50% of the shares so that you can direct the business; **to lose control of a business** = to find that you have less than 50% of the shares in a company, and so are not longer able to direct it; *the family lost control of its business* **(b)** restricting or checking something, making sure that something is kept in check; **under control** = kept in check; *expenses are kept under tight control*; *the company is trying to bring its overheads back under control*; **out of control** = not kept in check; *costs have got out of control*; **budgetary control** =

keeping check on spending according to a planned budget; **credit control** = checking that customers pay on time and do not exceed their credit limits; **quality control** = making sure that the quality of a product is good; **stock control** *US* **inventory control** = making sure that the correct level of stock is maintained (to be able to meet demand while keeping the costs of holding stock to a minimum) **(c)** **exchange controls** = government restrictions on changing the local currency into foreign currency; *the government has imposed exchange controls*; *they say the government is going to lift exchange controls*; **price controls** = legal measures to prevent prices rising too fast **(d)** **control group** = small group which is used to check a sample group; **control key** = key on a computer keyboard which works part of a program; **control systems** = systems used to check that a computer system is working correctly **2** *verb* **(a) to control a business** = to direct a business; *the business is controlled by a company based in Luxembourg*; *the company is controlled by the majority shareholder* **(b)** to make sure that something is kept in check or is not allowed to develop; *the government is fighting to control inflation or to control the rise in the cost of living* (NOTE: **controlling - controlled**)

controlled [kən'trəʊld] *adjective* ruled, kept in check; **government-controlled** = ruled by a government; **controlled economy** = economy where the most business activity is directed by orders from the government

controller [kən'trəʊlə] *noun* **(a)** person who controls (especially the finances of a company); **credit controller** = member of staff whose job is to try to get payment of overdue invoices; **stock controller** = person who notes movements of stock and makes sure that enough stock is kept to satisfy orders **(b)** *US* chief accountant in a company

controlling [kən'trəʊlɪŋ] *adjective* **to have a controlling interest in a company** = to own more than 50% of the shares so that you can direct how the company is run

convene [kən'viːn] *verb* to ask people to come together; *to convene a meeting of shareholders*

convenience [kən'viːnjəns] *noun* **at your earliest convenience** = as soon as you find it possible; **convenience foods** = food which is prepared by the shop before it is sold, so that it needs only heating to be made ready to eat; **convenience store** = small store selling food or household goods, open until late at night, or even 24 hours per day; **ship sailing under a flag of convenience** = flying the flag of a country which may have no ships of its own but allows ships of other countries to be registered in its ports

> the nation's largest convenience store chain has expanded the range of bills it takes payments for to include gas and telephone services
>
> *Nikkei Weekly*

convenient [kən'viːnjənt] *adjective* suitable or handy; *a bank draft is a convenient way of sending money abroad*; *is 9.30 a convenient time for the meeting?*

convenor [kən'viːnə] *noun* trade unionist who organizes union meetings

conversion [kən'vɜːʃən] *noun* change **(a) conversion of funds** = using money which does not belong to you for a purpose for which it is not supposed to be used **(b) conversion price** = price at which preference shares are converted into ordinary shares; **conversion rate** = rate at which a currency is changed into a foreign currency

convert [kən'vɜːt] *verb* **(a)** to change money of one country for money of another; *we converted our pounds into Swiss francs* **(b) to convert funds to your own use** = to use someone else's money for yourself

convertibility [kənvɜːtə'bɪləti] *noun* ability to exchange one currency for another easily

convertible [kən'vɜːtəbl] *adjective* **convertible currency** = currency which can be exchanged for another easily; **convertible debentures** *or* **convertible loan stock** = debentures or loan stock which can be exchanged for ordinary shares at a later date

conveyance [kən'veɪəns] *noun* legal document which transfers a property from the seller to the buyer

conveyancer [kən'veɪənsə] *noun* person who draws up a conveyance

conveyancing [kən'veɪənsɪŋ] *noun* legally transferring a property from a seller to a buyer; **do-it-yourself conveyancing** = drawing up a legal conveyance without the help of a lawyer

cooling off period ['kuːlɪŋ ɒf 'piːriəd] *noun* (i) during an industrial dispute, a period when negotiations have to be carried on and no action can be taken by either side; (ii) period when a person is allowed to think about something which he has agreed to buy on hire-purchase and possibly change his mind; (iii) period of ten days during which a person who has signed a life assurance policy may cancel it

co-op ['kəʊɒp] *noun* = CO-OPERATIVE, 2

co-operate [kəʊ'ɒpəreɪt] *verb* to work together; *the regional governments are co-operating in the fight against piracy*; *the two firms have co-operated on the computer project*

co-operation [kəʊɒpə'reɪʃən] *noun* working together; *the project was completed ahead of schedule with the co-operation of the workforce*

co-operative [kəʊ'ɒpərətɪv] **1** *adjective* willing to work together; *the workforce has not been co-operative over the management's productivity plan*; **co-operative society** = society where the customers and workers are partners and share the profits **2** *noun* business run by a group of workers who are the owners and who share the profits; *he works for an agricultural co-operative*; *they set up a workers' co-operative to run the factory*

co-opt [kəʊ'ɒpt] *verb* **to co-opt someone onto a committee** = to ask someone to join a committee without being elected

co-owner ['kəʊ'əʊnə] *noun* person who owns something with another person; *the two sisters are co-owners of the property*

co-ownership [ˈkəʊˈəʊnəʃɪp] *noun* arrangement where two people own a property or where partners or workers have shares in a company

copartner [kəʊˈpɑːtnə] *noun* person who is a partner in a business with another person

copartnership [kəʊˈpɑːtnəʃɪp] *noun* arrangement where partners or workers have shares in the company

cope [kəʊp] *verb* to manage to do something; *the new assistant manager coped very well when the manager was on holiday*; *the warehouse is trying to cope with the backlog of orders*

copier [ˈkɒpɪə] *noun* = COPYING MACHINE, PHOTOCOPIER machine which makes copies of documents; **copier paper** = special paper used in photocopiers; **plain paper copier** = copier which uses ordinary white paper, not special copier paper

coproprietor [kəʊprəˈpraɪətə] *noun* person who owns a property with another person or several other people

coproperty [kəʊˈprɒpəti] *noun* ownership of property by two or more people together

copy [ˈkɒpi] **1** *noun* **(a)** document which is made to look the same as another; **carbon copy** = copy made with carbon paper; **certified copy** = document which is certified as being the same as another; **file copy** = copy of a document which is filed in an office for reference; **copy paper** = special paper used in photocopiers **(b)** any document; **fair copy** *or* **final copy** = document which is written or typed with no changes or mistakes; **hard copy** = printout of a text which is on a computer; **rough copy** = draft of a document which, it is expected, will have changes made to it; **top copy** = first or top sheet of a document which is typed with carbon copies **(c)** **publicity copy** = text of a proposed advertisement before it is printed; *she writes copy for a travel firm*; **knocking copy** = advertising material which criticizes competing products **(d)** a book, a newspaper; *have you kept yesterday's copy of the 'Times'?*; *I read it in the office copy of 'Fortune'*; *where is my copy of the*

telephone directory? **2** *verb* to make a second document which is like the first; *he copied the company report at night and took it home*

copyholder [ˈkɒpihəʊldə] *noun* frame on which a document can be put, which stands next to a typewriter or keyboard, so that the operator can read the text to be copied more easily

copying machine [ˈkɒpiɪŋ məˈʃiːn] *noun* machine which makes copies of documents

copyright [ˈkɒpiraɪt] **1** *noun* legal right (lasting for a number of years after the death of a writer) which a writer has to publish his own work and not to have it copied; **Copyright Act** = Act of Parliament making copyright legal, and controlling the copying of copyright material; **copyright law** = laws concerning copyright; **work which is out of copyright** = work by a writer who has been dead for seventy years; **work still in copyright** = work by a living writer, or by a writer who died less than seventy years ago; **infringement of copyright** *or* **copyright infringement** = act of illegally copying a work which is in copyright; **copyright holder** = person who owns a copyright (and who can expect to receive royalties from it); **copyright notice** = note in a book showing who owns the copyright and the date of ownership **2** *verb* to confirm the copyright of a written work by inserting a copyright notice and publishing the work **3** *adjective* covered by the laws of copyright; *it is illegal to photocopy a copyright work*

copyrighted [ˈkɒpiraɪtɪd] *adjective* in copyright

copy typing [ˈkɒpi ˈtaɪpɪŋ] *noun* typing documents from handwritten originals, not from dictation

copy typist [ˈkɒpi ˈtaɪpɪst] *noun* person who types documents from handwritten originals, not from dictation

copywriter [ˈkɒpiraɪtə] *noun* person who writes advertisements

corner [ˈkɔːnə] **1** *noun* **(a)** place where two streets or two walls join; *the Post Office is on the corner of the High Street and London Road*; **corner shop** = small general store in a town on a street corner

(b) place where two sides join; *the box has to have specially strong corners*; *the corner of the crate was damaged* **(c)** situation where one person or a group controls the supply of a certain commodity; *the syndicate tried to create a corner in the silver market* **2** *verb* to **corner the market** = to own most or all of the supply of a certain commodity and so control the price; *the syndicate tried to corner the market in silver*

corp *US* = CORPORATION

corporate ['kɔːpərət] *adjective* referring to a whole company; **corporate image** = idea which a company would like the public to have of it; **corporate plan** = plan for the future work of a whole company; **corporate planning** = planning the future work of a whole company; **corporate profits** = profits of a corporation; **corporate raider** = person or company which buys a stake in a company before making a hostile takeover bid

> the prime rate is the rate at which banks lend to their top corporate borrowers
> *Wall Street Journal*

> corporate profits for the first quarter showed a 4 per cent drop from last year
> *Financial Times*

> if corporate forecasts are met, sales will exceed $50 million next year
> *Citizen (Ottawa)*

corporation [kɔːpə'reɪʃən] *noun* **(a)** large company; **finance corporation** = company which provides money for hire purchase; **corporation tax (CT)** = tax on profits and capital gains made by companies, calculated before dividends are paid; **Advance Corporation Tax (ACT)** = tax paid by a company in advance of its main tax payments; it is paid when dividends are paid to shareholders and appears on the tax voucher attached to a dividend warrant; **mainstream corporation tax** = tax paid by a company on its profits (the ACT is set against this) **(b)** *US* company which is incorporated in the United States; **corporation income tax** = tax on profits made by incorporated

companies **(c)** *GB* municipal authority; **corporation loan** = loan issued by a local authority

> COMMENT: a corporation is formed by registration with the Registrar of Companies under the Companies Act (in the case of public and private companies) or other Acts of Parliament (in the case of building societies and charities)

correct [kə'rekt] **1** *adjective* accurate or right; *the published accounts do not give a correct picture of the company's financial position* **2** *verb* to remove mistakes from something; *the accounts department have corrected the invoice*; *you will have to correct all these typing errors before you send the letter*

correction [kə'rekʃən] *noun* **(a)** making something correct; change which makes something correct; *he made some corrections to the text of the speech*; **correction fluid** = white liquid which is put on a typed document to correct mistakes **(b)** *(stock exchange)* **technical correction** = situation where a share price or a currency moves up or down because it was previously too low or too high

> there were fears in October that shares were overvalued and bears were ready to enter the market. This only proved to be a small correction
> *Investors Chronicle*

correspond [kɒrɪs'pɒnd] *verb* **(a)** to **correspond with someone** = to write letters to someone **(b)** to **correspond with something** = to fit or to match something

correspondence [kɒrɪs'pɒndəns] *noun* letters which are exchanged; **business correspondence** = letters concerned with a business; **to be in correspondence with someone** = to write letters to someone and receive letters back; **correspondence clerk** = clerk whose responsibility it is to answer correspondence

correspondent [kɒrɪs'pɒndənt] *noun* **(a)** person who writes letters **(b)** journalist who writes articles for a newspaper on specialist subjects; *the 'Times' business correspondent*; *he is the Paris correspondent of the 'Telegraph'*

corrupt [kə'rʌpt] **1** *adjective* **(a)** (person, especially an official) who takes bribes; referring to the taking of bribes; *they accused the minister's assistant of corrupt practices* **(b)** (data on a computer disk) which is faulty and therefore cannot be used **2** *verb* to make data unusable; *the faulty disk drive corrupted our files*

corruption [kə'rʌpʃn] *noun* paying money or giving a favour to someone (usually an official) so that he does what you want; *bribery and corruption are difficult to control*

cost [kɒst] **1** *noun* **(a)** amount of money which has to be paid for something; *what is the cost of a first class ticket to New York?*; *computer costs are falling each year*; *we cannot afford the cost of two cars*; **to cover costs** = to produce enough money in sales to pay for the costs of production; *the sales revenue barely covers the costs of advertising or the advertising costs*; **to sell at cost** = to sell at a price which is the same as the cost of manufacture or the wholesale cost; **direct costs** = all costs (e.g. materials, labour and expenses) which can be directly related to the making of a product; **fixed costs** = business costs which do not change with the quantity of the product made; **historic(al) cost** = actual purchase cost of something which was bought some time ago; **indirect costs** = costs which are not directly related to the making of a product (such as cleaning, rent, administration); **labour costs** = cost of hourly-paid workers employed to make a product; **manufacturing costs** *or* **production costs** = costs of making a product; **operating costs** *or* **running costs** = cost of the day-to-day organization of a company; **variable costs** = production costs which increase with the quantity of the product made (such as wages, raw materials) **(b)** **cost accountant** = accountant who gives managers information about their business costs; **cost accounting** = specially prepared accounts of manufacturing and sales costs; **cost analysis** = calculating in advance what a new product will cost; **cost centre** = person or group whose costs can be itemized and to which costs can be allocated in accounts; **cost, insurance and**

freight (CIF) = estimate of a price, which includes the cost of the goods, the insurance and the transport charges; **cost price** = selling price which is the same as the price which the seller paid for the item (i.e. either the manufacturing cost or the wholesale price); **cost of sales** = all the costs of a product sold, including manufacturing costs and the staff costs of the production department **(c)** **costs** = expenses involved in a court case; **to pay costs** = to pay the expenses of a court case; *the judge awarded costs to the defendant*; *costs of the case will be borne by the prosecution* **2** *verb* **(a)** to have a price; *how much does the machine cost?*; *this cloth costs £10 a metre* **(b)** **to cost a product** = to calculate how much money will be needed to make a product, and so work out its selling price

cost-benefit analysis ['kɒst'benɪfɪt ə'næləsɪs] *noun* comparing the costs and benefits of different possible ways of using available resources

cost-cutting ['kɒst'kʌtɪŋ] *noun* reducing costs; *we have taken out the second telephone line as a cost-cutting exercise*

cost-effective ['kɒstɪ'fektɪv] *adjective* which gives value, especially when compared with its cost; *we find advertising in the Sunday newspapers very cost-effective*

cost-effectiveness ['kɒstɪ'fektɪvnəs] *noun* being cost-effective; *can we calculate the cost-effectiveness of air freight against shipping by sea?*

costing ['kɒstɪŋ] *noun* calculation of the manufacturing costs, and so the selling price of a product; *the costings give us a retail price of $2.95*; *we cannot do the costing until we have details of all the production expenditure*

costly ['kɒstli] *adjective* expensive, costing a lot of money

cost of living ['kɒst əv 'lɪvɪŋ] *noun* money which has to be paid for food, heating, rent, etc.; **to allow for the cost of living in the salary adjustments**; **cost-of-living allowance** = addition to normal salary to cover increases in the cost of living; **cost-of-living bonus** = extra money paid to meet the increase in the cost of living; **cost-of-living increase** = increase in salary to allow it to keep up with the increased cost of living; **cost-of-living index** = way of measuring the cost of living which is shown as a percentage increase on the figure for the previous year (similar to the consumer price index, but including other items such as the interest on mortgages)

cost plus ['kɒst 'plʌs] *noun* system of calculating a price, by taking the cost of production of goods or services and adding a percentage to cover the supplier's overheads and margin; *we are charging for the work on a cost plus basis*

cost-push inflation ['kɒst'pʊʃ ɪn'fleɪʃən] *noun* inflation caused by increased wage demands which lead to higher prices and in turn lead to further wage demands

cottage industry ['kɒtɪdʒ 'ɪndəstri] *noun* production of goods, or other type of work, carried out by workers in their homes

council ['kaʊnsl] *noun* official group chosen to run something or to advise on a problem; **consumer council** = group representing the interests of consumers; **town council** = representatives elected to run a town

counsel ['kaʊnsl] **1** *noun* lawyer acting for one of the parties in a legal action; *defence counsel*; *prosecution counsel*; *GB* **Queen's Counsel (QC)** = senior lawyer **2** *verb* to advise; **he counselled caution** = he advised us to act carefully

counselling *US* **counseling** ['kaʊnsəlɪŋ] *noun* giving advice; **debt counselling** = advising people in debt as to the best way of arranging their finances to pay off their debts

count [kaʊnt] *verb* **(a)** to add figures together to make a total; *he counted up the sales for the six months to December* **(b)** to include; *did you count my trip to New York as part of my sales expenses?*

counter ['kaʊntə] *noun* long flat surface in a shop for displaying and selling goods; **over the counter** = legally; **goods sold over the counter** = retail sales of goods in shops; *some drugs are sold over the counter, but others need to be recommended by a doctor*; **over-the-counter sales** = legal selling of shares which are not listed in the official Stock Exchange list (usually carried out by telephone); **under the counter** = illegally; **under-the-counter sales** = black market sales; **bargain counter** = counter where things are sold cheaply; **check-in counter** = place where plane passengers have to check in; **ticket counter** = place where tickets are sold; **trade counter** = shop in a factory or warehouse where goods are sold to retailers; **glove counter** = section of a shop where gloves are sold; **counter staff** = sales staff who serve behind counters

counter- ['kaʊntə] *prefix* against

counterbid ['kaʊntəbɪd] **1** *noun* higher bid in reply to a previous bid; *when I bid £20 he put in a counterbid of £25* **2** *verb* to make a higher bid in reply to a previous bid; *when I bid £20 he counterbid £25*

counter-claim ['kaʊntəkleɪm] **1** *noun* claim for damages made in reply to a previous claim; *Jones claimed £25,000 in damages against Smith, and Smith entered a counter-claim of £50,000 for loss of office* **2** *verb* to put in a counter-claim; *Jones claimed £25,000 in damages and Smith counter-claimed £50,000 for loss of office*

counterfeit ['kaʊntəfɪt] **1** *adjective* false or imitation (money); *shops in the area have been asked to look out for counterfeit £20 notes* **2** *verb* to make imitation money

counterfoil ['kaʊntəfɔɪl] *noun* slip of paper kept after writing a cheque, an invoice or a receipt, as a record of the deal which has taken place

countermand ['kaʊntəmɑːnd] *verb* to **countermand an order** = to say that an order must not be carried out

counter-offer ['kaʊntər'ɒfə] *noun* higher (or lower) offer made in reply to another offer; *Smith Ltd made an offer of £1m for the property, and Blacks replied with a counter-offer of £1.4m*

```
the company set about paring
costs   and   improving   the
design of its product. It came
up with a price cut of 14%, but
its  counter-offer  -  for  an
```

order that was to have provided 8% of its workload next year - was too late and too expensive

Wall Street Journal

counterpart ['kaʊntəpɑːt] *noun* person who has a similar job in another company; **John is my counterpart in Smith's** = he has the same post as I have here

counterparty ['kaʊntəpɑːti] *noun* the other party in a deal

counter-productive
['kaʊntəprə'dʌktɪv] *adjective* which has the opposite effect to what you expect; *increasing overtime pay was counter-productive, the workers simply worked more slowly*

countersign ['kaʊntəsaɪn] *verb* to sign a document which has already been signed by someone else; *all our cheques have to be countersigned by the finance director; the sales director countersigns all my orders*

countervailing duty ['kaʊntəveɪlɪŋ 'djuːti] *noun* duty imposed by a country on imported goods, where the price of the goods includes a subsidy from the government in the country of origin

counting house ['kaʊntɪŋ 'haʊs] *noun (old-fashioned)* department dealing with cash

count on ['kaʊnt ɒn] *verb* to expect something to happen; *they are counting on getting a good response from the TV advertising; do not count on a bank loan to start your business*

country ['kʌntri] *noun* (a) land which is separate and governs itself; *the contract covers distribution in the countries of the EU; some African countries export oil; the Organization of Petroleum Exporting Countries; the managing director is out of the country* = he is on a business trip abroad (b) land which is not near a town; *distribution is difficult in country areas; his territory is mainly the country, but he is based in the town*

couple ['kʌpl] *noun* two things or people taken together; *we only have enough stock for a couple of weeks; a couple of the directors were ill, so the board meeting was cancelled;* **the negotiations lasted a couple of hours** = the negotiations went on for about two hours

coupon ['kuːpɒn] *noun* (a) piece of paper used in place of money; **gift coupon** = coupon from a store which is given as a gift and which must be exchanged in that store (b) piece of paper which replaces an order form; **coupon ad** = advertisement with a form attached, which is to be cut out and returned to the advertiser with your name and address if you want further information about the product advertised; **reply coupon** = form attached to a coupon ad, which must be filled in and returned to the advertiser (c) **interest coupon** = slip of paper attached to a government bond certificate which can be cashed to provide the annual interest; **cum coupon** = with a coupon attached or before interest due on a security is paid; **ex coupon** = without the interest coupons or after interest has been paid

courier ['kʊrɪə] **1** *noun* (a) person or company which arranges to carry parcels or take messages from one place another in a town (b) person who goes with a party of tourists to guide them on a package tour **2** *verb* to send by courier; *we will courier the package to your hotel*

course [kɔːs] *noun* (a) **in the course of** = during or while something is happening; *in the course of the discussion, the managing director explained the company's expansion plans; sales have risen sharply in the course of the last few months* (b) series of lessons; *she has finished her secretarial course; the company has paid for her to attend a course for trainee sales managers* (c) **of course** = naturally; *of course the company is interested in profits; are you willing to go on a sales trip to Australia? - of course!*

court [kɔːt] *noun* place where a judge listens to a case and decides legally which of the parties in the argument is right; **court case** = legal action or trial; **court order** = legal order made by a court, telling someone to do or not to do something; **to take someone to court** = to tell someone to appear in court to settle an argument; **a settlement was reached out of court** *or* the two parties reached an out-of-court settlement = the dispute was settled between the two parties privately without continuing the court case

covenant ['kʌvənənt] **1** *noun* legal contract; **deed of covenant** = official signed agreement to pay someone a sum of money each year **2** *verb* to agree to pay a sum of money each year by contract; *to covenant to pay £10 per annum*

Coventry ['kɒvəntri] **to send someone to Coventry** = to refuse to speak to or to have any dealings with someone, especially a fellow-worker; *after he told the management about the thefts, the other workers sent him to Coventry*

cover ['kʌvə] **1** *noun* **(a)** thing put over a machine, etc., to keep it clean; *put a cover over your PC when the office is being redecorated; she always keeps a cover over the typewriter* **(b)** insurance cover = protection guaranteed by an insurance policy; *do you have cover against theft?*; **to operate without adequate cover** = without being protected by insurance; **to ask for additional cover** = to ask the insurance company to increase the amount for which you are insured; **full cover** = insurance against all risks; **cover note** = letter from an insurance company giving details of an insurance policy and confirming that the policy exists (NOTE: the American English for this is **binder**) **(c)** security to guarantee a loan; *do you have sufficient cover for this loan?* **(d)** *(in restaurant)* **cover charge** = charge for a place at the table in addition to the charge for food **(e)** **dividend cover** = ratio of profits to dividend **(f)** **to send something under separate cover** = in a separate envelope; **to send a magazine under plain cover** = in an ordinary envelope with no company name printed on it **2** *verb* **(a)** to put something over a machine, etc., to keep it clean; *don't forget to cover your PC when they are repainting the office* **(b)** **cover a risk** = to be protected by insurance against a risk; **to be fully covered** = to have insurance against all risks; *the insurance covers fire, theft and loss of work* **(c)** to have enough money to pay; to ask for security against a loan which you are making; **the damage was covered by**

the insurance = the insurance company paid for the damage; **to cover a position** = to have enough money to be able to pay for a forward purchase **(d)** to earn enough money to pay for costs, expenses, etc.; *we do not make enough sales to cover the expense of running the shop; breakeven point is reached when sales cover all costs; the dividend is covered four times* = profits are four times the dividend paid out

three export credit agencies have agreed to provide cover for large projects in Nigeria
Business Times (Lagos)

coverage ['kʌvərɪdʒ] *noun* **(a)** press coverage *or* media coverage = reports about something in the newspapers, on TV, etc.; *the company had good media coverage for the launch of its new model* **(b)** *US* protection guaranteed by insurance; *do you have coverage against fire damage?*

covering letter *or* **covering note** ['kʌvərɪŋ 'letə *or* 'kʌvərɪŋ 'nəʊt] *noun* letter or note sent with documents to say why you are sending them

cowboy ['kaʊbɔɪ] *noun* workman who does bad work and charges a high price; *the people we got in to repaint the office were a couple of cowboys*; **cowboy outfit** = company which does bad work and charges high prices

Cr *or* **CR** = CREDIT

crane [kreɪn] *noun* machine for lifting heavy objects; *the container slipped as the crane was lifting it onto the ship; they had to hire a crane to get the machine into the factory*

crash [kræʃ] **1** *noun* **(a)** accident to a car, plane, train, etc.; *the car was damaged in the crash; the plane crash killed all the passengers or all the passengers were killed in the plane crash* **(b)** financial collapse; *the financial crash caused several bankruptcies; he lost all his money in the crash of 1929* **2** *verb* **(a)** to hit something and be damaged; *the plane crashed into the mountain; the lorry crashed into a tree* **(b)** to collapse financially; *the company crashed with debts of over £1 million*

crate [kreɪt] **1** *noun* large wooden box; *a crate of oranges* **2** *verb* to put goods into crates

create [krɪ'eɪt] *verb* to make something new; *by acquiring small unprofitable companies he soon created a large manufacturing group*; *the government scheme aims at creating new jobs for young people*

he insisted that the tax advantages he directed towards small businesses will help create jobs and reduce the unemployment rate

Toronto Star

creation [krɪ'eɪʃən] *noun* making; **job creation scheme** = government-backed scheme to make work for the unemployed

creative accounting [krɪ'eɪtɪv ə'kaʊntɪŋ] *noun* adaptation of a company's figures to present a better picture than is correct (to appear to make a company more attractive to a potential buyer, or for some other reason which may not be strictly legal)

COMMENT: 'creative accounting' is the term used to cover a number of accounting practices which, although legal, may be used to mislead banks, investors and shareholders about the profitability or liquidity of a business

credere ['kreɪdəri] *see* DEL CREDERE

credit ['kredɪt] **1** *noun* **(a)** period of time a customer is allowed before he has to pay a debt incurred for goods or services; *to give someone six months' credit*; *to sell on good credit terms*; **extended credit** = credit on very long repayment terms; **interest-free credit** = arrangement to borrow money without paying interest on the loan; **long credit** = terms allowing the borrower a long time to pay; **open credit** = credit given to good customers without security; **short credit** = terms allowing the customer only a short time to pay; **credit account** = account which a customer has with a shop which allows him to buy goods and pay for them later; **credit agency** *US* **credit bureau** = company which reports on the creditworthiness of customers to show whether they should be allowed credit; **credit bank** = bank which lends money;

credit control = check that customers pay on time and do not owe more than their credit limit; **credit controller** = member of staff whose job is to try to get payment of overdue invoices; **credit facilities** = arrangement with a bank or supplier to have credit so as to buy goods; **credit freeze** *or* **credit squeeze** = period when lending by banks is restricted by the government; **letter of credit (L/C)** = letter from a bank, allowing someone credit and promising to repay at a later date; **irrevocable letter of credit** = letter of credit which cannot be cancelled; **credit limit** = fixed amount which is the most a customer can owe on credit; **he has exceeded his credit limit** = he has borrowed more money than he is allowed; **to open a line of credit** *or* **a credit line** = to make credit available to someone; **credit rating** = amount which a credit agency feels a customer should be allowed to borrow; **credit sale** = sale where the purchaser will pay for the goods bought at a later date; **on credit** = without paying immediately; *to live on credit*; *we buy everything on sixty days credit*; *the company exists on credit from its suppliers* **(b)** amount entered in accounts to show a decrease in assets or expenses or an increase in liabilities, revenue or capital (in accounts, credits are entered in the right-hand column); *(compare* DEBIT) *to enter £100 to someone's credit*; *to pay in £100 to the credit of Mr Smith*; **debits and credits** = figures which are entered in the accounts to record increases or decreases in assets, expenses, liabilities, revenue or capital; **credit balance** = balance in an account showing that more money has been received than is owed by the company; *the account has a credit balance of £1,000*; **credit column** = right-hand column in accounts showing money received; **credit entry** = entry on the credit side of an account; **credit note (C/N)** = note showing that money is owed to a customer; *the company sent the wrong order and so had to issue a credit note*; **credit side** = right-hand side of accounts showing money received; **account in credit** = account where the credits are higher than the debits; **bank credit** = loans or overdrafts from a bank to a customer;

tax credit = part of a dividend on which the company has already paid advance corporation tax which is deducted from the shareholder's income tax charge **2** *verb* to put money into someone's account; to note money received in an account; *to credit an account with £100 or to credit £100 to an account*

credit card ['kredɪt 'kɑːd] *noun* plastic card which allows you to borrow money and to buy goods without paying for them immediately (you pay the credit card company at a later date)

creditor ['kredɪtə] *noun* person or company that is owed money (a company's creditors are its liabilities); **creditors** = list of all liabilities in a set of accounts, including overdrafts, amounts owing to other companies in the group, trade creditors, payments received on account for goods not yet supplied, etc.; **trade creditors** = companies which are owed money by a company (the amount owed to trade creditors is shown in the annual accounts); **creditors' meeting** = meeting of all persons to whom an insolvent company owes money, to decide how to obtain the money owed

credit union ['kredɪt 'juːnjən] *noun US* group of people who pay in regular deposits or subscriptions which earn interest and are used to make loans to other members of the group

creditworthiness ['kredɪtwɜːðɪnəs] *noun* ability of a customer to pay for goods bought on credit

creditworthy ['kredɪtwɜːði] *adjective* able to buy goods on credit; *we will do some checks on him to see if he is creditworthy*

crew [kruː] *noun* group of people who work on a plane, ship, etc.; *the ship carries a crew of 250*

crime [kraɪm] *noun* act which is against the law; *crimes in supermarkets have risen by 25%*

criminal ['krɪmɪnl] *adjective* illegal; *misappropriation of funds is a criminal act*; **criminal action** = court case brought by the state against someone who is charged with a crime

crisis ['kraɪsɪs] *noun* serious economic situation where decisions have to be taken rapidly; *the government stepped in to try to resolve the international crisis*; *withdrawals from the bank have reached crisis level*; *the crisis in the mortgage banks has caused problems for the central bank*; **crisis management** = management of a business or a country's economy during a period of crisis; **to take crisis measures** = to take severe measures rapidly to stop a crisis developing (NOTE: plural is **crises**)

critical path analysis ['krɪtɪkəl 'pɑːθ ə'næləsɪs] *noun* analysis of the way a project is organized in terms of the minimum time it will take to complete, calculating which parts can be delayed without holding up the rest of the project

criticize ['krɪtɪsaɪz] *verb* to say that something or someone is wrong or is working badly, etc.; *the MD criticized the sales manager for not improving the volume of sales*; *the design of the new catalogue has been criticized*

CRO = COMPANIES REGISTRATION OFFICE

crore [krɔː] *noun (in India)* ten million (NOTE: one crore equals 100 lakh)

> the company clocked a sales turnover of Rs.7.09 crore and earned a profit after tax of Rs.10.39 lakh on an equity base of Rs.14 lakh
>
> *Business India*

> the turnover for the nine months ended December 31 registered a 6.26 per cent increase to Rs. 87.91 crores from Rs. 82.73 crores in the corresponding period last year
>
> *The Hindu*

cross [krɒs] *verb* **(a)** to go across; *Concorde only takes three hours to cross the Atlantic*; *to get to the bank, you turn left and cross the street at the post office* **(b) to cross a cheque** = to write two lines across a cheque to show that it has to be paid into a bank; **crossed cheque** = cheque which has to be paid into a bank

COMMENT: crossed cheques have the words 'A/C payee' printed in the space between the two vertical lines: all British cheques are now printed in this way. This means that the cheque can only be paid into a bank, and only into the account of the person whose name is written on it - it cannot be endorsed to a third party

cross holding   or   **cross shareholding** ['krɒs 'həʊldɪŋ] *noun* situation where two companies own shares in each other in order to stop each from being taken over; *the two companies have protected themselves from takeover by a system of cross holdings*

the unveiling of the tax reform plans last week drove Frankfurt's index of leading shares sharply higher amid speculation of a wave of industrial restructuring, as companies unravelled e x t e n s i v e cross-shareholdings

Financial Times

cross off ['krɒs 'ɒf] *verb* to remove something from a list; *he crossed my name off his list; you can cross him off our mailing list*

cross out ['krɒs 'aʊt] *verb* to put a line through something which has been written; *she crossed out £250 and put in £500*

cross rate ['krɒs 'reɪt] *noun* exchange rate between two currencies expressed in a third currency

crude (oil) ['kruːd 'ɔɪl] *noun* raw petroleum, taken from the ground; *the price for Arabian crude has slipped*

cubic ['kjuːbɪk] *adjective* measured in volume by multiplying length, depth and width; *the crate holds six cubic metres*; **cubic measure** = volume measured in cubic feet or metres (NOTE: cubic is written in figures as $6m^3$ = six cubic metres; $10ft^3$ = ten cubic feet)

cum [kʌm] *preposition* with; **cum dividend** = price of a share including the next dividend still to be paid; **cum coupon** = with a coupon attached

cumulative ['kjuːmjʊlətɪv] *adjective* which is added automatically each year; **cumulative interest** = interest which is added to the capital each year; **cumulative preference share** *US* **cumulative preferred stock** = preference share which will have the dividend paid at a later date even if the company is not able to pay a dividend in the current year

currency ['kʌrənsi] *noun* money in coins and notes which is used in a particular country; **convertible currency** = currency which can easily be exchanged for another; **foreign currency** = currency of another country; **foreign currency account** = bank account in the currency of another country (e.g. a dollar account in a British bank); **foreign currency reserves** = a country's reserves in currencies of other countries; **hard currency** = currency of a country which has a strong economy, and which can be changed into other currencies easily; *to pay for imports in hard currency; to sell raw materials to earn hard currency*; **legal currency** = money which is legally used in a country; **soft currency** = currency of a country with a weak economy, which is cheap to buy and difficult to exchange for other currencies; **currency backing** = gold or securities which maintain the international strength of a currency; **currency note** = bank note (NOTE: **currency** has no plural when it refers to the money of one country: **he was arrested trying to take currency out of the country**)

today's wide daily variations in exchange rates show the instability of a system based on a single currency, namely the dollar

Economist

the level of currency in circulation increased to N4.9 billion in the month of August

Business Times (Lagos)

current ['kʌrənt] *adjective* referring to the present time; **current assets** = assets used by a company in its ordinary work (such as materials, finished products, cash); **current cost accounting (CCA)** = method of accounting which notes the cost of replacing assets at current prices, rather than valuing assets at their original cost; **current liabilities** = debts which a company has to pay within the next accounting period; **current price** = today's price; **current rate of exchange** = today's rate of exchange; **current yield** = dividend calculated as a percentage of the price paid per share

---

crude oil output plunged during the past month and is likely to remain at its current level for the near future

Wall Street Journal

---

customers' current deposit and current accounts also rose to $655.31 million at the end of December

Hongkong Standard

---

current account ['kʌrənt ə'kaunt] *noun* **(a)** account in an bank from which the customer can withdraw money when he wants (current accounts do not always pay interest); *to pay money into a current account* (NOTE: the American equivalent is a **checking account) (b)** account of the balance of payments of a country relating to the sale or purchase of raw materials, goods and invisibles

---

a surplus in the current account is of such vital importance to economists and currency traders because the more Japanese goods that are exported, the more dollars overseas customers have to pay for these products. That pushes up the value of the yen

Nikkei Weekly

---

currently ['kʌrəntli] *adverb* at the present time; *we are currently negotiating with the bank for a loan*

curriculum vitae (CV) [kə'rikjuləm 'viːtaɪ] *noun* summary of a person's life story showing details of education and work experience; *candidates should send a letter of application with a curriculum vitae to the personnel officer* (NOTE: the plural is **curriculums** or **curricula vitae**. Note also that the American English is **résumé**)

curve [kɜːv] *noun* line which bends round; *the graph shows an upward curve*; **learning curve** = gradual process of learning (as shown on an imaginary scale);

sales curve = graph showing how sales increase or decrease

cushion ['kuʃən] *noun* money which allows a company to pay interest on its borrowings or to survive a loss; *we have sums on deposit which are a useful cushion when cash flow is tight*

custom ['kʌstəm] *noun* **(a)** use of a shop by regular shoppers; **to lose someone's custom** = to do something which makes a regular customer go to another shop; **custom-built** or **custom-made** = made specially for one customer; *he drives a custom-built Rolls Royce* **(b)** the customs of the trade = the general way of working in a certain trade; *it is the custom of the book trade to allow unlimited returns for credit*

customer ['kʌstəmə] *noun* company or person who buys goods or services; *the shop was full of customers*; *can you serve this customer first please?*; *he is a regular customer of ours*; **customer appeal** = what attracts customers to a product; **customer service department** = department which deals with customers and their complaints and orders

customize ['kʌstəmaɪz] *verb* to change something to fit the special needs of a customer; *we use customized computer terminals*

customs ['kʌstəmz] *plural noun* **H.M. Customs and Excise** = the British government department which organizes the collection of taxes on imports (and also collects VAT); an office of this department at a port or airport; **to go through customs** = to pass through the area of a port or airport where customs officials examine goods; **to take something through customs** = to carry something illegal through the customs area without declaring it; *he was stopped by customs*; *her car was searched by customs*; **customs barrier** = customs duty intended to prevent imports; **customs broker** = person or company which takes goods through customs for a shipping company; **customs clearance** = document given by customs to a shipper to show that customs duty has been paid and the goods can be shipped; *to wait for customs clearance*; **customs declaration**

= statement showing goods being imported on which duty will have to be paid; *to fill in a customs (declaration) form*; **customs duty** = tax paid on goods brought into or taken out of a country; **the crates had to go through a customs examination** = the crates had to be examined by customs officials; **customs formalities** = declaration of goods by the shipper and examination of them by customs; **customs officers** *or* **customs officials** = people working for customs; **customs tariff** = list of duties to be paid on imported goods; **customs union** = agreement between several countries that goods can travel between them, without paying duty, while goods from other countries have to pay special duties

cut [kʌt] **1** *noun* **(a)** sudden lowering of a price, salary or numbers of jobs; *price cuts or cuts in prices*; **job cuts** = reductions in the number of jobs; **he took a cut in salary** *or* **a salary cut** = he accepted a lower salary **(b)** share in a payment; *he introduces new customers and gets a cut of the salesman's commission* **2** *verb* **(a)** to lower suddenly; *we are cutting prices on all our models*; **to cut (back) production** = to reduce the quantity of products made; *the company has cut back its sales force*; *we have taken out the second telephone line in order to try to cut costs* **(b)** to reduce the number of something; **to cut jobs** = to reduce the number of jobs by making people redundant; **he cut his losses** = he stopped doing something which was creating a loss (NOTE: **cutting - cut - has cut**)

---

state-owned banks cut their prime rates a percentage point to 11%

---

cutback [ˈkʌtbæk] *noun* reduction; *cutbacks in government spending*

cut down (on) [ˈkʌt ˈdaʊn ɒn] *verb* to reduce suddenly the amount of something used; *the government is cutting down on welfare expenditure*; *the office is trying to cut down on electricity consumption*; *we have installed networked computers to cut down on paperwork*

cut in [ˈkʌt ˈɪn] *verb (informal)* **to cut someone in on a deal** = to give someone a share in the profits of a deal

cut-price [kʌtˈpraɪs] *adjective* sold at a cheaper price than usual; *he made his money selling cut-price goods in the local market*; *you can get cut-price petrol in petrol stations near the border*; **cut-price store** = store selling cut-price goods

cut-throat competition [ˈkʌtθrəʊt kɒmpəˈtɪʃn] *noun* sharp competition which cuts prices and offers high discounts

cutting [ˈkʌtɪŋ] *noun* **(a)** cost cutting = reducing costs; *we have made three secretaries redundant as part of our cost-cutting programme*; **price cutting** = sudden lowering of prices; **price-cutting war** = competition between companies to get a larger market share by cutting prices **(b)** press cutting agency = company which cuts out references to a client from newspapers and magazines and sends them on to him; **press cuttings** = references to a client or person or product cut out of newspapers or magazines; *we have a file of press cuttings on our rivals' products*

CV [ˈsiːˈviː] *noun* = CURRICULUM VITAE; *please apply in writing, enclosing a current CV*

CWO = CASH WITH ORDER

cwt [ˈhʌndrədweɪt] = HUNDREDWEIGHT

cycle [ˈsaɪkl] *noun* period of time when something leaves its original position and then returns to it; **economic cycle** *or* **trade cycle** *or* **business cycle** = period during which trade expands, then slows down and then expands again

cyclical [ˈsɪklɪkəl] **1** *adjective* which happens in cycles; **cyclical factors** = way in which a trade cycle affects businesses **2** *noun* **cyclicals** = shares which move up and down in cycles

---

consumer cyclicals such as general retailers should in theory suffer from rising interest rates. And food retailers in particular have cyclical exposure without price power

Dd

daily ['deɪli] *adjective* done every day; **daily consumption** = amount used each day; **daily production of cars** = number of cars produced each day; **daily sales returns** = reports of sales made each day; **a daily newspaper** *or* **a daily** = newspaper which is produced every day

damage ['dæmɪdʒ] **1** *noun* **(a)** harm done to things; **fire damage** = damage caused by a fire; **storm damage** = damage caused by a storm; **to suffer damage** = to be harmed; *we are trying to assess the damage which the shipment suffered in transit*; **to cause damage** = to harm something; *the fire caused damage estimated at £100,000*; **damage survey** = survey of damage done **(b) damages** = money claimed as compensation for harm done; *to claim £1000 in damages*; *to be liable for damages*; *to pay £25,000 in damages*; **to bring an action for damages against someone** = to take someone to court and claim damages **2** *verb* to harm; *the storm damaged the cargo*; *they are holding a sale of stock which has been damaged by water*

damaged ['dæmɪdʒd] *adjective* which has suffered damage or which has been harmed; *goods damaged in transit*; **fire-damaged goods** = goods harmed in a fire

damp down ['dæmp 'daʊn] *verb* to reduce; *to damp down demand for domestic consumption of oil*

D & B = DUN & BRADSTREET

danger ['deɪndʒə] *noun* **(a)** possibility of being harmed or killed; *the old machinery poses a danger to the workforce* **(b)** likelihood, possibility; **there is no danger of the sales force leaving** = it is not likely that the sales force will leave; **in danger of** = which may easily happen; *the company is in danger of being taken over*; *she is in danger of being made redundant*

danger money ['deɪndʒə 'mʌni] *noun* extra money paid to workers in dangerous jobs; *the workforce has stopped work and asked for danger money*

dangerous ['deɪndʒərəs] *adjective* which can be harmful; **dangerous job** = job where the workers may be killed or hurt

data ['deɪtə] *noun* information (letters or figures) available on computer; **data acquisition** = gathering information about a subject; **data bank** *or* **bank of data** = store of information in a computer; **data capture** = act of putting information onto a computer (by keyboarding or by scanning); **data processing** = selecting and examining data in a computer to produce special information (NOTE: **data** is usually singular: **the data is easily available**)

database ['deɪtəbeɪs] *noun* store of information in a computer system; *we can extract the lists of potential customers from our database*

date [deɪt] **1** *noun* **(a)** number of day, month and year; *I have received your letter of yesterday's date*; **date stamp** = rubber stamp for marking the date on letters received; **date of receipt** = date when something is received; **sell-by date** = date on a food packet which is the last date when the food can be sold and is still guaranteed to be good **(b) to date** = up to now; **interest to date** = interest up to the present time **(c) up to date** = current, recent or modern; *an up-to-date computer system*; **to bring something up to date** = to add the latest information to something; **to keep something up to date** = to keep adding information to something so that it is always up to date; *we spend a lot of time keeping our mailing list up to date* **(d) out of date** = old-fashioned, no longer modern; *their computer system is years out of date*; *they are still using out-of-date machinery* **(e) maturity date** = date when a government stock will mature; **date of bill** = date when a bill will mature **2** *verb* to put a date on a document; *the cheque was dated March 24th*; *you forgot to date the cheque*; **to date a cheque forward** = to put a later date than the present one on a cheque

dated [ˈdeɪtɪd] *adjective* with a date written on it; *thank you for your letter dated June 15th*; **long-dated bill** = bill which is payable more than three months from now; **short-dated bill** = bill which is payable within a few days

dawn raid [ˈdɔːn ˈreɪd] *noun* sudden planned purchase of a large number of a company's shares at the beginning of a day's trading (up to 15% of a company's shares may be bought in this way, and the purchaser must wait for seven days before purchasing any more shares; sometimes a dawn raid is the first step towards a takeover of the target company)

day [deɪ] *noun* **(a)** period of 24 hours; *there are thirty days in June*; *the first day of the month is a public holiday*; **settlement day** = day when accounts have to be settled; **three clear days** = three whole working days; *to give ten clear days' notice*; *allow four clear days for the cheque to be paid into the bank* **(b)** period of work from morning to night; *she took two days off* = she did not come to work for two days; *he works three days on, two days off* = he works for three days, then has two days' holiday; **to work an eight-hour day** = to spend eight hours at work each day; **day shift** = shift which works during the daylight hours such as from 8 a.m. to 5.30 p.m.; *there are 150 men on the day shift*; *he works the day shift*; **day release** = arrangement where a company allows a worker to go to college to study for one or two days each week; *the junior sales manager is attending a day release course*

day book [ˈdeɪ ˈbʊk] *noun* book with an account of sales and purchases made each day; **sales day book (SDB)** = book in

which non-cash sales are recorded with details of customer, invoice, amount and date; these details are later posted to each customer's account in the sales ledger

day-to-day [ˈdeɪtəˈdeɪ] *adjective* ordinary, which goes on all the time; *he organizes the day-to-day running of the company*; *sales only just cover the day-to-day expenses*

day trader [ˈdeɪ ˈtreɪdə] *noun* person who buys shares and sells them within the same day

day trading [ˈdeɪ ˈtreɪdɪŋ] *noun* buying shares and selling them within the same day

day worker [ˈdeɪ ˈwɜːkə] *noun* person who works the day shift

DCF = DISCOUNTED CASH FLOW

dead [ded] *adjective* **(a)** not alive; *six people were dead as a result of the accident*; *the founders of the company are all dead* **(b)** not working; **dead account** = account which is no longer used; **the line went dead** = the telephone line suddenly stopped working; **dead loss** = total loss; *the car was written off as a dead loss*; **dead capital** *or* **dead money** = money which is not invested to make a profit; **dead season** = time of year when there are few tourists about

deadline [ˈdedlaɪn] *noun* date by which something has to be done; **to meet a deadline** = to finish something in time; *we've missed our October 1st deadline*

deadlock [ˈdedlɒk] **1** *noun* point where two sides in a dispute cannot agree; *the negotiations have reached a deadlock*; **to break a deadlock** = to find a way to start discussions again after being at a point where no agreement was possible **2** *verb* to be unable to agree to continue negotiations; **talks have been deadlocked for ten days** = after ten days the talks have not produced any agreement

deadweight [ˈdedweɪt] *noun* heavy goods like coal, iron or sand; **deadweight cargo** = heavy cargo which is charged by weight, not by volume; **deadweight capacity** *or* **deadweight tonnage** = largest amount of cargo which a ship can carry safely

deal [di:l] **1** *noun* **(a)** business agreement, affair or contract; *to arrange a deal or to set up a deal or to do a deal*; *to sign a deal*; *the sales director set up a deal with a Russian bank*; *the deal will be signed tomorrow*; *they did a deal with an American airline*; **to call off a deal** = to stop an agreement; *when the chairman heard about the deal he called it off*; **cash deal** = sale done for cash; **package deal** = agreement where several different items are agreed at the same time; *they agreed a package deal, which involves the construction of the factory, training of staff and purchase of the product* **(b)** **a great deal** *or* **a good deal of something** = a large quantity of something; *he has made a good deal of money on the stock market*; *the company lost a great deal of time asking for expert advice* **2** *verb* **(a)** **to deal with** = to organize; *leave it to the filing clerk - he'll deal with it*; **to deal with an order** = to work to supply an order **(b)** to trade, to buy and sell; **to deal with someone** = to do business with someone; **to deal in leather** *or* **to deal in options** = to buy and sell leather or options; **he deals on the Stock Exchange** = his work involves buying and selling shares on the Stock Exchange for clients

dealer ['di:lə] *noun* person who buys and sells; *an old-established dealer in tobacco or tobacco dealer*; **foreign exchange dealer** = person who buys and sells foreign currencies; **retail dealer** = person who sells to the general public; **wholesale dealer** = person who sells in bulk to retailers

dealership ['di:ləʃɪp] *noun* **(a)** authorization to sell certain products or services **(b)** business run by an authorized dealer; *he has a Volkswagen dealership*

dealing ['di:lɪŋ] *noun* **(a)** buying and selling on the Stock Exchange, commodity markets or currency markets; **fair dealing** = legal trade, legal buying and selling of shares; **foreign exchange dealing** = buying and selling foreign currencies; **forward dealings** = buying or selling commodities forward; **insider dealing** = illegal buying or selling of shares by staff of a company or other persons who have secret information about the company's

plans; **option dealing** = buying and selling share options **(b)** buying and selling goods; **to have dealings with someone** = to do business with someone

dear [dɪə] *adjective* **(a)** expensive, costing a lot of money; *property is very dear in this area*; **dear money** = money which has to be borrowed at a high interest rate **(b)** way of starting a letter by addressing someone; **Dear Sir** *or* **Dear Madam** = addressing a man or woman whom you do not know, or addressing a company; **Dear Sirs** = addressing a company; **Dear Mr Smith** *or* **Dear Mrs Smith** *or* **Dear Miss Smith** = addressing a man or woman whom you know; **Dear James** *or* **Dear Julia** = addressing a friend or a person you do business with often

COMMENT: first names are commonly used between business people in the UK; they are less often used in other European countries (France and Germany, for example), where business letters tend to be more formal

death [deθ] *noun* act of dying; **death benefit** = insurance benefit paid to the family of someone who dies in an accident at work; **death in service** = insurance benefit or pension paid when someone dies while employed by a company; *US* **death duty** *or* **death tax** = tax paid on the property left by a dead person (NOTE: the British equivalent is **inheritance tax**)

debenture [dɪ'bentʃə] *noun* agreement to repay a debt with fixed interest using the company's assets as security; *the bank holds a debenture on the company*; **convertible debenture** = debenture which can be converted into ordinary shares at a certain date; **mortgage debenture** = debenture where the lender can be repaid by selling the company's property; **debenture issue** *or* **issue of debentures** = borrowing money against the security of the company's assets; **debenture bond** = (i) certificate showing that a debenture has been issued; (ii) *US* unsecured loan; **debenture capital** *or* **debenture stock** = capital borrowed by a company, using its fixed assets as security; **debenture holder** = person who holds a debenture for money lent; **debenture register** *or* **register of debentures** = list of debenture holders of a company

> COMMENT: in the UK, debentures are always secured on the company's assets; in the USA, debenture bonds are not secured

debit ['debɪt] **1** *noun* money which a company owes, an entry in accounts which shows an increase in assets or expenses or a decrease in liabilities, revenue or capital (entered in the left-hand side of an account); *compare* CREDIT; **debits and credits** = money which a company owes and money it receives, figures which are entered in the accounts to record increases or decreases in assets, expenses, liabilities, revenue or capital; **debit balance** = balance in an account, showing that the company owes more money than it has received; **debit card** = plastic card, similar to a credit card, but which debits the holder's account immediately through an EPOS system; **debit column** = left-hand column in accounts showing the money paid or owed to others; **debit entry** = entry on the debit side of an account; **debit side** = left-hand side of an account showing the money paid or owed to others; **debit note** = note showing that a customer owes money; *we undercharged Mr Smith and had to send him a debit note for the extra amount*; **direct debit** = system where a customer allows a company to charge costs to his bank account automatically and where the amount charged can be increased or decreased with the agreement of the customer; *I pay my electricity bill by direct debit* **2** *verb* **to debit an account** = to charge an account with a cost; *his account was debited with the sum of £25*

debitable ['debɪtəbl] *adjective* which can be debited

debt [det] *noun* **(a)** money owed for goods or services; *the company stopped trading with debts of over £1 million*; **to be in debt** = to owe money; **he is in debt to the tune of £250,000** = he owes £250,000; **to get into debt** = to start to borrow more money than you can pay back; **the company is out of debt** = the company does not owe money any more; **to pay back a debt** = to pay all the money owed; **to pay off a debt** = to finish paying money owed; **to service a debt** = to pay interest on a debt; *the company is having problems in servicing its debts*; **bad debt** = debt which will not be paid (usually because the debtor has gone out of business) and which has to be written off in the accounts; *the company has written off £30,000 in bad debts*; **secured debts** *or* **unsecured debts** = debts which are guaranteed or not guaranteed by assets; **debt collecting** *or* **collection** = collecting money which is owed; **debt collection agency** = company which collects debts for a commission; **debt collector** = person who collects debts; **debts due** = money owed which is due for repayment **(b) funded debt** = part of the British National Debt which pays interest, but where there is no date for repayment of the principal; **the National Debt** = money borrowed by a government in selling gilts, National Savings Certificates, etc.

debtor ['detə] *noun* person who owes money; **debtors** = all money owed to a company as shown in the accounts; **trade debtors** = debtors who owe money to a company in the normal course of that company's trading; **debtor side** = debit side of an account; **debtor nation** = country whose foreign debts are larger than money owed to it by other countries

> the United States is now a debtor nation for the first time since 1914, owing more to foreigners than it is owed itself
> *Economist*

debug [diː'bʌg] *verb* to remove errors from a computer program (NOTE: **debugging - debugged**)

deceit *or* **deception** [dɪ'siːt or dɪ'sepʃən] *noun* making a wrong statement to someone in order to trick him into paying money; *he obtained £10,000 by deception*

decentralization [diːsentrəlaɪ'zeɪʃn] *noun* organization from various points, away from the centre; *the decentralization of the buying departments*

decentralize [diː'sentrəlaɪz] *verb* to organize from various points, away from the centre; *the group has a policy of decentralized purchasing so that each division is responsible for its own purchasing*

decide [dɪ'saɪd] *verb* to make up your mind to do something; *to decide on a course of action*; *to decide to appoint a new managing director*

deciding [dɪ'saɪdɪŋ] *adjective* **deciding factor** = most important factor which influences a decision

decile ['desaɪl] *noun* one of a series of nine figures below which one tenth or several tenths of the total fall; **sixth decile** = number below which sixty percent of numbers fall; *this group falls within the sixth decile of consumers*

decimal ['desɪməl] *noun* **decimal system** = system based on the number 10; **correct to three places of decimals** = correct to three figures after the decimal point (e.g. 3.485)

decimalization [desɪməlaɪ'zeɪʃn] *noun* changing to a decimal system

decimalize ['desɪməlaɪz] *verb* to change to a decimal system

decimal point ['desɪməl 'pɔɪnt] *noun* dot which indicates the division between the whole unit and its smaller parts (such as 4.75)

COMMENT: the decimal point is used in the UK and USA. In most European countries a comma is used to indicate a decimal, so 4,75% in Germany means 4.75% in the UK

decision [dɪ'sɪʒən] *noun* making up your mind to do something; *it took the committee some time to come to a decision or to reach a decision*; **decision-making** = act of coming to a decision; **the decision-making processes** = ways in which decisions are reached; **decision maker** = person who has to decide; **decision tree** = model for decision-making, showing the possible outcomes of different decisions

deck [dek] *noun* flat floor in a ship; **deck cargo** = cargo carried on the open top deck of a ship; **deck hand** = ordinary sailor on a cargo ship

declaration [deklə'reɪʃən] *noun* official statement; **declaration of bankruptcy** = official statement that someone is bankrupt; **declaration of income** = statement declaring income to the tax office; **customs declaration** = statement declaring goods brought into a country on which customs duty should be paid; **VAT declaration** = statement declaring VAT income to the VAT office

declare [dɪ'kleə] *verb* to make an official statement, to announce to the public; *he was declared bankrupt*; *the company declared an interim dividend of 10p per share*; **to declare goods to customs** = to state that you are importing goods which are liable to duty; *customs officials asked him if he had anything to declare*; **to declare an interest** = to state in public that you own shares in a company being investigated, that you are related to someone who can benefit from your contacts, etc.

declared [dɪ'kleəd] *adjective* which has been made public or officially stated; **declared value** = value of goods entered on a customs declaration

decline [dɪ'klaɪn] **1** *noun* gradual fall; *the decline in the value of the franc*; *a decline in buying power*; *the last year has seen a decline in real wages* **2** *verb* to fall slowly; *shares declined in a weak market*; *imports have declined over the last year*; *the economy declined during the last government*

Saudi oil production has declined by three quarters to around 2.5m barrels a day

Economist

this gives an average monthly decline of 2.15 per cent during the period

Business Times (Lagos)

share prices disclosed a weak tendency right from the onset of business and declined further, showing losses over a broad front

The Hindu

decontrol [diːkən'trəul] *verb* to stop controls; **to decontrol the price of petrol** = to stop controlling the price of petrol so that it can be priced freely by the market (NOTE: **decontrolling - decontrolled**)

decrease 1 ['diːkriːs] *noun* fall or reduction; *the decrease in the prices of consumer goods is reflected in the fall in the cost of living*; *exports have registered a decrease*; *sales show a 10% decrease on last year* **2** [dɪ'kriːs] *verb* to fall or to become less; *imports are decreasing*; *the value of the pound has decreased by 5%*

decreasing [dɪ'kriːsɪŋ] *adjective* which is falling; *the decreasing influence of the finance director*

deduct [dɪ'dʌkt] *verb* to remove money from a total; *to deduct £3 from the price*; *to deduct a sum for expenses*; *after deducting costs the gross margin is only 23%*; *expenses are still to be deducted*; **tax deducted at source** = tax which is removed from a salary, interest payment or dividend payment on shares before the money is paid

deductible [dɪ'dʌktəbl] *adjective* which can be deducted; **tax-deductible** = which can be deducted from an income before tax is paid; **these expenses are not tax-deductible** = tax has to be paid on these expenses

deduction [dɪ'dʌkʃən] *noun* removing of money from a total, money removed from a total; *net salary is salary after deduction of tax and social security*; **deductions from salary** *or* **salary deductions** *or* **deductions at source** = money which a company removes from salaries to give to the government as tax, national insurance contributions, etc.; **tax deductions** = (i) money removed from a salary to pay tax; (ii) *US* business expenses which can be claimed against tax

deed [diːd] *noun* legal document or written agreement; **deed of assignment** = document which legally transfers a property from a debtor to a creditor; **deed of covenant** = signed legal agreement to pay someone a sum of money every year; **deed of partnership** = agreement which sets up a partnership; **deed of transfer** = document which transfers the ownership of shares; **title deeds** = document showing who owns a property; *we have deposited the deeds of the house in the bank*

deep discount ['diːp 'dɪskaʊnt] *noun* very large discount

as the group's shares are already widely held, the listing will be via an introduction. It will also be accompanied by a deeply discounted £25m rights issue, leaving the company cash positive
Sunday Times

when it needed to make its financial results look good, it shipped a lot of inventory. It did this by offering deep discounts to distributors
Forbes

defalcation [diːfæl'keɪʃən] *noun* illegal use of money by someone who is not the owner but who has been trusted to look after it

default [dɪ'fɔːlt] **1** *noun* **(a)** failure to carry out the terms of a contract, especially failure to pay back a debt; **in default of payment** = with no payment made; **the company is in default** = the company has failed to carry out the terms of the contract **(b) by default** = because no one else will act; **he was elected by default** = he was elected because all the other candidates withdrew **2** *verb* to fail to carry out the terms of a contract, especially to fail to pay back a debt; *there was a major financial crisis when the bank defaulted*; **to default on payments** = not to make payments which are due under the terms of a contract

defaulter [dɪ'fɔːltə] *noun* person who defaults

defeat [dɪ'fiːt] **1** *noun* loss of a vote; *the chairman offered to resign after the defeat of the proposal at the AGM* **2** *verb* to beat someone or something in a vote; *the proposal was defeated by 10 votes to 23*; *he was heavily defeated in the ballot for union president*

defect ['diːfekt] *noun* something which is wrong or which stops a machine from working properly; *a computer defect or a defect in the computer seems to be the cause of the problem*

defective [dɪ'fektɪv] *adjective* **(a)** faulty, not working properly; *the machine broke* *down because of a defective cooling system* **(b)** not legally valid; *his title to the property is defective*

defence US **defense** [dɪˈfens] *noun* **(a)** protecting someone or something against attack; *the merchant bank is organizing the company's defence against the takeover bid* **(b)** fighting a lawsuit on behalf of a defendant; **defence counsel** = lawyer who represents the defendant in a lawsuit

defend [dɪˈfend] *verb* to fight to protect someone or something which is being attacked; *the company is defending itself against the takeover bid*; *he hired the best lawyers to defend him against the tax authorities*; **to defend a lawsuit** = to appear in court to state your case when accused of something

defendant [dɪˈfendənt] *noun* person who is sued or who is accused of doing something to harm someone (NOTE: the other side in a case is the **claimant**)

defer [dɪˈfɜː] *verb* to put back to a later date, to postpone; *we will have to defer payment until January*; *the decision has been deferred until the next meeting* (NOTE: **deferring - deferred**)

deferment [dɪˈfɜːmənt] *noun* postponement, putting back to a later date; *deferment of payment*; *deferment of a decision*

deferred [dɪˈfɜːd] *adjective* put back to a later date; **deferred creditor** = person who is owed money by a bankrupt but who is paid only after all other creditors; **deferred payment** = (i) money paid later than the agreed date; (ii) payment for goods by instalments over a long period; **deferred stock** = shares which receive a dividend after all other dividends have been paid

deficiency [dɪˈfɪʃənsi] *noun* lack; money lacking; *there is a £10 deficiency in the petty cash*; **to make up a deficiency** = to put money into an account to balance it

deficit [ˈdefɪsɪt] *noun* amount by which spending is higher than income; **the accounts show a deficit** = the accounts show a loss; **to make good a deficit** = to put money into an account to balance it; **balance of payments deficit** *or* **trade deficit** = situation when a country imports

more than it exports; **deficit financing** = planning by a government to borrow money to cover the shortfall between tax income and expenditure

deflate [dɪˈfleɪt] *verb* **to deflate the economy** = to reduce activity in the economy by cutting the supply of money

deflation [dɪˈfleɪʃən] *noun* **(a)** general reduction in economic activity; *the oil crisis resulted in worldwide deflation* **(b)** **price deflation** = gradual fall in prices because of increased competition; *compare* DISINFLATION

> the reluctance of people to spend is one of the main reasons behind 26 consecutive months of price deflation, a key economic ill that has led to price wars, depressed the profit margins of state enterprises and hit incomes among the rural population
> *Financial Times*

deflationary [dɪˈfleɪʃnəri] *adjective* which can cause deflation; *the government has introduced some deflationary measures in the budget*

> the strong dollar's deflationary impact on European economies as national governments push up interest rates
> *Duns Business Month*

defraud [dɪˈfrɔːd] *verb* to cheat someone to get money (NOTE: you **defraud someone of something**)

defray [dɪˈfreɪ] *verb* to provide money to pay (costs); *the company agreed to defray the costs of the exhibition*

degearing [diːˈɡɪərɪŋ] *noun* reduction in gearing, reducing a company's loan capital in relation to the value of its ordinary shares

delay [dɪˈleɪ] **1** *noun* time when someone or something is later than planned; *there was a delay of thirty minutes before the AGM started or the AGM started after a thirty minute delay*; *we are sorry for the delay in supplying your order or in replying to your letter* **2** *verb* to be late; to make someone late; *he was delayed because his taxi had an accident*; *the* *company has delayed payment of all invoices*

del credere agent [del 'kreɪdəri 'eɪdʒənt] *noun* agent who receives a high commission because he guarantees payment by customers

delegate ['delɪgət] **1** *noun* person who represents others at a meeting; *the management refused to meet the trade union delegates* **2** *verb* to pass authority or responsibility to someone else; *to delegate authority*; **he cannot delegate** = he wants to control everything himself and refuses to give up any of his responsibilities to his subordinates

delegation [delɪ'geɪʃən] *noun* **(a)** group of delegates; *a Chinese trade delegation is visiting the UK*; *the management met a union delegation* **(b)** act of passing authority or responsibility to someone else

delete [dɪ'liːt] *verb* to cut out words in a document; *they want to delete all references to credit terms from the contract*; *the lawyers have deleted clause two*

deliver [dɪ'lɪvə] *verb* to transport goods to a customer; **goods delivered free** *or* **free delivered goods** = goods transported to the customer's address at a price which includes transport costs; **goods delivered on board** = goods transported free to the ship or plane but not to the customer's warehouse; **delivered price** = price which includes packing and transport

delivery [dɪ'lɪvəri] *noun* **(a)** delivery of goods = transport of goods to a customer's address; *we have a pallet of parcels awaiting delivery*; *the store offers free delivery or delivery free to addresses within 2km*; *allow 28 days for delivery*; *delivery is not allowed for or is not included*; **delivery note** = list of goods being delivered, given to the customer with the goods; **delivery order** = instructions given by the customer to the person holding his goods, to tell him to deliver them; **the store has a delivery service to all parts of the town** = the store will deliver goods to all parts of the town; **delivery time** = number of days before something will be delivered; **delivery van** = goods van for delivering goods to retail customers; **express delivery** = very fast delivery; *US* **General Delivery** = system where letters can be addressed to someone at a post office, where they can be collected (NOTE: British English for this is **poste restante**); **recorded delivery** = mail service where the letters are signed for by the person receiving them; *we sent the documents (by) recorded delivery*; **cash on delivery (c.o.d.)** = payment in cash when the goods are delivered; **to take delivery of goods** = to accept goods when they are delivered; *we took delivery of the stock into our warehouse on the 25th* **(b)** goods being delivered; *we take in three deliveries a day*; *there were four items missing in the last delivery* **(c)** transfer of a bill of exchange

demand [dɪ'mɑːnd] **1** *noun* **(a)** asking for payment; **payable on demand** = which must be paid when payment is asked for; **demand bill** = bill of exchange which must be paid when payment is asked for; *US* **demand deposit** = money in a bank account which can be taken out when you want it by writing a cheque; **final demand** = last reminder from a supplier, after which he will sue for payment **(b)** need for goods at a certain price; *there was an active demand for oil shares on the stock market*; **to meet a demand** *or* **to fill a demand** = to supply what is needed; *the factory had to increase production to meet the extra demand*; *the factory had to cut production when demand slackened*; *the office cleaning company cannot keep up with the demand for its services*; **there is not much demand for this item** = not many people want to buy it; **this book is in great demand** *or* **there is a great demand for this book** = many people want to buy it; **effective demand** = actual demand for a product which can be paid for; **demand price** = price at which a certain quantity of goods will be bought; **supply and demand** = amount of a product which is available and the amount which is wanted by customers; **law of supply and demand** = general rule that the amount of a product which is available is related to the needs of potential customers **2** *verb* to ask for something and expect to get it; *she demanded a refund*; *the suppliers are* *demanding immediate payment of their outstanding invoices*

> spot prices are now relatively stable in the run-up to the winter's peak demand
>
> *Economist*

> the demand for the company's products remained strong throughout the first six months of the year with production and sales showing significant increases
>
> *Business Times (Lagos)*

> growth in demand is still coming from the private rather than the public sector
>
> *Lloyd's List*

demand-led inflation [dɪˈmɑːndled ɪnˈfleɪʃən] *noun* inflation caused by rising demand which cannot be met

demarcation dispute [diːmɑːˈkeɪʃən dɪsˈpjuːt] *noun* argument between different trade unions over who shall do different parts of a job; *production of the new car was held up by demarcation disputes*

demerge [diːˈmɜːdʒ] *verb* to separate a company into various separate parts

demerger [diːˈmɜːdʒə] *noun* separation of a company into several separate parts (especially used of companies which have grown by acquisition)

demise [dɪˈmaɪz] *noun* (a) death; *on his demise the estate passed to his daughter* (b) granting of a property on a lease

demonetization [diːmʌnɪtaɪˈzeɪʃn] *noun* stopping a coin or note being used as money

demonetize [diːˈmʌnətaɪz] *verb* to stop a coin or note being used as money

demonstrate [ˈdemənstreɪt] *verb* to show how something works; *he was demonstrating a new tractor when he was killed*; *the managers saw the new stock control system being demonstrated*

demonstration [demənsˈtreɪʃən] *noun* showing how something works; *we went to a demonstration of new laser equipment*; **demonstration model** = piece of equipment used in demonstrations and later sold off cheaply

demonstrator [ˈdemənstreɪtə] *noun* person who demonstrates pieces of equipment

demote [dɪˈməʊt] *verb* to give someone a less important job; *he was demoted from manager to salesman*; *her salary was reduced when she was demoted*

demotion [dɪˈməʊʃən] *noun* giving someone a less important job; *he was very angry at his demotion*

demurrage [dɪˈmʌrɪdʒ] *noun* money paid to a customer when a shipment is delayed at a port or by customs

demutalization [dɪˈmjutjʊaɪaɪˈzeɪʃn] *noun* changing the status of a building society from being mutual to normal share ownership

denationalization [ˈdiːnæʃnəlaɪˈzeɪʃn] *noun* act of denationalizing; *the denationalization of the aircraft industry*

denationalize [diːˈnæʃənəlaɪz] *verb* to put a nationalized industry back into private ownership; *the government has plans to denationalize the steel industry*

denomination [dɪnɒmɪˈneɪʃən] *noun* unit of money (on a coin, banknote or stamp); *we collect coins of all denominations for charity*; *small denomination notes are not often counterfeited*

depart [dɪˈpɑːt] *verb* (a) to leave; *the plane departs from Paris at 11.15* (b) to **depart from normal practice** = to act in a different way from the normal way of doing things

department [dɪˈpɑːtmənt] *noun* (a) specialized section of a large company; *she phoned the complaints department*; *design department is responsible for the shop window displays*; *the order was passed to our export department*; **accounts department** = section which deals with money paid or received; **dispatch department** = department which deals with the packing and sending of goods to customers; **legal department** = section of a company dealing with legal matters; **marketing department** = section of a company dealing with marketing and sales; **new issues department** = section of a bank which deals with issues of new shares; **personnel department** = section of a company dealing with the staff; **head of department** _or_ **department head** _or_ **department manager** = person in charge of a department **(b)** section of a large store selling one type of product; _you will find beds in the furniture department_; **budget department** = department in a large store which sells cheaper goods **(c)** section of the British government containing several ministries; **Department of Employment (DoE)** = British government department which deals with employers, employees, training, etc.; **Department of Trade and Industry (DTI)** = British government department which deals with commerce, international trade, the stock exchange, etc.

departmental [diːpɑːt'mentl] _adjective_ referring to a department; **departmental manager** = manager of a department

department store [dɪ'pɑːtmənt 'stɔː] _noun_ large store with separate sections for different types of goods

departure [dɪ'pɑːtʃə] _noun_ **(a)** going away; _the plane's departure was delayed by two hours_; **departures** = part of an airport terminal which deals with passengers who are leaving; **departure lounge** = room in an airport where passengers wait to get on their planes **(b)** new venture, a new type of business; _selling records will be a departure for the local bookshop_ **(c)** departure from normal practice = doing something in a different way from the usual one

depend [dɪ'pend] _verb_ **(a) to depend on** = to need someone or something to exist; _the company depends on efficient service from its suppliers_; _we depend on government grants to pay the salary bill_ **(b)** to happen because of something; _the success of the launch will depend on the publicity campaign_; **depending on** = which varies according to something; _depending on the advertising budget, the new product will be launched on radio or on TV_

deposit [dɪ'pɒzɪt] **1** _noun_ **(a)** money placed in a bank for safe keeping or to earn interest; **certificate of deposit** = certificate from a bank to show that money has been deposited; **bank deposits** = all the money

placed in banks; _bank deposits are at an all-time high_; **fixed deposit** = deposit which pays a fixed interest over a fixed period; **deposit account** = bank account which pays interest but on which notice has usually to be given to withdraw money; **deposit at 7 days' notice** = money deposited which you can withdraw by giving seven days' notice; **deposit slip** = piece of paper stamped by the cashier to prove that you have paid money into your account **(b) safe deposit** = bank safe where you can leave jewellery or documents; **safe deposit box** = small box which you can rent, in which you can keep jewellery or documents in a bank's safe **(c)** money given in advance so that the thing which you want to buy will not be sold to someone else; _to pay a deposit on a watch_; _to leave £10 as deposit_ **2** _verb_ **(a)** to put documents somewhere for safe keeping; _to deposit shares with a bank_; _we have deposited the deeds of the house with the bank_; _he deposited his will with his solicitor_ **(b)** to put money into a bank account; _to deposit £100 in a current account_

depositary [dɪ'pɒzɪtəri] _noun US_ person or corporation which can place money or documents for safekeeping with a depository; _see also_ AMERICAN DEPOSITARY RECEIPT (NOTE: do not confuse with **depository**)

depositor [dɪ'pɒzɪtə] _noun_ person who deposits money in a bank

depository [dɪ'pɒzɪtəri] _noun_ **(a) furniture depository** = warehouse where you can store household furniture **(b)** person or company with whom money or documents can be deposited (NOTE: do not confuse with **depositary**)

depot ['depəu] _noun_ **(a)** central warehouse for goods; _freight depot_; _goods depot_; _oil storage depot_ **(b)** centre for transport; _bus depot_

depreciate [dɪ'priːʃieɪt] _verb_ **(a)** to reduce the value of assets in accounts; _we depreciate our company cars over three years_ **(b)** to lose value; _share which has depreciated by 10% over the year_; _the pound has depreciated by 5% against the dollar_ this involved reinvesting funds on items which could be depreciated against income for three years

Australian Financial Review

buildings are depreciated at two per cent per annum on the estimated cost of construction

Hongkong Standard

the euro's downward drift sparked alarmed reactions from the European Central Bank which has seen the new currency depreciate by almost 15% since its launch

Times

depreciation [dɪpriːʃiˈeɪʃən] *noun* **(a)** reduction in value of an asset; **depreciation rate** = rate at which an asset is depreciated each year in the accounts; **accelerated depreciation** = system of depreciation which reduces the value of assets at a high rate in the early years to encourage companies, because of tax advantages, to invest in new equipment; **annual depreciation** = reduction in the book value of an asset at a certain rate per year; *see also* STRAIGHT LINE DEPRECIATION **(b)** loss of value; *a share which has shown a depreciation of 10% over the year; the depreciation of the pound against the dollar*

COMMENT: various methods of depreciating assets are used, such as the 'straight line method', where the asset is depreciated at a constant percentage of its cost each year and the 'reducing balance method', where the asset is depreciated at a constant percentage which is applied to the cost of the asset after each of the previous years' depreciation has been deducted

depress [dɪˈpres] *verb* to reduce; *reducing the money supply has the effect of depressing demand for consumer goods*

depressed [dɪˈprest] *adjective* **depressed area** = part of a country suffering from depression; **depressed market** = market where there are more goods than customers

depression [dɪˈpreʃən] *noun* period of economic crisis with high unemployment and loss of trade; *the country entered a period of economic depression*; **the Great Depression** = the world economic crisis of 1929-1933

dept [dɪˈpɑːtmənt] = DEPARTMENT

deputy [ˈdepjuti] *noun* person who takes the place of another; *to act as deputy for someone or to act as someone's deputy*; *he is deputy manager of the accounts department*; *her title is deputy managing director*

deputize [ˈdepjutaɪz] *verb* to deputize for someone = to take the place of someone who is absent; *he deputized for the chairman who had a cold*

deregulate [diːˈregjuleɪt] *verb* to remove government controls from an industry; *the US government deregulated the banking sector in the 1980s*

deregulation [diːregjuˈleɪʃn] *noun* reducing government control over an industry; *the deregulation of the airlines*

after the slump in receipts last year that followed liner shipping deregulation in the US, carriers are probably still losing money on their transatlantic services. But with a possible contraction in capacity and healthy trade growth, this year has begun in a much more promising fashion than last

Lloyd's List

derivatives [dɪˈrɪvətɪvz] *noun* any forms of traded security, such as option contracts, which are derived from ordinary bonds and shares, exchange rates or stock market indices

other trading scandals have been the result of poor judgement or plain incompetence, exacerbated by the rise of derivatives – financial instruments that enable traders to take ever larger bets with smaller and smaller stakes. Derivatives mean that a single employee can expose a financial institution to huge risks

Times

COMMENT: also called 'derivative instruments', they can be bought or sold on stock exchanges or futures exchanges

describe [dɪ'skraɪb] *verb* to say what someone or something is like; *the leaflet describes the services the company can offer; the managing director described the company's difficulties with cash flow*

description [dɪ'skrɪpʃən] *noun* words which show what something is like; **false description of contents** = wrongly stating the contents of a packet to trick customers into buying it; **job description** = official document from the management which says what a job involves; **trade description** = description of a product to attract customers

design [dɪ'zaɪn] **1** *noun* planning or drawing of a product before it is built or manufactured; **industrial design** = design of products made by machines (such as cars and refrigerators); **product design** = design of consumer products; **design department** = department in a large company which designs the company's products or its advertising; **design studio** = independent firm which specializes in creating designs **2** *verb* to plan or to draw something before it is built or manufactured; *he designed a new car factory; she designs garden furniture*

designer [dɪ'zaɪnə] *noun* person who designs; *she is the designer of the new computer*; **designer clothes** = clothes which have been designed by a famous designer, with his or her name printed on them

designate ['dezɪgnət] *adjective* (person) who has been appointed to a job but who has not yet started work; *the chairman designate* (NOTE: always follows a noun)

desk [desk] *noun* **(a)** writing table in an office, usually with drawers for stationery; *desk diary; desk drawer; desk light*; **a three-drawer desk** = desk with three drawers; **desk pad** = pad of paper kept on a desk for writing notes; **desk research** = looking for information which is in printed sources, such as directories **(b) cash desk** *or* **pay desk** = place in a store where you pay for goods bought; *please pay at the desk* **(c)** section of a newspaper; **the City desk** = the department in a British newspaper which deals with business news

desk-top publishing (DTP) ['desktɒp 'pʌblɪʃɪŋ] *noun* writing, designing and printing of documents in an office, using a computer, a printer and special software

despatch [dɪ'spætʃ] = DISPATCH

destination [destɪ'neɪʃən] *noun* place to which something is sent, to which something is going; *the ship will take ten weeks to reach its destination*; **final destination** *or* **ultimate destination** = place reached at the end of a journey after stopping at several places en route

detail ['diːteɪl] **1** *noun* small part of a description; *the catalogue gives all the details of our product range; we are worried by some of the details in the contract*; **in detail** = giving many particulars; *the catalogue lists all the products in detail* **2** *verb* to list in detail; *the catalogue details the payment arrangements for overseas buyers; the terms of the licence are detailed in the contract*

detailed ['diːteɪld] *adjective* in detail; **detailed account** = account which lists every item

determine [dɪ'tɜːmɪn] *verb* to fix, to arrange or to decide; *to determine prices or quantities; conditions still to be determined*

Deutschmark ['dɔɪtʃmɑːk] *noun* currency used with the euro in Germany (NOTE: also called a **mark;** when used with a figure, usually written **DM** before the figure: **DM250** (say 'two hundred and fifty Deutschmarks')

devaluation [diːvæljʊ'eɪʃən] *noun* reduction in value of a currency against other currencies; *the devaluation of the franc*

devalue [diː'vælju:] *verb* to reduce the value of a currency against other currencies; *the pound has been devalued* *by 7%; the government has devalued the pound by 7%*

develop [dɪ'veləp] *verb* **(a)** to plan and produce; *to develop a new product* **(b)** to plan and build an area; *to develop an industrial estate*

developed country [dɪ'veləpt 'kʌntri] *noun* country which has an advanced manufacturing system

> developed countries would gain $135 billion a year and developing countries, such as the former centrally planned economies of Eastern Europe, would gain $85 billion a year. The study also notes that the poorest countries would lose an annual $7 billion
>
> *Times*

developer [dɪ'veləpə] *noun* **a property developer** = person who plans and builds a group of new houses or new factories

developing country *or* **developing nation** [dɪ'veləpɪŋ 'kʌntri *or* dɪ'veləpɪŋ 'neɪʃən] *noun* country which is not yet fully industrialized

development [dɪ'veləpmənt] *noun* **(a)** planning the production of a new product; *we spend a great deal on research and development* **(b)** industrial development = planning and building of new industries in special areas; **development area** *or* **development zone** = area which has been given special help from a government to encourage businesses and factories to be set up there

device [dɪ'vaɪs] *noun* small useful machine; *he invented a device for screwing tops on bottles*

devise [dɪ'vaɪz] **1** *noun* giving freehold land to someone in a will **2** *verb* to give freehold property to someone in a will

> COMMENT: giving of other types of property is a **bequest**

devisee [dɪvaɪ'ziː] *noun* person who receives freehold property in a will

diagram ['daɪəgræm] *noun* drawing which shows something as a plan or a map; *diagram showing sales locations; he drew a diagram to show how the*

decision-making processes work; *the paper gives a diagram of the company's organizational structure;* **flow diagram** = diagram showing the arrangement of work processes in a series

diagrammatic [daɪəgrə'mætɪk] *adjective* **in diagrammatic form** = in the form of a diagram; *the chart showed the sales pattern in diagrammatic form*

diagrammatically [daɪəgrə'mætɪkəli] *adverb* using a diagram; *the chart shows the sales pattern diagrammatically*

dial ['daɪəl] *verb* to call a telephone number on a telephone; *to dial a number; to dial the operator;* **to dial direct** = to contact a phone number without asking the operator to do it for you; *you can dial New York direct from London* (NOTE: British English is **dialling - dialled,** but American spelling is **dialing - dialed**)

dialling ['daɪəlɪŋ] *noun* act of calling a telephone number; **dialling code** = special series of numbers which you use to make a call to another town or country; **dialling tone** = noise made by a telephone to show that it is ready for you to dial a number; **international direct dialling (IDD)** = calling telephone numbers in other countries direct without the help of an operator

diary ['daɪəri] *noun* book in which you can write notes or appointments for each day of the week; *she notes her boss's engagements in his desk diary*

dictaphone ['dɪktəfəʊn] *noun* trademark for a brand of dictating machine

dictate [dɪk'teɪt] *verb* to say something to someone who then writes down your words; *to dictate a letter to a secretary; he was dictating orders into his pocket dictating machine;* **dictating machine** = machine which records text that someone dictates, which a secretary can play back and type out

dictation [dɪk'teɪʃən] *noun* act of dictating; **to take dictation** = to write down what someone is saying; *the secretary was taking dictation from the managing director;* **dictation speed** = number of words per minute which a secretary can write down in shorthand

differ ['dɪfə] *verb* not to be the same as something else; *the two products differ considerably - one has an electric motor, the other runs on oil*

difference ['dɪfrəns] *noun* way in which two things are not the same; *what is the difference between these two products?*; *differences in price or price differences*

different ['dɪfrənt] *adjective* not the same; *our product range is quite different in design from that of our rivals*; *we offer ten models each in six different colours*

differential [dɪfə'renʃəl] **1** *adjective* which shows a difference; **differential tariffs** = different tariffs for different classes of goods **2** *noun* **price differential** = difference in price between products in a range; **wage differentials** = differences in salary between workers in similar types of jobs; **to erode wage differentials** = to reduce differences in salary gradually

difficult ['dɪfɪkʌlt] *adjective* not easy; *the company found it difficult to sell into the European market*; *the market for secondhand computers is very difficult at present*

difficulty ['dɪfɪkʌlti] *noun* problem, thing which is not easy; *they had a lot of difficulty selling into the European market*; *we have had some difficulties with customs over the export of computers*

digit ['dɪdʒɪt] *noun* single number; **a seven-digit phone number** = a phone number with seven figures; *the seven-digit numbers are being replaced by eight digits*

digital ['dɪdʒɪtl] *adjective* **digital clock** = clock which shows the time as a series of figures (such as 12:05:23); **digital computer** = computer which calculates on the basis of numbers

dilution [daɪ'luːʃən] *noun* **dilution of equity** or **of shareholding** = situation where the ordinary share capital of a company has been increased but without an increase in the assets, so that each share is worth less than before

dime [daɪm] *noun US (informal)* ten cent coin

diminish [dɪ'mɪnɪʃ] *verb* to become smaller; *our share of the market has diminished over the last few years*; **law of**

diminishing returns = general rule that as more factors of production (land, labour and capital) are added to the existing factors, so the amount they produce is proportionately smaller

dip [dɪp] **1** *noun* sudden small fall; *last year saw a dip in the company's performance* **2** *verb* to fall in price; *shares dipped sharply in yesterday's trading* (NOTE: **dipping - dipped**)

diplomat or **diplomatist** ['dɪpləmæt or dɪ'pləʊmətɪst] *noun* person (such as an ambassador) who is the official representative of his country in another country

diplomatic [dɪplə'mætɪk] *adjective* referring to diplomats; **diplomatic immunity** = being outside the control of the laws of the country you are living in because of being a diplomat; *he claimed diplomatic immunity to avoid being arrested*; **to grant someone diplomatic status** = to give someone the rights of a diplomat

direct [daɪ'rekt] **1** *verb* to manage or to organize; *he directs our South-East Asian operations*; *she was directing the development unit until last year* **2** *adjective* straight, with no interference; **direct action** = strike, go-slow, etc.; **direct cost** = production cost of a product; **direct labour costs** = cost of the workers employed which can be allocated to a product (not including materials or overheads); **direct debit** = system where a customer allows a company to charge costs to his bank account automatically and where the amount charged can be increased or decreased with the agreement of the customer; *I pay my electricity bill by direct debit*; **direct selling** = selling a product direct to the customer without going through a shop; **direct taxation** = tax, such as income tax, which is paid direct to the government; *the government raises more money by direct taxation than by indirect* **3** *adverb* straight, with no third party involved; *we pay income tax direct to the government*; **to dial direct** = to contact a phone number yourself without asking the operator to do it for you; *you can dial New York direct from London if you want*

after five years of explosive
growth, fuelled by the boom in
financial services, the
direct marketing world is
becoming a lot more
competitive

Marketing Workshop

direct marketing is all about
targeting the audience,
individualising the message
and getting a response

PR Week

direction [daɪˈrekʃən] *noun* **(a)**
organizing or managing; *he took over the
direction of a multinational group* **(b)**
directions for use = instructions showing
how to use something

directly [daɪˈrektli] *adverb* **(a)**
immediately; *he left for the airport
directly after receiving the telephone
message* **(b)** straight, with no third party
involved; *we deal directly with the
manufacturer, without using a wholesaler*

direct mail [ˈdaɪrekt ˈmeɪl] *noun* selling
a product by sending publicity material to
possible buyers through the post; *these
calculators are only sold by direct mail;
the company runs a successful direct-mail
operation*; **direct-mail advertising** =
advertising by sending leaflets to people
through the post

all of those who had used
direct marketing techniques
had used direct mail, 79% had
used some kind of telephone
technique and 63% had tried
off-the-page selling

Precision marketing

director [daɪˈrektə] *noun* **(a)** person
appointed by the shareholders to help run a
company; **managing director** = director
who is in charge of the whole company;
chairman and managing director =
managing director who is also chairman of
the board of directors; **board of directors**
= all the directors of a company; **directors'
report** = annual report from the board of
directors to the shareholders; **directors'
salaries** = salaries of directors (which have
to be listed in the company's profit and loss
account); **associate director** = director
who attends board meetings but has not
been elected by the shareholders;

executive director = director who actually
works full-time in the company;
non-executive director = director who
attends board meetings only to give advice;
outside director = director who is not
employed by the company **(b)** person who
is in charge of a project, an official
institute, etc.; *the director of the
government research institute; she was
appointed director of the trade association*

COMMENT: directors are elected by
shareholders at the AGM, though they
are usually chosen by the chairman or
chief executive. A board will consist of
a chairman (who may be
non-executive), a chief executive or
managing director, and a series of
specialist directors in change of
various activities of the company
(such as a finance director, production
director or sales director). The
company secretary will attend board
meetings, but need not be a director.
Apart from the executive directors,
who are in fact employees of the
company, there may be several
non-executive directors, appointed
either for their expertise and contacts,
or as representatives of important
shareholders such as banks. The
board of an American company may
be made up of a large number of
non-executive directors and only one
or two executive officers; a British
board has more executive directors

the research director will
manage and direct a team of
business analysts reporting
on the latest developments in
retail distribution
throughout the UK

Times

directorate [daɪˈrektərət] *noun* group of
directors

directorship [daɪˈrektəʃɪp] *noun* post of
director; *he was offered a directorship
with Smith Ltd*

what benefits does the
executive derive from his
directorship? In the first
place compensation has
increased sharply in recent
years

Duns Business Month

directory [daɪˈrektəri] *noun* list of people or businesses with information about their addresses and telephone numbers; **classified directory** = list of businesses grouped under various headings, such as computer shops or newsagents; **commercial directory** *or* **trade directory** = book which lists all the businesses and business people in a town; **street directory** = list of people living in a street; map of a town which lists all the streets in alphabetical order in an index; **telephone directory** = book which lists all people and businesses in alphabetical order with their phone numbers; *to find his address you will have to look up his number in the telephone directory; her number is in the London directory*

disallow [dɪsəˈlaʊ] *verb* not to accept a claim for insurance; *he claimed £2,000 for fire damage, but the claim was disallowed*

disaster [dɪˈzɑːstə] *noun* (a) very bad accident; *ten people died in the air disaster* (b) financial collapse; **the company is heading for disaster** *or* **is on a disaster course** = the company is going to collapse; **the advertising campaign was a disaster** = the advertising campaign was very bad, did not have the required effect (c) accident in nature; *a storm disaster on the south coast; flood disaster damage*

disastrous [dɪˈzɑːstrəs] *adjective* very bad; *the company suffered a disastrous drop in sales*

disburse [dɪsˈbɜːs] *verb* to pay money

disbursement [dɪsˈbɜːsmənt] *noun* payment of money

discharge [dɪsˈtʃɑːdʒ] **1** *noun* (a) **discharge in bankruptcy** = being released from bankruptcy after paying your debts (b) payment of debt; **in full discharge of a debt** = paying a debt completely; **final discharge** = final payment of what is left of a debt (c) **in discharge of his duties as director** = carrying out his duties as director **2** *verb* (a) **to discharge a bankrupt** = to release someone from bankruptcy because he has paid his debts (b) **to discharge a debt** *or* **to discharge your liabilities** = to pay a debt or your liabilities in full (c) to dismiss or to sack; *to discharge an employee*

disciplinary procedure [dɪsɪˈplɪnəri prəˈsiːdʒə] *noun* way of warning a worker officially that he is breaking rules or that he is working badly

disclaimer [dɪsˈkleɪmə] *noun* legal refusal to accept responsibility

disclose [dɪsˈkləʊz] *verb* to tell details; *the bank has no right to disclose details of my account to the tax office*

disclosure [dɪsˈkləʊʒə] *noun* act of telling details; *the disclosure of the takeover bid raised the price of the shares*

discontinue [dɪskənˈtɪnjuː] *verb* to stop stocking, selling or making (a product); *these carpets are a discontinued line*

discount [ˈdɪskaʊnt] **1** *noun* (a) percentage by which a full price is reduced to a buyer by the seller; **to give a discount on bulk purchases**; **to sell goods at a discount** *or* **at a discount price** = to sell goods below the normal price; **basic discount** = normal discount without extra percentages; *we give 25% as a basic discount, but can add 5% for cash payment*; **quantity discount** *or* **volume discount** = discount given to people who buy large quantities; **10% discount for quantity purchases** = you pay 10% less if you buy a large quantity; **10% discount for cash** *or* **10% cash discount** = you pay 10% less if you pay in cash; **trade discount** = discount given to a customer in the same trade (b) **discount house** = (i) financial company which specializes in discounting bills; (ii) shop which specializes in selling cheap goods bought at a high discount; **discount rate** = percentage taken when a bank buys bills; **discount store** = shop which specializes in cheap goods bought at a high discount (c) **shares which stand at a discount** = shares which are lower in price than their face value **2** *verb* (a) to reduce prices to increase sales (b) **to discount bills of exchange** = to sell bills of exchange for less than the value written on them in order to cash them before their maturity date; **to discount invoices** = to obtain a cash advance from a discounter against the value of invoices (c) **shares are discounting a rise in the dollar** = shares have risen in advance of a rise in the dollar price; **discounted value** = difference between the face value of a share and its lower market price

> pressure on the Federal Reserve Board to ease monetary policy and possibly cut its discount rate mounted yesterday
>
> *Financial Times*

> banks refrained from quoting forward US/Hongkong dollar exchange rates as premiums of 100 points replaced the previous day's discounts of up to 50 points
>
> *South China Morning Post*

discountable [dɪsˈkaʊntəbl] *adjective* which can be discounted; *these bills are not discountable*

discounted cash flow (DCF)

[dɪsˈkaʊntɪd ˈkæʃfləʊ] *noun* calculating the forecast return on capital investment by discounting future cash flows from the investment, usually at a rate equivalent to the company's minimum required rate of return

> COMMENT: discounting is necessary because it is generally accepted that money held today is worth more than money to be received in the future. The effect of discounting is to reduce future income or expenses to their 'present value'. Once discounted, future cash flows can be compared directly with the initial cost of a capital investment which is already stated in present value terms. If the present value of income is greater than the present value of costs the investment can be said to be worthwhile

discounter [dɪsˈkaʊntə] *noun* person or company which discounts bills or invoices, or sells goods at a discount

> invoice discounting is an instant finance raiser. Cash is advanced by a factor or discounter against the value of invoices sent out by the client company. Debt collection is still in the hands of the client company, which also continues to run its own bought ledger
>
> *Times*

> a 100,000 square-foot warehouse generates ten times the volume of a discount retailer; it can turn its inventory over 18 times a year, more than triple a big discounter's turnover
>
> *Duns Business Month*

discover [dɪsˈkʌvə] *verb* to find something new; *we discovered that our agent was selling our rival's products at the same price as ours*; *the auditors discovered some errors in the accounts*

discrepancy [dɪsˈkrepənsi] *noun* situation where figures are not correct; **there is a discrepancy in the accounts** = there is an error; **statistical discrepancy** = amount by which sets of figures differ

discretion [dɪsˈkreʃən] *noun* being able to decide correctly what should be done; **I leave it to your discretion** = I leave it for you to decide what to do; **at the discretion of someone** = if someone decides; *membership is at the discretion of the committee*

discretionary [dɪsˈkreʃənəri] *adjective* which can be done if someone wants; **the minister's discretionary powers** = powers which the minister could use if he thought he should do so; **discretionary account** = a client's account with a stockbroker, where the broker invests and sells at his own discretion; **on a discretionary basis** = way of managing a client's funds, where the fund manager uses his discretion to do as he wants, without the client giving him any specific instructions

discrimination [dɪskrɪmɪˈneɪʃən] *noun* treating people in different ways because of class, religion, race, language, colour or sex; **sexual discrimination** *or* **sex discrimination** *or* **discrimination on grounds of sex** = treating men and women in different ways

discuss [dɪsˈkʌs] *verb* to talk about a problem; *they spent two hours discussing the details of the contract*; *the committee discussed the question of import duties on cars*; *the board will discuss wage rises at its next meeting*; *we discussed delivery schedules with our suppliers*

discussion [dɪsˈkʌʃən] *noun* talking about a problem; *after ten minutes' discussion the board agreed the salary increases*; *we spent the whole day in discussions with our suppliers*

diseconomies of scale
[dɪsiːˈkɒnəmiːz əv ˈskeɪl] *noun* situation where increased production actually increases unit cost

> COMMENT: after having increased production using the existing workforce and machinery, giving economies of scale, the company finds that in order to increase production further it has to employ more workers and buy more machinery, leading to an increase in unit cost

disembark [dɪsɪmˈbɑːk] *verb* to get off a boat or plane

disembarkation [dɪsɪmbɑːˈkeɪʃn] *noun* getting off a boat or plane; **disembarkation card** = card which allows you to get off a plane or boat, and return after a short time

disenfranchise [dɪsɪnˈfræntʃaɪz] *verb* to take away someone's right to vote; *the company has tried to disenfranchise the ordinary shareholders*

dishonour *US* **dishonor** [dɪsˈɒnə] *verb* **to dishonour a bill** = not to pay a bill; **dishonoured cheque** = cheque which the bank will not pay because there is not enough money in the account to pay it

disinflation [dɪsɪnˈfleɪʃən] *noun* reducing inflation in the economy by increasing tax, reducing the level of money supply, etc.; *compare* DEFLATION

disinvest [dɪsɪnˈvest] *verb* to reduce investment by not replacing capital assets when they wear out

disinvestment [dɪsɪnˈvestmənt] *noun* reduction in capital assets by not replacing them when they wear out

disk [dɪsk] *noun* round flat object, used to store information in computers; **floppy disk** = small disk for storing information through a computer; **hard disk** = solid disk in a sealed case which will store a large amount of computer information; **disk drive** = part of a computer which makes a disk spin round in order to read it or store information on it

diskette [dɪsˈket] *noun* small floppy disk; *he sent a diskette of the accounts to his accountant*

dismiss [dɪsˈmɪs] *verb* **to dismiss an employee** = to remove an employee from a job; *he was dismissed for being late*

dismissal [dɪsˈmɪsəl] *noun* removal of an employee from a job; **constructive dismissal** = situation where an employee does not leave his job voluntarily, but because of pressure from the management; **unfair dismissal** = removing someone from a job for reasons which are not fair; **wrongful dismissal** = removing someone from a job for reasons which are wrong; **dismissal procedures** = correct way of dismissing someone according to the contract of employment

dispatch [dɪsˈpætʃ] **1** *noun* **(a)** sending of goods to a customer; *the strike held up dispatch for several weeks*; **dispatch department** = department which deals with the packing and sending of goods to customers; **dispatch note** = note saying that goods have been sent; **dispatch rider** = motorcyclist who delivers messages or parcels in a town **(b)** goods which have been sent; *the weekly dispatch went off yesterday* **2** *verb* to send goods to customers; *the goods were dispatched last Friday*

dispatcher [dɪsˈpætʃə] *noun* **(a)** person who sends goods to customers **(b)** *US* person responsible for the route schedules of taxis, buses, trucks, etc.

dispenser [dɪsˈpensə] *noun* machine which automatically provides something (an object, a drink, some food), often when money is put in; **automatic dispenser**; **towel dispenser**; **cash dispenser** = machine which gives out money when a special card is inserted and instructions given

display [dɪsˈpleɪ] **1** *noun* showing of goods for sale; *the shop has several car models on display*; *an attractive display of kitchen equipment*; **display advertisement** = advertisement which is well designed or printed in bold type to attract attention; **display cabinet** *or* **display**

case = piece of furniture with a glass top or glass doors for showing goods for sale; **display material** = posters, photographs, etc., to be used to attract attention to goods which are for sale; **display pack** *or* **display box** = special box for showing goods for sale; *the watches are prepacked in plastic display boxes*; **display stand** *or* **display unit** = special stand for showing goods for sale; **visual display unit (VDU)** *or* **visual display terminal** = screen attached to a computer which shows the information stored in the computer **2** *verb* to show; *the company was displaying three new car models at the show*

disposable [dɪsˈpəʊzəbl] *adjective* **(a)** which can be used and then thrown away; *the machine serves soup in disposable paper cups* **(b)** **disposable personal income** = income left after tax and national insurance have been deducted

disposal [dɪsˈpəʊzəl] *noun* sale; *the company has started a systematic disposal of its property portfolio*; **lease** *or* **business for disposal** = lease or business for sale

dispose [dɪsˈpəʊz] *verb* to dispose of = to get rid of or to sell cheaply; *to dispose of excess stock*; *he is planning to dispose of his business in the new year*

dispute [dɪsˈpjuːt] **1** *noun* industrial disputes *or* labour disputes = arguments between management and workers; **to adjudicate** *or* **to mediate in a dispute** = to try to settle a dispute between other parties; **disputes procedure** = formal way of resolving disputes between a trade union and management **2** *verb* to argue that something is wrong; *he disputed the bill*

disqualification [dɪskwɒlɪfɪˈkeɪʃn] *noun* making someone disqualified to do something

Even 'administrative offences' can result in disqualification. A person may be disqualified for up to five years following persistent breach of company legislation in terms of failing to file returns, accounts and other documents with the Registrar

Accountancy

disqualify [dɪsˈkwɒlɪfaɪ] *verb* to make a person unqualified to do something, such as to be a director of a company

dissolution [dɪsəˈluːʃən] *noun* ending (of a partnership)

dissolve [dɪˈzɒlv] *verb* to bring to an end; *to dissolve a partnership*

distrain [dɪˈstreɪn] *verb* to seize (goods) to pay for debts

distress [dɪˈstres] *noun* taking someone's goods to pay for debts; *US* **distress merchandise** = goods sold cheaply to pay a company's debts; **distress sale** = sale of goods at low prices to pay a company's debts

distribute [dɪˈstrɪbjuːt] *verb* **(a)** to share out dividends; *profits were distributed among the shareholders* **(b)** to send out goods from a manufacturer's warehouse to retail shops; *Smith Ltd distributes for several smaller companies*; *all orders are distributed from our warehouse near Oxford*

distribution [dɪstrɪˈbjuːʃən] *noun* **(a)** act of sending goods from the manufacturer to the wholesaler and then to retailers; *stock is held in a distribution centre which deals with all order processing*; *distribution costs have risen sharply over the last 18 months*; *he has several years' experience as distribution manager*; **channels of distribution** *or* **distribution channels** = ways of sending goods from the manufacturer to the retailer; **distribution network** = series of points or small warehouses from which goods are sent all over a country **(b)** **distribution slip** = paper attached to a document or a magazine showing all the people in an office who should read it

distributive [dɪˈstrɪbjutɪv] *adjective* referring to distribution; **distributive trades** = all business involved in the distribution of goods

distributor [dɪˈstrɪbjutə] *noun* company which sells goods for another company which makes them; **exclusive distributor** *or* **sole distributor** = retailer who is the only one in an area who is allowed by the manufacturer to sell a certain product; **a network of distributors** = a series of distributors spread all over a country

distributorship [dɪ'strɪbjʊtəʃɪp] *noun* position of being a distributor for a company

district ['dɪstrɪkt] *noun* section of a country or of a town; *district manager*; the **commercial district** *or* **the business district** = part of a town where offices and shops are located

diversification [daɪvɜːsɪfɪ'keɪʃən] *noun* adding another quite different type of business to a firm's existing trade; **product diversification** *or* **diversification into new products** = adding new types of products to the range already made

diversify [daɪ'vɜːsɪfaɪ] *verb* (a) to add new types of business to existing ones; *the company is planning to diversify into new products* (b) to invest in different types of shares or savings so as to spread the risk of loss

divest [daɪ'vest] *verb* **to divest oneself of something** = to get rid of something; *the company had divested itself of its US interests*

divide [dɪ'vaɪd] *verb* to cut into separate sections; *the country is divided into six sales areas*; *the two companies agreed to divide the market between them*

dividend ['dɪvɪdend] *noun* percentage of profits paid to shareholders; **to raise** *or* **to increase the dividend** = to pay out a higher dividend than in the previous year; **to maintain the dividend** = to keep the same dividend as in the previous year; **to pass the dividend** = to pay no dividend; **final dividend** = dividend paid at the end of a financial year; **dividend forecast** = forecast of the amount of an expected dividend; **forecast dividend** *or* **prospective dividend** = dividend which a company expects to pay at the end of the current year; **interim dividend** = dividend paid at the end of a half-year; **dividend cover** = the ratio of earnings after tax to dividend; **the dividend is covered four times** = the profits are four times the dividend; **dividend warrant** = cheque which makes payment of a dividend; **dividend yield** = dividend expressed as a percentage of the price of a share; **cum dividend** = share sold with the dividend still to be paid; **ex dividend** = share sold

after the dividend has been paid; **the shares are quoted ex dividend** = the share price does not include the right to the dividend

---

COMMENT: the dividend is calculated as the proportion of profits a company can pay to its shareholders after tax has been paid, always keeping some of the profit back to reinvest in the company's products or activities. Large companies usually pay dividends twice a year, once after the half-year results have been declared (called the 'interim dividend') and gain when the final results are published

---

divider [dɪ'vaɪdə] *noun* (a) sheet of coloured cardboard which fits into a ring binder to separate different series of sheets of paper (b) **room divider** = moveable low wall, which can be used to make a 'room' in an open-plan office

division [dɪ'vɪʒən] *noun* (a) main section of a large company; *marketing division*; *production division*; *retail division*; *she has taken over responsibility for the hotel division*; *he is in charge of one of the major divisions of the company* (b) company which is part of a large group; *Smith's is now a division of the Brown group of companies*

divisional [dɪ'vɪʒənl] *adjective* referring to a division; *a divisional director*; *the divisional headquarters*

DIY ['diːaɪ'waɪ] = DO-IT-YOURSELF

DM *or* **D-mark** = DEUTSCHMARK, MARK

dock [dɒk] **1** *noun* harbour, place where ships can load or unload; *loading dock*; *a dock worker*; *the dock manager*; *the docks* = part of a town where the harbour is; **dock dues** = money paid by a ship going into or out of a dock, used to keep the dock in good repair **2** *verb* (a) to go into dock; *the ship docked at 17.00* (b) to remove money from someone's wages; *we will have to dock his pay if he is late for work again*; *he had £20 docked from his pay for being late*

docker ['dɒkə] *noun* person who works in a dock

docket ['dɒkɪt] *noun* list of contents of a package which is being sent

dockyard ['dɒkjɑːd] *noun* place where ships are built

doctor ['dɒktə] *noun* specialist who examines people when they are sick to see how they can be made well; **company doctor** = (i) doctor who works for a company and looks after sick workers; (ii) specialist businessman who rescues businesses which are in difficulties; *the staff are all sent to see the company doctor once a year*; **doctor's certificate** = document written by a doctor to say that a worker is ill and cannot work; *he has been off sick for ten days and still has not sent in a doctor's certificate*

document ['dɒkjumənt] *noun* paper with writing on it; *he left a file of documents in the taxi*; *she asked to see the documents relating to the case*

documentary [dɒkju'mentəri] *adjective* in the form of documents; *documentary evidence*; *documentary proof*

documentation [dɒkjumen'teɪʃən] *noun* all documents referring to something; *please send me the complete documentation concerning the sale*

DoE = DEPARTMENT OF EMPLOYMENT

dog [dɒg] *noun* product that has a low market share and a low growth rate, and so is likely to be dropped from the company's product line

dogsbody ['dɒgzbɒdi] *noun (informal)* person who does all types of work in an office for very low wages

do-it-yourself ['duːɪtjə'self] *adjective* done by an ordinary person, not by a skilled worker; **do-it-yourself conveyancing** = drawing up a legal conveyance by the person selling a property, without the help of a lawyer; **do-it-yourself magazine** = magazine with articles on work which the average person can do to repair or paint his or her house

dole [dəʊl] *noun* money given by the government to unemployed people; **he is receiving dole payments** *or* **he is on the dole** = he is receiving unemployment benefits; **dole queues** = lines of people waiting to collect the dole

dollar ['dɒlə] *noun* **(a)** unit of currency used in the USA and other countries, such as Australia, Bahamas, Barbados, Bermuda, Brunei, Canada, Fiji, Hong Kong, Jamaica, New Zealand, Singapore, Zimbabwe; *the US dollar rose 2%*; *they sent a cheque for fifty Canadian dollars*; *it costs six Australian dollars*; **a five dollar bill** = a banknote for five dollars **(b)** *(in particular)* the currency used in the USA; **dollar area** = area of the world where the US dollar is the main trading currency; **dollar balances** = a country's trade balances expressed in US dollars; **dollar crisis** = fall in the exchange rate for the US dollar; **dollar gap** *or* **dollar shortage** = situation where the supply of US dollars is not enough to satisfy the demand for them from overseas buyers; **dollar stocks** = shares in US companies (NOTE: usually written $ before a figure: **$250**. The currencies used in different countries can be shown by the initial letter of the country: **C$** (Canadian dollar) **A$** (Australian dollar), etc.)

domestic [də'mestɪk] *adjective* referring to the home market, the market of the country where the business is situated; *domestic sales have increased over the last six months*; **domestic consumption** = consumption on the home market; *domestic consumption of oil has fallen sharply*; **domestic market** = market in the country where a company is based; *they produce goods for the domestic market*; **domestic production** = production of goods for domestic consumption; **domestic trade** = trade within the home market

domicile ['dɒmɪsaɪl] **1** *noun* country where someone lives or where a company's office is registered **2** *verb* **he is domiciled in Denmark** = he lives in Denmark officially; **bills domiciled in France** = bills of exchange which have to be paid in France

door [dɔː] *noun* piece of wood, metal, etc., which closes the entrance to a building or room; *the finance director knocked on the chairman's door and walked in*; *the sales manager's name is on his door*; *the* store opened its doors on June 1st = the store started doing business on June 1st

door-to-door ['dɔːtə'dɔː] *adjective* going from one house to the next, asking the occupiers to buy something or to vote for someone; *we have 200 door-to-door salesmen*; *door-to-door selling is banned in this part of the village*

dormant ['dɔːmənt] *adjective* not active; **dormant account** = bank account which is no longer used

dossier ['dɒsɪeɪ] *noun* file of documents

dot [dɒt] *noun* small round spot; *the order form should be cut off along the line shown by the row of dots*

dot com ['dɒt'kɒm] *see* .COM

dot-matrix printer ['dɒtmeɪtrɪks 'prɪntə] *noun* cheap printer which makes letters by printing many small dots (the quality is not as good as laser printers or inkjet printers)

dotted line ['dɒtɪd 'laɪn] *noun* line made of a series of dots; *please sign on the dotted line*; *do not write anything below the dotted line*

double ['dʌbl] **1** *adjective* **(a)** twice as large, two times the size; *their turnover is double ours*; **to be on double time** = to earn twice the usual wages for working on Sundays or other holidays; **double-entry bookkeeping** = system of bookkeeping where both debit and credit entries are recorded in the accounts at the same time (e.g., when a sale is credited to the sales account the purchaser's debt is debited to the debtors account); **double taxation** = taxing the same income twice; **double taxation agreement** = agreement between two countries that a person living in one country shall not be taxed in both countries on the income earned in the other country **(b)** **in double figures** = with two figures, from 10 to 99; *inflation is in double figures*; *we have had double-figure inflation for some years* **2** *verb* to become twice as big; to make something twice as big; *we have doubled our profits this year or our profits have doubled this year*; *the company's borrowings have doubled*

double-book ['dʌbl'bʊk] *verb* to let the same hotel room, plane seat, etc., to more

than one person at a time; *we had to change our flight as we were double-booked*

double-booking ['dʌbl'bʊkɪŋ] *noun* letting by a travel agent of the same hotel room or the same plane seat to more than one person at a time

doubtful ['daʊtfəl] *adjective* which is not certain; **doubtful debt** = debt which may never be paid; **doubtful loan** = loan which may never be repaid

Dow Jones Index ['daʊ 'dʒəʊnz 'ɪndeks] any of several indices published by the Dow Jones Co., based on prices on the New York Stock Exchange

Dow Jones Industrial Average (DJIA) ['daʊ 'dʒəʊnz ɪn'dʌstrɪəl 'ævrɪdʒ] index of share prices on the New York Stock Exchange, based on a group of thirty major corporations; *the Dow Jones Average rose ten points*; *general optimism showed in the rise on the Dow Jones Average*

down [daʊn] **1** *adverb & preposition* in a lower position, to a lower position; *the inflation rate is gradually coming down*; *shares are slightly down on the day*; *the price of petrol has gone down*; **to pay money down** = to make a deposit; *he paid £50 down and the rest in monthly instalments* **2** *verb* **to down tools** = to stop working; *the entire workforce downed tools in protest*

downgrade [daʊn'greɪd] *verb* to reduce the importance of someone or of a job; *his job was downgraded in the company reorganization*

download [daʊn'ləʊd] *verb* to load data or a program onto a computer from another computer

down market ['daʊnmɑːkɪt] *adverb & adjective* cheaper, appealing to a less wealthy section of the population; *the company has adopted a down-market image*; **the company has decided to go down market** = the company has decided to make products which appeal to a wider section of the public (NOTE: the opposite is **up market**)

down payment ['daʊn 'peɪmənt] *noun* part of a total payment made in advance; *he made a down payment of $100*

downside ['daʊnsaɪd] *noun* **downside factor** *or* **downside risk** = possibility of making a loss (in an investment); **the sales force have been asked to give downside forecasts** = they have been asked for pessimistic forecasts (NOTE: the opposite is **upside**)

downsizing ['daʊnsaɪzɪŋ] *noun* reducing the size of something, especially reducing the number of people employed in a company to make it more profitable

down time ['daʊn 'taɪm] *noun* time when a machine is not working because it is broken, being mended, etc.; time when a worker cannot work because machines have broken down, because components are not available, etc.

downtown ['daʊntaʊn] *noun, adjective & adverb* in the central business district of a town; *his office is in downtown New York*; *she works in a downtown store*; *they established a business downtown*

downturn ['daʊntɜːn] *noun* movement towards lower prices, sales or profits; *a downturn in the market price*; *the last quarter saw a downturn in the economy*

downward ['daʊnwəd] *adjective* towards a lower position; *the downward movement of shares continued during the day*

downwards ['daʊnwədz] *adverb* towards a lower position; *the company's profits have moved downwards over the last few years*

dozen ['dʌzn] *noun* twelve; *to sell in sets of one dozen*; **cheaper by the dozen** = the product is cheaper if you buy twelve at a time

Dr *or* **DR 1** = DEBTOR **2** = DRACHMA

drachma ['drækmə] *noun* currency used in Greece (NOTE: usually written **Dr** before a figure: **Dr22bn**)

draft [drɑːft] **1** *noun* **(a)** order for money to be paid by a bank; *we asked for payment by banker's draft*; **to make a draft on a bank** = to ask a bank to pay money for you; **sight draft** = bill of exchange which is payable when it is presented **(b)** first rough plan or document which has not been finished; *a draft of the contract* *or* *the draft contract is waiting for the MD's comments*; *he drew up the draft agreement on the back of an envelope*; *the first draft of the contract was corrected by the managing director*; *the finance department has passed the final draft of the accounts*; **rough draft** = plan of a document which may have changes made to it before it is complete **2** *verb* to make a first rough plan of a document; *to draft a letter*; *to draft a contract*; *the contract is still being drafted* *or* *is still in the drafting stage*

drafter ['drɑːftə] *noun* person who makes a draft; *the drafter of the agreement*

drafting ['drɑːftɪŋ] *noun* act of preparing the draft of a document; *the drafting of the contract took six weeks*

drain [dreɪn] **1** *noun* gradual loss of money flowing away; *the costs of the London office are a continual drain on our resources* **2** *verb* to remove something gradually; *the expansion plan has drained all our profits*; *the company's capital resources have drained away*

draw [drɔː] *verb* **(a)** to take money away; *to draw money out of an account*; **to draw a salary** = to have a salary paid by the company; *the chairman does not draw a salary* **(b)** to write a cheque; *he paid the invoice with a cheque drawn on an Egyptian bank* (NOTE: **drawing - drew - has drawn**)

drawback ['drɔːbæk] *noun* **(a)** thing which is not convenient or likely to cause problems; *one of the main drawbacks of the scheme is that it will take six years to complete* **(b)** paying back customs duty when imported goods are then re-exported

draw down ['drɔː 'daʊn] *verb* to draw money which is available under a credit agreement

drawee [drɔː'iː] *noun* person or bank asked to make a payment by a drawer

drawer ['drɔːə] *noun* person who writes a cheque or a bill asking a drawee to pay money to a payee; **the bank returned the cheque to drawer** = the bank would not pay the cheque because the person who wrote it did not have enough money in the account to pay it

drawing ['drɔːɪŋ] *noun* **(a) drawing account** = current account, account from which the customer may take money when he wants; *see also* SPECIAL DRAWING RIGHTS **(b) drawing pin** = pin with a flat head for attaching a sheet of paper to something hard; *she used drawing pins to pin the poster to the door* (NOTE: American English is **thumbtack**)

draw up ['drɔː 'ʌp] *verb* to write a legal document; *to draw up a contract or an agreement; to draw up a company's articles of association*

drift [drɪft] *verb* to move slowly; *shares drifted lower in a dull market; strikers are drifting back to work*

drive [draɪv] **1** *noun* **(a)** energy, energetic way of working; **economy drive** = vigorous effort to save money or materials; **sales drive** = vigorous effort to increase sales; *he has a lot of drive* = he is very energetic in business **(b)** part of a machine which makes other parts work; **disk drive** = part of a computer which makes the disk spin round in order to store information on it **2** *verb* **(a)** to make a car, lorry, etc., go in a certain direction; *he was driving to work when he heard the news on the car radio; she drives a company car* **(b)** *he drives a hard bargain* = he is a difficult person to negotiate with (NOTE: **driving - drove - has driven**)

driving licence *US* **driver's license** ['draɪvɪŋ 'laɪsəns *or* 'draɪvəz 'laɪsəns] *noun* document which allows someone to drive a car, a truck, etc.; *applicants for the job should hold a valid driving licence*

drop [drɒp] **1** *noun* fall; *sales show a drop of 10%; the drop in prices resulted in no significant increase in sales* **2** *verb* **(a)** to fall; *sales have dropped by 10% or have dropped 10%; the pound dropped three points against the dollar* **(b)** not to keep in a product range; *we have dropped these items from the catalogue because they've been losing sales steadily for some time* (NOTE: **dropping - dropped**)

drop ship ['drɒp 'ʃɪp] *verb* to deliver a large order direct to a customer

drop shipment ['drɒp 'ʃɪpmənt] *noun* delivery of a large order from the manufacturer direct to a customer's shop or warehouse without going through an agent or wholesaler

drug [drʌg] *noun* medicine; **a drug on the market** = product which is difficult to sell because it has already been sold in large quantities and the market is saturated

dry [draɪ] *adjective* not wet; **dry goods** = cloth, clothes and household goods; **dry measure** = way of calculating loose dry produce (such as corn)

DTI ['diːtiːˈaɪ] = DEPARTMENT OF TRADE AND INDUSTRY

DTP = DESK-TOP PUBLISHING

dubious ['djuːbɪəs] *adjective* doubtful, probably not legal; *dubious business practices can cause a collapse of market confidence*

duck *see* LAME DUCK

dud [dʌd] *adjective & noun (informal)* false, not good (coin or banknote); *the £50 note was a dud*; **dud cheque** = cheque which the bank refuses to pay because the person writing it has not enough money in his account to pay it

due [djuː] *adjective* **(a)** owed; *sum due from a debtor; a bond due for repayment*; **to fall due** *or* **to become due** = to be ready for payment; **bill due on May 1st** = bill which has to be paid on May 1st; **balance due to us** = amount owed to us which should be paid **(b)** expected to arrive; *the plane is due to arrive at 10.30 or is due at 10.30* **(c)** **in due form** = written in the correct legal form; *receipt in due form; contract drawn up in due form*; **after due**

consideration of the problem = after thinking seriously about the problem (**d**) caused by; *supplies have been delayed due to a strike at the manufacturers*; *the company pays the wages of staff who are absent due to illness*

> many expect the US economic indicators for April, due on this Thursday, to show faster economic growth
>
> *Australian Financial Review*

dues ['dju:z] *plural noun* (**a**) regular subscription payments made by a union member to the union; **dock dues** *or* **port dues** *or* **harbour dues** = payment which a ship makes to the harbour authorities for the right to use the harbour (**b**) orders taken but not supplied until new stock arrives; **to release dues** = to dispatch back orders when new stock arrives; *we have recorded thousands of dues for that item and our supplier cannot supply it*

dull [dʌl] *adjective* not exciting, not full of life; **dull market** = market where little business is done

dullness ['dʌlnəs] *noun* being dull; *the dullness of the market*

duly ['dju:li] *adverb* (**a**) properly; *duly authorized representative* (**b**) as was expected; *we duly received his letter of 21st October*

dummy ['dʌmi] *noun* imitation product to test the reaction of potential customers to its design; **dummy pack** = empty pack for display

dump [dʌmp] *verb* **to dump goods on a market** = to get rid of large quantities of excess goods cheaply in an overseas market

> a serious threat lies in the 400,000 tonnes of subsidized beef in European cold stores. If dumped, this meat will have disastrous effects in Pacific Basin markets
>
> *Australian Financial Review*

dump bin ['dʌmp 'bɪn] *noun* display container like a large box which is filled with goods for sale

dumping ['dʌmpɪŋ] *noun* act of getting rid of excess goods cheaply in an overseas market; *the government has passed anti-dumping legislation*; *dumping of goods on the European market is banned*; **panic dumping of sterling** = rush to sell sterling at any price because of possible devaluation

Dun & Bradstreet (D&B) ['dʌn ən 'brædstri:t] organization which produces reports on the financial rating of companies; it also acts as a debt collection agency

duplicate 1 ['dju:plɪkət] *noun* copy; *he sent me the duplicate of the contract*; **duplicate receipt** *or* **duplicate of a receipt** = copy of a receipt; **in duplicate** = with a copy; **receipt in duplicate** = two copies of a receipt; *to print an invoice in duplicate* **2** ['dju:plɪkeɪt] *verb* (**a**) *(of a bookkeeping entry)* **to duplicate with another** = to repeat another entry or to be the same as another entry (**b**) **to duplicate a letter** = to make a copy of a letter

duplicating ['dju:plɪkeɪtɪŋ] *noun* copying; **duplicating machine** = machine which makes copies of documents; **duplicating paper** = special paper to be used in a duplicating machine

duplication [dju:plɪ'keɪʃən] *noun* copying of documents; **duplication of work** = work which is done twice without being necessary

duplicator ['dju:plɪkeɪtə] *noun* machine which makes copies of documents

durable ['djuərəbl] **1** *adjective* **durable goods** = goods which will be used for a long time (such as washing machines or refrigerators); **durable effects** = effects which will be felt for a long time; *the strike will have durable effects on the economy* **2** *noun* **consumer durables** = goods bought by the public which will be used for a long time (such as washing machines or refrigerators)

dust cover ['dʌst 'kʌvə] *noun* cover which is put over a machine (such as a typewriter, or a computer) to keep dust off

Dutch [dʌtʃ] *adjective* **Dutch auction** = auction where the auctioneer offers an item for sale at a high price and then gradually reduces the price until someone makes a bid; **to go Dutch** = to share the bill in a restaurant

dutiable ['djuːtjəbl] *adjective* **dutiable goods** *or* **dutiable items** = goods on which a customs duty has to be paid

duty ['djuːti] *noun* **(a)** tax which has to be paid; *traders are asking the government to take the duty off alcohol or to put a duty on cigarettes*; **ad valorem duty** = duty calculated on the sales value of the goods; **customs duty** *or* **import duty** = tax on goods imported into a country; **excise duty** = tax on goods (such as alcohol and petrol) which are produced in the country; **goods which are liable to duty** = goods on which customs or excise tax has to be paid; **duty-paid goods** = goods where the duty has been paid; **stamp duty** = tax on legal documents (such as the conveyance of a property to a new owner); **estate duty** *US* **death duty** = tax paid on the property left by a dead person **(b)** work which has to be done; **night duty** = period of work during the night; **on duty** = doing official work which is part of your job; *she has been on duty all day; two security guards were on duty at the time of the theft*

Canadian and European negotiators agreed to a deal under which Canada could lower its import duties on $150 million worth of European goods
Globe and Mail (Toronto)

the Department of Customs and Excise collected a total of N79m under the new advance duty payment scheme
Business Times (Lagos)

duty-free ['djuːti'friː] *adjective & adverb* sold with no duty to be paid; *he bought a duty-free watch at the airport or he bought the watch duty-free*; **duty-free shop** = shop at an airport or on a ship where goods can be bought without paying duty

Ee

e- [iː] *prefix* referring to electronics or the Internet

e.& o.e. = ERRORS AND OMISSIONS EXCEPTED

eager [ˈiːgə] *adjective* wanting to do something; *the management is eager to get into the Far Eastern markets*; *our salesmen are eager to see the new product range*

early [ˈɜːli] **1** *adjective* **(a)** before the usual time; **early closing day** = weekday when some shops in a town close in the afternoon; **at your earliest convenience** = as soon as possible; **at an early date** = very soon; **to take early retirement** = to leave a job with a pension before the usual age for retirement; **early withdrawal** = withdrawing money from a deposit account before due date **(b)** at the beginning of a period of time; *he took an early flight to Paris*; **we hope for an early resumption of negotiations** = we hope negotiations will start again soon; **to take early retirement** = to retire from work before the usual age **2** *adverb* before the usual time; *the mail left early*; *he retired early and bought a house in Cornwall*

earmark [ˈɪəmɑːk] *verb* to reserve for a special purpose; *to earmark funds for a project*; *the grant is earmarked for computer systems development*

earn [ɜːn] *verb* **(a)** to be paid money for working; *to earn £500 a week*; *our agent in Paris certainly does not earn his commission*; **earned income** = income from wages, salaries, pensions, etc. (as opposed to 'unearned' income from investments) **(b)** to produce interest or dividends; *what level of dividend do these shares earn?*; *account which earns interest at 10%*

earnest [ˈɜːnɪst] *noun* money paid as a down payment

earning [ˈɜːnɪŋ] *noun* **earning capacity** *or* **earning power** = amount of money someone should be able to earn; *he is such a fine dress designer that his earning power is very large*; **earning potential** = amount of money a person should be able to earn; amount of dividend a share should produce

earnings [ˈɜːnɪŋz] *plural noun* **(a)** salary or wages, profits and dividends or interest received; **compensation for loss of earnings** = payment to someone who has stopped earning money or who is not able to earn money; **invisible earnings** = foreign currency earned by a country in providing services (such as banking, tourism), not in selling goods **(b)** money which is earned in interest or dividend; **earnings per share** *or* **earnings yield** = money earned in dividends per share, shown as a percentage of the market price of one share; **gross earnings** = earnings before tax and other deductions; **retained earnings** = profits which are not paid out to shareholders as dividend; *see also* PRICE/EARNINGS RATIO

the US now accounts for more than half of our world-wide sales. It has made a huge contribution to our earnings turnaround

Duns Business Month

last fiscal year the chain reported a 116% jump in earnings, to $6.4 million or $1.10 a share

Barrons

ease [iːz] *verb* to fall a little; *the share index eased slightly today*

easement ['iːzmənt] *noun* right which someone has to use land belonging to someone else (such as for a path across someone's land to a garage)

easily ['iːzɪli] *adverb* (a) without any difficulty; *we passed through customs easily* (b) much, a lot (compared to something else); *he is easily our best salesman*; *the firm is easily the biggest in the market*

easy ['iːzi] *adjective* (a) not difficult; **easy terms** = terms which are not difficult to accept, price which is easy to pay; *the shop is let on very easy terms*; **the loan is repayable in easy payments** = with very small sums paid back regularly; **easy money** = (i) money which can be earned with no difficulty; (ii) loan available on easy repayment terms; **easy money policy** = government policy of expanding the economy by making money more easily available (b) **easy market** = market where few people are buying, so prices are low; *the Stock Exchange was easy yesterday*; **share prices are easier** = prices have fallen slightly

e-business ['iːˈbɪznəs] *noun* the business of dealing with other businesses over the Internet; *e-business is a rising part of the economy*

> the enormous potential of e-business is that it can automate the link between suppliers and customers
>
> *Investors Chronicle*

EC ['iːˈsiː] = EUROPEAN COMMUNITY (NOTE: now called the **European Union (EU)**)

ECB ['iːˈsiːˈbiː] = EUROPEAN CENTRAL BANK

ECGD ['iːsiːdʒiːˈdiː] = EXPORT CREDIT GUARANTEE DEPARTMENT

echelon ['eʃəlɒn] *noun* group of people of a certain grade in an organization; *the upper echelons of industry*

e-commerce ['iːˈkɒmɜːs] *noun* system of buying and selling goods and services over the Internet

> the problem is that if e-commerce takes just a 3 per cent slice of the market that would be enough to reduce margins to ribbons
>
> *Investors Chronicle*

> the new economy requires new company structures. He believes that other blue-chip organizations are going to find that new set-ups would be needed to attract and retain the best talent for e-commerce
>
> *Times*

econometrics [iːkɒnəˈmetrɪks] *plural noun* study of the statistics of economics, using computers to analyse these statistics and make forecasts using mathematical models (NOTE: takes a singular verb)

economic [iːkəˈnɒmɪk] *adjective* (a) which provides enough money; *the flat is let at an economic rent*; *it is hardly economic for the company to run its own warehouse*; **economic order quantity (EOQ)** = quantity of stocks which a company should hold, calculated on the basis of the costs of warehousing, of lower unit costs because of higher quantities purchased, the rate at which stocks are used, and the time it takes for suppliers to deliver new orders (b) referring to the financial state of a country; *economic planners are expecting a comsumer-led boom*; *the government's economic policy is in ruins after the devaluation*; *the economic situation is getting worse*; *the country's economic system needs more regulation*; **economic crisis** *or* **economic depression** = situation where a country is in financial collapse; *the government has introduced import controls to solve the current economic crisis*; **economic cycle** = period during which trade expands, then slows down, then expands again; **economic development** = expansion of the commercial and financial situation; *the economic development of the region has totally changed since oil was discovered there*; **economic growth** = increase in the national income; *the country enjoyed a period of economic growth in the 1980s*; **economic indicators** = statistics which show how the economy is going to perform in the short or long term (unemployment rate, overseas trade, etc.); **economic sanctions** = restrictions on trade with a country in order to make its government change policy; *the western nations imposed economic sanctions on the country*

> each of the major issues on the agenda at this week's meeting is important to the government's success in overall economic management
>
> *Australian Financial Review*

economical [i:kə'nɒmɪkəl] *adjective* which saves money or materials or which is cheap; **economical car** = car which does not use much petrol; **economical use of resources** = using resources as carefully as possible

economics [i:kə'nɒmɪks] *noun* **(a)** study of production, distribution, selling and use of goods and services **(b)** study of financial structures to show how a product or service is costed and what returns it produces; *I do not understand the economics of the coal industry* (NOTE: takes a singular verb)

> believers in free-market economics often find it hard to sort out their views on the issue
>
> *Economist*

economist [ɪ'kɒnəmɪst] *noun* person who specializes in the study of economics; *an agricultural economist*

economize [ɪ'kɒnəmaɪz] *verb* to **economize on petrol** = to save petrol

economy [ɪ'kɒnəmi] *noun* **(a)** being careful not to waste money or materials; **an economy measure** = an action to save money or materials; **to introduce economies** *or* **economy measures into the system** = to start using methods to save money or materials; **economies of scale** = making a product more profitable by manufacturing it in larger quantities so that each unit costs less to make; *(compare* DISECONOMIES) **economy car** = car which does not use much petrol; **economy class** = cheapest class on a plane; *to travel economy class*; **economy drive** = campaign to save money or materials;

economy size = large size, large packet which is a bargain **(b)** financial state of a country, way in which a country makes and uses its money; *the country's economy is in ruins*; **black economy** = work which is paid for in cash or goods, but not declared to the tax authorities; **capitalist economy** = system where each person has the right to invest money, to work in business, to buy and sell with no restrictions from the state; **controlled economy** = system where business activity is controlled by orders from the government; **free market economy** = system where the government does not interfere in business activity in any way; **mixed economy** = system which contains both nationalized industries and private enterprise; **planned economy** = system where the government plans all business activity

> the European economies are being held back by rigid labor markets and wage structures, huge expenditures on social welfare programs and restrictions on the free movement of goods
>
> *Duns Business Month*

edge [edʒ] **1** *noun* **(a)** side of a flat thing; *he sat on the edge of the managing director's desk*; *the printer has printed the figures right to the edge of the printout* **(b)** advantage; *having a local office gives us a competitive edge over Smith Ltd*; **to have the edge on a rival company** = to be slightly more profitable or to have a slightly larger share of the market than a rival **2** *verb* to move a little; *prices on the stock market edged upwards today*; *sales figures edged downwards in January*

> the leading index edged down slightly for the week ended May 13, its first drop in six weeks
>
> *Business Week*

> the evidence suggests that U.S. companies have not lost their competitive edge over the last 20 years
>
> *Harvard Business Review*

editor ['edɪtə] *noun* person in charge of a newspaper or a section of a newspaper; *the editor of the 'Times'*; **the City editor** =

business and finance editor of a British newspaper

editorial [edɪˈtɔːrɪəl] **1** *adjective* referring to an editor; **editorial board** = group of editors (on a newspaper, etc.) **2** *noun* main article in a newspaper, written by the editor

EDP [ˈiːdiːˈpiː] = ELECTRONIC DATA PROCESSING

EEA [ˈiːiːˈeɪ] = EUROPEAN ECONOMIC AREA

EEC [ˈiːiːˈsiː] = EUROPEAN ECONOMIC COMMUNITY (NOTE: now called the **European Union (EU)**)

effect [ɪˈfekt] **1** *noun* **(a)** result; *the effect of the pay increase was to raise productivity levels* **(b)** terms of a contract which take effect *or* come into effect from **January 1st** = terms which start to operate on January 1st; **prices are increased 10% with effect from January 1st** = new prices will apply from January 1st; **to remain in effect** = to continue to be applied **(c)** meaning; **clause to the effect that** = clause which means that; **we have made provision to this effect** = we have put into the contract terms which will make this work **(d)** **personal effects** = personal belongings **2** *verb* to carry out; **to effect a payment** = to make a payment; **to effect customs clearance** = to clear something through customs; **to effect a settlement between two parties** = to bring two parties together and make them agree to a settlement

effective [ɪˈfektɪv] *adjective* **(a)** real; **effective control of a company** = situation where someone owns a large number of shares in a company, but less than 50%, and so in effect controls the company because no other single shareholder can outvote him; **effective demand** = actual demand for a product which can be paid for; **effective yield** = actual yield shown as a percentage of the price paid **(b)** **effective date** = date on which a rule or a contract starts to be applied; **clause effective as from January 1st** = clause which starts to be applied on January 1st **(c)** which works or which produces results; *advertising in the Sunday papers is the most effective way of selling*; *see* COST-EFFECTIVE

effectiveness [ɪˈfektɪvnəs] *noun* working or producing results; *I doubt the effectiveness of television advertising*; *see* COST-EFFECTIVENESS

effectual [ɪˈfektʃʊəl] *adjective* which produces a correct result

efficiency [ɪˈfɪʃənsi] *noun* ability to work well or to produce the right result or the right work quickly; *the bus system is run with a high degree of efficiency*; *a business efficiency exhibition*; *we called in an efficiency expert to report on ways of increasing profitability*

increased control means improved efficiency in purchasing, shipping, sales and delivery
Duns Business Month

efficient [ɪˈfɪʃənt] *adjective* able to work well or to produce the right result quickly; *the efficient working of a system*; *he needs an efficient secretary to look after him*; *efficient machine*

efficiently [ɪˈfɪʃəntli] *adverb* in an efficient way; *she organized the sales conference very efficiently*

efflux [ˈeflʌks] *noun* flowing out; *the efflux of capital to North America*

effort [ˈefət] *noun* using the mind or body to do something; *the salesmen made great efforts to increase sales*; *thanks to the efforts of the finance department, overheads have been reduced*; *if we make one more effort, we should clear the backlog of orders*

EFT = ELECTRONIC FUNDS TRANSFER

EFTA [ˈeftə] = EUROPEAN FREE TRADE ASSOCIATION

EFTPOS [ˈeftˈpɒs] = ELECTRONIC FUNDS TRANSFER AT POINT OF SALE

e.g. [ˈiːˈdʒiː] for example, such as; *the contract is valid in some countries (e.g. France and Belgium) but not in others*

EGM [ˈiːdʒiːˈem] = EXTRAORDINARY GENERAL MEETING

eighty/twenty rule [ˈeɪtɪˈtwentɪ ˈruːl] *noun* rule that a small percentage of customers may account for a large percentage of sales; *see also* PARETO'S LAW

800 number [eɪt'hʌndrəd 'nʌmbə] *US* toll-free number, telephone number beginning with the digits 800, on which calls can be made free of charge, such as to reply to an ad (the supplier pays for them, not the caller) (NOTE: the British equivalent is the **0800 number**)

elastic [ɪ'læstɪk] *adjective* which can expand or contract easily because of small changes in price

elasticity [ɪlæs'tɪsəti] *noun* ability to change easily; **elasticity of supply and demand** = changes in supply and demand of an item depending on its market price

elect [ɪ'lekt] *verb* to choose someone by a vote; *to elect the officers of an association*; *she was elected president*

-elect [ɪ'lekt] *suffix* person who has been elected but has not yet started the term of office; *she is the president-elect* (NOTE: the plural is **presidents-elect**)

election [ɪ'lekʃən] *noun* act of electing; *the election of officers of an association*; *the election of directors by the shareholders*; **general election** = choosing of representatives by all the voters in a country

electric [ɪ'lektrɪk] *adjective* referring to electricity; worked by electricity; *an electric typewriter*

electrical [ɪ'lektrɪkəl] *adjective* referring to electricity; *the engineers are trying to repair an electrical fault*

electricity [elek'trɪsəti] *noun* current used to make light, heat or power; *the electricity was cut off this morning, so the computers could not work*; *our electricity bill has increased considerably this quarter*; *electricity costs are an important factor in our overheads*

electronic [elek'trɒnɪk] *adjective* referring to computers and electronics; **electronic banking** = using computers to carry out banking transactions, such as withdrawals through cash dispensers, transfer of funds at point of sale, etc.; **electronic data processing (EDP)** = selecting and examining data stored in a computer to produce information;

electronic engineer = engineer who specializes in electronic machines; **electronic funds transfer (EFT)** = system for transferring money from one account to another electronically (as when using a smart card); **electronic funds transfer at point of sale (EFTPOS)** = system for transferring money directly from the purchaser's account to the seller's, when a sale is made using a plastic card; **electronic mail** *or* **email** = system of sending messages from one computer terminal to another, via telephone lines; **electronic point of sale (EPOS)** = system where sales are charged automatically to a customer's credit card and stock is controlled by the shop's computer

electronics [elek'trɒnɪks] *plural noun* applying the scientific study of electrons to produce manufactured products, such as computers, calculators or telephones; *the electronics industry*; *an electronics specialist or expert*; *an electronics engineer* (NOTE: takes a singular verb)

element ['elɪmənt] *noun* basic part; *the elements of a settlement*

elevator ['elɪveɪtə] *noun US* lift, a machine which carries passengers or goods from one floor to another in a building; *take the elevator to the 26th floor*

eligibility [elɪdʒə'bɪləti] *noun* being eligible; *the chairman questioned her eligibility to stand for re-election*

eligible ['elɪdʒəbl] *adjective* person who can be chosen; *she is eligible for re-election*; **eligible bill** *or* **eligible paper** = bill which will be accepted by the Bank of England or the US Federal Reserve, and which can be used as security against a loan

eliminate [ɪ'lɪmɪneɪt] *verb* to remove; *to eliminate defects in the system*; *using a computer should eliminate all possibility of error*

email ['iː'meɪl] **1** *noun* **(a)** system of sending messages from one computer terminal to another, via a modem and telephone lines; *you can contact me by phone or email if you want*; **email address** = series of letters and full stops which make up an address for email; *I'll give you my email address*; *my email address is:*

peter@pcp.co.uk (**b**) message sent by this means; *I had six emails from him today* **2** *verb* to send a message from one computer to another, using a modem and telephone lines; *she emailed her order to the warehouse*; *I emailed him about the meeting*

emailing ['i:'meɪlɪŋ] *noun* sending something by email

embargo [em'bɑːgəʊ] **1** *noun* (**a**) government order which stops a type of trade; **to lay** *or* **put an embargo on trade with a country** = to say that trade with a country must not take place; *the government has put an embargo on the export of computer equipment*; **to lift an embargo** = to allow trade to start again; *the government has lifted the embargo on the export of computers*; **to be under an embargo** = to be forbidden (**b**) period of time during which certain information in a press release must not be published (NOTE: plural is **embargoes**) **2** *verb* (**a**) to stop trade, not to allow trade; *the government has embargoed trade with the Eastern countries* (**b**) not to allow publication of information for a period of time; *the news of the merger has been embargoed until next Wednesday*

> the Commerce Department is planning to loosen export controls for products that have been embargoed but are readily available elsewhere in the West
> *Duns Business Month*

embark [ɪm'bɑːk] *verb* (**a**) to go on a ship; *the passengers embarked at Southampton* (**b**) **to embark on** = to start; *the company has embarked on an expansion programme*

embarkation [embɑː'keɪʃən] *noun* going on to a ship or plane; **port of embarkation** = port at which you get on to a ship; **embarkation card** = card given to passengers getting on to a plane or ship

embezzle [ɪm'bezl] *verb* to use money which is not yours, or which you are looking after for someone; *he was sent to prison for six months for embezzling his clients' money*

embezzlement [ɪm'bezlmənt] *noun* act of embezzling; *he was sent to prison for six months for embezzlement*

embezzler [ɪm'bezlə] *noun* person who embezzles

emergency [ɪ'mɜːdʒənsi] *noun* dangerous situation where decisions have to be taken quickly; **the government declared a state of emergency** = the government decided that the situation was so dangerous that the police or army had to run the country; **to take emergency measures** = to take action rapidly to stop a crisis developing; *the company had to take emergency measures to stop losing money*; **emergency reserves** = ready cash held in case it is needed suddenly

emoluments [ɪ'mɒljʊmənts] *plural noun* pay, salary or fees, or the earnings of directors who are not employees (NOTE: American English uses the singular **emolument**)

employ [ɪm'plɔɪ] *verb* to give someone regular paid work; **to employ twenty staff** = to have twenty people working for you; **to employ twenty new staff** = to give work to twenty new people

> 70 per cent of Australia's labour force was employed in service activity
> *Australian Financial Review*

employed [ɪm'plɔɪd] **1** *adjective* (**a**) in regular paid work; **he is not gainfully employed** = he has no regular paid work; **self-employed** = working for yourself; *he worked in a bank for ten years but now is self-employed* (**b**) (money) used profitably; **return on capital employed (ROCE)** = profit shown as a percentage of capital employed **2** *plural noun* people who are working; *the employers and the employed*; **the self-employed** = people who work for themselves

employee [emplɔɪ'iː] *noun* worker, a person employed by a company; *employees of the firm are eligible to join a profit-sharing scheme*; *relations between management and employees have improved*; *the company has decided to take on new employees*; **employee share ownership plan (ESOP)** *US* **employee stock ownership plan** = scheme which allows employees to obtain shares in the company for which they work (though tax may be payable if the shares are sold to employees at a price which is lower than the current market price)

---

companies introducing robotics think it important to involve individual employees in planning their introduction

Economist

---

employer [ɪmˈplɔɪə] *noun* person or company which has regular workers and pays them; **employers' organization** *or* **association** = group of employers with similar interests; **employer's contribution** = money paid by an employer towards a worker's pension

employment [ɪmˈplɔɪmənt] *noun* regular paid work; **full employment** = situation where everyone in a country who can work has a job; **full-time employment** = work for all of a working day; *to be in full-time employment*; **part-time employment** = work for part of a working day or only one or two days per week; **seasonal employment** = job which is available at certain times of the year only (such as in a ski resort); **temporary employment** = work which does not last for more than a few months; **to be without employment** = to have no work; **to find someone alternative employment** = to find another job for someone; **conditions of employment** = terms of a contract where someone is employed; **contract of employment** *or* **employment contract** = contract between management and an employee showing all the conditions of work; **security of employment** = feeling by a worker that he has the right to keep his job until he retires; **employment office** *or* **bureau** *or* **agency** = office which finds jobs for people; **employment protection** = protecting employees against unfair dismissal

---

the blue-collar unions are the people who stand to lose most in terms of employment growth

Sydney Morning Herald

---

emporium [emˈpɔːrɪəm] *noun* large shop (NOTE: plural is **emporia**)

empower [ɪmˈpaʊə] *verb* to give someone the power to do something; *she was empowered by the company to sign the contract*

emptor [ˈemptə] *see* CAVEAT

empty [ˈempti] **1** *adjective* with nothing inside; *the envelope is empty*; *you can take that filing cabinet back to the storeroom as it is empty*; *start the computer file with an empty workspace* **2** *verb* to take the contents out of something; *she emptied the filing cabinet and put the files in boxes*; *he emptied the petty cash box into his briefcase*

empties [ˈemptiz] *plural noun* empty bottles or cases; **returned empties** = empty bottles which are taken back to a shop to get back a deposit paid on them

encash [ɪnˈkæʃ] *verb* to cash a cheque, to exchange a cheque for cash

encashable [ɪnˈkæʃəbl] *adjective* which can be cashed

encashment [ɪnˈkæʃmənt] *noun* act of exchanging for cash

enc *or* **encl** = ENCLOSURE note put on a letter to show that a document is enclosed with it

enclose [ɪnˈkləʊz] *verb* to put something inside an envelope with a letter; *to enclose an invoice with a letter*; *I am enclosing a copy of the contract*; *a letter was lost which was enclosing a cheque*; *please find the cheque enclosed herewith*

enclosure [ɪnˈkləʊʒə] *noun* document enclosed with a letter; *letter with enclosures*

encourage [ɪnˈkʌrɪdʒ] *verb* **(a)** to make it easier for something to happen; *the general rise in wages encourages consumer spending*; *leaving your credit cards on your desk encourages people to steal or encourages stealing*; *the company is trying to encourage sales by giving large discounts* **(b)** to help someone to do something by giving advice; *he encouraged me to apply for the job*

encouragement [ɪnˈkʌrɪdʒmənt] *noun* giving advice to someone to help him to succeed; *the designers produced a very* marketable product, thanks to the encouragement of the sales director

end [end] **1** *noun* **(a)** final point, last part; *at the end of the contract period*; **at the end of six months** = after six months have passed; **account end** = the end of an accounting period; **month end** *or* **year end** = the end of a month or financial year, when accounts have to be drawn up; **end product** = manufactured product, made at the end of a production process; *after six months' trial production, the end product is still not acceptable*; **end user** = person who actually uses a product; *the company is creating a computer with the end user in mind*; **to come to an end** = to finish; *our distribution agreement comes to an end next month* **(b)** **in the end** = at last, after a lot of problems; *in the end the company had to pull out of the US market*; *in the end they signed the contract at the airport*; *in the end the company had to call in the police* **(c)** **on end** = for a long time, with no breaks; *the discussions continued for hours on end*; *the workforce worked at top speed for weeks on end to finish the order on time* **2** *verb* to finish; *the distribution agreement ends in July*; *the chairman ended the discussion by getting up and walking out of the room*

end in ['end 'ɪn] *verb* to have as a result; *the AGM ended in the shareholders fighting on the floor*

endorse [ɪn'dɔːs] *verb* **(a)** **to endorse a bill** *or* **a cheque** = to sign a bill or a cheque on the back to show that you accept it **(b)** to note details of driving offences on a driver's licence

COMMENT: by endorsing a cheque (i.e., signing it on the back), a person whose name is on the front of the cheque is passing ownership of it to another party, such as the bank, which can then accept it and pay him cash for it. If a cheque is deposited in an account, it does not need to be endorsed. Cheques can also be endorsed to another person: a cheque made payable to Mr A. Smith can be endorsed by Mr Smith on the back, with the words: 'Pay to Brown Ltd', and then his signature. This has the effect of making the cheque payable to

Brown Ltd, and to no one else. Most cheques are now printed as crossed cheques with the words 'A/C Payee' printed in the space between the two vertical lines. These cheques can only be paid to the person whose name is written on the cheque and cannot be endorsed

endorsee [endɔː'siː] *noun* person whose name is written on a bill or a cheque as having the right to cash it

endorsement [ɪn'dɔːsmənt] *noun* **(a)** act of endorsing; signature on a document which endorses it **(b)** note on an insurance policy which adds conditions to the policy

endorser [ɪn'dɔːsə] *noun* person who endorses a bill which is then paid to him

endowment [ɪn'daʊmənt] *noun* giving money to provide a regular income; **endowment insurance** *or* **endowment policy** = insurance policy where a sum of money is paid to the insured person on a certain date, or to his heirs if he dies earlier; **endowment mortgage** = mortgage backed by an endowment policy

COMMENT: the borrower pays interest on the mortgage in the usual way, but does not repay the capital; the endowment assurance (a life insurance) is taken out to cover the total capital sum borrowed, and when the assurance matures the capital is paid off, and a further lump sum is usually available for payment to the borrower; a mortgage where the borrower repays both interest and capital is called a 'repayment mortgage'

end up ['end 'ʌp] *verb* to finish; *we ended up with a bill for £10,000*

energetic [enə'dʒetɪk] *adjective* with a lot of energy; *the salesmen have made energetic attempts to sell the product*

energy ['enədʒi] *noun* **(a)** force or strength; *he hasn't the energy to be a good salesman*; *they wasted their energies on trying to sell cars in the German market* **(b)** power from electricity, petrol, etc.; *we try to save energy by switching off the lights when the rooms are empty*; *if you reduce the room temperature to eighteen degrees, you will save energy*

energy-saving ['enədʒi 'seɪvɪŋ] *adjective* which saves energy; *the company is introducing energy-saving measures*

enforce [ɪn'fɔːs] *verb* to make sure something is done or is obeyed; *to enforce the terms of a contract*

enforcement [ɪn'fɔːsmənt] *noun* making sure that something is obeyed; *enforcement of the terms of a contract*

engage [ɪn'geɪdʒ] *verb* (a) to engage someone to do something = to make someone do something legally; *the contract engages us to a minimum annual purchase* (b) to employ; *we have engaged the best commercial lawyer to represent us*; *the company has engaged twenty new salesmen* (c) to be engaged in = to be busy with; *he is engaged in work on computers*; *the company is engaged in trade with Africa*

engaged [ɪn'geɪdʒd] *adjective* busy (telephone); *you cannot speak to the manager - his line is engaged*; **engaged tone** = sound made by a telephone when the line dialled is busy; *I tried to phone the complaints department but got only the engaged tone*

engagement [ɪn'geɪdʒmənt] *noun* (a) agreement to do something; **to break an engagement to do something** = not to do what you have legally agreed; *our agents broke their engagement not to sell our rivals' products* (b) **engagements** = arrangements to meet people; *I have no engagements for the rest of the day*; *she noted the appointment in her engagements diary*

engine ['endʒɪn] *noun* machine which drives something; *a car with a small engine is more economical than one with a large one*; *the lift engine has broken down again - we shall just have to walk up to the 4th floor*

engineer [endʒɪ'nɪə] *noun* person who looks after technical equipment; **civil engineer** = person who specializes in the construction of roads, bridges, railways, etc.; **consulting engineer** = engineer who gives specialist advice; **product engineer** = engineer in charge of the equipment for making a product; **project engineer** = engineer in charge of a project; **programming engineer** = engineer in charge of programming a computer system

engineering [endʒɪ'nɪərɪŋ] *noun* science of technical equipment; **civil engineering** = construction of roads, bridges, railways, etc.; **the engineering department** = section of a company dealing with equipment; **an engineering consultant** = an engineer who gives specialist advice

enquire, enquiry [ɪn'kwaɪə or ɪn'kwaɪəri] = INQUIRE, INQUIRY

en route [ɒn 'ruːt] *adverb* on the way; *the tanker sank when she was en route to the Gulf*

entail [ɪn'teɪl] **1** *noun* legal condition which passes ownership of a property only to certain persons **2** *verb* to involve; *itemizing the sales figures will entail about ten days' work*

enter ['entə] *verb* (a) to go in; *they all stood up when the chairman entered the room*; *the company has spent millions trying to enter the do-it-yourself market* (b) to write; *to enter a name on a list*; *the clerk entered the interest in my bank book*; *to enter up an item in a ledger*; **to enter a bid for something** = to offer (usually in writing) to buy something; **to enter a caveat** = to warn legally that you have an interest in a case, and that no steps can be taken without your permission

enter into ['entə 'ɪntuː] *verb* to begin; *to enter into relations with someone*; *to enter into negotiations with a foreign government*; *to enter into a partnership with a friend*; *the company does not want to enter into any long-term agreement*

entering ['entərɪŋ] *noun* act of writing items in a record

enterprise ['entəpraɪz] *noun* (a) system of carrying on a business; **free enterprise** = system of business free from government interference; **private enterprise** = businesses which are owned privately, not nationalized; *the project is completely funded by private enterprise*; **enterprise zone** = area of the country where businesses are encouraged to develop by offering special conditions such as easy planning permission for buildings, reduction in the business rate, etc. (b) business; **a small-scale enterprise** = a small business; **a state enterprise** = a state-controlled company; *bosses of state enterprises are appointed by the government*

entertain [entə'teɪn] *verb* **(a)** to offer meals, hotel accommodation, theatre tickets, etc., to business visitors **(b)** to be ready to consider (a proposal); *the management will not entertain any suggestions from the union representatives*

entertainment [entə'teɪnmənt] *noun* offering meals, etc., to business visitors; **entertainment allowance** = money which a manager is allowed by his company to spend on meals with visitors; **entertainment expenses** = money spent on giving meals to business visitors

entitle [ɪn'taɪtl] *verb* to give the right to something; **he is entitled to a discount** = he has the right to be given a discount

entitlement [ɪn'taɪtlmənt] *noun* right; **holiday entitlement** = number of days' paid holiday which a worker has the right to take; *she has not used up all her holiday entitlement*; **pension entitlement** = amount of pension which someone has the right to receive when he or she retires

entrance ['entrəns] *noun* **(a)** way in, going in; *the taxi will drop you at the main entrance*; *deliveries should be made to the London Road entrance* **(b)** **entrance (charge)** = money which you have to pay to go in; *entrance is £1.50 for adults and £1 for children*

entrepot ['ɒntrəpəʊ] *noun* **entrepot port** = town with a large international commercial port dealing in re-exports; **entrepot trade** = exporting of imported goods

entrepreneur [ɒntrəprə'nɜː] *noun* person who directs a company and takes commercial risks

entrepreneurial [ɒntrəprə'nɜːrɪəl] *adjective* taking commercial risks; *an entrepreneurial decision*

entrust [ɪn'trʌst] *verb* **to entrust someone with something** *or* **to entrust something to someone** = to give someone the responsibility for looking after something; *he was entrusted with the keys to the office safe*

entry ['entri] *noun* **(a)** written information put in an accounts ledger; **credit entry** *or* **debit entry** = entry on the credit or debit side of an account; **single-entry bookkeeping** = recording only one entry per transaction (usually in the cash book); **double-entry bookkeeping** = system of bookkeeping where both debit and credit entries are recorded in the accounts at the same time (e.g., when a sale is credited to the sales account the purchaser's debt is debited to the debtors account); **to make an entry in a ledger** = to write in details of a transaction; **contra entry** = entry made in the opposite side of an account to offset an earlier entry; **to contra an entry** = to enter a similar amount on the opposite side of the account **(b)** act of going in; place where you can go in; *to pass a customs entry point*; *entry of goods under bond*; **entry charge** = money which you have to pay before you go in; **entry visa** = visa allowing someone to go into a country; **multiple entry visa** = entry visa which allows someone to enter a country as often as he or she likes

envelope ['envələʊp] *noun* flat paper cover for sending letters; **airmail envelope** = very light envelope for airmail letters; **aperture envelope** = envelope with a hole in it so that the address on the letter inside can be seen; **window envelope** = envelope with a hole covered with film so that the address on the letter inside can be seen; **sealed envelope** = envelope where the flap has been stuck down to close it; *to send the information in a sealed envelope*; *see also* SELF-SEAL; **a stamped addressed envelope (s.a.e.)** = an envelope with your own address written on it and a stamp stuck on it to pay for return postage; *please send a stamped addressed envelope for further details and our latest catalogue*; **unsealed envelope** = envelope where the flap has been pushed into the back of the envelope to close it, and has not been stuck down

EOC ['iː'əʊ'siː] = EQUAL OPPORTUNITIES COMMISSION

EOQ ['iː'əʊ'kjuː] = ECONOMIC ORDER QUANTITY

epos *or* **EPOS** ['i:pɒs] = ELECTRONIC POINT OF SALE

equal ['i:kwəl] **1** *adjective* exactly the same; *male and female workers have equal pay*; **Equal Opportunities Commission (EOC)** = government body set up to make sure that no discrimination exists in employment; **equal opportunities programme** = programme to avoid discrimination in employment (NOTE: the American equivalent is **affirmative action**); **equal pay** = paying the same rate to men and women who do the same job **2** *verb* to be the same as; *production this month has equalled our best month ever* (NOTE: **equalling - equalled** but American spelling is **equaling - equaled**)

equality [ɪ'kwɒlətɪ] *noun* state of being equal; **equality of opportunity** = situation where everyone, regardless of sex, race, class, etc., has the same opportunity to get a job

equalization [i:kwəlaɪ'zeɪʃən] *noun* process of making equal

equalize ['i:kwəlaɪz] *verb* to make equal; *to equalize dividends*

equally ['i:kwəlɪ] *adverb* in the same way; *costs will be shared equally between the two parties*; *they were both equally responsible for the disastrous launch*

equip [ɪ'kwɪp] *verb* to provide with machinery; *to equip a factory with new machinery*; *the office is fully equipped with word-processors*

equipment [ɪ'kwɪpmənt] *noun* machinery and furniture required to make a factory or office work; *office equipment or business equipment*; *an office equipment supplier*; *an office equipment catalogue*; **capital equipment** = equipment which a factory or office uses to work; **heavy equipment** = large machines, such as for making cars or for printing

equities ['ekwətɪz] *plural noun* ordinary shares

equity ['ekwətɪ] *noun* **(a)** right to receive dividends as part of the profit of a company in which you own shares **(b) equity** *or* **shareholders' equity** = the value of a company which is the property of its ordinary shareholders (the company's assets less its liabilities); **equity capital** = nominal value of the issued shares in a company

COMMENT: 'equity' (also called 'capital' or 'shareholders' equity' or 'shareholders' capital' or 'shareholders' funds') is the current net value of the company including the nominal value of the shares in issue. After several years a company would expect to increase its net worth above the value of the starting capital. 'Equity capital' on the other hand is only the nominal value of the shares in issue

equivalence [ɪ'kwɪvələns] *noun* being equivalent

equivalent [ɪ'kwɪvələnt] *adjective* **to be equivalent to** = to have the same value as, to be the same as; *the total dividend paid is equivalent to one quarter of the pretax profits*

eraser [ɪ'reɪzə] *noun* small piece of hard rubber used to remove text which has been written in pencil

ergonomics [ɜ:gə'nɒmɪks] *plural noun* study of people at work and their working conditions (NOTE: takes a singular verb)

ergonomist [ɜ:'gɒnəmɪst] *noun* scientist who studies people at work and tries to improve their working conditions

erode [ɪ'rəʊd] *verb* to wear away gradually; **to erode wage differentials** = to reduce gradually differences in salary between different grades

error ['erə] *noun* mistake; *he made an error in calculating the total*; *the secretary must have made a typing error*; **clerical error** = mistake made in an office; **computer error** = mistake made by a computer; **margin of error** = number of mistakes which are accepted in a document or in a calculation; **errors and omissions excepted (e. & o.e.)** = words written on an invoice to show that the company has no responsibility for mistakes in the invoice; **error rate** = number of mistakes per thousand entries or per page; **in error** *or* **by error** = by mistake; *the letter was sent to the London office in error*

escalate ['eskəleɪt] *verb* to increase steadily

escalation [eskə'leɪʃən] *noun* **escalation of prices** = steady increase in prices; **escalation clause** = ESCALATOR CLAUSE

escalator clause ['eskəleɪtə 'klɔːz] *noun* clause in a contract allowing for regular price increases because of increased costs, or regular wage increases because of the increased cost of living

escape [ɪs'keɪp] *noun* getting away from a difficult situation; **escape clause** = clause in a contract which allows one of the parties to avoid carrying out the terms of the contract under certain conditions

escrow ['eskrəʊ] *noun* **in escrow** = held in safe keeping by a third party; **document held in escrow** = document given to a third party to keep and to pass on to someone when money has been paid; *US* **escrow account** = account where money is held in escrow until a contract is signed or until goods are delivered, etc.

escudo [es'kjʊdəʊ] *noun* currency used with the euro in Portugal

ESOP = EMPLOYEE SHARE OWNERSHIP PLAN

espionage [espɪə'nɑːʒ] *noun* **industrial espionage** = trying to find out the secrets of a competitor's work or products, usually by illegal means

essential [ɪ'senʃəl] *adjective* very important; *it is essential that an agreement be reached before the end of the month*; *the factory is lacking essential spare parts*

essentials [ɪ'senʃəlz] *plural noun* goods or products which are very important

establish [ɪs'tæblɪʃ] *verb* to set up, to open; *the company has established a branch in Australia*; *the business was established in Scotland in 1823*; *it is a young company - it has been established for only four years*; **to establish oneself in business** = to become successful in a new business

establishment [ɪs'tæblɪʃmənt] *noun* **(a)** commercial business; *he runs an important printing establishment* **(b)** **establishment charges** = cost of people and property in a company's accounts **(c)** number of people working in a company; **to be on the establishment** = to be a full-time employee; **office with an establishment of fifteen** = office with a budgeted staff of fifteen

estate [ɪs'teɪt] *noun* **(a)** **real estate** = property (land or buildings); **estate agency** = office which arranges for the sale of property; **estate agent** = person in charge of an estate agency **(b)** **industrial estate** *or* **trading estate** = area of land near a town built specially with factories and warehouses **(c)** property left by a dead person; **estate duty** = tax on property left by a dead person

estimate **1** ['estɪmət] *noun* **(a)** calculation of probable cost, size or time of something; **rough estimate** = very approximate calculation; **at a conservative estimate** = calculation which probably underestimates the final figure; *their turnover has risen by at least 20% in the last year, and that is a conservative estimate*; *these figures are only an estimate* = these are not the final accurate figures; *can you give me an estimate of how much time was spent on the job?* **(b)** calculation of how much something is likely to cost, given to a client so as to get him to make an order; *before we can give the grant we must have an estimate of the total costs involved*; *to ask a builder for an estimate for building the warehouse*; **to put in an estimate** = to give someone a written calculation of the probable costs of carrying out a job; *three firms put in estimates for the job* **2** ['estɪmeɪt] *verb* **(a)** to calculate the probable cost, size or time of something; *to estimate that it will cost £1m* *or* *to estimate costs at £1m*; *we estimate current sales at only 60% of last year*; **estimated time of arrival (ETA)** = time when an aircraft, a coach or a group of tourists is expected to arrive **(b)** **to estimate for a job** = to state in writing the future costs of carrying out a piece of work so that a client can make an order; *three firms estimated for the refitting of the offices*

estimated ['estɪmeɪtɪd] *adjective* calculated approximately; *costs were slightly more than the estimated figure*

estimation [estɪ'meɪʃən] *noun* approximate calculation

estimator ['estɪmeɪtə] *noun* person whose job is to calculate estimates for carrying out work

ETA = ESTIMATED TIME OF ARRIVAL

etc. [ɪt'setrə] and so on; *the import duty is to be paid on luxury items including cars, watches, etc.*

EU ['iː'juː] = EUROPEAN UNION; *EU ministers met today in Brussels*; *the USA is increasing its trade with the EU*

euro ['juərəu] *noun* currency adopted as legal tender in several European countries from January 1st, 1999; *many articles are priced in euros*; *what's the exchange rate for the euro?*; **euro account** = bank account in euros (NOTE: written before numbers: €250: say: 'two hundred and fifty euros')

cross-border mergers in the European Union have shot up since the introduction of the euro

Investors Chronicle

COMMENT: the countries which are joined together in the European Monetary Union and adopted the euro as their common currency in 1999 are: Austria, Belgium, Finland, France, Germany, Ireland, Italy, Luxembourg, the Netherlands, Portugal, and Spain. The conversion of these currencies to the euro was fixed on 1st January 1999

Euro- ['juərəu] *prefix* referring to Europe or the European Union

Eurobond ['juərəubɒnd] *noun* long-term bearer bond issued by an international corporation or government outside its country of origin and sold to purchasers who pay in a eurocurrency (sold on the Eurobond market)

Eurocard ['juərəukɑːd] cheque card used when writing Eurocheques

Eurocheque ['juərəutʃek] *noun* cheque which can be cashed in any European bank (the Eurocheque system is based in Brussels)

Eurocurrency ['juərəukʌrənsi] *noun* any currency used for trade within Europe but outside its country of origin, the eurodollar being the most important; *a Eurocurrency loan*; *the Eurocurrency market*

Eurodollar ['juərəudɒlə] *noun* US dollar in a European bank, used for trade within Europe; *a Eurodollar loan*; *the Eurodollar markets*

Euroland ['juərəulænd] *noun* the European countries which use the euro as a common currency, seen as a group

Euromarket ['juərəumɑːkɪt] *noun* the European Union seen as a potential market for sales

Europe ['juərəp] *noun* **(a)** the continent of Europe, the part of the world to the west of Asia, from Russia to Ireland; *most of the countries of Western Europe are members of the EU*; *Poland is in eastern Europe, and Greece, Spain and Portugal are in southern Europe* **(b)** the same area, but not including the UK; *holidays in Europe are less popular than last year* **(c)** the European Union (including the UK); *Canadian exports to Europe have risen by 25%* **(d)** other EU countries but not including the UK; *British sales to Europe have increased this year*

European [juərə'piːən] *adjective* referring to Europe; *they do business with several European countries*; the **European Parliament** = the parliament with members (MEPs) from each country of the EU

European Central Bank (ECB)

[juərə'piən 'sentrəl 'bæŋk] *noun* central bank for most of the countries in the European Union, those which have accepted European Monetary Union and have the euro as their common currency

the ECB begins with some $300 billion of foreign exchange

> reserves, far more than any
> other central bank
>
> *Investors Chronicle*

> any change in the European
> bank's statutes must be
> agreed and ratified by all EU
> member nations
>
> *The Times*

European Commission [juərə'piːən kə'mɪʃn] *noun* the administration of the European Union, made up of members nominated by each member state (NOTE: also called the **Commission of the European Community**)

European Economic Area (EEA) [juərə'piːən iːkə'nɒmɪk 'eərɪə] agreement on trade between the EU and the members of EFTA

European Free Trade Association (EFTA) [juərə'piːən 'friː 'treɪd əsəusi'eɪʃn] group of countries (Iceland, Liechtenstein, Norway and Switzerland) formed to encourage freedom of trade between its members, and linked with the EU in the European Economic Area

European Monetary Union (EMU) ['juərəpiːən 'mʌnɪtəri 'juːnɪən] the process by which some of the member states of the EU joined together to adopt the euro as their common currency on 1st January 1999

European Regional Development Fund (ERDF) [juərə'piːən 'riːdʒənəl diː'veləpmənt 'fʌnd] fund set up to provide grants to underdeveloped parts of Europe

European Social Charter [juərə'piːən səuʃl 'tʃɑːtə] charter for workers, drawn up by the EU in 1989, by which workers have the right to a fair wage, to equal treatment for men and women, a safe work environment, training, freedom of association and collective bargaining, provision for disabled workers, freedom of movement from country to country, guaranteed standards of living both for the working population as well as for retired people, etc. (Note that there is no machinery for enforcing the Social Charter)

European Union (EU) [juərə'piːən 'juːnɪən] (formerly called the European Economic Community (EEC) or the Common Market) a group of European countries linked together by the Treaty of Rome, basing their cooperation on the four fundamental freedoms of movement: of goods, capital, people and services

> COMMENT: the European Community was set up in 1957 and changed its name to the European Union when it adopted the Single Market. It has now grown to include fifteen member states. These are: Austria, Belgium, Denmark, Finland, France, Germany, Greece, Ireland, Italy, Luxembourg, the Netherlands, Portugal, Spain, Sweden and the United Kingdom; other countries are negotiating to join. The member states of the EU are linked together by the Treaty of Rome in such a way that trade is more free, that money can be moved from one country to another freely, that people can move from one country to another more freely, and that people can work more freely in other countries of the group

Eurozone ['juərəuzəun] *noun* the European countries which use the euro as a common currency, seen as a group

> the European Central Bank left the door open yesterday for a cut in Eurozone interest rates
>
> *Financial Times*

> a sustained recovery in the euro will require either a sharp slowdown in US growth or a rise in inflation and interest rates in the eurozone beyond that already discounted
>
> *Investors Chronicle*

evade [ɪ'veɪd] *verb* to try to avoid something; **to evade tax** = to try illegally to avoid paying tax

evaluate [ɪ'væljueɪt] *verb* to calculate a value; *to evaluate costs*

evaluation [ɪvælju'eɪʃən] *noun* calculation of value; **job evaluation** = examining different jobs within an organization to see what skills and qualifications are needed to carry them out; **performance evaluation** = examining how well an employee is doing his job

evasion [ɪ'veɪʒən] *noun* avoiding; **tax evasion** = illegally trying not to pay tax

evidence ['evɪdəns] *noun* written or spoken report at a trial; **documentary evidence** = evidence in the form of documents; **the secretary gave evidence against her former employer** = the secretary was a witness, and her report suggested that her former employer was guilty; **the secretary gave evidence for her former employer** = the secretary was a witness, and her report suggested that her former employer was not guilty

ex [eks] *preposition & prefix* **(a)** out of, from; **price ex warehouse** = price for a product which is to be collected from the manufacturer's or agent's warehouse and so does not include delivery; **price ex works** *or* **ex factory** = price not including transport from the maker's factory **(b) ex coupon** = bond without the interest coupon; **share quoted ex dividend** = share price not including the right to receive the next dividend; *the shares went ex dividend yesterday* **(c)** formerly; *Mr Smith, the ex-chairman of the company*

exact [ɪg'zækt] *adjective* very correct; *the exact time is 10.27; the salesgirl asked me if I had the exact sum, since the shop had no change*

exactly [ɪg'zæktli] *adverb* very correctly; *the total cost was exactly £6,500*

examination [ɪgzæmɪ'neɪʃən] *noun* **(a)** looking at something very carefully to see if it is acceptable; **customs examination** = looking at goods or baggage by customs officials **(b)** test to see if someone has passed a course; *he passed his accountancy examinations; she came first in the final examination for the course; he failed his proficiency examination and so had to leave his job*

examine [ɪg'zæmɪn] *verb* **(a)** to look at someone or something very carefully to see if it can be accepted or to see if it is faulty; *customs officials asked to examine the inside of the car; the police are examining the papers from the managing director's safe* **(b)** to test someone to see if he or she has a passed a course

example [ɪg'zɑːmpl] *noun* something chosen to show; *the motor show has many examples of energy-saving cars on display;* **for example** = to show one thing out of many; *the government wants to encourage exports - for example, it gives free credit to exporters*

exceed [ɪk'siːd] *verb* to be more than; *discount not exceeding 15%; last year costs exceeded 20% of income for the first time;* **he has exceeded his credit limit** = he has borrowed more money than he is allowed

excellent ['eksələnt] *adjective* very good; *the quality of the firm's products is excellent, but its sales force is not large enough*

except [ɪk'sept] *preposition & conjunction* not including; *VAT is levied on all goods and services except books, newspapers and children's clothes; sales are rising in all markets except the Far East*

excepted [ɪk'septɪd] *adverb* not including; **errors and omissions excepted (e. & o.e.)** = note on an invoice to show that the company has no responsibility for mistakes in the invoice

exceptional [ɪk'sepʃənl] *adjective* not usual, different; **exceptional items** = items which arise from normal trading but which are unusual because of their size or nature (they are shown separately in a note to the company's accounts)

excess 1 [ɪk'ses] *noun* amount which is more than what is allowed; *an excess of expenditure over revenue;* **in excess of** = above, more than; *quantities in excess of twenty-five kilos* **2** ['ekses] *adjective* **excess baggage** = extra payment at an airport for taking baggage which is heavier than the normal passenger's allowance; **excess capacity** = spare capacity which is not being used; **excess fare** = extra fare to be paid (such as for travelling first class with a second class ticket); **excess profits** = profit which is more than what is thought to be normal; **excess profits tax** = tax on excess profits

most airlines give business class the same baggage allowance as first class, which can save large sums in excess baggage

Business Traveller

control of materials provides manufacturers with an opportunity to reduce the amount of money tied up in excess materials

Duns Business Month

excessive [ɪkˈsesɪv] *adjective* too large; *excessive production costs made the product uneconomic*

exchange [ɪksˈtʃeɪndʒ] **1** *noun* **(a)** giving of one thing for another; **part exchange** = giving an old product as part of the payment for a new one; *to take a car in part exchange*; **exchange of contracts** = point in the sale of property when the buyer and the seller both sign the contract of sale which then becomes binding **(b) foreign exchange** = (i) exchanging the money of one country for that of another; (ii) money of another country; *the company holds more than £1m in foreign exchange*; **foreign exchange broker** = person who buys and sells foreign currency on behalf of other people; **foreign exchange market** = dealings in foreign currencies; *he trades on the foreign exchange market*; *foreign exchange markets were very active after the dollar devalued*; **rate of exchange** *or* **exchange rate** = price at which one currency is exchanged for another; *the current rate of exchange is $1.60 to the pound*; **exchange controls** = control by a government of the way in which its currency may be exchanged for foreign currencies; *the government had to impose exchange controls to stop the rush to buy dollars*; **exchange dealer** = person who buys and sells foreign currency; **exchange dealings** = buying and selling foreign currency; *GB* **Exchange Equalization Account** = account with the Bank of England used by the government when buying or selling foreign currency to influence the sterling exchange rate; **exchange premium** = extra cost above the normal rate for buying a foreign currency **(c) bill of exchange** = document which tells a bank to pay a person (usually used in foreign currency payments) **(d) Stock Exchange** = place where stocks and shares are bought and sold; *the company's shares are traded on the New York Stock Exchange*; *he works on the Stock Exchange*; **commodity exchange** = place where commodities are bought and sold **2** *verb* **(a) to exchange one article for another** = to give one thing in place of something else; *he exchanged his motorcycle for a car*; *if the trousers are too small you can take them back and exchange them for a larger pair*; *goods can be exchanged only on production of the sales slip* **(b) to exchange contracts** = to sign a contract when buying a property (done by both buyer and seller at the same time) **(c)** to change money of one country for money of another; *to exchange pesos for pounds*

under the barter agreements, Nigeria will export crude oil in exchange for trucks, food, planes and chemicals

Wall Street Journal

can free trade be reconciled with a strong dollar resulting from floating exchange rates

Duns Business Month

a draft report on changes in the international monetary system casts doubt on any return to fixed exchange-rate parities

Wall Street Journal

exchangeable [ɪksˈtʃeɪndʒəbl] *adjective* which can be exchanged

exchanger [ɪksˈtʃeɪndʒə] *noun* person who buys and sells foreign currency

Exchequer [ɪksˈtʃekə] *noun GB* **the Exchequer** = (i) fund of all money received by the government of the UK from taxes and other revenues; (ii) the British government's account with the Bank of England; (iii) the British government department dealing with public revenue; **the Chancellor of the Exchequer** = the chief British finance minister

excise 1 [ˈeksaɪz] *noun* **(a) excise duty** = tax on certain goods produced in a country (such as alcohol); *to pay excise duty on wine* **(b) Customs and Excise** *or* **Excise**

Department = government department which deals with taxes on imports and on products such as alcohol produced in the country; it also deals with VAT; *an Excise officer* **2** [ɪk'saɪz] *verb* to cut out; *please excise all references to the strike in the minutes*

exciseman ['eksaɪzmæn] *noun* person who works in the Excise Department

exclude [ɪks'kluːd] *verb* to keep out, not to include; *interest charges have been excluded from the invoice*; *damage by fire is excluded from the policy*

excluding [ɪks'kluːdɪŋ] *preposition* not including; *all salesmen, excluding those living in London, can claim expenses for attending the sales conference*

exclusion [ɪks'kluːʒən] *noun* act of not including; **exclusion clause** = clause in an insurance policy or warranty which says which items are not covered

exclusive [ɪks'kluːsɪv] *adjective* **(a)** **exclusive agreement** = agreement where a person is made sole agent for a product in a market; **exclusive right to market a product** = right to be the only person to market the product **(b) exclusive of** = not including; *all payments are exclusive of tax*; *the invoice is exclusive of VAT*

exclusivity [eksklu:'sɪvəti] *noun* exclusive right to market a product

excuse 1 [ɪks'kjuːs] *noun* reason for doing something wrong; *his excuse for not coming to the meeting was that he had been told about it only the day before*; *the managing director refused to accept the sales manager's excuses for the poor sales* = he refused to believe that there was a good reason for the poor sales **2** [ɪks'kjuːz] *verb* to forgive a small mistake; *she can be excused for not knowing the French for 'photocopier'*

ex-directory ['eksdaɪ'rektəi] *adjective* (telephone number) which is not printed in the telephone book; *he has an ex-directory number*

execute ['eksɪkjuːt] *verb* to carry out (an order)

execution [eksɪ'kjuːʃən] *noun* carrying out of an order; **stay of execution** = temporary stopping of a legal order; *the*

court granted the company a two-week stay of execution

executive [ɪg'zekjʊtɪv] **1** *adjective* which puts decisions into action; **executive committee** = committee which runs a society or a club; **executive director** = director who actually works full-time in the company (as opposed to a 'non-executive director'); **executive powers** = right to put decisions into action; *he was made managing director with full executive powers over the European operation* **2** *noun* person in a business who takes decisions, a manager or director; *sales executive*; *senior or junior executive*; **account executive** = employee who is the link between his company and certain customers; **chief executive** = executive director in charge of a company; **executive search** = looking for new managers for organizations, usually by approaching managers in their existing jobs and asking them if they want to work for different companies (NOTE: a more polite term for 'headhunting')

one in ten students commented on the long hours which executives worked
Employment Gazette

our executives are motivated by a desire to carry out a project to the best of their ability
British Business

executor [ɪg'zekjʊtə] *noun* person who sees that the terms of a will are carried out; *he was named executor of his brother's will*

executrix [ɪg'zekjʊtrɪks] *noun* female executor

exempt [ɪg'zempt] **1** *adjective* not covered by a law; not forced to obey a law; **exempt supplies** = products or services on which the supplier does not have to charge VAT; **exempt from tax** *or* **tax-exempt** = not required to pay tax; *as a non-profit-making organization we are exempt from tax* **2** *verb* to free something from having tax paid on it or from having to pay tax; *non-profit-making organizations are exempted from tax*;

food is exempted from sales tax; *the government exempted trusts from tax*

Companies with sales under $500,000 a year will be exempt from the minimum-wage requirements

Nation's Business

---

exemption [ɪɡˈzempʃən] *noun* act of exempting something from a contract or from a tax; **exemption from tax** *or* **tax exemption** = being free from having to pay tax; *as a non-profit-making organization you can claim tax exemption*

exercise [ˈeksəsaɪz] **1** *noun* use of something; **exercise of an option** = using an option, putting an option into action **2** *verb* to use; *the chairwoman exercised her veto to block the motion*; **to exercise an option** = to put an option into action; *he exercised his option to acquire sole marketing rights for the product*

ex gratia [eks ˈɡreɪʃə] *adjective* **an ex gratia payment** = payment made as a gift, with no other obligations

exhibit [ɪɡˈzɪbɪt] **1** *noun* **(a)** thing which is shown; *the buyers admired the exhibits on our stand* **(b)** single section of an exhibition; *the British Trade Exhibit at the International Computer Fair* **2** *verb* to **exhibit at the Motor Show** = to display new models of cars

exhibition [eksɪˈbɪʃən] *noun* showing goods so that buyers can look at them and decide what to buy; *the government has sponsored an exhibition of good design*; *we have a stand at the Ideal Home Exhibition*; *the agricultural exhibition grounds were growded with visitors*; **exhibition room** *or* **hall** = place where goods are shown so that buyers can look at them and decide what to buy; **exhibition stand** *US* **exhibition booth** = separate section of an exhibition where a company exhibits its products or services

exhibitor [ɪɡˈzɪbɪtə] *noun* person or company which shows products at an exhibition

exile [ˈeɡzaɪl] **1** *noun* **(a)** state of being sent away from your home country; *the ex-finance minister went into exile in Switzerland* (NOTE: no plural in this meaning) **(b)** person who is sent away from his own

country; **tax exile** = person who lives in a country where taxes are low in order to avoid paying tax at home **2** *verb* to send someone away from his home country as a punishment; *the former finance minister was exiled for life*

exist [ɪɡˈzɪst] *verb* to be; *I do not believe the document exists - I think it has been burnt*

exit [ˈeɡsɪt] *noun* way out of a building; *the customers all rushed towards the exits*; **fire exit** = door which leads to a way out of a building if there is a fire

ex officio [eks əˈfɪʃɪəʊ] *adjective & adverb* because of an office held; *the treasurer is ex officio a member or an ex officio member of the finance committee*

expand [ɪkˈspænd] *verb* to increase or to get bigger; to make something bigger; *an expanding economy*; *the company is expanding fast*; *we have had to expand our sales force*

expansion [ɪkˈspænʃən] *noun* increase in size; *the expansion of the domestic market*; *the company had difficulty in financing its current expansion programme*

---

inflation-adjusted GNP moved up at a 1.3% annual rate, its worst performance since the economic expansion began

Fortune

---

the businesses we back range from start-up ventures to established businesses in need of further capital for expansion

Times

---

the group is undergoing a period of rapid expansion and this has created an exciting opportunity for a qualified accountant

Financial Times

---

expect [ɪkˈspekt] *verb* to hope that something is going to happen; *we are expecting him to arrive at 10.45*; *they are expecting a cheque from their agent next week*; *the house was sold for more than the expected price*

he observed that he expected exports to grow faster than imports in the coming year
Sydney Morning Herald

American business as a whole has seen profits well above the levels normally expected at this stage of the cycle
Sunday Times

expectancy [ɪk'spektənsi] *noun* **life expectancy** = number of years a person is likely to live

expenditure [ɪk'spendɪtʃə] *noun* amounts of money spent; **below-the-line expenditure** = exceptional payments which are separated from a company's normal accounts; **capital expenditure** = money spent on fixed assets (such as property or machinery); **the company's current expenditure programme** = the company's spending according to the current plan; **heavy expenditure on equipment** = spending large sums of money on equipment (NOTE: no plural in British English, but American English often uses **expenditures**)

expense [ɪk'spens] *noun* **(a)** money spent; *it is not worth the expense*; *the expense is too much for my bank balance*; **at great expense** = having spent a lot of money; **he furnished the office regardless of expense** = without thinking how much it cost **(b) expense account** = money which a businessman is allowed by his company to spend on travelling and entertaining clients in connection with his business; *I'll put this lunch on my expense account*; *expense account lunches form a large part of our current expenditure*

expenses [ɪk'spensɪz] *plural noun* money paid to cover the costs incurred by someone when doing something; *the salary offered is £10,000 plus expenses*; **all expenses paid** = with all costs paid by the company; *the company sent him to San Francisco all expenses paid*; **to cut down on expenses** = to try to reduce spending; **allowable expenses** = business expenses which are allowed against tax; **business expenses** = money spent on running a business, not on stock or assets; **direct expenses** = expenses (excluding materials, labour or purchase of stock for

resale) which are incurred in making a product; **entertainment expenses** = money spent on giving meals to business visitors; **fixed expenses** = expenses which do not vary with different levels of production (such as rent, secretaries' salaries, insurance); **incidental expenses** = small amounts of money spent at various times, in addition to larger amounts; **indirect expenses** = expenses (excluding materials, labour or purchase of stock for resale) which are incurred by a business, but which cannot be allocated to any particular product; **legal expenses** = money spent on fees paid to lawyers; **overhead expenses** *or* **general expenses** *or* **running expenses** = money spent on the day-to-day cost of a business; **travelling expenses** = money spent on travelling and hotels for business purposes

expensive [ɪk'spensɪv] *adjective* which costs a lot of money; *first-class air travel is becoming more and more expensive*

experience [ɪk'spɪərɪəns] **1** *noun* having lived through various situations and therefore knowing how to make decisions; *he is a man of considerable experience*; *she has a lot of experience of dealing with German companies*; *he gained most of his experience in the Far East*; *some previous experience is required for this job* **2** *verb* to live through a situation; *the company experienced a period of falling sales*

experienced [ɪk'spɪərɪənst] *adjective* person who has lived through many situations and has learnt from them; *he is the most experienced negotiator I know*; *we have appointed a very experienced woman as sales director*

expert ['ekspɜːt] *noun* person who knows a lot about something; *an expert in the field of electronics* *or* *an electronics expert*; *the company asked a financial expert for advice* *or* *asked for expert financial advice*; **expert's report** = report written by an expert

expertise [ekspɜː'tiːz] *noun* specialist knowledge; *we hired Mr Smith because of his financial expertise* *or* *because of his expertise in the African market*

expiration [ekspɪ'reɪʃən] *noun* coming to an end; *expiration of an insurance policy*;

to repay before the expiration of the stated period; **on expiration of the lease** = when the lease comes to an end

expire [ɪk'spaɪə] *verb* to come to an end; *the lease expires in 2010*; **his passport has expired** = his passport is no longer valid

expiry [ɪk'spaɪəri] *noun* coming to an end; *expiry of an insurance policy*; **expiry date** = (i) date when something will end; (ii) the last date on which a credit card can be used

explain [ɪk'spleɪn] *verb* to give reasons for something; *he explained to the customs officials that the two computers were presents from friends*; *can you explain why the sales in the first quarter are so high?*; *the sales director tried to explain the sudden drop in unit sales*

explanation [eksplə'neɪʃən] *noun* reason for something; *the VAT inspector asked for an explanation of the invoices*; *at the AGM, the chairman gave an explanation for the high level of interest payments*

exploit [ɪk'splɔɪt] *verb* to use something to make a profit; *the company is exploiting its contacts in the Ministry of Trade*; *we hope to exploit the oil resources in the China Sea*

exploitation [eksplɔɪ'teɪʃn] *noun* unfair use of cheap labour to get work done; *the exploitation of migrant farm workers was only stopped when they became unionized*

explore [ɪk'splɔː] *verb* to examine carefully; *we are exploring the possibility of opening an office in London*

export 1 ['ekspɔːt] *noun* **(a) exports** = goods sent to a foreign country to be sold; *exports to Africa have increased by 25%* **(b)** action of sending goods to foreign countries to be sold; *50% of the company's profits come from the export trade or the export market*; **export department** = section of a company which deals in sales to foreign countries; **export duty** = tax paid on goods sent out of a country for sale; **export house** = company which specializes in the export of goods made by other manufacturers; **export licence** = government permit allowing something to be exported; *the government has refused*

an export licence for computer parts; **export manager** = person in charge of an export department in a company; **Export Credit Guarantee Department (ECGD)** = British government department which insures exports sold on credit (NOTE: usually used in the plural, but the singular form is used before a noun) **2** [ɪk'spɔːt] *verb* to send goods to foreign countries for sale; *50% of our production is exported*; *the company imports raw materials and exports the finished products*

exportation [ekspɔː'teɪʃən] *noun* act of sending goods to foreign countries for sale

exporter [eks'pɔːtə] *noun* person, company or country which sells goods in foreign countries; *a major furniture exporter*; *Canada is an important exporter of oil or an important oil exporter*

exporting [eks'pɔːtɪŋ] *adjective* which exports; **oil exporting countries** = countries which produce oil and sell it to other countries

exposition [ekspə'zɪʃən] *noun* US = EXHIBITION

exposure [ɪk'spəʊʒə] *noun* **(a)** publicity given to an organization or product; *our company has achieved more exposure since we decided to advertise nationally* **(b)** amount of risk which a lender runs; *he is trying to limit his exposure in the property market*

COMMENT: exposure can be the amount of money lent to a customer (a bank's exposure to a foreign country) or the amount of money which an investor may lose if his investments collapse (such as his exposure in the stock market)

it attributed the poor result to the bank's high exposure to residential mortgages, which showed a significant slowdown in the past few months
South China Morning Post

express [ɪk'spres] **1** *adjective* **(a)** rapid, very fast; *express letter*; *express delivery* **(b)** clearly shown in words; *the contract has an express condition forbidding sale in Africa* **2** *verb* **(a)** to put into words or diagrams; *this chart shows home sales* *expressed as a percentage of total turnover* **(b)** to send very fast; *we expressed the order to the customer's warehouse*

expressly [ɪkˈspresli] *adverb* clearly in words; *the contract expressly forbids sales to the United States*

ext = EXTENSION

extend [ɪkˈstend] *verb* **(a)** to make available, to give; *to extend credit to a customer* **(b)** to make longer; *to extend a contract for two years*; **extended credit** = credit allowing the borrower a very long time to pay; *we sell to Australia on extended credit*; **extended guarantee** = guarantee offered by a dealer on consumer durables, such as dishwashers, which goes beyond the time specified in the manufacturer's guarantee

extension [ɪkˈstenʃən] *noun* **(a)** allowing longer time; **to get an extension of credit** = to get more time to pay back; **extension of a contract** = continuing the contract for a further period **(b)** *(in an office)* individual telephone linked to the main switchboard; *can you get me extension 21?*; *extension 21 is engaged*; *the sales manager is on extension 53*

the White House refusal to ask for an extension of the auto import quotas

Duns Business Month

extensive [ɪkˈstensɪv] *adjective* very large, covering a wide area; *an extensive network of sales outlets*

external [ɪkˈstɜːnl] *adjective* **(a)** outside a country; **external account** = account in a British bank of someone who is living in another country; **external trade** = trade with foreign countries **(b)** outside a company; **external audit** = audit carried

out by an independent auditor; **external auditor** = auditor who carries out audits of a company's accounts but is not employed by that company; **external growth** = growth by buying other companies, rather than by expanding existing sales or products (NOTE: the opposite is **internal**)

extinguisher [ɪkˈstɪŋgwɪʃə] *noun* **fire extinguisher** = can (usually painted red) containing chemical foam which can be sprayed onto a fire to put it out

extra [ˈekstrə] **1** *adjective* which is added or which is more than usual; *there is no extra charge for heating*; *to charge 10% extra for postage*; *he had £25 extra pay for working on Sunday*; *service is extra* **2** *plural noun* **extras** = items which are not included in a price; *packing and postage are extras*

extract [ˈekstrækt] *noun* printed document which is part of a larger document; *he sent me an extract of the accounts*

extraordinary [ɪkˈstrɔːdənəri] *adjective* different from normal; **Extraordinary General Meeting (EGM)** = special meeting of shareholders to discuss an important matter which cannot wait until the next AGM (such as a change in the company's articles of association); *to call an Extraordinary General Meeting*; **extraordinary items** = items in accounts which do not appear each year; *the auditors noted several extraordinary items in the accounts*; *see also comment at* RESOLUTION

extremely [ɪkˈstriːmli] *adverb* very much; *it is extremely difficult to break into the US market*; *their management team is extremely efficient*

Ff

f. & f. = FIXTURES AND FITTINGS

face value ['feɪs 'vælju:] *noun* value written on a coin, banknote or share certificate

> travellers cheques cost 1% of their face value - some banks charge more for small amounts
>
> *Sunday Times*

facility [fə'sɪləti] *noun* **(a)** being able to do something easily; *we offer facilities for payment* **(b)** loan; **credit facilities** = arrangement with a bank or supplier to have credit so as to buy goods; **overdraft facility** = arrangement with a bank to have an overdraft **(c) facilities** = equipment or buildings which make it easy to do something; *our storage facilities are the best in the region*; *transport facilities in the area are not satisfactory*; *there are no facilities for handicapped visitors*; *there are no facilities for unloading or there are no unloading facilities* **(d)** *US* single large building; *we have opened our new warehouse facility*

facsimile [fæk'sɪməli] *noun* **facsimile (copy)** = exact copy of a document; *see also* FAX

fact [fækt] *noun* **(a)** something which is true and real; *the chairman asked to see all the facts on the income tax claim*; *the sales director can give you the facts and figures about the African operation*; **fact sheet** = sheet of paper giving information about a product or service which can be used for publicity purposes **(b) the fact of the matter is** = what is true is that; *the fact of the matter is that the product does not fit the market* **(c)** **in fact** = really; *the chairman blamed the finance director for the loss when in fact he was responsible for it himself*

fact-finding ['fækt 'faɪndɪŋ] *adjective* looking for information; **a fact-finding mission** = visit, usually by a group of people, to search for information about a problem; *the minister went on a fact-finding tour of the region*

factor ['fæktə] **1** *noun* **(a)** thing which is important or which influences; *the drop in sales is an important factor in the company's lower profits*; **cost factor** = problem of cost; **cyclical factors** = way in which a trade cycle affects businesses; **deciding factor** = most important factor which influences a decision; **load factor** = number of seats in a bus, plane or train which are occupied by passengers who have paid the full fare; **factors of production** = the three things needed to produce a product (land, labour and capital) **(b) by a factor of ten** = ten times **(c)** person or company which is responsible for collecting debts for companies, by buying debts at a discount on their face value **2** *verb* to buy debts from a company at a discount

> COMMENT: a factor collects a company's debts when due, and pays the creditor in advance part of the sum to be collected, so 'buying' the debt

> factors 'buy' invoices from a company, which then gets an immediate cash advance representing most of their value. The balance is paid when the debt is met. The client company is charged a fee as well as interest on the cash advanced
>
> *Times*

factoring ['fæktərɪŋ] *noun* business of buying debts at a discount; **factoring**

charges = cost of selling debts to a factor for a commission; **full factoring service** = service by which a factor operates a client's bought ledger and even takes on responsibility for his bad debts

factory ['fæktri] *noun* building where products are manufactured; *the company is proposing to close three of its factories with the loss of 200 jobs*; *the car factory is expanding*; *a shoe factory has been on this site for 200 years*; **the factory floor** = main works of a factory; **factory hand** *or* **factory worker** = person who works in a factory; **factory inspector** *or* **inspector of factories** = government official who inspects factories to see if they are well run; **the factory inspectorate** = all factory inspectors; **factory price** *or* **price ex factory** = price not including transport from the maker's factory; **factory unit** = single building on an industrial estate

fail [feɪl] *verb* (a) not to do something which you were trying to do; *the company failed to notify the tax office of its change of address* (b) to be unsuccessful; *the prototype failed its first test*; **the company failed** = the company went bankrupt; *he lost all his money when the bank failed*

failing ['feɪlɪŋ] **1** *noun* weakness; *the chairman has one failing - he goes to sleep at board meetings* **2** *preposition* if something does not happen; **failing instructions to the contrary** = unless someone gives opposite instructions; **failing prompt payment** = if the payment is not made on time; **failing that** = if that does not work; *try the company secretary, and failing that the chairman*

failure ['feɪljə] *noun* (a) breaking down or stopping; *the failure of the negotiations* (b) **failure to pay a bill** = not having paid the bill (c) **commercial failure** = financial collapse or bankruptcy; *he lost all his money in the bank failure*

fair [feə] **1** *noun* **trade fair** = large exhibition and meeting for advertising and selling a certain type of product; *to organize or to run a trade fair*; *the fair is open from 9 a.m. to 5 p.m.*; *the computer fair runs from April 1st to 6th*; *there are two trade fairs running in London at the same time - the carpet manufacturers'*

and the mobile telephones **2** *adjective* **(a)** honest, correct; **fair deal** = arrangement where both parties are treated equally; *the workers feel they did not get a fair deal from the management*; **fair dealing** = legal buying and selling of shares; **fair price** = good price for both buyer and seller; **fair trade** = (i) international business system where countries agree not to charge import duties on certain items imported from their trading partners; (ii) *US* = RESALE PRICE MAINTENANCE; **fair trading** *or* **fair dealing** = way of doing business which is reasonable and does not harm the consumer; *GB* **Office of Fair Trading** = government department which protects consumers against unfair or illegal business; **fair value** *US* **fair market value** = (i) price paid by a buyer who knows the value of what he is buying to a seller who also knows the value of what he is selling (i.e., neither is cheating the other); (ii) method of valuing the assets and liabilities of a business based on the amount for which they could be sold to independent parties at the time of valuation; **fair wear and tear** = acceptable damage caused by normal use; *the insurance policy covers most damage, but not fair wear and tear to the machine* **(b)** **fair copy** = document which is written or typed with no changes or mistakes

fairly ['feəli] *adverb* quite; *the company is fairly close to financial collapse*; *she is a fairly fast keyboarder*

faith [feɪθ] *noun* **to have faith in something** *or* **someone** = to believe that something or a person is good or will work well; *the salesmen have great faith in the product*; *the sales teams do not have much faith in their manager*; *the board has faith in the managing director's judgement*; **to buy something in good faith** = to buy something thinking that is of good quality, that it has not been stolen or that it is not an imitation

faithfully ['feɪθfəli] *adverb* **yours faithfully** = used as an ending to a formal business letter not addressed to a named person (NOTE: not used in American English)

fake [feɪk] **1** *noun* imitation, copy made for criminal purposes; *the painting was* *proved to be a fake* **2** *adjective* copied for criminal purposes; *the shipment came with fake documentation* **3** *verb* to make an imitation for criminal purposes; *faked documents*; *he faked the results of the test*

fall [fɔːl] **1** *noun* sudden drop, suddenly becoming smaller, sudden loss of value; *a fall in the exchange rate*; *a fall in the price of gold*; *a fall on the Stock Exchange*; *profits showed a 10% fall* **2** *verb* **(a)** to drop suddenly to a lower price; *shares fell on the market today*; *gold shares fell 10%* or *fell 45 cents on the Stock Exchange*; *the price of gold fell for the second day running*; *the pound fell against other European currencies* **(b)** to happen or to take place; *the public holiday falls on a Tuesday*; *payments which fall due* = payments which are now due to be made (NOTE: **falling - fell - has fallen**)

> market analysts described the falls in the second half of last week as a technical correction to the market
> *Australian Financial Review*

> for the first time since mortgage rates began falling in March a financial institution has raised charges on homeowner loans
> *Globe and Mail (Toronto)*

> interest rates were still falling as late as June, and underlying inflation remains below the government's target of 2.5 per cent
> *Financial Times*

fall away [fɔːl əˈweɪ] *verb* to become less; *hotel bookings have fallen away since the tourist season ended*

fall back [fɔːl ˈbæk] *verb* to become lower or cheaper after rising in price; *shares fell back in light trading*

fall back on [fɔːl ˈbæk ɒn] *verb* to have to use something kept for emergencies; *to fall back on cash reserves*; *the management fell back on the usual old excuses*

fall behind [fɔːl bɪˈhaɪnd] *verb* **(a)** to be late in doing something; *he fell behind with his mortgage repayments*; *the company has fallen behind with its*

deliveries = it is late with its deliveries **(b)** to be in a worse position than; *we have fallen behind our rivals* = we have fewer sales or make less profit than our rivals

falling [ˈfɔːlɪŋ] *adjective* which is growing smaller or dropping in price; *a falling market* = market where prices are coming down; *the falling pound* = the pound which is losing its value against other currencies

> falling profitability means falling share prices
> *Investors Chronicle*

fall off [fɔːl ˈɒf] *verb* to become lower, cheaper or less; *sales have fallen off since the tourist season ended*

fall out [fɔːl ˈaut] *verb* **the bottom has fallen out of the market** = sales have fallen below what previously seemed to be their lowest point

fall through [fɔːl ˈθruː] *verb* not to happen, not to take place; *the plan fell through at the last moment*

false [fɔːls] *adjective* not true, not correct; *to make a false entry in the balance sheet*; **false accounting** = criminal offence of changing, destroying or hiding accounting records for a dishonest purpose, such as to gain money; **false pretences** = doing or saying something to cheat someone; *he was sent to prison for obtaining money by false pretences*; **false weight** = weight on shop scales which is wrong and so cheats customers

falsification [fɔːlsɪfɪˈkeɪʃən] *noun* action of making false entries in accounts

falsify [ˈfɔːlsɪfaɪ] *verb* to change something to make it wrong; *he was accused of falsifying the accounts*

famous [ˈfeɪməs] *adjective* very well known; *the company owns a famous department store in the centre of London*

fancy [ˈfænsi] *adjective* **(a) fancy goods** = small attractive items **(b) fancy prices** = high prices; *I don't want to pay the fancy prices they ask in London shops*

fao = FOR THE ATTENTION OF

fare [feə] *noun* price to be paid for a ticket to travel; *train fares have gone up by 5%*; *the government is asking the airlines to* keep air fares down; **concessionary fare =** reduced fare for certain types of passenger (such as employees of the transport company); **full fare =** ticket for a journey by an adult paying the full price; **half fare** = half-price ticket for a child; **single fare** US **one-way fare =** fare for a journey from one place to another; **return fare** US **round-trip fare =** fare for a journey from one place to another and back again

farm [fɑːm] **1** *noun* property in the country where crops are grown, where animals are raised for sale; **fish farm =** place where fish are grown for food; **fur farm =** farm where animals are grown to be killed for their fur; **mixed farm =** farm which has both animals and crops **2** *verb* to own a farm; *he farms 150 acres*

farming [ˈfɑːmɪŋ] *noun* job of working on a farm, of raising animals for sale or of growing crops for food; *chicken farming*; *fish farming*; *mixed farming*

farm out [ˈfɑːm ˈaʊt] *verb* to **farm out work =** to hand over work for another person or company to do for you; *she farms out the office typing to various local bureaux*

fascia [ˈfeɪʃə] *noun* (i) board over a shop on which the name of the shop is written; (ii) board above an exhibition stand on which the name of the company represented is written

fast [fɑːst] *adjective & adverb* quick or quickly; *the train is the fastest way of getting to our supplier's factory*; *home computers sell fast in the pre-Christmas period*

fast-moving *or* fast-selling

[ˈfɑːstˈmuːvɪŋ *or* ˈfɑːstˈselɪŋ] *adjective* **fast-selling items =** items which sell fast; *some dictionaries are not fast-moving stock*

fault [fɔːlt] *noun* **(a)** being to blame for something which is wrong; *it is the stock controller's fault if the warehouse runs out of stock*; *the chairman said the lower sales figures were the fault of a badly motivated sales force* **(b)** wrong working; *the technicians are trying to correct a programming fault*; *we think there is a basic fault in the product design*

faulty [ˈfɔːlti] *adjective* which does not work properly; *faulty equipment was to blame for the defective products*; *they installed faulty computer programs*

favour US **favor** [ˈfeɪvə] **1** *noun* **(a)** as a **favour =** to help, to be kind to someone; *he asked the secretary for a loan as a favour* **(b)** **in favour of =** in agreement with, feeling that something is right; *six members of the board are in favour of the proposal, and three are against it* **2** *verb* to agree that something is right; to vote for something; *the board members all favour Smith Ltd as partners in the project*

favourable US **favorable** [ˈfeɪvərəbl] *adjective* which gives an advantage; **favourable balance of trade =** situation where a country's exports are more than the imports; **on favourable terms =** on specially good terms; *the shop is let on very favourable terms*

favourite US **favorite** [ˈfeɪvərɪt] *adjective* which is liked best; *this brand of chocolate is a favourite with the children's market*

fax [fæks] **1** *noun* **(a)** (i) system for sending the exact copy of a document via the telephone lines; (ii) document sent by this method; *can you confirm the booking by fax?*; *we received a fax of the order this morning* **(b)** **fax (machine) =** machine for sending or receiving faxes; **plain paper fax =** fax machine which uses ordinary white paper and not special fax paper; **fax paper =** special paper which is used in fax machines; **fax roll =** roll of fax paper **2** *verb* to send a message by fax; *the details of the offer were faxed to the brokers this morning*; *I've faxed the documents to our New York office*

COMMENT: banks will not accept fax messages as binding instructions (as for example, a faxed order for money to be transferred from one account to another)

feasibility [fiːzəˈbɪləti] *noun* ability to be done; *to report on the feasibility of a project*; **feasibility report =** report saying if something can be done; **to carry out a feasibility study on a project =** to carry out an examination of costs and profits to see if the project should be started

federal ['fedərəl] *adjective* referring to a system of government where a group of states are linked together in a federation; especially the central government of the United States; *most federal offices are in Washington*

federal examiners will determine which of the privately-insured savings and loans qualify for federal insurance

Wall Street Journal

since 1978 America has freed many of its industries from federal rules that set prices and controlled the entry of new companies

Economist

the Fed [ðə 'fed] *noun US (informal)* = FEDERAL RESERVE BOARD

indications of weakness in the US economy were contained in figures from the Fed on industrial production for April

Financial Times

the half-point discount rate move gives the Fed room to reduce the federal funds rate further if economic weakness persists. The Fed sets the discount rate directly, but controls the federal funds rate by buying and selling Treasury securities

Wall Street Journal

Federal Reserve (System) ['fedərəl rɪ'zɜːv] system of federal government control of the US banks, where the Federal Reserve Board regulates money supply, prints money, fixes the discount rate and issues government bonds

COMMENT: the Federal Reserve system is the central bank of the USA. The system is run by the Federal Reserve Board, under a chairman and seven committee members (or 'governors') who are all appointed by the President. The twelve Federal Reserve Banks act as lenders of last resort to local commercial banks. Although the board is appointed by the president, the whole system is relatively independent of the US government

Federal Reserve Bank ['fedərəl rɪ'zɜːv 'bæŋk] one of the twelve central banks in the USA which are owned by the state and directed by the Federal Reserve Board

Federal Reserve Board ['fedərəl rɪ'zɜːv 'bɔːd] government organization which runs the central banks in the USA

pressure on the Federal Reserve Board to ease monetary policy mounted yesterday with the release of a set of pessimistic economic statistics

Financial Times

federation [fedə'reɪʃən] *noun* group of societies, companies or organizations which have a central organization which represents them and looks after their common interests; *a federation of trades unions*; *the employers' federation*

fee [fiː] *noun* **(a)** money paid for work carried out by a professional person (such as an accountant, a doctor or a lawyer); *we charge a small fee for our services*; *the consultant's fee was much higher than we expected*; *director's fees* = money paid to a director as a lump sum, not a salary **(b)** money paid for something; *entrance fee or admission fee*; *registration fee*

feed [fiːd] **1** *noun* device which puts paper into a printer or into a photocopier; *the paper feed has jammed*; **continuous feed** = device which feeds continuous computer stationery into a printer; **sheet feed** = device which puts one sheet of paper at a time into a printer **2** *verb* to put information into a computer or paper into a printer (NOTE: **feeding - fed**)

feedback ['fiːdbæk] *noun* information, especially about people's reactions; *have you any feedback from the sales force about the customers' reaction to the new model?*

feelgood factor ['fiːlɡʊd 'fæktə] *noun* general feeling that everything is going well (leading to increased consumer spending)

feint [feɪnt] *noun* very light lines on writing paper

ferry ['feri] *noun* boat which takes passengers or goods across water; *we are going to take the night ferry to Belgium*; **car ferry** = ferry which carries cars; **passenger ferry** = ferry which only carries passengers

fetch [fetʃ] *verb* **(a)** to go to bring something; *we have to fetch the goods from the docks*; *it is cheaper to buy at a cash and carry warehouse, provided you have a car to fetch the goods yourself* **(b)** to be sold for a certain price; *to fetch a high price*; *it will not fetch more than £200*; *these machines fetch very high prices on the black market*

few [fjuː] *adjective & noun* **(a)** not many; *we sold so few of this item that we have discontinued the line; few of the staff stay with us more than six months* **(b)** a few = some; *a few of our salesmen drive Rolls-Royces*; *we get only a few orders in the period from Christmas to the New Year*

fiat money ['fiːæt 'mʌni] *noun* coins or notes which are not worth much as paper or metal, but are said by the government to have a value

fictitious assets [fik'tɪʃəs 'æsɪts] *noun* assets (such as prepayments) which do not have a resale value, but are entered as assets in the balance sheet

fiddle ['fidl] **1** *noun (informal)* cheating; *it's all a fiddle*; **he's on the fiddle** = he is trying to cheat **2** *verb (informal)* to cheat; *he tried to fiddle his tax returns*; *the salesman was caught fiddling his expense account*

fide *see* BONA FIDE

fiduciary [fi'djuːʃjəri] *adjective & noun* (person) in a position of trust; *directors have fiduciary duty to act in the best interests of the company*; **fiduciary deposits** = bank deposits which are managed for the depositor by the bank

field [fiːld] *noun* **(a)** piece of ground on a farm; *the cows are in the field* **(b)** in the **field** = outside the office, among the customers; *we have sixteen reps in the field*; **first in the field** = first company to bring out a product or to start a service; *Smith Ltd has a great advantage in being first in the field with a reliable electric car*; **field sales force** = salesmen working outside the company's offices, in the field; *after working for a year in the field sales force, he became field sales manager*; **field sales manager** = manager in charge of a group of salesmen; **field work** = examination of the situation among possible customers; *he had to do a lot of field work to find the right market for the product*

FIFO ['faɪfəʊ] = FIRST IN FIRST OUT

fifty-fifty ['fifti'fifti] *adjective & adverb* half; **to go fifty-fifty** = to share the costs equally; **he has a fifty-fifty chance of making a profit** = he has an equal chance of making a profit or a loss

figure ['figə] *noun* **(a)** number, cost written in numbers; *the figure in the accounts for heating is very high*; **he put a very low figure on the value of the lease** = he calculated the value of the lease as very low **(b)** **figures** = written numbers; **sales figures** = total sales; **to work out the figures** = to calculate; **his income runs into six figures** *or* **he has a six-figure income** = his income is more than £100,000; **in round figures** = not totally accurate, but correct to the nearest 10 or 100; *they have a workforce of 2,500 in round figures* **(c)** **figures** = results for a company; *the figures for last year* *or* *last year's figures*

file [faɪl] **1** *noun* **(a)** cardboard holder for documents, which can fit in the drawer of a filing cabinet; *put these letters in the customer file*; *look in the file marked 'Scottish sales'*; **box file** = cardboard box for holding documents **(b)** documents kept for reference; **to place something on file** = to keep a record of something; **to keep someone's name on file** = to keep someone's name on a list for reference; **file copy** = copy of a document which is kept for reference in an office; **card-index file** = information kept on filing cards; **US file card** = card with information written on it, used to classify information into the correct order (NOTE: the British English for this is **filing card**) **(c)** section of data on a computer (such as payroll, address list, customer accounts); *how can we protect our computer files?* **2** *verb* **(a)** **to file documents** = to put documents in order so that they can be found easily; *the correspondence is filed under 'complaints'* **(b)** to make an official request; **to file a petition in bankruptcy** = (i) to ask officially to be made bankrupt; (ii) to ask officially for someone else to be made bankrupt **(c)** to register something officially; *to file an application for a patent; to file a return to the tax office*

filing ['faɪlɪŋ] *noun* documents which have to be put in order; *there is a lot of filing to do at the end of the week; the manager looked through the week's filing to see what letters had been sent;* **filing basket** *or* **filing tray** = container kept on a desk for documents which have to be filed; **filing cabinet** = piece of furniture, made of metal, with wide deep drawers so that files (called 'suspension files') can be hooked inside them; *we need two more four-drawer filing cabinets;* **filing card** *US* **file card** = card with information written on it, used to classify information into the correct order; **filing clerk** = clerk who files documents; **filing system** = way of putting documents in order for reference

fill [fɪl] **1** *verb* **(a)** to make something full; *we have filled our order book with orders for Africa; the production department has filled the warehouse with unsellable products* **(b)** **to fill a gap** = to provide a product or service which is needed, but which no one has provided before; *the new range of small cars fills a gap in the market* **(c)** **to fill a post** *or* **a vacancy** = to find someone to do a job; *your application arrived too late - the post has already been filled*

filler ['fɪlə] *noun* something which fills a space; **stocking filler** = small item which can be used to put into a Christmas stocking; *see* SHELF FILLER

fill in ['fɪl 'ɪn] *verb* to write in the blank spaces in a form; *fill in your name and address in block capitals*

filling station ['fɪlɪŋ 'steɪʃən] *noun* place where you can buy petrol; *he stopped at the filling station to get some petrol before going on to the motorway*

fill out ['fɪl 'aʊt] *verb* to write the required information in the blank spaces in a form; *to get customs clearance you must fill out three forms*

fill up ['fɪl 'ʌp] *verb* **(a)** to make something completely full; *he filled up the car with petrol; my appointments book is completely filled up* **(b)** to finish writing on a form; *he filled up the form and sent it to the bank*

final ['faɪnl] *adjective* last, coming at the end of a period; *to pay the final instalment; to make the final payment; to put the final details on a document;* **final accounts** = accounts produced at the end of an accounting period, including the balance sheet and profit and loss account; **final date for payment** = last date by which payment should be made; **final demand** = last reminder from a supplier, after which he will sue for payment; **final discharge** = last payment of what is left of a debt; **final dividend** = dividend paid at the end of a financial year; **final product** = manufactured product, made at the end of a production process

finalize ['faɪnəlaɪz] *verb* to agree final details; *we hope to finalize the agreement tomorrow; after six weeks of negotiations the loan was finalized yesterday*

finally ['faɪnəli] *adverb* in the end; *the contract was finally signed yesterday; after weeks of trials the company finally accepted the computer system*

finance 1 ['faɪnæns] *noun* **(a)** money used by a company, provided by the shareholders or by loans; *where will they get the necessary finance for the project?;* **finance company** *or* **finance corporation** *or* **finance house** = company which provides money for hire-purchase; **finance market** = place where large sums of money can be lent or borrowed; **high finance** = lending, investing and borrowing of very large sums of money, organized by financiers **(b)** money (of a club, local authority, etc.); *she is the secretary of the local authority finance committee* **(c) finances** = money or cash which is available; *the bad state of the company's finances* **2** [fɪ'næns] *verb* to provide money to pay for something; *they* *plan to finance the operation with short-term loans*

> an official said that the company began to experience a sharp increase in demand for longer-term mortgages at a time when the flow of money used to finance these loans diminished
>
> *Globe and Mail*

Finance Act ['faɪnæns 'ækt] *noun GB* annual act of parliament which gives the government the power to obtain money from taxes as proposed in the Budget

Finance Bill ['faɪnæns 'bɪl] *noun GB* bill which lists the proposals in a chancellor's budget and which is debated before being voted into law as the Finance Act

financial [fɪ'nænʃəl] *adjective* concerning money; **financial adviser** = person or company which gives advice on financial matters for a fee; **financial assistance** = help in the form of money; **financial correspondent** = journalist who writes articles on money matters for a newspaper; **financial instrument** = document showing that money has been lent or borrowed, invested or passed from one account to another (such as a bill of exchange, share certificate, certificate of deposit, IOU, etc.); **financial intermediary** = (i) institution which takes deposits or loans from individuals and lends money to clients (banks, building societies, hire purchase companies, are all types of financial intermediaries); (ii) company which arranges insurance for a client, but is not itself an insurance company; **financial position** = state of a person's or company's bank balance (assets and debts); *he must think of his financial position*; **financial resources** = money which is available for investment; *a company with strong financial resources*; **financial risk** = possibility of losing money; *there is no financial risk in selling to East European countries on credit*; **financial statement** = document which shows the financial situation of a company; *the accounts department has prepared a financial statement for the shareholders*; **financial year** = the twelve months' period for a firm's accounts

financially [fɪ'nænʃəli] *adverb* regarding money; **company which is financially sound** = company which is profitable and has strong assets

Financial Services Act [fɪ'nænʃəl 'sɜːvɪsɪz 'ækt] Act of the British Parliament which regulates the offering of financial services to the general public and to private investors

Financial Services Authority (FSA) [fɪ'nænʃəl 'sɜːvɪsɪz ɔː'θɒrəti] government agency set up to regulate all financial services, such as banks, stockbrokers, unit trusts, pension companies, professional bodies, stock exchanges, etc., including the ombudsmen for these services

> the FSA has set up an independent ombudsman scheme covering all areas of financial services
>
> *Times*

Financial Times (FT) [faɪ'nænʃəl 'taɪmz] important British financial daily newspaper (printed on pink paper); **FT All-Share Index** = index based on the market price of about 840 companies listed on the London Stock Exchange (it includes the companies on the FTSE 100 Index, the 250 Index, plus companies in other indices) (NOTE: also simply called the **All-Share Index**); **FT-Stock Exchange 100 Share Index (FTSE 100** *or* **Footsie)** = index based on the prices of one hundred leading companies (this is the main London index); **FTSE Mid 250 Share Index** = index based on the market prices of 250 companies capitalized between £300m and £2.5bn (this is about 16% of the total stock market capitalization)

> the benchmark FTSE 100 index ended the session up 94.3 points
>
> *Times*

financier [faɪ'nænsɪə] *noun* person who lends large amounts of money to companies or who buys shares in companies as an investment

financing [fɪ'nænsɪŋ] *noun* providing money; *the financing of the project was done by two international banks*; **deficit financing** = planning by a government to borrow money to cover the shortfall between expenditure and income from taxation

find [faɪnd] *verb* **(a)** to get something which was not there before; *we are still trying to find backing for the project* **(b)** to make a legal decision in court; *the tribunal found that both parties were at fault*; **the judge found for the defendant** = the judge decided that the defendant was right (NOTE: **finding - found**)

findings ['faɪndɪŋz] *plural noun* **the findings of a commission of enquiry** = the recommendations of the commission

find time ['faɪnd 'taɪm] *verb* to make enough time to do something; *we must find time to visit the new staff sports club*; *the chairman never finds enough time to play golf*

fine [faɪn] **1** *noun* money paid because of something wrong which has been done; *he was asked to pay a $25,000 fine*; *we had to pay a £50 parking fine* **2** *verb* to punish someone by making him pay money; *to fine someone £2,500 for obtaining money by false pretences* **3** *adverb* very thin or very small; **we are cutting our margins very fine** = we are reducing our margins to the smallest possible **4** *adjective* **fine print** = very small characters often used in contracts to list exceptions and restrictions; *did you read the fine print on the back of the agreement?*

fine tune [faɪn 'tjuːn] *verb* to make small adjustments to (a plan or the economy) so that it works better

fine-tuning ['faɪn'tjuːnɪŋ] *noun* making small adjustments to interest rates, the tax bands, the money supply, etc., to improve a nation's economy

finish ['fɪnɪʃ] **1** *noun* **(a)** final appearance; *the product has an attractive finish* **(b)** end of a day's trading on the Stock Exchange; *oil shares rallied at the finish* **2** *verb* **(a)** to do something or to make something completely; *the order was finished in time*; *she finished the test before all the other candidates* **(b)** to come to an end; *the contract is due to finish next month*

finished ['fɪnɪʃt] *adjective* **finished goods** = manufactured goods which are ready to be sold

fink [fɪŋk] *noun US (informal)* worker hired to replace a worker who is on strike

fire ['faɪə] **1** *noun* thing which burns; *the shipment was damaged in the fire on board the cargo boat*; *half the stock was destroyed in the warehouse fire*; **to catch fire** = to start to burn; *the papers in the waste paper basket caught fire*; **fire damage** = damage caused by fire; *he claimed £250 for fire damage*; **fire-damaged goods** = goods which have been damaged in a fire; **fire door** = special door to prevent fire going from one part of a building to another; **fire escape** = door or stairs which allow people to get out of a building which is on fire; **fire extinguisher** = can (usually painted red) containing chemical foam which can be sprayed onto a fire to put it out; **fire hazard** *or* **fire risk** = situation or goods which could start a fire; *that warehouse full of paper is a fire hazard*; **fire insurance** = insurance against damage by fire; **fire sale** = (i) sale of fire-damaged goods; (ii) sale of anything at a very low price **2** *verb* **to fire someone** = to dismiss someone from a job; *the new managing director fired half the sales force*; **to hire and fire** = to employ new staff and dismiss existing staff very frequently

fireproof ['faɪəpruːf] *adjective* which cannot be damaged by fire; *we stored the papers in a fireproof safe*; *it is impossible to make the office completely fireproof*

firm [fɜːm] **1** *noun* business or partnership; *he is a partner in a law firm*; *a manufacturing firm*; *an important publishing firm* **2** *adjective* **(a)** which cannot be changed; *to make a firm offer for something*; *to place a firm order for two aircraft*; *they are quoting a firm price of £1.22 per unit* **(b)** not dropping in price, and possibly going to rise; *sterling was firmer on the foreign exchange markets*; *shares remained firm* **3** *verb* to remain at a price and seem likely to go up; *the shares firmed at £1.50*

COMMENT: strictly speaking, a 'firm' is a partnership or other trading organization which is not a limited company. In practice, it is better to use the term for unincorporated businesses such as 'a firm of accountants' or 'a firm of stockbrokers', rather than for 'a major aircraft construction firm' which is likely to be a plc

some profit-taking was noted, but underlying sentiment remained firm

Financial Times

firmness ['fɜːmnəs] *noun* being steady at a price, being likely to rise; *the firmness of the pound on foreign exchanges*

Toronto failed to mirror New York's firmness as a drop in gold shares on a falling bullion price left the market closing on a mixed note

Financial Times

firm up ['fɜːm 'ʌp] *verb* to finalize, to agree final details; *we expect to firm up the deal at the next trade fair*

first [fɜːst] **1** *noun* person or thing which is there at the beginning or which is earlier than others; *our company was one of the first to sell into the European market*; **first in first out (FIFO)** = (i) redundancy policy, where the people who have been working longest are the first to be made redundant; (ii) accounting policy where it is assumed that stocks in hand were purchased last, and that stocks sold during the period were purchased first; *compare* LIFO **2** *adjective* **first quarter** = three months' period from January to the end of March; **first half** *or* **first half-year** = six months' period from January to the end of June

first-class ['fɜːst'klɑːs] *adjective & noun* **(a)** top quality or most expensive; *he is a first-class accountant* **(b)** most expensive and comfortable type of travel or type of hotel; *I always travel first-class*; *first-class travel provides the best service*; *a first-class ticket to New York costs more than I can afford*; *the MD prefers to stay in first-class hotels*; **first-class mail =** *GB* most expensive mail service, designed to be faster *US* mail service for letters and postcards; *a first-class letter should get to Scotland in a day*

first-line ['fɜːst'laɪn] *adjective* **first-line management** = the managers who have immediate contact with the workers

fiscal ['fɪskəl] *adjective* referring to tax or to government revenues; *the government's fiscal policies*; **fiscal measures** = tax changes made by a government to improve the working of the economy; **fiscal year** = twelve-month period on which taxes are calculated (in the UK, April 6th to April 5th)

the standard measure of fiscal policy - the public sector borrowing requirement - is kept misleadingly low

Economist

last fiscal year the chain reported a 116% jump in earnings

Barron's

fit [fɪt] *verb* to be the right size for something; *the paper doesn't fit the typewriter* (NOTE: **fitting - fitted**)

fit in ['fɪt 'ɪn] *verb* to make something go into a space; *will the computer fit in that little space?*; *the chairman tries to fit in a game of golf every afternoon*; *my appointments diary is full, but I shall try to fit you in tomorrow afternoon*

fit out ['fɪt 'aʊt] *verb* to provide equipment or furniture for a business; *they fitted out the factory with a new computer system*; *the shop was fitted out at a cost of £10,000*; **fitting out of a shop** = putting shelves or counters in for a new shop

fittings ['fɪtɪŋz] *plural noun* items in a property which are sold with it but are not permanently fixed (such as carpets or shelves); *see also* FIXTURES

fix [fɪks] *verb* **(a)** to arrange, to agree; *to fix a budget*; *to fix a meeting for 3 p.m.*; *the date has still to be fixed*; *the price of gold was fixed at $300*; *the mortgage rate has been fixed at 8%* **(b)** to mend; *the technicians are coming to fix the telephone switchboard*; *can you fix the photocopier?*

coupons are fixed by reference to interest rates

at the time a gilt is first
issued
Investors Chronicle

fixed ['fɪkst] *adjective* permanent, which cannot be removed; **fixed assets** = property or machinery which a company owns and uses, but which the company does not buy or sell as part of its regular trade, including the company's investments in shares of other companies; **fixed capital** = capital in the form of buildings and machinery; **fixed costs** = costs paid to produce a product which do not increase with the amount of product made (such as rent); **fixed deposit** = deposit which pays a stated interest over a set period; **fixed expenses** = money which is spent regularly (such as on rent, electricity, telephone); **fixed income** = income which does not change (as from an annuity); **fixed-price agreement** = agreement where a company provides a service or a product at a price which stays the same for the whole period of the agreement; **fixed scale of charges** = rate of charging which cannot be altered

you must offer shippers and
importers fixed rates over a
reasonable period of time
Lloyd's List

fixed-interest ['fɪkst'ɪntrest] *adjective* which has an interest rate which does not vary; **fixed-interest investments** = investments producing an interest which does not change; **fixed-interest securities** = securities (such as government bonds) which produce an interest which does not change

fixer ['fɪksə] *noun (informal)* (a) person who has a reputation for arranging business deals (often illegally) (b) *US* house or car which is being sold cheaply as it needs repairing

fixing ['fɪksɪŋ] *noun* (a) arranging; *fixing of charges*; *fixing of a mortgage rate* (b) **price fixing** = illegal agreement between companies to charge the same price for competing products (c) **the London gold fixing** = system where the world price for gold is set each day in London

fixtures ['fɪkstʃəz] *plural noun* items in a property which are permanently attached to it (such as sinks and lavatories); **fixtures**

and fittings (f. & f.) = objects in a property which are sold with the property, both those which cannot be removed and those which can

fix up with ['fɪks ʌp 'wɪð] *verb* to arrange; *my secretary fixed me up with a car at the airport*; *can you fix me up with a room for tomorrow night?*

flag [flæg] **1** *noun* (a) piece of cloth with a design on it which shows which country it belongs to; *a ship flying a British flag*; **ship sailing under a flag of convenience** = ship flying the flag of a country which may have no ships of its own, but allows ships from other countries to be registered in its ports (b) mark which is attached to information in a computer so that the information can be found easily **2** *verb* to insert marks on information in a computer so that the information can be found easily (NOTE: **flagging - flagged**)

flagship ['flægʃɪp] *noun* key product in a range, the product on which the reputation of the producer most depends

flat [flæt] **1** *adjective* (a) (market prices) which do not fall or rise because of low demand; *the market was flat today* (b) fixed, not changing; **flat rate** = charge which always stays the same; *we pay a flat rate for electricity each quarter*; *he is paid a flat rate of £2 per thousand* **2** *adverb* in a blunt way; *he turned down the offer flat* **3** *noun* set of rooms for one family in a building with other sets of similar rooms; *he has a flat in the centre of town*; *she is buying a flat close to her office*; **company flat** = flat owned by a company and used by members of staff from time to time (NOTE: American English is **apartment**)

the government revised its
earlier reports for July and
August. Originally reported
as flat in July and declining
by 0.2% in August, industrial
production is now seen to have
risen by 0.2% and 0.1%
respectively in those months
Sunday Times

flat out ['flæt 'aʊt] *adverb* (a) working hard or at full speed; *the factory worked flat out to complete the order on time* (b)

US in a blunt way; *he refused the offer flat out*

flat pack ['flæt 'pæk] *noun* pack of goods in which a piece of furniture is sold in flat sections, which the purchaser then has to try to put together; *the shelves are sold as a flat pack*

flea market ['fli: 'mɑːkɪt] *noun* market, usually in the open air, for selling cheap secondhand goods; *I bought this clock in the local flea market*

fleet [fli:t] *noun* group of cars belonging to a company and used by its staff; *a company's fleet of representatives' cars*; **a fleet car** = car which is one of a fleet of cars; **fleet discount** = specially cheap price for purchase or rental of a company's cars; **fleet rental** = renting all a company's cars at a special price

flexibility [fleksə'bɪləti] *noun* being easily changed; *there is no flexibility in the company's pricing policy*

they calculate interest on their 'flexible' mortgage on an annual basis rather than daily. Charging annual interest makes a nonsense of the whole idea of flexibility which is supposed to help you pay off your mortgage more quickly

Financial Times

flexible ['fleksəbl] *adjective* which can be altered or changed; *we try to be flexible where the advertising budget is concerned*; *the company has adopted a flexible pricing policy*; **flexible working hours** = system where workers can start or stop work at different hours of the morning or evening provided that they work a certain number of hours per day or week; *we work flexible hours*

flexitime ['fleksɪtaɪm] *noun* system where workers can start or stop work at different hours of the morning or evening, provided that they work a certain number of hours per day or week; *we work flexitime*; *the company introduced flexitime working two years ago* (NOTE: American English also uses **flextime**)

flier *or* **flyer** ['flaɪə] *noun* **(a)** high flier = (i) person who is very successful or who is

likely to rise to a very important position; (ii) share whose market price is rising rapidly **(b)** small advertising leaflet designed to encourage customers to ask for more information about the product for sale

flight [flaɪt] *noun* **(a)** journey by an aircraft, leaving at a regular time; *flight AC 267 is leaving from Gate 46*; *he missed his flight*; *I always take the afternoon flight to Rome*; *if you hurry you will catch the six o'clock flight to Paris* **(b)** rapid movement of money out of a country because of a lack of confidence in the country's economic future; *the flight of capital from Europe into the USA*; *the flight from the peso into the dollar* **(c)** series of steps; **top-flight** = in the most important position, very efficient; *top-flight managers can earn very high salaries*

flipchart ['flɪptʃɑːt] *noun* stand with large sheets of paper clipped together (a way of showing information to a group of people; a speaker writes on a sheet of paper which can then be turned over to show the next sheet)

float [fləut] **1** *noun* **(a)** cash taken from a central supply and used for running expenses; *the sales reps have a float of £100 each*; **cash float** = cash put into the cash box at the beginning of the day to allow business to start; *we start the day with a £20 float in the cash desk* **(b)** starting a new company by selling shares in it on the Stock Exchange; *the float of the new company was a complete failure* **(c)** allowing a currency to settle at its own exchange rate, without any government intervention; **clean float** = floating a currency freely on the international markets, without any interference from the government; **dirty float** *or* **managed float** = floating a currency, where the government intervenes to regulate the exchange rate **2** *verb* **(a)** to float a company = to start a new company by selling shares in it on the Stock Exchange; **to float a loan** = to raise a loan on the financial market by asking banks and companies to subscribe to it **(b)** to let a currency find its own exchange rate on the international markets and not be fixed; *the government has let sterling float*; *the* *government has decided to float the pound*

floating ['fləʊtɪŋ] **1** *noun* **(a) floating of a company** = starting a new company by selling shares in it on the Stock Exchange **(b) the floating of the pound** = letting the pound find its own exchange rate on the international market **2** *adjective* which is not fixed; *floating exchange rates*; *the floating pound*; **floating rate** = (i) rate of interest on a loan which is not fixed, but can change with the current bank interest rates; (ii) exchange rate for a currency which can vary according to market demand, and is not fixed by the government

in a world of floating exchange rates the dollar is strong because of capital inflows rather than weak because of the nation's trade deficit

Duns Business Month

flood [flʌd] **1** *noun* large quantity; *we received a flood of orders*; *floods of tourists filled the hotels* **2** *verb* to fill with a large quantity of something; *the market was flooded with cheap imitations*; *the sales department is flooded with orders or with complaints*

floor [flɔː] *noun* **(a)** part of the room which you walk on; **floor space** = area of floor in an office or warehouse; *we have 3,500 square metres of floor space to let*; **floor stand** = display stand which stands on the floor, as opposed to one which stands on a table or counter; **the factory floor** = main works of a factory; **on the shop floor** = in the works, in the factory, among the ordinary workers; *the feeling on the shop floor is that the manager does not know his job*; **dealing floor** *or* **trading floor** = (i) area of a broking house where dealing in securities is carried out by phone, using monitors to display current prices and stock exchange transactions; (ii) part of a stock exchange where dealers trade in securities **(b)** all rooms on one level in a building; *the shoe department is on the first floor*; *her office is on the 26th floor*; *US* **floor manager** = person in charge of the sales staff in a department store (NOTE: the numbering of floors is different

in Britain and the USA. The floor at street level is the **ground floor** in Britain, but the **first floor** in the USA. Each floor in the USA is one number higher than the same floor in Britain) **(c)** bottom level of something (such as the lowest exchange rate which a government will accept for its currency or the lower limit imposed on an interest rate; the opposite is the 'ceiling' or 'cap'); **floor price** = lowest price, price which cannot go any lower

floorwalker ['flɔːwɔːkə] *noun* employee of a department store who advises the customers, and supervises the shop assistants in a department

flop [flɒp] **1** *noun* failure, not being a success; *the new model was a flop* **2** *verb* to fail, not to be a success; *the flotation of the new company flopped badly* (NOTE: flopping - flopped)

floppy disk *or* **floppy** ['flɒpi 'dɪsk] *noun* flat circular flexible disk onto which data can be stored in a magnetic form (a floppy disk cannot store as much data as a hard disk, but is easily removed, and is protected by a plastic sleeve)

florin ['flɒrɪn] *noun* another name for the Dutch guilder (NOTE: the abbreviation for the guilder is fl)

flotation [fləʊ'teɪʃən] *noun* **the flotation of a new company** = starting a new company by selling shares in it

flotsam ['flɒtsəm] *noun* **flotsam and jetsam** = rubbish floating in the water after a ship has been wrecked and rubbish washed on to the land

flourish ['flʌrɪʃ] *verb* to be prosperous, to do well in business; *the company is flourishing*; *trade with Estonia flourished*

flourishing ['flʌrɪʃɪŋ] *adjective* profitable; **flourishing trade** = trade which is expanding profitably; *he runs a flourishing shoe business*

flow [fləʊ] **1** *noun* **(a)** movement; *the flow of capital into a country*; *the flow of investments into Japan* **(b) cash flow** = cash which comes into a company from sales and goes out in purchases or overhead expenditure; **discounted cash flow (DCF)** = calculation of forecast sales of a product in current terms with reductions for current interest rates; **the company is suffering from cash flow problems** = cash income is not coming in fast enough to pay for the expenditure going out **2** *verb* to move smoothly; *production is now flowing normally after the strike*

flowchart *or* **flow diagram** ['fləutʃɑːt *or* 'fləu 'daɪəgræm] *noun* chart which shows the arrangement of work processes in a series

fluctuate ['flʌktjueɪt] *verb* to move up and down; *prices fluctuated between £1.10 and £1.25; the pound fluctuated all day on the foreign exchange markets*

fluctuating ['flʌktjueɪtɪŋ] *adjective* moving up and down; *fluctuating dollar prices*

fluctuation [flʌktjuˈeɪʃən] *noun* up and down movement; *the fluctuations of the yen; the fluctuations of the exchange rate*

fly [flaɪ] *verb* to move through the air in an aircraft; *the chairman is flying to Germany on business; the overseas sales manager flies about 100,000 miles a year visiting the agents*

fly-by-night ['flaɪbaɪˈnaɪt] *adjective* company which is not reliable or which might disappear to avoid paying debts; *I want a reputable builder, not one of these fly-by-night outfits*

FOB *or* **f.o.b.** ['efəuˈbiː] = FREE ON BOARD

fold [fəuld] *verb* **(a)** to bend a flat thing, so that part of it is on top of the rest; *she folded the letter so that the address was clearly visible* **(b)** *(informal)* **to fold (up)** = to stop trading; *the business folded up last December; the company folded with debts of over £1m*

-fold [fəuld] *suffix* times; **four-fold** = four times

---

the company's sales have nearly tripled and its profits have risen seven-fold since 1982

Barrons

---

folder ['fəuldə] *noun* cardboard envelope for carrying papers; *put all the documents in a folder for the chairman*

folio ['fəulɪəu] **1** *noun* page with a number, especially two facing pages in an

account book which have the same number **2** *verb* to put a number on a page

follow ['fɒləu] *verb* to come behind or to come afterwards; *the samples will follow by surface mail; we will pay £10,000 down, with the balance to follow in six months' time*

follow up ['fɒləu 'ʌp] *verb* to examine something further; *I'll follow up your idea of targeting our address list with a special mailing;* **to follow up an initiative** = to take action once someone else has decided to do something

follow-up letter ['fɒləuˈʌp 'letə] *noun* letter sent to someone who has not acted on the instructions in a previous letter, or to discuss in more detail points which were raised earlier

food [fuːd] *noun* things which are eaten; *he is very fond of Indian food; the food in the staff restaurant is excellent;* **US food stamp** = coupon issued by the US federal government to poor people so that they can buy food at a discounted price

foodstuffs ['fuːdstʌfs] *plural noun* **essential foodstuffs** = very important food, such as bread or rice

foolscap ['fuːlzkæp] *noun* large size of writing paper (13½ by 8½ inches); *the letter was on six sheets of foolscap;* **a foolscap envelope** = large envelope which takes foolscap paper

foot [fut] **1** *noun* **(a)** part of the body at the end of the leg; **on foot** = walking; *the reps make most of their central London calls on foot; the rush hour traffic is so bad that it is quicker to go to the office on foot* **(b)** bottom part; *he signed his name at the foot of the invoice* **(c)** measurement of length (= 30cm); *the table is six feet long; my office is ten feet by twelve* (NOTE: the plural is **feet** for (a) and (c); there is no plural for (b). In measurements, **foot** is usually written **ft** or **'** after figures: **10ft; 10'**. Note that the foot is now no longer officially used in the UK) **2** *verb* **(a)** **to foot the bill** = to pay the bill; *the director footed the bill for the department's Christmas party* **(b)** *US* **to foot up an account** = to add up a column of numbers

footfall ['futfɔːl] *noun* the number of customers who come into and walk round a shop

the small independent retailer who stocks up using cash and carries could be hit hard by the loss of footfall associated with any increase in smuggled goods

The Grocer

Footsie ['futsiː] = FINANCIAL TIMES-STOCK EXCHANGE 100 INDEX an index based on the prices of 100 leading companies (this is the main London index)

FOR ['efəu'ɑː] = FREE ON RAIL

'Forbes' 500 ['fɔːbz 'faɪv'hʌndrəd] list of the largest US corporations, published each year in 'Forbes' magazine

forbid [fə'bɪd] *verb* to tell someone not to do something, to say that something must not be done; *the contract forbids resale of the goods to the USA*; *the staff are forbidden to use the front entrance* (NOTE: **forbidding - forbade - forbidden**)

force [fɔːs] **1** *noun* **(a)** strength; **to be in force** = to be operating or working; *the rules have been in force since 1986*; **to come into force** = to start to operate or work; *the new regulations will come into force on January 1st* **(b)** group of people; **labour force** *or* **workforce** = all the workers in a company or in an area; *the management has made an increased offer to the labour force*; *we are opening a new factory in the Far East because of the cheap local labour force*; **sales force** = group of salesmen **(c)** **force majeure** = something which happens which is out of the control of the parties who have signed a contract (such as strike, war, storm) **2** *verb* to make someone do something; *competition has forced the company to lower its prices*

forced [fɔːst] *adjective* **forced sale** = sale which takes place because a court orders it or because it is the only way to avoid a financial crisis

force down [fɔːs 'daʊn] *verb* to make something become lower; **to force prices down** = to make prices come down; *competition has forced prices down*

force up [fɔːs 'ʌp] *verb* to make something become higher; **to force prices up** = to make prices go up; *the war forced up the price of oil*

forecast ['fɔːkɑːst] **1** *noun* description or calculation of what will probably happen in the future; *the chairman did not believe the sales director's forecast of higher turnover*; *we based our calculations on the forecast turnover*; **cash flow forecast** = forecast of when cash will be received or paid out; **population forecast** = calculation of how many people will be living in a country or in a town at some point in the future; **sales forecast** = calculation of future sales **2** *verb* to calculate or to say what will probably happen in the future; *he is forecasting sales of £2m*; *economists have forecast a fall in the exchange rate* (NOTE: **forecasting - forecast**)

forecasting ['fɔːkɑːstɪŋ] *noun* calculating what will probably happen in the future; **manpower forecasting** = calculating how many workers will be needed in the future, and how many will actually be available

foreclose [fɔː'kləuz] *verb* to sell a property because the owner cannot repay money which he has borrowed (using the property as security); *to foreclose on a mortgaged property*

foreclosure [fɔː'kləuʒə] *noun* act of foreclosing

foreign ['fɒrən] *adjective* not belonging to your own country; *foreign cars have flooded our market*; *we are increasing our trade with foreign countries*; **foreign currency** = money of another country; **foreign goods** = goods manufactured in other countries; **foreign investments** = money invested in other countries; **foreign money order** = money order in a foreign currency which is payable to someone living in a foreign country; **foreign trade** = trade with other countries

a sharp setback in foreign trade accounted for most of the winter slowdown

Fortune

foreigner ['fɒrənə] *noun* person from another country

foreign exchange ['fɒrən ɪks'tʃeɪndʒ] *noun* **(a)** exchanging the money of one country for that of another; **foreign exchange broker** *or* **dealer** = person who deals on the foreign exchange market; **foreign exchange dealing** = buying and selling foreign currencies; **the foreign exchange markets** = market where people buy and sell foreign currencies **(b)** foreign currencies; **foreign exchange reserves** = foreign money held by a government to support its own currency and pay its debts; **foreign exchange transfer** = sending of money from one country to another

---
the dollar recovered a little lost ground on the foreign exchanges yesterday

Financial Times

---
the treasury says it needs the cash to rebuild its foreign reserves which have fallen from $19 billion when the government took office to $7 billion in August

Economist

---

foreman *or* **forewoman** ['fɔːmən *or* 'fɔːwʊmən] *noun* skilled worker in charge of several other workers (NOTE: plural is **foremen** *or* **forewomen**)

forex *or* **Forex** ['fɔːreks] = FOREIGN EXCHANGE

---
the amount of reserves sold by the authorities were not sufficient to move the $200 billion Forex market permanently

Duns Business Month

---

forfaiting ['fɔːfɪtɪŋ] *noun* providing finance for exporters, where an agent (the forfaiter) accepts a bill of exchange from an overseas customer; he buys the bill at a discount, and collects the payments from the customer in due course

forfeit ['fɔːfɪt] **1** *noun* taking something away as a punishment; **forfeit clause** = clause in a contract which says that goods or a deposit will be taken away if the contract is not obeyed; **the goods were declared forfeit** = the court said that the goods had to be taken away from the person who was holding them **2** *verb* to have something taken away as a

punishment; **to forfeit a patent** = to lose a patent because payments have not been made; **to forfeit a deposit** = to lose a deposit which was left for an item because you have decided not to buy that item

forfeiture ['fɔːfɪtʃə] *noun* act of forfeiting a property

forge [fɔːdʒ] *verb* to copy money or a signature illegally, to make a document which looks like a real one; *he tried to enter the country with forged documents*

forgery ['fɔːdʒəri] *noun* **(a)** making an illegal copy; *he was sent to prison for forgery* **(b)** illegal copy; *the signature was proved to be a forgery*

forget [fə'get] *verb* not to remember; *she forgot to put a stamp on the envelope*; *don't forget we're having lunch together tomorrow* (NOTE: **forgetting - forgot - forgotten**)

fork-lift truck ['fɔːklɪft 'trʌk] *noun* type of small tractor with two metal arms in front, used for lifting and moving pallets

form [fɔːm] **1** *noun* **(a)** **form of words** = words correctly laid out for a legal document; **receipt in due form** = correctly written receipt **(b)** official printed paper with blank spaces which have to be filled in with information; *you have to fill in form A20*; *each passenger was given a customs declaration form*; *the reps carry pads of order forms*; **application form** = form which has to be filled in to apply for something; **claim form** = form which has to be filled in when making an insurance claim **2** *verb* to start to organize; *the brothers have formed a new company*

forma ['fɔːmə] *see* PRO FORMA

formal ['fɔːməl] *adjective* clearly and legally written; *to make a formal application*; *to send a formal order*

formality [fɔː'mæləti] *noun* something which has to be done to obey the law; **customs formalities** = declaration of goods by the shipper and examination of them by customs

formally ['fɔːməli] *adverb* in a formal way; *we have formally applied for planning permission for the new shopping precinct*

formation *or* **forming** [fɔː'meɪʃən *or* 'fɔːmɪŋ] *noun* act of organizing; *the formation of a new company*

former ['fɔːmə] *adjective* before, at an earlier time; *the former chairman has taken a job with a rival company*

formerly ['fɔːməli] *adverb* at an earlier time; *he is currently managing director of Smith Ltd, but formerly he worked for Jones Brothers*

fortnight ['fɔːtnaɪt] *noun* two weeks; *I saw him a fortnight ago*; *we will be on holiday during the last fortnight of July* (NOTE: not used in American English)

fortune ['fɔːtʃuːn] *noun* large amount of money; *he made a fortune from investing in oil shares*; *she left her fortune to her three children*

'Fortune' 500 ['fɔːtʃuːn 'faɪv'hʌndrəd] the 500 largest companies in the USA, as listed annually in 'Fortune' magazine

forward ['fɔːwəd] **1** *adjective* in advance, to be paid at a later date; **forward buying** *or* **buying forward** = buying shares, currency or commodities at today's price for delivery at a later date; **forward contract** = agreement to buy foreign currency, shares or commodities for delivery at a later date at a certain price; **forward market** = market for purchasing foreign currency, oil or commodities for delivery at a later date; **forward (exchange) rate** = rate for purchase of foreign currency at a fixed price for delivery at a later date; *what are the forward rates for the pound?*; **forward sales** = sales for delivery at a later date **2** *adverb* **(a) to date a cheque forward** = to put a later date than the present one on a cheque; **carriage forward** *or* **freight forward** = deal where the customer pays for transporting the goods; **charges forward** = charges which will be paid by the customer **(b) to buy forward** = to buy foreign currency before you need it, in order to be certain of the exchange rate; **to sell forward** = to sell foreign currency for delivery at a later date **(c)** balance **brought forward** *or* **carried forward** = balance which is entered in an account at the end of a period and is then taken to be the starting point of the next period **3** *verb*

to forward something to someone = to send something to someone; *to forward a consignment to Nigeria*; **please forward** *or* **to be forwarded** = words written on an envelope, asking the person receiving it to send it on to the person whose name is written on it

forwarder ['fɔːwədə] *noun* **(freight) forwarder** = person or company which arranges shipping and customs documents for several shipments from different companies, putting them together to form one large shipment

forwarding ['fɔːwədɪŋ] *noun* **(a)** arranging shipping and customs documents; **air forwarding** = arranging for goods to be shipped by air; **forwarding agent** = FORWARDER; **forwarding instructions** *or* **instructions for forwarding** = instructions showing how the goods are to be shipped and delivered **(b) forwarding address** = address to which a person's mail can be sent on

foul [faʊl] *adjective* **foul bill of lading** = bill of lading which says that the goods were in bad condition when received by the shipper

founder ['faʊndə] **1** *noun* person who starts a company; **founder's shares** = special shares issued to the person who starts a company **2** *verb* the collapse, to fail; *the project foundered for lack of funds*

four [fɔː] *number* **the four O's** = simple way of summarizing the essentials of a marketing operation, which are objects, objectives, organization and operations; **the four P's** = simple way of summarizing the essentials of the marketing mix, which are product, price, promotion and place

four-part ['fɔː'pɑːt] *adjective* paper (for computers or typewriters) with a top sheet for the original and three other sheets for copies; *four-part invoices*; *four-part stationery*

fourth quarter ['fɔːθ 'kwɔːtə] *noun* period of three months from 1st October to the end of the year

Fr = FRANC

fraction ['frækʃən] *noun* very small amount; *only a fraction of the new share issue was subscribed*

fractional ['frækʃənl] *adjective* very small; **fractional certificate** = certificate for part of a share

fragile ['frædʒaɪl] *adjective* which can be easily broken; *there is an extra premium for insuring fragile goods in shipment*

franc [fræŋk] *noun* currency used with the euro in France and Belgium, also in Switzerland and many other countries; *French francs or Belgian francs or Swiss francs; it costs twenty-five Swiss francs;* **franc account** = bank account in francs (NOTE: in English usually written Fr before the figure: **Fr2,500** (say: 'two thousand, five hundred francs'). Currencies of different countries can be shown by the initial letters of the countries: **FFr** (French francs); **SwFr** (Swiss francs); **BFr** (Belgian francs), etc.)

franchise ['fræntʃaɪz] **1** *noun* licence to trade using a brand name and paying a royalty for it; *he has bought a printing franchise or a hot dog franchise* **2** *verb* to sell licences for people to trade using a brand name and paying a royalty; *his sandwich bar was so successful that he decided to franchise it*

> many new types of franchised businesses will join the ranks of the giant chains of fast-food restaurants, hotels and motels and rental car agencies
>
> *Franchising Opportunities*

franchisee [fræntʃaɪˈziː] *noun* person who runs a franchise

franchiser ['fræntʃaɪzə] *noun* person who licenses a franchise

franchising ['fræntʃaɪzɪŋ] *noun* act of selling a licence to trade as a franchise; *he runs his sandwich chain as a franchising operation*

franchisor ['fræntʃaɪzə] *noun* = FRANCHISER

franco ['fræŋkəʊ] *adverb* free

frank [fræŋk] *verb* to stamp the date and postage on a letter; **franking machine** = machine which marks the date and postage

on letters so that the sender does not need to use stamps

fraud [frɔːd] *noun* making money by making people believe something which is not true; *he got possession of the property by fraud; he was accused of frauds relating to foreign currency;* **to obtain money by fraud** = to obtain money by saying or doing something to cheat someone; **fraud squad** = special police department which investigates frauds; **Serious Fraud Office (SFO)** = British government department in charge of investigating major fraud in companies

fraudulent ['frɔːdjʊlənt] *adjective* not honest, aiming to cheat people; *a fraudulent transaction;* **fraudulent misrepresentation** = making a false statement with the intention of tricking a customer

fraudulently ['frɔːdjʊləntli] *adverb* not honestly; *goods imported fraudulently*

free [friː] **1** *adjective & adverb* **(a)** not costing any money; *I have been given a free ticket to the exhibition; the price includes free delivery; all goods in the store are delivered free; catalogue sent free on request;* **carriage free** = the customer does not pay for the shipping; **free gift** = present given by a shop to a customer who buys a certain amount of goods; *there is a free gift worth £25 to any customer buying a washing machine;* **free paper** *or* **freesheet** = newspaper which is given away free, and which relies for its income on its advertising; **free sample** = sample given free to advertise a product; **free trial** = testing of a machine with no payment involved; *to ask for a piece of equipment on two weeks' free trial;* **free of charge** = with no payment to be made; **free on board (FOB)** = (i) price including all the seller's costs until the goods are on the ship for transportation; (ii) *US* price includes all the seller's costs until the goods are delivered to a certain place; **free on rail (FOR)** = price including all the seller's costs until the goods are delivered to the railway for shipment **(b)** with no restrictions; **free collective bargaining** = negotiations over wage increases and working conditions between the management and the trade unions; **free**

competition = being free to compete without government interference; **free currency** = currency which is allowed by the government to be bought and sold without restriction; **free enterprise** = system of business with no interference from the government; **free market economy** = system where the government does not interfere in business activity in any way; **free port** *or* **free trade zone** = port or area where there are no customs duties; **free of tax** *or* **tax-free** = with no tax having to be paid; *he was given a tax-free sum of £25,000 when he was made redundant*; *interest is paid free of tax or tax-free interest*; **interest-free credit** *or* **loan** = credit or loan where no interest is paid by the borrower; **free of duty** *or* **duty-free** = with no duty to be paid; *to import wine free of duty or duty-free*; **free trade** = system where goods can go from one country to another without any restrictions; *the government adopted a free trade policy*; **free trade area** = group of countries practising free trade; **free trader** = person who is in favour of free trade **(c)** not busy, not occupied; *are there any free tables in the restaurant?*; *I shall be free in a few minutes*; *the chairman always keeps Friday afternoon free for a game of bridge* **2** *verb* to make something available or easy; *the government's decision has freed millions of pounds for investment*

American business as a whole is increasingly free from heavy dependence on manufacturing
Sunday Times

can free trade be reconciled with a strong dollar resulting from floating exchange rates?
Duns Business Month

free traders hold that the strong dollar is the primary cause of the nation's trade problems
Duns Business Month

freebie ['fri:bi:] *noun (informal)* product or service supplied free of charge (especially a gift to an agent or journalist)

freehold property ['fri:həuld 'prɒpəti] *noun* property which the owner holds for ever and on which no rent is paid

freeholder ['fri:həuldə] *noun* person who owns a freehold property

freelance ['fri:lɑ:ns] **1** *adjective & noun* independent worker who works for several different companies but is not employed by any of them; *we have about twenty freelances working for us or about twenty people working for us on a freelance basis*; *she is a freelance journalist* **2** *adverb* selling your work to various firms, but not being employed by any of them; *he works freelance as a designer* **3** *verb* **(a)** to do work for several firms but not be employed by any of them; *she freelances for the local newspapers* **(b)** to send work out to be done by a freelancer; *we freelance work out to several specialists*

freelancer ['fri:lɑ:nsə] *noun* freelance worker

freely ['fri:li] *adverb* with no restrictions; *money should circulate freely within the EU*

freephone ['fri:fəun] *noun GB* system where one can telephone to reply to an advertisement *or* to place an order or to ask for information and the seller pays for the call

freepost ['fri:pəust] *noun GB* system where one can write to an advertiser to place an order or to ask for information to be sent, and the seller pays the postage

freesheet ['fri:ʃi:t] *noun* = FREE PAPER

freeze [fri:z] **1** *noun* **credit freeze** = period when lending by banks is restricted by the government; **wages and prices freeze** *or* **a freeze on wages and prices** = period when wages and prices are not allowed to be increased **2** *verb* to keep money, costs, etc., at their present level and not allow them to rise; *we have frozen expenditure at last year's level*; *to freeze wages and prices*; *to freeze credits*; *to freeze company dividends* (NOTE: **freezing - froze - has frozen**)

freeze out ['fri:z 'aut] *verb* **to freeze out competition** = to trade successfully and cheaply and so prevent competitors from operating

freight [freɪt] **1** *noun* **(a)** cost of transporting goods by air, sea or land; *at an auction, the buyer pays the freight*; **freight charges** *or* **freight rates** = money charged for transporting goods; *freight charges have gone up sharply this year*; **freight costs** = money paid to transport goods; **freight forward** = deal where the customer pays for transporting the goods **(b) air freight** = shipping of goods in an aircraft; *to send a shipment by air freight*; **air freight charges** *or* **rates** = money charged for sending goods by air **(c)** goods which are transported; **to take on freight** = to load goods onto a ship, train or truck; *US* **freight car** = railway wagon for carrying goods; **freight depot** = central point where goods are collected before being shipped; **freight elevator** = strong lift for carrying goods up and down inside a building; **freight forwarder** = person or company which arranges shipping and customs documents for several shipments from different companies, putting them together to form one large shipment; **freight plane** = aircraft which carries goods, not passengers; **freight train** = train used for carrying goods **2** *verb* **to freight goods** = to send goods; *we freight goods to all parts of the USA*

> the airline will allow freight forwarder customers to track and trace consignments on the airline's website
>
> *Lloyd's List*

freightage [ˈfreɪtɪdʒ] *noun* cost of transporting goods

freighter [ˈfreɪtə] *noun* **(a)** aircraft or ship which carries goods **(b)** person or company which organizes the transport of goods

freightliner [ˈfreɪtlaɪnə] *noun* train which carries goods in containers; *the shipment has to be delivered to the freightliner depot*

frequent [ˈfriːkwənt] *adjective* which comes, goes or takes place often; *there is a frequent ferry service to France*; *we send*

frequent faxes to New York; how frequent are the planes to Birmingham?

frequently [ˈfriːkwəntli] *adverb* often; *the photocopier is frequently out of use*; *we email our New York office very frequently - at least four times a day*

friendly society [ˈfrendli səˈsaɪəti] *noun* group of people who pay regular subscriptions to a fund which is used to help members of the group when they are ill or in financial difficulties

fringe benefits [ˈfrɪndʒ ˈbenɪfɪts] *plural noun* extra items given by a company to workers in addition to a salary (such as company cars, private health insurance)

front [frʌnt] *noun* **(a)** part of something which faces away from the back; *the front of the office building is on the High Street*; *the front page of the company report has a photograph of the managing director*; *our ad appeared on the front page of the newspaper* **(b) in front of** = before, on the front side of something; *they put up a 'for sale' sign in front of the factory*; *the chairman's name is in front of all the others on the staff list* **(c)** business or person used to hide an illegal trade; *his restaurant is a front for a drugs organization* **(d) money up front** = payment in advance; *they are asking for £10,000 up front before they will consider the deal*; *he had to put money up front before he could clinch the deal*

front-end loaded [ˈfrʌntend ˈlaʊdɪd] *adjective* (investment or insurance) where most of the management charges are incurred in the first year, and are not spread out over the whole period

front-line management [ˈfrʌntlaɪn ˈmænɪdʒmənt] *adjective* managers who have immediate contact with the workers

front man [ˈfrʌnt ˈmæn] *noun* person who seems honest but is hiding an illegal trade

frozen [ˈfrəʊzn] *adjective* not allowed to be changed or used; **frozen account** = bank account where the money cannot be moved or used because of a court order; **frozen assets** = a company's assets which by law cannot be sold because someone has a claim against them; **frozen credits** = credit in an account which cannot be moved; **his**

assets have been frozen by the court = the court does not allow him to sell his assets; *see also* FREEZE

frustrate [frʌs'treɪt] *verb* to prevent something (especially the terms of a contract) being fulfilled

FSA = FINANCIAL SERVICES AUTHORITY

ft [fʊt] = FOOT

FT ['ef'tiː] = FINANCIAL TIMES

fuel [fjʊəl] **1** *noun* material (like oil, coal, gas) used to give power; *the annual fuel bill for the plant has doubled over the last years*; *he has bought a car with low fuel consumption* **2** *verb* to add to; *market worries were fuelled by news of an increase in electricity charges*; *the rise in the share price was fuelled by rumours of a takeover bid* (NOTE: British spelling **fuelled - fuelling** but American spelling **fueled - fueling**)

fulfil *US* **fulfill** [fʊl'fɪl] *verb* to complete something in a satisfactory way; *the clause regarding payments has not been fulfilled*; **to fulfil an order** = to supply the items which have been ordered; *we are so understaffed that we cannot fulfil any more orders before Christmas*

fulfilment *US* **fulfillment** [fʊl'fɪlmənt] *noun* carrying something out in a satisfactory way; **order fulfilment** = supplying items which have been ordered

full [fʊl] *adjective* **(a)** with as much inside it as possible; *the train was full of commuters*; *is the container full yet?*; *we sent a lorry full of spare parts to our warehouse*; *when the disk is full, don't forget to make a backup copy* **(b)** complete, including everything; **we are working at full capacity** = we are doing as much work as possible; **full costs** = all the costs of manufacturing a product, including both fixed and variable costs; **full cover** = insurance cover against all risks; **in full discharge of a debt** = paying a debt completely; **full employment** = situation where all the people who can work have jobs; **full fare** = ticket for a journey by an adult at full price; **full price** = price with no discount; *he bought a full-price ticket*; **full-service banking** = banking offering a whole range of services

(including mortgages, loans, pensions, etc.) **(c)** **in full** = completely; *give your full name and address* or *your name and address in full*; *he accepted all our conditions in full*; **full refund** or **refund paid in full**; *he got a full refund when he complained about the service*; **full payment** or **payment in full** = paying all money owed

---

a tax-free lump sum can be
taken partly in lieu of a full
pension
Investors Chronicle

---

full-scale ['fʊl'skeɪl] *adjective* complete, very thorough; *the MD ordered a full-scale review of credit terms*

---

the administration launched a
full-scale investigation into
maintenance procedures
Fortune

---

full-time ['fʊl'taɪm] *adjective & adverb* working all the normal working time (i.e. about seven hours a day, five days a week); *she is in full-time work* or *she works full-time* or *she is in full-time employment*; *he is one of our full-time staff*; *she is a full-time official of the union*

full-timer ['fʊl'taɪmə] *noun* person who works full-time

fully ['fʊli] *adverb* completely; **fully-paid shares** = shares where the full face value has been paid; **fully paid-up capital** = all money paid for the issued capital shares

---

issued and fully paid capital
is $100 million
Hongkong Standard

---

function ['fʌŋkʃən] **1** *noun* **(a)** duty or job; **management function** or **function of management** = the duties of being a manager **(b)** special feature available on a computer; *the program had a spelling-checker function but no built-in text-editing function*; **function code** = computer code that controls an action rather than representing a character; **function key** = key switch that has been assigned a particular task or sequence of instructions (function keys often form a separate group of keys on the keyboard, and have specific functions attached to them. They may be labelled F1, F2, etc.) **2**

verb to work; *the advertising campaign is functioning smoothly*; *the new management structure does not seem to be functioning very well*

fund [fʌnd] **1** *noun* **(a)** money set aside for a special purpose; **contingency fund =** money set aside in case it is needed urgently; **pension fund =** money which provides pensions for retired members of staff; **the International Monetary Fund (IMF) =** (part of the United Nations) a type of bank which helps member states in financial difficulties, gives financial advice to members and encourages world trade **(b)** money invested in an investment trust as part of a unit trust or given to a financial adviser to invest on behalf of a client; **managed fund** *or* **fund of funds =** unit trust fund which is invested in specialist funds within the group and can be switched from one specialized investment area to another; **fund management =** dealing with the investment of sums of money on behalf of clients; **fund manager =** person who invests money on behalf of clients **2** *verb* to provide money for a purpose; **to fund a company =** to provide money for a company to operate; *the company does not have enough resources to fund its expansion programme*

the S&L funded all borrowers' development costs, including accrued interest

Barrons

funded [ˈfʌndɪd] *adjective* backed by long-term loans; *long-term funded capital;* **GB funded debt =** part of the National Debt which pays interest, but where there is no date for repayment of the principal

funding [ˈfʌndɪŋ] *noun* **(a)** providing money for spending; *the bank is providing the funding for the new product launch* **(b)** changing a short-term debt into a long-term loan; *the capital expenditure programme requires long-term funding*

funds *plural noun* **(a)** money which is available for spending; *the company has no funds to pay for the research programme*; **the company called for extra funds =** the company asked for more money; **to run out of funds =** to come to

the end of the money available; **public funds =** government money available for expenditure; *the cost was paid for out of public funds*; **conversion of funds =** using money which does not belong to you for a purpose for which it is not supposed to be used; **to convert funds to another purpose =** to use money for a wrong purpose; **to convert funds to your own use =** to use someone else's money for yourself; *see also* INSUFFICIENT **(b)** *GB* **the Funds =** government stocks and securities

small innovative companies have been hampered for lack of funds

Sunday Times

the company was set up with funds totalling NorKr 145m

Lloyd's List

funny money [ˈfʌni ˈmʌni] *noun* strange types of shares or bonds offered by companies or their brokers, which are not the usual forms of loan stock

furnish [ˈfɜːnɪʃ] *verb* **(a)** to supply or to provide; *the VAT office has asked up to furnish details of all our transactions since August* **(b)** to put furniture into an office or room; *he furnished his office with secondhand chairs and desks*; *the company spent £10,000 on furnishing the chairman's office*; **furnished accommodation =** flat, house, etc., which is let with furniture in it

furniture [ˈfɜːnɪtʃə] *noun* chairs, tables, beds, etc.; **office furniture =** chairs, desks, filing cabinets used in an office; *he deals in secondhand office furniture*; *an office furniture store*; **furniture depository =** warehouse where you can store the furniture from a house when you are not using it

further [ˈfɜːðə] **1** *adjective* **(a)** at a larger distance away; *the office is further down the High Street*; *the flight from Paris terminates in New York - for further destinations you must change to internal flights* **(b)** additional or extra; *further orders will be dealt with by our London office*; *nothing can be done while we are awaiting further instructions*; *the bank has asked for further details* *or* *particulars*; *he had borrowed £100,000 and then tried to borrow a further £25,000*; *the company is asking for further credit*; *he asked for a further six weeks to pay* (c) **further to** = referring to something in addition; **further to our letter of the 21st** = in addition to what we said in our letter; **further to your letter of the 21st** = here is information which you asked for in your letter; **further to our telephone conversation** = here is some information which we discussed **2** *verb* to help to grow, to promote; *he was accused of using his membership of the council to further his own interests*

future ['fju:tʃə] **1** *adjective* referring to time to come or to something which has not yet happened; **future delivery** = delivery at a later date **2** *noun* time which has not yet happened; *try to be more careful in future*; *in future all reports must be sent to Australia by air*

futures ['fju:tʃəz] *plural noun* trading in shares or commodities for delivery at a later date; *gold rose 5% on the commodity futures market yesterday*; **futures contract** = contract for the purchase of commodities for delivery at a date in the future

cocoa futures plummeted in November to their lowest levels in seven years
Business in Africa

COMMENT: a futures contract is a contract to purchase; if an investor is bullish, he will buy a contract, but if he feels the market will go down, he will sell one

Gg

g = GRAM

G5, G7, G8, G10 [dʒiː'faɪv or dʒiː'sevn or dʒiː'eɪt or dʒiː'ten] = GROUP OF FIVE, GROUP OF SEVEN, GROUP OF EIGHT, GROUP OF TEN; *see* GROUP

gain [geɪn] **1** *noun* **(a)** increase, becoming larger; **gain in experience** = getting more experience; **gain in profitability** = becoming more profitable **(b)** increase in profit, price or value; *oil shares showed gains on the Stock Exchange*; *property shares put on gains of 10%-15%*; **capital gain** = money made by selling fixed assets, shares, or certain other types of property (such as works of art, leases, etc.; if the asset is sold for less than its purchase price, the result is a capital loss); **capital gains tax** = tax paid on capital gains; **short-term gains** = increase in price made over a short period **2** *verb* **(a)** to get or to obtain; *he gained some useful experience working in a bank*; **to gain control of a business** = to buy more than 50% of the shares so that you can direct the business **(b)** to rise in value; *the dollar gained six points on the foreign exchange markets*

gainful ['geɪnfʊl] *adjective* **gainful employment** = employment which pays money

gainfully ['geɪnfʊli] *adverb* **gainfully employed** = working and earning money

gallon ['gælən] *noun* measure of liquids (= 4.5 litres); **the car does twenty-five miles per gallon** *or* **the car does twenty-five miles to the gallon** = the car uses one gallon of petrol in travelling twenty-five miles (NOTE: usually written **gal** after figures: **25gal**. Note also that the gallon is now no longer officially used in the UK)

galloping inflation ['gæləpɪŋ ɪn'fleɪʃən] *noun* very rapid inflation which is almost impossible to reduce

gap [gæp] *noun* empty space; **gap in the market** = opportunity to make a product or provide a service which is needed but which no one has sold before; *to look for or to find a gap in the market*; *this laptop has filled a real gap in the market*; **dollar gap** = situation where the supply of dollars is not enough to satisfy the demand for them from overseas buyers; **trade gap** = difference in value between a country's imports and exports

> these savings are still not great enough to overcome the price gap between American products and those of other nations
>
> *Duns Business Month*

garnishee [gɑːnɪ'ʃiː] *noun* person who owes money to a creditor and is ordered by a court to pay that money to a creditor of the creditor, and not to the creditor himself; **garnishee order** *US* **garnishment** = court order, making a garnishee pay money not to the debtor, but to a third party

gasoline ['gæsəliːn] *noun US* liquid, made from petroleum, used to drive a car engine (NOTE: British English is **petrol**)

gate [geɪt] *noun* **(a)** door leading into a field **(b)** door leading to an aircraft at an airport; *flight AZ270 is now boarding at Gate 23* **(c)** number of people attending a sports match; *there was a gate of 30,000 at the football final*

gather ['gæðə] *verb* **(a)** to collect together, to put together; *he gathered his papers together before the meeting started*; *she has been gathering information on import controls from* *various sources* **(b)** to understand, to find out; *I gather he has left the office*; *did you gather who will be at the meeting?*

gazump [gə'zʌmp] *verb* **he was gazumped** = his agreement to buy the house was cancelled because someone offered more money

gazumping [gə'zʌmpɪŋ] *noun* offering more money for a house than another buyer has done, so as to be sure of buying it

GDP   ['dʒiːdiː'piː]   =   GROSS DOMESTIC PRODUCT

gear [gɪə] *verb* **(a)** to link to or to connect with; **salary geared to the cost of living** = salary which rises as the cost of living increases **(b) a company which is highly geared** *or* **a highly-geared company** = company which has a high proportion of its funds from fixed-interest borrowings

gearing ['gɪərɪŋ] *noun* **(a)** ratio of capital borrowed by a company at a fixed rate of interest to the company's total capital **(b)** borrowing money at fixed interest which is then used to produce more money than the interest paid

COMMENT: high gearing (when a company is said to be 'highly geared') indicates that the level of borrowings is high when compared to its ordinary share capital; a lowly-geared company has borrowings which are relatively low. High gearing has the effect of increasing a company's profitability when the company's trading is expanding; if the trading pattern slows down, then the high interest charges associated with gearing will increase the rate of slowdown

gear up ['gɪər 'ʌp] *verb* to get ready; **to gear up for a sales drive** = to make all the plans and get ready for a sales drive; *the company is gearing itself up for expansion into the African market*

general ['dʒenərəl] *adjective* **(a)** ordinary, not special; **general expenses** = all kinds of minor expenses, money spent on the day-to-day costs of running a business; **general manager** = manager in charge of the administration of a company; **general office** = main administrative office of a company **(b)** dealing with everything or with everybody; **general audit** = examining all the books and accounts of a company; **general average** = sharing of the cost of lost goods between all parties to an insurance; **general election** = election of a government by all the voters in a country; **general meeting** = meeting of all the shareholders of a company; **Annual General Meeting (AGM)** = meeting of all the shareholders, when the company's financial situation is discussed with the directors; **Extraordinary General Meeting (EGM)** = special meeting of shareholders to discuss an important matter; **general strike** = strike of all the workers in a country **(c) general trading** = dealing in all types of goods; **general store** = small country shop which sells a large range of goods

generally ['dʒenərəli] *adverb* normally or usually; *the office is generally closed between Christmas and the New Year*; *we generally give a 25% discount for bulk purchases*

generous ['dʒenərəs] *adjective* (person) who is glad to give money; *the staff contributed a generous sum for the retirement present for the manager*

gentleman ['dʒentlmən] *noun* **(a)** 'gentlemen' = way of starting to talk to a group of men; *'good morning, gentlemen - if everyone is here, the meeting can start'*; *'well, gentlemen, we have all read the report from our Australian office'*; **'ladies and gentlemen'** = way of starting to talk to a group of women and men **(b)** man; **gentleman's agreement** *US* **gentlemen's agreement** = verbal agreement between two parties who respect each other; *they have a gentleman's agreement not to trade in each other's area*

genuine ['dʒenjuɪn] *adjective* true or real; *a genuine Picasso*; *a genuine leather purse*; **the genuine article** = real article, not an imitation; **genuine purchaser** = someone who is really interested in buying

genuineness ['dʒenjuɪnnəs] *noun* being real, not being an imitation

Gesellschaft [gə'zelʃɑːft] *German for* company; **Gesellschaft mit beschr„nkter Haftung (GmbH)** = private limited company

get [get] *verb* **(a)** to receive; *we got a letter from the solicitor this morning*; *when do you expect to get more stock?*; *he gets £250 a week for doing nothing*; *she got £5,000 for her car* **(b)** to arrive at a place; *the shipment got to Canada six weeks late*; *she finally got to the office at 10.30* (NOTE: **getting - got - has got** US **gotten**)

get across ['get ə'krɒs] *verb* to make someone understand something; *the manager tried to get across to the workforce why some people were being made redundant*

get along ['get ə'lɒŋ] *verb* to manage; *we are getting along quite well with only half the staff we had before*

get back ['get 'bæk] *verb* to receive something which you had before; *I got my money back after I had complained to the manager*; *he got his initial investment back in two months*

get on ['get 'ɒn] *verb* **(a)** to work, to manage; *how is the new secretary getting on?* **(b)** to succeed; *my son is getting on well - he has just been promoted*

get on with ['get 'ɒn wɪð] *verb* **(a)** to be friendly, to work well with someone; *she does not get on with her new boss* **(b)** to go on doing work; *the staff got on with the work and finished the order on time*

get out ['get 'aʊt] *verb* **(a)** to produce something; *the accounts department got out the draft accounts in time for the meeting* **(b)** to sell an investment; *he didn't like what he read in the company's annual report, so he got out before the company collapsed*

get out of ['get 'aʊt əv] *verb* to stop trading in (a product or an area); *the company is getting out of computers*; *we got out of the South American market*

get round ['get 'raʊnd] *verb* to avoid; *we tried to get round the embargo by shipping from Canada*

get through ['get 'θruː] *verb* **(a)** to speak to someone on the phone; *I tried to get through to the complaints department* **(b)** to be successful; *he got through his exams, so he is now a qualified engineer* **(c)** to try to make someone understand; *I could not get through to her that I had to be at the airport by 2.15*

gift [gɪft] *noun* thing given to someone; **gift coupon** *or* **gift token** *or* **gift voucher** = card, bought in a store, which is given as a present and which must be exchanged in that store for goods; *we gave her a gift token for her birthday*; **gift shop** = shop selling small items which are given as presents; **gift inter vivos** = present given to another living person; **free gift** = present given by a shop to a customer who buys a certain amount of goods

gift-wrap ['gɪft'ræp] *verb* to wrap a present in attractive paper; *do you want this book gift-wrapped?*

gift-wrapping ['gɪft'ræpɪŋ] *noun* **(a)** service in a store for wrapping presents for customers **(b)** attractive paper for wrapping presents

gilt-edged ['gɪlt'edʒd] *adjective* investment which is very safe; **gilt-edged stock** *or* **securities** = government securities

gilts [gɪlts] *plural noun GB* government securities

gimmick ['gɪmɪk] *noun* clever idea or trick; *a publicity gimmick*; *the PR people thought up this new advertising gimmick*

giro ['dʒaɪrəʊ] *noun* **(a)** **giro system** = banking system in which money can be transferred from one account to another without writing a cheque (the money is first removed from the payer's account and then credited to the payee's account; as opposed to a cheque payment, which is credited to the payee's account first and then claimed from the payer's account); *GB* **National Giro** = banking system which allows account holders to move money from one account to another free of cost; *a giro cheque*; *his giro account number*; *she put £25 into her giro account*; to pay by **bank giro transfer** **(b)** a giro cheque

Girobank ['dʒaɪrəʊbæŋk] *noun* bank in a giro system; *a National Girobank account*

give [gɪv] *verb* **(a)** to pass something to someone as a present; *the office gave him a clock when he retired* **(b)** to pass something to someone; *she gave the documents to the accountant*; *can you give me some information about the new* *mobile phone system?*; *do not give any details to the police* (c) to organize; *the company gave a party on a boat to publicize its new discount system* (NOTE: **giving - gave - has given**)

give away ['gɪv ə'weɪ] *verb* to give something as a free present; *we are giving away a pocket calculator with each £10 of purchases*

giveaway ['gɪvəweɪ] **1** *adjective* **giveaway paper** = newspaper which is given away free, and which relies for its income on its advertising; **to sell at giveaway prices** = to sell at very cheap prices **2** *noun* thing which is given as a free gift when another item is bought

global ['gləubəl] *adjective* (a) referring to the whole world; *we offer a 24-hour global delivery service* (b) referring to all of something; *the management proposed a global review of salaries*

glue [glu:] **1** *noun* material which sticks items together; *she put some glue on the back of the poster to fix it to the wall*; *the glue on the envelope does not stick very well* **2** *verb* to stick things together with glue; *he glued the label to the box*

glut [glʌt] **1** *noun* **a glut of produce** = too much produce, which is then difficult to sell; *a coffee glut or a glut of coffee*; **glut of money** = situation where there is too much money available to borrowers **2** *verb* to fill the market with something which is then difficult to sell; *the market is glutted with cheap cameras* (NOTE: **glutting - glutted**)

gm = GRAM

GmbH *German* = GESELLSCHAFT MIT BESCHRANKTER HAFTUNG

gnome [nəum] *noun* (*informal*) **the gnomes of Zurich** = important Swiss international bankers

if the Frankfurt gnomes put the interest rate brake on a government too carefree for too long about its debt-ridden fiscal policies, they did so out of concern for Germany's monetary stability
                                        Times

GNP ['dʒi:en'pi:] = GROSS NATIONAL PRODUCT

go [gəu] *verb* (a) to move from one place to another; *the cheque went to your bank yesterday*; *the plane goes to Frankfurt, then to Rome*; *he is going to our Lagos office* (b) to be placed; *the date goes at the top of the letter* (NOTE: **going - went - has gone**)

go-ahead ['gəuəhed] **1** *noun* **to give something the go-ahead** = to approve something, to say that something can be done; *his project got a government go-ahead*; *the board refused to give the go-ahead to the expansion plan* **2** *adjective* energetic, keen to do well; *he is a very go-ahead type*; *she works for a go-ahead clothing company*

goal [gəul] *noun* aim, something which you try to do; *our goal is to break even within twelve months*; *the company achieved all its goals*

go back on ['gəu 'bæk ɒn] *verb* not to do what has been promised; *two months later they went back on the agreement*

godown ['gəudaun] *noun* warehouse (in the Far East)

gofer ['gəufə] *noun* US person who does all types of work in an office for low wages

going ['gəuɪŋ] *adjective* (a) active or busy; **to sell a business as a going concern** = to sell a business as an active trading company; **it is a going concern** = the company is working (and making a profit) (b) **the going price** = the usual or current price, the price which is being charged now; *what is the going price for 1975 Volkswagen Beetles?*; **the going rate** = the usual or current rate of payment; *we pay the going rate for typists*; *the going rate for offices is £10 per square metre*

going to ['gəuɪŋ tu] *verb* **to be going to do something** = to be just about to start doing something; *the firm is going to open an office in New York next year*; *when are you going to answer my letter?*

go into ['gəu 'ɪntu] *verb* (a) **to go into business** = to start in business; *he went into business as a car dealer*; *she went into business in partnership with her son* (b) to examine carefully; *the bank wants to go into the details of the inter-company loans*

gold [gǝʊld] *noun* **(a)** very valuable yellow metal; *you can buy gold coins at certain Swiss banks*; *he has a licence to deal in gold*; **gold bullion** = bars of gold **(b) the country's gold reserves** = the country's store of gold kept to pay international debts; **the gold standard** = linking of the value of a currency to the value of a quantity of gold; **the pound came off the gold standard** = the pound stopped being linked to the value of gold **(c) gold point** = amount by which a currency which is linked to gold can vary in price **(d) gold shares** *or* **golds** = shares in gold mines

COMMENT: gold is the traditional hedge against investment uncertainties. People buy gold in the form of coins or bars, because they think it will maintain its value when other investments such as government bonds, foreign currency, property, etc., may not be so safe. Gold is relatively portable, and small quantities can be taken from country to country if an emergency occurs. This view, which is prevalent when the political situation is uncertain, has not been borne out in recent years, and gold has not maintained its value for some time

gold card [ˈgǝʊld ˈkɑːd] *noun* credit card issued to important customers (i.e., those with a certain level of income), which gives certain privileges, such as a higher spending limit than ordinary credit cards

golden [ˈgǝʊldǝn] *adjective* made of gold, like gold; **golden hallo** = cash inducement paid to someone to encourage him to change jobs and move to another company; **golden handcuffs** = contractual arrangement to make sure that a valued member of staff stays in his job, by which he is offered special financial advantages if he stays and heavy penalties if he leaves; **golden handshake** = large, usually tax-free, sum of money given to a director who resigns from a company before the end of his service contract; *when the company was taken over, the sales director received a golden handshake of £25,000*; **golden parachute** = special contract for a director of a company, which gives him advantageous financial terms if

he has to resign when the company is taken over; **golden share** = share in a privatized company which is retained by the government and carries special privileges (such as the right to veto foreign takeover bids)

goldmine [ˈgǝʊldmaɪn] *noun* mine which produces gold; **that shop is a little goldmine** = that shop is a very profitable business

gondola [ˈgɒndǝlǝ] *noun* display case in a supermarket on either side of which shoppers can pass

good [gʊd] *adjective* **(a)** not bad; **a good buy** = excellent item which has been bought cheaply; **to buy something in good faith** = to buy something thinking it is of good quality, that it has not been stolen or that it is not an imitation **(b) a good deal of** = a large quantity of; *we wasted a good deal of time discussing the arrangements for the AGM*; *the company had to pay a good deal for the building site*; **a good many** = very many; *a good many staff members have joined the union*

goods [gʊdz] *plural noun* **(a) goods and chattels** = moveable personal possessions **(b)** items which can be moved and are for sale; **goods in bond** = imported goods held by customs until duty is paid; **capital goods** = machinery, buildings and raw materials which are used to make other goods; **consumer goods** *or* **consumable goods** = goods bought by the general public and not by businesses; **dry goods** = cloth and clothes; **finished goods** = manufactured goods which are ready to be sold; **household goods** = items which are used in the home; **luxury goods** = expensive items which are not basic necessities; **manufactured goods** = items which are made by machine **(c) goods depot** = central warehouse where goods can be stored until they are moved; **goods train** = train for carrying freight

profit margins are lower in the industries most exposed to foreign competition - machinery, transportation equipment and electrical goods

Sunday Times

the minister wants people buying goods ranging from washing machines to houses to demand facts on energy costs

Times

goodwill ['gudwɪl] *noun* good reputation of a business; *he paid £10,000 for the goodwill of the shop and £4,000 for the stock*

> COMMENT: goodwill can include the trading reputation, the patents, the trade names used, the value of a 'good site', etc., and is very difficult to establish accurately. It is an intangible asset, and so is not shown as an asset in a company's accounts, unless it figures as part of the purchase price paid when acquiring another company

go on *verb* (a) ['gəu 'ɒn] to continue; *the staff went on working in spite of the fire*; *the chairman went on speaking for two hours* (b) ['gəu ɒn] to work with; *the figures for 1998 are all he has to go on*; *we have to go on the assumption that sales will not double next year* (NOTE: you go on **doing** something)

go out ['gəu 'aut] *verb* to go out of business = to stop trading; *the firm went out of business last week*

go-slow ['gəu'sləu] *noun* slowing down of production by workers as a protest against the management; *a series of go-slows reduced production*

govern ['gʌvən] *verb* to rule a country; *the country is governed by a group of military leaders*

governance ['gʌvənəns] *noun* the philosophy of ruling, whether a country or a company; **corporate governance** = theory of the way companies should be run

the chairman has committed the cardinal sin in corporate governance - he acted against the wishes and interests of the shareholders

Investors Chronicle

in two significant decisions, the Securities and Exchange Board of India today allowed trading of shares through the Internet and set a deadline

for companies to conform to norms for good corporate governance

The Hindu

government ['gʌvnmənt] *noun* (a) organization which administers a country; **central government** = main organization dealing with the affairs of the whole country; **local government** = organizations dealing with the affairs of a small area of the country; **provincial government** *or* **state government** = organization dealing with the affairs of a province or of a state (b) coming from the government, referring to the government; *government employees can belong to one of two unions*; *local government staff are to get a salary rise*; *government intervention* or *intervention by the government helped to solve the dispute*; *a government ban on the import of arms*; *a government investigation into organized crime*; *government officials prevented him leaving the country*; *government policy is outlined in the booklet*; *government regulations state that import duty has to be paid on luxury items*; *he invested all his savings in government securities*; **government support** = financial help given by the government; *the aircraft industry relies on government support*; **government annuity** = money paid each year by the government; **government bonds** *or* **government securities** = bonds or other securities issued by the government on a regular basis as a method of borrowing money for government expenditure; **government contractor** = company which supplies goods or services to the government on contract

governmental [gʌvən'mentl] *adjective* referring to a government

government-backed ['gʌvnmənt'bækt] *adjective* backed by the government

government-controlled ['gʌvnməntkən'trəuld] *adjective* under the direct control of the government; *advertisements cannot be placed in the government-controlled newspapers*

government-regulated
['gʌvnmənt'regjʊleɪtɪd] *adjective* regulated
by the government

government-sponsored
['gʌvnmənt'spɒnsəd] *adjective*
encouraged by the government and backed
by government money; *he is working in a
government-sponsored scheme to help
small businesses*

governor ['gʌvnə] *noun* **(a)** person in
charge of an important institution; **the
Governor of the Bank of England =**
person (nominated by the British
government) who is in charge of the Bank
of England (NOTE: the American equivalent is
the Chairman of the Federal Reserve Board)
(b) *US* one of the members of the Federal
Reserve Board

grace [greɪs] *noun* favour shown by
granting a delay; *to give a creditor a period
of grace or two weeks' grace*

grade [greɪd] **1** *noun* level or rank; *top
grade of civil servant*; *to reach the top
grade in the civil service*; **high-grade =** of
very good quality; *high-grade petrol*; **a
high-grade trade delegation =** a
delegation made up of important people;
low-grade = not very important, not of
very good quality; *a low-grade official
from the Ministry of Commerce*; *the car
runs well on low-grade petrol*; **top-grade
=** most important, of the best quality;
top-grade petrol **2** *verb* **(a)** to sort
something into different levels of quality;
to grade coal **(b)** to make something rise in
steps; **graded advertising rates =** rates
which become cheaper as you take more
advertising space; **graded tax =** (i) tax
which rises according to income; (ii) *US*
tax on property which is higher if the
property has not been kept in a good state
by the owner **(c)** **graded hotel =** good
quality hotel

gradual ['grædʊəl] *adjective* slow, step
by step; *1999 saw a gradual return to
profits*; *his CV describes his gradual rise
to the position of company chairman*

gradually ['grædʊəli] *adverb* slowly,
step by step; *the company has gradually
become more profitable*; *she gradually
learnt the details of the import-export
business*

graduate ['grædʒʊət] *noun* person who
has a degree from a university or college;
graduate entry = entry of graduates into
employment with a company; *the graduate
entry into the civil service*; **graduate
training scheme =** training scheme for
graduates; **graduate trainee =** person in a
graduate training scheme

graduated ['grædʒʊeɪtɪd] *adjective*
rising in steps; **graduated income tax =**
tax which rises in steps (each level of
income is taxed at a higher percentage);
graduated pension scheme = pension
scheme where the benefit is calculated as a
percentage of the salary of each person in
the scheme; **graduated taxation =** tax
system where the percentage of tax paid
rises as the income rises (also called
'progressive taxation')

gram *or* **gramme** [græm] *noun* measure
of weight (one thousandth of a kilo);
*first-class postage for letters is 26p for the
first 20 grams* (NOTE: usually written **g** or **gm**
with figures: **25g**)

grand [grænd] **1** *adjective* important;
grand plan = major plan; *he explained his
grand plan for redeveloping the factory
site*; **grand total =** final total made by
adding several subtotals **2** *noun (informal)*
one thousand pounds or dollars; *they
offered him fifty grand for the
information*

grant [grɑːnt] **1** *noun* money given by the
government to help pay for something; *the
laboratory has a government grant to
cover the cost of the development
programme*; *the government has
allocated grants towards the costs of the
scheme*; **grant-aided scheme =** scheme
which is funded by a government grant **2**
verb to agree to give someone something;
to grant someone a loan or a subsidy; *the
local authority granted the company an
interest-free loan to start up the new
factory*

| the budget grants a tax |
| exemption for $500,000 in |
| capital gains |
| *Toronto Star* |

graph [grɑːf] *noun* diagram which shows
statistics as a drawing; *to set out the results
in a graph*; *to draw a graph showing the*

rising profitability; *the sales graph shows a steady rise*; **graph paper** = special paper with many little squares, used for drawing graphs

gratia ['greɪʃə] *see* EX GRATIA

gratis ['grætɪs] *adverb* free, not costing anything; *we got into the exhibition gratis*

gratuity [grə'tjuːəti] *noun* tip, money given to someone who has helped you; *the staff are instructed not to accept gratuities*

great [greɪt] *adjective* large; **a great deal of** = very much; *he made a great deal of money on the Stock Exchange*; *there is a great deal of work to be done before the company can be made really profitable*

greenback ['griːnbæk] *noun US (informal)* dollar bill

> gold's drop this year is of the same magnitude as the greenback's 8.5% rise
> *Business Week*

green card ['griːn 'kɑːd] *noun* **(a)** special British insurance certificate to prove that a car is insured for travel abroad **(b)** work permit for a person going to live in the USA

green currency ['griːn 'kʌrənsiː] *noun* currency used in the EU for calculating agricultural payments; each country has an exchange rate fixed by the Commission, so there are 'green pounds', 'green francs', 'green marks', etc.

greenfield site ['griːnfiːld 'saɪt] *noun* site for a factory which is in the country, and not surrounded by other buildings; *compare* BROWNFIELD SITE

greenmail ['griːnmeɪl] *noun* making a profit by buying a large number of shares in a company, threatening to take the company over, and then selling the shares back to the company at a higher price

> he proposes that there should be a limit on greenmail, perhaps permitting payment of a 20% premium on a maximum of 8% of the stock
> *Duns Business Month*

Green Paper ['griːn 'peɪpə] *noun* report from the British government on proposals for a new law to be discussed in Parliament

green pound ['griːn 'paʊnd] *noun* value of the British pound as used in calculating agricultural prices and subsidies in the EU

grey market ['greɪ 'mɑːkɪt] *noun* unofficial market run by dealers, where new issues of shares are bought and sold before they officially become available for trading on the Stock Exchange (even before the share allocations are known)

grid [grɪd] *noun* system of numbered squares; **grid structure** = structure based on a grid

grievance ['griːvəns] *noun* complaint made by a trade union or a worker to the management; **grievance procedure** = way of presenting and settling complaints from a trade union to the management

> ACAS has a legal obligation to try and resolve industrial grievances before they reach industrial tribunals
> *Personnel Today*

gross [grəʊs] **1** *noun* twelve dozen (144); *he ordered four gross of pens* (NOTE: no plural) **2** *adjective* **(a)** total, with no deductions; **gross earnings** = total earnings before tax and other deductions; **gross income** *or* **gross salary** = salary before tax is deducted; **gross margin** = (i) percentage difference between the unit manufacturing cost and the received price; (ii) difference between the total interest paid by a borrower and the cost of the loan to the lender; **gross profit** = profit calculated as sales income less the cost of sales; **gross receipts** = total amount of money received before expenses are deducted; **gross tonnage** = total amount of space in a ship; **gross turnover** = total turnover including discounts, VAT charged, etc.; **gross weight** = weight of both the container and its contents; **gross yield** = profit from investments before the deduction of tax **(b)** **gross domestic product (GDP)** = annual value of goods sold and services paid for inside a country; **gross national product (GNP)** = annual value of goods and services in a country including income from other countries **3** *adverb* with no deductions; *his salary is paid gross* **4** *verb* to make a gross profit; *the group grossed £25m in 1999* news that gross national product increased only 1.3% in the first quarter of the year sent the dollar down on foreign exchange markets

Fortune

gross wool receipts for the selling season to end June appear likely to top $2 billion

Australian Financial Review

ground [graʊnd] *noun* (a) soil or earth; **the factory was burnt to the ground** = the factory was completely destroyed in a fire; **ground hostess** = woman who looks after passengers at the airport before they board the plane; **ground landlord** = person or company which owns the freehold of a property which is then leased and subleased; **ground lease** = first lease on a freehold building; **ground rent** = rent paid by a lessee to the ground landlord (b) **grounds** = basic reasons; *does he have good grounds for complaint?*; *there are no grounds on which we can be sued*; *what are the grounds for the demand for a pay rise?*

ground floor ['graʊnd 'flɔː] *noun* floor (in a shop or office) which is level with the ground; *the men's department is on the ground floor*; *he has a ground-floor office* (NOTE: in the USA this is the **first floor**)

group [gruːp] **1** *noun* (a) several things or people together; *a group of managers has sent a memo to the chairman complaining about noise in the office*; **group insurance** = insurance scheme where a group of employees are covered by one policy (b) several companies linked together in the same organization; *the group chairman or the chairman of the group*; *group turnover or turnover for the group*; **group accounts** = accounts for a holding company and its subsidiaries; **group results** = results of a group of companies taken together **2** *verb* **to group together** = to put several items together; *sales from six different agencies are grouped together under the heading 'European sales'*

Group of Five (G5) ['gruːp əv 'faɪv] central group of major industrial nations (France, Germany, Japan, UK and the USA), now expanded to form the G7

Group of Seven (G7) ['gruːp əv 'sevn] central group of major industrial nations (Canada, France, Germany, Italy, Japan, UK and the USA) who meet regularly to discuss problems of international trade and finance

Group of Eight (G8) ['gruːp əv 'eɪt] the G7 expanded to include Russia

Group of Ten (G10) ['gruːp əv 'ten] the major world economic powers working within the framework of the IMF: Belgium, Canada, France, Germany, Italy, Japan, Netherlands, Sweden, United Kingdom and the United States. There are in fact now eleven members, since Switzerland has joined the original ten. It is also called the 'Paris Club', since its first meeting was in Paris)

grow [grəʊ] *verb* to become larger; *the company has grown from a small repair shop to a multinational electronics business*; *turnover is growing at a rate of 15% per annum*; *the computer industry grew very rapidly in the 1980s* (NOTE: **growing - grew - has grown**)

the thrift had grown from $4.7 million in assets to $1.5 billion

Barrons

growth [grəʊθ] *noun* increase in size; **the company is aiming for growth** = is aiming to expand rapidly; **economic growth** = rate at which a country's national income grows; **a growth area** *or* **a growth market** = an area where sales are increasing rapidly; **a growth industry** = industry which is expanding rapidly; **growth rate** = speed at which something grows; **growth share** *or* **growth stock** = share which people think is likely to rise in value

a general price freeze succeeded in slowing the growth in consumer prices

Financial Times

growth in demand is still coming from the private rather than the public sector

Lloyd's List

population growth in the south-west is again reflected by the level of rental values

Lloyd's List

GST = GOODS AND SERVICES TAX
(the Canadian equivalent of VAT)

because the GST is applied only to fees for brokerage and appraisal services, the new tax does not appreciably increase the price of a resale home

Toronto Globe & Mail

guarantee [gærən'tiː] **1** *noun* **(a)** legal document which promises that a machine will work properly or that an item is of good quality; *certificate of guarantee or guarantee certificate*; *the guarantee lasts for two years*; *it is sold with a twelve-month guarantee*; **the car is still under guarantee** = is still covered by the maker's guarantee; **extended guarantee** = guarantee offered by a dealer on a product such as a dish-washer, which goes beyond the time specified in the manufacturer's guarantee (NOTE: also called a **warranty**) **(b)** promise that someone will pay another person's debts; **to go guarantee for someone** = to act as security for someone's debts **(c)** thing given as a security; *to leave share certificates as a guarantee* **2** *verb* **(a)** to give a promise that something will happen; **to guarantee a debt** = to promise that you will pay a debt made by someone else; **to guarantee an associate company** = to promise that an associate company will pay its debts; **to guarantee a bill of exchange** = to promise that the bill will be paid; **guaranteed minimum wage** = lowest wage which is legally guaranteed to workers (no employer can pay a worker less than this wage) **(b)** **the product is guaranteed for twelve months** = the manufacturer says that the product will work well for twelve months, and will mend it free of charge if it breaks down

guarantor [gærən'tɔː] *noun* person who promises to pay someone's debts; *he stood guarantor for his brother*

guess [ges] **1** *noun* calculation made without any real information; *the forecast of sales is only a guess*; **he made a guess at the pretax profits** = he tried to calculate roughly what the pretax profits would be; **it is anyone's guess** = no one really knows what is the right answer **2** *verb* **to guess (at) something** = to try to calculate something without any information; *they could only guess at the total loss*; *the sales director tried to guess the turnover of the Far East division*

guesstimate ['gestɪmət] *noun* (*informal*) rough calculation

guideline ['gaɪdlaɪn] *noun* unofficial suggestion from the government as to how something should be done; *the government has issued guidelines on increases in incomes and prices*; *the increase in the retail price breaks or goes against the government guidelines*

guild [gɪld] *noun* association of merchants or of shopkeepers; *a trade guild*; *the guild of master bakers*

guilder ['gɪldə] *noun* currency used with the euro in the Netherlands (also called the 'florin') (NOTE: usually written **fl** before or after figures: **fl25, 25fl**)

the shares, which eased 1.10 guilders to fl149.80 earlier in the session, were suspended during the final hour of trading

Wall Street Journal

guillotine ['gɪlətiːn] *noun* machine for cutting paper

guilty ['gɪlti] *adjective* (person) who has done something wrong; *he was found guilty of libel*; *the company was guilty of not reporting the sales to the auditors*

gum [gʌm] *noun* glue; *he stuck the label to the box with gum*

gummed [gʌmd] *adjective* with glue on it; **gummed label** = label with dry glue on it, which has to be made wet to make it stick

Hh

ha = HECTARE

haggle ['hægl] *verb* to discuss prices and terms and try to reduce them; *to haggle about or over the details of a contract*; *after two days' haggling the contract was signed*

half [hɑːf] **1** *noun* one of two equal parts into which something is divided; *the first half of the agreement is acceptable*; **the first half *or* the second half of the year** = the periods from January 1st to June 30th and from June 30th to December 31st; **we share the profits half and half** = we share the profits equally (NOTE: plural is **halves**) **2** *adjective* divided into two parts; **half a per cent *or* a half per cent** = 0.5%; **his commission on the deal is twelve and a half per cent** = 12.5%; **half a dozen *or* a half-dozen** = six; **to sell goods off at half price** = at 50% of the price for which they were sold before; **a half-price sale** = sale of all goods at half the price

economists believe the economy is picking up this quarter and will do better in the second half of the year
Sunday Times

half-dollar ['hɑːf'dɒlə] *noun US* fifty cents

half-year ['hɑːf'jɜː] *noun* six months of an accounting period; **first half-year *or* second half-year** = the first six months or the second six months of a company's accounting year; **to announce the results for the half-year to June 30th *or* the first half-year's results** = results for the period January 1st to June 30th; *we look forward to improvements in the second half-year*

half-yearly ['hɑːf'jɜːli] **1** *adjective* happening every six months; referring to a period of six months; *half-yearly accounts*; *half-yearly payment*; *half-yearly statement*; *a half-yearly meeting* **2** *adverb* every six months; *we pay the account half-yearly*

hallmark ['hɔːlmɑːk] **1** *noun* mark put on gold or silver items to show that the metal is of the correct quality **2** *verb* to put a hallmark on a piece of gold or silver; *a hallmarked spoon*

hammer ['hæmə] **1** *noun* **auctioneer's hammer** = wooden hammer used by an auctioneer to hit his desk, showing that an item has been sold; **to go under the hammer** = to be sold by auction; **all the stock went under the hammer** = all the stock was sold by auction **2** *verb* to hit hard; **to hammer the competition** = to attack and defeat the competition; **to hammer prices** = to reduce prices sharply

hammered ['hæməd] *adjective (on the London Stock Exchange)* **they were hammered** = the firm was removed from the Stock Exchange because it had failed

one of Britain's largest independent stockbrokers was hammered by the Stock Exchange yesterday, putting it out of business for good. The hammering leaves all clients of the firm in the dark about the value of their investments and the future of uncompleted financing deals
Guardian

hammering ['hæmərɪŋ] *noun* **(a)** beating; **the company took a hammering in Europe** = the company had large losses in Europe or lost parts of its European markets; **we gave them a hammering** = we beat them commercially **(b)** *(on the*

London Stock Exchange) removal of a member firm because it has failed

hammer out ['hæmə 'aʊt] *verb* **to hammer out an agreement** = to agree something after long and difficult negotiations; *the contract was finally hammered out*

hand [hænd] *noun* **(a)** part of the body at the end of each arm; **to shake hands** = to hold someone's hand when meeting to show you are pleased to meet him or to show that an agreement has been reached; *the two negotiating teams shook hands and sat down at the conference table*; **to shake hands on a deal** = to shake hands to show that a deal has been agreed **(b) by hand** = using the hands, not a machine; *these shoes are made by hand*; **to send a letter by hand** = to ask someone to carry and deliver a letter personally, not sending it through the post **(c) in hand** = kept in reserve; **balance in hand** *or* **cash in hand** = cash held to pay small debts and running costs; *we have £10,000 in hand*; **work in hand** = work which is in progress but not finished (NOTE: US English is **on hand**) **(d) goods left on hand** = unsold goods left with the retailer or manufacturer; *they were left with half the stock on their hands* **(e) to hand** = here or present; **I have the invoice to hand** = I have the invoice in front of me **(f) show of hands** = vote where people show how they vote by raising their hands; *the motion was carried on a show of hands* **(g) to change hands** = to be sold to a new owner; *the shop changed hands for £100,000* **(h) note of hand** = document where someone promises to pay money at a stated time without conditions; **in witness whereof, I set my hand** = I sign as a witness **(i)** worker; *to take on ten more hands*; **deck hand** = ordinary sailor on a ship; **factory hand** = worker in a factory

handbill ['hænbɪl] *noun* sheet of printed paper handed out to members of the public as an advertisement

handbook ['hænbʊk] *noun* book which gives instructions on how something is to be used; *the handbook does not say how you open the photocopier*; *look in the handbook to see if it tells you how to put the toner in*; **service handbook** = book which shows how to service a machine

hand in [hænd 'ɪn] *verb* to deliver (a letter) by hand; **he handed in his notice** *or* **he handed in his resignation** = he resigned

handle ['hændl] *verb* **(a)** to deal with something or to organize something; *the accounts department handles all the cash*; *we can handle orders for up to 15,000 units*; *they handle all our overseas orders* **(b)** to sell or to trade in (a sort of product); *we do not handle foreign cars*; *they will not handle goods produced by other firms*

handling ['hændlɪŋ] *noun* (i) moving something by hand; (ii) dealing with something; **handling charges** = money to be paid for packing and invoicing, for dealing with something in general or for moving goods from one place to another; *the bank adds on a 5% handling charge for changing travellers' cheques*; **materials handling** = moving materials from one part of a factory to another in an efficient way

> shipping companies continue to bear the extra financial burden of cargo handling operations at the ports
> *Business Times (Lagos)*

hand luggage ['hænd 'lʌɡɪdʒ] *noun* small cases which passengers can carry themselves (and so can take with them into a plane)

handmade [hæn'meɪd] *adjective* made by hand, not by machine; *he writes all his letters on handmade paper*

hand-operated ['hænd'ɒpəreɪtɪd] *adjective* worked by hand, not automatically; *a hand-operated machine*

handout ['hændaʊt] *noun* **(a)** publicity **handout** = information sheet which is given to members of the public **(b)** free gift; *the company exists on handouts from the government*

hand over ['hænd 'əʊvə] *verb* to pass something to someone; *she handed over the documents to the lawyer*; *he handed over to his deputy* = he passed his responsibilities to his deputy

handover ['hændəʊvə] *noun* passing of responsibilities to someone else; *the handover from the old chairman to the* *new went very smoothly; when the ownership of a company changes, the handover period is always difficult*

handshake ['hænʃeɪk] *noun* **golden handshake** = large, usually tax-free, sum of money given to a director who retires from a company before the end of his service contract; *the retiring director received a golden handshake of £250,000*

handwriting ['hændraɪtɪŋ] *noun* writing done by hand; **send a letter of application in your own handwriting** = written by you with a pen, and not typed

handwritten ['hændrɪtn] *adjective* written by hand, not typed; *it is more professional to send in a typed rather than a handwritten letter of application*

handy ['hændi] *adjective* useful or convenient; *they are sold in handy-sized packs*; *this small case is handy for use when travelling*

hang [hæŋ] *verb* to attach something to a hook, nail, etc.; *hang your coat on the hook behind the door; he hung his umbrella over the back of his chair* (NOTE: **hanging - hung**)

hang on ['hæŋ 'ɒn] *verb* to wait (while phoning); *if you hang on a moment, the chairman will be off the other line soon*

hang up ['hæŋ 'ʌp] *verb* to stop a telephone conversation by putting the telephone back on its hook; *when I asked him about the unpaid invoice, he hung up*

happen ['hæpən] *verb* to take place by chance; *the contract happened to arrive when the managing director was away on holiday; he happened to be in the shop when the customer placed the order*; **what has happened to?** = what went wrong with? what is the matter with? where is?; *what has happened to that order for Japan?*

happy ['hæpi] *adjective* very pleased; *we will be happy to supply you at 25% discount; the MD was not at all happy when the sales figures came in*

harbour *US* **harbor** ['hɑːbə] *noun* port, place where ships come to load or unload; **harbour dues** = payment which a ship makes to the harbour authorities for the right to use a harbour; **harbour installations** *or* **harbour facilities** = buildings or equipment in a harbour

hard [hɑːd] **1** *adjective* **(a)** strong, not weak; **to take a hard line in trade union negotiations** = to refuse to compromise with the other side **(b)** difficult; *these typewriters are hard to sell; it is hard to get good people to work on low salaries* **(c)** solid; **hard cash** = money in notes and coins which is ready at hand; *he paid out £100 in hard cash for the chair*; **hard copy** = printout of a text which is on a computer; *he made the presentation with diagrams and ten pages of hard copy*; **hard disk** = computer disk which has a sealed case and can store large quantities of information **(d)** **hard bargain** = bargain with difficult terms; **to drive a hard bargain** = to be a difficult negotiator; **to strike a hard bargain** = to agree a deal where the terms are favourable to you; **after weeks of hard bargaining** = after weeks of difficult discussions **(e)** **hard currency** = currency of a country which has a strong economy and which can be changed into other currencies easily; *exports which can earn hard currency; these goods must be paid for in hard currency; he insisted on a hard currency deal* **2** *adverb* with a lot of effort; *the sales team sold the new product range hard into the supermarkets; if all the workforce works hard, the order should be completed on time*

hard disks help computers
function more speedily and
allow them to store more
information
Australian Financial Review

few of the paper millionaires
sold out and transformed
themselves into hard cash
millionaires
Investors Chronicle

harden ['hɑːdn] *verb* **prices are hardening** = prices are settling at a higher price

hardening ['hɑːdnɪŋ] *noun* **a hardening of prices** = prices which are becoming settled at a higher level

hardness ['hɑːdnəs] *noun* **hardness of the market** = being strong, not being likely to fall

hard sell ['hɑːd 'sel] *noun* **to give a product the hard sell** = to make great efforts to persuade people to buy it; **he tried to give me the hard sell** = he put a lot of effort into trying to make me buy

hard selling ['hɑːd 'selɪŋ] *noun* act of selling by using great efforts; *a lot of hard selling went into that deal*

hardware ['hɑːdweə] *noun* **(a)** computer hardware = machines used in data processing, including the computers and printers, but not the programs; *a hardware maintenance contract* **(b)** military hardware = guns, rockets, tanks, etc. **(c)** solid goods for use in the house (such as frying pans or hammers); *a hardware shop*

harm [hɑːm] **1** *noun* damage done; *the recession has done a lot of harm to export sales* **2** *verb* to damage; *the bad publicity has harmed the company's reputation*

hatchet man ['hætʃɪt 'mæn] *noun* recently appointed manager, whose job is to make staff redundant and reduce expenditure

haul [hɔːl] *noun* distance travelled with a load of cargo; *it is a long haul from Birmingham to Athens*; **short-haul flight** = flight over a short distance (up to 1000km); **long-haul flight** = long-distance flight, especially one between continents

haulage ['hɔːlɪdʒ] *noun* **(a)** **road haulage** = moving of goods by road; **road haulage depot** = centre for goods which are being moved by road, and the lorries which carry them; **haulage contractor** = company which arranges for goods to be moved by road or rail under contract; **haulage costs** *or* **haulage rates** = cost or rates of transporting goods by road; **haulage firm** *or* **company** = company which transports goods by road **(b)** cost of transporting goods by road; *haulage is increasing by 5% per annum*

haulier ['hɔːljə] *noun* **road haulier** = company which transports goods by road

haven ['heɪvn] *noun* safe place; **tax haven** = country where taxes are low

which encourages companies to set up their main offices there

hawk [hɔːk] *verb* to sell goods from door to door or in the street; **to hawk something round** = to take a product, an idea or a project to various companies to see if one will accept it; *he hawked his idea for a plastic car body round all the major car constructors*

hawker ['hɔːkə] *noun* person who sells goods from door to door or in the street

hazard ['hæzəd] *noun* danger; **fire hazard** = situation or goods which could start a fire; *that warehouse full of wood and paper is a fire hazard*

head [hed] **1** *noun* **(a)** most important person; **head of department** *or* **department head** = person in charge of a department **(b)** most important, main; *the head porter will deal with your bags*; *ask the head waiter for a table*; **head buyer** = most important buyer in a department store; **head office** = main office, where the board of directors works and meets **(c)** top part, first part; *write the name of the company at the head of the list* **(d)** person; *representatives cost on average £25,000 per head per annum* **(e)** **heads of agreement** = draft agreement with not all the details complete **2** *verb* **(a)** to be the manager, to be the most important person; *we are looking for someone to head our sales department*; *he is heading a buying mission to China* **(b)** to be first; *the two largest oil companies head the list of stock market results*

headed paper ['hedɪd 'peɪpə] *noun* notepaper with the name of the company and its address printed on it (NOTE: American English is **letterhead**)

head for ['hed 'fɔː] *verb* to go towards; **the company is heading for disaster** = the company is going to collapse

headhunt ['hedhʌnt] *verb* to look for managers and offer them jobs in other companies; **he was headhunted** = he was approached by a headhunter and offered a new job (NOTE: also called **executive search**)

headhunter ['hedhʌntə] *noun* person or company which looks for top managers and offers them jobs in other companies

heading ['hedɪŋ] *noun* **(a)** words at the top of a piece of text; *items are listed under several headings*; *look at the figure under the heading 'Costs 98-99'* **(b)** letter **heading** *or* **heading on notepaper** = name and address of a company printed at the top of a piece of notepaper

headlease ['hedliːs] *noun* lease from a freehold owner to a lessee

headline inflation ['hedlaɪn ɪn'fleɪʃn] *noun* British inflation figure which includes all items (such as mortgage interest and local taxes, which are not included in the inflation figures for other countries)

the UK economy is at the uncomfortable stage in the cycle where two years of tight money are having the desired effect on demand: output is falling and unemployment is rising, but headline inflation and earnings are showing no sign of decelerating
Sunday Times

headquarters (HQ) [hed'kwɔːtəz] *plural noun* main office, where the board of directors meets and works; *the company's headquarters are in New York*; **divisional headquarters** = main office of a division of a company; **to reduce headquarters staff** = to have fewer people working in the main office

head up ['hed 'ʌp] *verb* to be in charge of; *he has been appointed to head up our European organization*

reporting to the deputy managing director, the successful candidate will be responsible for heading up a team which provides a full personnel service
Times

health [helθ] *noun* **(a)** being fit and well, not ill; *GB* **Health and Safety at Work Act** = Act of Parliament which rules how the health of workers should be protected by the companies they work for; **health insurance** = insurance which pays the cost of treatment for illness, especially when travelling abroad; **a private health scheme** = insurance which will pay for the cost of treatment in a private hospital, not a state one **(b) to give a company a clean bill of health** = to report that a company is trading profitably

the main US banks have been forced to pull back from international lending as nervousness continues about their financial health
Financial Times

financial health, along with a dose of independence, has largely sheltered Japan's pharmaceutical companies from a global wave of consolidation. Those assets, however, are expected to soon lure foreign suitors too powerful to resist
Nikkei Weekly

healthy ['helθi] *adjective* **a healthy balance sheet** = balance sheet which shows a good profit; **the company made some very healthy profits** *or* **a very healthy profit** = made a large profit

hear [hɪə] *verb* **(a)** to sense a sound with the ears; *you can hear the printer in the next office*; *the traffic makes so much noise that I can't hear my phone ringing* **(b)** to have a letter or a phone call from someone; *we have not heard from them for some time*; *we hope to hear from the lawyers within a few days* (NOTE: **hearing - heard**)

heavily ['hevəli] *adverb* **he is heavily in debt** = he has many debts; **they are heavily into property** = they have large investments in property; **the company has had to borrow heavily to repay its debts** = the company has had to borrow large sums of money

the steel company had spent heavily on new equipment
Fortune

heavy ['hevi] *adjective* **(a)** large, in large quantities; *a programme of heavy investment overseas*; *he had heavy losses on the Stock Exchange*; *the company is a heavy user of steel* *or* *a heavy consumer of electricity*; *the government imposed a heavy tax on luxury goods*; *heavy costs* *or*

heavy expenditure = spending large sums of money **(b)** which weighs a lot; *the Post Office refused to handle the package because it was too heavy*; **heavy goods vehicle (HGV)** = large lorry used for carrying big loads; **heavy industry** = industry which deals in heavy raw materials (such as coal) or makes large products (such as ships or engines); **heavy machinery** = large machines **(c)** (share) which is has such a high price that small investors are reluctant to buy it (in which case the company may decide to split the shares so as to make them more attractive: in the UK, a share price of £10.00 is considered 'heavy', though many shares have higher prices than this)

> heavy selling sent many blue chips tumbling in Tokyo yesterday
>
> *Financial Times*

hectare ['hekteə] *noun* measurement of area of land (= 2.47 acres) (NOTE: usually written **ha** after figures: **16ha**)

hectic ['hektɪk] *adjective* wild, very active; *a hectic day on the Stock Exchange*; *after last week's hectic trading, this week has been very calm*

hedge [hedʒ] **1** *noun* protection against a possible loss (by taking an action which is the opposite of an action taken earlier); **a hedge against inflation** = investment which should increase in value more than the increase in the rate of inflation; *he bought gold as a hedge against exchange losses* **2** *verb* to hedge your bets = to make investments in several areas so as to be protected against loss in one of them; **to hedge against inflation** = to buy investments which will rise in value faster than the increase in the rate of inflation

> during the 1970s commercial property was regarded by investors as an alternative to equities, with many of the same inflation-hedge qualities
>
> *Investors Chronicle*

> the move saved it from having to pay its creditors an estimated $270 million owed in connection with hedge contracts which began working

against the company when the price of gold rose unexpectedly during September

> *Business in Africa*

hedge fund ['hedʒ 'fʌnd] *noun* partnership open to a small number of rich investors, which invests in equities, currency futures and derivatives and may produce high returns but carries a very high risk

> COMMENT: originally, hedge funds were funds planned to protect equity investments against possible falls on the stock market. Nowadays the term is applied to funds which take speculative positions in financial futures or equities, and are usually highly-geared: in other words, they do nothing to 'hedge' their holdings

> much of what was described as near hysteria was the hedge funds trying to liquidate bonds to repay bank debts after losing multi-million dollar bets on speculations that the yen would fall against the dollar
>
> *Times*

> hedge funds generally have in common an ability to sell short (that is, sell stocks you do not own), and to increase growth prospects - and risk - by borrowing to enhance the fund's assets
>
> *Money Observer*

> the stock is a hedge fund - limited by the Securities and Exchange Commission to only wealthy individuals and qualified institutions
>
> *Smart Money*

hedging ['hedʒɪŋ] *noun* buying investments at a fixed price for delivery later, so as to protect oneself against possible loss

height [haɪt] *noun* **(a)** measurement of how tall or high something is; *what is the height of the desk from the floor?*; *he measured the height of the room from floor to ceiling* **(b)** highest point; *it is difficult to find hotel rooms at the height of the tourist season*

heir [eə] *noun* person who will receive property when someone dies; *his heirs split the estate between them*

heiress ['eəres] *noun* female heir

helicopter ['helɪkɒptə] *noun* aircraft with a large horizontal propeller on top which allows it to lift straight off the ground; *he took the helicopter from the airport to the centre of town; it is only a short helicopter flight from the centre of town to the factory site*

helipad ['helɪpæd] *noun* small area where helicopters can land or take off (such as on the roof of a building)

heliport ['helɪpɔːt] *noun* small airport for helicopters

help [help] **1** *noun* thing which makes it easy to do something; *she finds the word-processor a great help in sending out chasers; the company was set up with financial help from the government; her assistant is not much help in the office - he can't type or drive* **2** *verb* to make it easy for something to be done; *he helped the salesman carry his case of samples; the computer helps in the rapid processing of orders or helps us to process orders rapidly; the government helps exporting companies with easy credit* (NOTE: you help someone *or* something **to do** something)

hereafter [hɪər'ɑːftə] *adverb* from this time on

hereby [hɪə'baɪ] *adverb* in this way, by this letter; *we hereby revoke the agreement of January 1st 1982*

hereditament [herɪ'dɪtəmənt] *noun* property, including land and buildings

herewith [hɪə'wɪð] *adverb* together with this letter; *please find the cheque enclosed herewith*

hesitate ['hezɪteɪt] *verb* not to be sure what to do next; *the company is hesitating about starting up a new computer factory; she hesitated for some time before accepting the job*

HGV ['eɪtʃ'dʒiː'viː] = HEAVY GOODS VEHICLE

hidden ['hɪdn] *adjective* which cannot be seen; **hidden asset** = asset which is valued much less in the company's accounts than its true market value; **hidden reserves** =

reserves which are not easy to identify in the company's balance sheet (reserves which are illegally kept hidden are called 'secret reserves'); **hidden defect in the program** = defect which was not noticed when the program was tested

high [haɪ] **1** *adjective* **(a)** tall; *the shelves are 30 cm high; the door is not high enough to let us get the machines into the building; they are planning a 30-storey high office block* **(b)** large, not low; *high overhead costs increase the unit price; high prices put customers off; they are budgeting for a high level of expenditure; investments which bring in a high rate of return; high interest rates are killing small businesses;* **high finance** = lending, investing and borrowing of very large sums of money organized by financiers; **high flier** = (i) person who is very successful or who is likely to get a very important job; (ii) share whose market price is rising rapidly; **high sales** = large amount of revenue produced by sales; **high taxation** = taxation which imposes large taxes on incomes or profits; **highest tax bracket** = the group which pays the most tax; **high volume (of sales)** = large number of items sold **(c) highest bidder** = person who offers the most money at an auction; *the tender will be awarded to the highest bidder; the property was sold to the highest bidder;* **a decision taken at the highest level** = decision taken by the most important person or group **2** *adverb* **prices are running high** = prices are above their usual level **3** *noun* point where prices or sales are very large; *share prices have dropped by 10% since the high of January 2nd; the highs and lows on the Stock Exchange;* **sales volume has reached an all-time high** = has reached the highest point it has ever been at

> in a leveraged buyout the
> acquirer raises money by
> selling high-yielding
> debentures to private
> investors
>
> *Fortune*

high-grade ['haɪgreɪd] *adjective* of very good quality; *high-grade petrol*; **a high-grade trade delegation** = a delegation made up of very important people

> the accepted wisdom built
> upon for well over 100 years
> that government and
> high-grade corporate bonds
> were almost riskless
>
> *Forbes Magazine*

high-income ['haɪ'ɪnkʌm] *adjective* which gives a large income; *high-income shares*; *a high-income portfolio*

high-level ['haɪ'levl] *adjective* **(a)** very important; **a high-level meeting** *or* **delegation** = meeting or delegation of the most important people (such as ministers, managing directors); **a high-level decision** = decision taken by the most important person or group **(b) high-level language** = programming language which uses normal words and figures

highlighter ['haɪlaɪtə] *noun* felt-tip pen with transparent ink in bright colours (pink, red, orange, etc.) and a wide felt tip, used to put a thick line of transparent colour to mark text in a document

highly ['haɪli] *adverb* very; **highly-geared company** = company which has a high proportion of its funds from fixed-interest borrowings; **highly-paid** = earning a large salary; **highly-placed** = occupying an important post; *the delegation met a highly-placed official in the Trade Ministry*; **highly-priced** = with a large price; **she is highly thought of by the managing director** = the managing director thinks she is very competent

high pressure ['haɪ 'preʃə] *noun* strong force by other people to make you do something; **working under high pressure** = working with a manager telling you what to do and to do it quickly or with customers asking for supplies urgently; **high-pressure salesman** = salesman who forces the customer to buy something he or she does not really need; **high-pressure sales techniques** *or* **high-pressure selling** = forcing a customer to buy something he or she does not really want

high-quality ['haɪ'kwɒləti] *adjective* of very good quality; *high-quality goods*; *high-quality steel*

High Street ['haɪ 'striːt] *noun* main shopping street in a British town; *the High Street shops*; *a High Street bookshop*; **the High Street banks** = main British banks which accept deposits from individual customers

hike [haɪk] **1** *noun US* increase; **pay hike** = increase in salary **2** *verb US* to increase; *the union hiked its demand to $3 an hour*

hire ['haɪə] **1** *noun* **(a)** paying money to rent a car, boat or piece of equipment for a time; **car hire firm** *or* **equipment hire firm** = company which owns cars or equipment and lends them to customers for a payment; **hire car** = car which has been rented; *he was driving a hire car when the accident happened* **(b) 'for hire'** = sign on a taxi showing it is empty **(c)** *US* **for hire contract** = freelance contract; **to work for hire** = to work freelance **2** *verb* **(a) to hire staff** = to engage new staff to work for you; **to hire and fire** = to employ new staff and dismiss existing staff frequently; *we have hired the best lawyers to represent us*; *they hired a small company to paint the offices* **(b) to hire a car** *or* **a crane** = to pay money to use a car or a crane for a time; *he hired a truck to move his furniture* **(c) to hire out cars** *or* **equipment** = to lend cars or equipment to customers who pay for their use

hired ['haɪəd] *adjective* **a hired car** = car which has been rented

hire purchase (HP) ['haɪə 'pɜːtʃəs] *noun* system of buying something by paying a sum regularly each month; *to buy a refrigerator on hire purchase*; **to sign a hire-purchase agreement** = to sign a contract to pay for something by instalments; **hire-purchase company** = company which provides money for hire purchase (NOTE: US English uses **to buy on the installment plan**)

COMMENT: an agreement to hire a piece of equipment, etc., involves two parties: the hirer and the owner. The equipment remains the property of the owner while the hirer is using it. Under a hire-purchase agreement, the equipment remains the property of the owner until the hirer has complied with the terms of the agreement (i.e., until he has paid all monies due)

hiring ['haɪərɪŋ] *noun* employing; *hiring of new personnel has been stopped*

historic *or* **historical** [hɪs'tɒrɪk *or* hɪs'tɒrɪkəl] *adjective* which goes back over a period of time; **historic(al) cost** = actual purchase cost of something which was bought some time ago; **historical figures** = figures which were current in the past

COMMENT: by tradition, a company's accounts are usually prepared on the historic(al) cost principle, i.e. that assets are costed at their purchase price; with inflation, such assets are undervalued, and current-cost accounting or replacement-cost accounting may be preferred

the Federal Reserve Board has eased interest rates in the past year, but they are still at historically high levels
Sunday Times

the historic p/e for the FTSE all-share index is 28.3 and the dividend yield is barely 2 per cent. Both indicators suggest that the stock markets are very highly priced
Times

hit [hɪt] **1** *noun* action of accessing a website; *we are averaging over 3,500 hits a day* **2** *verb* **(a)** to knock against something; *he hit his head against the table*; **we have hit our export targets** = we have reached our targets **(b)** to hurt or to damage; *the company was badly hit by the falling exchange rate*; *our sales of summer clothes have been hit by the bad weather*; *the new legislation has hit the small companies hardest* (NOTE: **hitting - hit)**

hive off ['haɪv 'ɒf] *verb* to split off part of a large company to form a smaller subsidiary; *the new managing director hived off the retail sections of the company*

hoard [hɔːd] *verb* to buy and store food in case of need; to keep cash instead of investing it

hoarder ['hɔːdə] *noun* person who buys and stores food in case of need

hoarding ['hɔːdɪŋ] *noun* **(a) hoarding of supplies** = buying large quantities of money or food to keep in case of need **(b) advertisement hoarding** = large board for posters **(c)** *US* temporary fence put up around a construction site

as a result of hoarding, rice has become scarce with prices shooting up
Business Times (Lagos)

hold [həʊld] **1** *noun* bottom part of a ship or aircraft, in which cargo is carried **2** *verb* **(a)** to own or to keep; *he holds 10% of the company's shares*; **you should hold these shares - they look likely to rise** = you should keep these shares and not sell them **(b)** to contain; *the carton holds twenty packets*; *each box holds 250 sheets of paper*; *a bag can hold twenty kilos of sugar* **(c)** to make something happen; *to hold a meeting or a discussion*; *the computer show will be held in London next month*; *board meetings are held in the boardroom*; *the AGM will be held on March 24th*; *the receiver will hold an auction of the company's assets*; *the accountants held a review of the company's accounting practices* **(d)** *(on telephone)* **hold the line please** = please wait; *the chairman is on the other line - will you hold?* (NOTE: **holding - held)**

as of last night, the bank's shareholders no longer hold any rights to the bank's shares
South China Morning Post

hold back ['həʊld 'bæk] *verb* to wait, not to go forward; **investors are holding back until after the Budget** = investors are waiting until they hear the details of the Budget before they decide whether to buy or sell; *he held back from signing the* lease until he had checked the details = he delayed signing the lease until he had checked the details; **payment will be held back until the contract has been signed** = payment will not be made until the contract has been signed

hold down [ˈhəʊld ˈdaʊn] *verb* **(a)** to keep at a low level; *we are cutting margins to hold our prices down* **(b) to hold down a job** = to manage to do a difficult job

> real wages have been held down; they have risen at an annual rate of only 1% in the last two years
> *Sunday Times*

holder [ˈhəʊldə] *noun* **(a)** person who owns or keeps something; *holders of government bonds or bondholders; holder of stock or of shares in a company; holder of an insurance policy or policy holder;* **credit card holder** = person who has a credit card; **debenture holder** = person who holds a debenture for money lent **(b)** thing which keeps something, which protects something; **card holder** *or* **message holder** = frame which protects a card or a message; **credit card holder** = plastic wallet for keeping credit cards

holding [ˈhəʊldɪŋ] *noun* **(a)** group of shares owned; *he has sold all his holdings in the Far East; the company has holdings in German manufacturing companies* **(b) cross holdings** = situation where two companies own shares in each other in order to stop each from being taken over; *the two companies have protected themselves from takeover by a system of cross holdings*

holding company [ˈhəʊldɪŋ ˈkʌmpni] *noun* (i) company which owns more than 50% of the shares in another company; (ii) company which exists only or mainly to own shares in subsidiary companies; *see also* SUBSIDIARY (NOTE: the American English for this is a **proprietary company**)

hold on [ˈhəʊld ˈɒn] *verb* to wait, not to change; **the company's shareholders should hold on and wait for a better offer** = they should keep their shares and not sell them

hold out for [ˈhəʊld ˈaʊt ˈfɔː] *verb* to wait and ask for; **you should hold out for a 10% pay rise** = do not agree to a pay rise of less than 10%

hold over [ˈhəʊld ˈəʊvə] *verb* to postpone, to put back to a later date; *discussion of item 4 was held over until the next meeting*

hold to [ˈhəʊld ˈtuː] *verb* not to allow something to change; **we will try to hold him to the contract** = we will try to stop him going against the contract; **the government hopes to hold wage increases to 5%** = the government hopes that wage increases will not be more than 5%

hold up [ˈhəʊld ˈʌp] *verb* **(a)** to stay at a high level; *share prices have held up well*; *sales held up during the tourist season* **(b)** to delay; *the shipment has been held up at customs*; *payment will be held up until the contract has been signed*; *the strike will hold up dispatch for some weeks*

hold-up [ˈhəʊldʌp] *noun* delay; *the strike caused hold-ups in the dispatch of goods*

holiday [ˈhɒlədeɪ] *noun* **(a) bank holiday** = weekday which is a public holiday when the banks are closed; *New Year's Day is a bank holiday*; **public holiday** = day when all workers rest and enjoy themselves instead of working; **statutory holiday** = holiday which is fixed by law; *the office is closed for the statutory Christmas holiday* **(b)** period when a worker does not work, but rests, goes away and enjoys himself; *to take a holiday or to go on holiday; when is the manager taking his holidays?*; *my secretary is off on holiday tomorrow; he is away on holiday for two weeks*; **the job carries five weeks' holiday** = one of the conditions of the job is that you have five weeks' holiday; **the summer holidays** = holidays taken by the workers in the summer when the weather is good and children are not at school; **holiday entitlement** = number of days' paid holiday which a worker has the right to take; **holiday pay** = salary which is still paid during the holiday (NOTE: American English is **vacation**) **(c) tax holiday** = period when a new business is exempted from paying tax

hologram ['hɒləgræm] *noun* three-dimensional picture which is used on credit cards as a means of preventing forgery

home [həum] *noun* **(a)** place where a person lives; *please send the letter to my home address, not my office*; **home banking** = system of banking using a personal computer in your own home to carry out various financial transactions (such as paying invoices, checking your bank account) **(b) home country** = country where a company is based; **home sales** *or* **sales in the home market** = sales in the country where a company is based; **home-produced products** = products manufactured in the country where the company is based **(c)** house; **new home sales** = sales of new houses; **home loan** = loan by a bank or a building society to a person buying a house

homegrown ['həumgrəun] *adjective* which has been developed in a local area or in a country where the company is based; *a homegrown computer industry*; *India's homegrown car industry*

homemade ['həummeɪd] *adjective* made in a home; *homemade jam*

homeowner ['həuməunə] *noun* person who owns a private house or flat; **homeowner's insurance policy** = insurance policy covering a house and its contents and the personal liability of the people living in it

homeward ['həumwəd] *adjective* going towards the home country; *the ship is carrying homeward freight*; *the liner left Buenos Aires on her homeward journey*

homewards ['həumwədz] *adverb* towards the home country; *cargo homewards*

homeworker ['həum'wʌkə] *noun* person who works at home for a company

hon = HONORARY; **hon sec** = honorary secretary

honest ['ɒnɪst] *adjective* respected, saying what is right; **to play the honest broker** = to act for the parties in a negotiation to try to make them agree to a solution

honestly ['ɒnɪstli] *adverb* saying what is right, not cheating; *they acted completely honestly with us*

honorarium [ɒnə'reərɪəm] *noun* money paid to a professional person, such as an accountant or a lawyer, when he does not ask for a fee (NOTE: plural is **honoraria**)

honorary ['ɒnərəri] *adjective* person who is not paid a salary; *she is honorary secretary of the tennis club*; *he is honorary president of the translators' association*; **honorary member** = member who does not have to pay a subscription

honour *US* **honor** ['ɒnə] *verb* to pay something because it is owed and is correct; **to honour a bill**; **to honour a signature** = to pay something because the signature is correct

hope [həup] *verb* to expect, to want something to happen; *we hope to be able to dispatch the order next week*; *he is hoping to break into the US market*; *they had hoped the TV commercials would help sales*

horizontal [hɒrɪ'zɒntl] *adjective* flat, going from side to side, not up and down; **horizontal integration** = joining similar companies in the same type of business, taking over a company in the same line of business; **horizontal communication** = communication between workers at the same level

horse trading ['hɔːs 'treɪdɪŋ] *noun* hard bargaining which ends with someone giving something in return for a concession from the other side

hostess ['həustəs] *noun* woman who looks after passengers or clients; **air hostess** *US* **airline hostess** = woman who looks after passengers in a plane; **ground hostess** = woman who looks after passengers before they get into the plane

hostile bid ['hɒstaɪl 'bɪd] *noun* takeover bid where the board of the target company does not recommend it to the shareholders and tries to fight it (NOTE: also called a **contested takeover**)

about 6%, hardly enough to
block a hostile bid

Fortune

Europe gets used to hostile
takeover bids fought on the
basis of shareholder value

Investors Chronicle

while hostile takeovers still
inspire fear in Japan,
friendly takeovers are likely
to become more common

Nikkei Weekly

hot [hɒt] *adjective* (**a**) very warm; *the staff complain that the office is too hot in the summer and too cold in the winter*; *the drinks machine sells coffee, tea and hot soup*; *switch off the machine if it gets too hot* (**b**) not safe, very bad; **to make things hot for someone** = to make it difficult for someone to work or to trade; *customs officials are making things hot for drug smugglers*; **hot money** = money which is moved from country to country to get the best interest rates; **he is in the hot seat** = his job involves making many difficult decisions

hotel [həʊˈtel] *noun* building where you can rent a room for a night, or eat in a restaurant; *his hotel bills were paid by the insurance company*; *she put her hotel expenses on her expense account*; *hotel staff had instructions not to let him into the hotel*; **hotel accommodation** = rooms available in hotels; *all hotel accommodation has been booked up for the exhibition*; **hotel chain** *or* **chain of hotels** = group of hotels owned by the same company; **the hotel trade** = business of running hotels

hotelier [həʊˈtelɪə] *noun* person who owns or manages a hotel

hour [ˈaʊə] *noun* (**a**) period of time lasting sixty minutes; **to work a thirty-five hour week** = to work seven hours a day each weekday; **we work an eight-hour day** = we work for eight hours a day, e.g. from 8.30 to 5.30 with one hour for lunch (**b**) sixty minutes of work; *he earns £14 an hour*; *we pay £16 an hour*; **to pay by the hour** = to pay people a fixed amount of money for each hour worked (**c**) **banking hours** = time when a bank is open for its

customers; *you cannot get money out of a bank outside banking hours*; **office hours** = time when an office is open; *do not make private phone calls during office hours*; **outside hours** *or* **out of hours** = when the office is not open; *he worked on the accounts out of hours*; **the shares rose in after-hours trading** = in trading after the Stock Exchange had closed

hourly [ˈaʊəli] *adverb* per hour; **hourly-paid workers** = workers paid at a fixed rate for each hour worked; **hourly rate** = amount of money paid for an hour worked

despite the Fed's
long-standing fears that low
unemployment will raise wage
costs, average hourly
earnings grew by just 3.6 per
cent in the year to November

Investors Chronicle

house [haʊs] *noun* (**a**) building in which someone lives; **house property** = private houses or flats, not shops, offices or factories; **house agent** = estate agent who deals in buying or selling houses or flats (**b**) company; *the largest London finance house*; *he works for a broking house or a publishing house*; **clearing house** = central office where clearing banks exchange cheques; **discount house** = financial company which specializes in discounting bills; **export house** = company which specializes in the export of goods manufactured by other companies; **house journal** *or* **house magazine** *US* **house organ** = magazine produced for the workers or shareholders in a company to give them news about the company; **house style** = a company's own design which is used in all its products, including packaging, stationery, etc.; **house telephone** = internal telephone for calling from one office to another (**c**) **the House** = the London Stock Exchange

household [ˈhaʊshəʊld] *noun* people living in a house; **household expenses** = money spent on running a private house; **household goods** = goods which are used in a house; **household insurance policy** = insurance policy covering a house and its contents and the personal liability of the people living in it; **household name** =

brand name which is recognised by a large number of consumers

householder ['haʊshəʊldə] *noun* person who owns a private house or flat

house starts *or* **housing starts** ['haʊs 'stɑːts or 'haʊzɪŋ 'stɑːts] *plural noun* number of new private houses or flats of which the construction has begun during a year

house-to-house ['haʊstə'haʊs] *adjective* going from one house to the next, asking people to buy something or to vote for someone; *he trained as a house-to-house salesman; house-to-house selling is banned in this area*

HP ['eɪtʃ'piː] = HIRE PURCHASE

HQ ['eɪtʃ'kjuː] = HEADQUARTERS

human resources ['hjuːmən rɪ'sɔːsɪz] *noun* workers which a company has available (seen from the point of view of their skills and experience)

---

effective use and management of human resources hold the key to future business development and success

Management Today

---

hundredweight ['hʌndrədweɪt] *noun* weight of 112 pounds (about fifty kilos) (NOTE: usually written **cwt** after figures: **20cwt**)

hungry ['hʌŋgri] *adjective* wanting more sales, a bigger share of the market, etc.; *after the cutbacks in staff, the company is leaner and hungrier*

hurry ['hʌri] **1** *noun* doing things fast; *there is no hurry for the figures, we do not need them until next week*; **in a hurry** = very fast; *the sales manager wants the report in a hurry* **2** *verb* to do something, to make something or to go very fast; *the production team tried to hurry the order through the factory; the chairman does not want to be hurried into making a decision; the directors hurried into the meeting*

hurry up [hʌri 'ʌp] *verb* to make something go faster; *can you hurry up that order - the customer wants it immediately?*

hurt [hɜːt] *verb* to harm or to damage; *the bad publicity did not hurt our sales; sales of summer clothes were hurt by the bad weather; the company has not been hurt by the recession* (NOTE: **hurting - hurt**)

hype [haɪp] **1** *noun* excessive claims made in advertising; *all the hype surrounding the launch of the new soap* **2** *verb* to make excessive claims in advertising

hyper- ['haɪpə] *prefix meaning* very large

hyperinflation ['haɪpərɪn'fleɪʃn] *noun* inflation which is so rapid that it is almost impossible to reduce

hypermarket ['haɪpəmɑːkɪt] *noun* very large supermarket, usually on the outside of a large town

Ii

ice [aɪs] *noun* **to put something on ice** = to file a plan or document as the best way of forgetting about it; *the whole expansion plan was put on ice*

IDD = INTERNATIONAL DIRECT DIALLING

idea [aɪ'dɪə] *noun* thing which you think of; *one of the salesman had the idea of changing the product colour; the chairman thinks it would be a good idea to ask all directors to itemize their expenses*

ideal [aɪ'dɪəl] *adjective* perfect, very good for something; *this is the ideal site for a new hypermarket*

Ideal Home Exhibition [aɪ'dɪəl 'həʊm eksɪ'bɪʃən] *noun* annual exhibition in London showing new houses, new kitchens, etc.

idle ['aɪdl] *adjective* **(a)** not working; *2,000 employees were made idle by the recession* **(b) idle machinery** *or* **machines lying idle** = machinery not being used; **idle time** = period of time when a machine is available for production but not doing anything **(c) idle capital** = capital not being used productively; **money lying idle** *or* **idle money** = money which is not being used to produce interest, which is not invested in business

i.e. ['aɪ'i: or 'ðæt'ɪz] that is; *the largest companies, i.e. Smith's and Brown's, had a very good first quarter; the import restrictions apply to expensive items, i.e. items costing more than $2,500*

illegal [ɪ'li:gəl] *adjective* not legal, against the law; *he was stopped at the airport and illegal weapons were seized* ; **illegal contract** = contract which cannot be enforced in law (such as a contract to commit a crime)

illegality [ɪlɪ'gælətɪ] *noun* being illegal

illegally [ɪ'li:gəlɪ] *adverb* against the law; *he was accused of illegally importing arms into the country*

illicit [ɪ'lɪsɪt] *adjective* not legal or not permitted; *illicit sale of alcohol*; *trade in illicit alcohol*

illiquid [ɪ'lɪkwɪd] *adjective* (i) (asset) which is not easy to change into cash; (ii) (company) which has no cash

ILO ['aɪel'əʊ] = INTERNATIONAL LABOUR ORGANIZATION

image ['ɪmɪdʒ] *noun* general idea which the public has of a product or of a company; *they are spending a lot of advertising money to improve the company's image*; *the company has adopted a down-market image*; **brand image** = picture which people have in their minds of a product associated with the brand name; **corporate image** = idea which a company would like the public to have of it; **to promote the corporate image** = to publicize a company so that its reputation is improved

IMF ['aɪem'ef] = INTERNATIONAL MONETARY FUND

imitate ['ɪmɪteɪt] *verb* to do what someone else does; *they imitate all our sales gimmicks*

imitation [ɪmɪ'teɪʃən] **1** *noun* thing which copies another; **beware of imitations** = be careful not to buy low quality goods which are made to look like other more expensive items **2** *adjective* which copies something; *he was caught selling imitation Rolex watches in Oxford Street*

immediate [ɪ'mi:djət] *adjective* happening at once; *he wrote an immediate* *letter of complaint; your order will receive immediate attention*

immediately [ɪ'miːdjətli] *adverb* at once; *he immediately placed an order for 2,000 boxes; as soon as he heard the news he immediately faxed his office; can you phone immediately you get the information?*

immovable [ɪ'muːvəbl] *adjective* which cannot be moved; **immovable property** = houses and other buildings on land

immunity [ɪ'mjuːnəti] *noun* protection against arrest; **diplomatic immunity** = being outside a country's laws because of being a diplomat; **he was granted immunity from prosecution** = he was told he would not be prosecuted

impact ['ɪmpækt] *noun* shock or strong effect; *the impact of new technology on the cotton trade; the new design has made little impact on the buying public*

```
the    strong    dollar's
deflationary   impact   on
European    economies    as
governments push up interest
rates    to    support    their
sinking currencies
                Duns Business Month
```

imperfect [ɪm'pɜːfikt] *adjective* not perfect; *they are holding a sale of imperfect items; to check a batch for imperfect products*

imperfection [ɪmpə'fekʃən] *noun* item or part of an item which is not perfect; *to check a batch for imperfections*

impersonal [ɪm'pɜːsnl] *adjective* without any personal touch, as if done by machines; *an impersonal style of management*

implement ['ɪmplɪmənt] **1** *noun* tool or instrument used to do some work; *we don't have the right implements for this type of work* **2** *verb* to put into action; *to implement an agreement*

implementation [ɪmplɪmen'teɪʃən] *noun* putting into action; *the implementation of new rules*

import 1 ['ɪmpɔːt] *noun* **(a) imports** = goods brought into a country from abroad for sale; *imports from Poland have risen to $1m a year; invisible imports* =

services (such as banking, tourism and insurance) which are paid for in foreign currency; **visible imports** = real goods which are imported **(b) import ban** = forbidding imports; *the government has imposed an import ban on arms*; **import duty** = tax on goods imported into a country; **import levy** = tax on imports, especially in the EU a tax on imports of farm produce from outside the EU; **import licence** *or* **import permit** = government licence or permit which allows goods to be imported; **import quota** = fixed quantity of a particular type of goods which the government allows to be imported; *the government has imposed an import quota on cars*; **import restrictions** = action taken by a government to reduce the level of imports (by imposing quotas, duties, etc.); **import surcharge** = extra duty charged on imported goods, to try to prevent them from being imported and to encourage local manufacture (NOTE: usually used in the plural, but the singular form is used before a noun) **2** [ɪm'pɔːt] *verb* to bring goods from abroad into a country for sale; *the company imports television sets from Japan; this car was imported from France; the union organized a boycott of imported cars*

```
European   manufacturers   rely
heavily   on   imported   raw
materials   which   are   mostly
priced in dollars
                Duns Business Month
```

importation [ɪmpɔː'teɪʃən] *noun* act of importing; *the importation of arms is forbidden*

importer [ɪm'pɔːtə] *noun* person or company which imports goods; *a major London cigar importer; the company is a big importer of foreign cars*

import-export ['ɪmpɔːt 'ekspɔːt] *noun & adjective* dealing with both bringing foreign goods into a country and sending locally made goods abroad; *Rotterdam is an important centre for the import-export trade; he works in import-export*

importing [ɪm'pɔːtɪŋ] **1** *adjective* which imports; *oil-importing countries; an importing company* **2** *noun* act of bringing foreign goods into a country for sale; *the* *importing of arms into the country is illegal*

importance [ɪmˈpɔːtəns] *noun* having a value; mattering a lot; *the bank attaches great importance to the deal*

important [ɪmˈpɔːtənt] *adjective* which matters a lot; *he left a pile of important papers in the taxi*; *she has an important meeting at 10.30*; *he was promoted to a more important job*

each of the major issues on the agenda at this week's meeting is important to the government's success in overall economic management

Australian Financial Review

impose [ɪmˈpəʊz] *verb* to put a tax or a duty on goods; *to impose a tax on bicycles*; *they tried to impose a ban on smoking*; *the government imposed a special duty on oil*; *customs have imposed a 10% tax increase on luxury items*; *the unions have asked the government to impose trade barriers on foreign cars*

imposition [ɪmpəˈzɪʃən] *noun* putting a tax or duty on goods or services

impossible [ɪmˈpɒsəbl] *adjective* which cannot be done; *getting skilled staff is becoming impossible*; *government regulations make it impossible for us to export*

impound [ɪmˈpaʊnd] *verb* to take something away and keep it until a tax is paid; *customs impounded the whole cargo*

impounding [ɪmˈpaʊndɪŋ] *noun* act of taking something and keeping it until a tax is paid

imprest system [ˈɪmprest ˈsɪstəm] *noun* system of controlling petty cash, where cash is paid out against a written receipt and the receipt is used to get more cash to bring the float to the original level

improve [ɪmˈpruːv] *verb* to make something better; to become better; *we are trying to improve our image with a series of TV commercials*; *they hope to improve the company's cash flow position*; *we hope the cash flow position will improve or we will have difficulty in paying our bills*; **export trade has improved sharply**

during the first quarter = export trade has increased

we also invest in companies whose growth and profitability could be improved by a management buyout

Times

improved [ɪmˈpruːvd] *adjective* better; *the union rejected the management's improved offer*

improvement [ɪmˈpruːvmənt] *noun* **(a)** getting better; *there is no improvement in the cash flow situation*; *sales are showing a sharp improvement over last year* **(b)** thing which is better; **an improvement on an offer** = making a better offer

the management says the rate of loss-making has come down and it expects further improvement in the next few years

Financial Times

improve on [ɪmˈpruːv ˈɒn] *verb* to do better than; **he refused to improve on his previous offer** = he refused to make a better offer

impulse [ˈɪmpʌls] *noun* sudden decision; **to do something on impulse** = to do something because you have just thought of it, not because it was planned; **impulse buyer** = person who buys something on impulse, not because he or she intended to buy it; **impulse buying** = buying things which you have just seen, not because you had planned to buy them; *the store puts racks of chocolates by the checkout to attract the impulse buyer*; **impulse purchase** = thing bought as soon as it is seen

IMRO [ˈɪmrəʊ] = INVESTMENT MANAGEMENT REGULATORY ORGANIZATION

in = INCH

inactive [ɪnˈæktɪv] *adjective* not active, not busy; **inactive account** = bank account which is not used (i.e., no deposits or withdrawals are made) over a period of time; **inactive market** = stock market with few buyers or sellers

Inc [ɪŋk or ɪnˈkɔːpəreɪtɪd] *US* = INCORPORATED

incentive [ɪnˈsentɪv] *noun* thing which encourages someone to work better; **staff incentives** = pay and better conditions offered to workers to make them work better; **incentive bonus** *or* **incentive payment** = extra pay offered to a worker to make him work better; **incentive scheme** = plan to encourage better work by paying higher commission or bonuses; *incentive schemes are boosting production*

some further profit-taking was seen yesterday as investors continued to lack fresh incentives to renew buying activity
Financial Times

a well-designed plan can help companies retain talented employees and offer enticing performance incentives - all at an affordable cost
Fortune

inch [ɪntʃ] *noun* measurement of length (= 2.54cm); *a 3½ inch disk* (NOTE: usually written **in** or **"** after figures: **2in** or **2"**. Note also that the inch is now no longer officially used in the UK)

incidental [ɪnsɪˈdentl] **1** *adjective* which is not important, but connected with something else; **incidental expenses** = small amounts of money spent at various times in addition to larger amounts **2** *noun* **incidentals** = incidental expenses

include [ɪnˈkluːd] *verb* to count something along with other things; *the charge includes VAT; the total comes to £1,000 including freight; the total is £140 not including insurance and freight; the account covers services up to and including the month of June*

inclusive [ɪnˈkluːsɪv] *adjective* which counts something in with other things; *inclusive of tax; not inclusive of VAT;* **inclusive sum** *or* **inclusive charge** = charge which includes all costs; **the conference runs from the 12th to the 16th inclusive** = it starts on the morning of the 12th and ends on the evening of the 16th

income [ˈɪnkʌm] *noun* **(a)** money which a person receives as salary or dividends; **annual income** = money received during a calendar year; **disposable income** = income left after tax and national insurance have been deducted; **earned income** = money received as a salary, wages, fees or rental income; **fixed income** = income which does not change from year to year; **gross income** = income before tax has been deducted; **net income** = income left after tax has been deducted; **private income** = income from dividends, interest or rent which is not part of a salary; **personal income** = income received by an individual person; **retained income** = profits which are not paid out to shareholders as dividends; **unearned income** = money received from interest or dividends; **lower income bracket** *or* **upper income bracket** = groups of people who earn low or high salaries considered for tax purposes; **he comes into the higher income bracket** = he is in a group of people earning high incomes and therefore paying more tax; **income shares** = shares in an investment trust which receive income from the investments, but do not benefit from the rise in capital value of the investments; **income units** = units in a unit trust, where the investor receives dividends in the form of income (as opposed to accumulation units where the dividend is left to accumulate as new units) **(b)** **government's incomes policy** = the government's ideas on how incomes should be controlled **(c)** money which an organization receives as gifts or from investments; *the hospital has a large income from gifts* **(d)** *US* **income statement** = a statement of company expenditure and sales which shows whether the company has made a profit or loss (NOTE: the British equivalent is the **profit and loss account**)

income tax [ˈɪnkʌm ˈtæks] *noun* **(a)** tax on a person's income (both earned and unearned); **income tax form** = form to be completed which declares all income to the tax office; **declaration of income** *or* **income tax return** = statement declaring income to the tax office; *see also* PAYE **(b)** *US* **corporate** *or* **corporation income tax** = tax paid on the income of a business there is no risk-free way of taking regular income from your money much higher than the rate of inflation

Guardian

incoming ['ɪnkʌmɪŋ] *adjective* **(a)** incoming call = phone call coming into the office from someone outside; **incoming mail** = mail which comes into an office **(b)** (someone) who has recently been elected or appointed; **the incoming board of directors** = the new board which is about to start working; *the incoming chairman or president*

incompetent [ɪn'kɒmpətənt] *adjective* who cannot work well; *the sales manager is quite incompetent*; *the company has an incompetent finance director*

inconvertible [ɪnkən'vɜːtəbl] *adjective* (currency) which cannot be easily converted into other currencies

incorporate [ɪn'kɔːpəreɪt] *verb* **(a)** to bring something in to form part of a main group; *income from the 1998 acquisition is incorporated into the accounts* **(b)** to form a registered company; *a company incorporated in the USA*; *an incorporated company*; *J. Doe Incorporated*

incorporation [ɪnkɔːpə'reɪʃən] *noun* act of incorporating a company

COMMENT: a corporation (a body which is legally separate from its members) is formed in one of three ways: 1) registration under the Companies Act (the normal method for commercial companies); 2) granting of a royal charter; 3) by a special Act of Parliament. A company is incorporated by drawing up a memorandum and articles of association, which are lodged with Companies House. In the UK, a company is either a private limited company (they print Ltd after their name) or a public limited company (they print Plc after their name). A company must be a Plc to obtain a Stock Exchange listing. In the USA, there is no distinction between private and public companies, and all are called 'corporations'; they put Inc. after their name

incorrect [ɪnkə'rekt] *adjective* wrong, not correct; *the minutes of the meeting were incorrect and had to be changed*

incorrectly [ɪnkə'rektli] *adverb* wrongly, not correctly; *the package was incorrectly addressed*

Incoterms ['ɪŋkəʊtɜːmz] *noun* standard definition (by the International Chamber of Commerce) of terms (such as 'FOB' or 'cif') used in international trade

increase 1 ['ɪŋkriːs] *noun* **(a)** growth, becoming larger; *there have been several increases in tax or tax increases in the last few years*; *there is an automatic 5% increase in price or price increase on January 1st*; *profits showed a 10% increase or an increase of 10% on last year*; **increase in the cost of living** = rise in the annual cost of living **(b)** higher salary; *increase in pay or pay increase*; *increase in salary or salary increase*; *the government hopes to hold salary increases to 3%*; **he had two increases last year** = his salary went up twice; **cost-of-living increase** = increase in salary to allow it to keep up with higher cost of living; **merit increase** = increase in pay given to a worker whose work is good **(c)** **on the increase** = growing larger, becoming more frequent; *stealing in shops is on the increase* **2** [ɪn'kriːs] *verb* **(a)** to grow bigger or higher; *profits have increased faster than the increase in the rate of inflation*; *exports to Africa have increased by more than 25%*; *the price of oil has increased twice in the past week*; **to increase in price** = to cost more; **to increase in size or in value** = to become larger or more valuable **(b)** **the company increased his salary to £20,000** = the company gave him a rise in salary to £20,000

turnover has potential to be increased to over 1 million dollars with energetic management and very little capital

Australian Financial Review

competition is steadily increasing and could affect profit margins as the company

tries to retain its market
share

Citizen (Ottawa)

increasing [ɪn'kriːsɪŋ] *adjective* which is
growing bigger; *increasing profits*; *the
company has an increasing share of the
market*

increasingly [ɪn'kriːsɪŋli] *adverb* more
and more; *the company has to depend
increasingly on the export market*

increment ['ɪŋkrɪmənt] *noun* regular
automatic increase in salary; **salary which
rises in annual increments of £1000 =**
each year the salary is increased by £1000

incremental [ɪŋkrɪ'mentl] *adjective*
which rises automatically in stages;
incremental cost = cost of making extra
units above the number already planned
(this may then include further fixed costs);
incremental increase = increase in salary
according to an agreed annual increment;
incremental scale = salary scale with
regular annual salary increases

incur [ɪŋ'kɜː] *verb* to make yourself liable
to; **to incur the risk of a penalty =** to make
it possible that you risk paying a penalty; **to
incur debts** *or* **costs =** to do something
which means that you owe money or that
you will have to pay costs; **the company
has incurred heavy costs to implement
the expansion programme =** the company
has had to pay large sums of money (NOTE:
incurring - incurred)

the company blames fiercely
competitive market conditions
in Europe for a £14m operating
loss last year, incurred
despite a record turnover

Financial Times

indebted [ɪn'detɪd] *adjective* owing
money to someone; *to be indebted to a
property company*

indebtedness [ɪn'detɪdnəs] *noun* state
of indebtedness = being in debt, owing
money

indemnification [ɪndemnɪfɪ'keɪʃən]
noun payment for damage

indemnify [ɪn'demnɪfaɪ] *verb* to pay for
damage; *to indemnify someone for a loss*

indemnity [ɪn'demnəti] *noun* guarantee
of payment after a loss; *he had to pay an*

indemnity of £100; **letter of indemnity =**
letter promising payment as compensation
for a loss

indent 1 ['ɪndent] *noun* **(a)** order placed
by an importer for goods from overseas; *he
put in an indent for a new stock of soap*
(b) line of typing which starts several
spaces from the left-hand margin **2**
[ɪn'dent] *verb* **(a) to indent for something**
= to put in an order for something; *the
department has indented for a new
computer* **(b)** to start a line of typing
several spaces from the left-hand margin;
indent the first line three spaces

indenture [ɪn'dentʃə] **1** *noun* **(a)
indentures** *or* **articles of indenture =**
contract by which an apprentice works for
a master for some years to learn a trade **(b)**
US formal agreement showing the terms of
a bond issue **2** *verb* to contract with an
apprentice who will work for some years to
learn a trade; *he was indentured to a
builder*

independent [ɪndɪ'pendənt] *adjective*
free, not controlled by anyone;
independent company = company which
is not controlled by another company;
independent trader *or* **independent shop**
= shop which is owned by an individual
proprietor, not by a chain; **the
independents =** shops or companies which
are owned by private individuals or
families

many independents took
advantage of the bank holiday
period when the big multiples
were closed

The Grocer

index ['ɪndeks] **1** *noun* **(a)** list of items
classified into groups or put in alphabetical
order; **index card =** small card used for
filing; **card index =** series of cards with
information written on them, kept in a
special order so that the information can be
found easily; **index letter** *or* **index number**
= letter or number of an item in an index
(b) regular statistical report which shows
rises and falls in prices, etc.; **growth index**
= index showing how something has
grown; **cost-of-living index =** way of
measuring the cost of living, shown as a
percentage increase on the figure for the

previous year; **retail price index** *US* **consumer price index** = index showing how prices of consumer goods have risen over a period of time, used as a way of measuring inflation and the cost of living; **wholesale price index** = index showing rises and falls of prices of manufactured goods as they leave the factory; **index number** = number which shows the percentage rise of something over a period of time **(c)** figure based on the current market price of certain shares on a stock exchange; **the Financial Times Index (FT Index)** = index which shows percentage rises or falls in shares prices on the London Stock Exchange based on a small group of major companies; **index fund** = investment fund consisting of shares in all the companies which are used to calculate a Stock Exchange index (NOTE: plural is **indexes** or **indices**) **2** *verb* to link a payment to an index; **indexed portfolio** = portfolio of shares in all the companies which form the basis of a stock exchange index

> the index of industrial production sank 0.2 per cent for the latest month after rising 0.3 per cent in March
> *Financial Times*

> an analysis of the consumer price index for the first half of the year shows that the rate of inflation went down by 12.9 per cent
> *Business Times (Lagos)*

indexation [ɪndek'seɪʃn] *noun* linking of something to an index; **indexation of wage increases** = linking of wage increases to the percentage rise in the cost of living

index-linked ['ɪndeks'lɪŋkt] *adjective* which rises automatically by the percentage increase in the cost of living; *his pension is index-linked*; *index-linked government bonds*

> two-year index-linked savings certificates now pay 3 per cent a year tax free, in addition to index-linking
> *Financial Times*

indicate ['ɪndɪkeɪt] *verb* to show; *the latest figures indicate a fall in the inflation rate*; *our sales for last year*

indicate a move from the home market to exports

indicator ['ɪndɪkeɪtə] *noun* thing which indicates; **government economic indicators** = statistics which show how the country's economy is going to perform in the short or long term; **leading indicator** = indicator (such as manufacturing order books) which shows a change in economic trends earlier than other indicators

> it reduces this month's growth in the key M3 indicator from about 19% to 12%
> *Sunday Times*

> we may expect the US leading economic indicators for April to show faster economic growth
> *Australian Financial Review*

> other indicators, such as high real interest rates, suggest that monetary conditions are extremely tight
> *Economist*

indirect [ɪndaɪ'rekt] *adjective* **(a)** not direct; **indirect expenses** *or* **costs** = costs which are not directly attached to the making of a product (such as cleaning, rent, administration); **indirect labour costs** = cost of paying workers which cannot be allocated to a cost centre (such as workers who are not directly involved in making a product, like secretaries in a typing pool, cleaners, etc.) **(b) indirect taxation** = tax which is paid to someone who then pays it to the government (such as sales tax or VAT); *the government raises more money by indirect taxation than by direct*

individual [ɪndɪ'vɪdjuəl] **1** *noun* one single person; *savings plan made to suit the requirements of the private individual* **2** *adjective* single, belonging to one person; *a pension plan designed to meet each person's individual requirements*; *we sell individual portions of ice cream*; *US* **Individual Retirement Account (IRA)** = private pension scheme, into which persons on lower incomes can make contributions (for people not covered by a company pension scheme)

inducement [ɪn'djuːsmənt] *noun* thing which helps to persuade someone to do something; *they offered him a company car as an inducement to stay*

induction [ɪn'dʌkʃən] *noun* starting a new person in a new job; **induction courses** *or* **induction training** = courses to train people starting new jobs

industrial [ɪn'dʌstrɪəl] **1** *adjective* referring to manufacturing work; **industrial accident** = accident which takes place at work; **to take industrial action** = to go on strike or go-slow; **industrial capacity** = amount of work which can be done in a factory or several factories; **industrial centre** = large town with many industries; *GB* **industrial court** *or* **industrial tribunal** = court which can decide in industrial disputes if both parties agree to ask it to judge between them; **industrial design** = design of products made by machines (such as cars, refrigerators); **industrial disputes** = arguments between management and workers; **industrial espionage** = trying to find out the secrets of a competitor's work or products, usually by illegal means; **industrial estate** *or* **industrial park** = area of land near a town specially for factories and warehouses; **industrial expansion** = growth of industries in a country or a region; **industrial injuries** = injuries which happen to workers at work; **industrial processes** = processes involved in manufacturing products in factories; **industrial relations** = relations between management and workers; **good industrial relations** = situation where management and workers understand each others' problems and work together for the good of the company; **industrial training** = training of new workers to work in an industry; **land zoned for light industrial use** = land where planning permission has been given to build small factories for light industry **2** *noun* **industrials** = shares in manufacturing companies

ACAS has a legal obligation to try and solve industrial grievances before they reach industrial tribunals
Personnel Today

Britain's industrial relations climate is changing
Personnel Today

indications of renewed weakness in the US economy were contained in figures on industrial production for April
Financial Times

industrialist [ɪn'dʌstrɪəlɪst] *noun* owner or director of a factory

industrialization [ɪndʌstrɪəlaɪ'zeɪʃən] *noun* changing of an economy from being based on agriculture to industry

industrialize [ɪn'dʌstrɪəlaɪz] *verb* to set up industries in a country which had none before; **industrialized societies** = countries which have many industries

central bank and finance ministry officials of the industrialized countries will continue work on the report
Wall Street Journal

industry ['ɪndəstri] *noun* **(a)** all factories, companies or processes involved in the manufacturing of products; *all sectors of industry have shown rises in output*; **basic industry** = most important industry of a country (such as coal, steel, agriculture); **a boom industry** *or* **a growth industry** = industry which is expanding rapidly; **heavy industry** = industry which deals in heavy raw materials (such as coal) or makes large products (such as ships or engines); **light industry** = industry making small products (such as clothes, books, calculators); **primary industry** = industry dealing with basic raw materials (such as coal, wood, farm produce); **secondary industry** = industry which uses basic raw materials to produce manufactured goods; **service industry** *or* **tertiary industry** = industry which does not produce raw materials or manufacture products but offers a service (such as banking, retailing, accountancy) **(b)** group of companies making the same type of product or offering the same type of service; *the aircraft industry; the building industry; the car industry; the food processing industry; the mining industry; the petroleum industry; the tourist industry* with the present overcapacity in the airline industry, discounting of tickets is widespread

Business Traveller

inefficiency [ɪnɪ'fɪʃənsi] *noun* lack of efficiency; *the report criticized the inefficiency of the sales staff*

inefficient [ɪnɪ'fɪʃənt] *adjective* not efficient, not doing a job well; *an inefficient sales director*

ineligible [ɪn'elɪdʒɪbl] *adjective* not eligible; **ineligible bills** = bills of exchange which cannot be discounted by a central bank

inertia selling [ɪ'nɜːʃjə 'selɪŋ] *noun* method of selling items by sending them when they have not been ordered and assuming that if the items are not returned, the person who has received them is willing to buy them

inexpensive [ɪnɪk'spensɪv] *adjective* cheap, not expensive

inexpensively [ɪnɪk'spensɪvli] *adverb* without spending much money

inferior [ɪn'fɪərɪə] *adjective* not as good as others; *inferior products or products of inferior quality*

inflate [ɪn'fleɪt] *verb* **(a) to inflate prices** = to increase prices without any reason; *tourists don't want to pay inflated London prices* **(b) to inflate the economy** = to make the economy more active by increasing the money supply

inflated [ɪn'fleɪtɪd] *adjective* **(a) inflated prices** = prices which are increased without any reason **(b) inflated currency** = currency which is too high in relation to other currencies

inflation [ɪn'fleɪʃən] *noun* situation where prices rise to keep up with increased production costs, with the result that the purchasing power of money falls; **we have 15% inflation** *or* **inflation is running at 15%** = prices are 15% higher than at the same time last year; *to take measures to reduce inflation*; **high interest rates tend to increase inflation**; **rate of inflation** *or* **inflation rate** = percentage increase in prices over a twelve-month period; **inflation-proof** = (pension, etc.) which is

index-linked, so that its value is preserved in times of inflation; **galloping inflation** *or* **runaway inflation** = very rapid inflation which it is almost impossible to reduce; **spiralling inflation** = inflation where price rises make workers ask for higher wages which then increase prices again

COMMENT: the inflation rate in the UK is calculated on a series of figures, including prices of consumer items; petrol, gas and electricity; interest rates, etc. This gives the 'underlying' inflation rate which can be compared to that of other countries. The calculation can also include mortgage interest and local taxes which give the 'headline' inflation figure; this is higher than in other countries because of these extra items. Inflation affects businesses, in that as their costs rise, so their profits may fall and it is necessary to take this into account when pricing products

the decision by the government to tighten monetary policy will push the annual inflation rate above the year's previous high

Financial Times

when you invest to get a return, you want a 'real' return – above the inflation rate

Investors Chronicle

the retail prices index rose 0.4 per cent in the month, taking the annual headline inflation rate to 1.7 per cent. The underlying inflation rate, which excludes mortgage interest payments, increased to an annual rate of 3.1 per cent

Times

inflationary [ɪn'fleɪʃnəri] *adjective* which tends to increase inflation; *inflationary trends in the economy*; **the economy is in an inflationary spiral** = in a situation where price rises encourage higher wage demands which in turn make prices rise; **anti-inflationary measures** = measures to reduce inflation

inflationary expectations
fell somewhat this month, but
remained a long way above the
actual inflation rate,
according to figures released
yesterday. The annual rate of
inflation measured by the
consumer price index has been
below 2 per cent for over 18
months

Australian Financial Review

inflow ['ɪnfləʊ] *noun* flowing in; **inflow of capital into the country** = capital which is coming into a country in order to be invested

the dollar is strong because
of capital inflows rather
than weak because of the trade
deficit

Duns Business Month

influence ['ɪnfluəns] **1** *noun* effect which is had on someone or something; *the price of oil has a marked influence on the price of manufactured goods*; *we are suffering from the influence of a high exchange rate* **2** *verb* to have an effect on someone or something; *the board was influenced in its decision by the memo from the managers*; *the price of oil has influenced the price of manufactured goods*; *high inflation is influencing our profitability*

influx ['ɪnflʌks] *noun* rushing in; *an influx of foreign currency into the country*; *an influx of cheap labour into the cities* (NOTE: plural is **influxes**)

the retail sector will also
benefit from the expected
influx of tourists

Australian Financial Review

inform [ɪn'fɔːm] *verb* to tell someone officially; *I regret to inform you that your tender was not acceptable*; *we are pleased to inform you that your offer has been accepted*; *we have been informed by the Department of Trade that new tariffs are coming into force*

information [ɪnfə'meɪʃən] *noun* **(a)** details which explain something; *please send me information on or about holidays in the USA*; *have you any information on or about deposit accounts?*; *I enclose this leaflet for your information*; *to disclose a piece of information*; *to answer a request for information*; *for further information, please write to Department 27*; **disclosure of confidential information** = telling someone information which should be secret; **flight information** = information about flight times; **tourist information** = information for tourists **(b) information technology (IT)** = working with computer data; **information retrieval** = storing and then finding data in a computer **(c) information bureau** *or* **information office** = office which gives information to tourists or visitors; **information officer** = person whose job is to give information about a company, an organization or a government department to the public; person whose job is to give information to other departments in the same organization; **information pack** = folder containing information about a product, tourist attraction, etc. (NOTE: no plural; for one item say **a piece of information**)

infrastructure ['ɪnfrəstrʌktʃə] *noun* **(a)** basic structure; **the company's infrastructure** = how the company is organized **(b)** basic services; **a country's infrastructure** = the road and rail systems of a country

infringe [ɪn'frɪndʒ] *verb* to break a law or a right; **to infringe a copyright** = to copy a copyright text illegally; **to infringe a patent** = to make a product which works in the same way as a patented product and not pay a royalty to the patent holder

infringement [ɪn'frɪndʒmənt] *noun* breaking a law or a right; *this infringement of customs regulations must be stopped*; **infringement of copyright** *or* **copyright infringement** = act of illegally copying a work which is in copyright; **infringement of patent** *or* **patent infringement** = act of illegally using, making or selling an invention which is patented, without the permission of the patent holder

ingot ['ɪŋgət] *noun* bar of gold or silver

inherit [ɪn'herɪt] *verb* to get something from a person who has died; *when her father died she inherited the shop*; *he inherited £10,000 from his grandfather*

inheritance [ɪn'herɪtəns] *noun* property which is received from a dead person; **inheritance tax** = tax on wealth or property inherited after the death of someone

in-house ['ɪn'haʊs] *adverb & adjective* working inside a company's building; *the in-house staff*; *we do all our data processing in-house*; **in-house training** = training given to staff at their place of work

initial [ɪ'nɪʃəl] **1** *adjective* first; starting; **initial capital** = capital which is used to start a business; *he started the business with an initial expenditure or initial investment of £500*; **initial sales** = first sales of a new product; *the initial response to the TV advertising has been very good* **2** *noun* **initials** = first letters of the words in a name; *what do the initials IMF stand for?*; *the chairman wrote his initials by each alteration in the contract he was signing* **3** *verb* to write your initials on a document to show you have read it and approved; *to initial an amendment to a contract*; *please initial the agreement at the place marked with an X*

> the founding group has
> subscribed NKr 14.5m of the
> initial NKr 30m share capital
> *Financial Times*

> career prospects are
> excellent for someone with
> potential, and initial salary
> is negotiable around $45,000
> per annum
> *Australian Financial Review*

initiate [ɪ'nɪʃɪeɪt] *verb* to start; *to initiate discussions*

initiative [ɪ'nɪʃɪətɪv] *noun* decision to start something; **to take the initiative** = to decide to do something; **to follow up an initiative** = to take action once someone else has decided to do something

inject [ɪn'dʒekt] *verb* **to inject capital into a business** = to put money into a business

injection [ɪn'dʒekʃən] *noun* **a capital injection of £100,000** *or* **an injection of £100,000 capital** = putting £100,000 into an existing business

injunction [ɪn'dʒʌŋkʃən] *noun* court order telling someone not to do something; *he got an injunction preventing the company from selling his car*; *the*

company applied for an injunction to stop their rival from marketing a similar product

injure ['ɪndʒə] *verb* to hurt (someone); *two workers were injured in the fire*

injured party ['ɪndʒəd 'pɑːti] *noun* party in a court case which has been harmed by another party

injury ['ɪndʒəri] *noun* hurt caused to a person; **injury benefit** = money paid to a worker who has been hurt at work; **industrial injuries** = injuries caused to workers at work

inking pad ['ɪŋkɪŋ 'pæd] *noun* small pad with ink on it, used for putting ink on a rubber stamp

inkjet printer ['ɪŋkdʒet 'prɪntə] *noun* printer which prints by sending a jet of ink onto the paper to form the characters (they give very good results, but cannot be used for multipart stationery)

inland ['ɪnlənd] *adjective* **(a)** inside a country; **inland postage** = postage for a letter to another part of the country; **inland freight charges** = charges for carrying goods from one part of the country to another; *US* **inland carrier** = company which transports goods from a port to a destination inside the country **(b)** *GB* the **Inland Revenue** = British government department dealing with taxes (income tax, corporation tax, capital gains tax, inheritance tax, etc.) but not duties, such as VAT, which are collected by the Customs and Excise; *he received a letter from the Inland Revenue* (NOTE: the American equivalent is the **Internal Revenue Service or IRS**)

innovate ['ɪnəveɪt] *verb* to bring in new ideas or new methods

innovation [ɪnə'veɪʃən] *noun* new idea, new method or new product

innovative ['ɪnəveɪtɪv] *adjective* (person or thing) which is new and makes changes

> small innovative companies in
> IT have been hampered for lack
> of funds
> *Sunday Times*

innovator ['ɪnəveɪtə] *noun* person who brings in new ideas and methods

input ['ɪmpʊt] **1** *noun* **(a) input of information** *or* **computer input** = data fed into a computer; **input lead** = lead for connecting the electric current to a machine **(b) inputs** = goods or services bought by a company and which may be liable to VAT; **input tax** = VAT paid on goods or services which a company buys **2** *verb* **to input information** = to put data into a computer (NOTE: **inputting - inputted**)

inquire [ɪŋ'kwaɪə] *verb* to ask questions about something; *he inquired if anything was wrong*; *she inquired about the mortgage rate*; **'inquire within'** = ask for more details inside the office or shop

inquire into [ɪŋ'kwaɪə 'ɪntʊ] *verb* to investigate, to try to find out about something; *we are inquiring into the background of the new supplier*

inquiry [ɪŋ'kwaɪəri] *noun* official question; *I refer to your inquiry of May 25th*; *all inquiries should be addressed to this department*

inquorate [ɪn'kwɔːreɪt] *adjective* without a quorum

COMMENT: if there is a quorum at a meeting, the meeting is said to be 'quorate'; if there aren't enough people present to make a quorum, the meeting is 'inquorate'

insert 1 ['ɪnsɜːt] *noun* thing which is put inside something; **an insert in a magazine mailing** *or* **a magazine insert** = advertising sheet put into a magazine when it is mailed **2** [ɪn'sɜːt] *verb* to put something in; *to insert a clause into a contract*; *to insert a publicity piece into a magazine mailing*

inside [ɪn'saɪd] **1** *adjective & adverb* in, especially in a company's office or building; *we do all our design work inside*; **inside information** = information which is passed from people working in a company to people outside (and which can be valuable to investors in the company); **inside worker** = worker who works in the office or factory (not in the open air, not a salesman) **2** *preposition* in; *there was nothing inside the container*; *we have a contact inside our rival's production department who gives us very useful information*

insider [ɪn'saɪdə] *noun* person who works in an organization and therefore knows its secrets; **insider dealings** *or* **insider trading** = illegal buying or selling of shares by staff of a company or other persons who have secret information about the company's plans

insolvency [ɪn'sɒlvənsi] *noun* not being able to pay debts; **he was in a state of insolvency** = he could not pay his debts

hundreds of thrifts found themselves on the brink of insolvency after a deregulation programme prompted them to enter dangerous financial waters
Times

insolvent [ɪn'sɒlvənt] *adjective* not able to pay debts; **he was declared insolvent** = he was officially stated to be insolvent

COMMENT: a company is insolvent when its liabilities are higher than its assets; if this happens it must cease trading

inspect [ɪn'spekt] *verb* to examine in detail; *the gas board is sending an engineer to inspect the central heating system*; *inspectors from the DTI have come to inspect the accounts*; **to inspect products for defects** = to look at products in detail to see if they have any defects

inspection [ɪn'spekʃən] *noun* close examination of something; **to make an inspection** *or* **to carry out an inspection of a machine** *or* **an installation**; *the inspection of a product for defects*; **to carry out a tour of inspection** = to visit various places, offices or factories to inspect them; **to issue an inspection order** = to order an official inspection; **VAT inspection** = visit by officials of the Customs and Excise Department to see if a company is correctly reporting its VAT; **inspection stamp** = stamp placed on something to show it has been inspected

inspector [ɪn'spektə] *noun* official who inspects; **inspector of factories** *or* **factory inspector** = government official who inspects factories to see if they are safely run; **inspector of taxes** *or* **tax inspector** = official of the Inland Revenue who examines tax returns and decides how much tax people should pay; **inspector of weights and measures** = government official who inspects weighing machines and goods sold in shops to see if the quantities and weights are correct

inspectorate [ɪn'spektərət] *noun* all inspectors; **the factory inspectorate** = all inspectors of factories

inst [ɪnst] = INSTANT; **your letter of the 6th inst** = your letter of the 6th of this month

instability [ɪnstə'bɪlətɪ] *noun* being unstable, moving up and down; **period of instability in the money markets** = period when currencies fluctuate rapidly

install [ɪn'stɔːl] *verb* to put (a machine) into an office or into a factory; *we are planning to install the new machinery over the weekend*; *they must install a new data processing system because the old one cannot cope with the mass of work involved*

installation [ɪnstə'leɪʃən] *noun* **(a)** machines, equipment and buildings; *harbour installations were picketed by striking dockers*; *the fire seriously damaged the oil installations* **(b)** putting new machines into an office or a factory; *to supervise the installation of new equipment*

instalment *US* **installment**
[ɪn'stɔːlmənt] *noun* part of a payment which is paid regularly until the total amount is paid; *the first instalment is payable on signature of the agreement*; **the final instalment is now due** = the last of a series of payments should be paid now; **to pay £25 down and monthly instalments of £20** = to pay a first payment of £25 and the rest in payments of £20 each month; **to miss an instalment** = not to pay an instalment at the right time

installment plan *or* **installment sales** *or* **installment buying**
[ɪn'stɔːlmənt 'plæn or seɪlz or baɪɪŋ] *noun US* system of buying something by paying a sum regularly each month; *to buy a car on an installment plan* (NOTE: the British English equivalent is **hire purchase or HP**)

instance ['ɪnstəns] *noun* particular example or case; *in this instance we will overlook the delay*

instant ['ɪnstənt] *adjective* **(a)** immediately available; *instant credit is available to current account holders*; **instant access account** = deposit account which pays interest and from which you can withdraw money immediately without penalty **(b)** this month; **our letter of the 6th instant** = our letter of the 6th of this current month

institute ['ɪnstɪtjuːt] **1** *noun* **(a)** official organization; **research institute** = organization set up to do research **(b)** professional body which represents its members; *the Institute of Chartered Accountants* **2** *verb* to start; *to institute proceedings against someone*

institution [ɪnstɪ'tjuːʃən] *noun* organization or society set up for a particular purpose; **financial institution** = bank, investment trust or insurance company whose work involves lending or investing large sums of money

institutional [ɪnstɪ'tjuːʃənl] *adjective* referring to a financial institution; **institutional buying** *or* **selling** = buying or selling shares by financial institutions; **institutional investors** = financial institutions who invest money in securities

> during the 1970s commercial property was regarded by big institutional investors as an alternative to equities
> *Investors Chronicle*

instruct [ɪn'strʌkt] *verb* **(a)** to give an order to someone; **to instruct someone to do something** = to tell someone officially to do something; *he instructed the credit controller to take action* **(b)** to instruct a solicitor = to give information to a solicitor and to ask him to start legal proceedings on your behalf

instruction [ɪn'strʌkʃən] *noun* order which tells what should be done or how something is to be used; *he gave instructions to his stockbroker to sell the shares immediately*; **to await instructions** = to wait for someone to tell you what to do; **to issue instructions** = to tell everyone what to do; **in accordance with** *or* **according to instructions** = as the instructions show; **failing instructions to the contrary** = unless someone tells you to do the opposite; **forwarding instructions** *or* **shipping instructions** = details of how goods are to be shipped and delivered

instructor [ɪnˈstrʌktə] *noun* person who shows how something is to be done

instrument [ˈɪnstrʊmənt] *noun* (a) tool or piece of equipment; *the technician brought instruments to measure the output of electricity* (b) legal document; **financial instrument** = document showing that money has been lent or borrowed, invested or passed from one account to another (such as a bill of exchange, share certificate, certificate of deposit, IOU, etc.); **negotiable instrument** = document (such as a bill of exchange or a cheque) which can be exchanged for cash

insufficient funds [ɪnsəˈfɪʃənt ˈfʌndz] *noun US* not enough money in a checking account to pay a cheque that has been presented

insurable [ɪnˈʃʊərəbl] *adjective* which can be insured

insurance [ɪnˈʃʊərəns] *noun* (a) agreement that in return for regular payments (called 'premiums'), a company will pay compensation for loss, damage, injury or death; **to take out an insurance against fire** = to pay a premium, so that if a fire happens, compensation will be paid; **to take out an insurance on the house** = to pay a premium, so that if the house is damaged compensation will be paid; **the damage is covered by the insurance** = the insurance company will pay for the damage; *repairs will be paid for by the insurance*; **to pay the insurance on a car** = to pay premiums to insure a car (b) **accident insurance** = insurance which will pay if an accident takes place; **car insurance** *or* **motor insurance** = insuring a car, the driver and passengers in case of accident; **comprehensive insurance** = insurance which insures you against all risks which are likely to happen; **endowment insurance** = insurance where a sum of money is paid to the insured person on a certain date or to his heirs if he dies before that date; **fire insurance** = insurance against damage by fire; **general insurance** = insurance covering theft, loss, damage, etc. (but not life insurance);

household insurance = insuring a house and its contents against damage; **life insurance** = insurance which pays a sum of money when someone dies, or at a certain date if he is still alive (NOTE: for life insurance, British English prefers to use **life assurance**); **medical insurance** = insurance which pays the cost of medical treatment, especially when travelling abroad; **term insurance** = life assurance which covers a person's life for a period of time (at the end of the period, if the person is still alive he receives nothing from the insurance); **third-party insurance** = insurance to cover damage to any person who is not one of the people named in the insurance contract (that is, not the insured person nor the insurance company); **whole-life insurance** = insurance where the insured person pays a fixed premium each year and the insurance company pays a sum when he or she dies (also called 'whole-of-life assurance') (c) **insurance agent** *or* **insurance broker** = person who arranges insurance for clients; **insurance certificate** = document from an insurance company showing that an insurance policy has been issued; **insurance claim** = asking an insurance company to pay for damage; **insurance company** = company whose business is to receive payments and pay compensation for loss or damage; **insurance contract** = agreement by an insurance company to insure; **insurance cover** = protection guaranteed by an insurance policy; **insurance policy** = document which shows the conditions of an insurance; **insurance premium** = payment made by the insured person to the insurer (d) *GB* **National Insurance** = state insurance, organized by the government, which pays for medical care, hospitals, unemployment benefits, etc.; **National Insurance contributions (NIC)** = money paid by a worker and the employer each month to the National Insurance

insure [ɪnˈʃʊə] *verb* to have a contract with a company where, if regular small payments are made, the company will pay compensation for loss, damage, injury or death; *to insure a house against fire*; *to insure someone's life*; *he was insured for £100,000*; *to insure baggage against loss*;

to insure against bad weather; *to insure against loss of earnings*; **the life insured** = the person whose life is covered by a life assurance; **the sum insured** = the largest amount of money that an insurer will pay under an insurance (NOTE: for life insurance, British English prefers to use **assure**)

insurer [ɪnˈʃʊərə] *noun* company which insures (NOTE: for life insurance, British English prefers to use **assurer**)

intangible [ɪnˈtændʒəbl] *adjective* which cannot be touched; **intangible fixed assets** = assets which have a value, but which cannot be seen (such as goodwill, copyrights, patents or trademarks)

integrate [ˈɪntɪgreɪt] *verb* to link things together to form one whole group

integration [ɪntɪˈgreɪʃən] *noun* bringing several businesses together under a central control; **horizontal integration** = joining similar companies in the same type of business or taking over a company in the same line of business as yourself; **vertical integration** = joining business together which deal with different stages in the production or sale of the same product

COMMENT: in a case of horizontal integration, a large supermarket might take over another smaller supermarket chain; on the other hand, if a supermarket takes over a food packaging company the integration would be vertical

intellectual property [ɪntɪˈlektjʊəl ˈprɒpəti] *noun* ownership of something (a copyright, patent or design) which is intangible (it is in the mind of the inventor and cannot be seen or touched)

intend [ɪnˈtend] *verb* to plan or to expect to do something; *the company intends to open an office in New York next year*; *we intend to offer jobs to 250 unemployed young people*

intensive [ɪnˈtensɪv] *adjective* **intensive farming** = farming small areas of expensive land, using machines and fertilizers to obtain high crops; **capital-intensive industry** = industry which needs a large amount of capital investment in plant to make it work; **labour-intensive industry** = industry which needs large numbers of workers, where labour costs are high in relation to turnover

intent [ɪnˈtent] *noun* what is planned; **letter of intent** = letter which states what a company intends to do if something happens

inter- [ˈɪntə] *prefix* between; **inter-bank loan** = loan from one bank to another; **the inter-city rail services are good** = train services between cities are good; **inter-company dealings** = dealings between two companies in the same group; **inter-company comparisons** = comparing the results of one company with those of another in the same product area

interest [ˈɪntrəst] **1** *noun* **(a)** special attention; *the MD takes no interest in the staff club*; *the buyers showed a lot of interest in our new product range* **(b)** payment made by a borrower for the use of money, calculated as a percentage of the capital borrowed; **high interest** *or* **low interest** = interest at a high or low percentage; **interest charges** = cost of paying interest; **interest rate** *or* **rate of interest** = percentage charge for borrowing money; **interest-free credit** *or* **loan** = credit or loan where no interest is paid by the borrower; *the company gives its staff interest-free loans* **(c)** money paid as income on investments or loans; *the bank pays 10% interest on deposits*; *to receive interest at 5%*; *the loan pays 5% interest*; *deposit which yields* or *gives* or *produces* or *bears 5% interest*; *account which earns interest at 10%* or *which earns 10% interest*; **simple interest** = interest calculated on the capital only, and not added to it; **compound interest** = interest which is added to the capital and then earns interest itself; **accrual of interest** = automatic addition of interest to capital; **accrued interest** = interest which is accumulating and is due for payment at a later date; **back interest** = interest which has not yet been paid; **fixed interest** = interest which is paid at a set rate; **interest-bearing deposits** = deposits which produce interest; **fixed-interest investments** = investments producing an interest which does not change **(d)** part of the ownership of something, such as money invested in a company giving a financial share in it; **beneficial interest** = situation where someone is allowed to occupy or receive rent from a house without owning it; **he has a controlling interest in the company** = he owns more than 50% of the shares and so can direct how the company is run; **life interest** = situation where someone benefits from a property as long as he or she is alive; **majority interest** *or* **minority interest** = situation where someone owns a majority or a minority of shares in a company; *he has a majority interest in a supermarket chain*; **to acquire a substantial interest in the company** = to buy a large number of shares in a company; **to declare an interest** = to state in public that you own shares in a company **2** *verb* to attract someone's attention; *he tried to interest several companies in his new invention*; **interested in** = paying attention to; *the managing director is interested only in increasing profitability*

since last summer American interest rates have dropped by between three and four percentage points

Sunday Times

a lot of money is said to be tied up in sterling because of the interest-rate differential between US and British rates

Australian Financial Review

interested party ['intrestid 'pɑːti] *noun* person or company with a financial interest in a company

interesting ['intrəstiŋ] *adjective* which attracts attention; *they made us a very interesting offer for the factory*

interface ['intəfeis] **1** *noun* link between two different computer systems or pieces of hardware **2** *verb* to meet and act with; *the office PCs interface with the computer at head office*

interfere [intə'fiə] *verb* to get involved, to try to change something which is not your concern

interference [intə'fiərəns] *noun* the act of interfering; *the sales department*

complained of continual interference from the accounts department

interim ['intərim] *noun* **interim dividend** = dividend paid at the end of a half-year; **interim payment** = payment of part of a dividend; **interim report** = report given at the end of a half-year; **in the interim** = meanwhile, for the time being

the company plans to keep its annual dividend unchanged at ¥7.5 per share, which includes a ¥3.75 interim payout

Financial Times

intermediary [intə'miːdjəri] *noun* person who is the link between parties who do not agree or who are negotiating; *he refused to act as an intermediary between the two directors*; **financial intermediary** = (i) institution which takes deposits or loans from individuals and lends money to clients; (ii) person or company which arranges insurance for a client, but is not itself an insurance company

COMMENT: banks, building societies, hire purchase companies are all types of financial intermediaries

internal [in'tɜːnl] *adjective* **(a)** inside a company; **we decided to make an internal appointment** = we decided to appoint an existing member of staff to the post, and not bring someone in from outside the company; **internal audit** = audit carried out by a department within the company; **internal audit department** *or* **internal auditor** = department or member of staff who examines the internal accounting controls of the company he works for; **internal telephone** = telephone which is linked to other phones in an office **(b)** inside a country; **an internal flight** = flight to a town inside the same country *US* **Internal Revenue Service (IRS)** = government department which deals with tax; **internal trade** = trade between various parts of a country (NOTE: the opposite is **external**)

internally [in'tɜːnəli] *adverb* inside a company; **the job was advertised internally** = the job was advertised inside the company, but not in a public place such as a newspaper

international [ɪntə'næʃənl] *adjective* working between countries; **international call** = telephone call to another country; **international dialling code** = number used to make a telephone call to another country; **international direct dialling (IDD)** = system by which you can telephone direct to a number in another country without going through the operator; **international law** = laws governing relations between countries; **international (postal) reply coupon** = coupon which can be used in another country to pay the postage of replying to a letter; *he enclosed an international reply coupon with his letter*; **international trade** = trade between different countries

International Labour Organization (ILO) [ɪntə'næʃənl 'leɪbə ɔːgənaɪ'zeɪʃn] section of the United Nations, an organization which tries to improve working conditions and workers' pay in member countries

International Monetary Fund (IMF) [ɪntə'næʃənl 'mʌnɪtri 'fʌnd] part of the United Nations, a type of bank which helps member states in financial difficulties, gives financial advice to members and encourages world trade

Internet ['ɪntənet] *noun* international network linking thousands of computers using telephone links; *much of our business is done on the Internet; Internet sales form an important part of our turnover; he searched the Internet for information on cheap tickets to the USA*

> they predict a tenfold increase in sales via internet or TV between 1999 and 2004
>
> *Investors Chronicle*

> in two significant decisions, the Securities and Exchange Board of India today allowed trading of shares through the Internet and set a deadline for companies to conform to norms for good corporate governance
>
> *The Hindu*

interpret [ɪn'tɜːprɪt] *verb* to translate what someone has said into another language; *my assistant knows Greek, so he will interpret for us*

interpreter [ɪn'tɜːprɪtə] *noun* person who translates what someone has said into another language; *my secretary will act as interpreter*

Interstate Commerce Commission (ICC) ['ɪntəsteɪt 'kɒmɜːs kə'mɪʃn] *noun US* federal agency which regulates business activity involving two or more of the states in the USA

intervene [ɪntə'viːn] *verb* to try to make a change in a system; **to intervene in a dispute** = to try to settle a dispute

intervention [ɪntə'venʃən] *noun* acting to make a change in a system; *the government's intervention in the foreign exchange markets; the central bank's intervention in the banking crisis; the government's intervention in the labour dispute;* **intervention price** = price at which the EU will buy farm produce which farmers cannot sell, in order to keep prices high

interview ['ɪntəvjuː] **1** *noun* **(a)** talking to a person who is applying for a job; *we called six people for interview; I have an interview next week* or *I am going for an interview next week* **(b)** asking a person questions as part of an opinion poll **2** *verb* to talk to a person applying for a job to see if he or she is suitable; *we interviewed ten candidates, but did not find anyone suitable*

interviewee [ɪntəvjuː'iː] *noun* person who is being interviewed

interviewer ['ɪntəvjuːə] *noun* person who is conducting the interview

inter vivos ['ɪntə 'vaɪvəs] *Latin phrase* meaning 'between living people'; **gift inter vivos** = gift given to another living person

intestacy [ɪn'testəsi] *noun* dying without having made a will

intestate [ɪn'testət] *adjective* **to die intestate** = to die without having made a will

> COMMENT: when someone dies intestate, the property automatically goes to the parents or siblings of an

unmarried person or, if married, to the surviving partner, unless there are children

in transit ['ɪn 'trænzɪt] *adverb* **goods in transit** = goods being transported

in tray ['ɪn 'treɪ] *noun* basket on a desk for letters or memos which have been received and are waiting to be dealt with

introduce [ɪntrə'djuːs] *verb* to make someone get to know a new person or thing; **to introduce a client** = to bring in a new client and make him known to someone; **to introduce a new product on the market** = to produce a new product and launch it on the market

introduction [ɪntrə'dʌkʃən] *noun* **(a)** letter making someone get to know another person; *I'll give you an introduction to the MD - he is an old friend of mine* **(b)** bringing into use; **the introduction of new technology** = putting new machines (usually computers) into a business or industry

introductory offer [ɪntrə'dʌktəri 'ɒfə] *noun* special price offered on a new product to attract customers

invalid [ɪn'vælɪd] *adjective* not valid, not legal; *this permit is invalid*; *claim which has been declared invalid*

invalidate [ɪn'vælɪdeɪt] *verb* to make something invalid; *because the company has been taken over, the contract has been invalidated*

invalidation [ɪnvælɪ'deɪʃən] *noun* making invalid

invalidity [ɪnvə'lɪdəti] *noun* being invalid; *the invalidity of the contract*

invent [ɪn'vent] *verb* to make something which has never been made before; *she invented a new type of computer terminal*; *who invented shorthand?*; *the chief accountant has invented a new system of customer filing*

invention [ɪn'venʃən] *noun* thing which has been invented; *he tried to sell his latest invention to a US car manufacturer*

inventor [ɪn'ventə] *noun* person who invents something; *he is the inventor of the all-plastic car*

inventory ['ɪnvəntri] **1** *noun* **(a)** *(especially US)* stock, the goods in a warehouse or shop; *to carry a high inventory*; *to aim to reduce inventory*; **inventory control** = system of checking that there is not too much stock in a warehouse, but just enough to meet requirements; **to take inventory** = to count and record the quantity of each item in a warehouse or shop (NOTE: the word 'inventory' is used in the USA where British English uses the word 'stock'. So, the American 'inventory control' is 'stock control' in British English) **(b)** list of the contents of a house for sale, of an office for rent, etc.; *to draw up an inventory of fixtures*; **to agree the inventory** = to agree that the inventory is correct **2** *verb* to make a list of stock or contents

> a warehouse needs to tie up less capital in inventory and with its huge volume spreads out costs over bigger sales
> *Duns Business Month*

invest [ɪn'vest] *verb* **(a)** to put money into shares, bonds, a building society, etc., hoping that it will produce interest and increase in value; *he invested all his money in unit trusts*; *she was advised to invest in real estate or in government bonds*; **to invest abroad** = to put money into shares or bonds in overseas countries **(b)** to spend money on something which you believe will be useful; *to invest money in new machinery*; *to invest capital in a new factory*

> we have substantial venture capital to invest in good projects
> *Times*

investigate [ɪn'vestɪgeɪt] *verb* to examine something which may be wrong; *the Serious Fraud Office has been asked to investigate his share dealings*

investigation [ɪnvestɪ'geɪʃən] *noun* examination to find out what is wrong; *to conduct an investigation into irregularities in share dealings*

investigator [ɪn'vestɪgeɪtə] *noun* person who investigates; *government investigator*

investment [ɪnˈvestmənt] *noun* **(a)**
placing of money so that it will increase in
value and produce interest; *they called for
more government investment in new
industries*; *investment in real estate has
produced a very good return*; *she was
advised to make investments in oil
companies*; **return on investment (ROI)**
= interest or dividends shown as a
percentage of the money invested **(b)**
shares, bonds, deposits bought with
invested money; **long-term investment** *or*
short-term investment = shares, etc.,
which are likely to increase in value over a
long or short period; **safe investment** =
shares, etc., which are not likely to fall in
value; **blue-chip investments** = risk-free
shares of good companies; **quoted
investments** = investments which are
listed on a Stock Exchange; **he is trying to
protect his investments** = he is trying to
make sure that the money he has invested is
not lost **(c) investment adviser** = person
who advises people on what investments to
make; **investment company** *or* **investment
trust** = company whose shares can be
bought on the Stock Exchange, and whose
business is to make money by buying and
selling stocks and shares; **investment
grant** = government grant to a company to
help it to invest in new machinery;
investment income = income (such as
interest and dividends) from investments;
**Investment Management Regulatory
Organization (IMRO)** = organization
which regulates managers of investment
funds, such as pension funds, now part of
the FSA

---

investment trusts, like unit
trusts, consist of portfolios
of shares and therefore
provide a spread of
investments

Investors Chronicle

---

investment companies took the
view that prices had reached
rock bottom and could only go
up

Lloyd's List

---

investor [ɪnˈvestə] *noun* person who
invests money; **the small investor** *or* **the
private investor** = person with a small
sum of money to invest; **the institutional**

investor = organization (like a pension
fund or insurance company) with large
sums of money to invest

invisible [ɪnˈvɪzəbl] **1** *adjective* **invisible
assets** = assets which have a value but
which cannot be seen (such as goodwill or
patents); **invisible earnings** = foreign
currency earned by a country by providing
services, not selling goods; **invisible
imports** *or* **invisible exports** *or* **invisible
trade** = services which are paid for in
foreign currency or earn foreign currency
without actually selling a product (such as
banking, insurance or tourism) (NOTE: the
opposite is **visible**) **2** *plural noun* **invisibles**
= invisible imports and exports

invitation [ɪnvɪˈteɪʃən] *noun* asking
someone to do something; *to issue an
invitation to someone to join the board*;
*they advertised the invitation to tender for
a contract* *or* *to subscribe a new issue*

invite [ɪnˈvaɪt] *verb* to ask someone to do
something; *to ask for something*; *to invite
someone to an interview*; *to invite
someone to join the board*; *to invite
shareholders to subscribe a new issue*; *to
invite tenders for a contract*

invoice [ˈɪnvɔɪs] **1** *noun* **(a)** note asking
for payment for goods or services supplied;
your invoice dated November 10th; *they
sent in their invoice six weeks late*; *to
make out an invoice for £250*; *to settle* *or*
to pay an invoice; **the total is payable
within thirty days of invoice** = the total
sum has to be paid within thirty days of the
date on the invoice; **VAT invoice** = invoice
which includes VAT **(b) invoice clerk** =
office worker who deals with invoices;
invoice price = price as given on an
invoice (including discount and VAT);
total invoice value = total amount on an
invoice, including transport, VAT, etc. **2**
verb to send an invoice to someone; *to
invoice a customer*; *we invoiced you on
November 10th* = we sent you the invoice
on November 10th

invoicing [ˈɪnvɔɪsɪŋ] *noun* sending of
invoices; *all our invoicing is done by
computer*; **invoicing department** =
department in a company which deals with
preparing and sending invoices; **invoicing
in triplicate** = preparing three copies of

invoices; **VAT invoicing** = sending of an invoice including VAT

inward ['ınwəd] *adjective* towards the home country; **inward bill** = bill of lading for goods arriving in a country; **inward investment** = investment by foreign companies in your home country; **inward mission** = visit to your home country by a group of foreign businessmen

IOU ['aıəu'ju:] *noun* (= I OWE YOU) signed document promising that you will pay back money borrowed; *I have a pile of IOUs which need paying*

IRA ['aıɑːr'eı] *US* = INDIVIDUAL RETIREMENT ACCOUNT

irrecoverable [ırı'kʌvərəbl] *adjective* which cannot be recovered; **irrecoverable debt** = debt which will never be paid

irredeemable [ırı'di:məbl] *adjective* which cannot be redeemed; **irredeemable bond** = government bond which has no date of maturity and which therefore provides interest but can never be redeemed at full value (in the UK, the War Loan is irredeemable)

irregular [ı'regjulə] *adjective* not correct; not done in the correct way; *the shipment arrived with irregular documentation*; *this procedure is highly irregular*

irregularity [ıregju'lærəti] *noun* (a) not being regular; not being on time; *the irregularity of the postal deliveries* (b) **irregularities** = things which are not done in the correct way and which are possibly illegal; *to investigate irregularities in the share dealings*

> the group, which asked for its shares to be suspended last week after the discovery of accounting irregularities, is expected to update investors about its financial predicament by the end of this week
> *Times*

irrevocable [ı'revəkəbl] *adjective* which cannot be changed; **irrevocable acceptance** = acceptance which cannot be withdrawn; **irrevocable letter of credit** = letter of credit which cannot be cancelled or changed

IRS ['aıɑːr'es] *US* = INTERNAL REVENUE SERVICE

island site *or* **island display** ['aılənd 'saıt *or* dıs'pleı] *noun* exhibition stand separated from others; *there are only two island sites at the exhibition and we have one of them*; *an island site means that visitors can approach the stand from several directions*

issue ['ıʃu:] **1** *noun* (a) number of a newspaper or magazine; *we have an ad in the January issue of the magazine* (b) giving out new shares; **bonus issue** *or* **scrip issue** = new shares given free to shareholders; **issue of debentures** *or* **debenture issue** = borrowing money by giving debentures to lenders; **issue of new shares** *or* **share issue** = selling new shares in a company to the public; **rights issue** = giving shareholders the right to buy more shares at a lower price; **new issues department** = section of a bank which deals with issues of new shares in companies; **issue price** = price of shares when they are offered for sale for the first time (c) problem being discussed; *to bring up the question of VAT will only confuse the issue* **2** *verb* to put out or to give out; *to issue a letter of credit*; *to issue shares in a new company*; *to issue a writ against someone*; *the government issued a report on London's traffic*

> the rights issue should overcome the cash flow problems
> *Investors Chronicle*

> the company said that its recent issue of 10.5 per cent convertible preference shares at A$8.50 a share has been oversubscribed
> *Financial Times*

issued ['ıʃu:d] *adjective* **issued capital** = amount of capital which is given out as shares to shareholders; **issued price** = price of shares in a new company when they are offered for sale for the first time

> issued and fully paid capital is $100 million
> *Hongkong Standard*

issuing ['ıʃuıŋ] *noun* which organizes an issue of shares; **issuing bank** *or* **issuing**

house = bank which organizes the selling of shares in a new company

IT ['aɪ'tiː] = INFORMATION TECHNOLOGY

item ['aɪtəm] *noun* **(a)** thing for sale; **cash items** = goods sold for cash; **we are holding orders for out of stock items** = for goods which are not in stock; *please find enclosed an order for the following items from your catalogue* **(b)** piece of information; **the items on a profit and loss account** = the different entries on a profit and loss account; **exceptional items** = items which arise from normal trading but which are unusual because of their size or nature (they are shown separately in a note to the company's accounts); **extraordinary items** = items in accounts which do not appear each year; **item of expenditure** = goods or services which have been paid for and appear in the accounts **(c)** point on a list; **we will now take item four on the agenda** = we will now discuss the fourth point on the agenda

itemize ['aɪtəmaɪz] *verb* to make a detailed list of things; *itemizing the sales figures will take about two days*; **itemized account** = detailed record of money paid or owed; *US* **itemized deductions** = deductions from a person's taxable income which are listed on his tax return; **itemized invoice** = invoice which lists each item separately; **itemized statement** = bank statement where each transaction is recorded in detail

itinerant worker [ɪ'tɪnərənt 'wɜːkə] *noun* worker who moves from place to place, looking for work

itinerary [aɪ'tɪnərəri] *noun* list of places to be visited on one journey; *a salesman's itinerary*

Jj

jam [dʒæm] **1** *noun* blocking; **traffic jam** = situation where there is so much traffic on the road that it moves only very slowly; *there were huge traffic jams on motorways leading out of the capital* **2** *verb* to stop working or to be blocked; *the paper feed has jammed*; *the switchboard was jammed with calls* (NOTE: **jamming - jammed**)

janitor ['dʒænɪtə] *noun US* person who looks after a building, making sure it is clean and that the rubbish is cleared away (NOTE: British English is **caretaker**)

J curve ['dʒeɪ 'kɜːv] *noun* line on a graph shaped like a letter 'J', with an initial short fall, followed by a longer rise (used to describe the effect of a falling exchange rate on a country's balance of trade)

jetsam ['dʒetsəm] *noun* **flotsam and jetsam** = rubbish floating in the water after a ship has been wrecked and rubbish washed on to the land

jettison ['dʒetɪzn] *verb* to throw cargo from a ship into the sea to make the ship lighter

Jiffy bag® ['dʒɪfi 'bæg] *noun* trade name for a padded bag, used for sending items by post; *she sent the diskettes in a Jiffy bag*

jingle ['dʒɪŋgl] *noun* **advertising jingle** *or* **publicity jingle** = short and easily remembered tune or song to advertise a product on television, etc.

JIT = JUST-IN-TIME

job [dʒɒb] *noun* **(a)** piece of work; **to do a job of work** = to be given a job of work to do; **to do odd jobs** = to do various pieces of work; *he does odd jobs for us around the house*; **odd-job-man** = person who does various pieces of work; **to be paid by the job** = to be paid for each piece of work

done **(b)** order being worked on; *we are working on six jobs at the moment*; *the shipyard has a big job starting in August* **(c)** regular paid work; *he is looking for a job in the computer industry*; *he lost his job when the factory closed*; *she got a job in a factory*; *he is going to apply for a job in an office*; **office job** *or* **white-collar job** = job in an office; **to give up your job** = to resign from your work; **to look for a job** = to try to find work; **to retire from your job** = to leave work and take a pension; **to be out of a job** = to have no work **(d) job analysis** = detailed examination and report on the duties of a job; **job application** *or* **application for a job** = asking for a job in writing; *you have to fill in a job application form*; **job centre** = government office which lists jobs which are vacant; **job classification** = describing jobs listed under various classes; **job creation scheme** = government-backed plan to make work for the unemployed; **job description** = official document from the management which says what a job involves; **job evaluation** = examining different jobs within an organization to see what skills and qualifications are needed to carry them out; **job losses** = jobs which no longer exist because workers have been made redundant; **job satisfaction** = a worker's feeling that he is happy in his place of work and pleased with the work he does; **job security** = feeling which a worker has that he has a right to keep his job, or that he will stay in his job until he retires; **job sharing** = situation where a job is shared by more than one person, each working part-time; **job specification** = very detailed description of what is involved in a job; **job title** = name given to a person in a certain job; *her job title is*

'Chief Buyer'; **on-the-job training** = training given to workers at their place of work; **off-the-job training** = training given to workers away from their place of work (i.e. at a college) **(e) job lot** = group of miscellaneous items sold together; *he sold the household furniture as a job lot* **(f)** difficulty; *they will have a job to borrow the money they need for the expansion programme*; *we had a job finding a qualified secretary*

> he insisted that the tax advantages he directed toward small businesses will help create jobs
>
> *Toronto Star*

jobber ['dʒɒbə] *noun* **(a)** *(formerly on the London Stock Exchange)* **(stock) jobber** = person who bought and sold shares from other traders **(b)** *US* wholesaler; **rack jobber** = wholesaler who sells goods by putting them on racks in retail shops

> warehouse clubs buy directly from manufacturers, eliminating jobbers and wholesale middlemen
>
> *Duns Business Month*

jobbing ['dʒɒbɪŋ] *noun* **(a)** *(formerly on the London Stock Exchange)* **(stock) jobbing** = buying and selling shares from other traders **(b)** doing small pieces of work; **jobbing gardener** *or* **jobbing printer** = person who does odd jobs in the garden or who does small printing jobs

jobclub ['dʒɒbklʌb] *noun* organization which helps its members to find jobs; *since joining the jobclub she has improved her interview techniques and gained self-confidence*

jobless ['dʒɒbləs] *noun* people with no jobs, the unemployed (NOTE: takes a plural verb)

> the contradiction between the jobless figures and latest economic review
>
> *Sunday Times*

join [dʒɔɪn] *verb* **(a)** to put things together; *the offices were joined together by making a door in the wall*; *if the paper is too short to take all the accounts, you can join an extra piece on the bottom* **(b)** **to join a firm** = to start work with a

company; *he joined on January 1st* = he started work on the January 1st **(c) to join an association** *or* **a group** = to become a member of an association or a group; *all the staff have joined the company pension plan*; *he was asked to join the board*; *Smith Ltd has applied to join the trade association*

joint [dʒɔɪnt] *adjective* **(a)** combined, with two or more organizations linked together; **joint commission of inquiry** *or* **joint committee** = commission or committee with representatives of various organizations on it; **joint discussions** = discussions between management and workers before something is done; **joint management** = management done by two or more people; **joint venture** = very large business project where two or more companies join together, often forming a new joint company to manage the project **(b) joint account** = bank account for two people; *most married people have joint accounts so that they can each take money out when they want it*; **joint-stock bank** = bank which is a public company quoted on the Stock Exchange; **joint-stock company** = a company which issues shares to those who have contributed capital to it **(c)** one of two or more people who work together or who are linked; *they are joint beneficiaries of the will*; *she and her brother are joint managing directors*; *the two countries are joint signatories of the treaty*; **joint ownership** = owning of a property by several owners

jointly ['dʒɔɪntli] *adverb* together with one or more other people; *to own a property jointly*; *to manage a company jointly*; *they are jointly liable for damages*

journal ['dʒɜːnl] *noun* **(a)** book with the account of sales and purchases made each day; **sales journal** = sales day book, the book in which non-cash sales are recorded with details of customer, invoice, amount and date (these details are later posted to each customer's account in the sales ledger) **(b)** magazine; **house journal** = magazine produced for the workers in a company to give them news about the company; **trade journal** = magazine produced for people or companies in a certain trade

journalist ['dʒɜːnəlɪst] *noun* person who writes for a newspaper

journey ['dʒɜːni] *noun* long trip, especially a trip done by a salesman; *he planned his journey so as to visit all his accounts in two days*; **journey order** = order given by the shopkeeper to a salesman when he calls; **journey planning** = planning what calls a salesperson will make and how he or she will reach them most efficiently, giving priority to the more profitable accounts

journeyman ['dʒɜːnɪmən] *noun US* skilled craftsman who has completed his apprenticeship

judge [dʒʌdʒ] **1** *noun* person who decides in a legal case; *the judge sent him to prison for embezzlement* **2** *verb* to decide; *the chairman judged it was time to call an end to the discussion*

judgement *or* **judgment** ['dʒʌdʒmənt] *noun* legal decision or official decision; **to pronounce judgement** *or* **to give your judgement on something** = to give an official or legal decision about something; **judgment debtor** = debtor who has been ordered by a court to pay a debt (NOTE: the spelling **judgment** is used by lawyers)

judicial [dʒuːˈdɪʃəl] *adjective* referring to the law; **judicial processes** = the ways in which the law works

jumble sale ['dʒʌmbl 'seɪl] *noun* sale of odd secondhand items organized by a club or organization to raise money

jump [dʒʌmp] **1** *noun* sudden rise; *a jump in the cost-of-living index*; *there was a jump in unemployment figures in December* **2** *verb* **(a)** to go up suddenly; *oil prices have jumped since the war started*; *share values jumped on the Stock Exchange* **(b)** to go away suddenly; **to jump bail** = not to appear in court after having been released on bail; **to jump the gun** = to start to do something too early or before you should; **to jump the queue** = to go in front of someone who has been

waiting longer; *they jumped the queue and got their export licence before we did*; **to jump ship** = to leave a ship where you work as a sailor and not to go back

jumpy ['dʒʌmpi] *adjective* nervous or excited; **the market is jumpy** = the stock market is nervous and share prices are likely to fluctuate

junior ['dʒuːnjə] **1** *adjective* younger or lower in rank; **junior clerk** = clerk, usually young, who has lower status than a senior clerk; **junior executive** *or* **junior manager** = young manager in a company; **junior partner** = person who has been made a partner more recently than others; **John Smith, Junior** = the younger John Smith (i.e. the son of John Smith, Senior) **2** *noun* **(a)** barrister who is not a Queen's counsel **(b)** **office junior** = young man or woman who does all types of work in an office

junk [dʒʌŋk] *noun* rubbish, useless items; *you should throw away all that junk*; **junk bonds** = bonds raised as debentures on the security of a company which is the subject of a takeover bid; **junk mail** = unsolicited advertising material sent through the post and thrown away immediately by the people who receive it

> the big US textile company is running deep in the red, its junk bonds are trading as low as 33 cents on the dollar
> *Wall Street Journal*

jurisdiction [dʒʊərɪsˈdɪkʃn] *noun* **within the jurisdiction of the court** = in the legal power of a court

just-in-time (JIT) ['dʒʌstɪnˈtaɪm] *noun* **just-in-time (JIT) production** = making goods to order just before they are needed, so as to avoid having too many goods in stock; **just-in-time (JIT) purchasing** = purchasing system where goods are purchased immediately before they are needed, so as to avoid carrying high levels of stock

Kk

K [keɪ] *abbreviation* one thousand; **'salary: £20K+'** = salary more than £20,000 per annum

KD = KNOCKDOWN

keen [kiːn] *adjective* **(a)** eager or active; **keen competition** = strong competition; *we are facing some keen competition from European manufacturers*; **keen demand** = wide demand; *there is a keen demand for home computers* **(b) keen prices** = prices which are kept low so as to be competitive; *our prices are the keenest on the market*

keep [kiːp] *verb* **(a)** to go on doing something; *they kept working, even when the boss told them to stop*; *the other secretaries complain that she keeps singing when she is typing* **(b)** to do what is necessary; **to keep an appointment** = to be there when you said you would be; **to keep the books of a company** *or* **to keep a company's books** = to note the accounts of a company accurately **(c)** to hold items for sale or for information; **we always keep this item in stock** = we always have this item in our warehouse or shop; **to keep someone's name on file** = to have someone's name on a list for reference **(d)** to hold things at a certain level; *we must keep our mailing list up to date*; *to keep spending to a minimum*; *the price of oil has kept the pound at a high level*; *the government is encouraging firms to keep prices low*; *lack of demand for typewriters has kept prices down* (NOTE: **keeping - kept**)

keep back [kiːp bæk] *verb* to hold on to something which you could give to someone; *to keep back information or to keep something back from someone*; *to keep £10 back from someone's salary*

keeping [kiːpɪŋ] *noun* **safe keeping** = being looked after carefully; *we put the documents into the bank for safe keeping*

keep on [kiːp ɒn] *verb* to continue to do something; *the factory kept on working in spite of the fire*; *we keep on receiving orders for this item although it was discontinued two years ago*

keep up [kiːp ʌp] *verb* to hold at a certain high level; *we must keep up the turnover in spite of the recession*; *she kept up a rate of sixty words per minute for several hours*

Keogh plan [kiːəʊ plæn] *noun* US private pension system allowing self-employed businessmen and professionals to set up pension and retirement plans for themselves

key [kiː] **1** *noun* **(a)** piece of metal used to open a lock; *we have lost the keys to the computer room*; **key money** = premium paid when taking over the keys of a flat or office which you are renting **(b)** part of a computer or typewriter which you press with your fingers; *there are sixty-four keys on the keyboard*; **control key** = key on a computer which works part of a program; **function key** = key switch that has been assigned a particular task or sequence of instructions (function keys often form a separate group of keys on the keyboard, and have specific functions attached to them. They may be labelled F1, F2, etc.); **shift key** = key which makes a typewriter or computer move to capital letters **(c)** important; *key factor*; *key industry*; *key personnel*; *key post*; *key staff* **2** *verb* **to key in data** = to put information into a computer

he gave up the finance job in
September to devote more time

to his global responsibilities as chairman and to work more closely with key clients

Times

keyboard ['kiːbɔːd] **1** *noun* part of a typewriter or computer with keys which are pressed to make letters or figures; **qwerty keyboard** = English language keyboard, where the first letters are Q-W-E-R-T-Y; *the computer has a normal qwerty keyboard* **2** *verb* to press the keys on a keyboard to type something; *he is keyboarding our address list*

keyboarder ['kiːbɔːdə] *noun* person who types information into a computer

keyboarding ['kiːbɔːdɪŋ] *noun* act of typing on a keyboard; *keyboarding costs have risen sharply*

keyed *adjective* which has a key; **keyed advertisement** = advertisement which asks customers to reply in writing to a particular address, or to a particular department, which will indicate the magazine in which the advertisement appeared and so help the advertiser gauge the effectiveness of using that magazine

keypad ['kiːpæd] *noun* small keyboard; **numeric keypad** = part of a computer keyboard which is a programmable set of numbered keys

kg = KILOGRAM

kickback ['kɪkbæk] *noun* illegal commission paid to someone (especially a government official) who helps in a business deal

killing ['kɪlɪŋ] *noun (informal)* huge profit; *he made a killing on the stock market*

kilo *or* **kilogram** ['kiːləʊ *or* 'kɪləgræm] *noun* measure of weight (= one thousand grams); *packets weighing more than 2kg must go by parcel post* (NOTE: written **kg** after figures: **20kg**)

kilobyte ['kɪləbaɪt] *noun* unit of storage in a computer (= 1,024 bytes)

kilometre *US* **kilometer** [kɪ'lɒmɪtə] *noun* measure of length (= one thousand metres); **the car does fifteen kilometres to the litre** = the car uses a litre of petrol to travel fifteen kilometres (NOTE: written **km** after figures: **70km**)

kind [kaɪnd] *noun* sort or type; *the printer produces two kinds of printout*; *our drinks machine has three kinds of cold drinks*; **payment in kind** = payment made by giving goods or food, but not money

king-size ['kɪŋ'saɪz] *adjective* extra large container of a product (usually comparatively economical to buy)

kiosk ['kiːɒsk] *noun* small wooden shelter, for selling goods out of doors; *she had a newspaper kiosk near the station for 20 years*; **telephone kiosk** = shelter with a public telephone in it; *there are two telephone kiosks outside the post office*

kite [kaɪt] **1** *noun* **(a) to fly a kite** = to put forward a proposal to try to interest people; **kite flier** = person who tries to impress by putting forward a proposal; **kite-flying** = trying to impress by putting forward grand plans **(b)** *GB* **kite mark** = mark on goods to show they meet official standards **2** *verb* **(a)** *US* to write cheques on one account (which may not have any money in it) and deposit them in another, withdrawing money from the second account before the cheques are cleared **(b)** *GB* to use stolen credit cards or cheque books

kitty ['kɪti] *noun* money which has been collected by a group of people to be used later (such as for an office party)

km = KILOMETRE

knock [nɒk] *verb* **(a)** to hit something; *he knocked on the door and went in*; *she knocked her head on the filing cabinet* **(b) to knock the competition** = to hit competing firms hard by vigorous selling; **knocking copy** = advertising material which criticizes competing products

knock down [nɒk 'daʊn] *verb* **to knock something down to a bidder** = to sell something at an auction; *the furniture was knocked down to him for £100*

knockdown ['nɒkdaʊn] *noun* **(a) knockdown (KD) goods** = goods sold in parts, which must be assembled by the buyer **(b) knockdown prices** = very low prices; *he sold me the car at a knockdown price*

knock off ['nɒk 'ɒf] *verb* **(a)** to stop work; *we knocked off at 3p.m. on Friday* **(b)** to reduce a price by an amount; *he knocked £10 off the price for cash*

knock-on effect ['nɒk'ɒn ɪ'fekt] *noun* effect which an action will have on other situations; *the strike by customs officers has had a knock-on effect on car production by slowing down exports of cars*

knot [nɒt] *noun* measure of speed used to show the speed of a ship or of the wind

> COMMENT: one knot is one nautical mile per hour

know [nəʊ] *verb* **(a)** to learn, to have information about something; *I do not know how a computer works*; *does he know how long it takes to get to the airport?*; *the managing director's secretary does not know where he is*; *he knows the African market very well* **(b)** to have met someone; *do you know Mr Jones, our new sales director?* (NOTE: knowing - known)

know-how ['nəʊhaʊ] *noun* knowledge about how something works or how something is made; *to acquire computer know-how* or *electronic know-how*; **know-how fund** = fund created by the UK government to provide technical training and advice to countries of Eastern Europe

knowledge ['nɒlɪdʒ] *noun* what is known; **he had no knowledge of the contract** = he did not know that the contract existed

krona ['krəʊnə] *noun* currency used in Sweden and Iceland

krone ['krəʊnə] *noun* currency used in Denmark and Norway

LI

label ['leɪbl] **1** *noun* **(a)** piece of paper or card attached to something to show its price *or* an address or instructions for use; **gummed label** = label with dry glue on it, which has to be made wet to make it stick; **self-sticking label** *or* **sticky label** = label with glue on it, ready to stick on an item; **tie-on label** = label with a piece of string attached so that it can be tied on to an item; **a sheet of computer labels** = a sheet of sticky labels which can be printed with addresses in a printer **(b) address label** = label with an address on it; **price label** = label showing a price; **quality label** = label which states the quality of something **(c) own label goods** = goods specially produced for a store with the store's name on them **2** *verb* to attach a label to something; **an incorrectly labelled parcel** = a parcel with the wrong information on the label (NOTE: British English **labelling - labelled** but American spelling **labeling - labeled**)

labelling ['leɪblɪŋ] *noun* putting a label on something; **labelling department** = section of a factory where labels are attached to the product; **labelling program** = word-processing program which allows you to print addresses from an address list onto labels

laboratory [lə'bɒrətri] *noun* place where scientific research is carried out; *the product was developed in the company's laboratories*; *all products are tested in our own laboratories*

labour *US* **labor** ['leɪbə] *noun* **(a)** heavy work; **manual labour** = work done by hand; **to charge for materials and labour** = to charge for both the materials used in a job and also the hours of work involved;

labour costs *or* **labour charges** = cost of the workers employed to make a product (not including materials or overheads); **direct labour (costs)** = cost of the workers employed which can be allocated to a product (not including materials or overheads); **indirect labour (costs)** = cost of paying workers which cannot be allocated to a cost centre (such as workers who are not directly involved in making a product, like secretaries in a typing pool, cleaners, etc.); **labour is charged at £5 an hour** = each hour of work costs £5 **(b)** workers, the workforce; **casual labour** = workers who are hired for a short period; **cheap labour** = workers who do not earn much money; **local labour** = workers recruited near a factory, not brought in from somewhere else; **organized labour** = workers who are members of trade unions; **skilled labour** = workers who have special knowledge or qualifications; **labour force** = all workers; *the management has made an increased offer to the labour force*; *we are setting up a factory in the Far East because of the cheap labour force available*; **labour market** = number of workers who are available for work; **25,000 young people have left school and have come on to the labour market** = 25,000 people have left school and become available for work; **labour shortage** *or* **shortage of labour** = situation where there are not enough workers to fill jobs; **labour-intensive industry** = industry which needs large numbers of workers or where labour costs are high in relation to turnover **(c) labour disputes** = arguments between management and workers; **labour laws** *or* **labour legislation** = laws relating to the employment of workers; **labour relations** = relations between management and workers; *US* **labor union** = organization which represents workers who are its members in discussions about wages and conditions of work with management (NOTE: British English is **trade union**) **(d) International Labour Organization (ILO)** = section of the United Nations which tries to improve working conditions and workers' pay in member countries

the possibility that British goods will price themselves back into world markets is doubtful as long as sterling labour costs continue to rise faster than in competitor countries
Sunday Times

70 per cent of Australia's labour force is employed in service activity
Australian Financial Review

European economies are being held back by rigid labor markets and wage structures
Duns Business Month

labourer ['leɪbərə] *noun* person who does heavy work; **agricultural labourer** = person who does heavy work on a farm; **casual labourer** = manual worker who can be hired for a short period; **manual labourer** = person who does heavy work with his hands

labour-saving ['leɪbə'seɪvɪŋ] *adjective* which saves you doing hard work; *a labour-saving device*

lack [læk] **1** *noun* not having enough; **lack of data** *or* **lack of information** = not having enough information; *the decision has been put back for lack of up-to-date information*; **lack of funds** = not enough money; *the project was cancelled because of lack of funds* **2** *verb* not to have enough of something; *the company lacks capital*; **the sales staff lack motivation** = the sales staff are not motivated enough

ladder ['lædə] *noun* series of steps made of wood or metal which can be moved about, and which you can climb; *you will need a ladder to look into the machine*; **promotion ladder** = series of steps by which people can be promoted; *by being*

appointed sales manager, he moved several steps up the promotion ladder

laden ['leɪdn] *adjective* loaded; **fully-laden ship** = ship with a full cargo; **ship laden in bulk** = ship which has a loose cargo (such as corn) which is not packed in containers

lading ['leɪdɪŋ] *noun* loading, putting goods on a ship; **bill of lading** = list of goods being shipped, which the transporter gives to the person sending the goods to show that they have been loaded

Laffer curve ['læfə 'kɜ:v] *noun* chart showing that cuts in tax rates increase output in the economy

laid up ['leɪd 'ʌp] *adjective* **(a)** *(ship)* not used because there is no work; *half the shipping fleet is laid up by the recession* **(b)** (person who is) unable to work because of illness or injury; *half the staff are laid up with flu*

laissez-faire economy ['leseɪ'feə ɪ'kɒnəmi] *noun* economy where the government does not interfere because it believes it is right to let the economy run itself

lakh [læk] *noun (in India)* one hundred thousand (NOTE: ten lakh equal one crore)

lame duck ['leɪm 'dʌk] *noun* **(a)** company which is in financial difficulties; *the government has refused to help lame duck companies* **(b)** official who has not been re-elected and is finishing his term of office; *a lame-duck president*

land [lænd] **1** *noun* area of earth; **land agent** = person who runs a farm or a large area of land for someone; **land bank** = undeveloped land which belongs to a property developer; *GB* **land register** = register of land, showing who owns it and what buildings are on it; **land registration** = system of registering land and its owners; **land registry** = government office where land is registered; **land taxes** = taxes on the amount of land someone owns **2** *verb* **(a)** to put goods or passengers onto land after a voyage by sea or by air; *the ship landed some goods at Mombasa*; *the plane stopped for thirty minutes at the local airport to land passengers and mail*; **landed costs** = costs of goods which have been delivered to a port, unloaded and passed through customs **(b)** to come down to earth after a flight; *the plane landed ten minutes late*

landing ['lændɪŋ] *noun* **(a)** action of bringing a plane down to land; **landing card** = card given to passengers who have passed customs and can land from a ship or an aircraft; **landing charges** = payment for putting goods on land and paying customs duties; **landing order** = permit which allows goods to be unloaded into a bonded warehouse without paying customs duty **(b)** **soft landing** = change in economic strategy to curb inflation, which has only minor effects on the bulk of the population

landlady ['lænleɪdi] *noun* woman who owns a property which she lets; *we pay our rent direct to the landlady every week*

landlord ['lænlɔːd] *noun* person or company which owns a property which is let; **ground landlord** = person or company which owns the freehold of a property which is then let and sublet; *our ground landlord is an insurance company*

landowner ['lændəunə] *noun* person who owns large areas of land

language ['læŋgwɪdʒ] *noun* words spoken or written by people in a certain country; *the managing director conducted the negotiations in three languages*; **programming language** = system of signs, letters and words used to instruct a computer; *what language does the program run on?*

lapse [læps] **1** *noun* **a lapse of time** = a period of time which has passed **2** *verb* to stop being valid, to stop being active; *the guarantee has lapsed*; **to let an offer lapse** = to allow time to pass so that an offer is no longer valid

laptop ['læptɒp] *noun* small portable computer which you can hold on your knees to work; *I take my laptop with me so that I can write reports on the train*; *our reps all have laptops on which they can key their orders and email them back to the warehouse*

large [lɑːdʒ] *adjective* very big or important; *our company is one of the largest suppliers of computers to the government*; *he is our largest customer*;

why has she got an office which is larger than mine?

largely ['lɑːdʒli] *adverb* mainly or mostly; *our sales are largely in the home market*; *they have largely pulled out of the American market*

large-scale ['lɑːdʒ'skeɪl] *adjective* working in a big way, with large numbers of people or large amounts of money involved; *large-scale investment in new technology*; *large-scale redundancies in the construction industry*

laser printer ['leɪzə 'prɪntə] *noun* computer printer which uses a laser source to print high-quality dot matrix characters on paper; **laser cartridge** = cartridge of toner for a laser printer; **laser paper** = paper used in a laser printer

last [lɑːst] **1** *adjective & adverb* **(a)** coming at the end of a series; *out of a queue of twenty people, I was served last*; *this is our last board meeting before we move to our new offices*; *we finished the last items in the order just two days before the promised delivery date*; **last quarter** = period of three months to the end of the financial year **(b)** most recent or most recently; *where is the last batch of invoices?*; *the last ten orders were only for small quantities*; **last week** or **last month** or **last year** = the week, month or year before this one; *last week's sales were the best we have ever had*; *the sales managers have been asked to report on last month's drop in unit sales*; *last year's accounts have to be ready by the AGM* **(c)** the week or month or year before last = the week, month or year before the one before this; *last year's figures were bad, but they were an improvement on those of the year before last* **2** *verb* to go on, to continue; *the boom started in the 1980s and lasted until the early 1990s*; *the discussions over redundancies lasted all day*

last in first out (LIFO) ['lɑːst 'ɪn 'fɜːst 'aut] *noun* **(a)** redundancy policy, where the people who have been most recently appointed are the first to be made redundant **(b)** accounting method where stock is valued at the price of the earliest purchases (it is assumed that the most recently purchased stock is sold first)

late [leɪt] **1** *adjective* **(a)** after the time stated or agreed; *we apologize for the late arrival of the plane from Amsterdam*; **there is a penalty for late delivery** = if delivery is later than the agreed date, the supplier has to pay a fine **(b)** at the end of a period of time; **latest date for signature of the contract** = the last acceptable date for signing the contract **(c) latest** = most recent; *he always drives the latest model of car*; *here are the latest sales figures* **2** *adverb* after the time stated or agreed; *the shipment was landed late*; *the plane was two hours late*

late-night ['leɪt'naɪt] *adjective* happening late at night; *the stores are open for late-night shopping on Thursdays*; *he had a late-night meeting at the airport*; *their late-night negotiations ended in an agreement which was signed at 3 a.m.*

launch [lɔːntʃ] **1** *verb* to put a new product on the market (usually spending money on advertising it); *they launched their new car model at the motor show*; *the company is spending thousands of pounds to launch a new brand of soap* **2** *noun* act of putting a new product on the market; *the launch of the new model has been put back three months*; *the company is geared up for the launch of the new brand of soap*; *the management has decided on a September launch date*

launching ['lɔːntʃɪŋ] *noun* act of putting a new product on the market; **launching costs** = costs of publicity for a new product; **launching date** = date when a new product is officially shown to the public for the first time; **launching party** = party held to advertise the launching of a new product

launder ['lɔːndə] *verb* to pass illegal profits, money from selling drugs, money which has not been taxed, etc., into the normal banking system; *to launder money through an offshore bank*

it has since emerged that the bank was being used to launder drug money and some of its executives have been given lengthy jail sentences

Times

law [lɔː] *noun* **(a) laws** = rules by which a country is governed and the activities of people and organizations controlled; **labour laws** = laws concerning the employment of workers **(b) law** = all the laws of a country taken together; **civil law** = laws relating to arguments between individuals and the rights of individuals; **commercial law** = laws regarding business; **company law** = laws which refer to the way companies work; **contract law** *or* **the law of contract** = laws relating to private agreements; **copyright law** = laws concerning the protection of copyright; **criminal law** = laws relating to crime; **international law** = laws referring to the way countries deal with each other; **maritime law** *or* **the law of the sea** = laws referring to ships, ports, etc.; **law courts** = place where a judge listens to cases and decides who is right legally; **to take someone to law** = to tell someone to appear in court to settle an argument; **inside the law** *or* **within the law** = obeying the laws of a country; **against** *or* **outside the law** = not according to the laws of a country; *the company is possibly operating outside the law*; **to break the law** = to do something which is not allowed by law; *he is breaking the law by trading without a licence*; *you will be breaking the law if you try to take that computer out of the country without an export licence* **(c)** general rule; **law of supply and demand** = general rule that the amount of a product which is available is related to the needs of the possible customers; **law of diminishing returns** = general rule that as more factors of production (land, labour and capital) are added to the existing factors, so the amount they produce is proportionately smaller

lawful ['lɔːful] *adjective* acting within the law; **lawful practice** = action which is permitted by the law; **lawful trade** = trade which is allowed by law

lawfully ['lɔːfuli] *adverb* acting within the law

lawsuit ['lɔːsuːt] *noun* case brought to a court; **to bring a lawsuit against someone** = to tell someone to appear in court to settle an argument; **to defend a lawsuit** = to appear in court to state your case

lawyer ['lɔːjə] *noun* person who has studied law and can act for people on legal business; **commercial lawyer** *or* **company lawyer** = person who specializes in company law or who advises companies on legal problems; **international lawyer** = person who specializes in international law; **maritime lawyer** = person who specializes in laws concerning ships

lay [leɪ] *verb* to put; **to lay an embargo on trade with a country** = to forbid trade with a country (NOTE: **laying - laid**)

lay off ['leɪ 'ɒf] *verb* **(a) to lay off workers** = to dismiss workers for a time (until more work is available); *the factory laid off half its workers because of lack of orders* **(b) to lay off risks** = to protect oneself against risk in one investment by making other investments

> the company lost $52 million last year, and has laid off close to 2,000 employees
> *Toronto Star*

lay-off ['leɪɒf] *noun* action of dismissing a worker for a time; *the recession has caused hundreds of lay-offs in the car industry*

lay out ['leɪ 'aʊt] *verb* to spend money; *we had to lay out half our cash budget on equipping the new factory*

layout ['leɪaʊt] *noun* arrangement of the inside of a building; *they have altered the layout of the offices*

lay up ['leɪ 'ʌp] *verb* to stop using a ship because there is no work; *half the shipping fleet is laid up by the recession*; *see also* **LAID UP**

> while trading conditions for the tanker are being considered, it is possible that the ship could be laid up
> *Lloyd's List*

lazy ['leɪzi] *adjective* (person) who does not want to work; *she is too lazy to do any overtime*; *he is so lazy he does not even send in his expense claims on time*

lb = pound

LBO = LEVERAGED BUYOUT

L/C = LETTER OF CREDIT

LDT = LICENSED DEPOSIT-TAKER

lead [liːd] *verb* **(a)** to be the first, to be in front; *the company leads the market in cheap computers* **(b)** to be the main person in a group; *she will lead the trade mission to Nigeria; the tour of American factories will be led by the minister* (NOTE: **leading - led**)

leader ['liːdə] *noun* **(a)** person who manages or directs others; *the leader of the construction workers' union* *or* *the construction workers' leader; she is the leader of the trade mission to Nigeria; the minister was the leader of the party of industrialists on a tour of American factories* **(b)** product which sells best; **a market leader** = product which sells most in a market, company which has the largest share of a market; **loss-leader** = article which is sold very cheaply to attract customers **(c)** important share, a share which is often bought or sold on the Stock Exchange

> market leaders may benefit from scale economies or other cost advantages; they may enjoy a reputation for quality simply by being at the top, or they may actually produce a superior product that gives them both a large market share and high profits
> *Accountancy*

leading ['liːdɪŋ] *adjective* most important; *leading industrialists feel the end of the recession is near; leading shares rose on the Stock Exchange; leading shareholders in the company forced a change in management policy; they are the leading company in the field*; **leading indicator** = indicator (such as manufacturing order books) which shows a change in economic trends earlier than other indicators

lead time ['liːd 'taɪm] *noun* time between deciding to place an order and receiving the product; *the lead time on this item is more than six weeks*

lead (up) to [liːd 'ʌp tʊ] *verb* to come before and be the cause of; *the discussions led to a big argument between the management and the union; we received a series of approaches leading up to the takeover bid*

leaflet ['li:flət] *noun* sheet of paper giving information, used to advertise something; *to mail leaflets or to hand out leaflets describing services*; *they made a leaflet mailing to 20,000 addresses*

leak [li:k] *verb* to pass on a secret; *information on the contract was leaked to the press*; *they discovered the sales director was leaking information to a rival company*

leakage ['li:kɪdʒ] *noun* amount of goods lost in storage (by going bad, by being stolen or by escaping from the container)

lean [li:n] *adjective* slim (and efficient); *after the cutbacks in staff, the company is leaner and hungrier*; **lean management** = style of management, where few managers are employed, allowing decisions to be taken rapidly; **lean production** = production methods using few workers

leap-frogging ['li:p'frɒgɪŋ] *adjective* **leap-frogging pay demands** = pay demands where each section of workers asks for higher pay to do better than another section, which then asks for further increases in turn

lease [li:s] **1** *noun* **(a)** written contract for letting or renting a building, a piece of land or a piece of equipment for a period against payment of a fee; *to rent office space on a twenty-year lease*; **long lease** = lease which runs for fifty years or more; *to take an office building on a long lease*; **short lease** = lease which runs for up to two or three years; *we have a short lease on our current premises*; **full repairing lease** = lease where the tenant has to pay for all repairs to the property; **headlease** = lease from the freeholder to a tenant; **sublease** or **underlease** = lease from a tenant to another tenant; **the lease expires** or **runs out next year** = the lease comes to an end next year; **on expiration of the lease** = when the lease comes to an end **(b) to hold an oil lease in the North Sea** = to have a lease on a section of the North Sea to explore for oil **2** *verb* **(a)** to let or rent offices, land or machinery for a period; *to lease offices to small firms*; *to lease equipment* **(b)** to use an office, land or machinery for a time and pay a fee; *to lease*

an office from an insurance company; *all our company cars are leased*

lease back ['li:s 'bæk] *verb* to sell a property or machinery to a company and then take it back on a lease; *they sold the office building to raise cash, and then leased it back on a twenty-five year lease*

lease-back ['li:sbæk] *noun* arrangement where property is sold and then taken back on a lease; *they sold the office building and then took it back under a lease-back arrangement*

leasehold ['li:shəʊld] *noun & adjective* possessing property on a lease, for a fixed time; *we are currently occupying a leasehold property*; *the company has some valuable leaseholds*; *to buy a property leasehold*

leaseholder ['li:shəʊldə] *noun* person who holds a property on a lease

leasing ['li:sɪŋ] *noun* which leases or which is using equipment under a lease; *the company has branched out into car leasing*; *an equipment-leasing company*; *to run a copier under a leasing arrangement*; *see also* LESSEE

leave [li:v] **1** *noun* permission to be away from work; **six weeks' annual leave** = six weeks' holiday each year; **leave of absence** = being allowed to be away from work; **maternity leave** = permission given to a woman to be away from work to have a baby; **sick leave** = period when a worker is away from work because of illness; **to go on leave** or **to be on leave** = to be away from work; *she is away on sick leave or on maternity leave* **2** *verb* **(a)** to go away from; *he left his office early to go to the meeting*; *the next plane leaves at 10.20* **(b)** to resign; *he left his job and bought a farm* (NOTE: **leaving - left**)

leave out ['li:v 'aʊt] *verb* not to include; *she left out the date on the letter*; *the contract leaves out all details of marketing arrangements*

-led [led] *suffix* which is led by something; *an export-led boom*; *the consumer-led rise in sales*

ledger ['ledʒə] *noun* book in which accounts are written; **bought ledger** or **purchase ledger** = book in which purchases are recorded; **bought ledger clerk** *or* **sales ledger clerk** = office worker who deals with the bought ledger or the sales ledger; **nominal ledger** *or* **general ledger** = book which records a company's transactions in the various accounts (normally, all accounts except those relating to debtors, creditors and cash, which are kept in separate ledgers); **payroll ledger** = list of staff and their salaries; **sales ledger** = book in which sales are noted; **stock ledger** = book which records quantities and values of stock

left [left] *adjective* on the side of the body which usually has the weaker hand, not right; *the numbers run down the left side of the page*; *put the debits in the left column*; *see also* LEAVE

left-hand ['lefthænd] *adjective* belonging to the left side; *the debits are in the left-hand column in the accounts*; *he keeps the personnel files in the left-hand drawer of his desk*

left luggage office ['left 'lʌgɪdʒ 'ɒfɪs] *noun* room where suitcases can be left while passengers are waiting for a plane or train (NOTE: American English uses **baggage room**)

legacy ['legəsi] *noun* property given by someone to someone else at his death

legal ['liːgəl] *adjective* **(a)** according to the law, allowed by the law; *the company's action was completely legal* **(b)** referring to the law; **to take legal action** = to sue someone, to take someone to court; **to take legal advice** = to ask a lawyer to advise about a legal problem; **legal adviser** = person who advises clients about the law; *GB* **Legal Aid scheme** = British government scheme where a person with very little money can have legal representation and advice paid for by the state; **legal claim** = statement that someone owns something legally; *he has no legal claim to the property*; **legal costs** *or* **legal charges** *or* **legal expenses** = money spent on fees to lawyers; **legal currency** = money which is legally used in a country; **legal department** *or* **legal section** = section of a company dealing with legal matters; **legal expert** = person who knows a lot about the law; **legal holiday** = day

when banks and other businesses are closed; **legal tender** = coins or notes which can be legally used to pay a debt (small denominations cannot be used to pay large debts)

legality [lɪ'gæləti] *noun* being allowed by law; *there is doubt about the legality of the company's action in dismissing him*

legalization [liːgəlaɪ'zeɪʃən] *noun* making something legal; *the campaign for the legalization of cannabis*

legalize ['liːgəlaɪz] *verb* to make something legal

legally ['liːgəli] *adverb* according to the law; **the contract is legally binding** = according to the law, the contract has to be obeyed; **the directors are legally responsible** = the law says that the directors are responsible

legatee [legə'tiː] *noun* person who receives property from someone who has died

legislation [ledʒɪs'leɪʃən] *noun* laws; **labour legislation** = laws concerning the employment of workers

lend [lend] *verb* to allow someone to use something for a period; *to lend something to someone or to lend someone something*; *he lent the company money or he lent money to the company*; *to lend money against security*; *the bank lent him £50,000 to start his business* (NOTE: **lending - lent**)

lender ['lendə] *noun* person who lends money; **lender of last resort** = central bank which lends money to commercial banks

lending ['lendɪŋ] *noun* act of letting someone use money for a time; **lending limit** = limit on the amount of money a bank can lend

length [leŋθ] *noun* **(a)** measurement of how long something is; *the boardroom table is twelve feet in length*; *inches and centimetres are measurements of length* **(b) to go to great lengths to get something** = to do anything (even commit a crime) to get something; *they went to considerable lengths to keep the project secret*

less [les] **1** *adjective* smaller than, of a smaller size or of a smaller value; *we do not grant credit for sums of less than £100*; *he sold it for less than he had paid for it* **2** *preposition* minus, with a sum removed; *purchase price less 15% discount*; *interest less service charges*

lessee [le'siː] *noun* person who has a lease or who pays money for a property he leases

lessor [le'sɔː] *noun* person who grants a lease on a property

let [let] **1** *verb* to lend a house, an office or a farm to someone for a payment; **to let an office** = to allow someone to use an office for a time in return for payment of rent; **offices to let** = offices which are available to be leased by companies (NOTE: **letting - let**) **2** *noun* period of the lease of a property; *they took the office on a short let*

let-out clause ['letaut 'klɔːz] *noun* clause which allows someone to avoid doing something in a contract; *he added a let-out clause to the effect that the payments would be revised if the exchange rate fell by more than 5%*

letter ['letə] *noun* **(a)** piece of writing sent from one person or company to another to ask for or to give information; **business letter** = letter which deals with business matters; **circular letter** = letter sent to many people; **covering letter** = letter sent with documents to say why they are being sent; **follow-up letter** = letter sent to someone after a previous letter or after a visit; **private letter** = letter which deals with personal matters; **standard letter** = letter which is sent without change to various correspondents **(b)** **letter of acknowledgement** = letter which says that something has been received; **letters of administration** = letter given by a court to allow someone to deal with the estate of someone who has died; **letter of allotment** *or* **allotment letter** = letter which tells someone how many shares in a new company he has been allotted; **letter of application** = letter in which someone applies for a job; **letter of appointment** = letter in which someone is appointed to a job; **letter of comfort** = letter supporting someone who is trying to get a loan; **letter**

of complaint = letter in which someone complains; **letter of indemnity** = letter promising payment of compensation for a loss; **letter of intent** = letter which states what a company intends to do if something happens; **letters patent** = official document which gives someone the exclusive right to make and sell something which he has invented; **letter of reference** = letter in which an employer recommends someone for a new job **(c)** **air letter** = special thin blue paper which when folded can be sent by air without an envelope; **airmail letter** = letter sent by air; **express letter** = letter sent very fast; **registered letter** = letter which is noted by the post office before it is sent, so that compensation can be claimed if it is lost **(d)** **to acknowledge receipt by letter** = to write a letter to say that something has been received **(e)** written or printed sign (such as A, B, C, etc.); *write your name and address in block letters or in capital letters*

letterhead ['letəhed] *noun* **(a)** name and address of a company printed at the top of a piece of notepaper **(b)** *US* sheet of paper with the name and address of the company printed on it (NOTE: British English is **headed paper**)

letter of credit (L/C) ['letə əv 'kredɪt] *noun* document issued by a bank on behalf of a customer authorizing payment to a supplier when the conditions specified in the document are met (this is a common method of guaranteeing payment by overseas customers); **irrevocable letter of credit** = letter of credit which cannot be cancelled or changed

letting ['letɪŋ] *noun* **letting agency** = agency which deals in property to let; **furnished lettings** = furnished property to let

level ['levl] **1** *noun* position where high is large and low is small; *low levels of productivity or low productivity levels*; *to raise the level of employee benefits*; *to lower the level of borrowings*; **high level of investment** = large amount of money invested; **a decision taken at the highest level** = decision taken by the most important person or group; **low-level** = not very important; *a low-level delegation*; **high-level** = very important; *a high-level* meeting or decision; **decisions taken at managerial level** = decisions taken by managers; **manning levels** or **staffing levels** = number of people required in each department of a company to do the work efficiently **2** verb **to level off** or **to level out** = to stop rising or falling; *profits have levelled off over the last few years*; *prices are levelling out* (NOTE: **levelling - levelled** but American spelling **leveling - leveled**)

---

figures from the Fed on
industrial production for
April show a decline to levels
last seen in June 1984
Sunday Times

---

applications for mortgages
are running at a high level
Times

---

employers having got their
staff back up to a reasonable
level are waiting until the
scope for overtime working is
exhausted before hiring
Sydney Morning Herald

---

leverage ['li:vərɪdʒ] *noun* **(a)** influence which you can use to achieve an aim; *he has no leverage over the chairman* **(b)** ratio of capital borrowed by a company at a fixed rate of interest to the company's total capital (also called 'gearing') **(c)** borrowing money at fixed interest which is then used to produce more money than the interest paid; *see* COMMENT *at* GEARING

leveraged buyout (LBO) ['li:vərɪdʒd 'baɪaʊt] *noun* buying all the shares in a company by borrowing money against the security of the shares to be bought

---

the offer came after
management had offered to
take the company private
through a leveraged buyout
for $825 million
Fortune

---

lever-arch file ['li:vəːɑːtʃ 'faɪl] *noun* type of ring binder, where you lift up one side of the rings with a lever, place the document on the prongs of the other side and then close the rings together again

levy ['levi] **1** *noun* money which is demanded and collected by the government; **capital levy** = tax on the value of a person's property and possessions; **import levy** = tax on imports, especially in the EU a tax on imports of farm produce from outside the EU; **levies on luxury items** = taxes on luxury items; **training levy** = tax to be paid by companies to fund the government's training schemes **2** *verb* to demand payment of a tax or an extra payment and to collect it; *the government has decided to levy a tax on imported cars*; *to levy a duty on the import of luxury items*; **to levy members for a new club house** = to ask members of the club to pay for the new building

---

royalties have been levied at
a rate of 12.5% of full
production
Lloyd's List

---

liability [laɪə'bɪləti] *noun* **(a)** being legally responsible for damage, loss, etc.; **to accept liability for something** = to agree that you are responsible for something; **to refuse liability for something** = to refuse to agree that you are responsible for something; **contractual liability** = legal responsibility for something as stated in a contract; **employers' liability insurance** = insurance to cover accidents which may happen at work, and for which the company may be responsible; **limited liability** = situation where someone's liability for debt is limited by law; **limited liability company** = company where a shareholder is responsible for repaying the company's debts only to the face value of the shares he owns **(b)** **liabilities** = debts of a business; *the balance sheet shows the company's assets and liabilities*; **current liabilities** = debts which a company should pay within the next accounting period; **long-term liabilities** = debts which are not due to be paid for some time; **he was not able to meet his liabilities** = he could not pay his debts; **to discharge your liabilities in full** = to pay everything which you owe

liable ['laɪəbl] *adjective* **(a)** **liable for** = legally responsible for; *the customer is liable for breakages*; *the chairman was personally liable for the company's debts* **(b)** **liable to** = which is officially due to be paid; *goods which are liable to stamp duty*

libel ['laɪbəl] **1** *noun* untrue written statement which damages someone's character; **action for libel** *or* **libel action** = case in a law court where someone says that another person has written a libel **2** *verb* **to libel someone** = to damage someone's character in writing (NOTE: **libelling - libelled** but American spelling **libeling - libeled.** Compare SLANDER)

licence *US* **license** ['laɪsəns] *noun* **(a)** official document which allows someone to do something; **driving licence** *US* **driver's license** = document which allows someone to drive a car, a truck, etc.; *applicants for the job should hold a valid driving licence*; **import licence** *or* **export licence** = official documents which allow goods to be exported or imported; **liquor licence** = government document allowing someone to sell alcohol; **off licence** = licence to sell alcohol to be drunk away from the place where it is bought; *shop which sells alcohol for drinking at home* **(b)** **goods manufactured under licence** = goods made with the permission of the owner of the copyright or patent

license ['laɪsəns] **1** *noun US* = LICENCE **2** *verb* to give someone official permission to do something; *licensed to sell beers, wines and spirits*; *to license a company to manufacture spare parts*; *she is licensed to run an employment agency*; **licensed deposit-taker (LDT)** *or* **licensed institution** = deposit-taking institution, such as a building society, bank or friendly society, which is licensed to receive money on deposit from private individuals and to pay interest on it

licensee [laɪsən'siː] *noun* person who has a licence, especially a licence to sell alcohol or to manufacture something

licensing ['laɪsənsɪŋ] *noun* which refers to licences; **a licensing agreement** = agreement where a person or company is granted a licence to manufacture something or to use something, but not an outright sale; **licensing authorities** = local authorities which have the right to grant licences to sell alcohol; **licensing laws** = laws relating to the sale of alcohol; **licensing hours** = hours of the day when alcohol can be sold

licensor ['laɪsensə] *noun* person who licenses someone

lien [liːn] *noun* legal right to hold someone's goods and keep them until a debt has been paid; **general lien** = holding goods or property until a debt has been paid; **particular lien** = right of a person to keep possession of another person's property until debts relating to that property have been paid

lieu [ljuː] *noun* **in lieu of** = instead of; **she was given two months' salary in lieu of notice** = she was given the salary and asked to leave immediately

life [laɪf] *noun* **(a)** time when a person is alive; **for life** = for as long as someone is alive; *his pension gives him a comfortable income for life*; **life annuity** *or* **annuity for life** = annual payments made to someone as long as he is alive; **life assurance** *or* **life insurance** = insurance which pays a sum of money when someone dies, or at a certain date if he is still alive; **the life assured** *or* **the life insured** = the person whose life has been covered by the life assurance; **life expectancy** = number of years a person is likely to live; **life interest** = interest in a property which stops when a person dies **(b)** period of time something exists; *the life of a loan*; *during the life of the agreement*; **shelf life of a product** = length of time during which a product can stay in the shop and still be good to use

lifeboat ['laɪfbəʊt] *noun* boat used to rescue passengers from sinking ships; **lifeboat operation** = rescue of a company (especially of a bank) which is in difficulties

LIFO = LAST IN FIRST OUT

lift [lɪft] **1** *noun* machine which takes people or goods from one floor to another in a building; *he took the lift to the 27th floor*; *the staff could not get into their office when the lift broke down* (NOTE: American English is **elevator**) **2** *verb* to take away, to remove; *the government has lifted the ban on imports from Japan*; *to lift trade barriers*; *the minister has lifted the embargo on the export of computers to certain countries*

light [laɪt] *adjective* **(a)** not heavy; **shares fell back in light trading** = shares lost value on a day when there was little business done on the Stock Exchange; **light industry** = industry which makes small products (such as clothes, books, calculators) **(b) light pen** = type of pen which, when passed over a bar code, can read it and pass information in it back to a central computer

lighter ['laɪtə] *noun* boat used to take cargo from a cargo ship to shore

limit ['lɪmɪt] **1** *noun* point at which something ends, point where you can go no further; **to set limits to imports** *or* **to impose import limits** = to allow only a certain amount of imports; **age limit** = top age at which you are allowed to do a job; *there is an age limit of thirty-five on the post of buyer*; **credit limit** = largest amount of money which a customer can borrow; **he has exceeded his credit limit** = he has borrowed more money than he is allowed; **lending limit** = restriction on the amount of money a bank can lend; **time limit** = maximum time which can be taken to do something; *to set a time limit for acceptance of the offer*; **weight limit** = maximum weight; *the packet is over the weight limit for letter post, so it will have to go by parcel post* **2** *verb* to stop something from going beyond a certain point; **the banks have limited their credit** = the banks have allowed their customers only a certain amount of credit; **each agent is limited to twenty-five units** = each agent is allowed only twenty-five units to sell

---

the biggest surprise of 1999 was the rebound in the price of oil. In the early months of the year commentators were talking about a fall to $5 a barrel but for the first time in two decades, the oil exporting countries got their act together, limited production and succeeded in pushing prices up

Financial Times

---

limitation [lɪmɪ'teɪʃən] *noun* **(a)** act of allowing only a certain quantity of something; **limitation of liability** = making someone liable for only a part of the damage or loss; **time limitation** =

restricting the amount of time available; *the contract imposes limitations on the number of cars which can be imported* **(b) statute of limitations** = law which allows only a certain amount of time (a few years) for someone to claim damages or property

limited ['lɪmɪtɪd] *adjective* restricted, not open; **limited company** *or* **limited liability company** = company where each shareholder is responsible for repaying the company's debts only to the face value of the shares he owns (NOTE: shortened to **Ltd**); **private limited company** = (i) company with a small number of shareholders whose shares are not traded on the Stock Exchange; (ii) subsidiary company whose shares are not listed on the Stock Exchange, while those of its parent company are (NOTE: shortened to **Ltd**); **Public Limited Company** = company whose shares can be bought on the Stock Exchange (NOTE: written as **Plc**); **limited market** = market which can take only a certain quantity of goods; **limited partner** = partner in a limited partnership (he is only liable for the amount of capital he has put into the firm, and takes no part in the management of the firm); **limited partnership** = registered business where the liability of the partners is limited to the amount of capital they have each provided to the business and where the partners may not take part in the running of the business

limiting ['lɪmɪtɪŋ] *adjective* which limits; *a limiting clause in a contract*; *the short holiday season is a limiting factor on the hotel trade*

line [laɪn] *noun* **(a)** long mark; *paper with thin blue lines*; *I prefer notepaper without any lines*; *he drew a thick line across the bottom of the column to show which figure was the total* **(b) shipping line** *or* **airline** = large shipping or aircraft company which carries passengers or cargo; *profits of major airlines have been affected by the rise in fuel prices* **(c) line of business** *or* **line of work** = type of business or work; **line of product** *or* **product line** = series of different products which form a group, all made by the same company; *we do not stock that line*; *computers are not one of our best-selling lines*; *they produce an interesting line in* *garden tools*; **line of shares** = large block of shares sold as one deal on the stock exchange **(d)** row of letters or figures on a page; **bottom line** = last line in accounts, showing the net profit; *the boss is interested only in the bottom line*; **to open a line of credit** *or* **a credit line** = to make credit available to someone **(e)** **assembly line** *or* **production line** = production system where the product (such as a car) moves slowly through a factory with new sections added to it as it goes along; *he works on the production line or he is a production line worker in the car factory* **(f)** **line chart** *or* **line graph** = chart or graph using lines to indicate values; **line printer** = machine which prints information from a computer one line at a time **(g)** **line of command** *or* **line management** *or* **line organization** = organization of a business where each manager is responsible for doing what his superior tells him to do **(h)** **telephone line** = wire along which telephone messages travel; **the line is bad** = it is difficult to hear clearly what someone is saying; **a crossed line** = when two telephone conversations get mixed; **the line is engaged** = the person is already speaking on the phone; **the chairman is on the other line** = the chairman is speaking on his second telephone; **outside line** = line from an internal office telephone system to the main telephone exchange

---

cash paid for overstocked lines, factory seconds, slow sellers, etc.
Australian Financial Review

---

lined [laɪnd] *adjective* with lines; *he prefers lined paper for writing notes*

liner ['laɪnə] *noun* large passenger ship; *cruise liners call at Miami regularly*

link [lɪŋk] *verb* to join or to attach to something else; *to link pensions to inflation*; *to link bonus payments to productivity*; *his salary is linked to the cost of living*; *see also* INDEX-LINKED

liquid ['lɪkwɪd] *adjective* **liquid assets** = cash, or bills which can easily be changed into cash; **to go liquid** = to convert as many assets as possible into cash

liquidate ['lɪkwɪdeɪt] *verb* **to liquidate a company** = to close a company and sell its

assets; **to liquidate a debt** = to pay a debt in full; **to liquidate stock** = to sell stock to raise cash

liquidation [lɪkwɪ'deɪʃən] *noun* **(a)** **liquidation of a debt** = payment of a debt **(b)** closing of a company and selling of its assets; **the company went into liquidation** = the company was closed and its assets sold; **compulsory liquidation** = liquidation which is ordered by a court; **voluntary liquidation** = situation where a company itself decides it must close

liquidator ['lɪkwɪdeɪtə] *noun* person named to supervise the closing of a company which is in liquidation

liquidity [lɪ'kwɪdəti] *noun* having cash or assets which can be changed into cash; **liquidity crisis** = not having enough ash or other liquid assets

lira ['lɪərə] *noun* currency used with the euro in Italy; *the book cost 2,700 lira or L2,700* (NOTE: **lira** is usually written **L** before figures: **L2,700**)

list [lɪst] **1** *noun* **(a)** several items written one after the other; *they have an attractive list of products or product list*; *I can't find that item on our stock list*; *please add this item to the list*; *she crossed the item off her list*; **address list** *or* **mailing list** = list of names and addresses of people and companies; **black list** = list of goods, companies or countries which are banned for trade; **picking list** = list of items in a customer's order, but listed according to where they can be found in the warehouse **(b)** catalogue; **list price** = price as given in a catalogue; **price list** = sheet giving prices of goods for sale **2** *verb* **(a)** to write a series of items one after the other; *to list products by category*; *to list representatives by area*; *to list products in a catalogue*; *the catalogue lists ten models of fax machine* **(b)** **listed company** = company whose shares can be bought or sold on the Stock Exchange; **listed securities** = shares which can be bought or sold on the Stock Exchange, shares which appear on the official Stock Exchange list

listing ['lɪstɪŋ] *noun* **(a)** **Stock Exchange listing** = being on the official list of shares which can be bought or sold on the Stock Exchange; *the company is planning to* obtain a Stock Exchange listing (b) computer listing = printout of a list of items taken from the data stored in a computer; listing paper = paper made as a long sheet, used in computer printers

literature ['lɪtrətʃə] *noun* written information about something; *please send me literature about your new product range*

litigant ['lɪtɪgənt] *noun* person who brings a lawsuit against someone

litigation [lɪtɪ'geɪʃən] *noun* the bringing of a lawsuit against someone

litre *US* **liter** ['liːtə] *noun* measure of liquids; **the car does fifteen kilometres to the litre** *or* **fifteen kilometres per litre** = the car uses one litre of petrol to travel fifteen kilometres (NOTE: usually written l after figures: 25l)

lively ['laɪvli] *adjective* **lively market** = active stock market, with many shares being bought or sold

livery ['lɪvri] *noun* a company's own special design, used on uniforms, vehicles, etc.

living ['lɪvɪŋ] *noun* **cost of living** = money which a person has to pay for rent, food, heating, etc.; **cost-of-living allowance** = addition to normal salary to cover increases in the cost of living; **cost-of-living index** = way of measuring the cost of living which is shown as a percentage increase on the figure for the previous year; **he does not earn a living wage** = he does not earn enough to pay for essentials (food, heat, rent); **standard of living** *or* **living standards** = quality of personal home life (amount of food, clothes bought, size of the family car, etc.); *living standards fell as unemployment rose*

Lloyd's [lɔɪdz] *noun* central London insurance market; **Lloyd's Register** = classified list showing details of all the ships in the world and estimates of their condition; **ship which is A1 at Lloyd's** = ship in very good condition

COMMENT: Lloyd's is an old-established insurance market; the underwriters who form Lloyd's are divided into syndicates, each made up of active underwriters who arrange the business and non-working underwriters (called 'names') who stand surety for any insurance claims which may arise

load [ləʊd] **1** *noun* **(a)** goods which are transported; **load of a lorry** *or* **of a container** = goods carried by a lorry or in a container; **lorry-load** *or* **container-load** = amount of goods carried on a lorry or in a container; *a container-load of spare parts is missing*; *they delivered six lorry-loads of coal*; **commercial load** = amount of goods or number of passengers which a bus, train or plane has to carry to make a profit; **maximum load** = largest weight of goods which a lorry or plane can carry; **load-carrying capacity** = amount of goods which a lorry is capable of carrying; **load factor** = number of seats in a bus, train or plane which are occupied by passengers who have paid the full fare **(b)** **workload** = amount of work which a person has to do; *he has difficulty in coping with his heavy workload* **2** *verb* **(a)** to load a lorry *or* a ship = to put goods into a lorry or a ship for transporting; *to load cargo onto a ship*; *a truck loaded with boxes*; *a ship loaded with iron*; **fully loaded ship** = ship which is full of cargo **(b)** *(of ship)* to take on cargo; *the ship is loading a cargo of wood* **(c)** to put a program into a computer; *load the word-processing program before you start keyboarding* **(d)** *(insurance)* to put charges into a certain period or into certain payments; **back-end loaded** = (insurance or investment scheme) where commission is only charged when the investor withdraws his money from the scheme; **front-end loaded** = (insurance or investment scheme) where most of the management charges are incurred in the first year of the investment or insurance

loading ['ləʊdɪŋ] *noun* **loading bay** = section of road in a warehouse where lorries can drive in to be loaded; **loading dock** = part of a harbour where ships can load or unload; **loading ramp** = raised platform which makes it easier to load goods onto a lorry

load line ['ləʊd 'laɪn] *noun* line painted on the side of a ship to show where the water should reach for maximum safety if the ship is fully loaded (NOTE: also called **Plimsoll line** on British ships)

loan [ləʊn] **1** *noun* money which has been lent; **loan capital** = part of a company's capital which is a loan to be repaid at a later date; **loan stock** = money lent to a company at a fixed rate of interest; **convertible loan stock** = money which can be exchanged for shares at a later date; **bank loan** = money lent by a bank; **bridging loan** *US* **bridge loan** = short-term loan to help someone buy a new house when he has not yet sold his old one; **government loan** = money lent by the government; **home loan** = loan by a bank or building society to help someone buy a house; **short-term loan** *or* **long-term loan** = loans which have to be repaid within a few weeks or some years; **soft loan** = loan (from a company to an employee or from one government to another) with no interest payable; **unsecured loan** = loan made with no security **2** *verb* to lend; *the truck has been loaned by the local haulage company*

> over the last few weeks, companies raising new loans from international banks have been forced to pay more, and an unusually high number of attempts to syndicate loans among banks has failed
> *Financial Times*

lobby ['lɒbi] **1** *noun* group of people who try to influence MPs, members of town councils, etc.; **the energy-saving lobby** = people who try to persuade MPs to pass laws to save energy **2** *verb* to try to influence members of parliament, members of town councils, etc.; *the group lobbied the chairmen of all the committees*

local ['ləʊkəl] **1** *adjective* referring to a particular area, especially one near where a factory or an office is based; **local authority** = elected section of government which runs a small area of the country; **local call** = telephone call to a number in the same area as the person making the call; **local currency** = the currency of a particular country where a transaction is being carried out; *because of the weakness of the local currency, all payments are in*

dollars; **local government** = elected administrative bodies which run areas of the country; **local labour** = workers who are recruited near a factory, and are not brought there from a distance; **local time** = the time in the country where something is happening; *if it is 12.00 noon in London, it will be 5 o'clock in the morning local time* **2** *noun US* branch of a trade union

> each cheque can be made out for the local equivalent of £100 rounded up to a convenient figure
> *Sunday Times*

> the business agent for Local 414 of the Store Union said his committee will recommend that the membership ratify the agreement
> *Toronto Star*

> EC regulations insist that customers can buy cars anywhere in the EC at the local pre-tax price
> *Financial Times*

locally ['ləʊkəli] *adverb* in the area near where an office or factory is based; *we recruit all our staff locally*

locate [ləʊ'keɪt] *verb* to be located = to be in a certain place; *the warehouse is located near to the motorway*

location [lə'keɪʃən] *noun* place where something is; **the company has moved to a new location** = the company has moved to a new office or a different town

lock [lɒk] **1** *noun* device for closing a door or box so that it can be opened only with a key; *the lock is broken on the petty cash box*; *I have forgotten the combination of the lock on my briefcase* **2** *verb* to close a door with a key, so that it cannot be opened; *the manager forgot to lock the door of the computer room*; *the petty cash box was not locked*

locking up ['lɒkɪŋ 'ʌp] *noun* **the locking up of money in stock** = investing money in stock so that it cannot be used for other, possibly more profitable, investments

lock out ['lɒk 'aʊt] *verb* **to lock out workers** = to shut the factory door so that workers cannot get in and so force them not to work until the conditions imposed by the management are met

lockout ['lɒkaʊt] *noun* industrial dispute where the management will not let the workers into the factory until they have agreed to the management's conditions

lock up ['lɒk 'ʌp] *verb* **(a) to lock up a shop** *or* **an office** = to close and lock the door at the end of the day's work **(b) to lock up capital** = to have capital invested in such a way that it cannot be used for other investments

lock-up shop *or* **lock-up premises** ['lɒkʌp 'ʃɒp or 'premɪsɪz] *noun* shop or other commercial building which has no living accommodation and which the proprietor locks at night when it is closed

lodge [lɒdʒ] *verb* **to lodge a complaint against someone** = to make an official complaint about someone; **to lodge money with someone** = to deposit money with someone; **to lodge securities as collateral** = to put securities into a bank to be used as collateral for a loan

log [lɒg] *verb* to write down all that happens; **to log phone calls** = to note all details of phone calls made; **to log on** = to start a computer program by entering a password, and various other instructions; **to log off** = to stop work on a computer program and close down the program (NOTE: **logging - logged**)

I have just been trying to log onto a website for one hour - from 8.00 am to 9.00 am - to buy some shares. Their server just can't cope with the Monday morning rush to buy
Investors Chronicle

logo ['lɒgəʊ] *noun* symbol, design or group of letters used by a company as a mark on its products and in advertising

long [lɒŋ] **1** *adjective* for a large period of time; **long credit** = credit terms which allow the borrower a long time to pay; **in the long term** = over a long period of time; **to take the long view** = to plan for a long period before current investment becomes profitable **2** *noun* **longs** = government stocks which mature in over fifteen years' time

long-dated ['lɒŋ'deɪtɪd] *adjective* **long-dated bills** = bills which are payable in more than three months' time

long-distance ['lɒŋ'dɪstəns] *adjective* **a long-distance call** = telephone call to a number which is not near; **long-distance flight** = flight to a destination which is a long way away

longhand ['lɒŋhænd] *noun* handwriting where the words are written out in full and not typed or in shorthand; *applications should be written in longhand and sent to the personnel officer*

long-haul flight ['lɒŋhɔːl 'flaɪt] *noun* long-distance flight, especially one between continents

long-range ['lɒŋ'reɪndʒ] *adjective* for a long period of time in the future; **long-range economic forecast** = forecast which covers a period of several years

long-standing ['lɒŋ'stændɪŋ] *adjective* which has been arranged for a long time; *long-standing agreement*; **long-standing customer** *or* **customer of long standing** = person who has been a customer for many years

long-term ['lɒŋ'tɜːm] *adjective* **on a long-term basis** = for a long period of time; **long-term debts** = debts which will be repaid many years later; **long-term forecast** = forecast for a period of over three years; **long-term loan** = loan to be repaid many years later; **long-term objectives** = aims which will take years to achieve

land held under long-term leases is not amortized
Hongkong Standard

the company began to experience a demand for longer-term mortgages when the flow of money used to finance these loans diminished
Globe and Mail (Toronto)

loophole ['luːphəʊl] *noun* **to find a loophole in the law** = to find a means of legally avoiding the law; **to find a tax loophole** = to find a means of legally not paying tax because capital gains are not taxed but money taken out in profits is taxed, owners of businesses will be using accountants and tax experts to find loopholes in the law

Toronto Star

loose [luːs] *adjective* not packed together; **loose change** = money in coins; **to sell loose potatoes** *or* **to sell potatoes loose** = to sell potatoes in quantities which are separately weighed, not in previously weighed packets

loose-leaf book ['luːsliːf 'bʊk] *noun* book with loose pages which can be taken out and fixed back in again on rings

loosen ['luːsən] *verb* to make less strict; *the government has loosened the rules about the import of foodstuffs*

lorry ['lɒri] *noun GB* large motor vehicle for carrying goods; *he drives a five-ton lorry*; **heavy lorry** = very large lorry which carries heavy loads; **lorry driver** = person who drives a lorry (NOTE: American English is **truck**)

lose [luːz] *verb* **(a)** not to have something any more; **to lose an order** = not to get an order which you were hoping to get; *during the strike, the company lost six orders to American competitors*; **to lose control of a company** = to find that you have less than 50% of the shares and so are no longer able to direct the company; **to lose customers** = to have fewer customers; *their service is so slow that they have been losing customers*; *she lost her job when the factory closed* = she was made redundant **(b)** to have less money; *he lost £25,000 in his father's computer company* **(c)** to drop to a lower price; *the dollar lost two cents against the yen*; *gold shares lost 5% on the market yesterday*; *the pound has lost value* = the pound is worth less (NOTE: **losing - lost**)

lose out ['luːz 'aʊt] *verb* to suffer as a result of something; *the company has lost out in the rush to make cheap PCs*

loss [lɒs] *noun* **(a)** not having something any more; **loss of customers** = not keeping customers because of bad service, high prices, etc.; **loss of an order** = not getting an order which was expected; **the**

company suffered a loss of market penetration = the company found it had a smaller share of the market; **compensation for loss of earnings** = payment to someone who has stopped earning money or who is not able to earn money; **compensation for loss of office** = payment to a director who is asked to leave a company before his contract ends; **job losses** = jobs which no longer exist because workers have been made redundant **(b)** having less money than before, not making a profit; **the company suffered a loss** = the company did not make a profit; **to report a loss** = not to show a profit in the accounts at the end of the year; *the company reported a loss of £1m on the first year's trading*; **capital loss** = loss made by selling assets; **the car was written off as a dead loss** *or* **a total loss** = the car was so badly damaged that the insurers said it had no value; **paper loss** = loss made when an asset has fallen in value but has not been sold; **trading loss** = situation where the company's receipts are less than its expenditure; **at a loss** = making a loss, not making any profit; *the company is trading at a loss*; *he sold the shop at a loss*; **to cut your losses** = to stop doing something which was losing money **(c)** being worth less or having a lower value; *shares showed losses of up to 5% on the Stock Exchange* **(d)** weighing less; **loss in weight** = goods which weigh less than when they were packed; **loss in transport** = amount of weight which is lost while goods are being transported **(e)** damage to property or destruction of property, which is then subject to an insurance claim; **loss adjuster** = person who calculates how much insurance should be paid on a claim; **the cargo was written off as a total loss** = the cargo was so badly damaged that the insurers said it had no value

against losses of FFr 7.7m two years ago, the company made a net profit of FFr 300,000 last year

Financial Times

loss-leader ['lɒs'liːdə] *noun* article which is sold at a loss to attract customers; *we use these cheap films as a loss-leader*

lot [lɒt] *noun* **(a)** large quantity; *a lot of people or lots of people are out of work* **(b)** group of items sold together at an auction; *to bid for lot 23*; *at the end of the auction half the lots were unsold* **(c)** group of shares which are sold; *to sell a lot of shares*; *to sell shares in small lots* **(d)** US piece of land, especially one to be used for redevelopment; *they bought a lot and built a house*; **parking lot** = area for parking cars

lottery ['lɒtəri] *noun* game where numbered tickets are sold and prizes given for some of the numbers; **the National Lottery** = British lottery which takes place twice a week, where you try to forecast a series of numbers; *she won over £2m on the lottery*; *he buys a lottery ticket every week*

lounge [laʊndʒ] *noun* comfortable room; **departure lounge** = room in an airport where passengers wait to board their planes; **transit lounge** = room in an airport where passengers wait for connecting flights

low [ləʊ] **1** *adjective* small, not high; *low overhead costs keep the unit cost low*; *we try to keep our wages bill low*; *the company offered him a mortgage at a low rate of interest*; *the pound is at a very low rate of exchange against the dollar*; *our aim is to buy at the lowest price possible*; *shares were at their lowest for two years*; **low sales** = small amount of money produced by sales; **low volume of sales** = small number of items sold; **the tender will go to the lowest bidder** = the contract will be awarded to the person who offers the best terms **2** *noun* point where prices or sales are very small; *sales have reached a new low*; *the highs and lows on the stock market*; **shares have hit an all-time low** = shares have reached their lowest price ever

> after opening at 79.1 the index touched a peak of 79.2 and then drifted to a low of 78.8
>
> *Financial Times*

> the pound which had been as low as $1.02 earlier this year, rose to $1.30
>
> *Fortune*

lower ['ləʊə] **1** *adjective* smaller, less high; *a lower rate of interest*; *sales were lower in December than in November* **2** *verb* to make smaller or less expensive; *to lower prices to secure a larger market share*; *industrialists have asked the bank to lower interest rates*

> Canadian and European negotiators agreed to a deal under which Canada could keep its quotas but lower its import duties
>
> *Globe and Mail (Toronto)*

lowering ['ləʊərɪŋ] *noun* making smaller or less expensive; *lowering the prices has resulted in increased sales*; *we hope to achieve low prices with no lowering of quality*

low-grade ['ləʊgreɪd] *adjective* not very important, not of very good quality; *a low-grade official from the Ministry of Commerce*; *the car runs best on low-grade petrol*

low-level ['ləʊ'levl] *adjective* **(a)** not very important; *a low-level delegation visited the ministry*; *a low-level meeting decided to put off making a decision* **(b)** **low-level computer language** = programming language similar to machine code

low-pressure ['ləʊ'preʃə] *adjective* **low-pressure sales** = sales where the salesman does not force someone to buy, but only encourages him to do so

low-quality ['ləʊ'kwɒləti] *adjective* not of good quality; *they tried to sell us some low-quality steel*

loyalty ['lɔɪəlti] *noun* **brand loyalty** = feeling of a customer who always buys the same brand of product; **customer loyalty** = feeling of customers who always shop at the same shop

Ltd ['lɪmɪtɪd] = LIMITED

luggage ['lʌgɪdʒ] *noun* suitcases, bags for carrying clothes when travelling; **hand luggage** *or* **cabin luggage** = small cases which passengers can take with them into the cabin of a plane or ship; **free luggage allowance** = amount of luggage which a passenger can take with him free of charge; **luggage trolley** = metal holder on wheels, on which luggage can be moved easily in an airport, train station, etc.) (NOTE: no plural; to show one suitcase, etc., say **a piece of luggage**. Note also that American English prefers to use the word **baggage**)

lull [lʌl] *noun* quiet period; *after last week's hectic trading this week's lull was welcome*

lump [lʌmp] *noun* **(a) lump sum =** money paid in one single amount, not in several small sums; *when he retired he was given a lump-sum bonus*; *she sold her house and invested the money as a lump sum* **(b)** the **Lump** *or* **Lump labour =** self-employed workers who are paid a lump sum for a day's work or for the amount of work completed (often with a view to avoiding tax)

lunch [lʌntʃ] *noun* meal eaten in the middle of the day; *the hours of work are from 9.30 to 5.30 with an hour off for lunch*; *the chairman is out at lunch*; **business lunch =** meeting between businessmen where they have lunch together to discuss business deals

lunch hour *or* **lunchtime** [ˈlʌntʃ ˈauə or ˈlʌnʃtaɪm] *noun* time when people have lunch; *the office is closed during the lunch hour or at lunchtimes*

luncheon voucher [ˈlʌnʃən ˈvautʃə] *noun* ticket given by an employer to a worker in addition to his wages, which can be exchanged for food in a restaurant

luxury [ˈlʌkʃəri] *noun* expensive thing which is not necessary but which is good to have; *luxury items or luxury goods are taxed very heavily*; *a black market in luxury articles*

Mm

m = METRE, MILE, MILLION

M0 [ˈem ˈnɔːt] narrowest measure of money supply, including coins and notes in circulation plus the deposits of commercial banks with the Bank of England

Bank of England calculations of notes in circulation suggest that the main component of the narrow measure of money supply, M0, is likely to have risen by 0.4 per cent after seasonal adjustments

Times

M1 [ˈem ˈwʌn] measure of money supply, including all coins and notes plus personal money in current accounts

M2 [ˈem ˈtuː] measure of money supply, including coins and notes and personal money in current and deposit accounts

M3 [ˈem ˈθriː] measure of money supply, including coins and notes, personal money in current and deposit accounts, government deposits and deposits in currencies other than sterling; **£M3** = British measure of sterling money supply, including coins and notes, personal money in current and deposit accounts and government deposits

machine [məˈʃiːn] *noun* (a) device which works with power from a motor; **adding machine** = machine which adds numbers; **copying machine** *or* **duplicating machine** = machine which makes copies of documents; **dictating machine** = machine which records what someone dictates, which a typist can then play back and type out; **automatic vending machine** = machine which provides food or drink when money is put in it; **machine shop** = place where working machines are placed;

machine tools = tools worked by motors, used to work on wood or metal **(b) machine-made** *or* **machine-produced** = manufactured by a machine, not by people **(c) machine code** *or* **machine language** = instructions and information shown as a series of figures (0 and 1) which can be read by a computer; **machine-readable codes** = sets of signs or letters (such as bar codes, post codes) which a computer can read

machinery [məˈʃiːnəri] *noun* **(a)** machines; **idle machinery** *or* **machinery lying idle** = machines not being used; **machinery guards** = pieces of metal to prevent workers from getting hurt by the moving parts of a machine **(b)** organization or system; *the local government machinery* *or* *the machinery of local government is slow to act; the administrative machinery of a university; the machinery for awarding government contracts*

machinist [məˈʃiːnɪst] *noun* person who works a machine

macro- [ˈmækrəʊ] *prefix* very large, covering a wide area

macroeconomics [ˈmækrəʊiːkəˈnɒmɪks] *noun* study of the economics of a whole area, a whole industry, a whole group of the population, or a whole country, in order to help in economic planning; *compare* MICROECONOMICS

Madam [ˈmædəm] *noun* formal way of addressing a woman, especially one whom you do not know; **Dear Madam** = beginning of a letter to a woman whom you do not know; **Madam Chairman** = way of addressing a woman who is in the chair at a meeting

made [meɪd] *adjective* produced or manufactured; *made in Japan or Japanese made*; *see also* MAKE

magazine [mægə'ziːn] *noun* paper, usually with pictures, which comes out regularly, every month or every week; **computer magazine** = magazine with articles on computers and programs; **do-it-yourself magazine** = magazine with articles on work which the average person can do to repair or paint the house; **house magazine** = magazine produced for the workers in a company to give them news of the company's affairs; **trade magazine** = magazine produced for people or companies in certain trades; **travel magazine** = magazine with articles on holidays and travel; **women's magazine** = magazine aimed at the women's market; **magazine insert** = advertising sheet put into a magazine when it is mailed or sold; **to insert a leaflet in a specialist magazine** = to put an advertising leaflet into a magazine before it is mailed or sold; **magazine mailing** = sending of copies of a magazine by post to subscribers

magnate ['mægneɪt] *noun* important businessman; *a shipping magnate*

magnetic [mæg'netɪk] *adjective* **magnetic card** = plastic card with a strip of magnetic recording material on its surface, allowing data to be stored (used in automatic cash dispensers); **magnetic strip** = black strip on credit cards and cashpoint cards, on which personal information about the account is recorded; **magnetic tape** *or* **mag tape** = plastic tape for recording information

mail [meɪl] **1** *noun* **(a)** system of sending letters and parcels from one place to another; *to put a letter in the mail*; *the cheque was lost in the mail*; *the invoice was put in the mail yesterday*; *mail to some of the islands in the Pacific can take six weeks*; **by mail** = using the postal services, not sending something by hand or by messenger; **to send a package by surface mail** = to send a package by land or sea, not by air; **by sea mail** = sent by post abroad, using a ship; **to receive a sample by air mail** = by post using a plane; **we sent the order by first-class mail** = by the most expensive mail service,

designed to be faster; **electronic mail** *or* **email** = system of sending messages from one computer to another, using the telephone lines **(b)** letters sent or received; *has the mail arrived yet?*; *to open the mail*; *your cheque arrived in yesterday's mail*; *my secretary opens my mail as soon as it arrives*; *the receipt was in this morning's mail*; **incoming mail** = mail which arrives; **outgoing mail** = mail which is sent out; **mail room** = room in an office where incoming letters are sorted and sent to each department, and where outgoing mail is collected for sending **(c)** **direct mail** = selling a product by sending publicity material to possible buyers through the post; *the company runs a successful direct-mail operation*; *these calculators are sold only by direct mail*; **direct-mail advertising** = advertising by sending leaflets to people by post; **mail shot** = leaflets sent by mail to possible customers **2** *verb* to send something by post; *to mail a letter*; *we mailed our order last Wednesday*

mail box ['meɪl 'bɒks] *noun* **(a)** one of several boxes where incoming mail is put in a large building; box for putting letters, etc., which you want to post **(b)** number where email messages are received

mailer ['meɪlə] *noun* packaging made of folded cardboard, used to mail items which need protection; *a diskette mailer*

mailing ['meɪlɪŋ] *noun* sending something in the post; *the mailing of publicity material*; **direct mailing** = sending of publicity material by post to possible buyers; **mailing list** = list of names and addresses of people who might be interested in a product, list of names and addresses of members of a society; *his name is on our mailing list*; *to build up a mailing list*; **to buy a mailing list** = to pay a society, etc., money to buy the list of members so that you can use it to mail publicity material; **mailing piece** = leaflet suitable for sending by direct mail; **mailing shot** = leaflets sent by mail to possible customers; **mailing tube** = stiff cardboard or plastic tube, used for mailing large pieces of paper (such as posters)

mail merge ['meɪl 'mɜːdʒ] *noun* word-processing program that allows a standard form letter to be printed out to a series of different names and addresses

mail-order ['meɪl'ɔːdə] *noun* system of buying and selling from a catalogue, placing orders and sending goods by mail; *we bought our kitchen units by mail-order*; **mail-order business** *or* **mail-order firm** *or* **mail-order house** = company which sells a product by mail; **mail-order catalogue** = catalogue from which a customer can order items to be sent by mail

main [meɪn] *adjective* most important; *our main office is in Birmingham*; *the main building houses our admin and finance departments*; *one of our main customers has gone into receivership*; US **Main Street** = most important street in a town, where the shops and banks are

mainframe ['meɪnfreɪm] *noun* large computer; *the office PCs interface with the mainframe computer in the company headquarters*

mainly ['meɪnli] *adverb* mostly; usually; *their sales are mainly in the home market*; *we are interested mainly in buying children's gift items*

mainstream corporation tax (MCT) ['meɪnstriːm kɒpəˈreɪʃn 'tæks] *noun* total tax paid by a company on its profits (less any advance corporation tax, which a company has already paid when distributing profits to its shareholders in the form of dividends)

maintain [meɪn'teɪn] *verb* **(a)** to keep something going or working; *we try to maintain good relations with our customers*; *his trip aims to maintain contact with his important overseas markets* **(b)** to keep something working at the same level; *the company has maintained the same volume of business in spite of the recession*; *the interest rate has been maintained at 5%*; **to maintain a dividend** = to pay the same dividend as the previous year

maintenance ['meɪntənəns] *noun* **(a)** keeping things going or working; *maintenance of contacts is important for a salesman*; *it is essential to ensure the maintenance of supplies to the factory* **(b)** keeping a machine in good working order;

maintenance contract = contract by which a company keeps a piece of equipment in good working order; *we offer a full maintenance service*

> responsibilities include the maintenance of large computerized databases
> *Times*

> the federal administration launched a full-scale investigation into the airline's maintenance procedures
> *Fortune*

majeure [mæ'ʒɜː] *see* **FORCE MAJEURE**

major ['meɪdʒə] *adjective* important; **major shareholder** = shareholder with a large number of shares

> if the share price sinks much further the company is going to look tempting to any major takeover merchant
> *Australian Financial Review*

> monetary officials have reasoned that coordinated greenback sales would be able to drive the dollar down against other major currencies
> *Duns Business Month*

> a client base which includes many major commercial organizations and nationalized industries
> *Times*

majority [mə'dʒɒrəti] *noun* larger group than all others; **majority of the shareholders** = more than 50% of the shareholders; **the board accepted the proposal by a majority of three to two** = three members of the board voted to accept and two voted against; **majority vote** *or* **majority decision** = decision made after a vote according to the wishes of the largest group; **majority shareholding** *or* **majority interest** = group of more than half of all the shares in a company; **a majority shareholder** = person who owns more than half the shares in a company

make [meɪk] **1** *noun* type of product manufactured; *Japanese makes of cars are* *now manufactured in Europe*; *a standard make of equipment*; *what make is the new computer system* or *what is the make of the new computer system?* **2** *verb* **(a)** to produce, to manufacture; *these computers are made in the USA*; *the workmen spent ten weeks making the table*; *the factory makes three hundred cars a day* **(b)** to agree; to do an action; **to make a deal** or **to make an agreement** = to agree to do something; **to make a bid for something** = to offer to buy something; **to make a payment** = to pay; **to make a deposit** = to pay money as a deposit **(c)** to earn; *he makes £50,000 a year* or *£25 an hour* **(d)** to increase in value; *the shares made $2.92 in today's trading* **(e)** to make a profit = to have more money after a deal; **to make a loss** = to have less money after a deal; **to make a killing** = to make a very large profit (NOTE: **making - made**)

make good ['meɪk 'gʊd] *verb* **(a)** to repair; to compensate for; *the company will make good the damage*; *to make good a loss* **(b)** to be a success; **a local boy made good** = local person who has become successful

make out ['meɪk 'aʊt] *verb* to write; *to make out an invoice*; *the bill is made out to Smith & Co.*; **to make out a cheque to someone** = to write someone's name on a cheque

make over ['meɪk 'əʊvə] *verb* to transfer property legally; *to make over the house to your children*

maker ['meɪkə] *noun* person or company which makes something; *a major car maker*; *a furniture maker*; **decision maker** = person who decides, who takes decisions; *see also* MARKETMAKER

make up ['meɪk 'ʌp] *verb* **(a)** to compensate for something; **to make up a loss** or **to make up the difference** = to pay extra so that the loss or difference is covered **(b)** **to make up accounts** = to complete the accounts

make up for ['meɪk 'ʌp fɔ:] *verb* to compensate for something; **to make up for a short order** = to send items which were missing in the original order; **to make up for a late payment** = to pay more than is owed because the payment is late

making ['meɪkɪŋ] *noun* production of an item; *ten tons of concrete were used in the making of the wall*; **decision making** = act of coming to a decision

maladministration ['mælədmɪnɪs'treɪʃən] *noun* incompetent administration

malfunction [mæl'fʌŋkʃn] **1** *noun* not working properly; *the data was lost due to a software malfunction* **2** *verb* not to work properly; *some of the keys on the keyboard have started to malfunction*

mall [mɔ:l] *noun* **shopping mall** = enclosed covered area for shopping, with shops, restaurants, banks and other facilities

man [mæn] **1** *noun* person; an ordinary worker; *all the men went back to work yesterday* **2** *verb* to provide the workforce for something; *it takes six workers to man a shift*; *we need volunteers to man the exhibition on Sunday*; *the exhibition stand was manned by three salesgirls*; *see also* MANNED, MANNING (NOTE: that **to man** does not mean only using men)

manage ['mænɪdʒ] *verb* **(a)** to direct, to be in charge of; *to manage a department*; *to manage a branch office* **(b)** **to manage property** = to look after rented property for the owner; **managed fund** or **managed unit trust** = unit trust fund which is invested in specialist funds within the same group of unit trusts and can be switched from one specialized investment area to another **(c)** **to manage to** = to be able to do something; *did you manage to see the head buyer?*; *she managed to write six orders and take three phone calls all in two minutes*

```
the research director will
manage and direct a team of
graduate business analysts
reporting on consumer
behaviour throughout the UK
                          Times
```

manageable ['mænɪdʒəbl] *adjective* which can be dealt with easily; *difficulties which are still manageable*; *the problems are too large to be manageable*

management ['mænɪdʒmənt] *noun* **(a)** directing or running a business; *he studied management at university*; *good* *management or efficient management is essential in a large organization*; *bad management or inefficient management can ruin a business*; *a management graduate or a graduate in management*; **fund management** = dealing with the investment of sums of money on behalf of clients; **line management** = organization of a business where each manager is responsible for doing what his superior tells him to do; **portfolio management** = buying and selling shares by a person or by a specialist on behalf of a client; **product management** = directing the making and selling of a product as an independent item; **management accountant** = accountant who prepares specialized information for managers so that they can make decisions; **management accounts** = financial information prepared for a manager so that he can make decisions (including monthly or quarterly financial statements, often in great detail, with analysis of actual performance against the budget); **management committee** = committee which manages a club, a pension fund, etc.; **management consultant** = person who gives advice on how to manage a business; **management course** = training course for managers; **management by objectives** = way of managing a business by setting work targets for the managers and testing to see if they are achieved correctly and on time; **management team** = a group of managers working together; **management techniques** = ways of managing a business; **management training** = training managers by making them study problems and work out ways of solving them; **management trainee** = young person being trained to be a manager **(b)** group of managers or directors; *the management has decided to give an overall pay increase*; **senior management** or **top management** = the main directors of a company; **middle management** = the department managers of a company who carry out the policy set by the directors and organize the work of a group of workers; **management buyin (MBI)** = purchase of a subsidiary company by a group of outside directors; **management buyout (MBO)** = takeover of a subsidiary company by a

group of its employees (usually senior managers and directors)

> the management says that the rate of loss-making has come down and it expects further improvement in the next few years
>
> *Financial Times*

manager ['mænɪdʒə] *noun* **(a)** head of a department in a company; *she's a department manager in an engineering company*; *go and see the human resources manager if you have a problem*; *the production manager has been with the company for only two weeks*; *our sales manager started as a rep in London*; **accounts manager** = head of the accounts department; **area manager** = manager who is responsible for the company's work (usually sales) in an area; **general manager** = manager in charge of the administration in a large company **(b)** person in charge of a branch or shop; *Mr Smith is the manager of our local Lloyds Bank*; *the manager of our Lagos branch is in London for a series of meetings*; **bank manager** = person in charge of a branch of a bank; **branch manager** = person in charge of a branch of a company

> the No. 1 managerial productivity problem in America is managers who are out of touch with their people and out of touch with their customers
>
> *Fortune*

manageress [mænɪdʒə'res] *noun* woman who runs a shop, or a department

managerial [mænə'dʒɪərɪəl] *adjective* referring to managers; *all the managerial staff are sent for training every year*; **to be appointed to a managerial position** = to be appointed a manager; **decisions taken at managerial level** = decisions taken by managers

managership ['mænɪdʒəʃɪp] *noun* job of being a manager; *after six years, he was offered the managership of a branch in Scotland*

managing ['mænɪdʒɪŋ] *adjective* **managing director (MD)** = director who is in charge of a whole company;

chairman and managing director = managing director who is also chairman of the board of directors

mandate ['mændeɪt] *noun* **bank mandate** = written order allowing someone to sign cheques on behalf of a company

mandatory ['mændətəri] *adjective* which everyone must obey; *wearing a suit is mandatory for all managerial staff*; **mandatory meeting** = meeting which all members have to attend

> the wage talks are focusing on employment issues such as sharing of work among employees and extension of employment beyond the mandatory retirement age of 60 years
>
> *Nikkei Weekly*

man-hour ['mæn'aʊə] *noun* work done by one worker in one hour; *one million man-hours were lost through industrial action*

manifest ['mænɪfest] *noun* list of goods in a shipment; **passenger manifest** = list of passengers on a ship or plane

manilla [mə'nɪlə] *noun* thick brown paper; *a manilla envelope*

manipulate [mə'nɪpjʊleɪt] *verb* **to manipulate the accounts** = to make false accounts so that the company seems profitable; **to manipulate the market** = to work to influence share prices in your favour

manipulation [mənɪpjʊ'leɪʃən] *noun* **stock market manipulation** = trying to influence the price of shares

manipulator [mə'nɪpjʊleɪtə] *noun* **stock market manipulator** = person who tries to influence the price of shares in his own favour

manned [mænd] *adjective* with someone working on it; *the switchboard is manned twenty-four hours a day; the stand was manned by our sales staff* (NOTE: that **manned** does not mean only using men)

manning ['mænɪŋ] *noun* people who are needed to do a work process; **manning levels** = number of people required in each department of a company to do the work

efficiently; **manning agreement** *or* **agreement on manning** = agreement between the company and the workers about how many workers are needed for a certain job

manpower ['mænpaʊə] *noun* number of workers; **manpower forecasting** = forecasting how many workers will be needed, and how many will be available; **manpower planning** = planning to obtain the right number of workers in each job; **manpower requirements** = number of workers needed; **manpower shortage** *or* **shortage of manpower** = lack of workers

manual ['mænjʊəl] **1** *adjective* done by hand, done using the hands; **manual labour** *or* **manual work** = heavy work done by hand; **manual labourer** = person who does heavy work with his hands; **manual worker** = person who works with his hands **2** *noun* book of instructions; **operating manual** = book showing how to operate a machine; **service manual** = book showing how to service a machine

manually ['mænjʊəli] *adverb* done by hand, not by a machine; *invoices have had to be typed manually because the computer has broken down*

manufacture [mænjʊ'fæktʃə] **1** *verb* to make a product for sale, using machines; *manufactured goods*; *the company manufactures spare parts for cars* **2** *noun* making a product for sale, using machines; **products of foreign manufacture** = products made in foreign countries

manufacturer [mænjʊ'fæktʃərə] *noun* person or company which produces machine-made products; *foreign manufacturers have set up factories here*; *a big Indian cotton manufacturer*; **manufacturer's recommended price (MRP)** = price at which the manufacturer suggests the product should be sold on the retail market, though often reduced by the retailer; *all typewriters - 20% off the manufacturer's recommended price*

manufacturing [mænjʊ'fæktʃərɪŋ] *noun* producing machine-made products for sale; *we must try to reduce the manufacturing overheads*; *manufacturing processes are continually being updated*; **manufacturing capacity** =

amount of a product which a factory is capable of making; **manufacturing costs** = costs of making a product; **manufacturing industries** = industries which take raw materials and make them into finished products

margin ['mɑːdʒɪn] *noun* **(a)** difference between the money received when selling a product and the money paid for it; **gross margin** = percentage difference between the received price and the unit manufacturing cost or purchase price of goods for resale; **net margin** = percentage difference between received price and all costs, including overheads; **we are cutting our margins very fine** = we are reducing our margins to the smallest possible to be competitive; **our margins have been squeezed** = profits have been reduced because our margins have to be smaller to stay competitive **(b)** extra space or time allowed; **margin of error** = degree of inaccuracy or number of mistakes which are accepted in a document or in a calculation; **safety margin** = time or space allowed for something to be safe; **margin of safety** = units produced (or sales of such units) which are above the breakeven point

profit margins in the industries most exposed to foreign competition - machinery, transportation equipment and electrical goods - are significantly worse than usual

Australian Financial Review

marginal ['mɑːdʒɪnəl] *adjective* **(a)** **marginal cost** = cost of making a single extra unit above the number already planned; **marginal costing** = costing a product on the basis of its variable costs only, excluding fixed costs; **marginal pricing** = basing the selling price of a product on its variable costs of production plus a margin, but excluding fixed costs; **marginal rate of tax** = percentage of tax which a taxpayer pays at a higher rate (which is therefore paid on every further pound or dollar which he or she earns); **marginal revenue** = income from selling a single extra unit above the number already sold **(b)** not very profitable, hardly worth the money paid; *the return on investment*

is only marginal; **marginal land** = land which is almost not worth farming; **marginal purchase** = thing which a buyer feels is only just worth buying

pensioner groups claim that pensioners have the highest marginal rates of tax. Income earned by pensioners above $30 a week is taxed at 62.5 per cent, more than the highest marginal rate

Australian Financial Review

marine [məˈriːn] **1** *adjective* referring to the sea; **marine insurance** = insurance of ships and their cargoes; **marine underwriter** = person who insures ships and their cargoes **2** *noun* **the merchant marine** = all the commercial ships of a country

maritime ['mærɪtaɪm] *adjective* referring to the sea; **maritime law** = laws referring to ships, ports, etc.; **maritime lawyer** = lawyer who specializes in legal matters concerning ships and cargoes; **maritime trade** = transporting commercial goods by sea

mark [mɑːk] **1** *noun* **(a)** sign put on an item to show something; **assay mark** = hallmark, a mark put on gold or silver items to show that the metal is of the correct quality; *GB* **kite mark** = mark on goods to show that they meet official standards **(b)** money used with the euro in Germany; *the price is twenty-five marks*; *the mark rose against the dollar* (NOTE: usually written **DM** after a figure: **25DM**. Also called **Deutschmark, D-Mark**) **2** *verb* to put a sign on something; *to mark a product 'for export only'*; *article marked at £1.50*; *she used a black pen to mark the price on the book*

mark down ['mɑːk 'daʊn] *verb* to make lower; **to mark down a price** = to lower the price of something; *this range has been marked down to $24.99*; *we have marked all prices down by 30% for the sale*

mark-down ['mɑːkdaʊn] *noun* **(a)** reduction of the price of something to less than its usual price **(b)** percentage amount by which a price has been lowered; *we have used a 30% mark-down to fix the sale price*

marker pen ['mɑːkə 'pen] *noun* felt pen which makes a wide coloured mark

market ['mɑːkɪt] **1** *noun* **(a)** place (often in the open air) where farm produce is sold; *we bought these crabs in the fish market*; *the flower market is open on Sundays*; *there is an open-air market in the market square*; *here are this week's market prices for sheep*; **flea market** = market for secondhand goods; **market day** = day when a market is regularly held; *Tuesday is market day, so the streets are closed to traffic*; **market dues** = rent for a stall in a market **(b) the Common Market** = the European Union; **the single market** = the EU considered as one single market, with no tariff barriers between its member states **(c)** area where a product might be sold; group of people who might buy a product; **home** *or* **domestic market** = market in the country where the selling company is based; *sales in the home market rose by 22%* **(d)** possible sales of a certain type of product, demand for a certain type of product; *the market for PCs has risen sharply*; *we have 20% of the British car market*; *there is no market for electric typewriters*; **a growth market** = market where sales are likely to rise rapidly; **the labour market** = number of workers available for work; *25,000 graduates have come on to the labour market* = they have become available for work because they have left college; **the property market** = sales of houses **(e) the black market** = buying and selling goods in a way which is not allowed by law; *there is a flourishing black market in spare parts for cars*; **to pay black market prices** = to pay high prices to get items which are not easily available **(f) a buyer's market** = market where goods are sold cheaply because there is little demand; **a seller's market** = market where the seller can ask high prices because there is a large demand for the product **(g) closed market** = market where a supplier deals with only one agent or distributor and does not supply any others direct; **free market economy** = system where the government does not interfere in business activity in any way; **open market** = market where anyone can buy and sell **(h)** place where money or commodities are traded; **capital market** = place where

companies can look for investment capital; **commodity market** = place where commodities are bought or sold; **the foreign exchange markets** = places where currencies are bought or sold; **forward markets** = places where foreign currency or commodities can be bought or sold for delivery at a later date; **money market** *or* **finance market** = place where large sums of money are lent or borrowed **(i) stock market** = place where shares are bought and sold; *the market in oil shares was very active or there was a brisk market in oil shares*; **to buy shares in the open market** = to buy shares on the Stock Exchange, not privately; **over-the-counter market** = secondary market in shares which are not listed on the main Stock Exchange; *(of a company)* **to come to the market** = to apply for a Stock Exchange listing, by offering some of the existing shares for sale, or by floating it as a new company **(j) market analysis** = detailed examination and report on a market; **market capitalization** = value of a company calculated by multiplying the price of its shares on the Stock Exchange by the number of shares issued; **market economist** = person who specializes in the study of financial structures and the return on investments in the stock market; **market forces** = influences on the sales of a product; **market forecast** = forecast of prices on the stock market; **market leader** = company with the largest market share; *we are the market leader in home computers*; **market opportunities** = possibility of finding new sales in a market; **market penetration** *or* **market share** = percentage of a total market which the sales of a company cover; *we hope our new product range will increase our market share*; **market price** = price at which a product can be sold; **market rate** = normal price in the market; *we pay the market rate for secretaries or we pay secretaries the market rate*; **market research** = examining the possible sales of a product before it is put on the market; **market trends** = gradual changes taking place in a market; **market value** = value of a product or of a company if sold today **(k) down market** = less expensive; **up market** = more expensive; **to go up market** *or* **to go**

down market = to make products which appeal to a wealthy section of the market or to a wider, less wealthy, section of the market **(l) to be in the market for secondhand cars** = to look for secondhand cars to buy; **to come on to the market** = to start to be sold; *this soap has just come on to the market*; **to put something on the market** = to start to offer something for sale; *they put their house on the market*; *I hear the company has been put on the market*; **the company has priced itself out of the market** = the company has raised its prices so high that its products do not sell **2** *verb* to sell (products); *this product is being marketed in all European countries*

> after the prime rate cut yesterday, there was a further fall in short-term market rates
>
> *Financial Times*

> market analysts described the falls in the second half of last week as a technical correction to a market which had been pushed by demand to over the 900 index level
>
> *Australian Financial Review*

> market leaders may benefit from scale economies or other cost advantages; they may enjoy a reputation for quality simply by being at the top, or they may actually produce a superior product that gives them both a large market share and high profits
>
> *Accountancy*

marketability [mɑːkɪtəˈbɪləti] *noun* being able to be sold easily; *the marketability of shares in electronic companies*

marketable [ˈmɑːkɪtəbl] *adjective* which can be sold easily

marketing [ˈmɑːkɪtɪŋ] *noun* techniques used in selling a product (such as packaging, advertising, etc.); **marketing agreement** = contract by which one company will market another company's products; **marketing cost** = cost of selling a product, including advertising, packaging, etc.; **marketing department** =

department in a company which specializes in using marketing techniques to sell a product; **marketing manager** = person in charge of a marketing department; **marketing policy** *or* **marketing plans** = ideas of how the company's products are going to be marketed; *to plan the marketing of a new product*

> reporting to the marketing director, the successful applicant will be responsible for the development of a training programme for the new sales force
>
> *Times*

marketmaker [ˈmɑːkɪtmeɪkə] *noun* person who buys or sells shares on the stock market and offers to do so in a certain list of securities (a marketmaker operates a book, listing the securities he is willing to buy or sell, and makes his money by charging a commission on each transaction)

marketplace [ˈmɑːkɪtpleɪs] *noun* **(a)** open space in the middle of a town where a market is held; *you can park in the marketplace when there is no market* **(b)** place where goods are sold; *our salesmen find life difficult in the marketplace*; *what is the reaction to the new car in the marketplace? or what is the marketplace reaction to the new car?*

> most discounted fares are sold by bucket shops but in today's competitive marketplace any agent can supply them
>
> *Business Traveller*

mark up [ˈmɑːk ˈʌp] *verb* to increase; **to mark prices up** = to increase prices; *these prices have been marked up by 10%*

mark-up [ˈmɑːkʌp] *noun* **(a)** increase in price; *we put into effect a 10% mark-up of all prices in June* **(b)** amount added to the cost price to give the selling price; **we work to a 3.5 times mark-up** *or* **to a 350% mark-up** = we take the unit cost and multiply by 3.5 to give the selling price

mart [mɑːt] *noun* market, a place where things are sold; **auction mart** = auction rooms

mass [mæs] *noun* **(a)** large group of people; **mass marketing** = marketing which aims at reaching large numbers of people; **mass media** = means of communication which reach large numbers of people (such as radio, television, newspapers); **mass unemployment** = unemployment of large numbers of workers **(b)** large number; *we have a mass of letters or masses of letters to write*; *they received a mass of orders or masses of orders after the TV commercials*

mass-produce [ˈmæsprəˈdjuːs] *verb* to manufacture in large quantities; *to mass-produce cars*

mass production [ˈmæs prəˈdʌkʃən] *noun* manufacturing large quantities of products

master [ˈmɑːstə] *noun* **(a)** main; original; **master budget** = budget prepared by amalgamating budgets from various profit and cost centres (sales, production, marketing, administration, etc.) to provide a main budget for the whole company; **master copy of a file** = main copy of a computer file, kept for security purposes **(b)** captain of a cargo ship; *customs officers boarded the ship and arrested the master*

mate [meɪt] *noun* officer on a cargo ship below the rank of master

material [məˈtɪərɪəl] *noun* **(a)** substance which can be used to make a finished product; **building materials** = bricks, cement, etc., used in building; **raw materials** = basic materials such as wood, iron ore, crude petroleum, which have to be treated or processed in some way before they can be used; **synthetic materials** = substances made as products of a chemical process; **materials control** = system to check that a company has enough materials in stock to do its work; **material(s) cost** = cost of the materials used in making a product; **materials handling** = moving materials from one part of a factory to another in an efficient way **(b)** **display material** = posters, photographs, etc., which can be used to attract attention to goods which are for sale; **publicity material** = leaflets, adverts, etc., used in publicity (NOTE: no plural in this meaning)

maternity [məˈtɜːnəti] *noun* becoming a mother; **maternity benefit** = money paid by the National Insurance to a mother when she has her child; **maternity leave** = permission for a woman to be away from work to have a baby

matrix [ˈmeɪtrɪks] *see* DOT-MATRIX PRINTER

matter [ˈmætə] **1** *noun* **(a)** problem; *it is a matter of concern to the members of the committee* = the members of the committee are worried about it **(b)** **printed matter** = printed books, newspapers, publicity sheets, etc.; **publicity matter** = sheets, posters or leaflets used for publicity (NOTE: no plural in this meaning) **(c)** question or problem to be discussed; *the most important matter on the agenda*; *we shall consider first the matter of last month's fall in prices* **2** *verb* to be important; *does it matter if one month's sales are down?*

mature [məˈtjʊə] **1** *adjective* **mature economy** = fully developed economy **2** *verb* **bills which mature in three weeks' time** = bills which will be due for payment in three weeks

maturity [məˈtjʊərəti] *noun* **date of maturity** *or* **maturity date** = date when a government stock, an assurance policy or a debenture will become due for payment; **amount payable on maturity** = amount received by the insured person when the policy becomes mature

maximization [mæksɪmaɪˈzeɪʃən] *noun* making as large as possible; *profit maximization or maximization of profit*

maximize [ˈmæksɪmaɪz] *verb* to make as large as possible; *our aim is to maximize profits*

maximum [ˈmæksɪməm] **1** *noun* largest possible number, price or quantity; **up to a maximum of £10** = no more than £10; **to increase exports to the maximum** = as much as possible; *it is the maximum the insurance company will pay* (NOTE: plural is **maxima**) **2** *adjective* largest possible; *40% is the maximum income tax rate or maximum rate of tax*; *the maximum load for the truck is one ton*; *maximum production levels were reached last week*; **to increase production to the maximum level** = as much as possible

MB = MEGABYTE

MBI = MANAGEMENT BUYIN

MBO = MANAGEMENT BUYOUT

MCT = MAINSTREAM CORPORATION TAX

MD ['em'di:] = MANAGING DIRECTOR; *the MD is in his office*; *she was appointed MD of a property company*

mean [mi:n] **1** *adjective* average; *the mean annual increase in slaes is 3.20%*; **mean price** = average price of a share in a day's trading **2** *noun* average, a figure calculated by adding several figures together and dividing by the number of figures added; *unit sales are over the mean for the first quarter or above the first quarter mean*

means [mi:nz] *plural noun* **(a)** way of doing something; *air freight is the fastest means of getting stock to South America*; *do we have any means of copying all these documents quickly?* **(b)** money or resources; *the company has the means to launch the new product*; *such a level of investment is beyond the means of a small private company*; **means test** = inquiry into how much money someone earns to see if he is eligible for state benefits; **he has private means** = he has income from dividends, interest or rent which is not part of his salary

measure ['meʒə] **1** *noun* **(a)** way of calculating size or quantity; **cubic measure** = volume in cubic feet or metres, calculated by multiplying height, width and length; **dry measure** = way of calculating the quantity of loose dry goods (such as corn); **square measure** = area in square feet or metres, calculated by multiplying width and length; **inspector of weights and measures** = government inspector who inspects weighing machines and goods sold in shops to see if the quantities and weights are correct; **as a measure of the company's performance** = as a way of judging if the company's results are good or bad **(b)** **made to measure** = made specially to fit; *he has his clothes made to measure* **(c)** tape **measure** = long tape with centimetres or inches marked on it, used to measure how long something is **(d)** type of action; **to**

take measures to prevent something happening = to act to stop something happening; **to take crisis** *or* **emergency measures** = to act rapidly to stop a crisis developing; **an economy measure** = an action to save money; **fiscal measures** = tax changes made by the government to improve the working of the economy; **as a precautionary measure** = to prevent something taking place; **safety measures** = actions to make sure that something is safe **2** *verb* **(a)** to find out the size or quantity of something; to be of a certain size or quantity; *to measure the size of a package*; *a package which measures 10cm by 25cm or a package measuring 10cm by 25cm* **(b)** to measure the government's **performance** = to judge how well the government is doing

measurement ['meʒəmənt] *noun* **(a)** **measurements** = size (in inches, centimetres, etc.); *to write down the measurements of a package* **(b)** way of judging something; **performance measurement** *or* **measurement of performance** = way of calculating how something or someone (a share or a person) has performed; **measurement of profitability** = way of calculating how profitable something is

measuring tape ['meʒərɪŋ 'teɪp] *noun* long tape with centimetres or inches marked on it, used to measure how long something is

mechanic [mɪ'kænɪk] *noun* person who works with engines or machines; *he got a job as a car mechanic before going to college*

mechanical [mɪ'kænɪkəl] *adjective* worked by a machine; *a mechanical pump*

mechanism ['mekənɪzm] *noun* way in which something works; *a mechanism to slow down inflation*; *the company's discount mechanism*

mechanization [mekənaɪ'zeɪʃən] *noun* using machines in place of workers; *farm mechanization or the mechanization of farms*

mechanize ['mekənaɪz] *verb* to use machines in place of workers; *the country is aiming to mechanize its farming industry*

media ['miːdjə] *noun* **the media** *or* **the mass media** = means of communicating information to the public (such as television, radio, newspapers); *the product attracted a lot of interest in the media or a lot of media interest*; **media analysis** *or* **media research** = examining different types of media (such as the readers of newspapers, television viewers) to see which is best for promoting a certain type of product; **media coverage** = reports about something in the media; *we got good media coverage for the launch of the new model* (NOTE: **media** is followed by a singular or plural verb)

median ['miːdjən] *noun* point in the middle of a list of numbers

mediate ['miːdɪeɪt] *verb* to try to make the two sides in an argument come to an agreement; *the personnel director said she would try to mediate between the manager and his staff*; *the government offered to mediate in the dispute*

mediation [miːdɪ'eɪʃən] *noun* attempt by a third party to make the two sides in an argument agree; *the employers refused an offer of government mediation*; *the dispute was ended through the mediation of union officials*

mediator ['miːdɪeɪtə] *noun* **official mediator** = government official who tries to make the two sides in an industrial dispute agree

medical ['medɪkəl] *noun* referring to the study or treatment of illness; **medical certificate** = certificate from a doctor to show that a worker has been ill; **medical inspection** = examining a place of work to see if the conditions will not make the workers ill; **medical insurance** = insurance which pays the cost of medical treatment especially when travelling abroad; **medical officer of health** = person responsible for the health services in a town or other local area; *he resigned for medical reasons* = he resigned because he was too ill to work

medium ['miːdjəm] **1** *adjective* middle; average; *the company is of medium size* **2** *noun* **(a)** way of doing something, means of doing something; **advertising medium** = type of advertisement (such as a TV

commercial); *the product was advertised through the medium of the trade press* (NOTE: plural for this meaning is **media**) **(b)** **mediums** = government stocks which mature in seven to fifteen years' time

medium-sized ['miːdjəm'saɪzd] *adjective* **(a)** **a medium-sized company** = a company which is neither very large nor very small; *a medium-sized engineering company* **(b)** *(for UK tax purposes)* company which has a turnover of less than £5.75m and does not employ more than 250 staff (companies of this size can file modified accounts with the Registrar of Companies)

medium-term ['miːdjəm'tɜːm] *adjective* referring to a point between short term and long term; **medium-term forecast** = forecast for two or three years; **medium-term loan** = bank loan for three to five years

meet [miːt] *verb* **(a)** to come together with someone; *union leaders came to meet the negotiating committee*; *we met the agent at his hotel*; *the two sides met in the lawyer's office* **(b)** to be satisfactory for; *we must have a product which meets our requirements*; **to meet the demand for a new product** = to fill the demand for a product; **we will try to meet your price** = we will try to offer a price which is acceptable to you; **they failed to meet the deadline** = they were not able to complete in time **(c)** to pay for; *to meet someone's expenses*; *the company will meet your expenses*; *he was unable to meet his mortgage repayments* (NOTE: **meeting - met**)

meeting ['miːtɪŋ] *noun* **(a)** coming together of a group of people; **management meeting** = group of managers who meet; **staff meeting** = meeting of a group of staff or their representatives; **board meeting** = meeting of the directors of a company; **general meeting** *or* **meeting of shareholders** *or* **shareholders' meeting** = meeting of all the shareholders of a company, meeting of all the members of a society; **Annual General Meeting (AGM)** = meeting of all the shareholders when a company's financial situation is discussed with the directors; **Extraordinary General**

Meeting (EGM) = special meeting of shareholders to discuss an important matter which cannot wait until the next AGM (such as a change in the company's articles of association) **(b) to hold a meeting** = to organize a meeting of a group of people; *the meeting will be held in the committee room*; **to open a meeting** = to start a meeting; **to conduct a meeting** = to be in the chair for a meeting; **to close a meeting** = to end a meeting; **to address a meeting** = to speak to a meeting; **to put a resolution to a meeting** = to ask a meeting to vote on a proposal

in proportion to your holding you have a stake in every aspect of the company, including a vote in the general meetings
Investors Chronicle

meet with ['miːt 'wɪð] *verb* **(a)** *US* to come together with someone; **I hope to meet with him in New York** = I hope to meet him in New York **(b) his request met with a refusal** = his request was refused

megabyte (MB) ['megəbaɪt] *noun* storage unit in computers, equal to 1,048,576 bytes

member ['membə] *noun* **(a)** person who belongs to a group or a society; *members of a committee or committee members voted on the proposal*; *they were elected members of the board*; **ordinary member** = person who pays a subscription to belong to a group; **honorary member** = special person who does not have to pay a subscription **(b)** shareholder in a company; **members' voluntary winding up** = winding up of a company by the shareholders themselves **(c)** organization which belongs to a society; *the member states of the EU*; *the members of the United Nations*; *the member companies of a trade association*

it will be the first opportunity for party members and trade union members to express their views on the tax package
Australian Financial Review

membership ['membəʃɪp] *noun* **(a)** belonging to a group; *membership qualifications*; *conditions of membership*; *membership card*; *to pay your membership or your membership fees*; *Turkey has applied for membership of the EU* **(b)** all the members of a group; *the membership was asked to vote for the new president*; *the* **club's membership secretary** = committee member who deals with the ordinary members of a society; **the club has a membership of five hundred** = the club has five hundred members

the bargaining committee will recommend that its membership ratify the agreement at a meeting called for June
Toronto Star

memo ['meməʊ] *noun* short message sent from one person to another in the same organization; *she wrote a memo to the finance director*; *the sales manager is going to send a memo to all the sales representatives*; *according to your memo about debtors, the position is worse than last year*; *I sent the managing director a memo about your complaint*

memo pad ['meməʊ 'pæd] *noun* pad of paper for writing short notes

memorandum [memə'rændəm] *noun* short message; **memorandum (and articles) of association** = legal documents setting up a limited company and giving details of its name, aims, authorized share capital, conduct of meetings, appointment of directors, and registered office

memory ['meməri] *noun* facility for storing data in a computer; **random access memory (RAM)** = memory that allows access to any location in any order without having to access the rest of memory; **read only memory (ROM)** = memory device that has had data written into it when it is manufactured, and so can only be read but not written to

mention ['menʃən] *verb* to talk about something for a short time; *the chairman mentioned the work of the retiring managing director*; *can you mention to the secretary that the date of the next meeting has been changed?*

menu ['menjuː] *noun* list of options or programs available to the user of a computer program; **pop-up menu** *or*

pull-down menu = menu of options that can be displayed at any time, usually covering part of other text on the screen in the process

mercantile ['mɜːkəntaɪl] *adjective* commercial; **mercantile country** = country which earns income from trade; **mercantile law** = laws relating to business; **mercantile marine** = all the commercial ships of a country

merchandise ['mɜːtʃəndaɪs] *noun* goods which are for sale or which have been sold; *the merchandise is shipped through two ports*

---

fill huge warehouses with large quantities but limited assortments of top-brand, first-quality merchandise and sell the goods at rock-bottom prices

Duns Business Month

---

merchandize ['mɜːtʃəndaɪz] *verb* to sell goods by a wide variety of means, including display, advertising, sending samples, etc.; *to merchandize a product*

merchandizer ['mɜːtʃəndaɪzə] *noun* person or company which organizes the display and promotion of goods

merchandizing ['mɜːtʃəndaɪzɪŋ] *noun* organizing the display and promotion of goods for sale; *merchandizing of a product*; *merchandizing department*

merchant ['mɜːtʃənt] *noun* **(a)** businessman who buys and sells goods (especially imported goods) in bulk for retail sale; *coal merchant*; *tobacco merchant*; *wine merchant* **(b)** **merchant bank** = bank which arranges loans to companies and deals in international finance, buys and sells shares, launches new companies on the Stock Exchange but does not provide normal banking services to the general public; **merchant banker** = person who has a high position in a merchant bank; **merchant navy** *or* **merchant marine** = all the commercial ships of a country; **merchant ship** *or* **merchant vessel** = commercial ship, ship which carries a cargo **(c)** company, shop, etc., which accepts a certain type of credit card for purchases; **merchant number** = number of the merchant, printed at the top

of the report slip when depositing credit card payments

merchantman ['mɜːtʃəntmən] *noun* commercial ship

merge [mɜːdʒ] *verb* to join together; *the two companies have merged*; *the firm merged with its main competitor*

merger ['mɜːdʒə] *noun* joining together of two or more companies; *as a result of the merger, the company is the largest in the field*

merit ['merɪt] *noun* being good or efficient; **merit award** *or* **merit bonus** = extra money given to a worker because he has worked well; **merit increase** = increase in pay given to someone because his work is good; **merit rating** = judging how well a worker does his work, so that he can be paid according to merit

message ['mesɪdʒ] *noun* **(a)** piece of news which is sent to someone; *to send a message*; *I will leave a message with his secretary*; *can you give the director a message from his wife?*; *he says he never received the message*; **message board** = public noticeboard on which messages can be left (such as at a conference, or in a hotel lobby) **(b)** information given on a little screen on a computer, printer, fax machine, etc.; *we need more toner - the message is showing 'TONER LOW'*

messenger ['mesɪndʒə] *noun* person who brings a message; *he sent the package by special messenger or by motorcycle messenger*; **office messenger** = person who carries messages from one person to another in a large office; **messenger boy** = young man who carries messages

Messrs ['mesəz] *noun* plural form of Mr, used only in names of firms; *Messrs White, Ltd*

meter ['miːtə] **1** *noun* **(a)** device which measures the amount of something which has been used; *electricity meter*; *water meter* **(b)** *US* = METRE **2** *verb* to measure the amount of something which has been used

method ['meθəd] *noun* way of doing something; *they devised a new method of sending data*; *what is the best method of payment?*; *his organizing methods are out* of date; *their manufacturing methods or production methods are among the most modern in the country*; **time and method study** = examining the way in which something is done to see if a cheaper or quicker way can be found

metre *US* **meter** ['mi:tə] *noun* measure of length (= 3.4 feet) (NOTE: usually written **m** after figures: **the case is 2m wide by 3m long**)

metric ['metrɪk] *adjective* using the metre as a basic measurement; **metric ton** *or* **metric tonne** = 1000 kilograms; **the metric system** = system of measuring, using metres, litres and grams

mezzanine finance ['metsəni:n faɪ'næns] *noun* provision of finance for a company after the start-up finance has been provided

COMMENT: mezzanine finance is slightly less risky than start-up finance, since the company has usually already started trading; it is, however, unsecured; this type of finance is aimed at consolidating a company's trading position before it is floated on a stock exchange

mfg = MANUFACTURING

MFN = MOST FAVOURED NATION

mg = MILLIGRAM

mi = MILE

micro- ['maɪkrəu] *prefix* very small

microcomputer ['maɪkrəukəm'pju:tə] *noun* small computer for general use in the home or office

micro-economics ['maɪkrəui:kə'nɒmɪks] *noun* study of the economics of persons or single companies; *compare* MACROECONOMICS

microfiche ['maɪkrəufi:ʃ] *noun* index sheet, made of several microfilm photographs; *we hold our records on microfiche*

microfilm ['maɪkrəufɪlm] **1** *noun* roll of film on which a document is photographed in very small scale; *we hold our records on microfilm* **2** *verb* to make a very small scale photograph; *send the 1998 correspondence to be microfilmed or for microfilming*

microprocessor [maɪkrəu'prəusesə] *noun* central processing unit element, often contained on a single integrated circuit chip, which, when combined with other memory and I/O chips, will make up a microcomputer

mid- [mɪd] *prefix* middle; **from mid-1994** = from the middle of 1994; *the factory is closed until mid-July*

middle ['mɪdl] *adjective* in the centre, between two points; **middle management** = department managers in a company, who carry out the policy set by the directors and organize the work of a group of workers

middle-income ['mɪdl'ɪŋkʌm] *adjective* **people in the middle-income bracket** = people with average incomes, not very high or very low

middleman ['mɪdlmæn] *noun* businessman who buys from the manufacturer and sells to the public; *we sell direct from the factory to the customer and cut out the middleman* (NOTE: plural is **middlemen**)

middle-sized ['mɪdl'saɪzd] *adjective* neither small nor large; *a middle-sized company*

mid-month ['mɪd'mʌnθ] *adjective* taking place in the middle of the month; *mid-month accounts*

mid-week ['mɪd'wi:k] *adjective* which happens in the middle of a week; *the mid-week lull in sales*

mile [maɪl] *noun* measure of length (= 1.609 kilometres); **the car does twenty-five miles to the gallon** *or* **twenty-five miles per gallon** = the car uses one gallon of petrol to travel twenty-five miles (NOTE: can be shortened to **m** *or* **ml**; miles per gallon is usually written **mpg** after figures: **the car does 25mpg**)

mileage ['maɪlɪdʒ] *noun* **(a)** distance travelled in miles; **mileage allowance** = money allowed as expenses to someone who uses his own car for business travel; **the salesman's average annual mileage** = the number of miles which a salesman drives in a year **(b)** distance which can be driven in a rented car, which may be charged to the person renting the car; *the car comes with unlimited free mileage*

mill [mɪl] *noun* building where a certain type of material is processed or made; *after lunch the visitors were shown round the mill*; **cotton mill** = factory where raw cotton is processed; **paper mill** = factory where wood is made into paper

milligram ['mɪlɪgræm] *noun* one thousandth of a gram (NOTE: usually written **mg** after figures)

millilitre *US* **milliliter** ['mɪlɪliːtə] *noun* one thousandth of a litre (NOTE: usually written **ml** after figures)

millimetre *US* **millimeter** ['mɪlɪmiːtə] *noun* one thousandth of a metre (NOTE: usually written **mm** after figures)

million ['mɪljən] number 1,000,000; *the company lost £10 million in the African market*; *our turnover has risen to $13.4 million* (NOTE: can be written **m** after figures: **$5m** (say 'five million dollars'); *see also* notes at BILLION, TRILLION

millionaire [mɪljə'neə] *noun* person who has more than one million pounds or dollars; **dollar millionaire** = person who has more than one million dollars; **paper millionaire** = person who owns shares which, if sold, would be worth one million pounds or dollars; **sterling millionaire** = person who has more than one million pounds sterling (NOTE: to be specific, you can say **dollar millionaire, peso millionaire, etc.**)

min = MINUTE, MINIMUM

mine [maɪn] **1** *noun* hole in the ground for digging out coal, gold, iron, etc.; *the mines have been closed by a strike*; *the main coal mines are in the west of the country*; *see also* GOLDMINE **2** *verb* to dig and bring out coal, gold, etc.; *the company is mining coal in the south of the country*; **mining concession** = right to use a piece of land for mining

mineral ['mɪnərəl] *noun* natural material (usually in the ground) which can be used; **mineral resources** = minerals (such as coal, iron ore, natural gas, etc.) which lie under the ground in a country and form part of the country's potential wealth; **mineral rights** = the right to extract minerals from the ground

mini- ['mɪni] *prefix* very small

minicomputer [mɪnɪkəm'pjuːtə] *noun* computer which is larger than a PC but smaller than a mainframe

minicontainer [mɪnɪkən'teɪnə] *noun* small container

minimal ['mɪnɪməl] *adjective* the smallest possible; *there was a minimal quantity of imperfections in the batch*; *the head office exercises minimal control over the branch offices*

minimarket [mɪnɪ'mɑːkɪt] *noun* very small self-service store

minimize ['mɪnɪmaɪz] *verb* to make something seem to be very small and not very important; *do not minimize the risks involved*; *he tends to minimize the difficulty of the project*

minimum ['mɪnɪməm] **1** *noun* smallest possible quantity, price or number; *to keep expenses to a minimum*; *to reduce the risk of a loss to a minimum* (NOTE: plural is **minima** or **minimums**) **2** *adjective* smallest possible; **minimum dividend** = smallest dividend which is legal and accepted by the shareholders; **minimum payment** = smallest payment necessary; **minimum quantity** = smallest quantity which is acceptable; **minimum stock level** = lowest level of stock in a warehouse (when this level is reached more stock has to be ordered); **minimum wage** = lowest hourly wage which a company can legally pay its workers; *the government has raised the minimum wage*

minister ['mɪnɪstə] *noun* member of a government who is in charge of a ministry; *a government minister*; *the Minister of Trade or the Trade Minister*; *the Minister of Foreign Affairs or the Foreign Minister* (NOTE: in the UK and USA, they are called **secretary: the Foreign Secretary, Secretary for Commerce**)

ministry ['mɪnɪstri] *noun* department in the government; *she works in the Ministry of Finance or the Finance Ministry*; *he is in charge of the Ministry of Information or of the Information Ministry*; *a ministry official or an official from the ministry* (NOTE: in the UK and the USA, important ministries are called **departments: the Department of Trade and Industry; the Commerce Department**)

minor ['mamə] *adjective* less important; *items of minor expenditure are not listed separately*; *the minor shareholders voted against the proposal*; **a loss of minor importance** = not a very serious loss

minority [mar'nɒrəti] *noun* number or quantity which is less than half of the total; *a minority of board members opposed the chairman*; **minority shareholding** *or* **minority interest** = group of shares which are less than one half of the shares in a company; **minority shareholder** = person who owns a group of shares but less than half of the shares in a company; **in the minority** = being fewer than half; *good salesmen are in the minority in our sales team*

mint [mɪnt] **1** *noun* factory where coins are made **2** *verb* to make coins

minus ['mamɔs] **1** *preposition* less, without; *net salary is gross salary minus tax and National Insurance deductions*; *gross profit is sales minus production costs* **2** *adjective* **the accounts show a minus figure** = show that more has been spent than has been received; **minus factor** = unfavourable factor; *to have lost sales in the best quarter of the year is a minus factor for the sales team* (NOTE: the opposite is **plus**)

minute ['mɪnɪt] **1** *noun* **(a)** one sixtieth part of an hour; *I can see you for ten minutes only*; *if you do not mind waiting, Mr Smith will be free in about twenty minutes' time* **(b)** **the minutes of the meeting** = notes of what happened at a meeting, written by the secretary; **to take the minutes** = to write notes of what happened at a meeting; **the chairman signed the minutes of the last meeting** = he signed them to show that they are a correct record of what was said and what decisions were taken; **this will not appear in the minutes of the meeting** = this is unofficial and will not be noted as having been said **2** *verb* to put something into the minutes of a meeting; *the chairman's remarks about the auditors were minuted*; **I do not want that to be minuted** *or* **I want that not to be minuted** = do not put that remark into the minutes of the meeting

minutebook ['mɪnɪtbʊk] *noun* book in which the minutes of a meeting are kept

misappropriate [mɪsə'prəʊprɪeɪt] *verb* to steal or to use illegally money which is not yours, but with which you have been trusted

misappropriation [mɪsəprəʊprɪ'eɪʃən] *noun* illegal use of money by someone who is not the owner but who has been trusted to look after it

misc = MISCELLANEOUS

miscalculate [mɪs'kælkjʊleɪt] *verb* to calculate wrongly; *the salesman miscalculated the discount, so we hardly broke even on the deal*

miscalculation [mɪskælkjʊ'leɪʃən] *noun* mistake in calculating

miscellaneous [mɪsə'leɪnjəs] *adjective* various, mixed, not all of the same sort; *miscellaneous items on the agenda*; *a box of miscellaneous pieces of equipment*; *miscellaneous expenditure is not itemized in the accounts*

miscount 1 ['mɪskaʊnt] *noun* mistake in counting **2** [mɪs'kaʊnt] *verb* to count wrongly; *the shopkeeper miscounted, so we got twenty-five bars of chocolate instead of two dozen*

misdirect [mɪsdaɪ'rekt] *verb* to give wrong directions

mismanage [mɪs'mænɪdʒ] *verb* to manage badly; *the company had been badly mismanaged under the previous MD*

mismanagement [mɪs'mænɪdʒmənt] *noun* bad management; *the company failed because of the chairman's mismanagement*

misrepresent [mɪsreprɪ'zent] *verb* to report facts wrongly; *our spokesman was totally misrepresented in the Sunday papers*

misrepresentation [mɪsreprɪzen'teɪʃən] *noun* wrongly reporting facts; **fraudulent misrepresentation** = giving someone wrong information in order to cheat him

Miss [mɪs] *noun* title given to a woman who is not married; *Miss Smith is our sales manager*

miss [mɪs] *verb* (a) not to hit; *the company has missed its profit forecast again*; *the sales team has missed its sales targets* (b) not to meet; *I arrived late, so missed most of the discussion*; *he missed the chairman by ten minutes* = he left ten minutes before the chairman arrived (c) to be late for; *he missed the last plane to Frankfurt*

mission ['mɪʃən] *noun* group of people going on a journey for a special purpose; **trade mission** = visit by a group of businessmen to discuss trade; *he led a trade mission to China*; **inward mission** = visit to your home country by a group of foreign businessmen; **outward mission** = visit by a group of businessmen to a foreign country; **a fact-finding mission** = visit to an area to search for information about a problem

mistake [mɪ'steɪk] **1** *noun* wrong action or wrong decision; **to make a mistake** = to do something wrong; *the shop made a mistake and sent the wrong items*; *there was a mistake in the address*; *she made a mistake in addressing the letter*; **by mistake** = in error, wrongly; *they sent the wrong items by mistake*; *she put my letter into an envelope for the chairman by mistake* **2** *verb* to think wrongly; **I mistook him for his brother** = I thought he was his brother (NOTE: **mistakes - mistaking - mistook** [mɪs'tʊk] - **has mistaken** [mɪs'teɪkən])

misunderstanding [mɪsʌndə'stændɪŋ] *noun* not understanding something correctly; *there was a misunderstanding over my tickets*

misuse [mɪs'juːs] *noun* wrong use; *misuse of funds or of assets*

mix [mɪks] **1** *noun* things put together; **product mix** = range of different products which a company has for sale; **sales mix** = sales and profitability of a wide range of different products **2** *verb* to put different things together; *I like to mix business with pleasure - why don't we discuss the deal over lunch?*

mixed [mɪkst] *adjective* (a) of different sorts, of different types together; **mixed economy** = system which contains both nationalized industries and private enterprise; **mixed farm** = farm which has both animals and crops (b) neither good nor bad

> prices closed on a mixed note after a moderately active trading session
>
> *Financial Times*

ml = MILLILITRE

mm = MILLIMETRE

MMC = MONOPOLIES AND MERGERS COMMISSION

mobile ['məʊbaɪl] **1** *adjective* which can move about; **mobile phone** = small telephone which you can carry about with you; **mobile shop** = van fitted out like a small shop which travels round selling groceries or vegetables; **mobile workforce** = workers who move from place to place to get work **2** *noun* mobile phone; *I managed to reach him on his mobile*; *as soon as she got on the train her mobile started ringing*

mobility [mə'bɪləti] *noun* being able to move from one place to another; **mobility of labour** = situation when workers agree to move from one place to another to get work

mobilize ['məʊbɪlaɪz] *verb* to bring together, especially to fight; **to mobilize capital** = to collect capital to support something; **to mobilize resources to defend a takeover bid** = to get the support of shareholders, etc., to stop a company being taken over

mock-up ['mɒkʌp] *noun* model of a new product for testing or to show to possible buyers; *the sales team were shown a mock-up of the new car*

mode [məʊd] *noun* way of doing something; **mode of payment** = way in which payment is made (such as cash or cheque)

model ['mɒdl] **1** *noun* (a) small copy of something to show what it will look like when finished; *he showed us a model of the new office building* (b) style or type of product; *this is the latest model*; *the model on display is last year's*; *he drives a 1990 model Range Rover*; **demonstration model** = piece of equipment used in demonstrations and then sold cheaply (c) person whose job is to wear new clothes to show them to possible buyers **(d) economic model** = computerized plan of a country's economic system, used for forecasting economic trends **2** *adjective* which is a perfect example to be copied; *a model agreement* **3** *verb* to wear new clothes to show them to possible buyers; *she has decided on a career in modelling* (NOTE: **modelling - modelled** but American spelling **modeling - modeled**)

modem ['məʊdem] *noun* device which links a computer to the telephone line, allowing data to be sent from one computer to another

moderate 1 ['mɒdərət] *adjective* not too large; *the trade union made a moderate claim*; *the government proposed a moderate increase in the tax rate* **2** *verb* ['mɒdəreɪt] to make smaller, to reduce; *the union was forced to moderate its claim*

modern ['mɒdən] *adjective* referring to the recent past or the present time; *it is a fairly modern invention - it was patented only in the 1980s*

modernization [mɒdənaɪ'zeɪʃən] *noun* making modern; *the modernization of the workshop*

modernize ['mɒdənaɪz] *verb* to make modern; *he modernized the whole product range*

modest ['mɒdɪst] *adjective* small; *oil shares showed modest gains over the week's trading*

modification [mɒdɪfɪ'keɪʃən] *noun* change; *the board wanted to make or to carry out modifications to the plan*; *the new model has had several important modifications*; *we asked for modifications to the contract*

modify ['mɒdɪfaɪ] *verb* to change or to make something fit a different use; *the management modified its proposals*; *this is the new modified agreement*; *the car will have to be modified to pass the government tests*; *the refrigerator was considerably modified before it went into production*; **modified accounts** = less detailed annual accounts which can be deposited with the Registrar of Companies by small or medium-sized companies

modular ['mɒdjʊlə] *adjective* made of various sections

momentum [mə'mentəm] *noun* movement forwards; **to gain** *or* **to lose momentum** = to move faster or more slowly; **the strike is gaining momentum** = more workers are joining the strike

monetarism ['mʌnɪtərɪzm] *noun* theory that the amount of money in the economy affects the level of prices, so that inflation can be controlled by regulating money supply

monetarist ['mʌnɪtərɪst] **1** *noun* person who believes in monetarism and acts accordingly **2** *adjective* according to monetarism; *monetarist theories*

monetary ['mʌnɪtəri] *adjective* referring to money or currency; **the government's monetary policy** = the government's policy relating to finance (bank interest rates, taxes, government expenditure and borrowing); **monetary standard** = fixing of a fixed exchange rate for a currency; **monetary targets** = figures such as the money supply, PSBR, etc., which are given as targets by the government when setting out its budget for the forthcoming year; **the international monetary system** = methods of controlling and exchanging currencies between countries; **the International Monetary Fund (IMF)** = (part of the United Nations) a type of bank which helps member states in financial difficulties, gives financial advice to members and encourages world trade; **monetary unit** = standard currency in a country (the pound, the dollar, the franc, etc.) or within a group of countries (the CFA franc, the euro, etc.)

> the decision by the government to tighten monetary policy will push the annual inflation rate above the year's previous high
>
> *Financial Times*

> it is not surprising that the Fed started to ease monetary policy some months ago
>
> *Sunday Times*

a draft report on changes in the international monetary system

Wall Street Journal

Monetary Policy Committee (MPC) ['mʌnɪtəri 'pɒlɪsi kə'mɪti]

committee of the Bank of England, chaired by the governor of the Bank, which has responsibility for setting interest rates independently of the British government; the aim is to set rates with a view to keeping inflation at a certain level, and avoiding deflation

Its Monetary Policy Committee (MPC) gets an opportunity to reveal whether it is still affected by the Christmas spirit when it meets this Wednesday

The Times

The Fed next meets to consider interest rates on February 3 and 4, just one day ahead of the February MPC meeting

The Times

money ['mʌni] *noun* **(a)** coins and notes used for buying and selling; **to earn money** = to have a salary; **to earn good money** = to have a large salary; **to lose money** = to make a loss, not to make a profit; **the company has been losing money for months** = the company has been working at a loss; **to get your money back** = to earn enough to cover your original investment; **to make money** = to make a profit; **to put money into the bank** = to deposit money into a bank account; **to put money into a business** = to invest money in a business; *he put all his redundancy money into a shop*; **to put money down** = to pay cash, especially as a deposit; *he put £25 down and paid the rest in instalments*; **call money** *or* **money at call** = money loaned for which repayment can be demanded without notice (used by commercial banks, placing money on very short-term deposit with discount houses); **cheap money** = money which can be borrowed at a low rate of interest; **danger money** = extra salary paid to workers in dangerous jobs; **dear money** = money which has to be borrowed at a high rate of interest; **easy money** = money which can be earned with no

difficulty; **hot money** = money which is moved from country to country to get the best returns; **paper money** = money in notes, not coins; **ready money** = cash or money which is immediately available; **money lying idle** = money not being used to produce interest; **they are worth a lot of money** = they are valuable **(b)** **money supply** = amount of money which exists in a country; **money markets** = markets for buying and selling short-term loans; *the international money markets are nervous*; **money rates** = rates of interest for borrowers or lenders **(c)** **money order** = document which can be bought for sending money through the post; **foreign money order** *or* **international money order** *or* **overseas money order** = money order in a foreign currency which is payable to someone living in a foreign country **(d)** **monies** = sums of money; *monies owing to the company*; *to collect monies due*

moneylender ['mʌnɪlendə] *noun* person who lends money at interest

money-making ['mʌni'meɪkɪŋ] *adjective* which makes money; *a money-making plan*

money-spinner ['mʌni'spɪnə] *noun* item which sells very well or which is very profitable; *the home delivery service has proved to be a real money- spinner*

monitor ['mɒnɪtə] **1** *noun* screen (like a TV screen) on a computer; *I'll just call up details of your account on the monitor*; *he brought up the information on the monitor* **2** *verb* to check or to examine how something is working; *he is monitoring the progress of sales*; *how do you monitor the performance of the sales reps?*

monopolization [mənɒpəlaɪ'zeɪʃən] *noun* making a monopoly

monopolize [mə'nɒpəlaɪz] *verb* to create a monopoly, to get control of all the means of supplying a product

monopoly [mə'nɒpəli] *noun* situation where one person or company controls all the market in the supply of a product; *to have the monopoly of alcohol sales or to have the alcohol monopoly*; *to be in a monopoly situation*; *the company has the absolute monopoly of imports of French wine*; *the factory has the absolute* *monopoly of jobs in the town*; **public monopoly** *or* **state monopoly** = situation where the state is the only supplier of a product or service (such as the Post Office, the coal industry, etc.); **Monopolies and Mergers Commission (MMC)** = government organization which examines takeover bids at the request of the Office of Fair Trading, to see if a successful bid would result in a monopoly and so harm the consumer by reducing competition (NOTE: **trust** is used more often in American English)

month [mʌnθ] *noun* one of twelve periods which make a year; *the company pays him £100 a month*; *he earns £2,000 a month*; *bills due at the end of the current month*; **calendar month** = whole month as on a calendar; **paid by the month** = paid once each month; **to give a customer two months' credit** = to allow a customer to pay not immediately, but after two months

month end [mʌnθ 'end] *noun* the end of a calendar month, when accounts have to be drawn up; *the accounts department are working on the month-end accounts*

monthly ['mʌnθli] **1** *adjective* happening every month, which is received every month; *we get a monthly statement from the bank*; *she makes monthly payments to the credit card company*; *he is paying for his car by monthly instalments*; *my monthly salary cheque is late*; **monthly ticket** = ticket for travel which is good for one month **2** *adverb* every month; *he asked if he could pay monthly by direct debit*; *the account is credited monthly*

moonlight ['muːnlaɪt] **1** *noun (informal)* **to do a moonlight flit** = to go away (at night) leaving many unpaid bills **2** *verb (informal)* to do a second job for cash (often in the evening) as well as a regular job

moonlighter ['muːnlaɪtə] *noun* person who moonlights

moonlighting ['muːnlaɪtɪŋ] *noun* doing a second job; *he makes thousands a year from moonlighting*

mooring(s) ['mʊərɪŋz] *noun* place where boats can be tied up in a harbour

morale [mə'rɑːl] *noun* confident feeling; *the manager gave us a pep talk to try to*

raise the morale of the workforce; *low morale has made everyone gloomy*; *morale among the lower-paid staff is low*; *the change of ownership has had an effect on staff morale*

moral right ['mɒrəl 'raɪt] *noun* right of an editor or illustrator, etc., to have some say in the publication of a work to which he has contributed, even if he does not own the copyright

moratorium [mɒrə'tɔːriəm] *noun* temporary stop to repayments of interest on loans or capital owed; *the banks called for a moratorium on payments* (NOTE: plural is **moratoria** or **moratoriums**)

mortality tables [mɔː'tæləti 'teɪblz] *plural noun* chart, used by insurers, which shows how long a person of a certain age can be expected to live on average

mortgage ['mɔːɡɪdʒ] **1** *noun* **(a)** (i) agreement where someone lends money to another person so that he can buy a property, the property being the security; (ii) money lent in this way; *to take out a mortgage on a house*; *to buy a house with a £200,000 mortgage*; **mortgage payments** = money paid each month as interest on a mortgage, plus repayment of a small part of the capital borrowed; **endowment mortgage** = mortgage backed by an endowment policy (the borrower pays interest on the mortgage in the usual way, but does not repay the capital; the endowment assurance (a life insurance) is taken out to cover the total capital sum borrowed, and when the assurance matures the capital is paid off, and a further lump sum is usually available for payment to the borrower); **first mortgage** = main mortgage on a property; **repayment mortgage** = mortgage where the borrower pays back both interest and capital over the period of the mortgage; **second mortgage** = further mortgage on a property which is already mortgaged; **to pay off a mortgage** = to pay back the principal and all the interest on a loan to buy a property **(b)** **mortgage bond** = certificate showing that a mortgage exists and that property is security for it; **mortgage debenture** = debenture where the lender can be repaid by selling the company's property; **mortgage famine** = situation where there is not enough money available to offer mortgages to house buyers; **mortgage queue** = list of people waiting for mortgages **2** *verb* to accept a loan with a property as security; *the house is mortgaged to the bank*; *he mortgaged his house to set up in business*; **to foreclose on a mortgaged property** = to sell a property because the owner cannot repay money which he has borrowed, using the property as security

---

mortgage payments account for just 20 per cent of the average first-time buyer's gross earnings against an average of 24 per cent during the past 15 years

Times

---

mortgage money is becoming tighter. Applications for mortgages are running at a high level and some building societies are introducing quotas

Times

---

for the first time since mortgage rates began falling a financial institution has raised charges on homeowner loans

Globe and Mail (Toronto)

---

mortgagee [mɔːgəˈdʒiː] *noun* person or company which lends money for someone to buy a property

mortgager *or* **mortgagor** [ˈmɔːgɪdʒə] *noun* person who borrows money to buy a property

most [məust] **1** *pronoun* very large amount or quantity; *most of the staff are graduates*; *most of our customers live near the factory*; *most of the orders come in the early part of the year* **2** *adjective* very large number of; *most orders are dealt with the same day*; *most salesmen have had a course of on-the-job training*

most favoured nation (MFN)

[ˈməust ˈfeɪvəd ˈneɪʃən] *noun* country which has the best trade terms; **most-favoured-nation clause** = agreement between two countries that each will offer the best possible terms in commercial contracts

mostly [ˈməustli] *adverb* mainly or generally; *the staff are mostly girls of twenty to thirty years of age*; *he works mostly in the London office*

motion [ˈməuʃən] *noun* **(a)** moving about; **time and motion study** = study in an office or factory of the time taken to do certain jobs and the movements workers have to make to do them **(b)** proposal which will be put to a meeting to vote on; *Mr Brown will propose or move a motion congratulating the board on the results*; *the meeting voted on the motion*; *to speak against or for a motion*; *the motion was carried or was defeated by 220 votes to 196*; **to table a motion** = to put forward a proposal for discussion by putting details of it on the table at a meeting

motivate [ˈməutɪveɪt] *verb* to encourage someone to do something, especially to work or to sell; **highly motivated sales staff** = sales staff who are very eager to sell

---

creative people aren't necessarily motivated by money or titles, they may not want a larger office or more work, they don't often want more responsibility. They want to see their ideas implemented

Nation's Business

---

motivation [məutɪˈveɪʃən] *noun* encouragement to staff; eagerness to work well or sell large quantities of a product; **the sales staff lack motivation** = the sales staff are not motivated enough

motive [ˈməutɪv] *noun* idea which makes someone do something; **profit motive** = idea that profit is the most import aim of a business

motor insurance [ˈməutə ɪnˈʃurəns] *noun* insuring a car, the driver and the passengers in case of accident

mountain [ˈmauntɪn] *noun* pile, large heap; *I have mountains of typing to do*; *there is a mountain of invoices on the sales manager's desk*

mounting [ˈmauntɪŋ] *adjective* increasing; *he resigned in the face of mounting pressure from the shareholders*; *the company is faced with mounting debts*

mount up ['maʊnt 'ʌp] *verb* to increase rapidly; *costs are mounting up*

mouse [maʊs] *noun* small moveable device for controlling the position of a cursor on a computer screen; **mouse mat** = soft plastic mat on which you move a mouse around

> you can use a mouse to access pop-up menus and a keyboard for a word-processor
>
> *Byte*

movable *or* **moveable** ['mu:vəbl] **1** *adjective* which can be moved; *all the moveable property has been seized by the bailiffs* **2** *plural noun* **moveables** = moveable property

move [mu:v] *verb* **(a)** to go from one place to another; *the company is moving from London Road to the centre of town; we have decided to move our factory to a site nearer the airport* **(b)** to be sold, to sell; *over Christmas the stock hardly moved at all but with the January sales it is finally starting to move; the salesmen will have to work hard if they want to move all that stock by the end of the month* **(c)** to propose formally that a motion be accepted by a meeting; *he moved that the accounts be agreed; I move that the meeting should adjourn for ten minutes*

movement ['mu:vmənt] *noun* **(a)** changing position, going up or down; *movements in the money markets; cyclical movements of trade;* **movements of capital** = changes of investments from one country to another; **stock movements** = passing of stock into or out of a warehouse; *all stock movements are logged by the computer* **(b)** group of people working towards the same aim; *the labour movement; the free trade movement*

mover ['mu:və] *noun* person who proposes a motion

MPC = MONETARY POLICY COMMITTEE

mpg ['empi:'dʒi:] = MILES PER GALLON

Mr ['mɪstə] *noun* title given to a man; *Mr Smith is the Managing Director*

MRP ['emɑ:'pi:] = MANUFACTURER'S RECOMMENDED PRICE

Mrs ['mɪsɪz] *noun* title given to a married woman; *the chair was taken by Mrs Smith*

Ms [məz] *noun* title given to a woman where it is not known if she is married, or where she does not want to show if she is married or not; *Ms Smith is the personnel officer*

multi- ['mʌltɪ] *prefix* referring to many things

multibillion [mʌltɪ'bɪljən] *adjective* referring to several billion pounds or dollars; *they signed a multibillion pound deal*

> factory automation is a multi-billion-dollar business
>
> *Duns Business Month*

multicurrency [mʌltɪ'kʌrənsi] *adjective* in several currencies; **multicurrency loan** = loan in several currencies

multilateral [mʌltɪ'lætərəl] *adjective* between several parties; *a multilateral agreement;* **multilateral trade** = trade between several countries

multimillion [mʌltɪ'mɪljən] *adjective* referring to several million pounds or dollars; *they signed a multimillion pound deal*

multimillionaire [mʌltɪmɪljə'neə] *noun* person who owns property or investments worth several million pounds or dollars

multinational [mʌltɪ'næʃənl] *noun* company which has branches or subsidiary companies in several countries; *the company has been bought by one of the big multinationals*

> the number of multinational firms has mushroomed in the past two decades. As their sweep across the global economy accelerates, multinational firms are posing pressing issues for nations rich and poor, and those in between
>
> *Australian Financial Review*

multipart stationery ['mʌltɪpɑ:t 'steɪʃənrɪ] *noun* stationery, such as invoices, with several sheets usually in different colours, attached together and printed together; *inkjet printers give very good results, but cannot print on multipart stationery*

multiple ['mʌltɪpl] **1** *adjective* many; **multiple entry visa** = visa which allows a visitor to enter a country many times; **multiple store** = one store in a chain of stores; **multiple ownership** = situation where something is owned by several parties jointly **2** *noun* **(a) share on a multiple of 5** = share with a P/E ratio of 5 (i.e. 5 is the result when dividing the current market price by the earnings per share) **(b)** company with stores in several different towns

---

many independents took advantage of the bank holiday period when the big multiples were closed

The Grocer

---

the multiple brought the price down to £2.49 in some stores. We had not agreed to this deal and they sold out very rapidly. When they reordered we would not give it to them. This kind of activity is bad for the brand and we cannot afford it

The Grocer

---

multiplication [mʌltɪplɪ'keɪʃən] *noun* act of multiplying; **multiplication sign** = sign used to show that a number is being multiplied by another

multiply ['mʌltɪplaɪ] *verb* **(a)** to calculate the sum of various numbers repeated a certain number of times; *if you multiply twelve by three you get thirty-six; square measurements are calculated by multiplying length by width* **(b)** to grow or to increase; *profits multiplied in the boom years*

municipal [mjʊ'nɪsɪpəl] *adjective* referring to a town; *we pay our municipal taxes by direct debit; the municipal offices are in the centre of the town*

Murphy's law ['mɜːfɪz 'lɔː] *noun* law, based on wide experience, which says that in commercial life if something can go wrong it will go wrong, or that when you are thinking that things are going right, they will inevitably start to go wrong

mutual ['mjuːtʃʊəl] *adjective* belonging to two or more people; **mutual (insurance) company** = company which belongs to insurance policy holders; *US* **mutual funds** = organizations which take money from small investors and invest it in stocks and shares for them, the investment being in the form of shares in the fund (NOTE: the British equivalent is a **unit trust**)

Nn

nail [neɪl] *noun* **to pay on the nail** = to pay promptly, to pay rapidly

naira [ˈnaɪrə] *noun* currency used in Nigeria (NOTE: no plural; naira is usually written N before figures: **N2,000** say 'two thousand naira')

name [neɪm] *noun* **(a)** word used to call a thing or a person; *I cannot remember the name of the managing director of Smith's Ltd; his first name is John, but I am not sure of his other names*; **brand name** = name of a particular make of product; **corporate name** = name of a large corporation; **under the name of** = using a particular name; **trading under the name of 'Best Foods'** = using the name 'Best Foods' as a commercial name, and not the name of the company **(b)** person who provides security for insurance arranged by a Lloyd's of London syndicate; *see comment at* LLOYD'S

named [ˈneɪmd] *adjective* **person named in the policy** = person whose name is given on an insurance policy as the person insured

narrow market [ˈnærəʊ ˈmɑːkɪt] *noun* market in a share where very few shares are available for sale, and where the price can vary sharply

NASDAQ [ˈnæzdæk] = NATIONAL ASSOCIATION OF SECURITIES DEALERS AUTOMATED QUOTATIONS; system which provides quotations via computer for the US electronic trading market, mainly in high tech stocks, and also for some large corporations listed on the NYSE, and publishes an index of stock price movements

nation [ˈneɪʃən] *noun* country and the people living in it; **most favoured nation** = country which has the best trade terms; **most-favoured-nation clause** = agreement between two countries that each will give the other the best possible trade terms in commercial contracts; **the United Nations** = organization which links almost all the countries of the world to promote good relations between them

national [ˈnæʃənl] *adjective* referring to a particular country; **national advertising** = advertising in every part of a country, not just in the capital; *we took national advertising to promote our new 24-hour delivery service; US* **national bank** = bank which is chartered by the federal government and is part of the Federal Reserve system (as opposed to a 'state bank'); **national campaign** = sales or publicity campaign in every part of a country; **the National Debt** = money borrowed by a government; *GB* **National Health Service** = scheme for free medical and hospital service for everyone, paid for by the National Insurance; **national income** = value of income from the sales of goods and services in a country; *GB* **National Insurance** = state insurance which pays for medical care, hospitals, unemployment benefits, etc.; **National Insurance contributions (NIC)** = money paid into the National Insurance scheme by the employer and the worker; **national newspapers** *or* **the national press** = newspapers which sell in all parts of a country; **gross national product (GNP)** = annual value of goods and services in a country including income from other countries; *GB* **National Savings** = government savings scheme for small investors (including a savings bank, savings certificates and premium bonds)

nationality [næʃə'næləti] *noun* **he is of British nationality** = he is a British citizen

nationalization [næʃənəlaɪ'zeɪʃən] *noun* taking over of private industry by the state

nationalize ['næʃənəlaɪz] *verb* to put a privately-owned industry under state ownership and control; *the government is planning to nationalize the banking system*

nationalized ['næʃənəlaɪzd] *adjective* **nationalized industry** = industry which was privately owned, but is now owned by the state

nationwide ['neɪʃənwaɪd] *adjective* all over a country; *the union called for a nationwide strike*; *we offer a nationwide delivery service*; *the new car is being launched with a nationwide sales campaign*

natural ['nætʃrəl] *adjective* **(a)** found in the earth; *the offices are heated by natural gas*; **natural resources** = raw materials (such as coal, gas, iron) which are found in the earth **(b)** not made by people; *they use only natural fibres for their best cloths* **(c)** normal; *it was natural for the shopkeeper to feel annoyed when the hypermarket was set up close to his shop*; **natural wastage** = losing workers because they resign or retire, not through redundancy or dismissal; *the company is hoping to avoid redundancies and reduce its staff by natural wastage*

nature ['neɪtʃə] *noun* kind or type; *what is the nature of the contents of the parcel?*; *the nature of his business is not known*

NAV = NET ASSET VALUE

navy ['neɪvi] *noun* **merchant navy** = all the commercial ships of a country

NB ['en'biː] = NOTE

NBV = NET BOOK VALUE

necessary ['nesəsəri] *adjective* which has to be done, which is needed; *it is necessary to fill in the form correctly if you are not to have difficulty at customs*; *is it really necessary for the chairman to have six personal assistants?*; *you must*

have all the necessary documentation before you apply for a subsidy

necessity [nɪ'sesəti] *noun* thing which is absolutely important, without which nothing can be done; *being unemployed makes it difficult to afford even the basic necessities*

negative ['negətɪv] *adjective* meaning 'no'; **the answer was in the negative** = the answer was 'no'; **negative cash flow** = situation where a company is spending more money than it receives; **negative equity** = situation where a house bought with a mortgage becomes less valuable than the money borrowed to buy it (because of falling house prices) (NOTE: the opposite is **positive**)

neglected [nɪ'glektɪd] *adjective* not well looked after; **neglected business** = company which has not been actively run by its owners and could therefore do better under more efficient management; **neglected shares** = shares which are not bought or sold often; *bank shares have been a neglected sector of the market this week*

negligence ['neglɪdʒəns] *noun* lack of proper care, not doing a duty; **criminal negligence** = not doing a duty with the result that harm is done to the interests of people

negligent ['neglɪdʒnt] *adjective* not taking proper care

negligible ['neglɪdʒəbl] *adjective* very small, not worth bothering about; **not negligible** = quite large

negotiable [nɪ'gəʊʃəbl] *adjective* **not negotiable** = which cannot be exchanged for cash; **'not negotiable'** = words written on a cheque to show that it can be paid only to a certain person; **negotiable cheque** = cheque made payable to bearer (i.e. to anyone who holds it); **negotiable instrument** = document (such as a bill of exchange, or cheque) which can be exchanged for cash

> initial salary is negotiable around $45,000 per annum
> *Australian Financial Review*

negotiate [nɪ'gəʊʃɪeɪt] *verb* **to negotiate with someone** = to discuss a problem formally with someone, so as to reach an agreement; *the management refused to negotiate with the union*; **to negotiate terms and conditions** *or* **to negotiate a contract** = to discuss and agree the terms of a contract; **he negotiated a £250,000 loan with the bank** = he came to an agreement with the bank for a loan of £250,000; **negotiating committee** = group of representatives of management or unions who negotiate a wage settlement

---

many of the large travel agency chains are able to negotiate even greater discounts

Duns Business Month

---

negotiation [nɪɡəʊʃɪ'eɪʃən] *noun* discussion of terms and conditions to reach an agreement; **contract under negotiation** = contract which is being discussed; **a matter for negotiation** = something which must be discussed before a decision is reached; **to enter into negotiations** *or* **to start negotiations** = to start discussing a problem; **to resume negotiations** = to start discussing a problem again, after talks have stopped for a time; **to break off negotiations** = to refuse to go on discussing a problem; **to conduct negotiations** = to negotiate; **negotiations broke down after six hours** = discussions stopped because no agreement was possible; **pay negotiations** *or* **wage negotiations** = discussions between management and workers about pay

---

after three days of tough negotiations, the company reached agreement with its 1,200 unionized workers

Toronto Star

---

negotiator [nɪ'ɡəʊʃɪeɪtə] *noun* **(a)** person who discusses with the aim of reaching an agreement; **an experienced union negotiator** = member of a union who has a lot of experience of discussing terms of employment with management **(b)** *GB* person who works in an estate agency

nest egg ['nest 'eɡ] *noun* money which someone has saved over a period of time (usually kept in an interest-bearing account, and intended for use after retirement)

net [net] **1** *adjective* **(a)** price, weight, pay, etc., after all deductions have been made; **net asset value (NAV)** *or* **net worth** = total value of a company after deducting the money owed by it (it is the value of shareholders' capital plus reserves and any money retained from profits); **net book value (NBV)** = value of an asset in a company's books (i.e., its original purchase price less any depreciation); **net cash flow** = difference between money coming in and money going out of a firm; **net earnings** *or* **net income** = total earnings of a business after tax and other deductions; **net income** *or* **net salary** = person's income which is left after taking away tax and other deductions; **net loss** = actual loss, after deducting overheads; **net margin** = net profit shown as a percentage of sales; **net price** = price of goods or services which cannot be reduced by a discount; **net profit** = result where income from sales is more than all expenditure; **net profit before tax** = profit of a company after expenses have been deducted but before tax has been paid; **net receipts** = receipts after deducting commission, tax, discounts, etc.; **net sales** = sales less damaged or returned items; **net weight** = weight of goods after deducting the weight of packaging material and container; **net yield** = profit from investments after deduction of tax **(b)** **terms strictly net** = payment has to be the full price, with no discount allowed (NOTE: the spelling **nett** is sometimes used on containers) **2** *noun* **the Net** = the Internet, international network linking thousands of computers using telephone links; *he searched the Net for information on cheap tickets to the USA* **3** *verb* to make a true profit; *to net a profit of £10,000* (NOTE: **netting - netted**)

---

out of its earnings a company will pay a dividend. When shareholders receive this it will be net, that is it will have had tax deducted at 30 per cent

Investors Chronicle

---

network ['netwɜːk] **1** *noun* system which links different points together; **a network of distributors** *or* **a distribution network** = series of points or warehouses from which goods are sent all over a country; **computer network** = computer system where several PCs are linked so that they all draw on the same database; **television network** = system of linked television stations covering the whole country **2** *verb* to link together in a network; **to network a television programme** = to send out the same television programme through several TV stations; **networked system** = computer system where several PCs are linked together so that they all draw on the same database or use the same server

new [njuː] *adjective* recent, not old; **under new management** = with a new owner; **new issue** = issue of new shares; **new issues department** = section of a bank which deals with issues of new shares; **new technology** = electronic instruments which have recently been invented

news [njuːz] *noun* information about things which have happened; *he always reads the business new or financial news first in the paper*; *financial markets were shocked by the news of the devaluation*; **news agency** = office which distributes news to newspapers and TV and radio stations; **news release** = sheet giving information about a new event which is sent to newspapers and TV and radio stations so that they can use it; *the company sent out a news release about the new managing director*

newsagent ['njuːzeɪdʒənt] *noun* person who runs a shop selling newspapers and magazines

newsletter ['njuːzletə] *noun* **company newsletter** = printed sheet or small newspaper giving news about a company

NIC = NATIONAL INSURANCE CONTRIBUTIONS

niche [niːʃ] *noun* special place in a market, occupied by one company (a 'niche company'); *they seem to have discovered a niche in the market*; **niche market** = small speciality market, where there is little competition

nickel ['nɪkl] *noun US* five cent coin

night [naɪt] *noun* **night safe** = safe in the outside wall of a bank where money and documents can be deposited at night using a special door; **night shift** = shift which works at night; *there are thirty men on the night shift*; *he works nights or he works the night shift*

Nikkei Average ['nɪkeɪ 'ævrɪdʒ] index of prices on the Tokyo Stock Exchange, based on about 200 leading shares

nil [nɪl] *noun* zero or nothing; *to make a nil return*; *the advertising budget has been cut to nil*

No. = NUMBER

no-claims bonus ['nəʊ'kleɪmz 'bəʊnəs] *noun* reduction of premiums on an insurance policy because no claims have been made

nominal ['nɒmɪnl] *adjective* **(a)** very small (payment); *we make a nominal charge for our services*; *they are paying a nominal rent* **(b)** **nominal share capital** = the total of the face value of all the shares which a company is authorized to issue according to its memorandum of association; **nominal ledger** = book which records a company's income and expenditure in general, but not debtors, creditors and cash, which are recorded in separate ledgers; **nominal value** = face value, the value written on a share, a coin or a banknote

nominate ['nɒmɪneɪt] *verb* to suggest someone or to name someone for a job; **to nominate someone to a post** = to appoint someone to a post without an election; **to nominate someone as proxy** = to name someone as your proxy

nomination [nɒmɪ'neɪʃən] *noun* act of nominating

nominee [nɒmɪ'niː] *noun* person who is nominated, especially someone who is appointed to deal with financial matters on your behalf; **nominee account** = account held on behalf of someone

COMMENT: shares can be purchased and held in nominee accounts so that the identity of the owner of the shares cannot be discovered easily

non- [nɒn] *prefix* not

non-acceptance [ˈnɒnəkˈseptəns] *noun* situation where the person who is to pay a bill of exchange does not accept it

non-contributory [ˈnɒnkənˈtrɪbjutəri] *adjective* **non-contributory pension scheme** = pension scheme where the employee does not make any contributions and the company pays everything; *the company pension scheme is non-contributory*

non-delivery [ˈnɒndɪˈlɪvəri] *noun* situation where something is not delivered

non-durables [ˈnɒnˈdjuərəblz] *plural noun* goods which are used up soon after they have been bought (such as food, newspapers)

non-executive director [ˈnɒnɪgˈzekjutɪv daɪˈrektə] *noun* director who attends board meetings and gives advice, but does not work full-time for the company

non-feasance [ˈnɒnˈfiːzəns] *noun* not doing something which should be done by law

non-negotiable instrument [ˈnɒnnɪˈgəuʃəbl ˈɪnstrəmənt] *noun* document (such as a crossed cheque) which cannot be exchanged for cash

non-payment [ˈnɒnˈpeɪmənt] *noun* **non-payment of a debt** = not paying a debt due

non profit-making organization *US* **non-profit corporation** [ˈnɒnˈprɒfitˈmeɪkɪŋ ɔːgənaɪˈzeɪʃən *or* ˈnɒnˈprɒfit kɔːpəˈreɪʃən] *noun* organization (such as a club) which is not allowed by law to make a profit; *non-profit-making organizations are exempted from tax*

non-recurring items [ˈnɒnrɪˈkɜːrɪŋ ˈaɪtəmz] *noun* special items in a set of accounts which appear only once

non-refundable [ˈnɒnrɪˈfʌndəbl] *adjective* which will not be refunded; *you will be asked to make a non-refundable deposit*

non-resident [ˈnɒnˈrezɪdənt] *noun* person who is not considered a resident of a country for tax purposes; *he has a non-resident bank account*

non-returnable [ˈnɒnrɪˈtɜːnəbl] *adjective* which cannot be returned; **non-returnable packing** = packing which is to be thrown away when it has been used and not returned to the sender

non-stop [ˈnɒnˈstɒp] *adjective & adverb* without stopping; *they worked non-stop to finish the audit on time*

non-sufficient funds [ˈnɒnsəˈfɪʃənt ˈfʌndz] *noun US* not having enough money in a bank account to pay a cheque drawn on that account

non-taxable [ˈnɒnˈtæksəbl] *adjective* which is not subject to tax; *lottery prizes are non-taxable*

non-union [ˈnɒnˈjuːnjən] *adjective* **company using non-union labour** = company employing workers who do not belong to trade unions

non-voting shares [ˈnɒnˈvəutɪŋ ˈʃeəz] *noun* shares which do not allow the shareholder to vote at meetings (also called 'A' shares)

norm [nɔːm] *noun* the usual quantity, the usual rate; *the output from this factory is well above the norm for the industry or well above the industry norm*

normal [ˈnɔːməl] *adjective* usual, which happens regularly; *normal deliveries are made on Tuesdays and Fridays; now that the strike is over we hope to resume normal service as soon as possible*; **under normal conditions** = if things work in the usual way; *under normal conditions a package takes two days to get to Copenhagen*

nosedive [ˈnəuzdaɪv] *verb* to fall very sharply; *the share price nosedived after the chairman was arrested*

nostro account [ˈnɒstrəu əˈkaunt] *noun* account which a bank has with a correspondent bank in another country; *see also* VOSTRO ACCOUNT

notary public [ˈnəutəri ˈpʌblɪk] *noun* lawyer who has the authority to witness documents and spoken statements, making them official (NOTE: plural is **notaries public**)

note [nəut] **1** *noun* **(a)** short document, short piece of information; **advice note** = written notice to a customer giving details of goods ordered and shipped but not yet delivered; **contract note** = note showing that shares have been bought or sold but not yet paid for; **cover note** = letter from an insurance company giving details of an insurance policy and confirming that the policy exists; **covering note** = letter sent with documents to explain why you are sending them; **credit note** = note showing that money is owed to a customer; **debit note** = note showing that a customer owes money; *we undercharged Mr Smith and had to send him a debit note for the extra amount*; **delivery note** = list of goods being delivered, given to the customer with the goods; **dispatch note** = note saying that goods have been sent; **note of hand** *or* **promissory note** = document stating that someone promises to pay an amount of money on a certain date **(b)** short letter; *they sent me a note about the deposit; I left a note on his desk; she left a note for the managing director with his secretary* **(c)** **bank note** *or* **currency note** = piece of printed paper money; *a counterfeit £20 note; he pulled out a pile of used notes* (NOTE: American English for this is **bill**) **2** *verb* to write down details of something and remember them; *we note that the goods were delivered in bad condition; your order has been noted and will be dispatched as soon as we have stock; your complaint has been noted*

notebook ['nəʊtbʊk] *noun* book for writing notes in; **shorthand notebook** = small notebook for taking shorthand dictation

notepad ['nəʊtpæd] *noun* pad of paper for writing short notes

notepaper ['nəʊtpeɪpə] *noun* **(a)** *GB* good quality paper for letters **(b)** *US* rough paper for writing notes

notice ['nəʊtɪs] *noun* **(a)** piece of written information; *the company secretary pinned up a notice about the pension scheme*; **copyright notice** = note in a book showing who owns the copyright and the date of ownership **(b)** official warning that a contract is going to end or that terms are going to be changed; **until further notice** = until different instructions are given; *you must pay £200 on the 30th of each month until further notice* **(c)** official written information that a worker is leaving his or her job on a certain date; **period of notice** = time stated in the contract of employment which the worker or company has to allow between resigning or being fired and the worker actually leaving his job; *we require three months' notice; he gave six months' notice; we gave him three months' wages in lieu of notice*; **she gave in** *or* **handed in her notice** = she resigned; **he is working out his notice** = he is working during the time between resigning and actually leaving the company **(d)** time allowed before something takes place; **at short notice** = with very little warning; *the bank manager will not see anyone at short notice*; **you must give seven days' notice of withdrawal** = you must ask to take money out of the account seven days before you want it **(e)** legal document (such as telling a tenant to leave property which he is occupying); **to give someone notice** *or* **to serve notice on someone** = to give someone a legal notice; **to give a tenant notice to quit** *or* **to serve a tenant with notice to quit** = to inform a tenant officially that he has to leave the premises by a certain date; *we have given our tenant notice to quit*

noticeboard ['nəʊtɪsbɔːd] *noun* board fixed to a wall where notices can be put up; *did you see the new list of prices on the noticeboard?*

notification [nəʊtɪfɪ'keɪʃən] *noun* informing someone

notify ['nəʊtɪfaɪ] *verb* to **notify someone of something** = to tell someone something formally; *they were notified of the arrival of the shipment*

notional ['nəʊʃnl] *adjective* probable but not known exactly; not quantifiable; **notional income** = invisible benefit which is not money or goods and services; **notional rent** = sum put into accounts as rent where the company owns the building it is occupying and so does not pay an actual rent

nought [nɔːt] number 0; *a million pounds can be written as '£1m' or as one and six noughts* (NOTE: **nought** is commoner in British English; in American English, **zero** is more usual)

null [nʌl] *adjective* which cannot legally be enforced; **the contract was declared null and void** = the contract was said to be not valid; **to render a decision null** = to make a decision useless, to cancel a decision

nullification [nʌlɪfɪ'keɪʃən] *noun* act of making something invalid

nullify ['nʌlɪfaɪ] *verb* to make something invalid, to cancel something

number ['nʌmbə] **1** *noun* **(a)** quantity of things or people; *the number of persons on the payroll has increased over the last year*; *the number of days lost through strikes has fallen*; *the number of shares sold during the month*; **a number of** = some; *a number of the staff will be retiring this year* **(b)** written figure; *please write your account number on the back of the cheque*; *if you have a complaint to make, always quote the batch number*; *he noted the cheque number in the ledger*; **box number** = reference number used when asking for mail to be sent to a post office or when asking for replies to an advertisement to be sent to the newspaper's offices; *please reply to Box No. 209*; **index number** = (i) number of something in an index; (ii) number showing the percentage rise of something over a period; **invoice number** *or* **order number** = the reference number printed on an invoice or order; **phone number** *or* **telephone number** = set of figures for a particular telephone; *he keeps a list of phone numbers in a little black book*; *the phone number is on the company notepaper*; **serial number** = number in a series; *this batch of shoes has the serial number 25-02* (NOTE: **number** is often written **No.** with figures: **Invoice No. 1234**) **2** *verb* to put a figure on a document; *to number an order*; *I refer to your invoice numbered 1234*; **numbered account** = bank account (usually in Switzerland) which is referred to only by a number, the name of the person holding it being kept secret

numeric *or* **numerical** [njʊ'merɪk or njʊ'merɪkl] *adjective* referring to numbers; **in numerical order** = in the order of figures (such as 1 before 2, 33 before 34); *file these invoices in numerical order*; **numeric data** = data in the form of figures; **numeric keypad** = part of a computer keyboard which is a programmable set of numbered keys

Oo

O's *see* FOUR

0800 number ['əʊ 'eɪt'hʌndrəd 'nʌmbə] telephone number which can be used to reply to advertisements (the supplier pays for the call, not the caller) (NOTE: the American equivalent is a **800 number**)

O & M = ORGANIZATION AND METHODS

OAP ['əʊeɪ'piː] = OLD AGE PENSIONER

oath [əʊθ] *noun* legal promise stating that something is true; **he was under oath** = he had promised in court to say what was true

object [əb'dʒekt] *verb* to refuse to do something, to say that you do not accept something; *to object to a clause in a contract* (NOTE: you object **to** something)

objection [əb'dʒekʃən] *noun* **to raise an objection to something** = to object to something; *the union delegates raised an objection to the wording of the agreement*

objective [əb'dʒektɪv] **1** *noun* something which you try to do; *the company has achieved its objectives*; *we set the sales forces certain objectives*; **long-term objective** *or* **short-term objective** = aim which you hope to achieve within a few years or a few months; **management by objectives** = way of managing a business by planning work for the managers to do and testing if it is completed correctly and on time **2** *adjective* considered from a general point of view not from that of the person involved; *you must be objective in assessing the performance of the staff*; *to carry out an objective survey of the market*

obligate ['ɒblɪgeɪt] *verb* **to be obligated to do something** = to have a legal duty to do something

obligation [ɒblɪ'geɪʃən] *noun* **(a)** duty to do something; **to be under an obligation to do something** = to feel it is your duty to do something; **there is no obligation to buy**; **to be under no obligation to do something**; **he is under no contractual obligation to buy** = he has signed no contract which forces him to buy; **to fulfil your contractual obligations** = to do what is stated in a contract; **two weeks' free trial without obligation** = the customer can try the item at home for two weeks without having to buy it at the end of the test **(b)** debt; **to meet your obligations** = to pay your debts

obligatory [ɒ'blɪgətəri] *adjective* necessary according to the law or rules; *each new member of staff has to pass an obligatory medical examination*

oblige [ə'blaɪdʒ] *verb* **to oblige someone to do something** = to make someone feel he must do something; *he felt obliged to cancel the contract*

o.b.o. ['əʊbiː'əʊ] = OR BEST OFFER

observe [ɒb'zɜːv] *verb* to obey (a rule or a law); *failure to observe the correct procedure will be punished*; *restaurants are obliged to observe the local fire regulations*

obsolescence [ɒbsə'lesəns] *noun* act of going out of date, and therefore becoming less useful and valuable; **built-in obsolescence** *or* **planned obsolescence** = method of ensuring continuing sales of a product by making it in such a way that it will soon become obsolete

obsolescent [ɒbsə'lesənt] *adjective* becoming out of date

obsolete ['ɒbsəli:t] *adjective* no longer used; *when the office was equipped with PCs the typewriters became obsolete*

> COMMENT: a product or asset may become obsolete because it is worn out, or because new products have been developed to replace it

obtain [əb'teɪn] *verb* to get; *to obtain supplies from abroad*; *we find these items very difficult to obtain*; *to obtain an injunction against a company*; *he obtained control by buying the founder's shareholding*

obtainable [əb'teɪnəbl] *adjective* which can be got; *prices fall when raw materials are easily obtainable*; *our products are obtainable in all computer shops*

occasional [ə'keɪʒənl] *adjective* which happens from time to time

occupancy ['ɒkjupənsi] *noun* act of occupying a property (such as a house, an office, a room in a hotel); **with immediate occupancy** = empty and available to be occupied immediately; **occupancy rate** = average number of rooms occupied in a hotel over a period of time shown as a percentage of the total number of rooms; *during the winter months the occupancy rate was down to 50%*

> while occupancy rates matched those of last year in July, August has been a much poorer month than it was the year before
>
> *Economist*

occupant ['ɒkjupənt] *noun* person or company which occupies a property

occupation [ɒkju'peɪʃən] *noun* (a) **occupation of a building** = act of occupying a building (b) job or work; *what is her occupation?*; *his main occupation is house building* (c) **occupations** = types of work; *people in professional occupations*

> employment in professional occupations increased by 40 per cent between 1974 and 1983, while the share of white-collar occupations in total employment rose from 44 per cent to 49 per cent
>
> *Sydney Morning Herald*

occupational [ɒkju'peɪʃənl] *adjective* referring to a job; **occupational accident** = accident which takes place at work; **occupational disease** = disease which affects people in certain jobs; **occupational hazards** = dangers which apply to certain jobs; *heart attacks are one of the occupational hazards of directors*; **occupational pension** = pension which is paid by the company by which a worker has been employed; **occupational pension scheme** = pension scheme where the worker gets a pension from a fund set up by the company he or she has worked for, which is related to the salary he or she was earning

occupier ['ɒkjupaɪə] *noun* person who lives in a property; **beneficial occupier** = person who occupies a property but does not own it fully; **owner-occupier** = person who owns the property in which he lives

occupy ['ɒkjupaɪ] *verb* (a) to live or work in a property (such as a house, an office, a hotel room); *all the rooms in the hotel are occupied*; *the company occupies three floors of an office block* (b) to **occupy a post** = to be employed in a job

odd [ɒd] *adjective* (a) **odd numbers** = numbers (like 17 or 33) which cannot be divided by two; *odd-numbered buildings or buildings with odd numbers are on the south side of the street* (b) **a hundred odd** = approximately one hundred; **keep the odd change** = keep the small change which is left over (c) one of a group; **an odd shoe** = one shoe of a pair; **we have a few odd boxes left** = we have a few boxes left out of the total shipment; **odd lot** = group of miscellaneous items for sale at an auction; **to do odd jobs** = to do various pieces of work (d) **odd sizes** = strange sizes which are not usual

odd-job-man ['ɒd'dʒɒbmæn] *noun* person who does various pieces of work

oddments ['ɒdmənts] *plural noun* items left over; *pieces of large items sold separately*

OECD ['əʊ'i:si:'di:] = ORGANIZATION FOR ECONOMIC CO-OPERATION AND DEVELOPMENT

> calling for a greater correlation between labour

market policies, social policies and education and training, the OECD warned that long-term unemployment would remain unacceptably high without a reassessment of labour market trends

Australian Financial Review

off [ɒf] **1** *adverb* **(a)** not working, not in operation; *the agreement is off; they called the strike off* **(b)** lower than (a previous price); *the shares closed 2% off; we give 5% off for quick settlement* **2** *preposition* **(a)** away from a price; *to take £25 off the price; we give 10% off our normal prices; these carpets are sold at £25 off the marked price* **(b)** not included; **items off balance sheet** *or* **off balance sheet assets** = financial items which do not appear in a company's balance sheet as assets (such as equipment acquired under an operating lease) **(c)** away from work; *to take time off work; we give the staff four days off at Christmas; it is the secretary's day off tomorrow*

its stock closed Monday at $21.875 a share in NYSE composite trading, off 56% from its high last July

Wall Street Journal

offer [ˈɒfə] **1** *noun* **(a)** statement that you are willing to pay a certain amount of money to buy something; *to make an offer for a company; he made an offer of £10 a share; we made a written offer for the house; £1,000 is the best offer I can make; to accept an offer of £1,000 for the car;* **the house is under offer** = someone has made an offer to buy the house and the offer has been accepted provisionally; **we are open to offers** = we are ready to discuss the price which we are asking; **cash offer** = being ready to pay in cash; **offer price** = price at which investors buy new shares or units in a unit trust (the opposite, i.e., the selling price, is called the 'bid price'; the difference between the two is the 'spread'); **or near offer** *US* **or best offer** = or an offer of a price which is slightly less than the price asked; *the car is for sale at £2,000 or near offer* (NOTE: often shortened to **o.n.o.** or **o.b.o.**) **(b)** statement that you are willing to sell

something; **offer for sale** = situation where a company advertises new shares for sale to the public as a way of launching the company on the Stock Exchange (the other ways of launching a company are a 'tender' or a 'placing'); **offer price** = price at which new shares are put on sale **(c) he received six offers of jobs** *or* **six job offers** = six companies told him he could have a job with them **(d) bargain offer** = sale of a particular type of goods at a cheap price; *this week's bargain offer - 30% off all carpet prices;* **introductory offer** = special price offered on a new product to attract customers; **special offer** = goods put on sale at a specially low price; *we have a range of men's shirts on special offer* **2** *verb* **(a) to offer someone a job** = to tell someone that he can have a job in your company; *he was offered a directorship with Smith Ltd* **(b)** to say that you are willing to pay a certain amount of money for something; *to offer someone £100,000 for his house; he offered £10 a share* **(c)** to say that you are willing to sell something; *we offered the house for sale; they are offering special prices on winter holidays in the USA*

offering [ˈɒfrɪŋ] *noun* action of stating that you are prepared to sell something at a certain price; **US initial public offering (IPO)** = offering new shares in a corporation for sale to the public as a way of launching the corporation on the Stock Exchange (NOTE: the British equivalent for this is an **offer for sale**)

shares of newly public companies posted their worst performance of the year last month as a spate of initial public offerings disappointed followers

Wall Street Journal

if the partnership supports a sale, a public offering of shares would be set for as early as the fourth quarter

Wall Street Journal

office [ˈɒfɪs] *noun* **(a)** set of rooms where a company works or where business is done; **branch office** = less important office, usually in a different town or country from the main office; **head office**

or **main office** = office building where the board of directors works and meets; *GB* **registered office** = office address of a company which is officially registered with the Companies' Registrar **(b) office block** *or* **a block of offices** = building which contains only offices; **office boy** = young man who works in an office, usually taking messages from one department to another; **office equipment** = furniture and machines needed to make an office work; **office hours** = time when an office is open; *open during normal office hours*; *do not telephone during office hours*; *the manager can be reached at home out of office hours*; **office junior** = young man or woman who does all types of work in an office; **office space** *or* **office accommodation** = space available for offices or occupied by offices; *we are looking for extra office space*; **office staff** = people who work in offices; **office supplies** = stationery and furniture used in an office; **an office supplies firm** = company which sells office supplies; **for office use only** = something which must only be used in an office; **office worker** = person who works in an office **(c)** room where someone works and does business; *come into my office*; *the manager's office is on the third floor* **(d) booking office** = office where you can book seats at a theatre or tickets for the railway; **box office** = office at a theatre where tickets can be bought; **employment office** = office which finds jobs for people; **general office** = main administrative office in a company; **information office** = office which gives information to tourists or visitors; **inquiry office** = office where someone can answer questions from members of the public; **ticket office** = office where tickets can be bought **(e)** *GB* government department; **the Foreign Office** = ministry dealing with foreign affairs; **the Home Office** = ministry dealing with the internal affairs of the country; **Office of Fair Trading (OFT)** = government department which protects consumers against unfair or illegal business; **Serious Fraud Office (SFO)** = government department in charge of investigating major fraud in companies **(f)** post or position; *he holds or performs the office of treasurer*; **high office** = important

position or job in the government or civil service; **compensation for loss of office** = payment to a director who is asked to leave a company before his contract ends

officer ['ɒfɪsə] *noun* **(a)** person who has an official position; **customs officer** = person working for the Customs and Excise Department; **fire safety officer** = person responsible for fire safety in a building; **information officer** = person who gives information about a company or about a government department to the public; **personnel officer** = person who deals with the staff, especially interviewing new workers; **training officer** = person who deals with the training of staff; **the company officers** *or* **the officers of a company** = the main executives or directors of a company **(b)** official (usually unpaid) of a club, society, etc.; *the election of officers of an association*

official [ə'fɪʃəl] **1** *adjective* **(a)** from a government department or organization; *she went to France on official business*; *he left official documents in his car*; *she received an official letter of explanation*; **speaking in an official capacity** = speaking officially; **to go through official channels** = to deal with officials, especially when making a request; **the official exchange rate** = exchange rate which is imposed by the government; *the official exchange rate is ten to the dollar, but you can get fifty on the black market* **(b)** done or approved by a director or by a person in authority; *this must be an official order - it is written on the company's headed paper*; **the strike was made official** = the local strike was approved by the main trade union office **(c) the official receiver** = government official who is appointed to close down a company which is in liquidation **2** *noun* person working in a government department; *airport officials inspected the shipment*; *government officials stopped the import licence*; **customs official** = person working for the Customs and Excise Department; **high official** = important person in a government department; **minor official** = person in a low position in a government department; *some minor official tried to stop my request for building permission*;

top official = very important person in a government department; **union officials** = paid organizers in a trade union

officialese [əfiʃə'liːz] *noun* language used in government documents which can be difficult to understand

officially [ə'fiʃəli] *adverb* in an official way; *officially he knows nothing about the problem, but unofficially he has given us a lot of advice about it*

officio [ə'fiʃɪəu] *see* EX OFFICIO

off-licence ['ɒf'laɪsəns] *noun* GB **(a)** licence to sell alcohol for drinking away from the place where you buy it **(b)** shop which sells alcohol for drinking at home

off-line ['ɒf'laɪn] *adverb* not connected to a network or central computer

offload [ɒf'ləud] *verb* to pass something which you do not want to someone else; **to offload excess stock** = to try to sell excess stock; **to offload costs onto a subsidiary company** = to try to get a subsidiary company to pay some charges so as to reduce tax (NOTE: you offload something **from** a thing or person **onto** another thing or person)

off-peak ['ɒf'piːk] *adjective* not during the most busy time; **during the off-peak period** = at the time when business is less busy; **off-peak tariff** *or* **rate** = lower charges used when the service is not busy

off-season **1** [ɒf'siːzn] *adjective* **off-season tariff** *or* **rate** = cheap fares which are charged in a season when there is less business **2** *noun* ['ɒfsiːzn] less busy season for travel (usually during the winter); *to travel in the off-season; air fares are cheaper in the off-season*

offset [ɒf'set] *verb* to balance one thing against another so that they cancel each other out; *to offset losses against tax; foreign exchange losses more than offset profits in the domestic market* (NOTE: **offsetting - offset**)

off-shore ['ɒf'ʃɔː] *adjective & adverb* **(a)** on an island or in the sea near to land; *an off-shore oil field; an off-shore oil platform* **(b)** on an island which is a tax haven; **off-shore fund** = fund which is based outside the UK, and usually in a country which has less strict taxation than in the UK, such as the Bahamas, etc.

off-the-job training ['ɒfðə'dʒɒb 'treɪnɪŋ] *noun* training given to workers away from their place of work (such as at a college or school)

off-the-shelf ['ɒfðə'ʃelf] *adjective & adverb* ready-made according to a regular design; **off-the-shelf company** = company which has already been registered by an accountant or lawyer, and which is ready for sale to someone who wants to begin trading quickly

OFT = OFFICE OF FAIR TRADING

oil [ɔɪl] *noun* natural liquid found in the ground, used to burn to give power; **oil-exporting countries** = countries which produce oil and sell it to others; **oil field** = area of land or sea under which oil is found; **oil-importing countries** = countries which import oil; **oil-producing countries** = countries which produce oil; **oil platform** *or* **oil rig** = large construction with equipment for making holes in the ground to find oil; **oil well** = hole in the ground from which oil is pumped

> the biggest surprise of 1999 was the rebound in the price of oil. In the early months of the year commentators were talking about a fall to $5 a barrel but for the first time in two decades, the oil exporting countries got their act together, limited production and succeeded in pushing prices up
>
> *Financial Times*

old [əuld] *adjective* having existed for a long time; *the company is 125 years old next year; we have decided to get rid of our old computer system and install a new one*

old age ['əuld 'eɪdʒ] *noun* period when a person is old; **old age pension** = state pension given to people over a certain age (currently to a man who is 65 or to a woman who is 60); **old age pensioner (OAP)** = person who receives the old age pension

old-established ['əuldɪs'tæblɪʃt] *adjective* (company or brand) which has been in existence for a long time; *the* *old-established family business was bought by a group of entrepreneurs*

old-fashioned ['əʊld'fæʃənd] *adjective* out of date, not modern; *he still uses an old-fashioned typewriter*

ombudsman ['ɒmbʊdzmən] *noun* an official who investigates complaints by the public against government departments or other large organizations (NOTE: plural is **ombudsmen**)

COMMENT: there are several ombudsmen: the main one is the Parliamentary Commissioner, who is a civil servant and investigates complaints against government departments. The Banking Ombudsman, the Investment Ombudsman, the Building Societies Ombudsman, the Pensions Ombudsman and the Insurance Ombudsman are independent officials who investigate complaints by the public against banks, financial advisers, building societies, pension funds or insurance companies. They are all regulated by the Financial Services Authority

radical changes to the disciplinary system, including appointing an ombudsman to review cases where complainants are not satisfied with the outcome, are proposed in a consultative paper the Institute of Chartered Accountants issued last month
Accountancy

omission [əʊ'mɪʃən] *noun* thing which has been omitted; **errors and omissions excepted (e. & o.e.)** = words written on an invoice to show that the company has no responsibility for mistakes in the invoice

omit [əʊ'mɪt] *verb* **(a)** to leave something out, not to put something in; *the secretary omitted the date when typing the contract* **(b)** not to do something; *he omitted to tell the managing director that he had lost the documents* (NOTE: **omitting - omitted**)

omnibus agreement ['ɒmnɪbəs ə'griːmənt] *noun* agreement which covers many different items

on [ɒn] *preposition* **(a)** being a member of a group; *to sit on a committee*; *she is on the boards of two companies*; *we have 250 people on the payroll*; *she is on our full-time staff* **(b)** in a certain way; *on a commercial basis*; *to buy something on approval*; *to buy a car on hire-purchase*; *to get a mortgage on easy terms*; **on average** = in general; *on average, £15 worth of goods are stolen every day* **(c)** at a time; *on weekdays*; *the shop is closed on Wednesday afternoons*; *the new car is being launched on May 24th* **(d)** doing something; *the director is on holiday*; *she is in the States on business*; *the switchboard operator is on duty from 6 to 9*

oncosts ['ɒnkɒsts] *plural noun* fixed costs, money paid in producing a product which does not rise with the quantity of the product made

one-man ['wɒn'mæn] *adjective* **one-man business** *or* **firm** *or* **company** *or* **operation** *or* **band** = business run by one person alone with no staff or partners

one-off ['wɒn'ɒf] *adjective* done or made only once; *one-off item*; *one-off deal*

onerous ['ɒnərəs] *adjective* heavy, needing a lot of effort or money; **the repayment terms are particularly onerous** = the loan is particularly difficult to pay back

one-sided ['wɒn'saɪdɪd] *adjective* which favours one side and not the other in a negotiation; *one-sided agreement*

one-way ['wɒn'weɪ] *adjective* **one-way ticket** = ticket for a journey from one place to another; *US* **one-way fare** = fare for a journey from one place to another; **one-way trade** = situation where one country sells to another, but does not buy anything in return

one-way street ['wɒn'weɪ 'striːt] *noun* street where the traffic is allowed to go only in one direction; *the shop is in a one-way street, which makes it very difficult for parking*

online ['ɒn 'laɪn] *adverb* linked directly to a mainframe computer; *the sales office is online to the warehouse*; *we get our data online from the stock control department*

there may be a silver lining for 'clicks-and-mortar' stores that have both an online and a high street presence. Many of these are accepting returns of goods purchased online at their traditional stores. This is a service that may make them more popular as consumers become more experienced online shoppers

Financial Times

a survey found that even among experienced users - those who shop online at least once a month - about 10% abandoned a planned purchase because of annoying online delays and procedures

Financial Times

some online brokers failed to foresee the huge increase in private dealing and had problems coping with the rising volume. It has been the year when private investors were able to trade online quickly, cheaply, and on the whole, with little bother

Financial Times

o.n.o. ['əʊen'əʊ] = OR NEAR OFFER

on-the-job training   ['ɒnðə'dʒɒb 'treɪnɪŋ] *noun* training given to workers at their place of work

OPEC ['əʊpek] = ORGANIZATION OF PETROLEUM EXPORTING COUNTRIES

open ['əʊpən] **1** *adjective* **(a)** at work, not closed; *the store is open on Sunday mornings*; *our offices are open from 9 to 6*; *they are open for business every day of the week* **(b)** ready to accept something; *the job is open to all applicants* = anyone can apply for the job; *we will keep the job open for you until you have passed your driving test* = we will not give the job to anyone else, and will wait until you have passed your test; **open to offers** = ready to accept a reasonable offer; *the company is open to offers for the empty factory* = the company is ready to discuss an offer which is lower than the suggested price **(c) open**

account = account where the supplier offers the purchaser unsecured credit; **open cheque** = cheque which is not crossed and can be cashed anywhere; **open credit** = bank credit given to good customers without security up to a certain maximum sum; **open market** = market where anyone can buy or sell; **to buy shares on the open market** = to buy shares on the Stock Exchange, not privately; **open ticket** = ticket which can be used on any date **2** *verb* **(a)** to start a new business working; *she has opened a shop in the High Street*; *we have opened an office in London* **(b)** to start work, to be at work; *the office opens at 9 a.m.*; *we open for business on Sundays* **(c)** to begin; **to open negotiations** = to begin negotiating; *he opened the discussions with a description of the product*; *the chairman opened the meeting at 10.30* **(d)** to start, to allow something to start; *to open a bank account*; *to open a line of credit*; *to open a loan* **(e) the shares opened lower** = share prices were lower at the beginning of the day's trading

after opening at 79.1 the index touched a peak of 79.2 and then drifted to a low of 78.8

Financial Times

open-ended *US* **open-end** ['əʊpən'endɪd or 'əʊpən'end] *adjective* with no fixed limit, with some items not specified; *they signed an open-ended agreement*; *US* **open-end mortgage** = mortgage where the borrower can increase the amount of the loan

opening ['əʊpənɪŋ] **1** *noun* **(a)** act of starting a new business; *the opening of a new branch*; *the opening of a new market or of a new distribution network* **(b) opening hours** = hours when a shop or business is open **(c) job openings** = jobs which are empty and need filling; *we have openings for office staff*; **a market opening** = possibility of starting to do business in a new market **2** *adjective* at the beginning, first; **opening balance** = balance at the beginning of an accounting period; **opening bid** = first bid at an auction; **opening entry** = first entry in an account; **opening price** = price at the start of the day's trading; **opening stock** = stock at the beginning of the accounting period

open-plan office ['əʊpənplæn 'ɒfɪs] *noun* large room divided into smaller working spaces with no fixed divisions between them

open up ['əʊpən 'ʌp] *verb* **to open up new markets** = to work to start business in markets where such business has not been done before

operate ['ɒpəreɪt] *verb* **(a)** to work; *the new terms of service will operate from January 1st; the rules operate on inland postal services* **(b) to operate a machine** = to make a machine work; *he is learning to operate the new telephone switchboard*

> the company gets valuable restaurant locations which will be converted to the family-style restaurant chain that it operates and franchises throughout most parts of the US
>
> *Fortune*

operating ['ɒpəreɪtɪŋ] *noun* general running of a business or of a machine; **operating budget** = forecast of income and expenditure over a period of time; **operating costs** *or* **operating expenses** = costs of the day-to-day organization of a company; **operating manual** = book which shows how to work a machine; **operating profit** *or* **operating loss** = profit or loss made by a company in its usual business; **operating system** = the main program which operates a computer

> the company blamed over-capacity and competitive market conditions in Europe for a £14m operating loss last year
>
> *Financial Times*

operation [ɒpə'reɪʃən] *noun* **(a)** business organization and work; *the company's operations in West Africa; he heads up the operations in Northern Europe;* **operations review** = examining the way in which a company or department works to see how it can be made more efficient and profitable; **a franchising operation** = selling licences to trade as a franchise **(b)** **Stock Exchange operation** = buying or

selling of shares on the Stock Exchange **(c) in operation** = working or being used; *the system will be in operation by June; the new system came into operation on January 1st*

> a leading manufacturer of business, industrial and commercial products requires a branch manager to head up its mid-western Canada operations based in Winnipeg
>
> *Globe and Mail (Toronto)*

operational [ɒpə'reɪʃənl] *adjective* **(a)** referring to how something works; **operational budget** = forecast of expenditure on running a business; **operational costs** = costs of running a business; **operational planning** = planning how a business is to be run; **operational research** = study of a company's way of working to see if it can be made more efficient and profitable **(b) the system became operational on June 1st** = the system began working on June 1st

operative ['ɒpərətɪv] **1** *adjective* **to become operative** = to start working; *the new system has been operative since June 1st* **2** *noun* person who operates a machine which makes a product; *a skilled operative can produce 250 units per hour*

operator ['ɒpəreɪtə] *noun* **(a)** person who works a machine; *a keyboard operator; a computer operator* **(b)** person who works a telephone switchboard; **switchboard operator; to call the operator** *or* **to dial the operator; to place a call through** *or* **via the operator (c)** *(on the Stock Exchange)* person who buys and sells shares hoping to make a quick profit **(d) tour operator** = person or company which organizes package tours

> a number of block bookings by American tour operators have been cancelled
>
> *Economist*

opinion [ə'pɪnjən] *noun* **(a)** **public opinion** = what people think about something; **opinion-leader** = person whose opinions influence others in society; *a pop-star is the ideal opinion-leader if the product is aimed at the teenage market;* **opinion poll** *or* **opinion research** = asking a sample group of people what their opinion is, so as to guess the opinion of the whole population; *opinion polls showed that the public preferred butter to margarine*; *before starting the new service, the company carried out nationwide opinion polls* **(b)** piece of expert advice; *the lawyers gave their opinion*; *to ask an adviser for his opinion on a case*

OPM ['əupiː'em] = OTHER PEOPLE'S MONEY

opportunity [ɒpə'tjuːnəti] *noun* situation where you can do something successfully; **investment opportunities** *or* **sales opportunities** = possibilities for making investments or sales which will be profitable; **a market opportunity** = possibility of going into a market for the first time; **employment opportunities** *or* **job opportunities** = new jobs being available; *the increase in export orders has created hundreds of job opportunities*

the group is currently undergoing a period of rapid expansion and this has created an exciting opportunity for a qualified accountant

Financial Times

oppose [ə'pəuz] *verb* to try to stop something happening; to vote against something; *a minority of board members opposed the motion*; *we are all opposed to the takeover*

opposite number ['ɒpəzɪt 'nʌmbə] *noun* person who has a similar job in another company; *John is my opposite number in Smith's* = John has the same job in Smith's as I have here

optimal ['ɒptɪməl] *adjective* best

optimism ['ɒptɪmɪzm] *noun* being sure that everything will work out well; *he has considerable optimism about sales possibilities in the Far East*; **market optimism** = feeling that the stock market will rise

optimistic [ɒptɪ'mɪstɪk] *adjective* feeling sure that everything will work out well; **he takes an optimistic view of the exchange rate** = he expects the exchange rate will go in his favour

optimum ['ɒptɪməm] *adjective* best; *the market offers optimum conditions for sales*

option ['ɒpʃən] *noun* **(a)** **option to purchase** *or* **to sell** = giving someone the possibility to buy or sell something within a period of time; **first option** = allowing someone to be the first to have the possibility of deciding something; **to grant someone a six-month option on a product** = to allow someone six months to decide if he wants to be the agent or if he wants to manufacture the product; **to take up an option** *or* **to exercise an option** = to accept the option which has been offered and to put it into action; *he exercised his option* or *he took up his option to acquire sole marketing rights to the product*; **I want to leave my options open** = I want to be able to decide what to do when the time is right; **to take the soft option** = to decide to do something which involves the least risk, effort or problems **(b)** *(Stock Exchange)* **call option** = option to buy shares at a certain price; **put option** = option to sell shares at a certain price; **share option** = right to buy or sell shares at a certain price at a time in the future; **stock option** = right to buy shares at a cheap price given by a company to its employees; **option contract** = right to buy or sell shares at a fixed price; **option dealing** *or* **option trading** = buying and selling share options; **traded options** = options to buy or sell shares at a certain price at a certain date in the future, which themselves can be bought or sold

optional ['ɒpʃənl] *adjective* which can be added if the customer wants; *the insurance cover is optional*; **optional extras** = items (such as a radio) which can be added (to a car) if wanted

order ['ɔːdə] **1** *noun* **(a)** arrangement of records (filing cards, invoices, etc.); **alphabetical order** = arrangement by the letters of the alphabet (A, B, C, etc.); **chronological order** = arrangement by the order of the dates; *the reports are filed in chronological order*; **numerical order** = arrangement by numbers; *put these invoices in numerical order* **(b)** working arrangement; **machine in full working order** = machine which is ready and able to work properly; **the telephone is out of order** = the telephone is not working; **is all the documentation in order?** = are all the documents valid and correct? **(c) pay to Mr Smith or order** = pay money to Mr Smith or as he orders; **pay to the order of Mr Smith** = pay money directly to Mr Smith or to his account **(d)** official request for goods to be supplied; *to give someone an order or to place an order with someone for twenty filing cabinets*; **to fill** or **to fulfil an order** = to supply items which have been ordered; *we are so understaffed we cannot fulfil any more orders before Christmas*; *to supply an order for twenty filing cabinets*; **purchase order** = official paper which places an order for something; **order fulfilment** = supplying items which have been ordered; **order number** = the reference number printed on an order; **order processing** = dealing with orders (entering details on a computer, printing out invoices, advice notes, dispatch notes, etc.); **terms: cash with order** = the goods will be supplied only if payment in cash is made at the same time as the order is placed; **items available to order only** = items which will be manufactured only if someone orders them; **on order** = ordered but not delivered; *this item is out of stock, but is on order*; **unfulfilled orders** or **back orders** or **outstanding orders** = orders received in the past and not yet supplied; **order book** = record of orders; **the company has a full order book** = it has enough orders to work at full capacity; **telephone orders** = orders received over the telephone; *since we mailed the catalogue we have had a large number of telephone orders*; **a pad of order forms** = a pad of blank forms for orders to be written on **(e)** item which has been ordered; *the order is to be delivered to our warehouse*; **order picking** = collecting various items in a warehouse to make up an order to be sent to a customer **(f)** instruction; **delivery order** = instructions given by the customer to the person holding his goods, telling him to deliver them **(g)** document which allows money to be paid to someone; *he sent us an order on the Chartered Bank*; **banker's order** or **standing order** = order written by a customer asking a bank to make a regular payment; *he pays his subscription by banker's order*; **money order** = document which can be bought for sending money through the post; **postal order** = document bought at a post office, as a method of paying small amounts of money by post **2** *verb* **(a)** to ask for goods to be supplied; *to order twenty filing cabinets to be delivered to the warehouse*; *they ordered a new Rolls Royce for the managing director* **(b)** to put in a certain way; *the address list is ordered by country*; *that filing cabinet contains invoices ordered by date*

ordinary ['ɔːdnri] *adjective* normal, not special; **ordinary member** = person who pays a subscription to belong to a group; **ordinary resolution** = resolution put before an AGM, usually referring to some general procedural matter, and which requires a simple majority of votes to be accepted; **ordinary shares** = normal shares in a company, which have no special bonuses or restrictions (NOTE: the American term is **common stock**); **ordinary shareholder** = person who owns ordinary shares in a company

organization [ɔːgənaɪˈzeɪʃən] *noun* **(a)** way of arranging something so that it works efficiently; *the chairman handles the organization of the AGM*; *the organization of the group is too centralized to be efficient*; *the organization of the head office into departments*; **organization and methods (O & M)** = examining how an office works, and suggesting how it can be made more efficient; **organization chart** = list of people working in various departments, showing how a company or office is organized; **line organization** = organization of a business where each manager is responsible for doing what his superior tells him to do **(b)** group or institution which is arranged for efficient work; **a government organization** = official body, run by the government; **a travel organization** = body representing companies in the travel business; **an employers' organization** = group of employers with similar interests

working with a client base
which includes many major

commercial organizations and nationalized industries

Times

organizational [ɔːgənaɪˈzeɪʃənl] *adjective* referring to the way in which something is organized; *the paper gives a diagram of the company's organizational structure*

Organization for Economic Co-operation and Development (OECD) organization representing the industrialized countries, aimed at encouraging international trade, wealth and employment in member countries, etc.

Organization of Petroleum Exporting Countries (OPEC) group of major countries who are producers and exporters of oil

organize [ˈɔːgənaɪz] *verb* to arrange something so that it works efficiently; *the company is organized into six profit centres*; *the group is organized by areas of sales*; **organized labour** = workers who are members of trade unions

we organize a rate with importers who have large orders and guarantee them space at a fixed rate so that they can plan their costs

Lloyd's List

governments are coming under increasing pressure from politicians, organized labour and business to stimulate economic growth

Duns Business Month

organizer [ˈɔːgənaɪzə] *noun* (a) person who arranges things efficiently; *address any queries about the venue to the conference organizer* (b) **personal organizer** *or* **electronic organizer** = very small pocket computer in which you can enter details of names, addresses, telephone numbers, appointments, meetings, etc.

organizing committee [ˈɔːgənaɪzɪŋ kəˈmɪti] *noun* group of people who arrange something; *he is a member of the organizing committee for the conference*

oriented *or* **orientated** [ˈɔːrientɪd or ˈɔːrienteɪtɪd] *adjective* working in a certain direction; **profit-oriented company** = company which does everything to make a profit; **export-oriented company** = company which produces goods mainly for export

origin [ˈɒrɪdʒɪn] *noun* where something comes from; *spare parts of European origin*; **certificate of origin** = document showing where goods were made; **country of origin** = country where a product is manufactured or where a food product comes from; *all produce must be labelled to show the country of origin*

original [əˈrɪdʒənl] **1** *adjective* which was used or made first; *they sent a copy of the original invoice*; *he kept the original receipt for reference* **2** *noun* first copy made; *send the original and file two copies*

originally [əˈrɪdʒənəli] *adverb* first, at the beginning

OS = OUTSIZE

O/S = OUT OF STOCK

other people's money (OPM) [ˈʌðə ˈpiːplz ˈmʌniː] money which a business 'borrows' from its creditors (such as by not paying invoices on schedule) and so avoids using its own funds

ounce [aʊns] *noun* measure of weight (= 28 grams) (NOTE: usually written **oz** after figures: **25oz**. Note also that the ounce is now no longer officially used in the UK)

out [aʊt] *adverb* (a) on strike; *the workers have been out on strike for four weeks*; *as soon as the management made the offer, the staff came out*; *the shop stewards called the workforce out* (b) to be out = to be wrong in calculating something; *the balance is £10 out*; *we are £20,000 out in our calculations* = we have £20,000 too much or too little (c) *US* away from work because of illness (NOTE: British English in this meaning is **off**)

outbid [aʊtˈbɪd] *verb* to offer a better price than someone else; *we offered £100,000 for the warehouse, but another company outbid us* (NOTE: **outbidding - outbid**)

outfit [ˈaʊtfɪt] *noun* small, sometimes badly run, company; *they called in a public relations outfit*; *he works for some finance outfit*

outflow ['aʊtfləʊ] *noun* **outflow of capital from a country** = capital which is sent out of a country for investment abroad

outgoing [aʊt'gəʊɪŋ] *adjective* **(a)** **outgoing mail** = mail which is being sent out **(b)** **the outgoing chairman** *or* **the outgoing president** = chairman or president who is about to retire

outgoings ['aʊtgəʊɪŋz] *plural noun* money which is paid out

out-house ['aʊt'haʊs] *adjective & adverb* working outside a company's buildings; *the out-house staff; we do all our data processing out-house*

outlay ['aʊtleɪ] *noun* money spent, expenditure; **capital outlay** = money spent on fixed assets (such as property, machinery, furniture); **for a modest outlay** = for a small sum; *for a modest outlay he was able to take control of the business*

outlet ['aʊtlet] *noun* place where something can be sold; **factory outlet** = shop where merchandise is sold direct to the public from the factory, usually at wholesale prices; **retail outlets** = shops which sell to the general public

outline ['aʊtlaɪn] **1** *noun* general description, without giving many details; *they drew up the outline of a plan or an outline plan*; **outline planning permission** = general permission to build a property on a piece of land, but not final because there are no details **2** *verb* to make a general description; *the chairman outlined the company's plans for the coming year*

outlook ['aʊtlʊk] *noun* view of what is going to happen in the future; *the economic outlook is not good; the stock market outlook is worrying*

American	demand	has
transformed	the	profit
outlook	for	many	European
manufacturers		

Duns Business Month

out of court ['aʊt əv 'kɔːt] *adverb & adjective* **a settlement was reached out of court** = a dispute was settled between two parties privately without continuing a court case; *they are hoping to reach an out-of-court settlement*

out of date ['aʊt əv 'deɪt] *adjective & adverb* old-fashioned, no longer modern; *their computer system is years out of date; they are still using out-of-date equipment*

out of pocket ['aʊt əv 'pɒkɪt] *adjective & adverb* having paid out money personally; *the deal has left me out of pocket*; **out-of-pocket expenses** = amount of money to pay a worker back for his own money which he has spent on company business

out of stock (O/S) ['aʊt əv 'stɒk] *adjective & adverb* with no stock left; *those books are temporarily out of stock; several out-of-stock items have been on order for weeks*

out of work ['aʊt əv 'wɜːk] *adjective & adverb* with no job; *the recession has put millions out of work; the company was set up by three out-of-work engineers*

outperform [aʊtpə'fɔːm] *verb* to do better than other companies

on the fairly safe assumption
that there is little to be
gained in attempting to find
the share or trust that
outperforms everything else,
there is every reason to buy
an index-tracking fund

Money Observer

output ['aʊtpʊt] **1** *noun* **(a)** amount which a company or a person or a machine produces; *output has increased by 10%; 25% of our output is exported*; **output per hour** = amount produced in one hour; **output bonus** = extra payment for increased production; **output tax** = VAT charged by a company on goods or services sold, and which the company pays to the government **(b)** information which is produced by a computer (NOTE: the opposite is **input**) **2** *verb* to produce (by a computer); *the printer will output colour graphics; that is the information outputted from the computer* (NOTE: **outputting - outputted**)

crude oil output plunged
during the last month and is
likely to remain near its
present level for the near
future

Wall Street Journal

outright ['aʊtraɪt] *adverb & adjective* completely; **to purchase something outright** *or* **to make an outright purchase** = to buy something completely, including all rights in it

outsell [aʊt'sel] *verb* to sell more than someone; *the company is easily outselling its competitors* (NOTE: **outselling - outsold**)

outside ['aʊtsaɪd] *adjective & adverb* **(a)** not in a company's office or building; **to send work to be done outside** = to send work to be done in other offices; **outside dealer** = person who is not a member of the Stock Exchange but is allowed to trade; **outside director** = director who is not employed by the company; **outside line** = line from an internal office telephone system to the main telephone exchange; *you dial 9 to get an outside line*; **outside worker** = worker who does not work in a company's offices **(b) outside office hours** = not during office hours, when the office is not open

outsize (OS) ['aʊtsaɪz] *noun* size which is larger than usual; **an outsize order** = a very large order

outsourcing ['aʊtsɔːsɪŋ] *noun* obtaining services from specialist bureaux or other companies, rather than employing full-time members of staff to provide them

organizations in the public and private sectors are increasingly buying in specialist services - or outsourcing - allowing them to cut costs and concentrate on their core business activities

Financial Times

outstanding [aʊt'stændɪŋ] *adjective* not yet paid or completed; **outstanding debts** = debts which are waiting to be paid; **outstanding orders** = orders received but not yet supplied; **what is the amount outstanding?** = how much money is still owed?; **matters outstanding from the previous meeting** = questions which were not settled at the previous meeting

COMMENT: note the difference between 'outstanding' and 'overdue'. If a debtor has 30 days credit, then his debts are outstanding until the end of

the 30 days, and they only become overdue on the 31st day

out tray ['aʊt 'treɪ] *noun* basket on a desk for letters or memos which have been dealt with and are ready to be dispatched

outturn ['aʊttɜːn] *noun* amount produced by a country or company

outvote [aʊt'vəʊt] *verb* to defeat in a vote; **the chairman was outvoted** = the majority voted against the chairman

outward ['aʊtwəd] *adjective* going away from the home country; *the ship is outward bound*; *on the outward voyage the ship will call in at the West Indies*; **outward cargo** *or* **outward freight** = goods which are being exported; **outward mission** = visit by a group of businessmen to a foreign country

outwork ['aʊtwɜːk] *noun* work which a company pays someone to do at home

outworker ['aʊtwɜːkə] *noun* person who works at home for a company

over ['əʊvə] **1** *preposition* **(a)** more than; *the carpet costs over £1000*; *packages not over 200 grams can be sent first class*; *the increase in turnover was over 25%* **(b)** compared with; *increase in output over last year*; *increase in debtors over the last quarter's figure* **(c)** during; *over the last half of the year profits doubled* **2** *adverb* **held over to the next meeting** = postponed, put back to the next meeting; **to carry over a balance** = to take a balance from the end of one page or period to the beginning of the next **3** *plural noun* **overs** = extra items above the agreed total; *the price includes 10% overs to compensate for damage*

over- ['əʊvə] *prefix* more than; **shop which caters to the over-60s** = shop which has goods which appeal to people who are more than sixty years old

overall [əʊvər'ɔːl] *adjective* covering or including everything; **although some divisions traded profitably, the company reported an overall fall in profits** = the company reported a general fall in profits; **overall plan** = plan which covers everything

overbook [əuvə'buk] *verb* to book more people than there are seats or rooms available; *the hotel or the flight was overbooked*

overbooking [əuvə'bukɪŋ] *noun* booking of more people than there are seats or rooms available

overborrowed [əuvə'bɒrəud] *adjective* (company) which has very high borrowings compared to its assets, and has difficulty in meeting its interest payments

overbought [əuvə'bɔːt] *adjective* having bought too much; **the market is overbought** = prices on the stock market are too high, because there have been too many people wanting to buy

> they said the market was overbought when the index was between 860 and 870 points
> *Australian Financial Review*

overcapacity [əuvəkə'pæsəti] *noun* unused capacity for producing something

> with the present overcapacity situation in the airline industry the discounting of tickets is widespread
> *Business Traveller*

overcapitalized [əuvə'kæpɪtəlaɪzd] *adjective* with more capital in a company than it needs

overcharge 1 ['əuvətʃɑːdʒ] *noun* charge which is higher than it should be; *to pay back an overcharge* **2** [əuvə'tʃɑːdʒ] *verb* to ask too much money; *they overcharged us for meals*; *we asked for a refund because we had been overcharged*

overdraft ['əuvədrɑːft] *noun* **(a)** *GB* amount of money which a company or person can withdraw from a bank account with the bank's permission, and which is more than there is in the account; *the bank has allowed me an overdraft of £5,000*; **overdraft facilities** = arrangement with a bank to have an overdraft; **we have exceeded our overdraft facilities** = we have taken out more than the overdraft allowed by the bank **(b)** *US* amount of a cheque which is more than the money in the account on which it is drawn (American banks do not offer overdraft facilities in the same way as British banks)

overdraw [əuvə'drɔː] *verb* to take out more money from a bank account than there is in it; **your account is overdrawn** *or* **you are overdrawn** = you have paid out more money from your account than you have in it (NOTE: **overdrawing - overdrew - overdrawn**)

overdue [əuvə'djuː] *adjective* which has not been paid on time; **interest payments are three weeks overdue** = interest payments which should have been made three weeks ago; *see note at* OUTSTANDING

overestimate [əuvər'estɪmeɪt] *verb* to think something is larger or worse than it really is; *he overestimated the amount of time needed to fit out the factory*; *they overestimated the costs of moving the offices to central London*

overextend [əuvərɪk'stend] *verb* **the company overextended itself** = the company borrowed more money than its assets would allow

overhead ['əuvəhed] **1** *adjective* **overhead costs** *or* **expenses** = money spent on the day-to-day cost of a business; **overhead budget** = plan of probable overhead costs **2** *noun* **overheads** *US* **overhead** = costs of the day-to-day running of a business; *the sales revenue covers the manufacturing costs but not the overheads*

> it ties up less capital in inventory and with its huge volume spreads out costs over bigger sales; add in low overhead (i.e. minimum staff, no deliveries, no credit cards) and a warehouse club can offer bargain prices
> *Duns Business Month*

overlook [əuvə'luk] *verb* **(a)** to look out over; *the Managing Director's office overlooks the factory* **(b)** not to pay attention to; *in this instance we will overlook the delay*

overmanning [əuvə'mænɪŋ] *noun* having more workers than are needed to do a company's work; *the MD's plan is to reduce overmanning*

overpaid [əuvəˈpeɪd] *adjective* paid too much; *our staff are overpaid and underworked*

overpay [əuvəˈpeɪ] *verb* to pay too much; *we overpaid the invoice by $245*

overpayment [əuvəˈpeɪmənt] *noun* paying too much

overproduce [əuvəprəˈdjuːs] *verb* to produce too much

overproduction [əuvəprəˈdʌkʃən] *noun* manufacturing too much of a product

overrated [əuvəˈreɪtɪd] *adjective* valued more highly than it should be; *the effect of the dollar on European business cannot be overrated*; *their 'first-class service' is very overrated*

overrider *or* **overriding commission** [ˈəuvəraɪdə or ˈəuvəraɪdɪŋ kəˈmɪʃən] *noun* special extra commission which is above all other commissions

overrun [əuvəˈrʌn] *verb* to go beyond a limit; *the construction company overran the time limit set to complete the factory* (NOTE: **overrunning - overran - overrun**)

overseas [əuvəˈsiːz] **1** *adjective* across the sea or to foreign countries; *an overseas call* = a phone call to another country; *the overseas division* = the section of a company dealing with trade with other countries; *overseas markets* = markets in foreign countries; *overseas trade* = trade with foreign countries **2** *noun* foreign countries; *the profits from overseas are far higher than those of the home division*

overseer [ˈəuvəsɪə] *noun* person who supervises other workers

oversell [əuvəˈsel] *verb* to sell more than you can produce; *he is oversold* = he has agreed to sell more product than he can produce; *the market is oversold* = stock market prices are too low, because there have been too many sellers (NOTE: **overselling - oversold**)

overspend [əuvəˈspend] *verb* to spend too much; *to overspend your budget* = to spend more money than is allowed in the budget (NOTE: **overspending - overspent**)

overspending [əuvəˈspendɪŋ] *noun* spending more than is allowed; *the board decided to limit the overspending by the production departments*

overstaffed [əuvəˈstɑːft] *adjective* with more workers than are needed to do the work of the company

overstock [əuvəˈstɒk] **1** *verb* to have more stock than is needed; **to be overstocked with spare parts** = to have too many spare parts in stock **2** *plural noun* US **overstocks** = more stock than is needed to supply orders; *we will have to sell off the overstocks to make room in the warehouse*

> Cash paid for your stock: any quantity, any products, overstocked lines, factory seconds
>
> *Australian Financial Review*

oversubscribe [əuvəsəbˈskraɪb] *verb* **the share offer was oversubscribed six times** = people applied for six times as many new shares as were available

over-the-counter [ˈəuvəðəˈkauntə] *adjective* **over-the-counter sales** = legal selling of shares which are not listed in the official Stock Exchange list; *this share is available on the over-the-counter market*

overtime [ˈəuvətaɪm] **1** *noun* hours worked more than the normal working time; *to work six hours' overtime*; *the overtime rate is one and a half times normal pay*; **overtime ban** = order by a trade union which forbids overtime work by its members; **overtime pay** = pay for extra time worked **2** *adverb* **to work overtime** = to work longer hours than in the contract of employment

overtrading [əuvəˈtreɪdɪŋ] *noun (of a company)* situation where a company expands too fast, so that it runs out of cash to pay for the products it sells

overvalue [əuvəˈvæljuː] *verb* to give a higher value than is right; **these shares are overvalued at £1.25** = the shares are worth less than the £1.25 for which they are selling; **the pound is overvalued against the dollar** = the exchange rate gives too many dollars to the pound, considering the strength of the two countries' economies (NOTE: the opposite is **undervalued**)

> the fact that sterling has been overvalued for the past three years shows that currencies can remain above

their fair value for very long
periods

Investors Chronicle

overweight [əʊvə'weɪt] *adjective* **the package is sixty grams overweight** = the package weighs sixty grams too much

overworked [əʊvə'wɜːkt] *adjective* having too much work to do; *our staff complain of being underpaid and overworked*

owe [əʊ] *verb* to have to pay money; *he owes the bank £250,000*; **they still owe the company for the stock they purchased last year** = they have still not paid for the stock

owing ['əʊɪŋ] *adjective* **(a)** which is owed; *money owing to the directors*; *how much is still owing to the company by its debtors?* **(b) owing to** = because of; *the plane was late owing to fog*; *I am sorry that owing to pressure of work, we cannot supply your order on time*

own [əʊn] *verb* to have or to possess; *he owns 50% of the shares*; **a wholly-owned subsidiary** = a subsidiary which belongs completely to the parent company; **a state-owned industry** = industry which is nationalized

own brand goods [əʊn 'brænd 'gʊdz] *noun* products specially packed for a store with the store's name on them

owner ['əʊnə] *noun* person who owns something; **sole owner** = person who owns something by himself; **owner-occupier** = person who owns and lives in a house; **goods sent at owner's risk** = situation where the owner has to insure the goods while they are being transported

ownership ['əʊnəʃɪp] *noun* act of owning something; **common** *or* **collective ownership** = situation where a business is owned by the workers who work in it; **joint ownership** = situation where two people own the same property; **public ownership** *or* **state ownership** = situation where an industry is nationalized; **private ownership** = situation where a company is owned by private shareholders; **the ownership of the company has passed to the banks** = the banks have become owners of the company

own label goods ['əʊn 'leɪbl 'gʊdz] *noun* goods specially produced for a store with store's name on them

oz = OUNCE(S)

Pp

P's *see* FOUR

PA ['piːˈeɪ] = PERSONAL ASSISTANT

p.a. = PER ANNUM

P&L = PROFIT AND LOSS

pack [pæk] **1** *noun* **(a) pack of items** = items put together in a container or shrink-wrapped for selling; *he bought a pack of cigarettes at the airport; we need two packs of envelopes*; **items sold in packs of 200** = sold in boxes containing 200 items; **blister pack** *or* **bubble pack** = type of packing where the item for sale is covered with a stiff plastic cover sealed to a card backing; **display pack** = specially attractive box for showing goods for sale; **dummy pack** = empty pack for display in a shop; **four-pack** *or* **six-pack** = box containing four or six items (often bottles) **(b)** folder containing documents about something; **information pack** = folder containing information about a product, tourist attraction, etc.; *the conference agenda or the agenda of the conference is in the information pack given to delegates* **2** *verb* to put things into a container for selling or sending; *to pack goods into cartons; your order has been packed and is ready for shipping; the computer is packed in expanded polystyrene before being shipped*

package ['pækɪdʒ] **1** *noun* **(a)** goods packed and wrapped for sending by mail; *the Post Office does not accept bulky packages; the goods are to be sent in airtight packages* **(b)** box or bag in which goods are sold; *instructions for use are printed on the package* **(c)** group of different items joined together in one deal; **pay package** *or* **salary package** *US* **compensation package** = salary and other benefits offered with a job; *the job carries an attractive salary package*; **package deal** = agreement where several different items are agreed at the same time; *we are offering a package deal which includes the whole office computer network system, staff training and hardware maintenance*; **package holiday** *or* **package tour** = holiday or tour where the hotel, travel and meals are all included in the price; *the travel company is arranging a package trip to the international trade fair* **(d)** different items of software sold together; *the computer is sold with accounting and word-processing packages; the company's area of specialization is accounts packages for small businesses* **2** *verb* **(a) to package goods** = to wrap and pack goods in an attractive way **(b) to package holidays** = to sell a holiday package including travel hotels and food

---

airlines offer special stopover rates and hotel packages to attract customers to certain routes
Business Traveller

---

the remuneration package will include an attractive salary, profit sharing and a company car
Times

---

airlines will book not only tickets but also hotels and car hire to provide a complete package
Business Traveller

---

in today's fast-growing packaged goods area many companies are discovering

that a well-recognized brand
name can be a priceless asset
Duns Business Month

packaging ['pækɪdʒɪŋ] *noun* **(a)** the
action of putting things into packages **(b)**
material used to protect goods which are
being packed; *the fruit is sold in airtight
packaging*; *bubble wrap and other
packaging material* **(c)** attractive material
used to wrap goods for display

packer ['pækə] *noun* person who packs
goods

packet ['pækɪt] *noun* small box of goods
for selling; *can you get me a packet of
cigarettes?*; *she bought a packet of
biscuits*; *we need two packets of filing
cards*; **item sold in packets of 20** = sold in
boxes containing 20 items each; **postal
packet** *or* **small packet** = small container
of goods sent by post

packing ['pækɪŋ] *noun* **(a)** action of
putting goods into boxes and wrapping
them for shipping; *what is the cost of the
packing?*; *packing is included in the
price*; **packing case** = large wooden box
for carrying easily broken items; **packing
charges** = money charged for putting
goods into boxes; **packing list** *or* **packing
slip** = list of goods which have been
packed, sent with the goods to show they
have been checked **(b)** material used to
protect goods; *the fruit is packed in
airtight packing*; **non-returnable packing**
= packing which is to be thrown away
when it has been used and not returned to
the sender

pad [pæd] *noun* **(a)** pile of sheets of paper
attached together on one side; **desk pad** =
pad of paper kept on a desk for writing
notes; **memo pad** *or* **note pad** = pad of
paper for writing memos or notes; **phone
pad** = pad of paper kept by a telephone for
noting messages **(b)** soft material like a
cushion; *the machine is protected by
rubber pads*; **inking pad** = cushion with
ink in it, used to put ink on a rubber stamp

paid [peɪd] *adjective* money has been
given **(a)** **paid holidays** = holidays where
the worker's wages are still paid even
though he is not working **(b)** **paid
assistant** = assistant who receives a salary
(c) (amount) which has been settled; *the*

order was sent carriage paid; **paid bills** =
bills which have been settled; *the invoice is
marked 'paid'*

paid-up ['peɪd'ʌp] *adjective* paid in full;
paid-up (share) capital = amount of
money paid for the issued capital shares (it
does not include called-up capital which
has not yet been paid for); **paid-up shares**
= shares which have been completely paid
for by the shareholders

pallet ['pælət] *noun* flat wooden base on
which goods can be stacked for easy
handling by a fork-lift truck (NOTE:
American English is **skid**)

palletize ['pælətaɪz] *verb* to put goods on
pallets; *palletized cartons*

pamphlet ['pæmflət] *noun* small booklet
of advertising material or of information

panel ['pænl] *noun* **(a)** flat surface
standing upright; **display panel** = flat area
for displaying goods in a shop window;
advertisement panel = specially designed
large advertising space in a newspaper **(b)**
panel of experts = group of people who
give advice on a problem; **consumer panel**
= group of consumers who report on goods
they have used so that the manufacturer can
improve the goods, or use the consumers'
reports in his advertising; **Panel on
Takeovers and Mergers** *or* **Takeover
Panel** = non-statutory body which
examines takeovers and applies the
Takeover Code

panic ['pænɪk] *noun & adjective* being
frightened; **panic buying** = rush to buy
something at any price because stocks may
run out or because the price may rise; *panic
buying of sugar or of dollars*; **panic selling
of sterling** = rush to sell sterling at any
price because of possible devaluation

paper ['peɪpə] *noun* **(a)** thin material for
writing on or for wrapping; **brown paper** =
thick paper for wrapping parcels; **carbon
paper** = sheet of paper with a black stuff on
one side used in a typewriter to make a
copy; *she put the carbon paper in the
wrong way round*; **copy paper** *or* **copier
paper** = special paper used in
photocopiers; **graph paper** = paper with
small squares printed on it, used for
drawing graphs; **headed paper** =
notepaper with the name and address of the

company printed on it; **lined paper** = paper with thin lines printed on it; **typing paper** = thin paper for use in a typewriter; **wrapping paper** = paper for wrapping **(b) paper bag** = bag made of paper; **paper feed** = device which puts paper into a printer or photocopier **(c) papers** = documents; *he sent me the relevant papers on the case*; *he has lost the customs papers*; *the office is asking for the VAT papers* **(d) on paper** = in theory; *on paper the system is ideal, but we have to see it working before we will sign the contract*; **paper loss** = loss made when an asset has fallen in value but has not been sold; **paper profit** = profit made when an asset has increased in value but has not been sold; **paper millionaire** = person who owns shares which, if he sold them, would make him a millionaire **(e)** document which can represent money (bills of exchange, promissory notes, etc.); **bankable paper** = document which a bank will accept as security for a loan; **negotiable paper** = document which can be transferred from one owner to another for money **(f) paper money** *or* **paper currency** = banknotes **(g)** newspaper; **trade paper** = newspaper aimed at people working in a certain industry; **free paper** *or* **giveaway paper** = newspaper which is given away free, and which relies for its income on its advertising

> the profits were tax-free and the interest on the loans they incurred qualified for income tax relief; the paper gains were rarely changed into spending money
> *Investors Chronicle*

paperclip ['peɪpəklɪp] *noun* piece of bent wire, used to hold pieces of paper together; *she keeps a box of paperclips in the drawer of her desk*

paperless office ['peɪpələs 'ɒfɪs] *noun* office where all work is done on computers, which should mean that less paper is used (in fact, such offices usually use far more paper than old-fashioned offices)

paperwork ['peɪpəwɜːk] *noun* office work, especially writing memos and filling

in forms; *exporting to Russia involves a large amount of paperwork*

par [pɑː] *adjective* equal, at the same price; **par value** = face value, the value printed on a share certificate; **shares at par** = shares whose market price is the same as their face value; **shares above par** *or* **below par** = shares with a market price higher or lower than their par value

parachute ['pærəʃuːt] *noun* **golden parachute** = large, usually tax-free, sum of money given to an executive who retires from a company before the end of his service contract

paragraph ['pærəgrɑːf] *noun* group of several lines of writing which makes a separate section; *the first paragraph of your letter or paragraph one of your letter*; *please refer to the paragraph in the contract on 'shipping instructions'*

parameter [pə'ræmɪtə] *noun* fixed limit; *the budget parameters are fixed by the finance director*; *spending by each department has to fall within certain parameters*

parastatal [pærə'steɪtl] *noun (in Africa)* large state-controlled organization

> the minister did reveal that the accumulated losses of major parastatals totalled $0.4 billion in mid-year
> *Business in Africa*

parcel ['pɑːsl] **1** *noun* **(a)** goods wrapped up in paper, plastic, etc., to be sent by post; *to do up goods into parcels*; **to tie up a parcel** = to fasten a parcel with string; **parcel delivery service** = private company which delivers parcels within a certain area; **parcels office** = office where parcels can be handed in for sending by mail; **parcel post** = mail service for sending parcels; *to send a box by parcel post*; **parcel rates** = charges for sending parcels by post **(b) parcel of shares** = group of shares (such as 50 or 100) which are sold as a group; *the shares are on offer in parcels of 50* **2** *verb* to wrap and tie to make a parcel; *to parcel up a consignment of books* (NOTE: **parcelling - parcelled** but American English **parceling - parceled**)

parent company ['peərənt 'kʌmpni] *noun* company which owns more than 50% of the shares of another company

Pareto's Law [pə'riːtəuz 'lɔː] *noun* the theory that a small percentage of a total is responsible for a large proportion of value or resources

> COMMENT: also called the 80/20 law, because 80/20 is the normal ratio between majority and minority figures: so 20% of accounts produce 80% of turnover; 80% of GDP enriches 20% of the population, etc.

pari passu ['pæri 'pæsuː] *Latin phrase* meaning 'equally'; *the new shares will rank pari passu with the existing ones*

Paris Club ['pærɪs 'klʌb] the Group of Ten, the major world economic powers working within the framework of the IMF (there are in fact eleven: Belgium, Canada, France, Germany, Italy, Japan, Netherlands, Sweden, Switzerland, United Kingdom and the United States. It is called the 'Paris Club' because its first meeting was in Paris)

parity ['pærəti] *noun* being equal; **the female staff want parity with the men** = they want to have the same rates of pay and conditions as the men; **the pound fell to parity with the dollar** = the pound fell to a point where one pound equalled one dollar

> the draft report on changes in the international monetary system casts doubt about any return to fixed exchange-rate parities
>
> *Wall Street Journal*

park [pɑːk] **1** *noun* open space with grass and trees; **business park** = group of small factories or warehouses, especially near a town; *he has rented a unit in the local business park*; **car park** = place where you can leave your car; *he left his car in the hotel car park*; *if the car park is full, you can park in the street for thirty minutes*; **industrial park** = area of land near a town specially set aside for factories and warehouses; **science park** = area near a town or university set aside for technological industries **2** *verb* to leave your car in a place while you are not using it; *the rep parked his car outside the shop*;

you cannot park here during the rush hour; *parking is difficult in the centre of the city*

Parkinson's law ['pɑːkɪnsnz 'lɔː] *noun* law, based on wide experience, that in business the amount of work increases to fill the time available for it

part [pɑːt] *noun* **(a)** piece or section; some; *part of the shipment was damaged*; *part of the workforce is on overtime*; *part of the expenses will be refunded* **(b)** **in part** = not completely; *to contribute in part to the costs* or *to pay the costs in part* **(c)** **spare part** = small piece of machinery to replace a part of a machine which is broken; *the photocopier will not work - we need to replace a part* or *a part needs replacing* **(d)** **part-owner** = person who owns something jointly with one or more other persons; *he is part-owner of the restaurant*; **part-ownership** = situation where two or more persons own the same property **(e)** **part exchange** = giving an old product as part of the payment for a new one; *they refused to take my old car as part exchange for the new one*; **part payment** = paying of part of a whole payment; *I gave him £250 as part payment for the car*; **part delivery** or **part order** or **part shipment** = delivering or shipping only some of the items in an order

partial ['pɑːʃəl] *adjective* not complete; **partial loss** = situation where only part of the insured property has been damaged or lost; **he got partial compensation for the damage to his house** = he was compensated for part of the damage; *US* **partial payment** = payment of part of a whole payment (NOTE: British English is **part payment**)

participation [pɑːtɪsɪ'peɪʃən] *noun* taking part; **worker participation** = situation where the workers take part in making management decisions

participative [pɑː'tɪsɪpeɪtɪv] *adjective* where both sides take part; *we do not treat management-worker relations as a participative process*

particular [pə'tɪkjulə] **1** *adjective* special, different from others; *the colour printer only works with a particular type of paper*; **particular average** = situation where part of a shipment is lost or damaged and the insurance costs are borne by the owner of the lost goods and not shared among all the owners of the shipment **2** *noun* **(a) particulars** = details; *sheet which gives particulars of the items for sale*; *the inspector asked for particulars of the missing car*; **to give full particulars of something** = to list all the known details about something **(b) in particular** = specially, as a special point; *fragile goods, in particular glasses, need special packing*

partly ['pɑːtli] *adverb* not completely; **partly-paid capital** = capital which represents partly-paid shares; **partly-paid up shares** = shares where the shareholders have not paid the full face value; **partly-secured creditors** = creditors whose debts are not fully covered by the value of the security

partner ['pɑːtnə] *noun* person who works in a business and has a share in it with other partners; *he became a partner in a firm of solicitors*; **active partner** *or* **working partner** = partner who works in a partnership; **junior partner** = person who has a small part of the shares in a partnership; **limited partner** = partner who is responsible for the debts of the firm only up to the amount of money which he or she has provided to the business; **senior partner** = person who has a large part of the shares in a partnership; **sleeping partner** = partner who has a share in a business but does not work in it

partnership ['pɑːtnəʃɪp] *noun* **(a)** unregistered business where two or more people (but not more than twenty) share the risks and profits according to a partnership agreement; *to go into partnership with someone*; *to join with someone to form a partnership*; **to offer someone a partnership** *or* **to take someone into partnership with you** = to have a working business and bring someone in to share it with you; **to dissolve a partnership** = to bring a partnership to an end **(b) limited partnership** = registered business where the liability of the partners is limited to the amount of capital they have each provided to the business and where the partners may not take part in the running of the business

part-time ['pɑːt'taɪm] *adjective & adverb* not working for the whole working day; *she works part-time*; *he is trying to find part-time work when the children are in school*; *a part-time worker*; *we are looking for part-time staff to work our computers*; **part-time work** *or* **part-time employment** = work for part of a working day

part-timer ['pɑːt'taɪmə] *noun* person who works part-time

party ['pɑːti] *noun* **(a)** company or person involved in a legal dispute or a legal agreement; *one of the parties to the suit has died*; *the company is not a party to the agreement* **(b) third party** = any person other than the two main parties involved in a contract (i.e., in an insurance contract, not the insurance company nor the person who is insured); **third party insurance** *or* **third party policy** = insurance to cover damage to any person who is not one of the people named in the insurance contract (that is, not the insured person nor the insurance company) **(c) working party** = group of experts who study a problem; *the government has set up a working party to study the problems of industrial waste*; *Professor Smith is the chairman of the working party on computers in society*

pass [pɑːs] **1** *noun* **(a)** permit to allow someone to go into a building; *you need a pass to enter the ministry offices*; *all members of staff must show a pass* **(b)** permit to allow someone to travel; **bus pass** = permit allowing someone (usually an old age pensioner) to travel by bus free **2** *verb* **(a) to pass a dividend** = to pay no dividend in a certain year **(b)** to approve; *the finance director has to pass an invoice before it is sent out*; *the loan has been passed by the board*; **to pass a resolution** = to vote to agree to a resolution; *the meeting passed a proposal that salaries should be frozen* **(c)** to be successful; *he passed his typing test*; *she has passed all her exams and now is a qualified accountant*

passage ['pæsɪdʒ] *noun* voyage by ship

passbook ['pɑːsbʊk] *noun* book given by a bank or building society which shows money which you deposit or withdraw from your savings account or building society account

---

instead of customers having transactions recorded in their passbooks, they will present plastic cards and have the transactions printed out on a receipt

Australian Financial Review

---

passenger ['pæsɪndʒə] *noun* person who travels in a train, bus, taxi, plane, etc., but is not the driver nor a member of the crew; **foot passenger** = passenger on a ferry who is not travelling with a car; **passenger terminal** = air terminal for people going on planes, not for cargo; **passenger train** = train which carries passengers but not freight

pass off ['pɑːs 'ɒf] *verb* **to pass something off as something else** = to pretend that it is another thing in order to cheat a customer; *he tried to pass off the wine as French, when in fact it came from outside the EU*

passport ['pɑːspɔːt] *noun* official document proving that you are a citizen of a country, which you have to show when you travel from one country to another; *we had to show our passports at the customs post*; *his passport is out of date*; *the passport officer stamped my passport*

password ['pɑːswɜːd] *noun* word or characters which identifies a user and allows him or her access to a computer system

patent ['peɪtənt or 'pætənt] **1** *noun* **(a)** official document showing that a person has the exclusive right to make and sell an invention; *to take out a patent for a new type of light bulb*; *to apply for a patent for a new invention*; **letters patent** = official term for a patent; **patent applied for** *or* **patent pending** = words on a product showing that the inventor has applied for a patent for it; **to forfeit a patent** = to lose a patent because payments have not been made; **to infringe a patent** = to make and sell a product which works in the same way as a patented product and not pay a royalty for it; **infringement of patent** *or* **patent infringement** = act of illegally making or selling a product which is patented **(b)**

patent agent = person who advises on patents and applies for patents on behalf of clients; **to file a patent application** = to apply for a patent; **patent medicine** = medicine which is registered as a patent; **patent office** = government office which grants patents and supervises them; **patent rights** = rights which an inventor holds under a patent **2** *verb* **to patent an invention** = to register an invention with the patent office to prevent other people from copying it

patented ['peɪtəntɪd or 'pætəntɪd] *adjective* which is protected by a patent

paternity leave [pə'tɜːnəti 'liːv] *noun* permission for a man to be away from work when his wife is having a baby

patron ['peɪtrən] *noun* regular customer (of a hotel, restaurant, etc.); *the car park is for the use of hotel patrons only*

pattern ['pætən] *noun* **(a) pattern book** = book showing examples of design **(b)** general way in which something usually happens; *the pattern of sales or sales pattern is quite different this year*; **pattern of trade** *or* **trading pattern** = general way in which trade is carried on; *the company's trading pattern shows high export sales in the first quarter and high home sales in the third quarter*

pawn [pɔːn] **1** *noun* **to put something in pawn** = to leave a valuable object with someone in exchange for a loan which has to be repaid if you want to take back the object; **to take something out of pawn** = to repay the loan and so get back the object; **pawn ticket** = receipt given by the pawnbroker for the object left in pawn **2** *verb* **to pawn a watch** = to leave a watch with a pawnbroker who gives a loan against it

pawnbroker ['pɔːnbrəʊkə] *noun* person who lends money against the security of valuable objects

pawnshop ['pɔːnʃɒp] *noun* pawnbroker's shop

pay [peɪ] **1** *noun* **(a)** salary or wages, money given to someone for regular work; **back pay** = salary which has not been paid; **basic pay** = normal salary without extra payments; **take-home pay** = pay left after tax and insurance have been deducted;

holidays with pay = holiday which a worker can take by contract and for which he is paid; **unemployment pay** = dole, money given by the government to someone who is unemployed **(b) pay cheque** = monthly cheque which pays a salary to a worker; **pay day** = day on which wages are paid to workers (usually Friday for workers paid once a week, and during the last week of the month for workers who are paid once a month); **pay negotiations** *or* **pay talks** = discussions between management and workers about pay increases; **pay packet** = envelope containing the pay slip and the cash pay; **pay rise** = increase in pay; **pay round** = annual series of wage bargaining negotiations in various industries; **pay slip** = piece of paper showing the full amount of a worker's pay, and the money deducted as tax, pension and National Insurance contributions **(c) pay desk** = place in a store where you pay for goods bought; **pay phone** = public telephone which works if you put coins into it **2** *verb* **(a)** to give money to buy an item or a service; *to pay £1,000 for a car; how much did you pay to have the office cleaned?*; **to pay in advance** = to give money before you receive the item bought or before the service has been completed; *we had to pay in advance to have the new telephone system installed*; **to pay in instalments** = to give money for an item by giving small amounts regularly; *we are buying the van by paying instalments of £500 a month*; **to pay cash** = to pay the complete sum in cash; **to pay by cheque** = to pay by giving a cheque, not by using cash or credit card; **to pay by credit card** = to pay, using a credit card and not a cheque or cash **(b)** to give money; **to pay on demand** = to pay money when it is asked for, not after a period of credit; **please pay the sum of £10** = please give £10 in cash or by cheque; **to pay a dividend** = to give shareholders a part of the profits of a company; *these shares pay a dividend of 1.5p*; **to pay interest** = to give money as interest on money borrowed or invested; *some building societies pay an interest of 10%* **(c)** to give a worker money for work done; *the workforce has not been paid for three weeks*; *we pay good wages for skilled*

workers; *how much do they pay you per hour?*; **to be paid by the hour** = to get money for each hour worked; **to be paid at piece-work rates** = to get money for each piece of work finished **(d)** to give money which is owed or which has to be paid; *he was late paying the bill*; *we phoned to ask when they were going to pay the invoice*; *you will have to pay duty on these imports*; *she pays tax at the highest rate* **(e) to pay a cheque into an account** = to deposit money in the form of a cheque (NOTE: **paying - paid**)

payable ['peɪəbl] *adjective* which is due to be paid; **payable in advance** = which has to be paid before the goods are delivered; **payable on delivery** = which has to be paid when the goods are delivered; **payable on demand** = which must be paid when payment is asked for; **payable at sixty days** = which has to be paid by sixty days after the date of invoice; **cheque made payable to bearer** = cheque which will be paid to the person who has it, not to any particular name written on it; **shares payable on application** = shares which must be paid for when you apply to buy them; **accounts payable** = money owed by a company; **bills payable** = bills which a debtor will have to pay; **electricity charges are payable by the tenant** = the tenant (and not the landlord) must pay for the electricity

pay as you earn (PAYE) ['peɪ æz ju 'ɜːn] *GB* tax system, where income tax is deducted from the salary before it is paid to the worker

pay-as-you-go ['peɪæzjʊ'gəʊ] **(a)** *US* = PAY AS YOU EARN **(b)** *GB* payment system where the purchaser pays in small instalments as he uses the service

pay back ['peɪ 'bæk] *verb* to give money back to someone; *banks are warning students not to take out loans which they cannot pay back; I lent him £50 and he promised to pay me back in a month; he has never paid me back the money he borrowed*

payback ['peɪbæk] *noun* paying back money which has been borrowed; **payback clause** = clause in a contract which states the terms for repaying a loan; **payback period** = period of time over which a loan is to be repaid or an investment is to pay for itself

pay-cheque *US* **paycheck** ['peɪtʃek] *noun* salary cheque given to an employee

pay down ['peɪ 'daʊn] *verb* **to pay money down** = to make a deposit; *he paid £50 down and the rest in monthly instalments*

PAYE ['piːeɪwaɪ'iː] = PAY AS YOU EARN

payee [peɪ'iː] *noun* person who receives money from someone, person whose name is on a cheque

payer ['peɪə] *noun* person who gives money to someone; **slow payer** = person or company which does not pay debts on time; *the company is well known as a slow payer*

paying ['peɪɪŋ] **1** *adjective* which makes a profit; *it is a paying business*; **it is not a paying proposition** = it is not a business which is going to make a profit **2** *noun* giving money; *the paying of the debt has been delayed*; **paying-in book** = book of forms for paying money into a bank account or a building society account; **paying-in slip** = form which is filled in when money is being deposited in a bank account or building society

payload ['peɪləʊd] *noun* cargo or passengers carried by a ship, train or plane for which payment is made

payment ['peɪmənt] *noun* **(a)** giving money; *we always ask for payment in cash or cash payment and not payment by cheque; the payment of interest or interest payment should be made on the 22nd of each month*; **payment on account** = paying part of the money owed; **full payment** *or* **payment in full** = paying all money owed; **payment on invoice** = paying money as soon as an invoice is received; **payment in kind** = paying by giving goods or food, but not money; **payment by results** = money given which increases with the amount of work done or goods produced **(b)** money paid; **back payment** = paying money which is owed; **deferred payment** = (i) money paid later than the agreed date; (ii) payment for goods by instalments over a period of time; *the company agreed to defer payments for three months*; **down payment** = part of a total payment made in advance; **repayable in easy payments** = repayable with small sums regularly; **incentive payments** = extra pay offered to a worker to make him work better; **balance of payments** = comparison between total receipts and payments arising from a country's international trade in goods, services and financial transactions

pay off ['peɪ 'ɒf] *verb* **(a)** to finish paying money which is owed; *he won the lottery and paid off his mortgage; she is trying to pay off the loan by monthly instalments* **(b)** to pay all the money owed to someone and terminate his employment; *when the company was taken over the factory was closed and all the workers were paid off*

payoff ['peɪɒf] *noun* **(a)** money paid to finish paying something which is owed, such as money paid to a worker when his employment is terminated **(b)** profit or reward; *one of the payoffs of a university degree is increased earning power*

the finance director of the group is to receive a payoff of about £300,000 after deciding to leave the company and pursue other business opportunities

Times

pay out ['peɪ 'aʊt] *verb* to give money; *the company pays out thousands of pounds in legal fees; we have paid out half our profits in dividends*

payout ['peɪaʊt] *noun* money paid to help a company in difficulties, a subsidy; *the company only exists on payouts from the government*

> after a period of recession followed by a rapid boost in incomes, many tax payers embarked upon some tax planning to minimize their payouts
>
> *Australian Financial Review*

payroll ['peɪrəʊl] *noun* list of people employed and paid by a company; money paid by a company in salaries; *the company has 250 on the payroll*; **payroll ledger** = list of staff and their salaries; **payroll tax** = tax on the people employed by a company; *US* **payroll deduction** = money taken from an employee's gross pay for taxes, social security and pension contributions

pay up ['peɪ 'ʌp] *verb* to give money which is owed; *the company only paid up when we sent them a letter from our solicitor*; *he finally paid up six months late*

pc = PER CENT

PC ['piː'siː] = PERSONAL COMPUTER

PCB = PETTY CASH BOOK

P/E ['piː'iː] *abbreviation* = PRICE/EARNINGS; **P/E ratio**; *see* PRICE/EARNINGS RATIO

peak [piːk] **1** *noun* highest point; *the shares reached their peak in January*; *the share index has fallen 10% since the peak in January*; *withdrawals from bank accounts reached a peak in the week before Christmas*; **peak period** = time of the day when most commuters are travelling or when most electricity is being used, etc.; **time of peak demand** = time when something is being used most; **peak output** = highest output; **peak year** = best year, year when the largest quantity of products was produced or when sales were highest **2** *verb* to reach the highest point; *productivity peaked in January*; *shares have peaked and are beginning to slip back*

pecuniary [pɪ'kjuːnjəri] *adjective* referring to money; **he gained no pecuniary advantage** = he made no profit

peddle ['pedl] *verb* to sell goods from door to door or in the street

peg [peg] *verb* to hold something at a certain point; **to peg prices** = to fix prices to stop them rising; **to peg wage increases to the cost-of-living index** = to limit increases in wages to the increases in the cost-of-living index (NOTE: **pegging - pegged)**

pen [pen] *noun* thing for writing with, using ink; **felt pen** = pen with a point made of hard cloth; **light pen** = type of pen which directs a beam of light which, when passed over a bar code, can read it and send information back to a computer; **marker pen** = pen which makes a wide coloured mark

penalize ['piːnəlaɪz] *verb* to punish or to fine; *to penalize a supplier for late deliveries*; *they were penalized for bad service*

penalty ['penlti] *noun* punishment (such as a fine) which is imposed if something is not done or is done incorrectly or illegally; **penalty clause** = clause which lists the penalties which will be imposed if the contract is not obeyed; *the contract contains a penalty clause which fines the company 1% for every week the completion date is late*

pence [pens] *see* PENNY

pencil ['pensəl] *noun* instrument for writing, made of a stick of wood, with black or coloured material in the centre; **pencil sharpener** = device for sharpening pencils

pending ['pendɪŋ] **1** *adjective* waiting; **pending tray** = basket on a desk for papers which cannot be dealt with immediately; **patent pending** = situation where an invention is put on the market before a patent is granted **2** *preposition* **pending advice from our lawyers** = while waiting for advice from our lawyers

penetrate ['penɪtreɪt] *verb* **to penetrate a market** = to get into a market and capture a share of it

penetration [penɪ'treɪʃən] *noun* **market penetration** = percentage of a total market which the sales of a company cover

penny ['peni] *noun* **(a)** *GB* small coin, of which one hundred make a pound (NOTE: written **p** after a figure: **26p; the plural is pence**) **(b)** *US (informal)* small coin, one cent (NOTE: plural in American English is **pennies**. In British English, say 'pee' for the coin, and 'pee' or 'pence' for the amount: **a five 'pee' coin; it costs ten 'pee'** *or* **ten 'pence'**. In American English, say **'pennies'** for coins and **'cents'** for the amount)

penny share *US* **penny stock** ['peni 'ʃeə or 'peni 'stɒk] *noun* very cheap share, costing about 10p or less than $1

> COMMENT: these shares can be considered as a good speculation, since buying even large numbers of them does not involve a large amount of money, and the share price of some companies can rise dramatically; the price can of course fall, but in the case of penny shares, the loss is not likely to be as much as with shares with a higher market value

pension ['penʃən] **1** *noun* **(a)** money paid regularly to someone who no longer works; **retirement pension** *or* **old age pension** = state pension given to a man who is over 65 or and woman who is over 60; **government pension** *or* **state pension** = pension paid by the state; **occupational pension** = pension which is paid by the company by which a worker has been employed; **portable pension** = pension entitlement which can be moved from one company to another without loss (as a worker changes jobs); **pension contributions** = money paid by an employer or worker into a pension fund **(b)** **pension plan** *or* **pension scheme** = plan worked out by an insurance company which arranges for a worker to pay part of his salary over many years and receive a regular payment when he retires; **company pension scheme** = pension which is organized by a company for its staff; *he decided to join the company's pension scheme*; **contributory pension scheme** = scheme where the worker has to pay a proportion of his salary; **graduated pension scheme** = pension scheme where

the benefit is calculated as a percentage of the salary of each person in the scheme; **non-contributory pension scheme** = scheme where the employer pays in all the money on behalf of the worker; **occupational pension scheme** = pension scheme where the worker gets a pension from a fund set up by the company he or she has worked for, which is related to the salary he or she was earning; **personal pension plan** = pension plan which applies to one worker only, usually a self-employed person, not to a group; **portable pension plan** = pension plan which a worker can carry from one company to another as he changes jobs **(c)** **pension entitlement** = amount of pension which someone has the right to receive when he retires; **pension fund** = fund which receives contributions from employers and employees, being the money which provides pensions for retired members of staff **2** *verb* **to pension someone off** = to ask someone to retire and take a pension

pensionable ['penʃənəbl] *adjective* able to receive a pension; **pensionable age** = age after which someone can stop working and take a pension

pensioner ['penʃənə] *noun* person who receives a pension; **old age pensioner** = person who receives the retirement pension

peppercorn rent ['pepəkɔːn 'rent] *noun* very small or nominal rent; *the charity pays only a peppercorn rent*; *to lease a property for* *or* *at a peppercorn rent*

PER = PRICE/EARNINGS RATIO

per [pɜː] *preposition* **(a)** as per = according to; **as per invoice** = as stated in the invoice; **as per sample** = as shown in the sample; **as per previous order** = according to the details given in our previous order **(b)** at a rate of; **per hour** *or* **per day** *or* **per week** *or* **per year** = for each hour, day, week or year; *the rate is £5 per hour*; *he makes about £250 per month*; *we pay £10 per hour* = we pay £10 for each hour worked; *the car was travelling at twenty-five miles per hour* = at a speed which covered 25 miles in one hour; **the earnings per share** = dividend received for each share; **the average sales per**

representative = the average sales achieved by one representative; **per head** = for each person; *allow £15 per head for expenses*; *representatives cost on average £50,000 per head per annum* **(c)** out of; *the rate of imperfect items is about twenty-five per thousand*; *the birth rate has fallen to twelve per hundred*

a 100,000 square-foot warehouse generates $600 in sales per square foot of space
Duns Business Month

per annum ['pər 'ænəm] *adverb* in a year; *what is their turnover per annum?*

per capita ['pə 'kæpɪtə] *adjective & adverb* for each person; **average income per capita** *or* **per capita income** = average income of one person; **per capita expenditure** = total money spent divided by the number of people involved

per cent ['pə 'sent] *adjective & adverb* out of each hundred or for each hundred; **10 per cent** = ten in every hundred; *what is the increase per cent?*; *fifty per cent of nothing is still nothing*

this would represent an 18 per cent growth rate - a slight slackening of the 25 per cent turnover rise in the first half
Financial Times

buildings are depreciated at two per cent per annum on the estimated cost of construction
Hongkong Standard

percentage [pə'sentɪdʒ] *noun* amount shown as part of one hundred; **percentage discount** = discount calculated at an amount per hundred; **percentage increase** = increase calculated on the basis of a rate for one hundred; **percentage point** = one per cent

state-owned banks cut their prime rates a percentage point to 11%
Wall Street Journal

a good percentage of the excess stock was taken up during the last quarter
Australian Financial Review

the Federal Reserve Board, signalling its concern about the weakening American economy, cut the discount rate by one-half percentage point to 6.5%
Wall Street Journal

percentile [pə'sentaɪl] *noun* one of a series of ninety-nine figures below which a certain percentage of the total falls

perfect 1 ['pɜːfɪkt] *adjective* completely correct, with no mistakes; *we check each batch to make sure it is perfect*; *she did a perfect typing test*; *(in economic theory)* **perfect competition** *or* **perfect market** = ideal market, where all products are equal in price and all customers are provided with all information about the products **2** [pə'fekt] *verb* to make something which is completely correct; *he perfected the process for making high grade steel*

perfectly ['pɜːfɪktli] *adverb* correctly, with no mistakes; *she keyboarded the data perfectly*

perform [pə'fɔːm] *verb* to do well or badly; **how did the shares perform?** = did the shares go up or down?; **the company** *or* **the shares performed badly** = the company's share price fell

performance [pə'fɔːməns] *noun* way in which someone or something acts; **the poor performance of the shares on the stock market** = the fall in the share price on the stock market; *last year saw a dip in the company's performance*; **as a measure of the company's performance** = as a way of judging if the company's results are good or bad; **performance of personnel against objectives** = how personnel have worked, measured against the objectives set; **performance fund** = fund invested in shares to provide capital growth, but probably with less dividend income than usual; **performance-related pay** = pay which is linked to good work by the employee; **performance review** = yearly interview between a manager and each worker to discuss how the worker has worked during the year; **earnings performance** = way in which shares earn dividends; **job performance** = doing a job well or badly

inflation-adjusted GNP edged
up at a 1.3% annual rate, its
worst performance since the
economic expansion began

Fortune

period ['pɪərɪəd] *noun* **(a)** length of time;
*for a period of time or for a period of
months or for a six-year period; sales over
a period of three months; sales over the
holiday period; to deposit money for a
fixed period* **(b) accounting period** =
period of time at the end of which the
firm's accounts are made up

periodic *or* **periodical** [pɪərɪ'ɒdɪk or
pɪərɪ'ɒdɪkəl] **1** *adjective* from time to time;
*a periodic review of the company's
performance* **2** *noun* **periodical** =
magazine which comes out regularly

peripherals [pə'rɪfərəlz] *plural noun*
items of hardware (such as terminals,
printers, monitors, etc.) which are attached
to a main computer system

perishable ['perɪʃəbl] **1** *adjective* which
can go bad or become rotten easily;
perishable goods or items or cargo **2** *plural
noun* **perishables** = goods which can go
bad easily

the survey, which covered
7,376 supermarkets run by 119
companies, found that sales
of food at the stores dropped
by 2.9%. That decline, also
the largest on record, was due
to increasing price awareness
among customers and the lower
price of perishables

Nikkei Weekly

perjure ['pɜːdʒə] *verb* **to perjure
yourself** = to tell lies when you have made
an oath to say what is true

perjury ['pɜːdʒəri] *noun* telling lies when
you have made an oath in court to say what
is true; *he was sent to prison for perjury;
she appeared in court on a perjury charge*

perk [pɜːk] *noun* extra item given by a
company to workers in addition to their
salaries (such as company cars, private
health insurance); *she earns a good salary
and in addition has all sorts of perks*

permanency ['pɜːmənənsi] *noun* being
permanent; *there is a lack of permanency
about the company*

permanent ['pɜːmənənt] *adjective*
which will last for a very long time or for
ever; *he has found a permanent job; she is
in permanent employment; the permanent
staff and part-timers*

permanently ['pɜːmənəntli] *adverb* for
ever; *the company is permanently in debt*

permission [pə'mɪʃən] *noun* being
allowed to do something; **written
permission** = document which allows
someone to do something; **verbal
permission** = telling someone that he is
allowed to do something; **to give someone
permission to do something** = to allow
someone to do something; *he asked the
manager's permission to take a day off*

permit 1 ['pɜːmɪt] *noun* official document
which allows someone to do something;
building permit = official document
which allows someone to build on a piece
of land; **export permit** *or* **import permit** =
official document which allows goods to be
exported or imported; **work permit** =
official document which allows someone
who is not a citizen to work in a country **2**
[pə'mɪt] *verb* to allow someone to do
something; *this document permits you to
export twenty-five computer systems; the
ticket permits three people to go into the
exhibition*

**perpetual inventory system
(PIS)** [pɜː'petjuəl 'ɪnventəri 'sɪstəm] *noun*
stock control system by which the stock is
continually counted as it moves into and
out of the warehouse, so avoiding having to
close the warehouse for annual stock
checks

per pro ['pɜː 'prəu] = PER
PROCURATIONEM; *the secretary
signed per pro the manager*

per procurationem ['pɜː
prɒkjuræsɪ'əunəm] *Latin phrase meaning*
'with the authority of'

perquisites ['pɜːkwɪzɪts] *plural noun* =
PERKS

person ['pɜːsn] *noun* **(a)** someone (a man
or a woman); *insurance policy which
covers a named person;* **the persons
named in the contract** = people whose
names are given in the contract; **the
document should be witnessed by a third
person** = someone who is not named in the

document should witness it **(b) in person** = someone himself or herself; **this important package is to be delivered to the chairman in person** = the package has to be given to the chairman himself (and not to his secretary, assistant, etc.); **he came to see me in person** = he himself came to see me

personal ['pɜːsənl] *adjective* **(a)** referring to one person; **personal allowances** = part of a person's income which is not taxed; **personal assets** = moveable assets which belong to a person; **personal call** = (i) telephone call where you ask the operator to connect you with a particular person; (ii) telephone call not related to business; *staff are not allowed to make personal calls during office hours*; **personal computer (PC)** = small computer which can be used at home; **personal effects** *or* **personal property** = things which belong to someone; **personal income** = income received by an individual person before tax is paid; **apart from the family shares, he has a personal shareholding in the company** = he has shares which he owns himself; **the car is for his personal use** = the car is for him to use himself **(b)** private; *the envelope was marked 'Personal'*; *I would like to see the managing director as soon as possible on a personal matter*; **personal assistant (PA)** = secretary who also helps the boss in various ways

Personal Identification Number (PIN) ['pɜːsənl aɪdentɪfɪ'keɪʃn 'nʌmbə] *noun* unique number allocated to the holder of a cash card or credit card, by which he or she can enter an automatic banking system, as, for example, to withdraw cash from a cash machine or to pay for something in a store

Personal Investment Authority (PIA) ['pɜːsənl ɪn'vestmənt ɔː'θɒrəti] self-regulatory body which regulates the activities of financial advisers, insurance brokers, etc., or others who give financial advice or arrange financial services for small clients

personalized ['pɜːsnəlaɪzd] *adjective* with the name or initials of a person printed on it; *he has a personalized briefcase*

personally ['pɜːsnəli] *adverb* in person; *he personally opened the envelope*; *she wrote to me personally*

personnel [pɜːsə'nel] *noun* people who work in a certain place or for a certain company; *the personnel of the warehouse or the warehouse personnel*; **the personnel department** = section of the company which deals with the staff; **personnel management** = organizing and training of staff so that they work well and profitably; **personnel manager** = head of the personnel department (NOTE: now replaced in some cases by **human resources:**; *human resources manager, human resources department*)

person-to-person call ['pɜːsntə'pɜːsn 'kɔːl] *noun* telephone call where you ask the operator to connect you with a named person

persuade [pə'sweɪd] *verb* to talk to someone and get him to do what you want; *after ten hours of discussion, they persuaded the MD to resign*; *we could not persuade the French company to sign the contract*

peseta [pə'seɪtə] *noun* currency used with the euro in Spain (NOTE: usually written **ptas** after a figure: **2,000ptas**)

peso ['peɪsəu] *noun* currency used in Mexico and many other countries such as Argentina, Bolivia, Chile, Colombia, Cuba, Dominican Republic, Philippines, and Uruguay

pessimism ['pesɪmɪzm] *noun* expecting that everything will turn out badly; *there is considerable pessimism about job opportunities*; **market pessimism** *or* **pessimism on the market** = feeling that the stock market prices will fall

pessimistic [pesɪ'mɪstɪk] *adjective* feeling sure that things will work out badly; **he takes a pessimistic view of the exchange rate** = he expects the exchange rate to fall

peter out ['piːtə 'aut] *verb* to come to an end gradually

```
economists believe the
economy is picking up this
quarter and will do better in
the second half of the year,
```

but most expect growth to peter out next year

Sunday Times

Peter principle ['pi:tə 'prɪnsəpl] *noun* law, based on wide experience, that people are promoted until they occupy positions for which they are incompetent

petition [pə'tɪʃən] **1** *noun* official request; **to file a petition in bankruptcy** = to ask officially to be made bankrupt, to ask officially for someone else to be made bankrupt **2** *verb* to make an official request; *he petitioned the government for a special pension*

petrocurrency ['petrəukʌrənsi] *noun* foreign currency which is earned by exporting oil

petrodollar ['petrəudɒlə] *noun* dollar earned by a country from exporting oil, then invested outside that country

petrol ['petrəl] *noun* liquid, made from petroleum, used to drive a car engine; *the car is very economic on petrol*; *we are looking for a car with a low petrol consumption* (NOTE: American English is **gasoline**)

petroleum [pə'trəuljəm] *noun* raw natural oil, found in the ground; **crude petroleum** = raw petroleum which has not been processed; **petroleum exporting countries** = countries which produce petroleum and sell it to others; **petroleum industry** = industry which uses petroleum to make other products (petrol, soap, etc.); **petroleum products** = products (such as petrol, soap, paint) which are made from crude petroleum; **petroleum revenues** = income from selling oil

petty ['peti] *adjective* not important; **petty cash** = small amount of money kept in an office to pay small debts; **petty cash book (PCB)** = book in which petty cash payments are noted; **petty cash box** = locked metal box in an office where the petty cash is kept; **petty cash voucher** = piece of paper on which cash expenditure is noted so that an employee can be reimbursed for what he has spent on company business; **petty expenses** = small sums of money spent

phase [feɪz] *noun* period, part of something which takes place; *the first phase of the expansion programme*

phase in ['feɪz 'ɪn] *verb* to bring something in gradually; *the new invoicing system will be phased in over the next two months*

the budget grants a tax exemption for $500,000 in capital gains, phased in over the next six years

Toronto Star

phase out ['feɪz 'aʊt] *verb* to remove something gradually; *Smith Ltd will be phased out as a supplier of spare parts*

phoenixism ['fi:nɪksɪzm] *noun* situation where phoenix companies can easily be set up

phoenix company ['fi:nɪks 'kʌmpni] *noun* company formed by the directors of a company which has gone into receivership, which trades in the same way as the first company, and in most respects (except its name) seems to be exactly the same as the first company

the prosecution follows recent calls for a reform of insolvency legislation to prevent directors from leaving behind a trail of debt while continuing to trade in phoenix companies - businesses which fold only to rise again, often under a slightly different name in the hands of the same directors and management

Financial Times

phone [fəun] **1** *noun* telephone, a machine used for speaking to someone over a long distance; *we had a new phone system installed last week*; **house phone** *or* **internal phone** = telephone for calling from one room to another in an office or hotel; **by phone** = using the telephone; *to place an order by phone*; **to be on the phone** = to be speaking to someone on the telephone; *she has been on the phone all morning*; *he spoke to the manager on the phone*; **phone book** = book which lists all people and businesses in alphabetical order with their telephone numbers; *look up his* address in the phone book; **phone call** = speaking to someone on the phone; **to make a phone call** = to speak to someone on the telephone; **to answer the phone** *or* **to take a phone call** = to reply to a call on the phone; **phone number** = set of figures for a particular telephone; *he keeps a list of phone numbers in a little black book; the phone number is on the company notepaper; can you give me your phone number?* **2** *verb* to phone someone = to call someone by telephone; *don't phone me, I'll phone you; his secretary phoned to say he would be late; he phoned the order through to the warehouse;* **to phone for something** = to make a phone call to ask for something; *he phoned for a taxi;* **to phone about something** = to make a phone call to speak about something; *he phoned about the January invoice*

phone back ['fəʊn 'bæk] *verb* to reply by phone; *the chairman is in a meeting, can you phone back in about half an hour?; Mr Smith called while you were out and asked if you would phone him back*

phonecard ['fəʊnkɑːd] *noun* special plastic card for use in public telephones

photocopier ['fəʊtəʊkɒpɪə] *noun* machine which makes a copy of a document by photographing and printing it

photocopy ['fəʊtəʊkɒpɪ] **1** *noun* copy of a document made by photographing and printing it; *make six photocopies of the contract* **2** *verb* to make a copy of a document by photographing and printing it; *she photocopied the contract*

photocopying ['fəʊtəʊkɒpiːɪŋ] *noun* making photocopies; *photocopying costs are rising each year;* **photocopying bureau** = office which photocopies documents for companies which do not possess their own photocopiers; **there is a mass of photocopying to be done** = there are many documents waiting to be photocopied

physical ['fɪzɪkl] *adjective* **physical inventory** = counting actual items of stock; **physical stock** = the actual items of stock held in a warehouse; **physical stock check** *or* **physical stocktaking** = counting actual

items of stock (and then checking this figure against stock records)

PIA = PERSONAL INVESTMENT AUTHORITY

pick [pɪk] **1** *noun* thing chosen; **take your pick** = choose what you want; **the pick of the group** = the best item in the group **2** *verb* to choose; *the board picked the finance director to succeed the retiring MD; the Association has picked Paris for its next meeting*

picket ['pɪkɪt] **1** *noun* striking worker who stands at the gate of a factory to try to persuade other workers not to go to work; **flying pickets** = pickets who travel round the country to try to stop workers going to work; **picket line** = line of pickets at the gate of a factory; *to man a picket line or to be on the picket line;* **to cross a picket line** = to go into a factory to work, even though pickets are trying to prevent workers from going in **2** *verb* **to picket a factory** = to put pickets at the gate of a factory to try to prevent other workers from going to work

picketing ['pɪkɪtɪŋ] *noun* act of standing at the gates of a factory to prevent workers going to work; **lawful picketing** = picketing which is allowed by law; **mass picketing** = picketing by large numbers of pickets who try to frighten workers who want to work; **peaceful picketing** = picketing which does not involve fighting; **secondary picketing** = picketing of another factory, not directly connected with the strike, to prevent it supplying a striking factory or receiving supplies from it

picking ['pɪkɪŋ] *noun* **order picking** = collecting various items in a warehouse to make up an order to be sent to a customer; **picking list** = list of items in an order, listed according to where they can be found in the warehouse

pick out ['pɪk 'aʊt] *verb* to choose (something or someone) out of a lot; *he was picked out for promotion by the chairman*

pick up ['pɪk 'ʌp] *verb* **(a)** to get better or to improve; *business or trade is picking up* **(b)** to fetch something or someone in a vehicle; *the company sent a driver to pick him up at the airport; we sent a courier to* *pick up the packet and deliver it to the designer*

pickup ['pɪkʌp] *noun* **pickup (truck)** = type of small van for transporting goods; **pickup and delivery service** = (i) service which takes goods from the warehouse and delivers them to the customer; (ii) service which takes something away for cleaning or servicing and returns it to the owner when finished

piece [piːs] *noun* small part of something; *to sell something by the piece*; *the price is 25p the piece*; **mailing piece** = leaflet suitable for sending by direct mail

piece rate ['piːs 'reɪt] *noun* rate of pay for a product produced or for a piece of work done and not paid for at an hourly rate; *to earn piece rates*

piecework ['piːswɜːk] *noun* work for which workers are paid for the products produced or the piece of work done and not at an hourly rate

pie chart ['paɪ 'tʃɑːt] *noun* diagram where information is shown as a circle cut up into sections of different sizes

pigeonhole ['pɪdʒɪnhəʊl] **1** *noun* one of a series of small spaces for filing documents or for putting letters for delivery to separate offices; *I looked in my pigeonhole but there were no letters for me* **2** *verb* to file a plan or document as the best way of forgetting about it; *the whole expansion plan was pigeonholed*

pile [paɪl] **1** *noun* lot of things put one on top of the other; *the Managing Director's desk is covered with piles of paper; she put the letter on the pile of letters waiting to be signed* **2** *verb* to put things on top of one another; *he piled the papers on his desk*

pile up ['paɪl 'ʌp] *verb* to put or get into a pile; *the invoices were piled up on the table; complaints are piling up about the after-sales service*

pilferage *or* **pilfering** ['pɪlfərɪdʒ or 'pɪlfərɪŋ] *noun* stealing small amounts of money or small items from an office or shop

pilot ['paɪlət] **1** *noun* **(a)** person who flies a plane or guides a ship into port; **pilot's case** = strong square leather case for carrying documents, used by salesmen to carry samples, order forms, etc. **(b)** used as a test, which if successful will then be expanded into a full operation; *the company set up a pilot project to see if the proposed manufacturing system was efficient; the pilot factory has been built to test the new production processes; he is directing a pilot scheme for training unemployed young people* **2** *verb* **(a)** to guide a ship into port **(b)** to test a project on a small number of people, to see if it will work in practice

PIN (number) ['pɪn 'nʌmbə] = PERSONAL IDENTIFICATION NUMBER

pin [pɪn] **1** *noun* sharp piece of metal for attaching papers together, etc.; **drawing pin** = pin with a flat head for attaching a sheet of paper to something hard; *she used drawing pins to pin the poster to the door* **2** *verb* to attach with a pin; *she pinned the papers together; pin your cheque to the application form*

pin money ['pɪn 'mʌni] *noun* small amount of money earned, used for personal expenditure; *she does some typing at home to earn some pin money*

pint [paɪnt] *noun* measure of liquids (= 0.568 of a litre)

pin up ['pɪn 'ʌp] *verb* to attach something with pins to a wall; *they pinned the posters up at the back of the exhibition stand*

pioneer [paɪə'nɪə] **1** *noun* first to do a type of work; **pioneer project** *or* **pioneer development** = project or development which is new and has never been tried before **2** *verb* to be the first to do something; *the company pioneered developments in the field of electronics*

piracy ['paɪərəsi] *noun* copying of patented inventions or copyright works

pirate ['paɪərət] **1** *noun* person who copies a patented invention or a copyright work and sells it; *a pirate copy of a book* **2** *verb* to copy a copyright work; *a pirated book* *or* *a pirated design; the designs for the new dress collection were pirated in the Far East*

pit [pɪt] *noun* **(a)** coal mine **(b)** *US* part of a stock exchange or of a commodities exchange where dealers trade (NOTE: also called the **trading floor**)

pitch [pɪtʃ] *noun* **sales pitch** = talk by a salesman to persuade someone to buy

pix [pɪks] *plural noun (informal)* pictures (used in advertising or design)

place [pleɪs] **1** *noun* **(a)** where something is or where something happens; **to take place** = to happen; *the meeting will take place in our offices*; **meeting place** = room or area where people can meet; **place of work** = office, factory, etc., where people work **(b)** position (in a competition); *three companies are fighting for first place in the home computer market* **(c)** job; *he was offered a place with an insurance company*; *she turned down three places before accepting the one we offered* **(d)** position in a text; *she marked her place in the text with a red pen*; *I have lost my place and cannot remember where I have reached in my filing* **2** *verb* **(a)** to put; **to place money in an account** = to deposit money; **to place a block of shares** = to find a buyer for a block of shares; **to place a contract** = to decide that a certain company shall have the contract to do work; **to place something on file** = to file something **(b) to place an order** = to order something; *he placed an order for 250 cartons of paper* **(c) to place staff** = to find jobs for staff; **how are you placed for work?** = have you enough work to do?

placement ['pleɪsmənt] *noun* finding work for someone; *the bureau specializes in the placement of former executives*

placing ['pleɪsɪŋ] *noun* finding a single buyer or a group of institutional buyers for a large number of shares in a new company or a company that is going public; **the placing of a line of shares** = finding a purchaser for a block of shares which was overhanging the market

plain [pleɪn] *adjective* **(a)** easy to understand; *we made it plain to the union that 5% was the management's final offer*; **the manager is a very plain-spoken man** = the manager says exactly what he thinks **(b)** simple; *the design of the package is in plain blue and white squares*; *we want the cheaper models to have a plain design* **(c) plain paper** = ordinary white paper; **plain**

paper copier = copier which uses ordinary white paper, not special copier paper; **plain paper fax** = fax machine which uses ordinary white paper and not special fax rolls

plain cover ['pleɪn 'kʌvə] *noun* **to send something under plain cover** = to send something in an ordinary envelope with no company name printed on it

plaintiff ['pleɪntɪf] *noun* person who starts an action against someone in the civil courts (NOTE: since April 1999, this term has been replaced by **claimant**)

plan [plæn] **1** *noun* **(a)** organized way of doing something; **contingency plan** = plan which will be put into action if something happens which no one expects to happen; **the government's economic plans** = the government's proposals for running the country's economy; **a Five-Year Plan** = proposals for running a country's economy over a five-year period **(b)** way of saving or investing money; *investment plan*; *pension plan*; *savings plan* **(c)** drawing which shows how something is arranged or how something will be built; *the designers showed us the first plans for the new offices*; **floor plan** = drawing of a floor in a building, showing where different departments are; **street plan** *or* **town plan** = map of a town showing streets and buildings **2** *verb* to organize carefully how something should be done; **to plan for an increase in bank interest charges** = to change a way of doing things because you think there will be an increase in bank interest charges; **to plan investments** = to propose how investments should be made (NOTE: **planning - planned**)

```
the benefits package is
attractive and the
compensation plan includes
base, incentive and car
allowance totalling $50,000+
```
Globe and Mail (Toronto)

plane [pleɪn] *noun* aircraft, a machine which flies in the air, carrying passengers or cargo; *I plan to take the 5 o'clock plane to New York*; *he could not get a seat on Tuesday's plane, so he had to wait until Wednesday*; *there are ten planes a day from London to Paris*

planned [plænd] *adjective* **planned economy** = system where the government plans all business activity

planner ['plænə] *noun* **(a)** person who plans; **the government's economic planners** = people who plan the future economy of the country for the government **(b) desk planner** *or* **wall planner** = book or chart which shows days, weeks and months so that the work of an office can be shown by diagrams

planning ['plænɪŋ] *noun* **(a)** organizing how something should be done, especially how a company should be run to make increased profits; *long-term planning or short-term planning*; **economic planning** = planning the future financial state of the country for the government; **corporate planning** = planning the future financial state of a company or group of companies; **manpower planning** = planning to get the right number of workers in each job **(b)** *GB* **planning permission** = official document allowing a person or company to plan new buildings on empty land; *to be refused planning permission*; *we are waiting for planning permission before we can start building*; *the land is to be sold with planning permission*; **the planning department** = section of a local government office which deals with requests for planning permission

---

buildings   are   closely
regulated   by   planning
restrictions

Investors Chronicle

---

plant [plɑːnt] *noun* **(a)** machinery; **plant-hire firm** = company which lends large machines (such as cranes and tractors) to building companies (NOTE: no plural in this meaning) **(b)** large factory; *they are planning to build a car plant near the river*; *to set up a new plant*; *they closed down six plants in the north of the country*; *he was appointed plant manager*

plastic money ['plæstɪk 'mʌni] *noun* credit cards and charge cards; **do you take plastic?** = can I pay by credit card?

platform ['plætfɔːm] *noun* high pavement in a station, so that passengers can get on or off trains; *the train for Birmingham leaves from Platform 12*; *the ticket office is on Platform 2*

PLC *or* **Plc** ['piːelˈsiː] = PUBLIC LIMITED COMPANY

plead [pliːd] *verb* **(a)** to speak on behalf of a client in court **(b)** to answer a charge in a criminal court; **to plead guilty** = to say at the beginning of a trial that you did commit the crime of which you are accused; **to plead not guilty** = to say at the beginning of a trial that you did not commit the crime of which you are accused

pledge [pledʒ] **1** *noun* object given to a pawnbroker as security for money borrowed; **to redeem a pledge** = to pay back a loan and interest and so get back the security; **unredeemed pledge** = pledge which the borrower has not claimed back by paying back his loan **2** *verb* **to pledge share certificates** = to deposit share certificates with the lender as security for money borrowed

plenary meeting *or* **plenary session** ['pliːnəri 'miːtɪŋ *or* 'pliːnəri 'seʃn] *noun* meeting at a conference when all the delegates meet together

Plimsoll Line ['plɪmsəl 'laɪn] *noun* line painted on the side of a ship to show where the water should reach for maximum safety if the ship is fully loaded (NOTE: also called a **load line**)

plough back *US* **plow back** ['plaʊ 'bæk] *verb* **to plough back profits into the company** = to invest the profits in the business (and not pay them out as dividends to the shareholders) by using them to buy new equipment or to create new products

plug [plʌg] **1** *noun* **(a)** device at the end of a wire for connecting a machine to the electricity supply; *the printer is supplied with a plug* **(b) to give a plug to a new product** = to publicize a new product **2** *verb* **(a) to plug in** = to attach a machine to the electricity supply; *the fax machine was not plugged in* **(b)** to publicize or to advertise; *they ran six commercials plugging holidays in Spain* **(c)** to block or to stop; *the company is trying to plug the drain on cash reserves* (NOTE: **plugging - plugged**)

plummet *or* **plunge** ['plʌmɪt or plʌndʒ] *verb* to fall sharply; *share prices plummeted or plunged on the news of the devaluation*

> in the first six months of this year secondhand values of tankers have plummeted by 40%
>
> *Lloyd's List*

> crude oil output plunged during the past month
>
> *Wall Street Journal*

plus [plʌs] **1** *preposition* **(a)** added to; *his salary plus commission comes to more than £45,000*; *production costs plus overheads are higher than revenue* **(b)** more than; **houses valued at £100,000 plus** = houses valued at over £100,000 **2** *adjective* favourable, good and profitable; *a plus factor for the company is that the market is much larger than they had originally thought*; **the plus side of the account** = the credit side of the account; **on the plus side** = this is a favourable point; *on the plus side, we must take into account the new product line* **3** *noun* a good or favourable point; *to have achieved £1m in new sales in less than six months is certainly a plus for the sales team* (NOTE: the opposite is **minus**)

p.m. *US* **P.M.** ['piː'em] *adverb* in the afternoon or in the evening, after 12 o'clock midday; *the train leaves at 6.50 p.m.*; *if you phone New York after 6 p.m. the calls are at a cheaper rate*

PO ['piː'əu] = POST OFFICE

pocket ['pɒkɪt] *noun* **(a)** **pocket calculator** *or* **pocket diary** = calculator or diary which can be carried in the pocket; **to be £25 in pocket** = to have made a profit of £25; **to be £25 out of pocket** = to have lost £25; **out-of-pocket expenses** = amount of money paid back to an employee for his own money which he has spent on company business **(b)** **pocket envelope** = type of envelope with the flap at the end, on the shorter side (an envelope with a flap along the longer side, is called a 'wallet envelope')

point [pɔɪnt] **1** *noun* **(a)** place or position; **point of sale (POS)** = place where a product is sold (such as a shop); **point of**

sale material = display material (such as posters, dump bins) to advertise a product where it is being sold; **breakeven point** = position at which sales cover costs but do not show a profit; **customs entry point** = place at a border between two countries where goods are declared to customs; **starting point** = place where something starts; **tax point** = date on which goods or services are supplied, which is the date when VAT becomes due **(b)** **decimal point** = dot which indicates the division between a whole unit and its smaller parts (such as 4.25); **percentage point** = 1 per cent; **half a percentage point** = 0.5 per cent; **the dollar gained two points** = the dollar increased in value against another currency by two hundredths of a cent; **the exchange fell ten points** = the stock market index fell by ten units **2** *verb* **to point out** = to show; *the report points out the mistakes made by the company over the last year*; *he pointed out that the results were better than in previous years*

> sterling M3, the most closely watched measure, rose by 13% in the year to August – seven percentage points faster than the rate of inflation
>
> *Economist*

> banks refrained from quoting forward US/Hongkong dollar exchange rates as premiums of 100 points replaced discounts of up to 50 points
>
> *South China Morning Post*

poison pill ['pɔɪzn 'pɪl] *noun* action taken by a company to make itself less attractive to a potential takeover bid

> COMMENT: in some cases, the officers of a company will vote themselves extremely high redundancy payments if a takeover is successful; or a company will borrow large amounts of money and give it away to the shareholders as dividends, so that the company has an unacceptably high level of borrowing

policy ['pɒlɪsi] *noun* **(a)** decisions on the general way of doing something; *the association attacked the government policy on wages or the government's wages policy*; *the government's prices policy or* incomes policy has been often mentioned in the press; *the country's economic policy seems to lack any direction*; **the government made a policy statement** *or* **made a statement of policy** = the government declared in public what its plans were; **budgetary policy** = policy of expected income and expenditure **(b) company policy** = the company's agreed plan of action, the company's way of doing things; *what is the company policy on credit?*; *it is against company policy to give more than thirty days' credit*; *our policy is to submit all contracts to the legal department* **(c) insurance policy** = document which shows the conditions of an insurance contract; **an accident policy** = an insurance contract against accidents; **all-risks policy** = insurance policy which covers risks of any kind, with no exclusions; **a comprehensive** *or* **an all-in policy** = an insurance which covers all risks; **contingent policy** = policy which pays out only if something happens (as if the person named in the policy dies before the person due to benefit); **endowment policy** = policy where a sum of money is paid to the insured person on a certain date, or to his estate if he dies earlier; **policy holder** = person who is insured by an insurance company; **to take out a policy** = to sign the contract for an insurance and start paying the premiums; *she took out a life insurance policy or a house insurance policy*; **the insurance company made out a policy** *or* **drew up a policy** = the company wrote the details of the contract on the policy

polite [pə'laɪt] *adjective* behaving in a pleasant way; *we insist on our salesgirls being polite to customers*; *we had a polite letter from the MD*

politely [pə'laɪtli] *adverb* in a pleasant way; *she politely answered the customers' questions*

political [pə'lɪtɪkəl] *adjective* referring to a certain idea of how a country should be run; **political levy** = part of the subscription of a member of a trade union which the union pays to support a political party; **political party** = group of people who believe a country should be run in a certain way

poll [pəul] **1** *noun* **opinion poll** = asking a sample group of people, taken at random, what they feel about something, so as to guess the opinion of the whole population; *opinion polls showed the public preferred butter to margarine*; *before starting the service the company carried out nationwide opinion polls* **2** *verb* **to poll a sample of the population** = to ask a sample group of people what they feel about something; **to poll the members of the club on an issue** = to ask the members for their opinion on an issue

pollster ['pəulstə] *noun* expert in understanding what polls mean

polystyrene [pɒlɪ'staɪriːn] *noun* **expanded polystyrene** = light solid plastic used for packing; *the computer is delivered packed in expanded polystyrene*

polythene ['pɒlɪθiːn] *noun* type of strong transparent plastic used in thin sheets; *the boxes are wrapped in polythene sheeting*; *we sell sweets in polythene bags*

pool [puːl] **1** *noun* **(a) typing pool** = group of typists, working together in a company, offering a secretarial service to several departments **(b)** unused supply; *a pool of unemployed labour or of expertise* **2** *verb* **to pool resources** = to put all resources together so as to be more powerful or profitable

poor [pɔː] *adjective* **(a)** without much money; *the company tries to help the poorest members of staff with soft loans*; *it is one of the poorest countries in the world* **(b)** not very good; *poor quality*; *poor service*; *poor turnround time of orders or poor order turnround time*

poorly ['pɔːli] *adverb* badly; *the offices are poorly laid out*; *the plan was poorly presented*; **poorly-paid staff** = staff with low wages

popular ['pɒpjulə] *adjective* liked by many people; *this is our most popular model*; *the South Coast is the most popular area for holidays*; **popular prices** = prices which are low and therefore liked

population [pɒpju'leɪʃən] *noun* number of people who live in a country or in a town; *Paris has a population of over three million*; *the working population is larger than ever before*; *population statistics* *show a rise in the 18-25 age group*; *population trends have to be taken into account when drawing up economic plans*; **floating population** = people who move from place to place

port ['pɔːt] *noun* **(a)** harbour, a place where ships come to load or unload; *the port of Rotterdam*; **inland port** = port on a river or canal; **to call at a port** = to stop at a port to load or unload cargo; **port authority** = organization which runs a port; **port of call** = port at which a ship often stops; **port charges** *or* **port dues** = payment which a ship makes to the port authority for the right to use the port; **port of embarkation** = port at which you get on a ship; **port installations** = buildings and equipment of a port; **commercial port** = port which has only goods traffic; **fishing port** = port which is used mainly by fishing boats; **free port** = port where there are no customs duties to be paid **(b)** part of a computer to which a lead can be attached; *attach the printer to the printer port*

portable ['pɔːtəbl] **1** *adjective* which can be carried; *a portable computer* *or* *a portable typewriter*; **portable pension** = pension rights which a worker can take with him from one company to another as he changes jobs **2** *noun* **a portable** = a computer or typewriter which can be carried; *he keys all his orders on his portable and then emails them to the office*

portfolio [pɔːt'fəʊljəʊ] *noun* **a portfolio of shares** = all the shares owned by someone; **portfolio management** = buying and selling shares to make profits for a person

portion ['pɔːʃən] *noun* small quantity, especially enough food for one person; *we serve ice cream in individual portions*

POS *or* **p.o.s.** ['piːəʊ'es] = POINT OF SALE

position [pə'zɪʃən] *noun* **(a)** situation or state of affairs; **what is the cash position?** = what is the state of the company's current account?; **bargaining position** = statement of position by one group during negotiations; **to cover a position** = to have enough money to pay for a forward purchase **(b)** job, paid work in a company;

to apply for a position as manager; *we have several positions vacant*; *all the vacant positions have been filled*; *she retired from her position in the accounts department*; **he is in a key position** = he has an important job

positive ['pɒzətɪv] *adjective* meaning 'yes'; *the board gave a positive reply*; **positive cash flow** = situation where more money is coming in than is being spent (NOTE: the opposite is **negative**)

> as the group's shares are already widely held, the listing will be via an introduction. It will also be accompanied by a deeply-discounted £25m rights issue, leaving the company cash positive
>
> *Sunday Times*

possess [pə'zes] *verb* to own; *the company possesses property in the centre of the town*; *he lost all he possessed in the collapse of his company*; *compare* REPOSSESS

possession [pə'zeʃən] *noun* **(a)** owning something; **the documents are in his possession** = he is holding the documents; **vacant possession** = being able to occupy a property immediately after buying it because it is empty; *the property is to be sold with vacant possession* **(b)** **possessions** = property, things owned; *they lost all their possessions in the fire*; *compare* REPOSSESSION

possibility [pɒsə'bɪləti] *noun* being likely to happen; *there is a possibility that the plane will be early*; *there is no possibility of the chairman retiring before next Christmas*

possible ['pɒsəbl] *adjective* which might happen; *the 25th and 26th are possible dates for our next meeting*; *it is possible that production will be held up by industrial action*; *there are two possible candidates for the job* = two candidates are good enough to be appointed

post [pəʊst] **1** *noun* **(a)** system of sending letters and parcels from one place to another; *to send an invoice by post*; *he put the letter in the post*; *the cheque was lost in the post*; *to send a reply by return of*

post = to reply to a letter immediately; **letter post** *or* **parcel post** = service for sending letters or parcels; **post room** = room in an office where the post is sorted and sent to each department or collected from each department for sending **(b)** letters sent or received; *has the post arrived yet?*; *my secretary opens the post as soon as it arrives*; *the receipt was in this morning's post*; *the letter did not arrive by first post this morning* (NOTE: American English only uses **mail** where British English uses both **mail** and **post**) **(c)** job, paid work in a company; *to apply for a post as cashier*; *we have three posts vacant*; *all our posts have been filled*; *we advertised three posts in the 'Times'* **2** *verb* **(a)** to send something by post; *to post a letter or to post a parcel* **(b)** **to post an entry** = to transfer an entry to an account; **to post up a ledger** = to keep a ledger up to date **(c) to post up a notice** = to put a notice on a wall or on a noticeboard **(d) to post an increase** = to let people know that an increase has taken place

> Toronto stocks closed at an all-time high, posting their fifth day of advances in heavy trading
>
> *Financial Times*

post- [pəʊst] *prefix* later; **post-balance sheet event** = something which happens after the date when the balance sheet is drawn up, and before the time when the balance sheet is officially approved by the directors, which affects a company's financial position

postage ['pəʊstɪdʒ] *noun* payment for sending a letter or parcel by post; *what is the postage for this airmail packet to China?*; **postage paid** = words printed on an envelope to show that the sender has paid the postage even though there is no stamp on it; **postage stamp** = small piece of paper attached to a letter or parcel to show that you have paid for it to be sent through the post (NOTE: usually called simply **a stamp**)

postal ['pəʊstəl] *adjective* referring to the post; **postal charges** *or* **postal rates** = money to be paid for sending letters or parcels by post; *postal charges are going up by 10% in September*; **postal order** =

document bought at a post office, as a method of paying small amounts of money by post

postcard ['pəʊskɑːd] *noun* piece of cardboard for sending a message by post (often with a picture on one side)

postcode ['pəʊskəʊd] *noun* letters and numbers used to indicate a town or street in an address on an envelope (NOTE: American English is **ZIP code**)

postdate [pəʊs'deɪt] *verb* to put a later date on a document; *he sent us a postdated cheque*; *his cheque was postdated to June*

poster ['pəʊstə] *noun* large notice or advertisement to be stuck up on a wall

poste restante ['pəʊst 'restɒnt] *noun* system where letters can be addressed to someone at a post office, where they can be collected; *send any messages to 'Poste Restante, Athens'* (NOTE: American English for this is **General Delivery**)

post free ['pəʊst 'friː] *adverb* without having to pay any postage; *the game is obtainable post free from the manufacturer*

Post-it® Notes ['pəʊstɪt 'nəʊts] *noun* trademark for small pieces of paper, partially sticky on one side, sold in pads (you write on a note and then stick it onto a document, a telephone, a computer monitor, etc.); *she left me a Post-it Note with the telephone number on my computer keyboard*

postmark ['pəʊsmɑːk] **1** *noun* mark stamped by the Post Office on a letter, covering the postage stamp, to show that the Post Office has accepted it; *letter with a London postmark* **2** *verb* to stamp a letter with a postmark; *the letter was postmarked New York*

post office ['pəʊst 'ɒfɪs] *noun* **(a)** (i) building where the postal services are based; (ii) shop where you can buy stamps, send parcels, etc.; *main post office*; **sub-post office** = small post office, usually part of a general store **(b) the Post Office** = national organization which deals with sending letters and parcels; *Post Office officials or officials of the Post Office*; *the Post Office van was collecting mail from the box*; **Post Office box number** *or* **PO**

box number = reference number given for delivering mail to a post office, so as not to give the actual address of the person who will receive it

travellers cheques cost 1% of their face value and can be purchased from any bank, main post offices, travel agents and several building societies

Sunday Times

postpaid [pəʊsˈpeɪd] *adjective* with the postage already paid; *the price is £5.95 postpaid*

postpone [pəʊsˈpəʊn] *verb* to arrange for something to take place later than planned; *he postponed the meeting to tomorrow*; *they asked if they could postpone payment until the cash situation was better*

postponement [pəʊsˈpəʊnmənt] *noun* arranging for something to take place later than planned; *I had to change my appointments because of the postponement of the board meeting*

post scriptum *or* **postscript (P.S.)** [ˈpəʊs ˈskrɪptəm or ˈpəʊskrɪpt] *Latin phrase meaning* 'after what has been written': an additional note at the end of a letter

potential [pəˈtenʃəl] **1** *adjective* possible; **potential customers** = people who could be customers; **potential market** = market which could be exploited; **the product has potential sales of 100,000 units** = the product will possibly sell 100,000 units; **he is a potential managing director** = he is the sort of man who could become managing director **2** *noun* possibility of becoming something; **share with a growth potential** *or* **with a potential for growth** = share which is likely to increase in value; **product with considerable sales potential** = product which is likely to have very large sales; **to analyze the market potential** = to examine the market to see how large it possibly is; **earning potential** = amount of money which someone should be able to earn, amount of dividend which a share is capable of earning

career prospects are excellent for someone with growth potential

Australian Financial Review

for sale: established general cleaning business; has potential to be increased to over 1 million dollar turnover

Australian Financial Review

pound [paʊnd] *noun* **(a)** measure of weight (= 0.45 kilos); *to sell oranges by the pound*; *a pound of oranges*; *oranges cost 50p a pound* (NOTE: usually written **lb** after a figure: **25lb**. Note also that the pound is now no longer officially used in the UK) **(b)** currency used in the UK and many other countries including Cyprus, Egypt, Ireland, Lebanon, Malta, Sudan and Syria **(c)** in particular, the currency of the UK; **pound sterling** = official term for the British currency; *a one pound coin*; *a ten pound note*; *it costs six pounds*; *the pound/dollar exchange rate* (NOTE: usually written **£** before a figure: **£25**)

poundage [ˈpaʊndɪdʒ] *noun* (i) rate charged per pound in weight; (ii) tax charged per pound in value

poverty [ˈpɒvəti] *noun* being poor; *he lost all his money and died in poverty*; **poverty trap** = situation where a poor person lives on government benefits and cannot afford to earn more money because he or she would then lose the benefits and be worse off

power [ˈpaʊə] *noun* **(a)** strength or ability; **purchasing power** = quantity of goods which can be bought by a group of people or with a sum of money; *the purchasing power of the school market*; *the purchasing power of the pound has fallen over the last five years*; **the power of a consumer group** = ability of a group to influence the government or manufacturers; **bargaining power** = strength of one person or group when discussing prices or wages; **borrowing power** = amount of money which a company can borrow; **earning power** = amount of money someone should be able to earn; *he is such a fine designer that his earning power is very large* **(b)** force; legal right; **executive power** = right to act as director or to put decisions into action; **power of attorney** = legal document which gives someone the right to act on someone's behalf in legal matters; **the full power of the law** = the full force of the law when applied; *we will apply the full power of the law to get possession of our property again*

p.p. ['pi:'pi:] *verb* = PER PROCURATIONEM; **to p.p. a letter** = to sign a letter on behalf of someone; *the secretary p.p.'d the letter while the manager was at lunch*

PR ['pi:'ɑ:] = PUBLIC RELATIONS; *a PR firm is handling all our publicity; he is working in PR; the PR people gave away 100,000 balloons*

practice ['præktɪs] *noun* **(a)** way of doing things; *his practice was to arrive at work at 7.30 and start counting the cash*; **business practices** *or* **industrial practices** *or* **trade practices** = ways of managing or working in business, industry or trade; **to depart from normal practice** = to act in a different way from the normal way of doing things; **restrictive practices** = ways of working which make people less free (such as stopping, by trade unions, of workers from doing certain jobs or not allowing customers a free choice of product); **sharp practice** = way of doing business which is not honest, but is not illegal; **code of practice** = rules drawn up by an association which the members must follow when doing business **(b) in practice** = when actually done; *the marketing plan seems very interesting, but what will it cost in practice?*

> the EC demanded international arbitration over the pricing practices of the provincial boards
>
> *Globe and Mail (Toronto)*

pre- [pri] *prefix* before; *a pre-stocktaking sale; there will be a pre-AGM board meeting or there will be a board meeting pre the AGM; the pre-Christmas period is always very busy*

precautionary [prɪ'kɔ:ʃnəri] *adjective* **as a precautionary measure** = in case something takes place

precautions [prɪ'kɔ:ʃənz] *plural noun* care taken to avoid something unpleasant; *to take precautions to prevent thefts in the office; the company did not take proper fire precautions*; **safety precautions** = actions to try to make sure that something is safe

precinct ['pri:sɪŋkt] *noun* **(a) pedestrian precinct** *or* **shopping precinct** = part of a town which is closed to traffic so that people can walk about and shop **(b)** *US* administrative district in a town

predatory ['predətəri] *adjective* which tries to destroy; **predatory pricing policy** = policy of reducing prices as low as possible to try to get market share from weaker competitors

predecessor ['pri:dɪsesə] *noun* person who had a job or position before someone else; *he took over from his predecessor last May; she is using the same office as her predecessor*

predict [prɪ'dɪkt] *verb* to say that something will certainly happen

pre-empt [prɪ'empt] *verb* to get an advantage by doing something quickly before anyone else; *they staged a management buyout to pre-empt a takeover bid*

pre-emptive [prɪ'emptɪv] *adjective* which has an advantage by acting early; **pre-emptive strike against a takeover bid** = rapid action taken to prevent a takeover bid; **a pre-emptive right** = (i) right of a government or of a local authority to buy a property before anyone else; (ii) *US* right of a shareholder to be first to buy a new stock issue

prefer [prɪ'fɜ:] *verb* to like something better than another thing; *we prefer the small corner shop to the large supermarket; most customers prefer to choose clothes themselves, rather than take the advice of the sales assistant*

preference ['prefrəns] *noun* thing which is preferred; *the customers' preference for small corner shops*; **preference shares** = shares (often with no voting rights) which receive their dividend before all other shares and which are repaid first (at face value) if the company is liquidated; **preference shareholders** = owners of preference shares; **cumulative preference share** = preference share where the dividend will be paid at a later date even if the company cannot pay a dividend in the current year

COMMENT: preference shares, because they have less risk than ordinary shares, normally carry no voting rights

preferential [prefə'renʃəl] *adjective* showing that something is preferred more than another; **preferential creditor** = creditor who must be paid first if a company is in liquidation; **preferential duty** *or* **preferential tariff** = special low rate of tax; **preferential terms** *or* **preferential treatment** = terms or way of dealing which is better than usual; *subsidiary companies get preferential treatment when it comes to subcontracting work*

preferred [prɪ'fɜːd] *adjective* **preferred creditor** = creditor who must be paid first if a company is in liquidation; **preferred shares** *US* **preferred stock** = shares which receive their dividend before all other shares, and which are repaid first (at face value) if the company is in liquidation; *US* **cumulative preferred stock** = preference share where the dividend will be paid at a later date even if the company cannot pay a dividend in the current year

pre-financing ['priːfaɪ'nænsɪŋ] *noun* financing in advance

prejudice ['predʒudɪs] **1** *noun* harm done to someone; **without prejudice** = without harming any interests (phrase spoken or written in letters when trying to negotiate a settlement, meaning that the negotiations cannot be referred to in court or relied upon by the other party if the discussions fail); **to act to the prejudice of a claim** = to do something which may harm a claim **2** *verb* to harm; *to prejudice someone's claim*

preliminary [prɪ'lɪmɪnəri] *adjective* early, happening before anything else; **preliminary discussion** *or* **a preliminary meeting** = discussion or meeting which takes place before the main discussion or meeting starts

preliminary indications of the level of business investment and activity during the March quarter will be available this week
Australian Financial Review

premises ['premɪsɪz] *plural noun* building and the land it stands on; **business premises** *or* **commercial premises** = building used for commercial use; **office premises** *or* **shop premises** = building which houses an office or shop; **lock-up premises** = shop which is locked up at night when the owner goes home; **licensed premises** = shop, restaurant or public house which is licensed to sell alcohol; **on the premises** = in the building; *there is a doctor on the premises at all times*

premium ['priːmjəm] *noun* **(a)** payment to encourage someone; **premium offer** = free gift offered to attract more customers **(b)** **insurance premium** = annual payment made by a person or a company to an insurance company; **additional premium** = payment made to cover extra items in an existing insurance; *you pay either an annual premium of £360 or twelve monthly premiums of £32* **(c)** amount to be paid to a landlord or a tenant for the right to take over a lease; *flat to let with a premium of £10,000; annual rent: £8,500, premium: £25,000* **(d)** extra charge; **exchange premium** = extra cost above the normal rate for buying foreign currency; *the dollar is at a premium*; **shares sold at a premium** = shares whose price is higher than their face value; *new shares whose market price is higher than their issue price* (NOTE: the opposite is **shares at a discount**) **(e)** *GB* **premium bonds** = government bonds, part of the national savings scheme, which pay no interest, but give the owner the chance to win a monthly prize **(f)** **premium quality** = top quality

greenmail, the practice of buying back stock at a premium from an acquirer who threatens a takeover
Duns Business Month

responsibilities include the production of premium quality business reports
Times

prepack *or* **prepackage** [priː'pæk or priː'pækɪdʒ] *verb* to pack something before putting it on sale; *the fruit are prepacked or prepackaged in plastic trays*; *the watches are prepacked in attractive display boxes*

prepaid [priː'peɪd] *adjective* paid in advance; **carriage prepaid** = note showing that the transport costs have been paid in advance; *the carriage charges are prepaid*; **prepaid reply card** = stamped addressed card which is sent to someone so that he can reply without paying the postage

prepay [priː'peɪ] *verb* to pay in advance (NOTE: **prepaying - prepaid**)

prepayment [priː'peɪmənt] *noun* payment in advance; **to ask for prepayment of a fee** = to ask for the fee to be paid before the work is done

present 1 ['preznt] *noun* thing which is given; *these calculators make good presents*; *the office gave her a present when she got married* **2** ['preznt] *adjective* **(a)** happening now; *the shares are too expensive at their present price*; *what is the present address of the company?* **(b)** being there when something happens; *only six directors were present at the board meeting* **3** [prɪ'zent] *verb* **(a)** to give someone something; *he was presented with a watch on completing twenty-five years' service with the company* **(b)** to bring or send and show a document; **to present a bill for acceptance** = to send a bill for payment by the person who has accepted it; **to present a bill for payment** = to send a bill to be paid

presentation [prezən'teɪʃən] *noun* **(a)** showing a document; **cheque payable on presentation** = cheque which will be paid when it is presented; **free admission on presentation of this card** = you do not pay to go in if you show this card **(b)** demonstration or exhibition of a proposed plan; *the manufacturer made a presentation of his new product line to possible customers*; *the distribution company made a presentation of the services they could offer*; *we have asked two PR firms to make presentations of proposed publicity campaigns*

present value (PV) ['preznt 'væljuː] *noun* **(a)** the value something has now; *in 1984 the pound was worth five times its present value* **(b)** (i) the value now of a specified sum of money to be received in the future, if invested at current interest rates; (ii) price which a share must reach in the future to be the equivalent of today's price, taking inflation into account

> COMMENT: the present value of a future sum of money is found by discounting that future sum, and can be used to decide how much money to invest now at current interest rates in order to receive the sum you want to have in a given number of years' time

preside [prɪ'zaɪd] *verb* to be chairman; *the MD will preside over the meeting*; *the meeting was held in the committee room, Mr Smith presiding*

president ['prezɪdənt] *noun* head of a company, a society or a club; *he was elected president of the sports club*; *A.B.Smith has been appointed president of the company*

> COMMENT: in the UK, president is sometimes a title given to a non-executive former chairman of a company; in the USA, the president is the main executive director of a company

press [pres] *noun* newspapers and magazines; *we plan to give the product a lot of press publicity*; *there was no mention of the new product in the press*; **the local press** = newspapers which are sold in a small area of the country; **the national press** = newspapers which sell in all parts of the country; *the new car has been advertised in the national press*; **trade press** = all magazines produced for people working in a certain trade; **press conference** = meeting where reporters from newspapers are invited to hear news of a new product, of a court case, of a takeover bid, etc.; **press coverage** = reports about something in the press; *we were very disappointed by the press coverage of the new car*; **press cutting** = piece cut out of a newspaper or magazine, which refers to an item which you find interesting; *we have kept a file of press* *cuttings about the new car*; **press office** = office in a company which deals with relations with the press, sends out press releases, organizes press conferences, etc.; **press officer** = person who works in a press office; **press release** = sheet giving news about something which is sent to newspapers and TV and radio stations so that they can use the information; *the company sent out a press release about the launch of the new car*

pressing ['presɪŋ] *adjective* urgent; **pressing engagements** = meetings which have to be attended; **pressing bills** = bills which have to be paid

pressure ['preʃə] *noun* something which forces you to do something; **he was under considerable financial pressure** = he was forced to act because he owed money; **to put pressure on someone to do something** = to try to force someone to do something; *the group tried to put pressure on the government to act*; *the banks put pressure on the company to reduce its borrowings*; **working under high pressure** = working with customers asking for supplies urgently or with a manager telling you to work faster; **high-pressure salesman** = salesman who forces a customer to buy something he does not really need; **pressure group** = group of people who try to influence the government, the local town council, etc.

prestige [pres'tiːʒ] *noun* importance because of high quality, high value, etc.; **prestige advertising** = advertising in high quality magazines to increase a company's reputation; **prestige product** = expensive luxury product; **prestige offices** = expensive offices in a good area of the town

presume [prɪ'zjuːm] *verb* to suppose something is correct; *I presume the account has been paid*; *the company is presumed to be still solvent*; *we presume the shipment has been stolen*

presumption [prɪ'zʌmʃən] *noun* thing which is assumed to be correct

pre-tax *or* **pretax** ['priːtæks] *adjective* before tax has been deducted or paid; **pretax profit** = profit before tax has been

paid; *the dividend paid is equivalent to one quarter of the pretax profit*

---

the company's goals are a growth in sales of up to 40 per cent, a rise in pre-tax earnings of nearly 35 per cent and a rise in after-tax earnings of more than 25 per cent

Citizen (Ottawa)

EC regulations which came into effect in July insist that customers can buy cars anywhere in the EC at the local pre-tax price

Financial Times

---

pretences *US* **pretenses** [prɪ'tensiz] *plural noun* **false pretences** = doing or saying something to cheat someone; *he was sent to prison for obtaining money by false pretences*

pretend [prɪ'tend] *verb* to act like someone else in order to trick, to act as if something is true when it really is not; *he got in by pretending to be a telephone engineer*; *the chairman pretended he knew the final profit*; *she pretended she had flu and asked to have the day off*

prevent [prɪ'vent] *verb* to stop something happening; *we must try to prevent the takeover bid*; *the police prevented anyone from leaving the building*; *we have changed the locks on the doors to prevent the former MD from getting into the building*

preventive [prɪ'ventɪv] *adjective* which tries to stop something happening; **to take preventive measures against theft** = to try to stop things from being stolen

previous ['priːvjəs] *adjective* which happens earlier; *he could not accept the invitation because he had a previous engagement* = because he had earlier accepted another invitation to go somewhere

previously ['priːvjəsli] *adverb* happening earlier; *previously our distribution was handled by Smith Ltd*; *his CV stated that he had previously been a salesman with Jones & Co*

price [praɪs] **1** *noun* **(a)** money which has to be paid to buy something; **agreed price**

= price which has been accepted by both the buyer and seller; **all-in price** = price which covers all items in a purchase (goods, insurance, delivery, etc.); **asking price** = price which the seller is hoping to be paid for the item when it is sold; **bargain price** = very cheap price; **catalogue price** *or* **list price** = price as marked in a catalogue or list; **competitive price** = low price aimed to compete with a rival product; **cost price** = selling price which is the same as the price which the seller paid for the item (either the manufacturing price or the wholesale price); **cut price** = very cheap price; **discount price** = full price less a discount; **factory price** *or* **price ex factory** = price not including transport from the maker's factory; **fair price** = good price for both buyer and seller; **firm price** = price which will not change; *they are quoting a firm price of $1.23 a unit*; **going price** *or* **current price** *or* **usual price** = the price which is being charged now; **to sell goods off at half price** = to sell goods at half the price at which they were being sold before; **market price** = price at which a product can be sold; **net price** = price which cannot be reduced by a discount; **retail price** = price at which the retailer sells to the final customer; **Retail Price(s) Index (RPI)** = index which shows how prices of consumer goods have increased or decreased over a period of time; **spot price** = price for immediate delivery of a commodity; *the spot price of oil on the commodity markets* **(b) price ceiling** = highest price which can be reached; **price control** = legal measures to stop prices rising too fast; **price cutting** = sudden lowering of prices; **price-cutting war** = competition between companies to get a larger market share by cutting prices; **prices and incomes policy** = government policy which tries to control both price rises and incomes; **price differential** = difference in price between products in a range; **price fixing** = illegal agreement between companies to charge the same price for competing products; **price label** *or* **price tag** = label which shows a price; *the takeover bid put a $2m price tag on the company*; **price list** = sheet giving prices of goods for sale; **price range** = series of

prices for similar products from different suppliers; **cars in the £8-9,000 price range** = cars of different makes, selling for between £8,000 and £9,000; **price-sensitive product** = product which will not sell if the price is increased; **price war** = competition between companies to get a larger market share by cutting prices **(c) to increase in price** = to become more expensive; *petrol has increased in price* *or* *the price of petrol has increased*; **to increase prices** *or* **to raise prices** = to make items more expensive; **we will try to meet your price** = we will try to offer a price which is acceptable to you; **to cut prices** = to reduce prices suddenly; **to lower prices** *or* **to reduce prices** = to make items cheaper **(d)** *(on the Stock Exchange)* **asking price** = price which sellers are asking for shares; **closing price** = price at the end of a day's trading; **opening price** = price at the start of a day's trading **2** *verb* to give a price to a product; *we have two used cars for sale, both priced at £5,000*; **competitively priced** = sold at a low price which competes with that of similar goods from other companies; **the company has priced itself out of the market** = the company has raised its prices so high that its products do not sell

---

that British goods will price themselves back into world markets is doubtful as long as sterling labour costs continue to rise

Sunday Times

---

the average price per kilogram for this season has been 300c

Australian Financial Review

European manufacturers rely heavily on imported raw materials which are mostly priced in dollars

Duns Business Month

---

after years of relying on low wages for their competitive edge, Spanish companies are finding that rising costs and the strength of the peseta are pricing them out of the market

Wall Street Journal

price/earnings ratio (P/E ratio *or* **PER)** ['praɪs'ɜːnɪŋz 'reɪʃəʊ] *noun* ratio between the current market price of a share and the earnings per share (the current dividend it produces) calculated by dividing the market price by the earnings per share; **these shares sell at a P/E ratio of 7** = they sell at 7 times their earnings

> COMMENT: the P/E ratio is an indication of the way investors think a company will perform in the future, as a high market price suggests that investors expect earnings to grow and this gives a high P/E figure; a low P/E figure implies that investors feel that earnings are not likely to rise

pricing ['praɪsɪŋ] *noun* giving a price to a product; **pricing policy** = a company's policy in giving prices to its products; *our pricing policy aims at producing a 35% gross margin*; **common pricing** = illegal fixing of prices by several businesses so that they all charge the same price; **competitive pricing** = putting a low price on a product so that it competes with similar products from other companies; **marginal pricing** = basing the selling price of a product on its variable costs of production plus a margin, but excluding fixed costs

primarily ['praɪmərəli] *adverb* mainly; *the company trades primarily in the South American market*

primary ['praɪməri] *adjective* basic; **primary commodities** = raw materials or food; **primary industry** = industry dealing with basic raw materials (such as coal, wood, farm produce); **primary products** = products (such as wood, milk, fish) which are basic raw materials

> farmers are convinced that primary industry no longer has the capacity to meet new capital taxes or charges on farm inputs
> *Australian Financial Review*

prime [praɪm] *adjective* **(a)** most important; **prime time** = most expensive advertising time for TV commercials; *we are putting out a series of prime-time commercials* **(b)** basic; **prime bills** = bills of exchange which do not involve any risk;

prime cost = cost involved in producing a product, excluding overheads

Prime Minister ['praɪm 'mɪnɪstə] *noun* head of a government; *the Australian Prime Minister or the Prime Minister of Australia*

prime rate *or* **prime** ['praɪm 'reɪt] *noun* US best rate of interest at which an American bank lends to its customers

> COMMENT: not the same as the British bank base rate, which is only a notional rate, as all bank loans in the UK are at a certain percentage point above the base rate

> the base lending rate, or prime rate, is the rate at which banks lend to their top corporate borrowers
> *Wall Street Journal*

priming ['praɪmɪŋ] *noun see* PUMP PRIMING

principal ['prɪnsəpl] **1** *noun* **(a)** person or company which is represented by an agent; *the agent has come to London to see his principals* **(b)** money invested or borrowed on which interest is paid; *we try to repay part of principal each month* (NOTE: do not confuse with **principle**) **2** *adjective* most important; *the principal shareholders asked for a meeting*; *the country's principal products are paper and wood*

> the company was set up with funds totalling NorKr 145m with the principal aim of making capital gains on the secondhand market
> *Lloyd's List*

principle ['prɪnsəpl] *noun* basic point or general rule; **in principle** = in agreement with a general rule; **agreement in principle** = agreement with the basic conditions of a proposal (NOTE: do not confuse with **principal**)

print [prɪnt] **1** *noun* words made (on paper) with a machine; **to read the small print** *or* **the fine print on a contract** = to read the conditions of a contract which are often printed very small so that people will not be able to read them easily **2** *verb* **(a)** to make letters on paper with a machine; *the health warning is printed on the front of* *the packet; we use a standard printed agreement for hire-purchase sales* **(b)** to write in capital letters; *please print your name and address on the top of the form*

printer ['prɪntə] *noun* machine which prints; **computer printer** = machine which prints information from a computer; **colour printer** = printer which prints material in colour; *all our publicity leaflets are printed on the colour printer here in the office*; **dot-matrix printer** = cheap printer which makes letters by printing many small dots (the quality is not as good as laser printers or inkjet printers); **inkjet printer** = printer which prints by sending a jet of ink onto the paper to form the characters (they give very good results, but cannot be used for multipart stationery); **laser printer** = computer printer which uses a laser source to print high-quality dot matrix characters on paper; **line printer** = machine which prints information from a computer, printing one line at a time (the quality is not as good as laser printers or inkjet printers but line printers are the only type which print on multipart stationery); **printer ribbon** = inked ribbon in a cartridge which is put into a line printer

print out ['prɪnt 'aʊt] *verb* to print information from a computer through a printer

printout ['prɪntaʊt] *noun* **computer printout** = printed copy of information from a computer; *the sales director asked for a printout of the agents' commissions*

prior ['praɪə] *adjective* earlier; **prior agreement** = agreement which was reached earlier; **without prior knowledge** = without knowing before; **prior charge** = (capital) ranking before other capital in terms of distributions of profits and repayment when a company goes into liquidation

priority [praɪ'ɒrəti] *noun* **to have priority** = to have the right to be first; **to have priority over** *or* **to take priority over something** = to be more important than something; *reducing overheads takes priority over increasing turnover; debenture holders have priority over ordinary shareholders*; **to give something top priority** = to make something the most important item

private ['praɪvət] *adjective* **(a)** belonging to a single person, not to a company or to the state; **letter marked 'private and confidential'** = letter which must not be opened by anyone other than the person it is addressed to; **private client** *or* **private customer** = client dealt with by a salesman as a person, not as a company; **private income** = income from dividends, interest or rents which is not part of a salary; **private investor** = ordinary person with money to invest; **private property** = property which belongs to a private person, not to the public **(b) in private** = away from other people; *he asked to see the managing director in private; in public he said the company would break even soon, but in private he was less optimistic* **(c) private limited company** = (i) company with a small number of shareholders whose shares are not traded on the Stock Exchange; (ii) subsidiary company whose shares are not listed on the Stock Exchange, while those of its parent company are **(d) private enterprise** = businesses which are owned by private shareholders, not by the state; *the project is funded by private enterprise*; **the private sector** = all companies which are owned by private shareholders, not by the state

in the private sector the total number of new house starts was 3 per cent higher than in the corresponding period last year, while public sector starts were 23 per cent lower

Financial Times

management had offered to take the company private through a leveraged buyout for $825 million

Fortune

privately ['praɪvətli] *adverb* away from other people; *the deal was negotiated privately*

privatization [praɪvɪtaɪ'zeɪʃən] *noun* selling a nationalized industry to private owners

privatize ['praɪvətaɪz] *verb* to sell a nationalized industry to private owners

PRO = **PUBLIC RELATIONS OFFICER**

pro [prəʊ] *preposition* for; **per pro** = with the authority of; *the secretary signed per pro the manager*; *see also* **PRO FORMA, PRO RATA, PRO TEM**

probable ['prɒbəbl] *adjective* likely to happen; *he is trying to prevent the probable collapse of the company*

probably ['prɒbəbli] *adverb* likely; *the MD is probably going to retire next year*; *this shop is probably the best in town for service*

probate ['prəʊbeɪt] *noun* legal acceptance that a document, especially a will, is valid; **grant of probate** = official document proving that a will is genuine, given to the executors so that they can act on the terms of the will; **the executor was granted probate** *or* **obtained a grant of probate** = the executor was told officially that the will was valid; **Probate Registry** = court which examines wills to see if they are valid

probation [prə'beɪʃən] *noun* period when a new worker is being tested before getting a permanent job; *he is on three months' probation*; *we will take her on probation*

probationary [prə'beɪʃənəri] *adjective* while someone is being tested; *we will take her for a probationary period of three months*; *after the probationary period the company decided to offer him a full-time contract*

problem ['prɒbləm] *noun* thing to which it is difficult to find an answer; *the company suffers from cash flow problems or staff problems*; **to solve a problem** = to find an answer to a problem; *problem solving is a test of a good manager*; **problem area** = area of a company's work which is difficult to run; *overseas sales is one of our biggest problem areas*

everyone blames the strong dollar for US trade problems, but they differ on what should be done

Duns Business Month

procedure [prə'siːdʒə] *noun* way in which something is done; **to follow the proper procedure**; **this procedure is very irregular** = this is not the proper way to do something; **accounting procedures** = set ways of doing the accounts of a company; **complaints procedure** *or* **grievance procedure** = way of presenting complaints formally from a trade union to a management; *the trade union has followed the correct complaints procedure*; **disciplinary procedure** = way of warning a worker that he is breaking the rules of a company; **dismissal procedures** = correct way to dismiss someone, following rules in the contract of employment; **disputes procedure** = formal way of resolving disputes between a trade union and management

proceed [prə'siːd] *verb* to go on, to continue; *the negotiations are proceeding slowly*; **to proceed against someone** = to start a legal action against someone; **to proceed with something** = to go on doing something; *shall we proceed with the committee meeting?*

proceedings [prə'siːdɪŋz] *plural noun* (a) **conference proceedings** = written report of what has taken place at a conference (b) **legal proceedings** = legal action or lawsuit; *we decided to take proceedings against our supplier*; *the court proceedings were adjourned*; **to institute proceedings against someone** = to start a legal action against someone

proceeds ['prəʊsiːdz] *plural noun* the **proceeds of a sale** = money received from a sale after deducting expenses; *he sold his shop and invested the proceeds in a computer repair business*

process ['prəʊses] **1** *noun* (a) **industrial processes** = the various stages involved in manufacturing products in factories; **decision-making processes** = ways in which decisions are reached (b) the **due processes of the law** = the formal work of a legal action **2** *verb* (a) **to process figures** = to sort out information to make it easily understood; *the sales figures are being processed by our accounts department*; *the data is being processed by our computer* (b) to deal with something in the usual routine way; *it usually takes at least* *two weeks to process an insurance claim*; *orders are processed in our warehouse*

processing ['prəʊsesɪŋ] *noun* **(a)** sorting of information; *the processing of information or of statistics by a computer*; **batch processing** = computer system, where information is collected into batches before being loaded into the computer; **data processing** *or* **information processing** = selecting and examining data in a computer to produce information in a special form; **word processing** *or* **text processing** = working with words, using a computer to produce, check and change texts, reports, letters, etc. **(b)** **the processing of a claim for insurance** = putting a claim for insurance through the usual office routine in the insurance company; **order processing** = dealing with orders

processor ['prəʊsesə] *noun* **word processor** = small computer which is used for working with words, to produce texts, reports, letters, etc.

procurement [prə'kjʊəmənt] *noun* action of buying equipment or raw materials for a company; *he is in charge of the materials procurement department*

produce 1 ['prɒdjuːs] *noun* foodstuffs grown on the land; *home produce*; *agricultural produce or farm produce* **2** [prə'djuːs] *verb* **(a)** to bring out; *he produced documents to prove his claim*; *the negotiators produced a new set of figures*; *the customs officer asked him to produce the relevant documents* **(b)** to make or to manufacture; *the factory produces cars or engines or books*; **to mass produce** = to make large quantities of a product **(c)** to give an interest; *investments which produce about 10% per annum*

producer [prə'djuːsə] *noun* company or country which manufactures; *country which is a producer of high quality watches*; *the company is a major car producer*; **producer prices** = prices of goods when they leave the manufacturer

producing [prə'djuːsɪŋ] *adjective* which produces; **producing capacity** = capacity to produce; **oil-producing country** = country which produces oil

product ['prɒdʌkt] *noun* **(a)** thing which is made or manufactured; **basic product** = main product made from a raw material; **by-product** = product made as a result of manufacturing a main product; **end product** *or* **final product** *or* **finished product** = product made at the end of a production process **(b)** manufactured item for sale; **product advertising** = advertising a particular named product, not the company which makes it; **product analysis** = examining each separate product in a company's range to see why it sells, who buys it, etc.; **product design** = design of consumer products; **product development** = improving an existing product line to meet the needs of the market; **product engineer** = engineer in charge of the equipment for making a product; **product liability** = liability of the maker of a product for negligence in the design or production of the product; **product line** *or* **product range** = series of different products made by the same company which form a group (such as cars in different models, pens in different colours, etc.); **product management** = directing the making and selling of a product as an independent item; **product mix** = group of quite different products made by the same company **(c)** **gross domestic product (GDP)** = annual value of goods sold and services paid for inside a country; **gross national product (GNP)** = annual value of goods and services in a country, including income from other countries

production [prə'dʌkʃən] *noun* **(a)** showing something; **on production of** = when something is shown; *the case will be released by customs on production of the relevant documents*; *goods can be exchanged only on production of the sales slip* **(b)** making or manufacturing of goods for sale; *production will probably be held up by industrial action*; *we are hoping to speed up production by installing new machinery*; **batch production** = production in batches; **domestic production** = production of goods in the home market; **mass production** = manufacturing of large quantities of goods; *the mass production of cars or of calculators*; **rate of production** *or*

production rate = speed at which items are made; **production cost** = cost of making a product; **production department** = section of a company which deals with the making of the company's products; **production line** = system of making a product, where each item (such as a car) moves slowly through the factory with new sections added to it as it goes along; *he works on the production line*; *she is a production line worker*; **production manager** = person in charge of the production department; **production unit** = separate small group of workers producing a certain product

productive [prə'dʌktɪv] *adjective* which produces; **productive capital** = capital which is invested to give interest; **productive discussions** = useful discussions which lead to an agreement or decision

productively [prə'dʌktɪvli] *adverb* in a productive way

productivity [prɒdʌk'tɪvəti] *noun* rate of output per worker or per machine in a factory; *bonus payments are linked to productivity*; *the company is aiming to increase productivity*; *productivity has fallen or risen since the company was taken over*; **productivity agreement** = agreement to pay a productivity bonus; **productivity bonus** = extra payments made to workers because of increased production per worker; **productivity drive** = extra effort to increase productivity

though there has been productivity growth, the absolute productivity gap between many British firms and their foreign rivals remains

profession [prə'feʃən] *noun* (a) work which needs special skills learnt over a period of time; *the managing director is an accountant by profession* (b) group of specialized workers; **the legal profession** = all lawyers; **the medical profession** = all doctors

professional [prə'feʃənl] **1** *adjective* (a) referring to one of the professions; *the accountant sent in his bill for professional*

services; *we had to ask our lawyer for professional advice on the contract*; **a professional man** = man who works in one of the professions (such as a lawyer, doctor, accountant); **professional qualifications** = documents showing that someone has successfully finished a course of study which allows him to work in one of the professions (b) expert or skilled; *his work is very professional*; *they did a very professional job in designing the new office* (c) doing work for money; *a professional tennis player*; **he is a professional troubleshooter** = he makes his living by helping companies to sort out their problems **2** *noun* skilled person, a person who does skilled work for money

one of the key advantages of an accountancy qualification is its worldwide marketability. Other professions are not so lucky: lawyers, for example, are much more limited in where they can work

proficiency [prə'fɪʃənsi] *noun* skill, being capable of doing something; *she has a certificate of proficiency in English*; *to get the job he had to pass a proficiency test*

proficient [prə'fɪʃənt] *adjective* capable of doing something well; *she is quite proficient in English*

profile ['prəʊfaɪl] *noun* brief description; *he asked for a company profile of the possible partners in the joint venture*; **customer profile** = description of an average customer for a product or service; *the customer profile shows our average buyer to be male, aged 25-30, and employed in the service industries*; **market profile** = basic characteristics of a particular market

the audience profile does vary greatly by period: 41.6% of the adult audience is aged 16 to 34 during the morning period, but this figure drops to 24% during peak viewing time

profit ['prɒfɪt] *noun* money gained from a sale which is more than the money spent; **clear profit** = profit after all expenses have been paid; *we made $6,000 clear profit on the deal*; **gross profit** *or* **gross trading profit** = profit calculated as sales income less the cost of the goods sold (i.e., without deducting any other expenses); **net profit** *or* **net trading profit** = result where income from sales is larger than all expenditure; **operating profit** = result where sales from normal business activities are higher than the costs; **trading profit** = result where the company' receipts are higher than its expenditure; **profit margin** = percentage difference between sales income and the cost of sales; **profit motive** = idea that profit is the most import aim of a business; **profits tax** *or* **tax on profits** = tax to be paid on profits; **profit before tax** *or* **pretax profit** = profit before any tax has been paid; **profit after tax** = profit after tax has been paid; **to take your profit** = to sell shares at a higher price than was paid for them, rather than to keep them as an investment; **to show a profit** = to make a profit and state it in the company accounts; *we are showing a small profit for the first quarter*; **to make a profit** = to have more money as a result of a deal; **to move into profit** = to start to make a profit; *the company is breaking even now, and expects to move into profit within the next two months*; **to sell at a profit** = to sell at a price which gives you a profit; **excess profit** = profit which is higher than what is thought to be normal; **excess profits tax** = tax on excess profits; **healthy profit** = quite a large profit; **paper profit** = profit on an asset which has increased in price but has not been sold; *he is showing a paper profit of £25,000 on his investment*

> because capital gains are not taxed and money taken out in profits and dividends is taxed, owners of businesses will be using accountants and tax experts to find loopholes in the law
>
> *Toronto Star*

> the bank transferred $5 million to general reserve compared with $10 million the previous year which made the

> consolidated profit and loss account look healthier
>
> *Hongkong Standard*

profitability [prɒfɪtə'bɪləti] *noun* **(a)** ability to make a profit; *we doubt the profitability of the project* **(b)** amount of profit made as a percentage of costs; **measurement of profitability** = way of calculating how profitable something is

profitable ['prɒfɪtəbl] *adjective* which makes a profit; *she runs a very profitable employment agency*

profitably ['prɒfɪtəbli] *adverb* making a profit; *the aim of every company must be to trade profitably*

profit and loss account (P&L account) ['prɒfɪt ənd 'lɒs ə'kaʊnt] *noun* statement of a company's expenditure and income over a period of time, almost always one calendar year, showing whether the company has made a profit or loss; **consolidated profit and loss account** = profit and loss accounts of the holding company and its subsidiary companies, grouped together into a single profit and loss account (NOTE: the American equivalent is the **profit and loss statement** or **income statement**)

profit centre ['prɒfɪt 'sentə] *noun* person or department which is considered separately for the purposes of calculating a profit; *we count the kitchen equipment division as a single profit centre*

profiteer [prɒfɪ'tɪə] *noun* person who makes too much profit, especially when goods are rationed or in short supply

profiteering [prɒfɪ'tɪərɪŋ] *noun* making too much profit

profit-making ['prɒfɪtmeɪkɪŋ] *adjective* which makes a profit; *the whole project was expected to be profit-making by 1998 but it still hasn't broken even*; **non profit-making** = (organization, such as a club) which is not allowed by law to make a profit; *non profit-making organizations are exempt from tax*

profit-sharing ['prɒfɪtʃeərɪŋ] *noun* arrangement where workers get a share of the profits of the company they work for; *the company runs a profit-sharing scheme*

profit-taking ['prɒfitteɪkɪŋ] *noun* selling investments to realize the profit, rather than keeping them; *share prices fell under continued profit-taking*

some profit-taking was seen yesterday as investors continued to lack fresh incentives to renew buying activity
Financial Times

pro forma ['prəʊ 'fɔːmə] **1** *Latin phrase meaning* 'for the sake of form'; **pro forma (invoice)** = invoice sent to a buyer before the goods are sent, so that payment can be made or that goods can be sent to a consignee who is not the buyer; *they sent us a pro forma*; *we only supply that account on pro forma* **2** *verb* to issue a pro forma invoice; *can you pro forma this order?*

program ['prəʊgræm] **1** *noun* **computer program** = instructions to a computer telling it to do a particular piece of work; *to buy a graphics program*; *the accounts department is running a new payroll program* **2** *verb* to write a program for a computer; **to program a computer** = to install a program in a computer; *the computer is programmed to print labels* (NOTE: **programming - programmed**)

programmable [prəʊ'græməbl] *adjective* which can be programmed

programme *US* **program** ['prəʊgræm] *noun* plan of things which will be done; *she is running the development programme* *or* *the research programme*; *the training programme sends all managers for retraining every year*; *to draw up a programme of investment* *or* *an investment programme*

programmer ['prəʊgræmə] *noun* **computer programmer** = person who writes computer programs

programming ['prəʊgræmɪŋ] *noun* **computer programming** = writing programs for computers; **programming engineer** = engineer in charge of programming a computer system; **programming language** = system of signs, letters and words used to instruct a computer

progress 1 ['prəʊgres] *noun* movement of work forward; *to report on the progress of the work* *or* *of the negotiations*; **to make a progress report** = to report how work is going; **in progress** = which is being done but is not finished; *negotiations in progress*; *work in progress*; **progress payments** = payments made as each stage of a contract is completed; *the fifth progress payment is due in March* **2** [prə'gres] *verb* to move forward, to go ahead; *the contract is progressing through various departments*

progress chaser ['prəʊgres 'tʃeɪsə] *noun* person whose job is to check that work is being carried out on schedule, that orders are being fulfilled on time, etc.

progressive [prə'gresɪv] *adjective* which moves forward in stages; **progressive taxation** = taxation system where tax levels increase as the income is higher (also called 'graduated taxation')

prohibitive [prə'hɪbɪtɪv] *adjective* with a price so high that you cannot afford to pay it; *the cost of redesigning the product is prohibitive*

project ['prɒdʒekt] *noun* **(a)** plan; *he has drawn up a project for developing new markets in Europe* **(b)** particular job of work which follows a plan; *we are just completing an engineering project in North Africa*; *the company will start work on the project next month*; **project analysis** = examining all costs or problems of a project before work on it is started; **project engineer** = engineer in charge of a project; **project manager** = manager in charge of a project

projected [prə'dʒektɪd] *adjective* planned or expected; **projected sales** = forecast of sales; *projected sales in Europe next year should be over £1m*

projection [prə'dʒekʃən] *noun* forecast of something which will happen in the future; *projection of profits for the next three years*; *the sales manager was asked to draw up sales projections for the next three years*

promise ['prɒmɪs] **1** *noun* saying that you will do something; **to keep a promise** = to do what you said you would do; *he says he will pay next week, but he never* *keeps his promises*; **to go back on a promise** = not to do what you said you would do; *the management went back on its promise to increase salaries across the board*; **a promise to pay** = a promissory note **2** *verb* to say that you will do something; *they promised to pay the last instalment next week*; *the personnel manager promised he would look into the grievances of the office staff*

promissory note [prəˈmɪsəri ˈnəʊt] *noun* document stating that someone promises to pay an amount of money on a certain date

promote [prəˈməʊt] *verb* **(a)** to give someone a more important job; *he was promoted from salesman to sales manager* **(b)** to advertise; **to promote a new product** = to increase the sales of a new product by a sales campaign *or* TV commercials or free gifts **(c) to promote a new company** = to organize the setting up of a new company

promoter [prəˈməʊtə] *noun* **company promoter** = person who organizes the setting up of a new company

promotion [prəˈməʊʃən] *noun* **(a)** moving up to a more important job; *promotion chances or promotion prospects*; *he ruined his chances of promotion when he argued with the managing director*; **to earn promotion** = to work hard and efficiently and so be promoted **(b) promotion of a product** = selling a new product by publicity, sales campaign, TV commercials or free gifts; *the promotion budget has been increased to £500,000*; *he is leading the promotion team in charge of the launch*; *we a running a special promotion offering two for the price of one* **(c)** promotion of a company = setting up a new company

promotional [prəˈməʊʃənl] *adjective* used in an advertising campaign; *the admen are using balloons as promotional material*; **promotional budget** = forecast cost of promoting a new product

prompt [prɒmpt] *adjective* rapid, done immediately; *we got very prompt service at the complaints desk*; *thank you for your prompt reply to my letter*; **prompt payment** = payment made rapidly;

prompt supplier = supplier who delivers orders rapidly

> they keep shipping costs low and can take advantage of quantity discounts and other allowances for prompt payment
> *Duns Business Month*

promptly [ˈprɒmptli] *adverb* rapidly; *he replied to my letter very promptly*

proof [pruːf] *noun* thing which shows that something is true; **documentary proof** = proof in the form of a document

-proof [pruːf] *suffix* which prevents something getting in or getting out or harming; *a dustproof cover*; *an inflation-proof pension*; *a soundproof studio*

prop = PROPRIETOR

property [ˈprɒpəti] *noun* **(a) (personal) property** = things which belong to a person; *the fire caused considerable damage to personal property*; *the management is not responsible for property left in the hotel rooms* **(b)** land and buildings; *property taxes are higher in the inner city*; *they are assessing damage to property or property damage after the storm*; *the commercial property market is booming*; **the office has been bought by a property company** = by a company which buys buildings to lease them; **property developer** = person who buys old buildings or empty land and builds new buildings for sale or rent; **the property market** = (i) the market in letting commercial properties; (ii) the market in developing commercial properties as investments; (iii) buying or selling residential properties by individual homeowners; **commercial property** = building used as offices or shops; **private property** = property which belongs to a private person and not to the public **(c)** a building; *we have several properties for sale in the centre of the town*

proportion [prəˈpɔːʃən] *noun* part (of a total); *a proportion of the pre-tax profit is set aside for contingencies*; *only a small proportion of our sales comes from retail shops*; **in proportion to** = showing how something is related to something else; *profits went up in proportion to the fall in* *overhead costs; sales in Europe are small in proportion to those in the USA*

proportional [prə'pɔːʃənl] *adjective* directly related; *the increase in profit is proportional to the reduction in overheads*

proportionately [prə'pɔːʃənətli] *adverb* in proportion

proposal [prə'pəuzəl] *noun* **(a)** suggestion, thing which has been suggested; *to make a proposal or to put forward a proposal to the board*; **the committee turned down the proposal** = the committee refused to accept what was suggested **(b)** official document with details of a property or person to be insured which is sent to the insurance company when asking for an insurance

propose [prə'pəuz] *verb* **(a)** to suggest that something should be done; **to propose a motion** = to ask a meeting to vote for a motion and explain the reasons for this; **to propose someone as president** = to ask a group to vote for someone to become president **(b)** **to propose to** = to say that you intend to do something; *I propose to repay the loan at £20 a month*

proposer [prə'pəuzə] *noun* person who proposes a motion at a meeting

proposition [prɒpə'zɪʃən] *noun* commercial deal which is suggested; **it will never be a commercial proposition** = it is not likely to make a profit

proprietary [prə'praiətəri] *adjective* **(a)** product (such as a medicine) which is made and owned by a company; **proprietary drug** = drug which is made by a particular company and marketed under a brand name **(b)** *US* **proprietary company** = company formed to invest in stock of other companies so as to control them (NOTE: British English for this **holding company**) **(c)** *(in South Africa and Australia)* **proprietary company** = private limited company

proprietor [prə'praiətə] *noun* owner; *the proprietor of a hotel or a hotel proprietor*

proprietress [prə'praiətrəs] *noun* woman owner; *the proprietress of an advertising consultancy*

pro rata ['prəu 'rɑːtə] *adjective & adverb* at a rate which varies according to the size

or importance of something; *when part of the shipment was destroyed we received a pro rata payment; the full-time pay is £500 a week and the part-timers are paid pro rata*; **dividends are paid pro rata** = dividends are paid according to the number of shares held

prosecute ['prɒsɪkjuːt] *verb* to bring (someone) to court to answer a criminal charge; *he was prosecuted for embezzlement*

prosecution [prɒsɪ'kjuːʃən] *noun* **(a)** act of bringing someone to court to answer a charge; *his prosecution for embezzlement* **(b)** people who prosecute someone; *the costs of the case will be borne by the prosecution*; **prosecution counsel** *or* **counsel for the prosecution** = lawyer acting for the prosecution

prospect ['prɒspekt] *noun* **(a)** **prospects** = possibilities for the future; **his job prospects are good** = he is very likely to find a job; **prospects for the market** *or* **market prospects are worse than those of last year** = sales in the market are likely to be lower than they were last year **(b)** possibility that something will happen; *there is no prospect of negotiations coming to an end soon* **(c)** person who may become a customer; *the salesmen were looking out for prospects*

prospective [prə'spektɪv] *adjective* which may happen in the future; **a prospective buyer** = someone who may buy in the future; *there is no shortage of prospective buyers for the computer*

prospectus [prə'spektəs] *noun* **(a)** document which gives information to attract buyers or customers; *the restaurant has girls handing out prospectuses in the street* **(b)** document which gives information about a company whose shares are being sold to the public for the first time (NOTE: plural is **prospectuses**)

```
when the prospectus emerges,
existing shareholders and any
prospective new investors can
find out more by calling the
free share information line;
they will be sent a leaflet.
Non-shareholders who register
in this way will receive a
prospectus when it is
```

published; existing shareholders will be sent one automatically

Financial Times

prosperity [prɒˈsperəti] *noun* being rich; **in times of prosperity** = when people are rich

prosperous [ˈprɒspərəs] *adjective* rich; *a prosperous shopkeeper; a prosperous town*

protect [prəˈtekt] *verb* to defend something against harm; *the workers are protected from unfair dismissal by government legislation; the computer is protected by a plastic cover; the cover is supposed to protect the machine from dust;* **to protect an industry by imposing tariff barriers** = to stop a local industry from being hit by foreign competition by stopping foreign products from being imported

protection [prəˈtekʃən] *noun* thing or legislation which protects; *the legislation offers no protection to part-time workers;* **consumer protection** = protecting consumers against unfair or illegal traders; **employment protection** = protecting employees against unfair dismissal

protectionism [prəˈtekʃənɪzm] *noun* protecting producers in the home country against foreign competitors by banning or taxing imports or by imposing import quotas

protective [prəˈtektɪv] *adjective* which protects; **protective cover** = cover which protects a machine; **protective tariff** = tariff which tries to ban imports to stop them competing with local products

pro tem [ˈprəʊ ˈtem] *adverb* temporarily, for a time

protest 1 [ˈprəʊtest] *noun* **(a)** statement or action to show that you do not approve of something; *to make a protest against high prices;* **sit-down protest** = action by members of the staff who occupy their place of work and refuse to leave; **in protest at** = showing that you do not approve of something; *the staff occupied the offices in protest at the low pay offer;* **to do something under protest** = to do something, but say that you do not approve of it **(b)** official document which proves

that a bill of exchange has not been paid **2** [prəˈtest] *verb* **(a) to protest against something** = to say that you do not approve of something; *the importers are protesting against the ban on luxury goods* (NOTE: British English is **to protest against something,** but American English is **to protest something) (b) to protest a bill** = to draw up a document to prove that a bill of exchange has not been paid

prototype [ˈprəʊtətaɪp] *noun* first model of a new machine before it goes into production; *the prototype car or prototype plane has had its first trial run; the company is showing the prototype of the new model at the exhibition*

provide [prəˈvaɪd] *verb* **(a) to provide for** = to allow for something which may happen in the future; *the contract provides for an annual increase in charges; £10,000 of expenses have been provided for in the budget* **(b)** to put money aside in accounts to cover expenditure or loss in the future; *£25,000 is provided against bad debts* **(c) to provide someone with something** = to supply something to someone; *each rep is provided with a company car; staff uniforms are provided by the hotel*

provided that *or* **providing** [prəˈvaɪdɪd ˈðæt or prəˈvaɪdɪŋ] *conjunction* on condition that; *the goods will be delivered next week provided or providing the drivers are not on strike*

provident [ˈprɒvɪdənt] *adjective* which provides benefits in case of illness, old age, etc.; *a provident fund; a provident society*

province [ˈprɒvɪns] *noun* **(a)** large division of a country; *the provinces of Canada* **(b) the provinces** = parts of any country away from the main capital town; *there are fewer retail outlets in the provinces than in the capital*

provincial [prəˈvɪnʃəl] *adjective* referring to a province or to the provinces; *a provincial government; a provincial branch of a national bank*

provision [prəˈvɪʒən] *noun* **(a) to make provision for** = to see that something is allowed for in the future; **there is no provision for** *or* **no provision has been made for car parking in the plans for the**

office block = the plans do not include space for cars to park **(b) provisions** = money put aside in accounts for anticipated expenditure where the timing or amount of expenditure is uncertain (if the expenditure is not certain to occur at all, then the money set aside is called a 'contingent liability'); *the bank has made a £2m provision for bad debts or a $5bn provision against Third World loans* **(c)** legal condition; **we have made provision to this effect** = we have put into the contract terms which will make this work **(d) provisions** = food

---

landlords can create short
lets of dwellings which will
be free from the normal
security of tenure provisions
Times

---

provisional [prə'vɪʒənl] *adjective* temporary, not final or permanent; *the sales department has been asked to make a provisional forecast of sales; the provisional budget has been drawn up for each department; they faxed their provisional acceptance of the contract*

provisionally [prə'vɪʒnəli] *adverb* not finally; *the contract has been accepted provisionally*

proviso [prə'vaɪzəu] *noun* condition; *we are signing the contract with the proviso that the terms can be discussed again after six months*

proxy ['prɒksi] *noun* **(a)** document which gives someone the power to act on behalf of someone else; *to sign by proxy;* **proxy form** *or* **proxy card** = form which a shareholder receives with his invitation to attend an AGM, which he fills in if he wants to appoint a proxy to vote for him on a resolution; **proxy vote** = votes made by proxy; *the proxy votes were all in favour of the board's recommendation* **(b)** person who acts on behalf of someone else; *she asked the chairman to act as proxy for her*

P.S. ['piː'es] *short for* = POST SCRIPTUM additional note at the end of a letter; *did you read the P.S. at the end of the letter?*

PSBR = PUBLIC SECTOR BORROWING REQUIREMENT

pt [paɪnt] = PINT

ptas [pə'seɪtəz] = PESETAS

Pte *(Singapore)* = PRIVATE LIMITED COMPANY

Pty = PROPRIETARY COMPANY

public ['pʌblɪk] **1** *adjective* **(a)** referring to all the people in general; **public holiday** = day when all workers rest and enjoy themselves instead of working; **public image** = idea which the people have of a company or a person; *the minister is trying to improve his public image;* **public transport** = transport (such as buses, trains) which is used by any member of the public; **public works** = large construction schemes which benefit the public in general (such as motorways, hospitals, etc.) **(b)** referring to the government or the state; **public expenditure** = spending of money by the local or central government; **public finance** = the raising of money by governments (by taxes or borrowing) and the spending of it; **public funds** = government money available for expenditure; **public ownership** = situation where an industry is nationalized **(c) the company is going public** = the company is going to place some of its shares for sale on the stock market so that anyone can buy them **2** *noun* **the public** *or* **the general public** = the people; **in public** = in front of everyone; *in public he said that the company would soon be in profit, but in private he was less optimistic*

publication [pʌblɪ'keɪʃən] *noun* **(a)** making something public; *the publication of the latest trade figures* **(b)** printed document which is to be sold or given to the public; *he asked the library for a list of government publications;* **the company has six business publications** = the company publishes six magazines or newspapers referring to business

publicity [pʌb'lɪsəti] *noun* attracting the attention of the public to products or services by mentioning them in the media; **publicity agency** *or* **publicity bureau** = office which organizes publicity for companies who do not have publicity departments; **publicity budget** = money allowed for expenditure on publicity; **publicity campaign** = period when planned publicity takes place; **publicity**

copy = text of an advertisement before it is printed; **publicity department** = section of a company which organizes the company's publicity; **publicity expenditure** = money spent on publicity; **publicity manager** = person in charge of a publicity department; **publicity matter** = sheets, posters or leaflets used for publicity

publicize ['pʌblɪsaɪz] *verb* to attract people's attention to a product for sale, a service or an entertainment; *the campaign is intended to publicize the services of the tourist board*; *we are trying to publicize our products by advertisements on buses*

Public Limited Company (Plc)
noun company in which the general public can invest and whose shares and loan stock can usually be bought and sold on the Stock Exchange (NOTE: also called a **Public Company**)

public relations (PR) ['pʌblɪk rɪ'leɪʃənz] *plural noun* keeping good relations between a company or a group and the public so that people know what the company is doing and can approve of it; *a public relations man explained the company's decision*; *he works in public relations*; *a public relations firm handles all our publicity*; a public relations exercise = a campaign to improve public relations; **public relations officer (PRO)** = person in an organization who is responsible for public relations activities

public sector ['pʌblɪk 'sektə] *noun* nationalized industries and services; *a report on wage rises in the public sector or on public sector wage settlements*; public sector borrowing requirement (PSBR) = amount of money which a government has to borrow to pay for its own spending

publish ['pʌblɪʃ] *verb* to have a document (such as a catalogue, book, magazine or newspaper) written and printed and then sell or give it to the public; *the society publishes its list of members annually*; *the government has not published the figures on which its proposals are based*; *the company publishes six magazines for the business market*

publisher ['pʌblɪʃə] *noun* person or company which publishes books, magazines, etc.

pull off ['pʊl 'ɒf] *verb (informal)* to succeed in negotiating a deal

pull out ['pʊl 'aʊt] *verb* to stop being part of a deal or agreement; *our Australian partners pulled out of the contract*

pump [pʌmp] *verb* to put something in by force; *venture capitalists have been pumping money into the company to keep it afloat*

> in each of the years 1986 to 1989, Japan pumped a net sum of the order of $100bn into foreign securities, notably into US government bonds
> *Financial Times Review*

pump priming ['pʌmp 'praɪmɪŋ] *noun* government investment in new projects which it hopes will benefit the economy

punch [pʌnʃ] **1** *noun* device for making holes (for instance, for making holes in sheets of paper so that they can be put into a ring binder) **2** *verb* to make holes in something; **punched card** = card with holes in it which a computer can read and store as information

punt [pʌnt] **1** *noun* **(a)** currency used with the euro in the Republic of Ireland (NOTE: also called **the Irish pound**) **(b)** *(informal)* gamble, bet; *that stock is worth a punt*; *he took a punt on the exchange rate falling* **2** *verb* to gamble or to bet (on something)

punter ['pʌntə] *noun (informal)* **(a)** person who gambles or who hopes to make money on the Stock Exchange; *the share price shot up as punters rushed to buy* **(b)** any customer; *the product looks attractive but will the punters like it?*

> if punters don't come in for their regular packet of cigarettes, then they are unlikely to make any impulse buys
> *The Grocer*

pup [pʌp] *noun (informal)* worthless item; *I've been sold a pup*

purchase ['pɜːtʃəs] **1** *noun* thing which has been bought; **to make a purchase** = to buy something; **purchase book** = records of purchases; **purchase ledger** = book in which expenditure is noted; **purchase order** = official order made out by a purchasing department for goods which a company wants to buy; *we cannot supply you without a purchase order number*; **purchase price** = price paid for something; **purchase tax** = tax paid on things which are bought; **bulk purchase** *or* **quantity purchase** = buying of large quantities of goods at low prices; **cash purchase** = purchase made in cash; **hire purchase** = system of buying something by paying a sum regularly each month; *he is buying a refrigerator on hire purchase*; **hire purchase agreement** = contract to pay for something by instalments **2** *verb* to buy; **to purchase something for cash** = to pay cash for something

purchaser ['pɜːtʃəsə] *noun* person or company which purchases; **the company is looking for a purchaser** = the company is trying to find someone who will buy it; *the company has found a purchaser for its warehouse*

purchasing ['pɜːtʃəsɪŋ] *noun* buying; **purchasing department** = section of a company which deals with buying of stock, raw materials, equipment, etc.; **purchasing manager** = head of a purchasing department; **purchasing officer** = person in a company or organization who is responsible for buying stock, raw materials, equipment, etc.; **purchasing power** = quantity of goods which can be bought by a group of people or with an amount of money; *the decline in the purchasing power of the pound*; **central purchasing** = purchasing organized by the main office for all departments or branches

purpose ['pɜːpəs] *noun* aim or plan; **we need the invoice for tax purposes** *or* **for the purpose of declaration to the tax authorities** = in order for it to be declared to the tax authorities

put [pʊt] **1** *noun* **put option** = right to sell shares at a certain price at a certain date (NOTE: the opposite, an option to purchase, is a **call option**) **2** *verb* to place or to fix; **the accounts put the stock value at £10,000** = the accounts state that the value of the stock is £10,000; **to put a proposal to the vote** = to ask a meeting to vote for or against the proposal; **to put a proposal to the board** = to ask the board to consider a suggestion (NOTE: **putting - put**)

put down ['pʊt 'daʊn] *verb* **(a)** to make a deposit; *to put down money on a house* **(b)** to write an item in a ledger or an account book; *to put down a figure for expenses*

put in ['pʊt 'ɪn] *verb* **to put an ad in a paper** = to have an ad printed in a newspaper; **to put in a bid for something** = to offer (usually in writing) to buy something; **to put in an estimate for something** = to give someone a written calculation of the probable costs of carrying out a job; **to put in a claim for damage** = to ask an insurance company to pay for damage; **the union put in a 6% wage claim** = the union asked for a 6% increase in wages

put into ['pʊt 'ɪntʊ] *verb* **to put money into a business** = to invest money in a business

put off ['pʊt 'ɒf] *verb* to arrange for something to take place later than planned; *the meeting was put off for two weeks*; *he asked if we could put the visit off until tomorrow*

put on ['pʊt 'ɒn] *verb* **to put an item on the agenda** = to list an item for discussion at a meeting; **to put an embargo on trade** = to forbid trade; **property shares put on gains of 10%-15%** = shares in property companies increased in value by 10%-15%

put out ['pʊt 'aʊt] *verb* to send out; *we are planning to put out most of the work to freelancers*; *we put all our typing out to a bureau*; **to put work out to contract** = to decide that work should be done by a company on a contract, rather than employ members of staff to do it

put up ['pʊt 'ʌp] *verb* **(a)** **who put up the money for the shop?** = who provided the investment money for the shop to start?; **to put something up for sale** = to advertise that something is for sale; *when he retired he decided to put his town flat up for sale* **(b)** to increase, to make higher; *the shop has put up all its prices by 5%*

PV = PRESENT VALUE

pyramid selling ['pɪrəmɪd 'selɪŋ] *noun* illegal way of selling goods or investments to the public, where each selling agent pays for the franchise to sell the product or service, and sells that right on to other agents, so that in the end the person who makes most money is the original franchisor, and sub-agents or investors lose all their investments

much of the population had committed their life savings to get-rich-quick pyramid investment schemes – where newcomers pay the original investors until the money runs out – which inevitably collapsed

Times

Qq

QC ['kjuː'siː] = QUEEN'S COUNSEL

qty ['kwɒntəti] = QUANTITY

quadruple [kwɒ'druːpl] *verb* to multiply four times; *the company's profits have quadrupled over the last five years*

quadruplicate [kwɒ'druːplɪkət] *noun* **in quadruplicate** = with the original and three copies; *the invoices are printed in quadruplicate*

qualification [kwɒlɪfɪ'keɪʃn] *noun* **(a)** proof that you have completed a specialized course of study; *you must have the right qualifications for the job*; **professional qualifications** = documents which show that someone has successfully finished a course of study which allows him to work in one of the professions **(b)** **period of qualification** = time which has to pass before someone qualifies for something **(c)** **auditors' qualification** = a form of words in a report from the auditors of a company's accounts, stating that in their opinion the accounts are not a true reflection of the company's financial position; *see also* QUALIFIED AUDIT REPORT

> personnel management is not an activity that can ever have just one set of qualifications as a requirement for entry into it
> *Personnel Management*

qualified ['kwɒlɪfaɪd] *adjective* **(a)** having passed special examinations in a subject; *she is a qualified accountant*; *we have appointed a qualified designer to supervise the decorating of the new reception area*; **highly qualified** = with very good results in examinations; *all our staff are highly qualified*; *they employ twenty-six highly qualified engineers* **(b)**

with some reservations or conditions; *qualified acceptance of a contract*; *the plan received qualified approval from the board* **(c)** **qualified accounts** = accounts which have been commented on by the auditors because they contain something with which the auditors do not agree; **qualified auditors' report** *or* **qualified audit report** *US* **qualified opinion** = report from a company's auditors which points out areas in the accounts with which the auditors do not agree or about which they are not prepared to express an opinion or where the auditors believe the accounts as a whole have not been prepared correctly or where they are unable to decide whether the accounts are correct or not

> applicants will be professionally qualified and ideally have a degree in Commerce and postgraduate management qualifications
> *Australian Financial Review*

qualify ['kwɒlɪfaɪ] *verb* **(a)** **to qualify for** = to be in the right position for, to be entitled to; *the company does not qualify for a government grant*; *she qualifies for unemployment benefit* **(b)** **to qualify as** = to follow a specialized course and pass examinations so that you can do a certain job; *she has qualified as an accountant*; *he will qualify as a solicitor next year* **(c)** **the auditors have qualified the accounts** = the auditors have found something in the accounts of the company which has made them unable to agree that they show a 'true and fair' view of the company's financial position

> federal examiners will also determine which of the

privately insured savings and loans qualify for federal insurance

qualifying ['kwɒlɪfaɪɪŋ] *adjective* **(a) qualifying period** = time which has to pass before something qualifies for a grant or subsidy, etc.; *there is a six-month qualifying period before you can get a grant from the local authority* **(b) qualifying shares** = number of shares which you need to earn to get a bonus issue or to be a director of the company, etc.

quality ['kwɒlɪti] *noun* **(a)** what something is like, how good or bad something is; *the bad quality of the service caused many complaints*; **we sell only quality farm produce** = we sell only farm produce of the best quality; *there is a market for good quality secondhand computers*; **high quality** *or* **top quality** = very best quality; *the store specializes in high quality imported items* **(b) quality control** = checking that the quality of a product is good; **quality controller** = person who checks the quality of a product

quango ['kwæŋgəʊ] *noun* official body, set up by a government to investigate or deal with a special problem

quantifiable ['kwɒntɪfaɪəbl] *adjective* which can be quantified; *the effect of the change in the discount structure is not quantifiable*

quantify ['kwɒntɪfaɪ] *verb* **to quantify the effect of something** = to show the effect of something in figures; *it is impossible to quantify the effect of the new legislation on our turnover*

quantity ['kwɒntəti] *noun* **(a)** amount or number of items; *a small quantity of illegal drugs*; *he bought a large quantity of spare parts* **(b)** large amount; *the company offers a discount for quantity purchase*; **quantity discount** = discount given to a customer who buys large quantities of goods **(c) to carry out a quantity survey** = to estimate the amount of materials and the cost of the labour required for a construction project; **quantity surveyor** = person who carries out a quantity survey

quart [kwɔːt] *noun* old measure of liquids or of loose goods, such as seeds (= 1.136 litres)

quarter ['kwɔːtə] *noun* **(a)** one of four equal parts (25%); *he paid only a quarter of the list price*; **a quarter of a litre** *or* **a quarter litre** = 250 millilitres; **a quarter of an hour** = 15 minutes; **three quarters** = 75%; *three quarters of the staff are less than thirty years old* **(b)** period of three months; *the instalments are payable at the end of each quarter*; **first quarter** = period of three months from January to the end of March; *the first quarter's rent is payable in advance*; **second quarter** = period of three months from April to the end of June; **third quarter** = period of three months from July to the end of September; **fourth quarter** *or* **last quarter** = period of three months from October to the end of the year; **quarter day** = day at the end of a quarter, when rents, fees, etc., should be paid **(c)** *US (informal)* 25 cent coin

COMMENT: in England, the quarter days are 25th March (Lady Day), 24th June (Midsummer Day), 29th September (Michaelmas Day) and 25th December (Christmas Day)

corporate profits for the first quarter showed a 4 per cent drop from last year's final three months

economists believe the economy is picking up this quarter and will do better still in the second half of the year

quarterly ['kwɔːtəli] *adjective & adverb* happening every three months, happening four times a year; *there is a quarterly charge for electricity*; *the bank sends us a quarterly statement*; *we agreed to pay the rent quarterly* *or* *on a quarterly basis*

quartile ['kwɔːtaɪl] *noun* one of a series of three figures below which 25%, 50% or 75% of the total falls; **second quartile** = number below which fifty percent of numbers fall; *this group falls within the second quartile*

quasi- ['kweɪzaɪ] *prefix* almost, which seems like; *a quasi-official body*

quay [kiː] *noun* place in a harbour where ships tie up; **price ex quay** = price of goods after they have been unloaded, not including transport from the harbour

query ['kwɪəri] **1** *noun* question; *the chief accountant had to answer a mass of queries from the auditors* **2** *verb* to ask a question about something, to suggest that something may be wrong; *the shareholders queried the payments to the chairman's son*

question ['kwestʃn] **1** *noun* **(a)** words which need an answer; *the managing director refused to answer questions about redundancies; the market research team prepared a series of questions to test the public's reactions to colour and price* **(b)** problem; *he raised the question of moving to less expensive offices; the main question is that of cost; the board discussed the question of redundancy payments* **2** *verb* **(a)** to ask questions; *the police questioned the accounts staff for four hours; she questioned the chairman on the company's investment policy* **(b)** to query, to suggest that something may be wrong; *we all question how accurate the computer printout is*

questionnaire [kwestʃə'neə] *noun* printed list of questions, especially used in market research; *to send out a questionnaire to test the opinions of users of the system; we were asked to answer* or *to fill in a questionnaire about holidays abroad*

queue [kjuː] **1** *noun* **(a)** line of people waiting one behind the other; *to form a queue* or *to join a queue; queues formed at the doors of the bank when the news spread about its possible collapse;* **dole queue** = line of people waiting to collect their unemployment money (NOTE: American English is **line**) **(b)** series of documents (such as orders, application forms) which are dealt with in order; **his order went to the end of the queue** = his order was dealt with last; **mortgage queue** = list of people waiting for mortgages **2** *verb* to form a line one after the other for something; *when food was rationed,*

people had to queue for bread; we queued for hours to get tickets; a list of companies queueing to be launched on the Stock Exchange

quick [kwɪk] *adjective* fast, not taking any time; *the company made a quick recovery; he is looking for a quick return on his investments; we are hoping for a quick sale*

quickly ['kwɪkli] *adverb* without taking much time; *the sale of the company went through quickly; the accountant quickly looked through the pile of invoices*

quid [kwɪd] *noun (slang)* one pound (in money)

quid pro quo ['kwɪd 'prəʊ 'kwəʊ] *noun* money paid or action carried out in return for something; *he agreed to repay the loan early, and as a quid pro quo the bank released the collateral*

quiet ['kwaɪət] *adjective* calm, not excited; *the market is very quiet; currency exchanges were quieter after the government's statement on exchange rates;* **on the quiet** = in secret; *he transferred the money to his bank account in Switzerland on the quiet*

quit [kwɪt] *verb* to resign, to leave (a job); *he quit after an argument with the managing director; several of the managers are quitting to set up their own company* (NOTE: **quitting - quit**)

quite [kwaɪt] *adverb* **(a)** more or less; *he is quite a good salesman; she can type quite fast; sales were quite satisfactory in the first quarter* **(b)** very or completely; *he is quite capable of running the department alone; the company is quite possibly going to be sold* **(c)** **quite a few** or **quite a lot** = many; *quite a few of our sales staff are women; quite a lot of orders come in the pre-Christmas period*

quorate ['kwɔːreɪt] *adjective* (meeting) with enough people to form a quorum

> COMMENT: if there is a quorum at a meeting, the meeting is said to be 'quorate'; if there aren't enough people present to make a quorum, the meeting is 'inquorate'

quorum ['kwɔːrəm] *noun* number of people who have to be present at a meeting to make it valid; **to have a quorum** = to have enough people present for a meeting to go ahead; *do we have a quorum?*

quota ['kwəʊtə] *noun* fixed amount of something which is allowed; **import quota** = fixed quantity of a particular type of goods which the government allows to be imported; *the government has imposed a quota on the importation of cars; the quota on imported cars has been lifted;* **quota system** = system where imports or supplies are regulated by fixing maximum amounts; **to arrange distribution through a quota system** = to arrange distribution by allowing each distributor only a certain number of items

Canada agreed to a new duty-free quota of 600,000 tonnes a year
Globe and Mail (Toronto)

quotation [kwəʊ'teɪʃn] *noun* **(a)** estimate of how much something will cost; *they sent in their quotation for the job; to ask for quotations for refitting the shop; his quotation was much lower than all the others; we accepted the lowest quotation* **(b)** **quotation on the Stock Exchange** *or* **Stock Exchange quotation** = listing of the price of a share on the Stock Exchange; **the company is going for a quotation on the Stock Exchange** = the company has applied to the Stock Exchange to have its shares listed; *we are seeking a stock market quotation*

quote [kwəʊt] **1** *verb* **(a)** to repeat words used by someone else; to repeat a reference number; *he quoted figures from the*

annual report; in reply please quote this number; when making a complaint please quote the batch number printed on the box; he replied, quoting the number of the account **(b)** to estimate, to say what costs may be; *to quote a price for supplying stationery; their prices are always quoted in dollars; he quoted me a price of £1,026; can you quote for supplying 20,000 envelopes?* **2** *noun (informal)* estimate of how much something will cost; *to give someone a quote for supplying computers; we have asked for quotes for refitting the shop; his quote was the lowest of three; we accepted the lowest quote*

banks operating on the foreign exchange market refrained from quoting forward US/Hongkong dollar exchange rates
South China Morning Post

quoted ['kwəʊtɪd] *adjective* **quoted company** = company whose shares can be bought or sold on the Stock Exchange; **quoted shares** = shares which can be bought or sold on the Stock Exchange

a Bermudan-registered company quoted on the Luxembourg stock exchange
Lloyd's List

qwerty *or* **QWERTY** ['kwɜːti] *noun* **qwerty keyboard** = English language keyboard for a typewriter or computer, where the first letters are Q-W-E-R-T-Y; *the computer has a normal qwerty keyboard*

Rr

R&D [ˈɑːrənˈdiː] = RESEARCH AND DEVELOPMENT; *the R&D department*; *the company spends millions on R&D*

rack [ræk] *noun* **(a)** frame to hold items for display; *put the birthday card display rack near the checkout*; *we need a bigger display rack for these magazines*; **rack jobber** = wholesaler who sells goods by putting them on racks in retail shops **(b)** **rack rent** = (i) very high rent; (ii) full yearly rent of a property let on a normal lease

racket [ˈrækɪt] *noun* illegal deal which makes a lot of money; *he runs a cut-price ticket racket*

racketeer [rækəˈtɪə] *noun* person who runs a racket

racketeering [rækəˈtɪərɪŋ] *noun* US crime of carrying on an illegal business to make money

> he was charged with 98 counts of racketeering and securities fraud and went on to serve two years in jail. He was banned for life from the securities industry
>
> *Times*

raid [reɪd] *noun* **dawn raid** = buying large numbers of shares in a company at the beginning of a day's trading (up to 15% of a company's shares may be bought in this way, and the purchaser must wait for seven days before purchasing any more shares; it is assumed that a dawn raid is the first step towards a takeover of the target company); **bear raid** = selling large numbers of shares to try to bring down prices

raider [ˈreɪdə] *noun* company which buys shares in another company before making a takeover bid

> bear raiding involves trying to depress a target company's share price by heavy selling of its shares, spreading adverse rumours or a combination of the two. As an added refinement, the raiders may sell short. The aim is to push down the price so that the raiders can buy back the shares they sold at a lower price
>
> *Guardian*

rail [reɪl] *noun* the railway, a system of travel using trains; *six million commuters travel to work by rail each day*; *we ship all our goods by rail*; *rail travellers are complaining about rising fares*; *rail travel is cheaper than air travel*; **free on rail (FOR)** = price including all the seller's costs until the goods are delivered to the railway for shipment

railhead [ˈreɪlhed] *noun* end of a railway line; *the goods will be sent to the railhead by lorry*

railway US **railroad** [ˈreɪlweɪ or ˈreɪlrəʊd] *noun* system using trains to carry passengers and goods; *the local railway station has frequent trains to London*; *they are planning to close the railway line as it isn't economic*; *the country's railway network is being modernized*

raise [reɪz] **1** *noun* US increase in salary; *he asked the boss for a raise*; *she is pleased - she has had her raise* (NOTE: British English is **rise**) **2** *verb* **(a)** to ask a meeting to discuss a question; *to raise a question or a point at a meeting*; *in answer to the questions raised by Mr Smith*; *the chairman tried to prevent the question of redundancies being raised* **(b)** to raise an

invoice = to write out or print out an invoice **(c)** to increase or to make higher; *the government has raised the tax levels*; *air fares will be raised on June 1st*; *the company raised its dividend by 10%*; *when the company raised its prices, it lost half of its share of the market* **(d)** to obtain (money) or to organize (a loan); *the company is trying to raise the capital to fund its expansion programme*; *the government raises more money by indirect taxation than by direct*; *where will he raise the money from to start up his business?*

> the company said yesterday that its recent share issue has been oversubscribed, raising A$225.5m
> *Financial Times*

> investment trusts can raise capital, but this has to be done as a company does, by a rights issue of equity
> *Investors Chronicle*

> over the past few weeks, companies raising new loans from international banks have been forced to pay more
> *Financial Times*

rake in ['reɪk 'ɪn] *verb* to gather together; **to rake in cash** *or* **to rake it in** = to make a lot of money

rake-off ['reɪkɒf] *noun* commission; *the group gets a rake-off on all the company's sales*; *he got a £100,000 rake-off for introducing the new business* (NOTE: plural is **rake-offs**)

rally ['ræli] **1** *noun* rise in price when the trend has been downwards; *shares staged a rally on the Stock Exchange*; *after a brief rally shares fell back to a new low* **2** *verb* to rise in price, when the trend has been downwards; *shares rallied on the news of the latest government figures*

> when Japan rallied, it had no difficulty in surpassing its previous all-time high, and this really stretched the price-earnings ratios into the stratosphere
> *Money Observer*

> bad news for the U.S. economy ultimately may have been the cause of a late rally in stock prices yesterday
> *Wall Street Journal*

RAM [ræm] = RANDOM ACCESS MEMORY

ramp [ræmp] *noun* **loading ramp** = raised platform which makes it easier to load goods onto a lorry

random ['rændəm] *adjective* done without making any special choice; **random access memory (RAM)** = computer memory that allows access to any location in any order without having to access the rest of memory; **random check** = check on items taken from a group without any special choice; **random error** = computer error which has no special reason; **random sample** = sample for testing taken without any choice; **random sampling** = choosing samples for testing without any special selection; **at random** = without special choice; *the chairman picked out two salesmen's reports at random*

range [reɪndʒ] **1** *noun* **(a)** series of items from which the customer can choose; *we offer a wide range of sizes or of styles*; *their range of products or product range is too narrow*; *we have the most modern range of models or model range on the market* **(b)** variation from small to large; *I am looking for something in the £6 - £8 price range*; *we make shoes in a wide range of prices* **(c)** type of variety; *this falls within the company's range of activities* **2** *verb* to vary, to be different; *the company sells products ranging from the cheap down-market pens to imported luxury items*; *the company's salary scale ranges from £8,000 for a trainee to £150,000 for the managing director*; *our activities range from mining in the USA to computer services in Scotland*

rank [ræŋk] **1** *noun* position in a company or an organization; *all managers are of equal rank*; **in rank order** = in order according to position of importance **2** *verb* **(a)** to classify in order of importance; *candidates are ranked in order of appearance* **(b)** to be in a certain position;

the non-voting shares rank equally with the voting shares; **all managers rank equally** = all managers have the same status in the company

rank and file ['ræŋk ənd 'faɪl] *noun* ordinary members (of a trade union, an association, etc.); *the rank and file of the trade union membership*; *the decision was not liked by the rank and file*; **rank-and-file members** = ordinary members

ranking ['ræŋkɪŋ] *adjective* in a certain position; *high-ranking official*; **he is the top-ranking** *or* **the senior-ranking official in the delegation** = the member of the delegation who occupies the highest official post

rapid ['ræpɪd] *adjective* fast or quick; **we offer a 5% discount for rapid settlement** = we take 5% off the price if the customer pays quickly

rapidly ['ræpɪdli] *adverb* quickly or fast; *the company rapidly ran up debts of over £1m*; *the new clothes shop rapidly increased sales*

rare [reə] *adjective* not common; *experienced salesmen are rare these days*; *it is rare to find a small business with good cash flow*

rarely ['reəli] *adverb* not often; *the company's shares are rarely sold on the Stock Exchange*; *the chairman is rarely in his office on Friday afternoons*

rata ['rɑːtə] *see* PRO RATA

rate [reɪt] **1** *noun* (a) money charged for time worked or work completed; **all-in rate** = price which covers all items in a purchase (such as delivery, tax and insurance, as well as the goods themselves); **fixed rate** = charge which cannot be changed; **flat rate** = charge which always stays the same; *a flat-rate increase of 10%*; *we pay a flat rate for electricity each quarter*; *he is paid a flat rate of £2 per thousand*; **freight rates** = charges for transporting goods; **full rate** = full charge, with no reductions; **the going rate** = the usual or the current rate of payment; **letter rate** *or* **parcel rate** = postage (calculated by weight) for sending a letter or a parcel; *it is more expensive to send a packet letter rate but it will get*

there quicker; **the market rate** = normal price in the market; *we pay the going rate or the market rate for typists*; *the going rate for offices is £10 per square foot*; **night rate** = cheap telephone calls at night; **reduced rate** = specially cheap charge; **rate card** = list of charges for advertising issued by a newspaper or magazine **(b)** **discount rate** = (i) interest rate used to calculate the discount on the sale of commercial bills to a central bank, such as the Bank of England; (ii) rate at which the face value of a bill of exchange is reduced when payment is made before the maturing date; (iii) percentage used in a discounting calculation, as when finding the present value of future income; **insurance rates** = amount of premium which has to be paid per £1000 of insurance **(c)** amount of money paid (shown as a percentage); **interest rate** *or* **rate of interest** = percentage charge for borrowing money; **rate of return** = amount of interest or dividend which comes from an investment, shown as a percentage of the money invested; **(bank) base rate** = basic rate of interest which a bank uses to calculate the actual rate of interest on loans to customers; *the Bank of England's Monetary Policy Committee decided to leave the base rate at 5.50%* **(d)** value of one currency against another; *what is today's rate or the current rate for the dollar?*; **cross rate** = exchange rate between two currencies expressed in a third currency; **exchange rate** *or* **rate of exchange** = rate at which one currency is exchanged for another; **to calculate costs on a fixed exchange rate** = to calculate costs on an exchange rate which does not change; **forward rate** = rate for purchase of foreign currency at a fixed price for delivery at a later date **(e)** amount, number or speed compared with something else; *the rate of increase in redundancies*; *the rate of absenteeism or the absenteeism rate always increases in fine weather*; **birth rate** = number of children born per 1,000 of the population; **call rate** = number of calls (per day or per week) which a salesman makes on customers; **depreciation rate** = rate at which an asset is depreciated each year in the company accounts; **error rate** = number of mistakes per thousand entries or per page; **rate of sales** = speed at which units are sold **(f) GB rates** = local taxes on property; **business rate** = tax levied on business property (NOTE: American English is **local property tax**) **2** *verb* **to rate someone highly** = to value someone, to think someone is very good

> state-owned banks cut their prime rate a percentage point to 11%
>
> *Wall Street Journal*

> the unions had argued that public sector pay rates had slipped behind rates applying in private sector employment
>
> *Australian Financial Review*

> royalties have been levied at a rate of 12.5% of full production
>
> *Lloyd's List*

> the minister is not happy that banks are paying low interest on current accounts of less than 10 per cent, but are charging rates of between 60 and 71 per cent on loans
>
> *Business in Africa*

rateable ['reɪtəbl] *adjective* **rateable value** = value of a property as a basis for calculating local taxes

ratepayer ['reɪtpeɪə] *noun* **business ratepayer** = business which pays local taxes on a shop, factory, etc.

ratification [rætɪfɪ'keɪʃən] *noun* official approval; *the agreement has to go to the board for ratification*

ratify ['rætɪfaɪ] *verb* to approve officially; *the agreement has to be ratified by the board*

rating ['reɪtɪŋ] *noun* **(a)** valuing of property; **rating officer** = official in a local authority who decides the rateable value of business premises **(b) credit rating** = amount which a credit agency feels a customer will be able to repay; **merit rating** = judging how well a worker does his work, so that he can be paid according to merit; **performance rating** = judging how well a share or a company has performed **(c) ratings** = estimated number of people who watch TV programmes; *the*

show is high in the ratings, which means it will attract good publicity

ratio ['reɪʃɪəʊ] *noun* proportion or quantity of something compared to something else; *the ratio of successes to failures*; *our product outsells theirs by a ratio of two to one*; **price/earnings ratio (P/E ratio)** = comparison between the market price of a share and the current dividend it produces; *the shares sell at a P/E ratio of 7*

ration ['ræʃən] *verb* to allow someone only a certain amount (of food or money); *to ration investment capital or to ration funds for investment*; **to ration mortgages** = to make only a certain amount of money available for house mortgages, and so restrict the number of mortgages which can be given; *mortgages are rationed for first-time buyers*

rationale [ræʃə'nɑːl] *noun* set of reasons for doing something; *I do not understand the rationale behind the decision to sell the warehouse*

rationalization [ræʃnəlaɪ'zeɪʃən] *noun* streamlining, making more efficient

rationalize ['ræʃnəlaɪz] *verb* to streamline, to make more efficient; *the rail company is trying to rationalize its freight services*

rationing ['ræʃənɪŋ] *noun* allowing only a certain amount of something to be sold; *there may be a period of food rationing this winter*; *building societies are warning of mortgage rationing*

rat race ['ræt 'reɪs] *noun* competition for success in business or in a career; *he decided to get out of the rat race and buy a small farm*

raw [rɔː] *adjective* in the original state, not processed; **raw data** = data as it is put into a computer, without being analyzed; **raw materials** = substances which have not been manufactured (such as wool, wood, sand)

> it makes sense for them to produce goods for sale back home in the US from plants in Britain where raw materials are relatively cheap
>
> *Duns Business Month*

Rd = ROAD

R/D = REFER TO DRAWER

re [riː] *preposition* about, concerning or referring to; *re your inquiry of May 29th*; *re: Smith's memo of yesterday*; *re: the agenda for the AGM*

re- [riː] *prefix* again

reach [riːtʃ] *verb* (**a**) to arrive at a place or at a point; *the plane reaches Hong Kong at midday*; *sales reached £1m in the first four months of the year*; *I did not reply because your letter never reached me* (**b**) to come to; **to reach an agreement** = to agree; **to reach an accommodation with creditors** = to agree terms for a settlement with creditors; **to reach a decision** = to decide; *the two parties reached an agreement over the terms for the contract*; *the board reached a decision about closing the factory*

react [rɪˈækt] *verb* **to react to** = to do or to say something in reply to what someone has done or said; *shares reacted sharply to the fall in the exchange rate*; *how will the chairman react when we tell him the news?*

reaction [rɪˈækʃən] *noun* change or action in reply to something said or done; *the reaction of the shares to the news of the takeover bid*; *his immediate reaction was to make half the workforce redundant*

read [riːd] *verb* to look at printed words and understand them; *the terms and conditions are printed in very small letters so that they are difficult to read*; *has the managing director read your report on sales in India?*; **can the computer read this information?** = can the computer take in this information and understand it or analyze it?

readable [ˈriːdəbl] *adjective* which can be read; **machine-readable codes** = sets of signs or letters (such as bar codes, post codes) which can be read and understood by a computer; **the data has to be presented in computer-readable form** = in a form which a computer can read

readjust [riːəˈdʒʌst] *verb* to adjust again; *to readjust prices to take account of the rise in the costs of raw materials*; *share prices readjusted quickly to the news of the devaluation*

readjustment [riːəˈdʒʌstmənt] *noun* act of readjusting; *a readjustment in pricing*; *after the devaluation there was a period of readjustment in the exchange rates*

read only memory (ROM) [ˈriːd ˈəʊnli ˈmeməri] *noun* computer memory device that has had data written into it when it is manufactured, and so can only be read but not written to

readvertise [ˈriːˈædvətaɪz] *verb* to advertise again; **to readvertise a post** = to put in a second advertisement for a vacant post; *all the candidates failed the test, so we will just have to readvertise*

readvertisement [ˈriːədˈvɜːtɪsmənt] *noun* second advertisement for a vacant post; *the readvertisement attracted only two new applicants*

ready [ˈredi] *adjective* (**a**) fit to be used or to be sold; *the order will be ready for delivery next week*; *the driver had to wait because the shipment was not ready*; **make-ready time** = time to get a machine ready to start production (**b**) **ready cash** = money which is immediately available for payment; *these items find a ready sale in the Middle East* = these items sell rapidly or easily in the Middle East

ready-made *or* **ready-to-wear** [redɪˈmeɪd *or* redɪtəˈweə] *adjective* (clothes) which are mass-produced, not made for each customer personally; *the ready-to-wear trade has suffered from foreign competition*

real [rɪəl] *adjective* (**a**) true, not an imitation; *his case is made of real leather or he has a real leather case*; *that car is a real bargain at £300* (**b**) (price, etc.) shown in terms of money adjusted for inflation; **real income** *or* **real wages** = income which is available for spending after tax, etc., has been deducted and after inflation has been taken into account; **in real terms** = actually or really; *prices have gone up by 3% but with inflation running at 5% that is a fall in real terms* (**c**) **real time** = time when a computer is working on the processing of data while the problem to which the data refers is actually taking place; *the website allows you to check* *share prices in real time* or *gives real time information on share prices*; **real-time system** = computer system where data is inputted directly into the computer which automatically processes it to produce information which can be used immediately **(d) real estate** = property (land or buildings); *he made his money from real estate deals in the 1980s; US* **real estate agent** = person who sells property for customers

---

real wages have been held down dramatically: they have risen as an annual rate of only 1% in the last two years

Sunday Times

---

sterling M3 rose by 13.5% in the year to August - seven percentage points faster than the rate of inflation and the biggest increase in real terms for years

Economist

Japan's gross national product for the April-June quarter dropped 0.4% in real terms from the previous quarter

Nikkei Weekly

---

on top of the cost of real estate, the investment in inventory and equipment to open a typical warehouse comes to around $5 million

Duns Business Month

---

realign [riːəˈlaɪn] *verb* to change the relationship between things; *to realign currencies*

realignment [rɪəˈlaɪnmənt] *noun* changing a system, so that different parts are in a different relationship to each other; **a currency realignment** = a change in the international exchange rates

realizable [rɪəˈlaɪzəbl] *adjective* **realizable assets** = assets which can be sold for money

realization [rɪəlaɪˈzeɪʃən] *noun* **(a)** gradual understanding; *the chairman's realization that he was going to be outvoted* **(b)** making real; **the realization of a project** = putting a project into action; *the plan moved a stage nearer realization*

when the contracts were signed **(c) realization of assets** = selling of assets for money

realize [ˈrɪəlaɪz] *verb* **(a)** to understand clearly; *he soon realized the meeting was going to vote against his proposal; the small shopkeepers realized that the hypermarket would take away some of their trade; when she went into the manager's office she did not realize she was going to be promoted* **(b)** to make something become real; **to realize a project** or **a plan** = to put a project or a plan into action; **(c)** to sell for money; *the company was running out of cash, so the board decided to realize some property* or *assets; the sale realized £100,000*

really [ˈrɪəli] *adverb* in fact; *the company is really making an acceptable profit; the office building really belongs to the chairman's father; the shop is really a general store, though it does carry some books*

realtor [ˈrɪəltə] *noun US* estate agent, person who sells real estate for customers

realty [ˈrɪəlti] *noun* property or real estate

reapplication [ˌriːæplɪˈkeɪʃən] *noun* second (or third, etc.) application

reapply [riːəˈplaɪ] *verb* to apply again; *when he saw that the job had still not been filled, he reapplied for it*

reappoint [ˈriːəˈpɔɪnt] *verb* to appoint someone again; *he was reappointed chairman for a further three-year period*

reappointment [ˈriːəˈpɔɪntmənt] *noun* being reappointed; *on her reappointment as chairman, she thanked the board for their support*

reason [ˈriːzn] *noun* explanation why something has happened; *the airline gave no reason for the plane's late arrival; the personnel officer asked him for the reason why he was late again; the chairman was asked for his reasons for closing the factory*

reasonable [ˈriːzənəbl] *adjective* **(a)** sensible or not annoyed; *the manager of the shop was very reasonable when she tried to explain that she had left her credit cards at home*; **no reasonable offer refused** = we will accept any offer which is not extremely low **(b)** moderate or not expensive; *the restaurant offers good food at reasonable prices*

reassess [riːəˈses] *verb* to assess again

reassessment [riːəˈsesmənt] *noun* new assessment

reassign [riːəˈsaɪn] *verb* to assign again

reassignment [riːəˈsaɪnmənt] *noun* new assignment

reassure [riːəˈʃʊə] *verb* **(a)** to make someone calm or less worried; *the markets were reassured by the government statement on import controls*; *the manager tried to reassure her that she would not lose her job* **(b)** to reinsure, to spread the risk of an insurance by asking another insurance company to cover part of it and receive part of the premium

rebate [ˈriːbeɪt] *noun* **(a)** reduction in the amount of money to be paid; *we are offering a 10% rebate on selected goods* **(b)** money returned to someone because he has paid too much; *he got a tax rebate at the end of the year*

rebound [rɪˈbaʊnd] *verb* to go back up again quickly; *the market rebounded on the news of the government's decision*

recall [rɪˈkɒl] *verb (of a manufacturer)* to ask for products to be returned because of possible faults; *they recalled 10,000 washing machines because of a faulty electrical connection*

recd = RECEIVED

receipt [rɪˈsiːt] **1** *noun* **(a)** paper showing that money has been paid or that something has been received; *he kept the customs receipt to show that he had paid duty on the goods*; *she lost her rent receipt*; *keep the receipt for items purchased in case you need to change them later*; *please produce your receipt if you want to exchange items*; *receipt book or book of receipts* = book of blank receipts to be filled in when purchases are made **(b)** act of receiving something; *to acknowledge receipt of a letter* = to write to say that you have received a letter; *we acknowledge receipt of your letter of the 15th*; *goods will be supplied within thirty days of receipt of order*; *invoices are payable within thirty days of receipt*; *on receipt of the notification, the company lodged an appeal* **(c)** *receipts* = money taken in sales; *to itemize receipts and expenditure*; *receipts are down against the same period of last year* **2** *verb* to stamp or to sign a document to show that it has been received, to stamp an invoice to show that it has been paid; *receipted invoices are filed in the ring binder*

> the public sector borrowing requirement is kept low by treating the receipts from selling public assets as a reduction in borrowing
> *Economist*

> gross wool receipts for the selling season to end June appear likely to top $2 billion
> *Australian Financial Review*

receivable [rɪˈsiːvəbl] *adjective* which can be received; **accounts receivable** = money owed to a company; **bills receivable** = bills which are due to be paid by a company's debtors

receivables [rɪˈsiːvəblz] *plural noun* money which is owed to a company

receive [rɪˈsiːv] *verb* to get something which has been delivered; *we received the payment ten days ago*; *the workers have not received any salary for six months*; *the goods were received in good condition*; *'received with thanks'* = words put on an invoice to show that a sum has been paid

receiver [rɪˈsiːvə] *noun* **(a)** person who receives something; *he signed as receiver of the shipment* **(b)** **official receiver** = government official who is appointed to run a company which is in financial difficulties, to pay off its debts as far as possible, and to close it down; *the court appointed a receiver for the company*; *the company is in the hands of the receiver*

receivership [rɪˈsiːvəʃɪp] *noun* **the company went into receivership** = the company was put into the hands of a receiver

> it suggests a classic case for receivership. There appear to be good businesses to be sold

to the right owner within a group that is terminally sick

Times

receiving [rɪ'siːvɪŋ] *noun* **(a)** act of getting something which has been delivered; **receiving clerk** = official who works in a receiving office; **receiving department** = section of a company which deals with incoming goods or payments; **receiving office** = office where goods or payments are received **(b) receiving order** = order from a court appointing a receiver to a company

recent ['riːsnt] *adjective* which happened not very long ago; *the company's recent acquisition of a chain of shoe shops*; *his recent appointment to the board*; *we will mail you our most recent catalogue*

recently ['riːsntli] *adverb* not very long ago; *the company recently started on an expansion programme*; *they recently decided to close the branch office in Australia*

reception [rɪ'sepʃən] *noun* place (in a hotel or office) where visitors register or say who they have come to see; **reception clerk** = person who works at a reception desk; **reception desk** = desk where customers or visitors check in

receptionist [rɪ'sepʃənɪst] *noun* person in a hotel or office who meets guests or clients, answers the phone, etc.

recession [rɪ'seʃən] *noun* fall in trade or in the economy; *the recession has reduced profits in many companies*; *several firms have closed factories because of the recession*

COMMENT: there are various ways of deciding if a recession is taking place: the usual one is when the GNP falls for three consecutive quarters

recipient [rɪ'sɪpɪənt] *noun* person who receives; *she is the recipient of an allowance from the company*

reciprocal [rɪ'sɪprəkəl] *adjective* applying from one country, person or company to another and vice versa; *we signed a reciprocal agreement or a reciprocal contract with a Russian company*; **reciprocal holdings** = situation where two companies own shares in each

other to prevent takeover bids; **reciprocal trade** = trade between two countries

reciprocate [rɪ'sɪprəkeɪt] *verb* to do the same thing to someone as he has just done to you; *they offered us an exclusive agency for their cars and we reciprocated with an offer of the agency for our buses*

in 1934 Congress authorized President Roosevelt to seek lower tariffs with any country willing to reciprocate

Duns Business Month

reckon ['rekən] *verb* **(a)** to calculate; *to reckon the costs at £25,000*; *we reckon the loss to be over £1m*; *they reckon the insurance costs to be too high* **(b) to reckon on** = to depend on, to expect something to happen; *they reckon on being awarded the contract*; *he can reckon on the support of the managing director*

reclaim [rɪ'kleɪm] *verb* to claim something which you owned before; *after he stopped paying the hire purchase instalments, the finance company tried to reclaim his car*

recognition [rekəg'nɪʃən] *noun* act of recognizing; **brand recognition** = ability of the consumer to recognize a brand on sight; **to grant a trade union recognition** = to recognize a trade union

recognize ['rekəgnaɪz] *verb* **(a)** to know someone or something because you have seen or heard them before; *I recognized his voice before he said who he was*; *do you recognize the handwriting on the letter?* **(b) to recognize a union** = to accept that a union can act on behalf of staff; *although more than half the staff had joined the union, the management refused to recognize it*; **recognized agent** = agent who is approved by the company for which he acts

recommend [rekə'mend] *verb* **(a)** to suggest that something should be done; *the investment adviser recommended buying supermarket shares*; *we do not recommend bank shares as a safe investment*; **manufacturer's recommended price (MRP)** *or* **recommended retail price (RRP)** = price which a manufacturer suggests the product should be sold at on the retail market, though often reduced by the retailer; *'all typewriters - 20% off MRP'* **(b)** to say that someone or something is good; *he recommended a shop in the High Street for shoes*; *I certainly would not recommend Miss Smith for the job*; *the board meeting recommended a dividend of 10p a share*; *can you recommend a good hotel in Amsterdam?*

---

the supermarkets have been fair with pricing - not trying to beat us down as many people might think. They are all selling at the recommended price which means the same as our smaller retail customers

The Grocer

---

recommendation [rekəmenˈdeɪʃən] *noun* saying that someone or something is good; *we appointed him on the recommendation of his former employer*

reconcile [ˈrekənsaɪl] *verb* to make two accounts or statements agree; *she is trying to reconcile one account with another or to reconcile the two accounts*

reconciliation [rekənsɪlɪˈeɪʃən] *noun* making two accounts or statements agree; **bank reconciliation** = making sure that the bank statements agree with the company's ledgers; **reconciliation statement** = statement which explains why two accounts do not agree

reconstruction [riːkənˈstrʌkʃən] *noun* **(a)** building again; *the economic reconstruction of an area after a disaster* **(b)** new way of organizing; **the reconstruction of a company** = restructuring the finances of a company by transferring the assets to a new company

record 1 [ˈrekɔːd] *noun* **(a)** report of something which has happened; *the chairman signed the minutes as a true record of the last meeting*; **for the record** *or* **to keep the record straight** = to note something which has been done; *for the record, I would like these sales figures to be noted in the minutes*; **on record** = correctly reported; *the chairman is on record as saying that profits are set to rise*; **off the record** = unofficially, in private; *he*

made some remarks off the record about the disastrous home sales figures **(b)** **records** = documents which give information; *the names of customers are kept in the company's records*; *we find from our records that our invoice number 1234 has not been paid* **(c)** description of what has happened in the past; *the salesman's record of service or service record*; *the company's record in industrial relations*; **track record** = success or failure of a company or salesman in the past; *he has a good track record as a salesman*; *the company has no track record in the computer market* **(d)** success which is better than anything before; **record sales** *or* **record losses** *or* **record profits** = sales, losses or profits which are higher than ever before; *last year was a record year for the company*; *sales last year equalled the record set in 1997*; *our top salesman has set a new record for sales per call*; **we broke our record for June** = we sold more than we have ever sold before in June **2** [rɪˈkɔːd] *verb* to note or to report; *the company has recorded another year of increased sales*; *your complaint has been recorded and will be investigated*; **recorded delivery** = mail service where the letters are signed for by the person receiving them

record-breaking [ˈrekɔːdˈbreɪkɪŋ] *adjective* which is better than anything which has happened before; *we are proud of our record-breaking profits last year*

recording [rɪˈkɔːdɪŋ] *noun* making of a note; *the recording of an order or of a complaint*

recoup [rɪˈkuːp] *verb* **to recoup your losses** = to get back money which you thought you had lost

recourse [rɪˈkɔːs] *noun* right of a lender to compel a borrower to repay money borrowed; **to decide to have recourse to the courts to obtain money due** = to decide in the end to sue someone to obtain money owed; **without recourse** = words used to show that the endorser of a bill (as an agent acting for a principal) is not responsible for paying it

recover [rɪˈkʌvə] *verb* **(a)** to get back something which has been lost; *he never* *recovered his money; the initial investment was never recovered; to recover damages from the driver of the car; to start a court action to recover property* **(b)** to get better, to rise; *the market has not recovered from the rise in oil prices; the stock market fell in the morning, but recovered during the afternoon*

recoverable [rɪˈkʌvərəbl] *adjective* which can be got back

recovery [rɪˈkʌvri] *noun* **(a)** getting back something which has been lost; *we are aiming for the complete recovery of the money invested; to start an action for recovery of property* **(b)** movement upwards of shares or of the economy; *the economy staged a recovery; the recovery of the economy after a slump;* **recovery shares** = shares which should be bought because they are likely to go up in value

recruit [rɪˈkruːt] *verb* **to recruit new staff** = to get new staff to join a company; *we are recruiting staff for our new store*

recruitment *or* **recruiting** [rɪˈkruːtmənt *or* rɪˈkruːtɪŋ] *noun* the **recruitment of new staff** = looking for new staff to join a company

rectification [rektɪfɪˈkeɪʃən] *noun* correction

rectify [ˈrektɪfaɪ] *verb* to correct something, to make something right; *to rectify an entry*

recurrent [rɪˈkʌrənt] *adjective* which happens again and again; *a recurrent item of expenditure; there is a recurrent problem in supplying this part*

recycle [ˈriːˈsaɪkl] *verb* to take waste material and process it so that it can be used again; **recycled paper** = paper made from waste paper

red [red] *noun* **in the red** = showing a debit or loss; *my bank account is in the red; the company went into the red in 1998; the company is out of the red for the first time since 1990*

redeem [rɪˈdiːm] *verb* **(a)** to pay off a loan or a debt; *to redeem a mortgage; to redeem a debt* **(b)** **to redeem a bond** = to sell a bond for cash

redeemable [rɪˈdiːməbl] *adjective* (bond) which can be sold for cash

redemption [rɪˈdempʃən] *noun* **(a)** repayment of a loan; **redemption date** = date on which a loan, etc., is due to be repaid; **redemption before due date** = paying back a loan before the date when repayment is due; **redemption value** = value of a security when redeemed; **redemption yield** = yield on a security including interest and its redemption value **(b)** repayment of a debt; *redemption of a mortgage*

redeploy [riːdɪˈplɔɪ] *verb* to move workers from one place to another, to give workers totally different jobs to do; *we closed the design department and redeployed the workforce in the publicity and sales departments*

redeployment [riːdɪˈplɔɪmənt] *noun* moving workers from one place to another

redevelop [riːdɪˈveləp] *verb* to knock down the buildings on a site, and build new ones

redevelopment [riːdɪˈveləpmənt] *noun* knocking down of existing buildings to replace them with new ones; *the redevelopment plan was rejected by the planning committee*

redistribute [riːdɪsˈtrɪbjut] *verb* to move items, work or money to different areas or people; *the government aims to redistribute wealth by taxing the rich and giving grants to the poor; the orders have been redistributed among the company's factories*

redistribution [riːdɪstrɪˈbjuːʃən] *noun* **redistribution of wealth** = sharing wealth among the whole population

redraft [riːˈdrɑːft] *verb* to draft again; *the whole contract had to be redrafted to take in the objections from the chairman*

red tape [ˈred ˈteɪp] *noun* official paperwork which takes a long time to complete; *the Hungarian joint venture has been held up by government red tape*

reduce [rɪˈdjuːs] *verb* to make smaller or lower; *we must reduce expenditure if we want to stay in business; they have reduced prices in all departments; we were expecting the government to reduce* *taxes not to increase them; we have made some staff redundant to reduce overmanning; prices have been reduced by 15%; carpets are reduced from £100 to £50; the company reduced output because of a fall in demand; the government's policy is to reduce inflation to 5%;* **to reduce staff** = to sack employees in order to have a smaller number of staff

reduced [rɪ'djuːst] *adjective* lower; *reduced prices have increased unit sales; prices have fallen due to a reduced demand for the goods*

reduction [rɪ'dʌkʃən] *noun* lowering (of prices, etc.); *price reductions have had no effect on our sales; we expect the new government to introduce tax reductions; the new MD has proposed a series of staff reductions; reduction of expenditure should help our cash flow; reduction in demand has led to the cancellation of several new projects; the company was forced to make job reductions*

redundancy [rɪ'dʌndənsi] *noun* **(a)** being no longer employed, because the job is no longer necessary; **redundancy package** = various benefits and payments given to a worker who is being made redundant; **redundancy payment** = payment made to a worker to compensate for losing his job; **voluntary redundancy** = situation where the worker asks to be made redundant, usually in return for a large payment **(b)** person who has lost a job because he is not needed any more; *the takeover caused 250 redundancies*

redundant [rɪ'dʌndənt] *adjective* **(a)** more than is needed, useless; *redundant clause in a contract; the new legislation has made clause 6 redundant* **(b) to make someone redundant** = to decide that a worker is not needed any more; **redundant staff** = staff who have lost their jobs because they are not needed any more

re-elect ['riːɪ'lekt] *verb* to elect again; *he was re-elected chairman*

re-election ['riːɪ'lekʃən] *noun* being elected again; **she is eligible to stand for re-election** = it is possible for her to be re-elected if she wants

re-employ ['riːɪm'plɔɪ] *verb* to employ someone again; *he came back to the factory hoping to be re-employed*

re-employment ['riːɪm'plɔɪmənt] *noun* employing someone again

re-engage ['riːɪn'geɪdʒ] *verb* **to re-engage staff** = to employ staff again

re-entry [riː'entri] *noun* coming back in again; **re-entry visa** *or* **permit** = visa which allows someone to leave a country and go back in again

re-examination ['riːɪgzæmɪ'neɪʃən] *noun* examining something which has already been examined before

re-examine ['riːɪg'zæmɪn] *verb* to examine something again

re-export 1 ['riː'ekspɔːt] *noun* exporting of goods which have been imported; *the port is a centre for the re-export trade; we import wool for re-export; the value of re-exports has increased* **2** [riː'eks'pɔːt] *verb* to export something which has been imported

re-exportation ['riːekspɔː'teɪʃən] *noun* exporting goods which have been imported

ref [ref] = REFERENCE

refer [rɪ'fɜː] *verb* **(a)** to mention, to deal with or to write about something; *we refer to your estimate of May 26th; he referred to an article which he had seen in the 'Times'; referring to your letter of June 4th* **(b)** to pass a problem on to someone else to decide; *the board has decided to refer the question to a committee; we have referred your complaint to our supplier* **(c)** **'refer to drawer' (R/D)** = words written on a cheque which a bank refuses to pay; **the bank referred the cheque to drawer** = the bank returned the cheque to person who wrote it because there was not enough money in the account to pay it (NOTE: **referring - referred**)

referee [refə'riː] *noun* person who can give a report on someone's character, ability, speed of work, etc.; *can I give your name as referee?; she gave the name of her boss as a referee; when applying please give the names of three referees*

reference ['refərəns] *noun* **(a) terms of reference** = areas which a committee or an inspector can deal with; *under the terms of* *reference of the committee, it cannot investigate complaints from the public*; *the committee's terms of reference do not cover exports* **(b)** mentioning, dealing with; *with reference to your letter of May 25th* **(c)** numbers or letters which make it possible to find a document which has been filed; *our reference: PC/MS 1234*; *thank you for your letter (reference 1234) please quote this reference in all correspondence*; *when replying please quote reference 1234* **(d)** written report on someone's character or ability, etc.; *to write someone a reference* or *to give someone a reference*; *to ask applicants to supply references*; **to ask a company for trade references** or **for bank references** = to ask for reports from traders or a bank on the company's financial status and reputation; **letter of reference** = letter in which an employer or former employer recommends someone for a job; *he enclosed letters of reference from his two previous employers* **(e)** person who reports on someone's character, ability, etc.; *to give someone's name as reference*; *please use me as a reference if you wish*

refinance [riːˈfaɪnæns] *verb* (i) to replace one source of finance with another; (ii) to extend a loan by exchanging it for a new one (normally done when the terms of the new loan are better)

refinancing [riːfaɪˈnænsɪŋ] *noun* **refinancing of a loan** = taking out a new loan to pay back a previous loan

the refinancing consisted of a two-for-five rights issue, which took place in September this year, to offer 55.8m shares at 2p and raise about £925,000 net of expenses

Accountancy

refit [riːˈfɪt] *verb* to fit out (a shop, factory or office) again; *the shop is being refitted* (NOTE: **refitting - refitted**)

refitting [riːˈfɪtɪŋ] *noun* fitting out (of a shop, factory or office) again; *the refitting of the shop is more expensive than we thought*; *refitting the conference room has disturbed the office routine*

reflate [rɪˈfleɪt] *verb* **to reflate the economy** = to stimulate the economy by

increasing the money supply or by reducing taxes, leading to increased inflation; *the government's attempts to reflate the economy were not successful*

reflation [rɪˈfleɪʃən] *noun* act of stimulating the economy by increasing the money supply or by reducing taxes

reflationary measures [rɪˈfleɪʃnəri ˈmeʃəz] *noun* acts which are likely to stimulate the economy

refresher course [rɪˈfreʃə ˈkɔːs] *noun* course of study to make you practise your skills again in order to improve them; *he went on a refresher course in programming*

refund 1 [ˈriːfʌnd] *noun* money paid back; *the shoes don't fit - I'm going to ask for a refund*; *she got a refund after she had complained to the manager*; **full refund** or **refund in full** = refund of all the money paid; *he got a full refund when he complained about the service* **2** [rɪˈfʌnd] *verb* to pay back money; *to refund the cost of postage*; *all money will be refunded if the goods are not satisfactory*

refundable [rɪˈfʌndəbl] *adjective* which can be paid back; *we ask for a refundable deposit of £20*; *the entrance fee is refundable if you purchase £5 worth of goods*

refusal [rɪˈfjuːzəl] *noun* saying no; **his request met with a refusal** = his request was refused; **to give someone first refusal of something** = to allow someone to be the first to decide if they want something or not; **blanket refusal** = refusal to accept many different items

refuse [rɪˈfjuːz] *verb* to say that you will not do something or will not accept something; *they refused to pay*; *the bank refused to lend the company any more money*; *he asked for a rise but it was refused*; *the loan was refused by the bank*; *the customer refused the goods* or *refused to accept the goods* (NOTE: you refuse **to do something** or refuse **something**)

regard [rɪˈgɑːd] *noun* **with regard to** = concerning or dealing with; *with regard to your request for unpaid leave*

regarding [rɪ'gɑːdɪŋ] *preposition* concerning or dealing with; *instructions regarding the shipment of goods to Africa*

regardless [rɪ'gɑːdləs] *adjective* **regardless of** = in spite of; **the chairman furnished his office regardless of expense** = without thinking of how much it would cost

region ['riːdʒən] *noun* **(a)** large area of a country; *his territory consists of all the eastern region of the country* **(b) in the region of** = about or approximately; *he was earning a salary in the region of £35,000*; *the house was sold for a price in the region of £300,000*

regional ['riːdʒənl] *adjective* referring to a region; **regional call** = phone call to a number within 56km of your own exchange; **regional planning** = planning the industrial development of a region

register ['redʒɪstə] **1** *noun* **(a)** official list; *to enter something in a register*; *keep a register up to date*; **companies' register** *or* **register of companies** = list of companies, showing their directors and registered addresses; **register of debentures** *or* **debenture register** = list of debenture holders of a company; **register of directors** = official list of the directors of a company which has to be sent to the Registrar of Companies; **land register** = list of pieces of land, showing who owns it and what buildings are on it; **Lloyd's Register** = classified list showing details of all the ships in the world and estimates of their condition; **register of shareholders** *or* **share register** = list of shareholders in a company with their addresses **(b)** large book for recording details (as in a hotel, where guests sign in, or in a registry where deaths are recorded) **(c) cash register** = machine which shows and adds the prices of items bought in a shop, with a drawer for keeping the cash received **2** *verb* **(a)** to write something in an official list; *to register a company you must pay a fee to Companies House*; *when a property is sold, the sale is registered at the Land Registry*; *you must register the trademark if you want to protect it* **(b)** to arrive at a hotel or at a conference, sign your name and write your address on a list; *they registered at the hotel under the name of*

Macdonald **(c)** to send (a letter) by registered post; *I registered the letter, because it contained some money*

registered ['redʒɪstəd] *adjective* **(a)** which has been noted on an official list; *registered share transaction*; **registered company** = company which has been officially set up and registered with the Registrar of Companies; **the company's registered office** = the head office of the company as noted in the register of companies; **registered trademark** = particular name, design, etc., which has been registered by the manufacturer and which cannot be used by other manufacturers **(b) registered post** *or* **registered mail** = system where a letter or parcel is noted by the post office before it is sent, so that compensation can be claimed if it is lost; *to send documents by registered mail* *or* *registered post*; *a registered letter* *or* *registered parcel*

registrar [redʒɪs'trɑː] *noun* person who keeps official records; **the registrar of a company** = the person who keep the share register of a company; **the Registrar of Companies** = government official whose duty is to ensure that companies are properly registered, and that, when registered, they file accounts and other information correctly (he is in charge of the Companies Registration Office or Companies House)

registration [redʒɪs'treɪʃən] *noun* **(a)** act of having something noted on an official list; *the registration of a trademark* *or* *of a share transaction*; **certificate of registration** *or* **registration certificate** = document showing that an item has been registered; **registration fee** = money paid to have something registered, money paid to attend a conference; **registration number** = official number (such as the number of a car) **(b) Companies Registration Office (CRO)** = office of the Registrar of Companies, the official organization where the records of companies must be deposited, so that they can be inspected by the public (NOTE: also called **Companies' House**); **land registration** = system of registering land and its owners

registry ['redʒɪstrɪ] *noun* **(a)** place where official records are kept; *GB* **Land Registry** = government office where details of land ownership and sales are kept; **registry office** = office where records of births, marriages and deaths are kept **(b) port of registry** = port where a ship is registered

regressive taxation [rɪ'gresɪv tæk'seɪʃn] *noun* system of taxation in which tax gets progressively less as income rises

regret [rɪ'gret] *verb* to be sorry; *I regret having to make so many staff redundant; we regret the delay in answering your letter; we regret to inform you of the death of the chairman* (NOTE: you **regret doing something** or **regret to do something** or **regret something**. Note also: **regretting - regretted**)

regular ['regjʊlə] *adjective* **(a)** which happens or comes at the same time each day, each week, each month or each year; *his regular train is the 12.45; the regular flight to Athens leaves at 06.00;* **regular customer** = customer who always buys from the same shop; **regular income** = income which comes in every week or month; *she works freelance so she does not have a regular income;* **regular staff** = full-time staff **(b)** ordinary or standard; *the regular price is $1.25, but we are offering them at 99c;* **regular size** = ordinary size (smaller than economy size, family size, etc.)

regularly ['regjʊləlɪ] *adverb* happening often each day, week, month or year; *the first train in the morning is regularly late*

regulate ['regjʊleɪt] *verb* **(a)** to adjust something so that it works well or is correct **(b)** to change or to maintain something by law; **prices are regulated by supply and demand** = prices are increased or lowered according to supply and demand; **government-regulated price** = price which is imposed by the government

regulation [regjʊ'leɪʃən] *noun* **(a)** act of making sure that something will work well; *the regulation of trading practices* **(b) regulations** = laws or rules; *the new government regulations on housing standards; fire regulations or safety*

regulations were not observed at the restaurant; regulations concerning imports and exports are set out in this leaflet

> EC regulations which came into effect in July insist that customers can buy cars anywhere in the EC at the local pre-tax price
>
> *Financial Times*

> a unit trust is established under the regulations of the Department of Trade, with a trustee, a management company and a stock of units
>
> *Investors Chronicle*

> fear of audit regulation, as much as financial pressures, is a major factor behind the increasing number of small accountancy firms deciding to sell their practices or merge with another firm
>
> *Accountancy*

regulator ['regjʊleɪtə] *noun* person whose job it is to see that regulations are followed

> the regulators have sought to protect investors and other market participants from the impact of a firm collapsing
>
> *Banking Technology*

regulatory [regjʊ'leɪtərɪ] *adjective* which applies regulations; **regulatory powers** = powers to enforce government regulations; *see* *also* SELF-REGULATORY

rehire ['riːhaɪə] *verb* to employ someone again; *I don't think it was a good idea to rehire those two workers*

reimburse [riːɪm'bɜːs] *verb* to **reimburse someone his expenses** = to pay someone back for money which he has spent; *you will be reimbursed for your expenses or your expenses will be reimbursed*

reimbursement [riːɪm'bɜːsmənt] *noun* paying back money; *reimbursement of expenses*

reimport 1 [riː'ɪmpɔːt] *noun* importing of goods which have been exported from the same country **2** ['riːɪm'pɔːt] *verb* to import goods which have been exported

reimportation [riːɪmpɔː'teɪʃən] *noun* importing goods which have been exported

reinstate [riːɪn'steɪt] *verb* to put someone back into a job from which he was dismissed; *the union demanded that the sacked workers should be reinstated*

reinstatement [riːɪn'steɪtmənt] *noun* putting someone back into a job from which he was dismissed

reinsurance [riːɪn'ʃuərəns] *noun* act of reinsuring

reinsure [riːɪn'ʃuə] *verb* to spread the risk of an insurance, by asking another insurance company to cover part of it and receive part of the premium

reinsurer [riːɪn'ʃuərə] *noun* insurance company which accepts to insure part of the risk for another insurer

reinvest [riːɪn'vest] *verb* to invest again; *he sold his shares and reinvested the money in government stocks*

reinvestment [riːɪn'vestmənt] *noun* **(a)** investing again in the same way as before **(b)** investing a company's earnings in its own business by using them to create new products for sale

many large U.S. corporations offer shareholders the option of reinvesting their cash dividend payments in additional company stock at a discount to the market price. But to some big securities firms these discount reinvestment programs are an opportunity to turn a quick profit
Wall Street Journal

reissue [riː'ɪʃuː] **1** *noun* issue of something again; thing which has been issued again; *this is a reissue of the government guidelines first issued in 1995* **2** *verb* to issue something again; *the company reissued its catalogue with a new price list*

reject 1 ['riːdʒekt] *noun* thing which has been thrown out because it is not of the usual standard; *sale of rejects or of reject items*; *to sell off reject stock*; **reject shop =**

shop which specializes in the sale of rejects **2** [rɪ'dʒekt] *verb* to refuse to accept, to say that something is not satisfactory; *the union rejected the management's proposals*; **the company rejected the takeover bid =** the directors recommended that the shareholders should not accept the bid

rejection [rɪ'dʒekʃən] *noun* refusal to accept; *the rejection of the company's offer meant that the negotiations had to start again*

related [rɪ'leɪtɪd] *adjective* connected or linked; *related items on the agenda*; **related company =** company in which another company makes a long-term capital investment in order to gain control or influence; **earnings-related pension =** pension which is linked to the size of the salary

relating to [rɪ'leɪtɪŋ 'tu] *adverb* referring to or connected with; *documents relating to the agreement*

relation [rɪ'leɪʃən] *noun* **(a) in relation to =** referring to or connected with; *he asked to see all documents in relation to the agreement* **(b) relations =** links (with other people or other companies); *we try to maintain good relations with our customers*; **to enter into relations with a company =** to start discussing a business deal with a company; **to break off relations with someone =** to stop dealing with someone; **industrial relations** *or* **labour relations =** relations between management and workers; *the company has a history of bad labour relations* **(c) public relations (PR) =** keeping good links between a company or a group and the public so that people know what the company is doing and approve of it; **public relations department (PR department) =** section of a company which deals with relations with the public; **public relations officer (PRO) =** official who deals with relations with the public

relative ['relətɪv] *adjective* which is compared to something; **relative error =** difference between an estimate and its correct value (divided by the estimate)

relatively ['relətɪvli] *adverb* more or less; *we have appointed a relatively new PR firm to handle our publicity*

release [rɪ'liːs] **1** *noun* (a) setting free; *release from a contract*; *release of goods from customs* (b) day release = arrangement where a company allows a worker to go to college to study for one day each week; *the junior sales manager is attending a day release course* (c) press release = sheet giving news about something which is sent to newspapers and TV and radio stations so that they can use the information in it; *the company sent out or issued a press release about the launch of the new car* (d) new releases = new CDs put on the market **2** *verb* (a) to free; *to release goods from customs*; *customs released the goods against payment of a fine*; *to release someone from a debt* (b) to make something public; *the company released information about the new mine in Australia*; *the government has refused to release figures for the number of unemployed women* (c) to put on the market; *they released several new CDs this month*; to release dues = to dispatch orders which had been piling up while a product was out of stock

> pressure to ease monetary policy mounted yesterday with the release of a set of pessimistic economic statistics
>
> *Financial Times*

> the national accounts for the March quarter released by the Australian Bureau of Statistics showed a real increase in GDP
>
> *Australian Financial Review*

relevant ['reləvənt] *adjective* which has to do with what is being discussed; *which is the relevant government department?*; *can you give me the relevant papers?*

reliability [rɪlaɪə'bɪləti] *noun* being reliable; *the product has passed its reliability tests*

reliable [rɪ'laɪəbl] *adjective* which can be trusted; *we are looking for a reliable bookkeeper to deal with the payroll*; *the sales manager is completely reliable*; *we have reliable information about our rival's sales*; *the company makes a very reliable product*

relief [rɪ'liːf] *noun* help; tax relief = allowing someone to pay less tax on certain parts of his income; *there is full tax relief on mortgage interest payments* = no tax is payable on income used to pay interest on a mortgage; mortgage (interest) relief = allowing someone to pay no tax on the interest payments on a mortgage up to a certain level; *see also* MORTGAGE; relief shift = shift which comes to take the place of another shift, usually the shift between the day shift and the night shift

relocate [riːlə'keɪt] *verb* to move to a different place; *the board decided to relocate the company in Scotland*; *when the company moved its headquarters, 1500 people had to be relocated*

relocation [riːlə'keɪʃn] *noun* moving to a different place; *we will pay all the staff relocation costs*

rely on [rɪ'laɪ 'ɒn] *verb* to depend on or to trust; *the chairman relies on the finance department for information on sales*; *we rely on part-time staff for most of our mail-order business*; *do not rely on the agents for accurate market reports*

remain [rɪ'meɪn] *verb* (a) to be left; *half the stock remained unsold*; *we will sell off the old stock at half price and anything remaining will be thrown away* (b) to stay; *she remained behind at the office after 6.30 to finish her work*

remainder [rɪ'meɪndə] **1** *noun* (a) things left behind; *the remainder of the stock will be sold off at half price* (b) remainders = new books sold cheaply; remainder merchant = book dealer who buys unsold new books from publishers at a very low price **2** *verb* to remainder books = to sell new books off cheaply; *the shop was full of piles of remaindered books*

remember [rɪ'membə] *verb* to bring back into your mind something which you have seen or heard or read before; *do you remember the name of the Managing Director of Smith Ltd?*; *I cannot remember the make of photocopier which he said was so good*; *did you remember to ask the switchboard to put my calls* *through to the boardroom?*; *she remembered seeing the item in a supplier's catalogue* (NOTE: you **remember doing something** which you did in the past; you **remember to do something** in the future)

remind [rɪ'maɪnd] *verb* to make someone remember; *I must remind my secretary to book the flight for New York*; *he reminded the chairman that the meeting had to finish at 6.30*

reminder [rɪ'maɪndə] *noun* letter to remind a customer that he has not paid an invoice; *to send someone a reminder*

remission [rɪ'mɪʃən] *noun* **remission of taxes** = refund of taxes which have been overpaid

remit 1 ['riːmɪt] *noun* task which a person or group is asked to deal with; *the new MD was appointed with the remit to improve the company's performance* **2** [rɪ'mɪt] *verb* to send (money); *to remit by cheque* (NOTE: **remitting - remitted**)

remittance [rɪ'mɪtəns] *noun* money which is sent; *please send remittances to the treasurer*; *the family lives on a weekly remittance from their father in the USA*

remnant ['remnənt] *noun* odd piece of a large item sold separately (used especially of items such as fabrics, carpets, etc.); *a remnant sale or a sale of remnants*

remortgage [riː'mɔːgɪdʒ] *verb* to mortgage a property which is already mortgaged; *the bank offered him better terms than the building society, so he decided to remortgage the house*

removal [rɪ'muːvəl] *noun* **(a)** moving to a new house or office; **removal** *or* **removals company** = company which specializes in moving the contents of a house or an office to a new building **(b)** sacking someone (usually a director) from a job; *the removal of the managing director is going to be very difficult*

remove [rɪ'muːv] *verb* to take something away; *we can remove his name from the mailing list*; *the government has removed the ban on imports from Japan*; *the minister has removed the embargo on the sale of computer equipment*; *two directors were removed from the board*

at the **AGM** = two directors were dismissed from the board

remunerate [rɪ'mjuːnəreɪt] *verb* to pay someone for doing something; *to remunerate someone for their services*

remuneration [rɪmjuːnə'reɪʃən] *noun* payment for services; *she has a monthly remuneration of £400*

COMMENT: remuneration can take several forms: the regular monthly salary cheque, a cheque or cash payment for hours worked or for work completed, etc.

remunerative [rɪ'mjuːnərətɪv] *adjective* (job) which pays well; *he is in a very remunerative job*

render ['rendə] *verb* **to render an account** = to send in an account; *please find enclosed payment per account rendered*

renew [rɪ'njuː] *verb* to continue something for a further period of time; *we have asked the bank to renew the bill of exchange*; *the tenant wants to renew his lease*; **to renew a subscription** = to pay a subscription for another year; **to renew an insurance policy** = to pay the premium for another year's insurance

renewal [rɪ'njuːəl] *noun* act of renewing; *renewal of a lease or of a subscription or of a bill*; *the lease is up for renewal next month*; *when is the renewal date of the bill?*; **renewal notice** = note sent by an insurance company asking the insured person to renew the insurance; **renewal premium** = premium to be paid to renew an insurance

rent [rent] **1** *noun* money paid to use an office, house or factory for a period of time; **high rent** *or* **low rent** = expensive or cheap rent; *rents are high in the centre of the town*; *we cannot afford to pay High Street rents*; *to pay three months' rent in advance*; **back rent** = rent owed; **the flat is let at an economic rent** = at a rent which covers all costs to the landlord; **ground rent** = rent paid by the main tenant to the ground landlord; **nominal rent** = very small rent; **rent control** = government regulation of rents; **income from rents** *or* **rent income** = income from letting offices, houses, etc. **2** *verb* **(a)** to pay money to hire an office, house, factory or piece of equipment for a period of time; *to rent an office or a car*; *he rents an office in the centre of town*; *they were driving a rented car when they were stopped by the police* **(b) to rent (out)** = to own a car, office, etc., and let it to someone for money; *we rented part of the building to an American company*

rental ['rentl] *noun* money paid to use an office, house, factory, car, piece of equipment, etc., for a period of time; *the car rental bill comes to over £1000 a quarter*; **rental income** *or* **income from rentals** = income from letting offices or houses, etc.; **car rental firm** = company which specializes in offering cars for rent; **fleet rental** = renting all a company's cars from the same company at a special price

top quality office furniture: short or long-term rental 50% cheaper than any other rental company
Australian Financial Review

until the vast acres of empty office space start to fill up with rent-paying tenants, rentals will continue to fall and so will values. Despite the very sluggish economic recovery under way, it is still difficult to see where the new tenants will come from
Australian Financial Review

renunciation [rɪnʌnsɪ'eɪʃən] *noun* act of giving up ownership of shares; **letter of renunciation** = form sent with new shares, which allows the person who has been allotted the shares to refuse to accept them and so sell them to someone else

reopen [riːˈəʊpən] *verb* to open again; *the office will reopen soon after its refit*

reopening [riːˈəʊpənɪŋ] *noun* opening again; *the reopening of the store after refitting*

reorder [riːˈɔːdə] **1** *noun* further order for something which has been ordered before; *the product has only been on the market ten days and we are already getting reorders*; **reorder level** = minimum amount of stock of an item which must be reordered when stock falls to this amount; **reorder quantity** = quantity of a product which is reordered, especially the economic order quantity (EOQ) **2** *verb* to place a new order for something; *we must reorder these items because stock is getting low*

reorganization [riːɔːgənaɪ'zeɪʃən] *noun* **(a)** new way of organizing; *his job was downgraded in the office reorganization or in the reorganization of the office* **(b)** action of organizing a company in a different way (as in the USA, when a bankrupt company applies to be treated under Chapter 11 to be protected from its creditors while it is being reorganized); **the reorganization of a company** *or* **a company reorganization** = restructuring the finances of a company

reorganize [riːˈɔːgənaɪz] *verb* to organize in a new way; *we have reorganized all our reps' territories*

rep [rep] **1** *noun* *(informal)* = REPRESENTATIVE; *to hold a reps' meeting*; *our reps make on average six calls a day*; **commission rep** = representative who is not paid a salary but receives a commission on sales **2** *verb* *(informal)* = REPRESENT; *he reps for two firms on commission* (NOTE: **repping - repped**)

repack [riːˈpæk] *verb* to pack again

repacking [riːˈpækɪŋ] *noun* packing again

repair [rɪˈpeə] **1** *noun* mending or making good something which was broken; *to carry out repairs to the machinery*; *his car is in the garage for repair* **2** *verb* to mend, to make good something which is broken; *the photocopier is being repaired*; **repairing lease** = lease where the tenant is responsible for repairs to the building which he is renting

repairer *or* **repair man** [rɪˈpeərə *or* rɪˈpeəmən] *noun* person who carries out repairs; *the repair man has come to mend the photocopier*

repay [rɪˈpeɪ] *verb* to pay back; *to repay money owed*; *the company had to cut back on expenditure in order to repay its debts*; **he repaid me in full** = he paid me back all the money he owed me (NOTE: **repaying - repaid**)

repayable [rɪ'peɪəbl] *adjective* which can be paid back; *loan which is repayable over ten years*

repayment [rɪ'peɪmənt] *noun* paying back; money which is paid back; *the loan is due for repayment next year*; **he fell behind with his mortgage repayments =** he was late in paying back the instalments on his mortgage; **repayment mortgage =** mortgage where the borrower pays back both interest and capital over the period of the mortgage (as opposed to an endowment mortgage, where only the interest is repaid, and an insurance is taken out to repay the capital at the end of the term of the mortgage)

repeat [rɪ'piːt] *verb* **(a)** to say something again; *he repeated his address slowly so that the salesgirl could write it down*; *when asked what the company planned to do, the chairman repeated 'Nothing'* **(b)** **to repeat an order =** to order something again

repeat order [rɪ'piːt 'ɔːdə] *noun* new order for something which has been ordered before; *the product has been on the market only ten days and we are already flooded with repeat orders*

replace [rɪ'pleɪs] *verb* to put someone or something in the place of something else; *the cost of replacing damaged stock is very high*; *the photocopier needs replacing*; *the company will replace any defective item free of charge*; *we are replacing all our salaried staff with freelancers*

replacement [rɪ'pleɪsmənt] *noun* **(a)** **replacement cost** *or* **cost of replacement =** cost of an item to replace an existing asset; **replacement value =** value of something for insurance purposes if it were to be replaced; *the computer is insured at its replacement value* **(b)** item which replaces something; *we are out of stock and are waiting for replacements* **(c)** person who replaces someone; *my secretary leaves us next week, so we are advertising for a replacement*

reply [rɪ'plaɪ] **1** *noun* answer; *there was no reply to my letter or to my phone call; I*

am writing in reply to your letter of the 24th; *the company's reply to the takeover bid*; **reply coupon =** form attached to a coupon ad which has to be filled in and returned to the advertiser; **international postal reply coupon =** coupon which can be used in another country to pay the postage of replying to a letter; *he enclosed an international reply coupon with his letter*; **reply paid card** *or* **letter =** card or letter to be sent back to the sender with a reply, the sender having already paid for the return postage **2** *verb* to answer; *he forgot to reply to the solicitor's letter*; *the company has replied to the takeover bid by offering the shareholders higher dividends*

repo = REPURCHASE AGREEMENT

report [rɪ'pɔːt] **1** *noun* **(a)** statement describing what has happened, describing a state of affairs; *the accountants are drafting a report on salary scales*; *to make a report or to present a report or to send in a report on market opportunities in the Far East*; *the sales manager reads all the reports from the sales team*; *the chairman has received a report from the insurance company*; **confidential report =** secret document which must not be shown to other people; **feasibility report =** document which says if something can be done; **financial report =** document which gives the financial position of a company or of a club, etc.; **progress report =** document which describes what progress has been made; **the treasurer's report =** document from the honorary treasurer of a society to explain the financial state of the society to its members **(b)** **the company's annual report** *or* **the chairman's report** *or* **the directors' report =** document sent each year by the chairman of a company or the directors to the shareholders, explaining what the company has done during the year and what its future prospects are (the directors' report is normally part of the annual report, but the chairman's report is optional) **(c)** **a report in a newspaper** *or* **a newspaper report =** article or news item; *can you confirm the report that the company is planning to close the factory?* **(d)** official document from a government committee; *the* government has issued a report on the *credit problems of exporters* **2** *verb* **(a)** to make a statement describing something; *the salesmen reported an increased demand for the product*; *he reported the damage to the insurance company*; *we asked the bank to report on his financial status*; *he reported seeing the absentee in a shop* **(b) to report to someone** = to be responsible to or to be under someone; *he reports direct to the managing director*; *the salesmen report to the sales director* **(c)** to go to a place or to attend; *she has been asked to report for an interview*; *please report to our London office for training*

a draft report on changes in the international monetary system

Wall Street Journal

responsibilities include the production of premium quality business reports

Times

the research director will manage a team of business analysts monitoring and reporting on the latest development in retail distribution

Times

the successful candidate will report to the area director for profit responsibility for sales of leading brands

Times

repossess [riːpəˈzes] *verb* to take back an item which someone is buying under a hire-purchase agreement, or a property which someone is buying under a mortgage, because the purchaser cannot continue the payments

repossession [riːpəˈzeʃn] *noun* act of repossessing; *repossessions are increasing as people find it difficult to meet mortgage repayments*

represent [reprɪˈzent] *verb* **(a)** to work for a company, showing goods or services to possible buyers; *he represents an American car firm in Europe*; *our French distributor represents several other competing firms* **(b)** to act for someone; *he*

sent his solicitor and accountant to *represent him at the meeting*; *three managers represent the workforce in discussions with the directors*

re-present [ˈriːprɪˈzent] *verb* to present something again; *he re-presented the cheque two weeks later to try to get payment from the bank*

representation [reprɪzenˈteɪʃən] *noun* **(a)** act of selling goods for a company; *we offered them exclusive representation in Europe*; *they have no representation in the USA* **(b)** having someone to act on your behalf; *the minority shareholders want representation on the board* **(c)** complaint made on behalf of someone; *the managers made representations to the board on behalf of the hourly-paid members of staff*

representative [reprɪˈzentətɪv] **1** *adjective* which is an example of what all others are like; *we displayed a representative selection of our product range*; *the sample chosen was not representative of the whole batch* **2** *noun* **(a) sales representative** = person who works for a company, showing goods or services for sale; *we have six representatives in Europe*; *they have vacancies for representatives to call on accounts in the north of the country* **(b)** company which works for another company, selling their goods; *we have appointed Smith & Co our exclusive representatives in Europe* **(c)** person who acts on someone's behalf; *he sent his solicitor and accountant to act as his representatives at the meeting*; *the board refused to meet the representatives of the workforce*

reprice [riːˈpraɪs] *verb* to change the price on an item (usually, to increase its price)

repudiate [rɪˈpjuːdɪeɪt] *verb* to refuse to accept; **to repudiate an agreement** = to refuse to continue with an agreement

repudiation [rɪpjuːdɪˈeɪʃən] *noun* refusal to accept

repurchase [ˈriːˈpɜːtʃəs] *verb* to buy something again, especially something which you have recently bought and then sold; **repurchase agreement** *or* **repo** = agreement, where a bank agrees to buy something and sell it back later (in effect, giving a cash loan to the seller; this is used especially to raise short-term finance)

reputable ['repjʊtəbl] *adjective* with a good reputation; *we only use reputable carriers*; *a reputable firm of accountants*

reputation [repjʊ'teɪʃən] *noun* opinion of someone or something held by other people; *company with a reputation for quality*; *he has a reputation for being difficult to negotiate with*

request [rɪ'kwest] **1** *noun* asking for something; *they put in a request for a government subsidy*; *his request for a loan was turned down by the bank*; on request = if asked for; *we will send samples on request or 'samples available on request'* **2** *verb* to ask for; *to request assistance from the government*; *I am sending a catalogue as requested*

require [rɪ'kwaɪə] *verb* **(a)** to ask for, to demand something; *to require a full explanation of expenditure*; *the law requires you to submit all income to the tax authorities* **(b)** to need; *the document requires careful study*; *to write the program requires a computer specialist*

requirement [rɪ'kwaɪəmənt] *noun* what is needed; **public sector borrowing requirement (PSBR)** = amount of money which a government has to borrow to pay for its own spending

requirements [rɪ'kwaɪəmənts] *plural noun* things which are needed; *we hope the items will meet the customer's requirements*; *if you will supply us with a list of your requirements, we shall see if we can meet them*; **these items are surplus to our requirements** = we do not need these items; **the requirements of a market** *or* **market requirements** = things which are needed by the market; **budgetary requirements** = spending or income needed to meet the budget forecasts; **manpower requirements** = number of workers needed

requisition [rekwɪ'zɪʃən] **1** *noun* official order for something; *what is the reference number of your latest requisition?*; **cheque requisition** = official note from a department to the company accounts staff asking for a cheque to be written **2** *verb* to put in an official order for something; to

ask for supplies to be sent; *we have requisitioned three truck to move the stock*

resale [riː'seɪl] *noun* selling goods which have been bought; *to purchase something for resale*; *the contract forbids resale of the goods to the USA*

resale price maintenance (RPM)

[riː'seɪl 'praɪs 'meɪntənəns] *noun* system where the price for an item is fixed by the manufacturer and the retailer is not allowed to sell it at a lower price

reschedule [riː'ʃedjuːl] *verb* **(a)** to arrange a new timetable for something; *he missed his plane, and all the meetings had to be rescheduled* **(b)** to arrange new credit terms for the repayment of a loan; *Third World countries which are unable to keep up the interest payments on their loans from western banks have asked for their loans to be rescheduled*

rescind [rɪ'sɪnd] *verb* to annul, to cancel; *to rescind a contract or an agreement*

rescue ['reskjuː] **1** *noun* saving someone or something from danger; **rescue operation** = arrangement by a group of people to save a company from collapse; *the banks planned a rescue operation for the company* **2** *verb* to save someone or something from danger; *the company nearly collapsed, but was rescued by the banks*

research [rɪ'sɜːtʃ] **1** *noun* trying to find out facts or information; **consumer research** = research into why consumers buy goods and what goods they may want to buy; **market research** = examining the possible sales of a product and the possible customers for it before it is put on the market; **research and development (R & D)** = scientific investigation which leads to making new products or improving existing products; *the company spends millions on research and development*; **research and development costs** = the costs involved in R & D; **research and development expenditure** = money spent on R & D; **scientific research** = study to try to find out information; *he is engaged in research into the packaging of the new product line*; *the company is carrying out research into finding a medicine to cure* *colds*; **research department** = section of a company which does research; **a research institute** *or* **organization** = place which exists only to carry out research; **research unit** = separate small group of research workers; **research worker** = person who works in a research department **2** *verb* to study, to try to find out information about something; *they are researching the market for the new product*

> COMMENT: research costs can be divided into (a) applied research, which is the cost of research leading to a specific aim, and (b) basic, or pure, research, which is research carried out without a specific aim in mind: these costs are written off in the year in which they are incurred. Development costs are the costs of making the commercial products based on the research

researcher [rɪˈsɜːtʃə] *noun* person who carries out research

resell [riːˈsel] *verb* to sell something which has just been bought; *the car was sold in June and the buyer resold it to an dealer two months later*

reseller [riːˈselə] *noun* person who sells something he has just bought

reservation [rezəˈveɪʃən] *noun* booking a seat, table or room; *I want to make a reservation on the train to Plymouth tomorrow evening*; **room reservations** = department in a hotel which deals with bookings for rooms; *can you put me through to reservations?*

reserve [rɪˈzɜːv] **1** *noun* **(a)** money from profits not paid as dividend, but kept back by a company in case it is needed for a special purpose; **bank reserves** = cash and securities held by a bank to cover deposits; **capital reserves** = money from profits, which forms part of the capital of a company and can be used for distribution to shareholders only when a company is wound up; **capitalization of reserves** = issuing free bonus shares to shareholders; **cash reserves** = a company's reserves in cash deposits or bills kept in case of urgent need; *the company was forced to fall back on its cash reserves*; *to have to draw on reserves to pay the dividend*; **contingency**

reserve *or* **emergency reserves** = money set aside in case it is needed urgently; **reserve for bad debts** = money kept by a company to cover debts which may not be paid; **hidden reserves** = reserves which are not easy to identify in the company's balance sheet (reserves which are illegally kept hidden are called 'secret reserves'); **sums chargeable to the reserve** = sums which can be debited to a company's reserves; **reserve fund** = profits in a business which have not been paid out as dividend but have been ploughed back into the business **(b) reserve currency** = strong currency held by other countries to support their own weaker currencies; **currency reserves** = foreign money held by a government to support its own currency and to pay its debts; **a country's foreign currency reserves** = a country's reserves in currencies of other countries; *the UK's gold and dollar reserves fell by $200 million during the quarter* **(c)** in reserve = kept to be used at a later date; *to keep something in reserve*; *we are keeping our new product in reserve until the launch date* **(d)** reserves = supplies kept in case of need; *our reserves of fuel fell during the winter*; *the country's reserves of gas or gas reserves are very large* **(e) reserve price** = lowest price which a seller will accept at an auction; *the painting was withdrawn when it did not reach its reserve* **2** *verb* to reserve a room *or* a table *or* a seat = to book a room, table or seat; to ask for a room, table or seat to be kept free for you; *I want to reserve a table for four people*; *can your secretary reserve a seat for me on the train to Glasgow?*

> COMMENT: the accumulated profits retained by a company usually form its most important reserve

residence [ˈrezɪdəns] *noun* **(a)** house or flat where someone lives; *he has a country residence where he spends his weekends* **(b)** act of living or operating officially in a country; **residence permit** = official document allowing a foreigner to live in a country; *he has applied for a residence permit*; *she was granted a residence permit for one year or a one-year residence permit*

resident ['rezɪdənt] *noun* person or company living or operating in a country; *the company is resident in France*; **non-resident** = person or company not officially resident in a country; *he has a non-resident account with a French bank*; *she was granted a non-resident visa*

residual [rɪ'zɪdjuəl] *adjective* remaining after everything else has gone

residue ['rezɪdjuː] *noun* money left over; *after paying various bequests the residue of his estate was split between his children*

resign [rɪ'zaɪn] *verb* to give up a job; *he resigned from his post as treasurer; he has resigned with effect from July 1st; she resigned as finance director*

resignation [rezɪg'neɪʃən] *noun* act of giving up a job; *he wrote his letter of resignation to the chairman*; **to hand in** *or* **to give in** *or* **to send in your resignation** = to resign from your job

resist [rɪ'zɪst] *verb* to fight against something, not to give in to something; *the chairman resisted all attempts to make him resign*; *the company is resisting the takeover bid*

resistance [rɪ'zɪstəns] *noun* showing that people are opposed to something; *there was a lot of resistance from the shareholders to the new plan*; *the chairman's proposal met with strong resistance from the banks*; **consumer resistance** = lack of interest by consumers in buying a new product; *the new product met no consumer resistance even though the price was high*

resolution [rezə'luːʃən] *noun* decision to be reached at a meeting; **to put a resolution to a meeting** = to ask a meeting to vote on a proposal; *the meeting passed or carried or adopted a resolution to go on strike; the meeting rejected the resolution or the resolution was defeated by ten votes to twenty*

COMMENT: there are three types or resolution which can be put to an AGM: the 'ordinary resolution', usually referring to some general procedural matter, and which requires a simple majority of votes; and the 'extraordinary resolution' and 'special resolution', such as a resolution to change a company's articles of association in some way, both of which need 75% of the votes before they can be carried

resolve [rɪ'zɒlv] *verb* to decide to do something; *the meeting resolved that a dividend should not be paid*

resources [rɪ'sɔːsɪz] *plural noun* **(a)** source of supply of something; **natural resources** = supplies of gas, oil, coal, etc., which are available in the ground; *the country is rich in natural resources*; we are looking for a site with good water resources = a site with plenty of water available **(b) financial resources** = supply of money for something; *the costs of the London office are a drain on the company's financial resources*; *the company's financial resources are not strong enough to support the cost of the research programme*; **the cost of the new project is easily within our resources** = we have quite enough money to pay for the new project

respect [rɪs'pekt] **1** *noun* **with respect to** = concerning **2** *verb* to pay attention to; *to respect a clause in an agreement*; *the company has not respected the terms of the contract*

respectively [rɪs'pektɪvli] *adverb* referring to each one separately; *Mr Smith and Mr Jones are respectively MD and Sales Director of Smith Ltd*

response [rɪ'spɒns] *noun* reply or reaction; *there was no response to our mailing shot; we got very little response to our complaints*

responsibility [rɪspɒnsə'bɪləti] *noun* **(a)** being responsible; *there is no responsibility on the company's part for loss of customers' property; the management accepts no responsibility for loss of goods in storage* **(b) responsibilities** = duties; *he finds the responsibilities of being managing director too heavy*

responsible [rɪ'spɒnsəbl] *adjective* **(a) responsible for** = directing, being in charge of; *he is responsible for all sales* **(b) responsible to someone** = being under someone's authority; *he is directly* *responsible to the managing director* **(c)** a **responsible job** = job where important decisions have to be taken or where the employee has many responsibilities; *he is looking for a responsible job in marketing*

rest [rest] *noun* what is left; *the chairman went home, but the rest of the directors stayed in the boardroom*; *we sold most of the stock before Christmas and hope to clear the rest in a sale*; *the rest of the money is invested in gilts*

restaurant ['restrənt] *noun* place where you can buy a meal; *he runs a French restaurant in New York*

restaurateur [restərə'tɜː] *noun* person who runs a restaurant, especially an up-market one

restitution [restɪ'tjuːʃən] *noun* **(a)** giving back (property); *the court ordered the restitution of assets to the company* **(b)** compensation, payment for damage or loss **(c)** *(in the EU)* **export restitution** = subsidies to European food exporters

restock [riː'stɒk] *verb* to order more stock; *to restock after the Christmas sales*

restocking [riː'stɒkɪŋ] *noun* ordering more stock

restraint [rɪ'streɪnt] *noun* control; **pay restraint** *or* **wage restraint** = keeping increases in wages under control; **restraint of trade** = (i) situation where a worker is not allowed to use his knowledge in another company if he changes jobs; (ii) attempt by companies to fix prices, create monopolies or reduce competition, which could affect free trade

restrict [rɪ'strɪkt] *verb* to limit or to impose controls on; *to restrict credit*; *we are restricted to twenty staff by the size of our offices*; *to restrict the flow of trade* *or* *to restrict imports*; **to sell into a restricted market** = to sell goods into a market where the supplier has agreed to limit sales to avoid competition

restriction [rɪ'strɪkʃən] *noun* limit or controlling; **import restrictions** *or* **restrictions on imports**; **to impose restrictions on imports** *or* **on credit** = to start limiting imports or credit; **to lift credit restrictions** *or* **import restrictions**

= to allow credit to be given freely *or* to allow imports to enter the country freely

restrictive [rɪ'strɪktɪv] *adjective* which limits; **restrictive trade practices** = arrangement between companies to fix prices, to share the market, etc.

restructure [riː'strʌktʃə] *verb* to reorganize the financial basis of a company

restructuring [riː'strʌktʃərɪŋ] *noun* reorganizing the financial basis (of a company)

result [rɪ'zʌlt] **1** *noun* **(a)** profit or loss account for a company at the end of a trading period; *the company's results for last year were an improvement on those of the previous year* **(b)** something which happens because of something else; *what was the result of the price investigation?*; *the company doubled its sales force with the result that the sales rose by 26%*; **the expansion programme has produced results** = has produced increased sales; **payment by results** = being paid for profits or increased sales **2** *verb* **(a)** **to result in** = to produce as a result; *the doubling of the sales force resulted in increased sales*; *the extra orders resulted in overtime work for all the factory staff* **(b)** **to result from** = to happen because of something; *the increase in debt resulted from the expansion programme*

the company has received the backing of a number of oil companies who are willing to pay for the results of the survey

Lloyd's List

some profit-taking was noted, but underlying sentiment remained firm in a steady stream of strong corporate results

Financial Times

resume [rɪ'zjuːm] *verb* to start again; *the discussions resumed after a two hour break*

résumé ['rezjʊmeɪ] *noun US* summary of a person's life story with details of education and work experience (NOTE: British English is **curriculum vitae**)

resumption [rɪ'zʌmpʃən] *noun* starting again; **we expect an early resumption of**

negotiations = we expect negotiations will start again soon

retail ['ri:teɪl] **1** *noun* sale of small quantities of goods to the general public; **retail dealer** = person who sells to the general public; **retail shop** *or* **retail outlet** = shop which sells goods to the general public; **the retail trade** = all people or businesses selling goods retail; **the goods in stock have a retail value of £1m** = the value of the goods if sold to the public is £1m, before discounts, etc., are taken into account **2** *adverb* **he sells retail and buys wholesale** = he buys goods in bulk at a wholesale discount and sells in small quantities to the public **3** *verb* **(a) to retail goods** = to sell goods direct to the public **(b)** to sell for a price; **these items retail at** *or* **for £2.50** = the retail price of these items is £2.50

retailer ['ri:teɪlə] *noun* person who runs a retail business, selling goods direct to the public

retailing ['ri:teɪlɪŋ] *noun* selling of full price goods to the public; *from car retailing the company branched out into car leasing*

retail price ['ri:teɪl 'praɪs] *noun* price at which the retailer sells to the final customer; **retail price(s) index (RPI)** = index which shows how prices of consumer goods have increased or decreased over a period of time

> COMMENT: in the UK, the RPI is calculated on a group of essential goods and services; it includes both VAT and mortgage interest; the US equivalent is the Consumer Price Index

retain [rɪ'teɪn] *verb* **(a)** to keep; *out of the profits, the company has retained £50,000 as provision against bad debts*; **retained income** = profit not distributed to the shareholders as dividend; *the balance sheet has £50,000 in retained income*; **retained profit** = amount of profit after tax which a company does not pay out as dividend to the shareholders, but keeps within the business **(b) to retain a lawyer to act for a company** = to agree with a lawyer that he will act for you (and pay him a fee in advance)

retainer [rɪ'teɪnə] *noun* money paid in advance to someone so that he will work for you, and not for someone else; *we pay him a retainer of £1,000*

retiral [rɪ'taɪərəl] *noun* US = RETIREMENT

retire [rɪ'taɪə] *verb* **(a)** to stop work and take a pension; *she retired with a £6,000 pension*; *the founder of the company retired at the age of 85*; *the shop is owned by a retired policeman* **(b)** to make a worker stop work and take a pension; *they decided to retire all staff over 50* **(c)** to come to the end of an elected term of office; *the treasurer retires from the council after six years*; *two retiring directors offer themselves for re-election*

retirement [rɪ'taɪəmənt] *noun* act of retiring from work; **to take early retirement** = to retire from work before the usual age; **retirement age** = age at which people retire (in the UK usually 65 for men and 60 for women); **retirement pension** = pension which someone receives when he retires

retrain [ri:'treɪn] *verb* to train someone for a new job, or to do the same job in a more efficient way; *she went back to college to be retrained*

retraining [ri:'treɪnɪŋ] *noun* act of training again; *the shop is closed for staff retraining*; *he had to attend a retraining session*

retrench [rɪ'trentʃ] *verb* to reduce expenditure or to shelve expansion plans because money is not available

retrenchment [rɪ'trentʃmənt] *noun* reduction of expenditure or of new plans; *the company is in for a period of retrenchment*

retrieval [rɪ'tri:vəl] *noun* getting back; **data retrieval** *or* **information retrieval** = getting information from the data stored in a computer; **retrieval system** = system which allows information to be retrieved

retrieve [rɪ'tri:v] *verb* **(a)** to get back (something) which has been lost; *the company is fighting to retrieve its market share* **(b)** to get back (information) which is stored in a computer; *all of the information was accidentally wiped off* the computer so we cannot retrieve our sales figures for the last month

retroactive [retrəʊˈæktɪv] *adjective* which takes effect from a time in the past; *the union is asking for a retroactive pay rise*; *they got a pay rise retroactive to last January*

---

salaries of civil servants should be raised by an average of 1.92% or about ¥6286 per month. The salary increases, retroactive from April of the current year, reflect the marginal rise in private sector salaries

Nikkei Weekly

---

retroactively [retrəʊˈæktɪvli] *adverb* going back to a time in the past

return [rɪˈtɜːn] **1** *noun* (a) going back or coming back; **return journey** = journey back to where you came from; **a return ticket** *or* **a return** = a ticket for a journey to a place and back again; *I want two returns to Edinburgh*; **return fare** = fare for a journey from one place to another and back again (b) sending back; **he replied by return of post** = he replied by the next post service back; **return address** = address to send back something; **these goods are all on sale or return** = if the retailer does not sell them, he sends them back to the supplier, and pays only for the items sold (c) profit or income from money invested; *we are buying technology shares because they bring in a quick return*; *what is the gross return on this line?*; **return on capital employed (ROCE)** = profit shown as a percentage of the capital in a business; **return on investment (ROI)** = relationship between profit and money invested in a project or company, usually expressed as a percentage; **rate of return** = amount of interest or dividend produced by an investment, shown as a percentage (d) **official return** = official report; **to make a return to the tax office** *or* **to make an income tax return** = to send a statement of income to the tax office; **to fill in a VAT return** = to complete the form showing VAT receipts and expenditure; **nil return** = report showing no sales, income, tax, etc.; **daily** *or* **weekly** *or* **quarterly sales return** = report of sales made each day or week or

quarter **2** *verb* (a) to send back; *to return unsold stock to the wholesaler*; *to return a letter to sender*; **returned empties** = empty bottles or containers which are sent back to a supplier (b) to make a statement; *to return income of £15,000 to the tax authorities*

---

with interest rates running well above inflation, investors want something that offers a return for their money

Business Week

Section 363 of the Companies Act 1985 requires companies to deliver an annual return to the Companies Registration Office. Failure to do so before the end of the period of 28 days after the company's return date could lead to directors and other officers in default being fined up to £2000

Accountancy

---

returnable [rɪˈtɜːnəbl] *adjective* which can be returned; *these bottles are not returnable*

returns [rɪˈtɜːnz] *plural noun* (a) profits or income from investment; *the company is looking for quick returns on its investment*; **law of diminishing returns** = general rule that as more factors of production (land, labour and capital) are added to the existing factors, so the amount they produce is proportionately smaller (b) unsold goods, especially books, newspapers or magazines, sent back to the supplier

revaluation [riːvæljuˈeɪʃən] *noun* act of revaluing; *the balance sheet takes into account the revaluation of the company's properties*; *the revaluation of the dollar against the euro*

revalue [riːˈvæljuː] *verb* to value something again (at a higher value than before); *the company's properties have been revalued*; *the dollar has been revalued against all world currencies*

revenue [ˈrevənjuː] *noun* (a) money received; *revenue from advertising* *or* *advertising revenue*; *oil revenues have* *risen with the rise in the dollar*; **revenue accounts** = accounts of a business which record money received as sales, commission, etc. **(b)** money received by a government in tax; **Inland Revenue** *US* **Internal Revenue Service** = government department which deals with tax; **revenue officer** = person working in the government tax offices

reversal [rɪ'vɜːsəl] *noun* change from being profitable to unprofitable; *the company suffered a reversal in the Far East*

reverse [rɪ'vɜːs] **1** *adjective* opposite, in the opposite direction; **reverse takeover** = takeover where the company which has been taken over ends up owning the company which has taken it over (the acquiring company's shareholders give up their shares in exchange for shares in the target company); **reverse charge call** = telephone call where the person receiving the call agrees to pay for it **2** *verb* **(a)** to change a decision to the opposite; *the committee reversed its decision on import quotas* **(b)** to reverse the charges = to make a phone call, asking the person receiving it to pay for it

the trade balance sank $17
billion, reversing last
fall's brief improvement

Fortune

reversion [rɪ'vɜːʃən] *noun* return of property to an original owner; **he has the reversion of the estate** = he will receive the estate when the present lease ends

reversionary [rɪ'vɜːʃənəri] *adjective* (property) which passes to another owner on the death of the present one; **reversionary annuity** = annuity paid to someone on the death of another person

review [rɪ'vjuː] **1** *noun* **(a)** general examination; *to conduct a review of distributors*; **financial review** = examination of an organization's finances; **wage review** *or* **salary review** = examination of salaries or wages in a company to see if the workers should earn more; **she had a salary review last April** = her salary was examined (and increased) in April **(b)** magazine, monthly or weekly journal; *we read it in last month's*

international business review **2** *verb* to examine something generally; **to review salaries** = to look at all salaries in a company to decide on increases; *his salary will be reviewed at the end of the year*; *the company has decided to review freelance payments in the light of the rising cost of living*; **to review discounts** = to look at discounts offered to decide whether to change them

revise [rɪ'vaɪz] *verb* to change something which has been calculated or planned; *sales forecasts are revised annually*; *the chairman is revising his speech to the AGM*

revival [rɪ'vaɪvəl] *noun* **revival of trade** = increase in trade after a recession

revive [rɪ'vaɪv] *verb* to make more lively; to increase (after a recession); *the government is introducing measures to revive trade*; *industry is reviving after the recession*

revoke [rɪ'vəʊk] *verb* to cancel; *to revoke a clause in an agreement*; *the quota on luxury items has been revoked*

revolving credit [rɪ'vɒlvɪŋ 'kredɪt] *noun* system where someone can borrow money at any time up to an agreed amount, and continue to borrow while still paying off the original loan

ribbon ['rɪbn] *noun* thin strip of material or plastic, with ink or carbon on it, used in typewriters or printers

rich [rɪtʃ] *adjective* **(a)** having a lot of money; *a rich stockbroker*; *a rich oil company* **(b)** having a lot of natural resources; *the country is rich in minerals*; *the oil-rich territory has attracted several international companies*

rid [rɪd] **to get rid of something** = to throw something away because it is useless; *the company is trying to get rid of all its old stock*; *our department has been told to get rid of twenty staff* (NOTE: **getting rid - got rid**)

rider ['raɪdə] *noun* additional clause; *to add a rider to a contract*

rig [rɪg] **1** *noun* **oil rig** = platform which holds the equipment for taking oil out of the earth **2** *verb* to arrange for a result to be changed; *they tried to rig the election of* *officers*; **to rig the market** = to make share prices go up or down so as to make a profit; **rigging of ballots** *or* **ballot-rigging** = trying to change the result of an election by altering or destroying voting papers (NOTE: **rigging - rigged**)

right [raɪt] **1** *adjective* **(a)** good or correct; *the chairman was right when he said the figures did not add up*; *this is not the right plane for Paris* **(b)** not left; *the credits are on the right side of the page* **2** *noun* **(a)** legal title to something; *there is no automatic right of renewal to this contract*; *she has a right to the property*; *he has no right to the patent*; *the staff have a right to know how the company is doing*; **foreign rights** = legal title to sell something (especially a book) in a foreign country; **right to strike** = legal title for workers to stop working if they have a good reason for it; **right of way** = legal title to go across someone's property **(b)** **rights issue** = giving shareholders the right to buy new shares usually at an advantageous price (the result being that if he or she takes up the offer, each shareholder still holds proportionately the same percentage of the company's shares as before)

rightful ['raɪtfʊl] *adjective* legally correct; **rightful claimant** = person who has a legal claim to something; **rightful owner** = legal owner

right-hand ['raɪthænd] *adjective* belonging to the right side; *the credit side is the right-hand column in the accounts*; *he keeps the address list in the right-hand drawer of his desk*; **right-hand man** = main assistant

ring [rɪŋ] **1** *noun* group of people who try to fix prices so as not to compete with each other and still make a large profit **2** *verb* to call using the telephone; *he rang (up) his stockbroker* (NOTE: **ringing - rang - has rung**)

ring back ['rɪŋ 'bæk] *verb* to telephone in reply to a phone call; *the managing director rang - can you ring him back?*

ring binder ['rɪŋ 'baɪndə] *noun* file with a stiff cover with rings in it which fit into special holes made in sheets of paper

rise [raɪz] **1** *noun* **(a)** increase or growing high; *a rise in the price of raw materials*;

oil price rises brought about a recession in world trade; *there has been a rise in sales of 10% or sales show a rise of 10%*; *salaries are increasing to keep up with the rises in the cost of living*; *the recent rise in interest rates has made mortgages dearer* **(b)** increase in salary; *she asked her boss for a rise*; *he had a 6% rise in January* (NOTE: American English for this is **raise**) **2** *verb* to move upwards or to become higher; *prices are rising faster than inflation*; *interest rates have risen to 15%* (NOTE: **rising - rose - has risen**)

the index of industrial production sank 0.2 per cent for the latest month after rising 0.3 per cent in March
Financial Times

the stock rose to over $20 a share, higher than the $18 bid
Fortune

customers' deposit and current accounts also rose to $655.31 million at the end of December
Hongkong Standard

the government reported that production in the nation's factories and mines rose 0.2% in September
Sunday Times

risk [rɪsk] *noun* **(a)** possible harm or chance of danger; **to run a risk** = to be likely to suffer harm; **to take a risk** = to do something which may make you lose money or suffer harm; **financial risk** = possibility of losing money; *there is no financial risk in selling to East European countries on credit*; *he is running the risk of overspending his promotion budget*; *the company is taking a considerable risk in manufacturing 25m units without doing any market research* **(b)** **risk capital** = capital for investment usually in high-risk projects, but which can also provide high returns (also called 'venture capital') **(c)** **at owner's risk** = situation where goods shipped or stored are insured by the owner, not by the transport company or the storage company; *goods left here are at owner's risk*; *the shipment was sent at owner's risk* **(d)** loss or damage against which you are insured; **fire risk** = situation or goods which could start a fire; *that warehouse full of paper is a fire risk* (e) **he is a good** *or* **bad risk** = it is not likely, it is very likely that the insurance company will have to pay out against claims where he is concerned

> remember, risk isn't volatility. Risk is the chance that a company's earnings power will erode - either because of a change in the industry or a change in the business that will make the company significantly less profitable in the long term
> *Fortune*

risk-free ['rɪsk'friː] *adjective* with no risk involved; *a risk-free investment*

> there is no risk-free way of taking regular income from your money higher than the rate of inflation and still preserving its value
> *Guardian*

> many small investors have also preferred to put their spare cash with risk-free investments such as building societies rather than take chances on the stock market. The returns on a host of risk-free investments have been well into double figures
> *Money Observer*

risky ['rɪski] *adjective* dangerous or which may cause harm; *he lost all his money in some risky ventures in South America*

> while the bank has scaled back some of its more risky trading operations, it has retained its status as a top-rate advisory house
> *Times*

rival ['raɪvəl] *noun* person or company which competes in the same market; *a rival company; to undercut a rival; we are analyzing the rival brands on the market*

road [rəʊd] *noun* (a) way used by cars, lorries, etc., to move from one place to

another; *to send or to ship goods by road; road transport costs have risen; the main office is in London Road; use the Park Road entrance to get to the buying department* (NOTE: in addresses, **Road** is usually shortened to **Rd**) (b) **on the road** = travelling; *the salesmen are on the road thirty weeks a year; we have twenty salesmen on the road*

robot ['rəʊbɒt] *noun* machine which can be programmed to work like a person; *the car is made by robots*

robotics [rəʊ'bɒtɪks] *noun* study of robots, making of robots (NOTE: takes a singular verb)

ROCE = RETURN ON CAPITAL EMPLOYED

rock [rɒk] *noun* **the company is on the rocks** = the company is in great financial difficulties

rock bottom ['rɒk 'bɒtəm] *noun* **rock-bottom prices** = the lowest prices possible; **sales have reached rock bottom** = sales have reached the lowest point possible

> investment companies took the view that secondhand prices had reached rock bottom and that levels could only go up
> *Lloyd's List*

rocket ['rɒkɪt] *verb* to rise fast; *investors are rushing to cash in on rocketing share prices; prices have rocketed on the commodity markets*

ROI = RETURN ON INVESTMENT

roll [rəʊl] **1** *noun* something which has been turned over and over to wrap round itself; *the desk calculator uses a roll of paper; we need to order some more rolls of fax paper* **2** *verb* (a) to make something go forward by turning it over or pushing it on wheels; *they rolled the computer into position* (b) **rolling account** = ROLLING SETTLEMENT; **rolling budget** = budget which moves forward on a regular basis (such as a budget covering a twelve-month period, which moves forward each month or quarter); **rolling settlement** = system of paying for shares bought on the stock exchange, where the buyer pays at the end of a certain number of days after the purchase is made

roll on/roll off (RORO) ['rəʊlɒn 'rəʊl'ɒf] *adjective* (ferry) where lorries and cars can drive straight into or off the boat

rolling plan ['rəʊlɪŋ 'plæn] *noun* plan which runs for a period of time and is updated regularly for the same period

rolling stock ['rəʊlɪŋ stɒk] *noun* wagons, etc., used on the railway

roll over ['rəʊl 'əʊvə] *verb* **to roll over credit** or **a debt** = to make credit available over a continuing period, to allow a debt to stand after the repayment date

> at the IMF in Washington, officials are worried that Japanese and US banks might decline to roll over the principal of loans made in the 1980s to Southeast Asian and other developing countries
> *Far Eastern Economic Review*

ROM [rɒm] = READ ONLY MEMORY

room [ruːm] *noun* **(a)** part of a building, divided off from other parts by walls; *the chairman's room is at the end of the corridor*; **conference room** = room where a small meeting can take place; **mail room** = section of a building where incoming letters are sorted and distributed to departments **(b)** bedroom in a hotel; *I want a room with bath for two nights*; **double room** = room with two beds, for two people; **room service** = arrangement in a hotel where food or drink can be served in a guest's bedroom **(c)** space; *the filing cabinets take up a lot of room*; *there is no more room in the computer file*

rotation [rəʊ'teɪʃən] *noun* taking turns; **to fill the post of chairman by rotation** = each member of the group is chairman for a period then gives the post to another member; **two directors retire by rotation** = two directors retire because they have been directors longer than any others, but can offer themselves for re-election

rouble *US* **ruble** ['ruːbl] *noun* currency used in Russia and Belarus

rough [rʌf] *adjective* **(a)** approximate, not very accurate; **rough calculation** or **rough estimate** = approximate answer; *I*

made some rough calculations on the back of an envelope **(b)** not finished; **rough copy** = draft of a document which will have changes made to it before it is complete; *he made a rough draft of the new design*

roughly ['rʌfli] *adverb* more or less; *the turnover is roughly twice last year's*; *the development cost of the project will be roughly £25,000*

rough out ['rʌf 'aʊt] *verb* to make a draft or a general design; *the finance director roughed out a plan of investment*

round [raʊnd] **1** *adjective* **(a)** in round figures = not totally accurate, but correct to the nearest 10 or 100 **(b)** round trip = journey from one place to another and back again; *she bought a round-trip ticket*; *the round-trip fare is twice the single fare* **2** *noun* series (of meetings); *a round of pay negotiations*

round down ['raʊnd 'daʊn] *verb* to decrease to the nearest full figure

round up ['raʊnd 'ʌp] *verb* to increase to the nearest full figure; *to round up the figures to the nearest pound*

> each cheque can be made out for the local equivalent of £100 rounded up to a convenient figure
> *Sunday Times*

route [ruːt] *noun* **(a)** way which is regularly taken; *companies were warned that normal shipping routes were dangerous because of the war*; **bus route** = normal way taken by a bus from one place to another **(b)** en route = on the way; *the tanker sank when she was en route to the Gulf*

routine [ruː'tiːn] **1** *noun* normal, regular way of doing something; *he follows a daily routine - he takes the 8.15 train to London, then the bus to his office, and returns by the same route in the evening*; *refitting the conference room has disturbed the office routine* **2** *adjective* normal, which happens regularly; *routine work*; *routine call*; *a routine check of the fire equipment*

royalty ['rɔɪəlti] *noun* money paid to an inventor, writer or the owner of land for the right to use his property (usually a certain percentage of sales, or a certain amount per sale); *the country will benefit from rising oil royalties*; *he is receiving royalties from his invention*

RPI [ɑːpiːˈaɪ] = RETAIL PRICE(S) INDEX

RPM = RESALE PRICE MAINTENANCE

RRP = RECOMMENDED RETAIL PRICE

RSVP [ˈɑːesviːˈpiː] = REPONDEZ S'IL VOUS PLAIT letters on an invitation asking the person invited to reply

rubber [ˈrʌbə] *noun* **(a)** elastic material made from the sap of a tropical tree; **rubber band** = thin ring of rubber for attaching things together; *put a rubber band round the filing cards to stop them falling on the floor; US* **rubber check** = cheque which cannot be cashed because the person writing it does not have enough money in the account to pay it (NOTE: the British equivalent is a **bouncing cheque**) **(b)** eraser, a small piece of rubber used to remove text which has been written in pencil

rubber stamp [ˈrʌbə ˈstæmp] **1** *noun* stamp with rubber letters or figures on it to put the date or a note on a document; *he stamped the invoice with the rubber stamp 'Paid'* **2** *verb* to agree to something without discussing it; *the board simply rubber stamped the agreement*

rule [ruːl] **1** *noun* **(a)** general way of conduct; **as a rule** = usually; *as a rule, we do not give discounts over 20%*; **company rules** = general way of working in a company; *it is a company rule that smoking is not allowed in the offices*; **rule of thumb** = easily remembered way of doing a simple calculation **(b) to work to rule** = to work strictly according to the rules agreed by the company and union, and therefore to work very slowly **2** *verb* **(a)** to give an official decision; *the commission of inquiry ruled that the company was in breach of contract*; *the judge ruled that the documents had to be deposited with the court* **(b)** to be in force or to be current; *prices which are ruling at the moment*

rulebook [ˈruːlbʊk] *noun* book which lists the rules by which the members of a union or self-regulatory organization must operate

ruler [ˈruːlə] *noun* strip of wood or plastic with measurements marked on it, used for measuring and drawing straight lines; *you need a ruler to draw straight lines*

ruling [ˈruːlɪŋ] **1** *adjective* in operation at the moment, current; *we will invoice at ruling prices* **2** *noun* decision; *the inquiry gave a ruling on the case*; *according to the ruling of the court, the contract was illegal*

run [rʌn] **1** *noun* **(a)** making a machine work; **a cheque run** = series of cheques processed through a computer; **a computer run** = period of work of a computer; **test run** = trial made on a machine **(b)** rush to buy something; *the Post Office reported a run on the new stamps*; **a run on the bank** = rush by customers to take deposits out of a bank which they think may close down; **a run on the pound** = rush to sell pounds and buy other currencies **(c)** regular route (of a plane or bus); *he flies the London-New York run* **2** *verb* **(a)** to be in force; *the lease runs for twenty years*; *the lease has only six months to run* **(b)** to amount to; *the costs ran into thousands of pounds* **(c)** to manage or to organize; *she runs a mail-order business from home*; *they run a staff sports club*; *he is running a multimillion-pound company* **(d)** to work on a machine; *do not run the photocopier for more than four hours at a time*; *the computer was running invoices all night* **(e)** *(of buses, trains, etc.)* to be working; *there is an evening plane running between Manchester and Paris*; *this train runs on weekdays* (NOTE: **running - ran - has run**)

business is booming for airlines on the London to Manchester run
Business Traveller

applications for mortgages are running at a high level
Times

with interest rates running well above inflation, investors want something that

offers a return for their money

runaway inflation [ˈrʌnəweɪ ɪnˈfleɪʃən] *noun* very rapid inflation, which is almost impossible to reduce

run down [ˈrʌn ˈdaʊn] *verb* **(a)** to reduce a quantity gradually; *we decided to run down stocks or to let stocks run down at the end of the financial year* **(b)** to slow down the business activities of a company before it is going to be closed; *the company is being run down*

run into [ˈrʌn ˈɪntʊ] *verb* **(a)** to run into debt = to start to have debts **(b)** to amount to; *costs have run into thousands of pounds*; *he has an income running into five figures* = he earns more than £10,000

running [ˈrʌnɪŋ] *noun* **(a)** running total = total carried from one column of figures to the next **(b)** running costs *or* running expenses *or* costs of running a business = money spent on the day-to-day cost of keeping a business going **(c)** the company has made a profit for six years running = the company has made a profit for six years one after the other

run out of [ˈrʌn ˈaʊt əv] *verb* to have nothing left, to use up all the stock; *we have run out of headed notepaper*; *the printer has run out of paper*

run up [ˈrʌn ˈʌp] *verb* to make debts go up quickly; *he quickly ran up a bill for £250*

rupee [ruːˈpiː] *noun* currency used in India, Mauritius, Nepal, Pakistan and Sri Lanka (NOTE: written **Rs** before the figure: **Rs. 250**)

rush [rʌʃ] **1** *noun* doing something rapidly; **rush hour** = time when traffic is worst, when everyone is trying to travel to work or from work back home; *the taxi was delayed in the rush hour traffic*; **rush job** = job which has to be done fast; **rush order** = order which has to be supplied fast **2** *verb* to make something go fast; *to rush an order through the factory*; *to rush a shipment to Africa*

Ss

sachet ['sæʃeɪ] *noun* small package or envelope containing a product in the form of liquid or powder; *the fish is packaged with a sachet of sauce*

sack [sæk] **1** *noun* **(a)** large bag made of strong cloth or plastic; *a sack of potatoes*; *we sell onions by the sack* **(b)** to get the **sack** = to be dismissed from a job **2** *verb* to **sack someone** = to dismiss someone from a job; *he was sacked after being late for work*

sackful ['sækful] *noun* large amount, the contents of a sack; *we got sackfuls of replies to our TV ad*

sacking ['sækɪŋ] *noun* dismissal from a job; *the union protested against the sackings*

SAE *or* **s.a.e.** = STAMPED ADDRESSED ENVELOPE

safe [seɪf] **1** *noun* heavy metal box which cannot be opened easily, in which valuable documents, money, etc., can be kept; *put the documents in the safe*; *we keep the petty cash in the safe*; **fireproof safe** = safe which cannot be harmed by fire; **night safe** = safe in the outside wall of a bank, where money and documents can be deposited at night, using a special door; **wall safe** = safe installed in a wall **2** *adjective* **(a)** out of danger; **keep the documents in a safe place** = in a place where they cannot be stolen or destroyed; **safe keeping** = being looked after carefully; *we put the documents into the bank for safe keeping* **(b) safe investments** = shares, etc., which are not likely to fall in value

safe deposit ['seɪf dɪ'pɒzɪt] *noun* bank safe where you can leave jewellery or documents

safe deposit box ['seɪf dɪ'pɒzɪt 'bɒks] *noun* small box which you can rent to keep jewellery or documents in a bank's safe

safeguard ['seɪfgɑːd] *verb* to protect; *the duty of the directors is to safeguard the interests of the shareholders*

safely ['seɪfli] *adverb* without being harmed; *the cargo was unloaded safely from the sinking ship*

safety ['seɪfti] *noun* **(a)** being free from danger or risk; **safety margin** = time or space allowed for something to be safe; **margin of safety** = units produced (or sales of such units) which are above the breakeven point; **to take safety precautions** *or* **safety measures** = to act to make sure something is safe; **safety regulations** = rules to make a place of work safe for the workers **(b) fire safety** = making a place of work safe for the workers in case of fire; **fire safety officer** = person in a company responsible for seeing that the workers are safe if a fire breaks out **(c) for safety** = to make something safe, to be safe; *put the documents in the cupboard for safety*; *to take a copy of the disk for safety*

sail [seɪl] *verb* to leave harbour; *the ship sails at 12.00*

sailing ['seɪlɪŋ] *noun* departure (of a ship); *there are no sailings to France because of the strike*

salaried ['sælərɪd] *adjective* earning a salary; *the company has 250 salaried staff*

salary ['sæləri] *noun* payment for work, made to an employee with a contract of employment, usually in the form of a monthly cheque; *she got a salary increase in June*; *the company froze all salaries for a six-month period*; **basic salary** = normal salary without extra payments; **gross salary** = salary before tax is deducted; **net salary** = salary which is left after deducting tax and national insurance contributions; **starting salary** = amount of payment for an employee when starting work; *he was appointed at a starting salary of £10,000*; **salary cheque** = monthly cheque by which an employee is paid; **salary cut** = sudden reduction in salary; **salary deductions** = money which a company removes from salaries to give to the government as tax, national insurance contributions, etc.; **salary review** = examination of salaries in a company to see if workers should earn more; *she had a salary review last April or her salary was reviewed last April*; **scale of salaries** *or* **salary scale** = list of salaries showing different levels of pay in different jobs in the same company; **the company's salary structure** = organization of salaries in a company, with different rates for different types of job

---

the union of hotel and
personal service workers has
demanded a new salary
structure and uniform
conditions of service for
workers in the hotel and
catering industry

Business Times (Lagos)

---

sale [seɪl] *noun* **(a)** act of selling, the act of giving an item or doing a service in exchange for money, or for the promise that money will be paid; **cash sale** = selling something for cash; **credit card sale** = selling something for credit, using a credit card; **firm sale** = sale which does not allow the purchaser to return the goods; **forced sale** = selling something because a court orders it or because it is the only thing to do to avoid a financial crisis; **sale and lease-back** = situation where a company sells a property to raise cash and then leases it back from the purchaser; **sale or return** = system where the retailer sends goods back if they are not sold, and pays the supplier only for goods sold; *we have taken 4,000 items on sale or return*; **bill of sale** = document which the seller gives to the buyer to show that a sale has taken place; **conditions of sale** = agreed ways in

which a sale takes place (such as discounts and credit terms) **(b) for sale** = ready to be sold; **to offer something for sale** *or* **to put something up for sale** = to announce that something is ready to be sold; *they put the factory up for sale*; *his shop is for sale*; *these items are not for sale to the general public* **(c) on sale** = ready to be sold in a shop; *these items are on sale in most chemists* **(d)** selling of goods at specially low prices; *the shop is having a sale to clear old stock*; *the sale price is 50% of the normal price*; **bargain sale** = sale of all goods in a store at cheap prices; **car boot sale** = type of flea market where you sell old items which you bring to the sale in your car, and sell from the back of the car; **clearance sale** = sale of items at low prices to get rid of the stock; **half-price sale** = sale of items at half the usual price; **jumble sale** = sale of old used household goods

saleability *US* **salability** [seɪlə'bɪlɪti] *noun* quality of an item which makes it easy to sell

saleable *US* **salable** ['seɪləbl] *adjective* which can easily be sold; *the company is not readily saleable in its present state*

saleroom ['seɪlrum] *noun* room where an auction takes place

sales [seɪlz] *noun* **(a)** (i) money received for selling something; (ii) number of items sold; *sales have risen over the first quarter*; **sales analysis** = examining the reports of sales to see why items have or have not sold well; **sales appeal** = quality which makes customers want to buy; **sales book** = record of sales; **book sales** = sales as recorded in the sales book; **sales budget** = plan of probable sales; **sales campaign** = planned work to achieve higher sales; **sales conference** *or* **sales meeting** = meeting of sales managers, representatives, publicity staff, etc., to discuss results and future sales plans; **cost of sales** = all the costs of a product sold, including manufacturing costs and the staff costs of the production department; **sales day book (SDB)** *or* **sales journal** = book in which non-cash sales are recorded with details of customer, invoice, amount and date; these details are later posted to each customer's account in the sales ledger; **sales department** = section of a company which deals in selling the company's products or services; **domestic sales** *or* **home sales** = sales in the home market; **sales drive** = vigorous work to increase sales; **sales executive** = person in a company in charge of sales; **sales figures** = total sales, or sales broken down by category; **sales force** = group of salesmen; **sales forecast** = estimate of future sales; **forward sales** = sales (of shares, commodities, foreign exchange) for delivery at a later date; **sales invoice** = invoice relating to a sale; **sales journal** = SALES DAY BOOK; **sales ledger** = book in which sales to each customer are posted; **sales ledger clerk** = office worker who deals with the sales ledger; **sales literature** = printed information (such as leaflets, prospectuses) which help sales; **sales manager** = person in charge of a sales department; **sales mix** = the quantity of different products sold by a single company; **sales pitch** = statements by a salesman to persuade a customer to buy; **sales quota** = amount of sales which a salesman is expected to make during a certain period; **sales report** = report made showing the number of items or amount of money received for selling stock; *in the sales reports all the European countries are bracketed together; US* **sales revenue** = income from sales of goods or services (NOTE: British English is **turnover**); **sales tax** = tax to be paid on each item sold; **sales volume** *or* **volume of sales** = number of units sold **(b)** **the sales** = period when major stores sell many items at specially low prices; *I bought this in the sales or at the sales or in the January sales*

---

the latest car sales for April show a 1.8 per cent dip from last year's total

Investors Chronicle

---

sales clerk ['seɪlz 'klɑːk] *noun US* person who sells goods to customers in a store

---

the wage agreement includes sales clerks and commission sales people in stores in Toronto

Toronto Star

---

salesgirl ['seɪlzgɜːl] *noun* girl who sells goods to customers in a store

saleslady ['seɪlzleɪdi] *noun* woman who sells goods to customers in a store

salesman ['seɪlzmən] *noun* **(a)** man who sells goods or services to members of the public; *he is the head salesman in the carpet department; his only experience is as a used car salesman;* **door-to-door salesman** = man who goes from one house to the next, asking people to buy something; **insurance salesman** = man who encourages clients to take out insurance policies **(b)** person who represents a company, selling its products or services to retail shops; *we have six salesmen calling on accounts in central London* (NOTE: plural is **salesmen**)

salesmanship ['seɪlzmənʃɪp] *noun* art of selling or of persuading customers to buy

saleswoman ['seɪlzwʊmən] *noun* woman in a shop who sells goods to customers (NOTE: plural is **saleswomen**)

salvage ['sælvɪdʒ] **1** *noun* **(a)** saving a ship or a cargo from being destroyed; **salvage money** = payment made by the owner of a ship or a cargo to the person who has saved it; **salvage value** *or* **scrap value** = the value of an asset if sold for scrap; **salvage vessel** = ship which specializes in saving other ships and their cargoes **(b)** goods saved from a wrecked ship, from a fire, etc.; *a sale of flood salvage items* (NOTE: no plural) **2** *verb* **(a)** to save goods or a ship from being wrecked; *we are selling off a warehouse full of salvaged goods* **(b)** to save something from loss; *the company is trying to salvage its reputation after the managing director was sent to prison for fraud; the receiver managed to salvage something from the collapse of the company*

same [seɪm] *adjective* being or looking exactly alike; **same-store sales** = sales for the same stores over an earlier period

---

it led the nation's department stores over the crucial Christmas season with an 11.7% increase in same-store sales

Fortune

---

its consistent double-digit same-store sales growth also

proves that it is not just adding revenue by adding new locations

Fortune

previously, only orders received by 11 a.m. via the Internet could be delivered the same day, and then only for a limited range of items. With fast packaging and inspection, same-day delivery is now possible anywhere in Tokyo

Nikkei Weekly

sample ['sɑːmpl] **1** *noun* **(a)** specimen, a small part of an item which is used to show what the whole item is like; *can you provide us with a sample of the cloth or a cloth sample?*; **check sample** = sample to be used to see if a whole consignment is acceptable; **free sample** = sample given free to advertise a product; **sample book** *or* **book of samples** = book showing samples of different types of cloth, paper, etc. **(b)** small group taken to show what a larger group is like; *we interviewed a sample of potential customers*; **a random sample** = a sample taken without any selection **2** *verb* **(a)** to test, to try something by taking a small amount; *to sample a product before buying it* **(b)** to ask a representative group of people questions to find out what the reactions of a much larger group would be; *they sampled 2,000 people at random to test the new perfume*

sampling ['sɑːmplɪŋ] *noun* **(a)** testing a product by taking a small amount; *sampling of EU produce*; **acceptance sampling** = testing a small sample of a batch to see if the whole batch is good enough to be accepted **(b)** testing the reactions of a small group of people to find out the reactions of a larger group of consumers; **random sampling** = choosing samples for testing without any special selection method; **sampling error** = difference between the results achieved in a survey using a small sample and what the results would be if you used the entire population

sanction ['sæŋkʃən] **1** *noun* **(a)** permission; *you will need the sanction of the local authorities before you can knock* down the office block **(b)** **economic sanctions** = restrictions on trade with a country in order to influence its political situation or in order to make its government change its policy; *to impose sanctions on a country*; *to lift sanctions from a country* **2** *verb* to approve; *the board sanctioned the expenditure of £1.2m on the development project*

members of the new Association of Coffee Producing Countries voted to cut their exports by 20 per cent to try to raise prices. The Association voted also on ways to enforce the agreement and to implement sanctions if it is breached

Times

sandwich ['sændwɪtʃ] *noun* **sandwich boards** = boards carried in front of and behind a person with advertisements on them; **sandwich course** = course of study where students spend a period of time working in a factory or office as part of a college course; *US* **sandwich lease** = lease held by someone who sublets the property he is leasing; **sandwich man** = man who carries sandwich boards

satisfaction [sætɪs'fækʃən] *noun* feeling of being happy, a good feeling; **customer satisfaction** = making a customer pleased with what he has bought; **job satisfaction** = a worker's feeling that he is happy in his place of work and pleased with the work he does

satisfy ['sætɪsfaɪ] *verb* **(a)** to satisfy a client = to make a client pleased with what he has purchased; **a satisfied customer** = a customer who has got what he wanted **(b)** to satisfy a demand = to fill a demand; *we cannot produce enough to satisfy the demand for the product*

saturate ['sætʃəreɪt] *verb* to fill something completely; *they are planning to saturate the market with cheap mobile phones*; *the market for home computers is saturated*

saturation [sætʃə'reɪʃən] *noun* filling completely; **saturation of the market** *or* **market saturation** = situation where the market has taken as much of the product as it can buy; **the market has reached saturation point** = the market is at a point where it cannot buy any more of the product; **saturation advertising** = highly intensive advertising campaign

save [seɪv] *verb* **(a)** to keep (money), not to spend (money); *he is trying to save money by walking to work; she is saving to buy a house* **(b)** not to waste, to use less; *to save time, let us continue the discussion in the taxi to the airport; the government is encouraging companies to save energy* **(c)** to store data on a computer disk; *don't forget to save your files when you have finished keyboarding them*

save-as-you-earn (SAYE) ['seɪvæzjuː'ɜːn] *noun GB* scheme where workers can save money regularly by having it deducted automatically from their wages and invested in National Savings

save on ['seɪv 'ɒn] *verb* not to waste, to use less; *by introducing shift work we find we can save on fuel*

saver ['seɪvə] *noun* person who saves money

save up ['seɪv 'ʌp] *verb* to put money aside for a special purpose; *they are saving up for a holiday in the USA*

saving ['seɪvɪŋ] **1** *noun* using less; *we are aiming for a 10% saving in fuel; the new heating system has produced remarkable savings in fuel* **2** *suffix* which uses less; **an energy-saving** *or* **labour-saving device** = machine which saves energy or labour; **time-saving** = which takes less time

savings ['seɪvɪŋz] *plural noun* money saved (i.e., money which is not spent); *he put all his savings into a deposit account*; *GB* **National Savings** = government scheme where small investors can invest in government savings certificates, premium bonds, etc.; **savings certificate** *US* **savings bond** = document showing that you have invested money in a government savings scheme (British savings certificates give an interest which is not taxable; in some cases, interest on US savings bonds is also tax exempt); **savings account** = bank account where you can put money in regularly and which pays interest, often at a higher rate than a deposit account

savings and loan (association) (S&L) ['seɪvɪŋz ən 'ləʊn əsəʊsɪ'eɪʃən] *noun US* financial association which accepts and pays interest on deposits from investors and lends money to people who are buying property; the loans are in the form of mortgages on the security of the property being bought (NOTE: the S&Ls are also called **thrifts**; the British equivalents are the building societies)

COMMENT: because of deregulation of interest rates in 1980, many S&Ls found that they were forced to raise interest on deposits to current market rates in order to secure funds, while at the same time they still were charging low fixed-interest rates on the mortgages granted to borrowers. This created considerable problems and many S&Ls had to be rescued by the Federal government

savings bank ['seɪvɪŋz 'bæŋk] *noun* bank where you can deposit money and receive interest on it

SAYE   ['eseɪwaɪ'iː]   = SAVE-AS-YOU-EARN

scab [skæb] *noun (informal)* worker who goes on working when there is a strike

scale [skeɪl] **1** *noun* **(a)** system which is graded into various levels; **scale of charges** *or* **scale of prices** = list showing various prices; **fixed scale of charges** = rate of charging which does not change; **scale of salaries** *or* **salary scale** = list of salaries showing different levels of pay in different jobs in the same company; *he was appointed at the top end of the salary scale*; **incremental scale** = salary scale with regular annual salary increases **(b)** **large scale** *or* **small scale** = working with large or small amounts of investment, staff, etc.; **to start in business on a small scale** = to start in business with a small staff, few products or little capital; **economies of scale** = making a product more economical by manufacturing it or buying it in larger quantities; **diseconomies of scale** = situation where increased production actually increases unit cost **(c)** **scales** = machine for weighing; **letter scale** *or* **letter scales** = special small scales for weighing letters **2** *verb* **to scale down** = to lower in proportion; **to scale up** = to increase in proportion

COMMENT: if a share issue is oversubscribed, applications may be scaled down; by doing this, the small investor is protected. So, in a typical case, all applications for 1,000 shares may receive 300; all applications for 2,000 shares may receive 500; applications for 5,000 shares receive 1,000, and applications for more than 5,000 shares will go into a ballot

scam [skæm] *noun (informal)* case of fraud; *many financial scams only come to light by accident*

scandal ['skændl] *noun* wrong action that produces a general feeling of public anger; *the government was brought down by the scandal over the slush funds*

> frauds have always been perpetrated, but the growth of the capital markets in the last 30 years has led to an explosion in trading scandals
> *Times*

scarce [skeəs] *adjective* not easily found, not common; *they specialize in the supply of scarce raw materials*; *reliable trained staff are scarce*

scarceness *or* **scarcity** ['skeəsnəs *or* 'skeəsəti] *noun* lack, being scarce; *the scarceness of trained staff*; *there is a scarcity of trained staff*; scarcity value = value of something because it is rare and there is a large demand for it

scenario [se'nɑːriəu] *noun* way in which a situation may develop

> on the upside scenario, the outlook is reasonably optimistic, bankers say, the worst scenario being that a scheme of arrangement cannot be achieved, resulting in liquidation
> *Irish Times*

schedule ['ʃedjuːl] **1** *noun* **(a)** timetable, plan of time drawn up in advance; **to be ahead of schedule** = to be early; **to be on schedule** = to be on time; **to be behind schedule** = to be late; *the project is on schedule*; *the building was completed ahead of schedule*; *I am sorry to say that*

we are three months behind schedule; *the managing director has a busy schedule of appointments*; *his secretary tried to fit me into his schedule* **(b)** list (especially additional documents attached to a contract); *please find enclosed our schedule of charges*; *schedule of territories to which a contract applies*; *see the attached schedule or as per the attached schedule* **(c)** list of interest rates; *GB* **tax schedules** = types of income as classified for tax **(d)** details of the items covered by an insurance, sent with the policy **2** *verb* **(a)** to list officially; *we offer a 10% reduction on scheduled prices or scheduled charges to selected customers* **(b)** to plan the time when something will happen; *the building is scheduled for completion in May*; **scheduled flight** = regular flight which is in the airline timetable; *he left for Helsinki on a scheduled flight*

COMMENT: the current British tax schedules are: **Schedule A:** rental income from land and buildings **Schedule C:** income from government stock **Schedule D:** profits of trade, profession, interest, etc., but not from employment **Schedule E:** salaries, wages, etc., from employment and pensions **Schedule F:** dividends from UK companies **(Schedule B** was formerly income from woodland)

scheduling ['ʃedjuːlɪŋ] *noun* drawing up a plan or a timetable

scheme [skiːm] *noun* plan, arrangement or way of working; *under the bonus scheme all employees get 10% of their annual pay as a Christmas bonus*; *he has joined the company pension scheme*; *we operate a profit-sharing scheme for managers*; **scheme of arrangement** = scheme drawn up by an individual to offer ways of paying his debts, and so avoid bankruptcy proceedings

science ['saiəns] *noun* study, knowledge based on observing and testing; **business science** *or* **management science** = the study of business or management techniques; *he has a master's degree in business science*; **science park** = area near a town or university set aside for technological industries

scope [skəʊp] *noun* opportunity or possibility; **there is scope for improvement in our sales performance** = the sales performance could be improved; *there is considerable scope for expansion into the export market*

scorched earth policy [ˈskɔːtʃt ˈɜːθ ˈpɒlɪsi] *noun* way of combating a takeover bid, where the target company sells valuable assets or purchases unattractive assets; *see also* **POISON PILL**

scrap [skræp] **1** *noun* material left over after an industrial process, and which still has some value (as opposed to waste, which has no value); *to sell a ship for scrap*; *its scrap value is £2,500*; **scrap dealer** *or* **scrap merchant** = person who deals in scrap; **scrap value** = the value of an asset if sold for scrap **2** *verb* **(a)** to give up, to stop working on; *we scrapped all our plans for expansion* **(b)** to throw (something) away as useless; *they had to scrap 10,000 spare parts* (NOTE: **scrapping - scrapped**)

screen [skriːn] **1** *noun* glass surface on which computer information, TV pictures, etc., can be shown; *he brought up the information on the screen*; *I'll just call up details of your account on the screen* **2** *verb* **to screen candidates** = to examine candidates to see if they are completely suitable

screening [ˈskriːnɪŋ] *noun* **the screening of candidates** = examining candidates to see if they are suitable

scrip [skrɪp] *noun* security (a share, bond, or the certificate issued to show that someone has been allotted a share or bond); **scrip issue** = issue of shares, where a company transfers money from reserves to share capital and issues free extra shares to the shareholders (the value of the company remains the same, and the total market value of shareholders' shares remains the same, the market price being adjusted to account for the new shares)

under the rule, brokers who fail to deliver stock within four days of a transaction are to be fined 1% of the transaction value for each day of missing scrip

Far Eastern Economic Review

scripophily [skrɪˈpɒfɪli] *noun* collecting old share certificates and bond certificates as a hobby and investment

scroll [skrəʊl] *verb* to move text up or down on a computer screen

SDB = SALES DAY BOOK

SDRs = SPECIAL DRAWING RIGHTS

sea [siː] *noun* large area of salt water; **by sea** = in a ship, not by air or land; *we send all bulky shipments by sea*; **by sea mail** = sent by post abroad, using a ship, not by air

seal [siːl] **1** *noun* **(a) common seal** *or* **company's seal** = metal stamp for stamping documents with the name of the company to show they have been approved officially; *to attach the company's seal to a document*; **contract under seal** = contract which has been legally approved with the seal of the company **(b)** piece of paper, metal or wax attached to close something, so that it can be opened only if the paper, metal or wax is removed or broken; **customs seal** = seal attached by a customs officer to a box, to show that the contents have not passed through customs **2** *verb* **(a)** to close something tightly; *the computer disks were sent in a sealed container*; **sealed envelope** = envelope where the back has been stuck down to close it; *the information was sent in a sealed envelope*; **sealed tenders** = tenders sent in sealed envelopes, which will all be opened at a certain time; *the company has asked for sealed bids for the warehouse* **(b)** to attach a seal, to stamp something with a seal; *customs sealed the shipment*

seaport [ˈsiːpɔːt] *noun* port by the sea

search [sɜːtʃ] *noun* examination of records by the lawyer acting for someone who wants to buy a property, to make sure that the vendor has the right to sell it

season [ˈsiːzn] *noun* **(a)** one of four parts which a year is divided into (spring, summer, autumn, winter) **(b)** a period of time when something usually takes place; **high season** = period when there are many travellers; **low season** = period when there are few travellers; *air fares are cheaper in* *the low season*; **tourist season** *or* **holiday season** = period when there are many people on holiday; **busy season** = period when a company is busy; **slack season** = period when a company is not very busy; **dead season** = time of year when there are few tourists about; **end of season sale** = selling goods cheaply when the season in which they would be used is over (such as summer clothes sold cheaply in the autumn)

seasonal ['si:zənl] *adjective* which lasts for a season or which only happens during a particular season; *the demand for this item is very seasonal*; *seasonal variations in sales patterns*; **seasonal adjustments** = changes made to figures to take account of seasonal variations; **seasonal demand** = demand which exists only during the high season; **seasonal employment** = job which is available at certain times of the year only (such as in a ski resort); **seasonal unemployment** = unemployment which rises and falls according to the season

seasonally ['si:znəli] *adverb* **seasonally adjusted figures** = statistics which are adjusted to take account of seasonal variations

season ticket ['si:zn 'tɪkɪt] *noun* rail or bus ticket which can be used for any number of journeys over a period (normally 1, 3, 6 or 12 months)

SEC = SECURITIES AND EXCHANGE COMMISSION

sec = SECRETARY; **hon sec** = honorary secretary

second 1 ['sekənd] *adjective* (thing) which comes after the first; **second half-year** = six month period from July to the end of December; **second mortgage** = further mortgage on a property which is already mortgaged; **second quarter** = three month period from April to the end of June **2** *verb* **(a)** ['sekənd] **to second a motion** = to be the first person to support a proposal put forward by someone else; *Mrs Smith seconded the motion or the motion was seconded by Mrs Smith* **(b)** [sɪ'kɒnd] to lend a member of staff to another company or to a government department, etc., for a fixed period of time; *he was*

seconded to the Department of Trade for two years

secondary ['sekəndri] *adjective* second in importance; **secondary banks** = companies which provide money for hire-purchase deals; **secondary industry** = industry which uses basic raw materials to make manufactured goods; **secondary picketing** = picketing of a second factory, which is not directly connected with a strike, to prevent it supplying a striking factory or receiving supplies from it

second-class ['sekənd'klɑ:s] *adjective & adverb* **(a)** less expensive or less comfortable way of travelling; *the group will travel second-class to Holland*; *the price of a second-class ticket is half that of a first class*; *I find second-class hotels are just as comfortable as the best ones* **(b)** **second-class mail** = *GB* less expensive, slower, mail service *US* mail service for sending newspapers and magazines; *a second-class letter is slower than a first-class*; *send it second-class if it is not urgent*

seconder ['sekəndə] *noun* person who seconds a proposal; *there was no seconder for the motion so it was not put to the vote*

second half ['sekənd 'hɑ:f] *noun* period of six months from 1st July to end of December; *the figures for the second half are up on those for the first part of the year*

secondhand [sekənd'hænd] *adjective & adverb* used, not new, which has been owned by someone before; *a secondhand car salesman*; *the secondhand car market or the market in secondhand cars*; *he bought the car secondhand, although it was almost new*; *look at the prices of secondhand cars or look at secondhand car prices*; **secondhand dealer** = dealer who buys and sells secondhand items

secondment [sɪ'kɒndmənt] *noun* being seconded to another job for a period; *he is on three years' secondment to an Australian college*

second-rate ['sekənd'reit] *adjective* not of good quality; *never buy anything second-rate*

seconds ['sekəndz] *plural noun* items which have been turned down by the quality controller as not being top quality; *the shop has a sale of seconds*

secret ['si:krət] *noun* & *adjective* (something) hidden, which is not known by many people; *the MD kept the contract secret from the rest of the board*; *they signed a secret deal with their main rivals*; **to keep a secret** = not to tell someone something which you know and no one else does

secretarial [sekrə'teəriəl] *adjective* referring to the work of a secretary; *she is taking a secretarial course*; *he is looking for secretarial work*; *we need extra secretarial help to deal with the mailings*; **secretarial college** = college which teaches typing, shorthand and word-processing

secretariat [sekrə'teəriət] *noun* important office and the officials who work in it; *the United Nations secretariat*

a debate has been going on over the establishment of a general secretariat for the G7. Proponents argue that this would give the G7 a sense of direction and continuity
Times

secretary ['sekrətri] *noun* **(a)** person who helps to organize work, types letters, files documents, arranges meetings, etc., for someone; *my secretary deals with incoming orders*; *his secretary phoned to say he would be late*; **secretary and personal assistant** *US* **executive secretary** = secretary to a top-level member of an organization (a director, or senior manager) **(b)** official of a company or society; **company secretary** = person who is responsible for a company's legal and financial affairs; **honorary secretary** = person who keeps the minutes and official documents of a committee or club, but is not paid a salary; *he was elected secretary of the committee* or *committee secretary*; **membership secretary** = committee member who deals with the ordinary members of a society **(c)** member of the government in charge of a department; *the Trade Secretary*; *the Foreign Secretary*; *US* **Secretary of the Treasury** or **Treasury Secretary** = senior

member of the government in charge of financial affairs

Secretary of State ['sekrətri əv 'steɪt] *noun* **(a)** *GB* member of the government in charge of a department; *the Secretary of State for Trade and Industry* **(b)** *US* senior member of the government in charge of foreign affairs (NOTE: the British equivalent is the **Foreign Secretary**)

section ['sekʃən] *noun* part of something; *you should read the last section of the report - it is very interesting*; **legal section** = department in a company dealing with legal matters

sector ['sektə] *noun* part of the economy or the business organization of a country; *all sectors of the economy suffered from the fall in the exchange rate*; *technology is a booming sector of the economy*; **public sector** = nationalized industries and public services; **public sector borrowing requirement (PSBR)** = amount of money which a government has to borrow to pay for its own spending; **private sector** = all companies which are owned by private shareholders, not by the state; *the expansion is funded completely by the private sector*; *salaries in the private sector have increased faster than in the public*

government services form a large part of the tertiary or service sector
Sydney Morning Herald

in the dry cargo sector, a total of 956 dry cargo vessels are laid up - 3% of world dry cargo tonnage
Lloyd's List

secure [sɪ'kjʊə] **1** *adjective* safe, which cannot change; **secure job** = job from which you are not likely to be made redundant; **secure investment** = investment where you are not likely to lose money **2** *verb* **(a) to secure a loan** = to pledge a property as a security for a loan **(b)** to get (something) safely into your control; *he is visiting several banks in an attempts to secure funds for his project*; *he secured the backing of an Australian group*

secured [sɪˈkjʊəd] *adjective* **secured creditor** = person who is owed money by someone, and can legally claim the same amount of the borrower's property if he fails to pay back the money owed; **secured debts** = debts which are guaranteed by assets; **secured loan** = loan which is guaranteed by the borrower giving valuable property as security

securities [sɪˈkjʊərətiz] *plural noun* investments in stocks and shares; certificates to show that someone owns stocks or shares; **gilt-edged securities** *or* **government securities** = investments in British government stock; **listed securities** = shares which can be bought or sold on the Stock Exchange, shares which appear on the official Stock Exchange list; **the securities market** = Stock Exchange, a place where stocks and shares can be bought or sold; **securities trader** = person whose business is buying and selling stocks and shares; *US* **Securities and Exchange Commission (SEC)** = the official body which regulates the securities markets in the USA; *GB* **Securities and Futures Authority (SFA)** = self-regulatory organization which regulates the trading in shares and futures, now part of the FSA

securitize [sɪˈkjʊrətaɪz] *verb* to make a loan into a security which can be traded (as by issuing an IOU for a loan)

security [sɪˈkjʊərəti] *noun* **(a)** **job security** = feeling which a worker has that he has a right to keep his job or that he will stay in his job until he retires; **security of employment** = feeling by a worker that he has the right to keep his job until he retires; **security of tenure** = right to keep a job or rented accommodation, provided that certain conditions are met **(b)** being protected against attack, etc.; **airport security** = actions taken to protect aircraft and passengers against attack; **security guard** = person who protects an office or factory against burglars; **office security** = protecting an office against theft **(c)** being secret; **security in this office is nil** = nothing can be kept secret in this office; **security printer** = printer who prints paper money, secret company documents, etc. **(d)** **social security** = money or help provided by the government to people who need it; *he lives on social security payments* **(e)** guarantee that someone will repay money borrowed; **to stand security for someone** = to guarantee that if the person does not repay a loan, you will repay it for him; *to give something as security for a debt*; *to use a house as security for a loan*; *the bank lent him £20,000 without security*

seed capital *or* **seed money** *or* **seedcorn** [ˈsiːd ˈkæpitəl *or* ˈsiːd ˈmʌni *or* ˈsiːdkɔːn] *noun* capital invested when a new project is starting up, before it is brought to the stock market

seek [siːk] *verb* to ask for; *they are seeking damages for loss of revenue*; **to seek an interview** = to ask if you can see someone; *she sought an interview with the minister* (NOTE: **seeking - sought**)

see-safe [ˈsiːˈseɪf] *adverb* agreement where a supplier will give credit for unsold goods at the end of a period if the retailer cannot sell them; *we bought the stock see-safe*

segment [ˈsegmənt] *noun* part of the area of sales of a large business

segmentation [segmenˈteɪʃn] *noun* division of a market or buyers into certain categories according to their buying habits

seize [siːz] *verb* to take hold of something, to take possession of something; *customs seized the shipment of books*; *the court ordered the company's funds to be seized*

seizure [ˈsiːʒə] *noun* taking possession of something; *the court ordered the seizure of the shipment or of the company's funds*

select [sɪˈlekt] **1** *adjective* of top quality, specially chosen; *our customers are very select*; *they offer a select range of merchandise* **2** *verb* to choose; **selected items are reduced by 25%** = some items have been reduced by 25%

selection [sɪˈlekʃən] *noun* **(a)** choice, the act of choosing; **selection board** *or* **selection committee** = committee which chooses a candidate for a job; **selection procedure** = general method of choosing a candidate for a job **(b)** thing which has been chosen; *here is a selection of our product line*

selective [sɪ'lektɪv] *adjective* which chooses; **selective strikes** = strikes in certain areas or at certain factories, but not everywhere

self [self] *pronoun* your own person; *(on cheques)* '**pay self**' = pay the person who has signed the cheque

self- [self] *prefix* referring to oneself

self-adhesive ['selfəd'hiːzɪv] *adjective* (label) which is already sticky and can be stuck on a surface without having to be licked (adhesive labels are sold stuck to a sheet of backing paper, and can be peeled off easily and stuck to an envelope, etc.)

self-assessment ['selfə'sesmənt] *noun* process of calculating how much tax you should pay and reporting it to the Inland Revenue on time; *self-assessment forms should be returned to the tax office by 31st January*

self-contained office ['selfkən'teɪnd 'ɒfɪs] *noun* office which has all facilities inside it, and its own entrance, so that it is separate from other offices in the same building

self-employed ['selfɪm'plɔɪd] **1** *adjective* working for yourself, not on the payroll of a company; *a self-employed engineer*; *he worked for a bank for ten years but now is self-employed* **2** *noun* the **self-employed** = people who work for themselves (NOTE: can be followed by a verb in the plural)

self-financed ['selffaɪ'nænst] *adjective* **the project is completely self-financed** = the project pays its development costs out of its own revenue, with no subsidies

self-financing ['selffaɪ'nænsɪŋ] **1** *noun* the financing of development costs, purchase of capital assets, etc., by a company from its own resources **2** *adjective* **the company is completely self-financing** = the company finances its development costs, capital assets, etc., from its own resources

self-made man ['selfmeɪd 'mæn] *noun* man who is rich and successful because of his work, not because he inherited money or position

self-regulation ['selfregjʊ'leɪʃən] *noun* regulation of an industry by itself, through

a committee which issues a rulebook and makes sure that members of the industry follow the rules (as in the case of the regulation of the Stock Exchange by the Stock Exchange Council)

self-regulatory ['selfregjʊ'leɪtəri] *adjective* (organization) which regulates itself; **Self-Regulatory Organization (SRO)** = organization which regulates the way in which its own members carry on their business

self-seal envelope ['self'siːl 'envələʊp] *noun* envelope which sticks closed when you press the flap down

self-service ['self'sɜːvɪs] *adjective & noun* **a self-service store** = shop where customers take goods from the shelves and pay for them at the checkout

self-sticking ['self'stɪkɪŋ] *adjective* (label) which is already sticky and can be stuck on a surface without having to be licked (self-sticking labels are sold stuck to a sheet of backing paper, and can be peeled off easily and stuck to an envelope, etc.)

self-sufficiency ['selfsə'fɪʃənsi] *noun* being self-sufficient

self-sufficient ['selfsə'fɪʃənt] *adjective* producing enough food or raw materials for its own needs; *the country is self-sufficient in oil*

self-supporting ['selfsə'pɔːtɪŋ] *adjective* which finances itself from its own resources, with no subsidies

sell [sel] **1** *noun* act of selling; **to give a product the hard sell** = to make great efforts to persuade customers to buy it; **he tried to give me the hard sell** = he put a lot of effort into trying to persuade me to buy his product; **soft sell** = persuading people to buy, by encouraging and not forcing them to do so **2** *verb* **(a)** to give goods in exchange for money; *the shop sells washing machines and refrigerators*; *they have decided to sell their house*; *they tried to sell their house for £100,000*; *to sell something on credit*; *her house is difficult to sell*; *their products are easy to sell*; **to sell forward** = to sell foreign currency, commodities, etc., for delivery at a later date **(b)** to be sold; *these items sell well in the pre-Christmas period*; *those packs sell for £25 a dozen* (NOTE: **selling - sold**)

sell-by date ['selbaɪ 'deɪt] *noun* date on a food packet which is the last date on which the food is guaranteed to be good

seller ['selə] *noun* **(a)** person who sells; *there were few sellers in the market, so prices remained high*; **seller's market** = market where the seller can ask high prices because there is a large demand for the product (NOTE: the opposite is a **buyer's market**) **(b)** thing which sells; *this book is a steady seller*; **best-seller** = item (especially a book) which sells very well

selling ['selɪŋ] **1** *noun* **direct selling** = selling a product direct to the customer without going through a shop; **Internet selling** = selling of goods or services over the Internet; **mail-order selling** = selling by taking orders and supplying a product by post; **selling costs** *or* **selling overheads** = amount of money to be paid for advertising, reps' commissions, etc., involved in selling something; **selling price** = price at which someone is willing to sell **2** *suffix* **fast-selling items** = items which sell quickly; **best-selling car** = car which sells better than other models

sell off ['sel 'ɒf] *verb* to sell goods quickly to get rid of them

sell out ['sel 'aʊt] *verb* **(a) to sell out of an item** = to sell all the stock of an item; *to sell out of a product line*; *we have sold out of plastic bags*; *this item has sold out* **(b)** to sell your business; *he sold out and retired to the seaside*

sellout ['selaʊt] *noun* **this item has been a sellout** = all the stock of the item has been sold

sell up ['sel 'ʌp] *verb* to sell a business and all the stock; *he sold up and bought a farm*

semi- ['semi] *prefix* half

semi-finished ['semɪ'fɪnɪʃt] *adjective* **semi-finished products** = products which are partly finished

semi-skilled ['semɪ'skɪld] *adjective* **semi-skilled jobs** = jobs which require some training or experience; **semi-skilled workers** = workers who have had some training

send [send] *verb* to make someone or something go from one place to another;

she sent a letter to our solicitors; *the order was sent to the warehouse*; *the company is sending him to Australia to be general manager of the Sydney office*; *send the letter airmail if you want it to arrive next week*; *the shipment was sent by rail* (NOTE: **sending - sent**)

send away for ['send ə'weɪ fə] *verb* to write asking for something to be sent to you; *we sent away for the new catalogue*

sender ['sendə] *noun* person who sends; **'return to sender'** = words on an envelope or parcel to show that it is to be sent back to the person who sent it

send for ['send 'fə] *verb* **(a)** to ask someone to come; to ask for something to be brought; *he sent for the chief accountant*; *she sent for the papers on the contract* **(b)** *US* to write to ask for something to be sent to you; *we sent for the new catalog* (NOTE: British English uses **send away for, send off for** in this meaning)

send in ['send 'ɪn] *verb* to send (a letter); *he sent in his resignation*; *she sent in an application*

send off ['send 'ɒf] *verb* to put (a letter) in the post

send off for ['send 'ɒf fə] *verb* to write asking for something to be sent to you; *we sent off for the new catalogue*

send on ['send 'ɒn] *verb* to post a letter which you have received, and address it to someone else; *he sent the letter on to his agent in Australia*

senior ['siːnjə] *adjective* **(a)** older; more important; (worker) who has been employed longer than another; **senior manager** *or* **senior executive** = manager or director who has a higher rank than others; **senior partner** = most important partner in a firm of solicitors or accountants; **John Smith, Senior** = the older John Smith (i.e. the father of John Smith, Junior) **(b)** (sum) which is repayable before others; **senior debts** = debts which must be repaid in preference to other debts (such as a first mortgage over a second mortgage)

seniority [siːnɪ'ɒrəti] *noun* being older; being an employee of the company longer; **the managers were listed in order of seniority** = the manager who had been an employee the longest was put at the top of the list

sensitive ['sensətɪv] *adjective* able to feel something sharply; *the market is very sensitive to the result of the elections*; **price-sensitive product** = product, for which demand will change significantly if its price is increased or decreased (products show an increased demand if the price falls and reduced demand if the price rises)

sentiment ['sentɪmənt] *noun* **market sentiment** = general feeling among investors or financial analysts on a stock market

> business sentiment in the service and restaurant sectors is recovering, although it is deteriorating in the retail sector due to a decline in customer numbers and falling prices
>
> *Nikkei Weekly*

COMMENT: 'sentiment' (either optimistic or pessimistic) can be influenced by external factors, and affects the prices of shares or the volume of business transacted

separate 1 ['seprət] *adjective* not together; **to send something under separate cover** = to send something in a different envelope **2** ['sepəreɪt] *verb* to divide; *the personnel are separated into part-timers and full-time staff*

separately ['seprətli] *adverb* not together; *each job was invoiced separately*

separation [sepə'reɪʃən] *noun* US leaving a job (resigning, retiring, or being fired or made redundant)

sequester *or* **sequestrate** [sɪ'kwestə or 'sekwəstreɪt] *verb* to take and keep (property) because a court has ordered it

sequestration [sekwes'treɪʃən] *noun* taking and keeping of property on the order of a court

sequestrator ['sekwəstreɪtə] *noun* person who takes and keeps property on the order of a court

serial number ['sɪərɪəl 'nʌmbə] *noun* number in a series; *this batch of shoes has the serial number 25-02*

series ['sɪəriːz] *noun* group of items following one after the other; *a series of successful takeovers made the company one of the largest in the trade* (NOTE: plural is **series**)

serious ['sɪərɪəs] *adjective* **(a)** bad; *the storm caused serious damage*; *the damage to the computer was not very serious* **(b)** thoughtful; *the management is making serious attempts to improve working conditions*

Serious Fraud Office (SFO) ['sɪərɪəs 'frɔːd 'ɒfɪs] *noun* British government department in charge of investigating major fraud in companies

seriously ['sɪərɪəsli] *adverb* **(a)** badly; *the cargo was seriously damaged by water* **(b)** in a thoughtful way; *we are taking the threat from our competitors very seriously*

servant ['sɜːvənt] *noun* person who is paid to work in someone's house; **civil servant** = person who works in the civil service

serve [sɜːv] *verb* **(a)** to deal with (a customer); **to serve a customer** = to take a customer's order and provide what he wants; **to serve in a shop** *or* **in a restaurant** = to deal with customers' orders **(b)** **to serve someone with a writ** *or* **to serve a writ on someone** = to give someone a writ officially, so that he has to receive it

server ['sɜːvə] *noun* computer or program which provides a function to a network; **file server** = computer connected to a network, running a network operating system software to manage accounts, files, etc.

service ['sɜːvɪs] **1** *noun* **(a)** working for a company, in a shop, etc.; **length of service** = number of years someone has worked; **service agreement** *or* **service contract** = contract between a company and a director showing all conditions of work **(b)** the work of dealing with customers; *the service in that restaurant is extremely slow* **(c)** payment for help for the customer; *to add on 10% for service*; **the bill includes service** = includes a charge added for the work involved; *is the service included?* **(d)** keeping a machine in good working order; *the machine has been sent* *in for service*; *the routine service of equipment*; **service contract** = contract by which a company keeps a piece of equipment in good working order; **after-sales service** = service of a machine carried out by the seller for the buyer; **service centre** = office or workshop which specializes in keeping machines in good working order; **service department** = section of a company which keeps customers' machines in good working order; **service engineer** = engineer who specializes in keeping machines in good working order; **service handbook** *or* **service manual** = book which shows how to service a machine; **service station** = garage where you can buy petrol and have small repairs done to a car **(e)** business of providing help in some form when it is needed; **answering service** = office which answers the telephone and takes messages for a company; **24-hour service** = help which is available for the whole day; **service bureau** = office which specializes in helping other offices; **service department** = department of a company which does not deal with production or sales (accounts, personnel, etc.); **service industry** = industry which does not make products, but offers a service (such as banking, insurance, transport) **(f) to put a machine into service** = to start using a machine **(g)** regular working of a public organization; *the postal service is efficient*; *the bus service is very irregular*; *we have a good train service to London*; **the civil service** = organization and personnel which administer a country; *you have to pass an examination to get a job in the civil service or to get a civil service job*; *he has a job in the civil service*; *civil service pensions are index-linked* **2** *verb* **(a)** to keep a machine in good working order; *the car needs to be serviced every six months*; *the computer has gone back to the manufacturer for servicing* **(b) to service a debt** = to pay interest on a debt; *the company is having problems in servicing its debts*

service charge ['sɜːvɪs 'tʃɑːdʒ] *noun* **(a)** charge added to the bill in a restaurant to pay for service; amount paid by tenants in a block of flats or offices for general maintenance, insurance, cleaning, etc. **(b)** *US* charges which a bank makes for carrying out work for a customer (NOTE: the British equivalent is **bank charges**)

session ['seʃən] *noun* meeting, a period when a group of people meets; *the morning session or the afternoon session will be held in the conference room*; **opening session** *or* **closing session** = first part or last part of a conference; **trading session** = one period (usually a day) during which trading takes place on a stock exchange

> statistics from the stock exchange show that customer interest in the equity market has averaged just under £700m in recent trading sessions
> *Financial Times*

set [set] **1** *noun* group of items which go together, which are used together or which are sold together; *a set of tools or a set of equipment*; **boxed set** = set of items sold together in a box **2** *adjective* fixed, which cannot be changed; *there is a set fee for all our consultants*; **set menu** = cheaper menu in a restaurant where there are only a few choices **3** *verb* to fix or to arrange; *we have to set a price for the new computer*; *the price of the calculator has been set low, so as to achieve maximum unit sales*; **the auction set a record for high prices** = the prices at the auction were the highest ever reached (NOTE: **setting - set**)

set against ['set ə'genst] *verb* to balance one group of figures against another group to try to make them cancel each other out; *to set the costs against the sales revenue*; *can you set the expenses against tax?*

set aside ['set ə'saɪd] *verb* to decide not to apply a decision; *the arbitrator's award was set aside on appeal*

set back ['set 'bæk] *verb* to make something late; *the project was set back six weeks by bad weather*

setback ['setbæk] *noun* stopping progress; *the company has suffered a series of setbacks over the past two years*; *the shares had a setback on the Stock Exchange*

a sharp setback in foreign
trade accounted for most of
the winter slowdown

Fortune

set out ['set 'aʊt] *verb* to put clearly in writing; *to set out the details in a report*

setting up costs *or* **setup costs** ['setɪŋ'ʌp 'kɒsts or 'setʌp 'kɒsts] *plural noun* costs of getting a machine or a factory ready to make a new product after finishing work on the previous one

settle ['setl] *verb* **(a) to settle an account** = to pay what is owed **(b) to settle a claim** = to agree to pay what is asked for; *the insurance company refused to settle his claim for storm damage*; **the two parties settled out of court** = the two parties reached an agreement privately without continuing the court case

settlement ['setlmənt] *noun* **(a)** payment of an account; **settlement date** = date when a payment has to be made; **settlement day** = day when accounts have to be settled; **our basic discount is 20% but we offer an extra 5% for rapid settlement** = we take a further 5% off the price if the customer pays quickly; **settlement in cash** *or* **cash settlement** = payment of an invoice in cash, not by cheque; **final settlement** = last payment which settles a debt; **rolling settlement** = system of paying for shares bought on the stock exchange, where the buyer pays at the end of a certain number of days after the purchase is made **(b)** agreement after an argument; **to effect a settlement between two parties** = to bring two parties together to make them agree

he emphasised that prompt
settlement of all forms of
industrial disputes would
guarantee industrial peace in
the country and ensure
increased productivity

Business Times (Lagos)

settle on ['setl 'ɒn] *verb* to leave property to someone when you die; *he settled his property on his children*

set up ['set 'ʌp] *verb* **(a)** to begin (something), to organize (something) new; *to set up an inquiry or a working party*; **to set up a company** = to start a company

legally **(b) to set up in business** = to start a new business; *he set up in business as an insurance broker*; *he set himself up as a freelance representative*

the concern announced that it
had acquired a third large
tanker since being set up

Lloyd's List

setup ['setʌp] *noun* **(a)** arrangement or organization; **the setup in the office** = the way the office is organized **(b)** commercial firm; *he works for a PR setup*

for sale: top quality office
furniture, which includes
executive desks, filing
cabinets, typewriters and
complete office setup

Australian Financial Review

several ['sevrəl] *adjective* more than a few, some; *several managers are retiring this year*; *several of our products sell well in Japan*

severally ['sevrəli] *adverb* separately, not jointly; **they are jointly and severally liable** = they are liable both as a group and as individuals

severance pay ['sevərəns 'peɪ] *noun* money paid as compensation to someone who is losing his job

severe [sɪ'vɪə] *adjective* bad or serious; *the company suffered severe losses in the European market*; *the government imposed severe financial restrictions*

severely [sɪ'vɪəli] *adverb* badly, in a serious way; *train services have been severely affected by snow*

SFA ['es 'ef 'eɪ] = SECURITES AND FUTURES AUTHORITY

SFO ['es 'ef 'əʊ] = SERIOUS FRAUD OFFICE

shady ['ʃeɪdi] *adjective* not honest; *the newspapers reported that he had been involved in several shady deals*

shake [ʃeɪk] *verb* **(a)** to move something quickly from side to side; **to shake hands** = to hold someone's hand when meeting to show you are pleased to meet them or to show that an agreement has been reached; *the two negotiating teams shook hands and sat down at the conference table*; **to shake hands on a deal** = to shake hands to show that a deal has been agreed **(b)** to surprise or to shock; *the markets were shaken by the company's results* (NOTE: shaking - shook - has shaken)

shakeout ['ʃeɪkaʊt] *noun* **(a)** change in an industry, where some companies fail and others gain more market share; *only three companies were left after the shakeout in the computer market* **(b)** reorganization in a company, where some people are left, but others go; *a shakeout in the top management*

shakeup ['ʃeɪkʌp] *noun* total reorganization; *the managing director ordered a shakeup of the sales departments*

shaky ['ʃeɪki] *adjective* not very sure or not very reliable; *the year got off to a shaky start*; *he only has the shakiest idea of what he should be doing*

share [ʃeə] **1** *noun* **(a)** to have a share in = to take part in, to contribute to; *to have a share in management decisions*; **market share** *or* **share of the market** = percentage of a total market which the sales of a company cover; *the company hopes to boost its market share*; *their share of the market has gone up by 10%* **(b)** one of many equal parts into which a company's capital is divided (the owners of shares are shareholders or, more formally, 'members'); *he bought a block of shares in Marks and Spencer*; *shares fell on the London market*; *the company offered 1.8m shares on the market*; **'A' shares** = ordinary shares with limited voting rights; **'B' shares** = ordinary shares with special voting rights (often owned by the founder of the company and his family); **bonus share** = extra share given to an existing shareholder; **deferred shares** = shares which receive a dividend only after all other dividends have been paid; **founder's shares** = special shares issued to the person who starts a company; **ordinary shares** = normal shares in a company, which have no special benefits or restrictions; **preference shares** = shares (often with no voting rights) which receive their dividend before all other shares and are repaid first (at face value) if the company goes into liquidation; **share allocation** *or* **share allotment** = sharing of a small number of

shares among a large number of people who have applied to buy them; **to allot shares** = to give a certain number of shares to people who have applied to buy them; **share capital** = value of the assets of a company held as shares; **share certificate** = document proving that someone owns shares; **share issue** = selling new shares in a company to the public; **share option** = right to buy or sell shares at a certain price at a time in the future (NOTE: American English often used the word **stock** where British English uses **share**. See the note at STOCK) **2** *verb* **(a)** to own or use something together with someone else; *it is very awkward having to share a telephone*; *I don't want to share an office with her because she smokes* **(b)** to divide something up among several people; *three companies share the market*; *to share computer time*; *to share the profits among the senior executives*; **to share information** *or* **to share data** = to give someone information which you have

> falling profitability means falling share prices
> *Investors Chronicle*

> the share of blue-collar occupations declined from 48 per cent to 43 per cent
> *Sydney Morning Herald*

shareholder ['ʃeəhəʊldə] *noun* person who owns shares in a company; *to call a shareholders' meeting*; **shareholders' equity** = a company's capital which is owned by its ordinary shareholders (note that preference shares are not equity capital; if the company is wound up none of the equity capital would be distributed to the preference shareholders); **majority shareholder** = person who owns more than half the shares in a company; **minority shareholder** = person who owns less than half the shares in a company; *the solicitor acting on behalf of the minority shareholders* (NOTE: American English is **stockholder**)

> as of last night the bank's shareholders no longer hold any rights to the bank's shares
> *South China Morning Post*

> the company said that its recent issue of 10.5%

convertible preference shares at A$8.50 has been oversubscribed, boosting shareholders' funds to A$700 million plus

Financial Times

shareholding ['ʃeəhəʊldɪŋ] *noun* group of shares in a company owned by one owner; **a majority shareholding** = group of shares which are more than half the total; **a minority shareholding** = group of shares which are less than half the total; *he acquired a minority shareholding in the company*; *she has sold all her shareholdings*; **dilution of shareholding** = situation where the ordinary share capital of a company has been increased, but without an increase in the assets so that each share is worth less than before (NOTE: American English is **stockholding**)

shareout ['ʃeəraʊt] *noun* dividing something among many people; *a shareout of the profits*

sharing ['ʃeərɪŋ] *noun* dividing up; **job sharing** = situation where a job is shared by more than one person, each working part-time; **profit sharing** = dividing profits among workers; *the company operates a profit-sharing scheme*; **time-sharing** = (i) owning a property in part, with the right to use it for a period each year; (ii) sharing a computer system with different users using different terminals

shark [ʃɑːk] *noun* **loan shark** = person who lends money at a very high interest rate

sharp [ʃɑːp] *adjective* **(a)** sudden; *there was a sharp rally on the stock market*; *last week's sharp drop in prices has been reversed* **(b) sharp practice** = way of doing business which is not honest, but not illegal

sharply ['ʃɑːpli] *adverb* suddenly; *shares dipped sharply in yesterday's trading*

sheet [ʃiːt] *noun* **(a) sheet of paper** = piece of paper; **sheet feed** = device which puts one sheet at a time into a computer printer or photocopier; **sales sheet** = paper which gives details of a product and explains why it is good; **time sheet** = paper showing when a worker starts work and when he leaves work in the evening **(b)**

balance sheet = statement of the financial position of a company at a particular time, such as the end of the financial year or the end of a quarter, showing the company's assets and liabilities; *the company's balance sheet for last year*; *the accountants prepared a balance sheet for the first half-year*

shelf [ʃelf] *noun* horizontal flat surface attached to a wall or in a cupboard on which items for sale are displayed; *the shelves in the supermarket were full of items before the Christmas rush*; **shelf filler** = person whose job it is to make sure that the shelves in a shop are kept full of items for sale; **shelf life of a product** = number of days or weeks when the product will stay on the shelf in the shop and still be good to use; **shelf space** = amount of space on shelves in a shop; **shelf wobbler** = card attached to the edge of a shelf or placed on a shelf in a shop to promote a product; **off-the-shelf company** = company which has already been registered by an accountant or lawyer, and which is ready for sale to someone who wants to begin trading quickly (NOTE: plural is **shelves**)

shell company ['ʃel 'kʌmpəni] *noun* company which does not trade, but exists only as a name with a quotation of the Stock Exchange (shell companies are bought by private companies as a means of obtaining a quotation on the Stock Exchange without having to go through a flotation)

shell companies, which can be used to hide investors' cash, figure largely throughout the twentieth century

Times

shelter ['ʃeltə] *noun* protected place; **tax shelter** = financial arrangement (such as a pension scheme) where investments can be made without tax

shelve [ʃelv] *verb* to postpone, to put back to another date; *the project was shelved*; *discussion of the problem has been shelved*

shelving ['ʃelvɪŋ] *noun* **(a)** rows of shelves, space on shelves; *we installed metal shelving in the household goods department* **(b)** postponing; *the shelving* *of the project has resulted in six redundancies*

shift [ʃɪft] **1** *noun* **(a)** group of workers who work for a period, and then are replaced by another group; period of time worked by a group of workers; **day shift** = shift worked during the daylight hours (from early morning to late afternoon); **night shift** = shift worked during the night; *there are 150 men on the day shift*; *he works the day shift or night shift*; *we work an 8-hour shift*; *the management is introducing a shift system or shift working*; **they work double shifts** = two groups of workers are working shifts together **(b)** movement or change; *a shift in the company's marketing strategy*; *the company is taking advantage of a shift in the market towards higher priced goods* **2** *verb* to move, to sell; *we shifted 20,000 items in one week*

shift key [ʃɪft 'kiː] *noun* key on a typewriter or computer which makes capital letters

shift work [ʃɪft 'wɜːk] *noun* system of work in a factory with shifts

shilling [ʃɪlɪŋ] *noun* currency used in Kenya

ship [ʃɪp] **1** *noun* large boat for carrying passengers and cargo on the sea; **cargo ship** = ship which carries cargo, not passengers; **container ship** = ship made specially to carry containers; **ship chandler** = person who supplies goods (such as food) to ships; **to jump ship** = to leave the ship on which you are working and not come back **2** *verb* to send (goods), but not always on a ship; *to ship goods to the USA*; *we ship all our goods by rail*; *the consignment of cars was shipped abroad last week*; **to drop ship** = to deliver a large order direct to a customer's shop or warehouse, without going through an agent (NOTE: **shipping - shipped**)

ship broker [ʃɪp 'brəʊkə] *noun* person who arranges shipping or transport of goods for customers on behalf of ship owners

shipment [ʃɪpmənt] *noun* goods sent; *two shipments were lost in the fire*; *a shipment of computers was damaged*; *we make two shipments a week to France*;

bulk shipment = shipments of large quantities of goods; **consolidated shipment** = goods from different companies grouped together into a single shipment; **drop shipment** = delivery of a large order from a manufacturer direct to a customer's shop or warehouse, without going through an agent

shipper [ʃɪpə] *noun* person who sends goods or who organizes the sending of goods for other customers

shipping [ʃɪpɪŋ] *noun* sending of goods; *shipping charges or shipping costs*; **shipping agent** = company which specializes in the sending of goods; **shipping clerk** = clerk who deals with shipping documents; **shipping company or shipping line** = company which owns ships; **shipping instructions** = details of how goods are to be shipped and delivered; **shipping note** = note which gives details of goods being shipped (NOTE: **shipping** does not always mean using a ship)

shipyard [ʃɪpjɑːd] *noun* factory where ships are built

shoot up [ʃuːt 'ʌp] *verb* to go up fast; *prices have shot up during the strike* (NOTE: **shooting - shot**)

shop [ʃɒp] **1** *noun* **(a)** place where goods are stored and sold; *a bookshop*; *a computer shop*; *an electrical goods shop*; *he has bought a shoe shop in the centre of town*; *she opened a women's wear shop*; *all the shops in the centre of town close on Sundays*; **retail shop** = shop where goods are sold only to the public; **the corner shop** = small privately owned general store; **shop assistant** = person who serves customers in a shop; **shop front** = part of a shop which faces the street, including the entrance and windows; **shop window** = window in a shop where goods are displayed so that customers can see them, place where goods or services can be exhibited (NOTE: American English usually uses **store** where British English uses **shop: a bookstore, a computer store, etc.**) **(b)** workshop, a place where goods are made; **machine shop** = place where working machines are kept; **repair shop** = small factory where machines are repaired; **on the shop floor** = in the factory, in the works or among the ordinary workers; *the feeling on the shop floor is that the manager does not know his job* **(c) closed shop** = system where a company agrees to employ only union members in certain jobs; *the union is asking the management to agree to a closed shop* **2** *verb* to shop **(for)** = to look for things in shops (NOTE: shopping - shopped)

shop around [ˈʃɒp əˈraʊnd] *verb* to go to various shops or suppliers and compare prices before making a purchase or before placing an order; *you should shop around before getting your car serviced*; *he is shopping around for a new computer*; *it pays to shop around when you are planning to ask for a mortgage*

shopkeeper [ˈʃɒpkiːpə] *noun* person who owns or runs a shop

shoplifter [ˈʃɒplɪftə] *noun* person who steals goods from shops

shoplifting [ˈʃɒplɪftɪŋ] *noun* stealing goods from shops

shopper [ˈʃɒpə] *noun* person who buys goods in a shop; *the store stays open to midnight to cater for late-night shoppers*; **shoppers' charter** = law which protects the rights of shoppers against shopkeepers who are not honest

shopping [ˈʃɒpɪŋ] *noun* **(a)** buying goods in a shop; goods bought in a shop; *to go shopping*; *to buy your shopping* or *to do your shopping in the local supermarket*; **window shopping** = looking at goods in shop windows, without buying anything; **shopping around** = looking at prices in various shops before buying what you want **(b) shopping basket** = basket for carrying shopping; *US* **shopping cart** = metal basket on wheels, used by shoppers to put their purchases in as they go round a supermarket (NOTE: the British English for this is **supermarket trolley**); *(Internet)* **shopping cart** *or* **shopping basket** = the electronic equivalent of a trolley you would use in your supermarket (as you browse around an online shopping web site, you can add products you want to buy to your shopping cart then, when you have finished selecting goods, you pay for them by typing in your credit card details); **shopping centre** = group of shops linked together with car

parks and restaurants; **shopping mall** = enclosed covered area for shopping, with shops, restaurants, banks and other facilities; **shopping precinct** = part of town where the streets are closed to traffic so that people can walk about and shop

shop-soiled [ˈʃɒpsɔɪld] *adjective* dirty because of having been on display in a shop; *these items are shop-soiled and cannot be sold at full price*

shop steward [ˈʃɒp ˈstjʊəd] *noun* elected trade union representative who reports workers' complaints to the management

shopwalker [ˈʃɒpwɔːkə] *noun* employee of a department store who advises the customers and supervises the shop assistants in a department

short [ʃɔːt] **1** *adjective* **(a)** for a small period of time; **short credit** = terms which allow the customer only a little time to pay; **in the short term** = in the near future, quite soon **(b)** not as much as should be; *the shipment was three items short*; **when we cashed up we were £10 short** = we had £10 less than we should have had; **to give short weight** = to sell something which is lighter than it should be **(c) short of** = with less than needed, with not enough of; *we are short of staff* or *short of money*; *the company is short of new ideas* **(d) to sell short** = to agree to sell something (such as shares) which you do not possess, but which you think you will be able to buy for less; **short selling** *or* **selling short** = arranging to sell something in the future which you think you can buy for less than the agreed selling price; **to borrow short** = to borrow for a short period **2** *noun* **shorts** = government stocks which mature in less than five years' time

shortage [ˈʃɔːtɪdʒ] *noun* lack, not having enough; *a chronic shortage of skilled staff*; *we employ part-timers to make up for staff shortages*; *the import controls have resulted in the shortage of spare parts*; **manpower shortage** *or* **shortage of manpower** = lack of workers; **there is no shortage of investment advice** = there are plenty of people who want to give advice on investments

shortchange [ˈʃɔːtˈtʃeɪndʒ] *verb* to give a customer less change than is right, either by mistake or in the hope that he will not notice

short-dated [ˈʃɔːtˈdeɪtɪd] *adjective* **short-dated bills** = bills which are payable within a few days; **short-dated securities** = government stocks which mature in less than five years time

shorten [ˈʃɔːtn] *verb* to make shorter; **to shorten a credit period** = to make a credit period shorter, so as to improve the company's cash position

shortfall [ˈʃɔːtfɔːl] *noun* amount which is missing which would make the total expected sum; *we had to borrow money to cover the shortfall between expenditure and revenue*

shorthand [ˈʃɔːthænd] *noun* rapid way of writing using a system of signs; **shorthand secretary** = secretary who takes dictation in shorthand; **shorthand typist** = typist who can take dictation in shorthand and then type it; **to take shorthand** = to write using shorthand; *he took down the minutes in shorthand*

shorthanded [ˈʃɔːtˈhændɪd] *adjective* without enough staff; *we are rather shorthanded at the moment*

short-haul flight [ˈʃɔːtˈhɔːl ˈflaɪt] *noun* flight over a short distance (up to 1,000 km)

shortlist [ˈʃɔːtlɪst] **1** *noun* list of some of the better people who have applied for a job, who can be asked to come for a test or an interview; *to draw up a shortlist*; *he is on the shortlist for the job* **2** *verb* to make a shortlist; *four candidates have been shortlisted*; *shortlisted candidates will be asked for an interview*

short-range [ˈʃɔːtˈreɪndʒ] *adjective* **short-range forecast** = forecast which covers a period of a few months

short-staffed [ˈʃɔːtˈstɑːft] *adjective* with not enough staff; *we are rather short-staffed at the moment*

short-term [ˈʃɔːtˈtɜːm] *adjective* for a short period; *to place money on short-term deposit*; *she is employed on a short-term contract*; **on a short-term basis** = for a short period; **short-term debts** = debts which have to be repaid within a few weeks; **short-term forecast** = forecast which covers a period of a few months; **short-term gains** = gains made over a short period (less than 12 months); **short-term loan** = loan which has to be repaid within a few weeks

short time [ˈʃɔːt ˈtaɪm] *noun* shorter working hours than usual; *to be on short time*; *the company has had to introduce short-time working because of lack of orders*

shot [ʃɒt] *noun* **mail shot** *or* **mailing shot** = leaflets sent by post to possible customers

show [ʃəʊ] **1** *noun* **(a)** exhibition or display of goods or services for sale; *motor show*; *computer show*; **show house** *or* **show flat** = house or flat built and furnished so that possible buyers can see what similar houses could be like **(b)** **show of hands** = vote where people show how they vote by raising their hands; *the motion was carried on a show of hands* **2** *verb* to make something be seen; *to show a gain* *or* *a fall*; *to show a profit* *or* *a loss* (NOTE: **showing - showed - has shown**)

showcard [ˈʃəʊkɑːd] *noun* piece of cardboard with advertising material, put near an item for sale

showcase [ˈʃəʊkeɪs] *noun* cupboard with a glass front or top to display items for sale

showroom [ˈʃəʊruːm] *noun* room where goods are displayed for sale; *car showroom*

shred [ʃred] *verb* to tear (paper) into thin strips, which can then be thrown away or used as packing material; *they sent a pile of old invoices to be shredded*; *she told the police that the manager had told her to shred all the documents in the file*

shredder [ˈʃredə] *noun* machine for shredding paper

shrink [ʃrɪŋk] *verb* to get smaller; *the market has shrunk by 20%*; *the company is having difficulty selling into a shrinking market* (NOTE: **shrinking - shrank - has shrunk**)

shrinkage [ˈʃrɪŋkɪdʒ] *noun* **(a)** amount by which something gets smaller; *to allow* *for shrinkage* (b) *(informal)* losses of stock through theft (especially by members of the staff of the shop)

shrink-wrapped [ˈʃrɪŋkˈræpt] *adjective* covered in tight plastic protective cover

shrink-wrapping [ˈʃrɪŋkˈræpɪŋ] *noun* act of covering (a book, fruit, record, etc.) in a tight plastic cover

shroff [ʃrɒf] *noun (in the Far East)* (i) accountant; (ii) accounts clerk

shut [ʃʌt] **1** *adjective* closed, not open; *the office is shut on Saturdays* **2** *verb* to close; *to shut a shop or a warehouse* (NOTE: **shutting - shut**)

shut down [ˈʃʌt ˈdaʊn] *verb* **to shut down a factory** = to make a factory stop working for a time; *the offices will shut down for Christmas; six factories have shut down this month*

shutdown [ˈʃʌtdaʊn] *noun* shutting of a factory

shutout [ˈʃʌtaʊt] *noun* locking of the door of a factory or office to stop the staff getting in

sick [sɪk] *adjective* ill, not well; **sick leave** = time when a worker is away from work because of illness; **sick pay** = pay paid to a worker who is sick, even if he cannot work

side [saɪd] *noun* **(a)** part of something near the edge; **credit side** = right-hand side of accounts showing money received; **debit side** = left-hand side of accounts showing money owed or paid **(b)** one of the surfaces of a flat object; *please write on one side of the paper only* **(c)** **on the side** = separate from your normal work, and hidden from your employer; *he works in an accountant's office, but he runs a construction company on the side; her salary is too small to live on, so the family lives on what she can make on the side*

sideline [ˈsaɪdlaɪn] *noun* business which is extra to your normal work; *he runs a profitable sideline selling postcards to tourists*

sight [saɪt] *noun* seeing; **bill payable at sight** = bill which must be paid when it is presented; **sight bill** *or* **sight draft** = bill of exchange which is payable at sight; **to buy something sight unseen** = to buy something without having inspected it

if your company needed a piece of equipment priced at about $50,000, would you buy it sight unseen from a supplier you had never met?

Nation's Business

sign [saɪn] **1** *noun* advertising board, notice which advertises something; *they have asked for planning permission to put up a large red shop sign; advertising signs cover most of the buildings in the centre of the town* **2** *verb* to write your name in a special way on a document to show that you have written it or approved it; *to sign a letter or a contract or a document or a cheque; the letter is signed by the managing director; our company cheques are not valid if they have not been signed by the finance director;* **the warehouse manager signed for the goods** = the manager signed a receipt to show that the goods had been received; **he signed the goods in** *or* **he signed the goods out** = he signed the stock report to show that the goods had arrived or had been dispatched

signatory [ˈsɪɡnətri] *noun* person who signs a contract, etc.; *you have to get the permission of all the signatories to the agreement if you want to change the terms*

signature [ˈsɪɡnətʃə] *noun* name written in a special way to show that a document has been authorized; *a pile of letters waiting for the managing director's signature; he found a pile of cheques on his desk waiting for signature; all our company's cheques need two signatures*

sign off [ˈsaɪn ˈɒf] *verb (of directors)* **to sign off the accounts** = to sign the final form of a company's accounts to show that they are approved, before sending them to Companies House

sign on [ˈsaɪn ˈɒn] *verb* to start work, by signing your name in the personnel office; **to sign on for the dole** = to register as unemployed

silent partner [ˈsaɪlənt ˈpɑːtnə] *noun* partner who has a share of the business but does not work in it

simple interest [ˈsɪmpl ˈɪntrəst] *noun* interest calculated on the capital invested only, and not added to it

sincerely [sɪn'sɪəli] *adverb* **Yours sincerely** *US* **Sincerely yours** = words used as an ending to a business letter addressed to a named person

sine die ['saɪni 'diːeɪ] *phrase* **to adjourn a case sine die** = to postpone the hearing of a case without fixing a new date for it

single ['sɪŋgl] *adjective* one alone **(a)** **single fare** *or* **single ticket** *or* **a single** = fare or ticket for one journey from one place to another; *I want two singles to London* **(b)** **single-entry bookkeeping** = method of bookkeeping where payments or sales are noted with only one entry per transaction (usually in the cash book); **in single figures** = less than ten; *sales are down to single figures*; *inflation is now in single figures*; **single-figure inflation** = inflation rising at less than 10% per annum; **single premium policy** = insurance policy where only one premium is paid rather than regular annual premiums; **single union agreement** = agreement between management and one union, that the union will represent all the workers in the company (whatever type of job they have) **(c)** **the single (European) market** = the EU considered as one single market, with no tariff barriers between its member states

sink [sɪŋk] *verb* **(a)** to go to the bottom of the water; *the ship sank in the storm and all the cargo was lost* **(b)** to go down suddenly; *prices sank at the news of the closure of the factory* **(c)** to invest money (into something); *he sank all his savings into a car-hire business* (NOTE: **sinking - sank - sunk**)

sinking fund ['sɪŋkɪŋ 'fʌnd] *noun* fund built up out of amounts of money put aside regularly to meet a future need, such as the repayment of a loan

sir [sɜː] *noun* **Dear Sir** = way of addressing a letter to a man whom you do not know or to a limited company; **Dear Sirs** = way of addressing a letter to a firm

sister ['sɪstə] *adjective* **sister company** = one of several companies which are part of the same group; **sister ship** = ship which is of the same design and belongs to the same company as another ship

sit-down ['sɪtdaʊn] *adjective* **sit-down protest** *or* **sit-down strike** = strike where the workers stay in their place of work and refuse to work or to leave

site [saɪt] **1** *noun* **(a)** place where something is built; *we have chosen a site for the new factory*; *the supermarket is to be built on a site near the station*; **building site** *or* **construction site** = place where a building is being constructed; *all visitors to the site must wear safety helmets*; **greenfield site** = site for a factory which is in the country, and not surrounded by other buildings; *(compare* **BROWNFIELD SITE)** **site engineer** = engineer in charge of a building being constructed **(b)** web site, a position on the Web, which is created by a company, organization or individual, and which anyone can visit; *how many hits did we have on our web site last week?* **2** *verb* **to be sited** = to be placed; *the factory will be sited near the motorway*

sit-in ['sɪtɪn] *noun* strike where the workers stay in their place of work and refuse to work or leave (NOTE: plural is **sit-ins**)

sitting tenant ['sɪtɪŋ 'tenənt] *noun* tenant who is occupying a building when the freehold or lease is sold; *the block of flats is for sale with four flats vacant and two with sitting tenants*

situated ['sɪtjʊeɪtɪd] *adjective* placed; *the factory is situated on the edge of the town*; *the office is situated near the railway station*

situation [sɪtjʊ'eɪʃən] *noun* **(a)** state of affairs; *financial situation of a company*; *the general situation of the economy* **(b)** job; **situations vacant** *or* **situations wanted** = list in a newspaper of vacancies for workers or of people wanting work **(c)** place where something is; *the factory is in a very pleasant situation by the sea*

size [saɪz] *noun* measurements of something, of how big something is or of how many there are of something; *what is the size of the container?*; *the size of the staff has doubled in the last two years*; *this packet is the maximum size allowed by the post office*

skeleton staff ['skelɪtn 'stɑːf] *noun* a few staff left to carry on essential work while most of the workforce is away

skid [skɪd] *noun US* flat wooden base on which goods can be stacked for easy handling by a fork-lift truck (NOTE: British English is **pallet)**

skill [skɪl] *noun* ability to do something because you have been trained; *she has acquired some very useful office management skills*; *he will have to learn some new skills if he is going to direct the factory*

> Britain's skills crisis has now reached such proportions that it is affecting the nation's economic growth
> *Personnel Today*

> we aim to add the sensitivity of a new European to the broad skills of the new professional manager
> *Management Today*

skilled [skɪld] *adjective* having learnt certain skills; **skilled workers** *or* **skilled labour** = workers who have special skills or who have had long training

slack [slæk] *adjective* not busy; *business is slack at the end of the week*; *January is always a slack period*

slacken off ['slækən 'ɒf] *verb* to become less busy; *trade has slackened off*

slander ['slɑːndə] **1** *noun* untrue spoken statement which damages someone's character; **action for slander** *or* **slander action** = case in a law court where someone says that another person had slandered him or her **2** *verb* **to slander someone** = to damage someone's character by saying untrue things about him or her; *compare* LIBEL

slash [slæʃ] *verb* to cut, to reduce sharply; *we have been forced to slash prices or credit terms*; *prices have been slashed in all departments*; *the bank has been forced to slash interest rates*

sleeper ['sliːpə] *noun* share which has not risen in value for some time, but which may suddenly do so in the future

sleeping partner ['sliːpɪŋ 'pɑːtnə] *noun* partner who has a share in the business but does not work in it

slide [slaɪd] *verb* to move down steadily; *prices slid after the company reported a loss* (NOTE: **sliding - slid)**

sliding ['slaɪdɪŋ] *adjective* which rises in steps; **a sliding scale of charges** = list of charges which rises gradually according to value, quantity, time, etc.

slight [slaɪt] *adjective* not very large, not very important; *there was a slight improvement in the balance of trade*; *we saw a slight increase in sales in February*

slightly ['slaɪtli] *adverb* not very much; *sales fell slightly in the second quarter*; *the Swiss bank is offering slightly better terms*

slip [slɪp] **1** *noun* **(a)** small piece of paper; **compliments slip** = piece of paper with the name of the company printed on it, sent with documents, gifts, etc., instead of a letter; **deposit slip** = piece of paper stamped by the cashier to prove that you have paid money into your account; **distribution slip** = paper attached to a document or to a magazine, showing all the people in an office who should read it; **pay slip** = piece of paper showing the full amount of a worker's pay, and the money deducted as tax, pension and insurance contributions; **paying-in slip** = printed form which is filled in when money is being deposited in a bank; **sales slip** = paper showing that an article was bought at a certain shop; *goods can be exchanged only on production of a sales slip* **(b)** mistake; *he made a couple of slips in calculating the discount* **2** *verb* to go down and back; *profits slipped to £1.5m*; *shares slipped back at the close* (NOTE: **slipping - slipped)**

> with long-term fundamentals reasonably sound, the question for brokers is when does cheap become cheap enough? The Bangkok and Taipei exchanges offer lower p/e ratios than Jakarta, but if Jakarta p/e ratios slip to the 16-18 range, foreign investors would pay more attention to it
> *Far Eastern Economic Review*

slip up ['slɪp 'ʌp] *verb* to make a mistake; *we slipped up badly in not signing the agreement with the Chinese company*

slip-up ['slɪpʌp] *noun* mistake; *there has been a slip-up in the customs documentation* (NOTE: plural is **slip-ups**)

slogan ['sləʊgən] *noun* **publicity slogan** = group of words which can be easily remembered, and which is used in publicity for a product; *we are using the slogan 'Smiths can make it' on all our publicity*

slot [slɒt] *noun* (a) period of time available for a TV or radio commercial; *they took six 30-second slots at peak viewing time* (b) **slot machine** = machine which provides drinks or cigarettes, plays music, etc., when a coin is put in it

slow [sləʊ] **1** *adjective* not going fast; *a slow start to the day's trading*; *the sales got off to a slow start, but picked up later*; *business is always slow after Christmas*; *they were slow to reply or slow at replying to the customer's complaints*; *the board is slow to come to a decision*; *there was a slow improvement in sales in the first half of the year* **2** *adverb* **to go slow** = to protest against management by working slowly

a general price freeze succeeded in slowing the growth in consumer prices
Financial Times

cash paid for stock: overstocked lines, factory seconds, slow sellers
Australian Financial Review

the fall in short-term rates suggests a slowing economy
Financial Times

slow down ['sləʊ 'daʊn] *verb* to stop rising, moving or falling; *inflation is slowing down*; *the fall in the exchange rate is slowing down*; *the management decided to slow down production*

slowdown ['sləʊdaʊn] *noun* becoming less fast, less busy; *a slowdown in the company's expansion*

slowly ['sləʊli] *adverb* not fast; *the company's sales slowly improved*; *we are slowly increasing our market share*

sluggish ['slʌgɪʃ] *adjective* not moving very fast; *the economy is still sluggish,*

and is taking a long time to get out of recession

the association said sluggish earnings by supermarkets are due to consumers' concern about income and job prospects
Nikkei Weekly

slump [slʌmp] **1** *noun* (a) rapid fall; *we experienced a slump in sales or a slump in profits*; *the slump in the value of the pound or the pound's slump on the foreign exchange markets* (b) period of economic collapse with high unemployment and loss of trade; *we are experiencing slump conditions*; *the Slump* = the world economic crisis of 1929 - 1933 **2** *verb* to fall fast; *profits have slumped*; *the pound slumped on the foreign exchange markets*

slush fund ['slʌʃ 'fʌnd] *noun* money kept to one side to give to people to persuade them to do what you want; *the government was brought down by the scandal over the slush funds*; *the party was accused of keeping a slush fund to pay foreign businessmen*

small [smɔːl] *adjective* not large; **small ads** = short private advertisements in a newspaper (selling small items, asking for jobs, etc.); **small businesses** = little companies with low turnover and few employees; **small businessman** = man who runs a small business; **small change** = loose coins; *GB* **small claims court** = court which deals with disputes over small amounts of money; **the small investor** = person who has a small amount of money to invest; **to read the small print on a contract** = to read the conditions of a contract which are often printed very small so that people will not be able to read them easily; **small shopkeepers** = owners of small shops

small company ['smɔːl 'kʌmpni] *noun* company with at least two of the following characteristics: turnover of less than £2.0m; fewer than 50 staff; net assets of less than £975,000 (small companies are allowed to file modified accounts with Companies House)

small-scale ['smɔːlskeɪl] *adjective* working in a small way, with few staff and not much money; **a small-scale enterprise** = a small business

smart card ['smɑːt 'kɑːd] *noun* credit card with a microchip, used for withdrawing money from ATMs, or for purchases at EFTPOS terminals

smash [smæʃ] *verb* to break (a record), to do better than (a record); *the factory is aiming to smash all production records this year*; *sales have smashed all records for the first half of the year*

smokestack industries ['sməʊkstæk 'ındʌstrɪz] *noun* heavy industries, such as steel-making

smuggle ['smʌgl] *verb* to take goods into a country without declaring them to customs; *they had to smuggle the spare parts into the country*

smuggler ['smʌglə] *noun* person who smuggles

smuggling ['smʌglɪŋ] *noun* taking goods illegally into a country; *he made his money in arms smuggling*

snap [snæp] *adjective* rapid or sudden; *the board came to a snap decision*; *they carried out a snap check or a snap inspection of the expense accounts*

snap up ['snæp 'ʌp] *verb* to buy something quickly; *to snap up a bargain*; *he snapped up 15% of the company's shares* (NOTE: **snapping - snapped**)

snip [snɪp] *noun (informal)* bargain; *these printers are a snip at £50*

soar [sɔː] *verb* to go up rapidly; *food prices soared during the cold weather*; *share prices soared on the news of the takeover bid or the news of the takeover bid sent share prices soaring*

social ['səʊʃəl] *adjective* referring to society in general; **social costs** = ways in which something will affect people; *the report examines the social costs of building the factory in the middle of the town*; **social security** = money from contributions paid to the National Insurance provided by the government to people who need it; *he gets weekly social security payments*; **the social system** = the way society is organized

society [sə'saɪəti] *noun* **(a)** way in which people in a country are organized; **consumer society** = type of society where consumers are encouraged to buy goods; **the affluent society** = type of society where most people are rich **(b)** club, group of people with the same interests; *he has joined a computer society*; **building society** = financial institution which accepts and pays interest on deposits, and lends money to people who are buying property against the security of the property which is being bought; **co-operative society** = organization where customers and workers are partners and share the profits; **friendly society** = group of people who pay regular subscriptions to a fund which is used to help members who are ill or in financial trouble

socio-economic ['səʊʃɪəʊiːkə'nɒmɪk] *adjective* referring to social and economic conditions; *the socio-economic system in capitalist countries*; **socio-economic groups** = groups in society divided according to income and position

soft [sɒft] *adjective* not hard; **soft currency** = currency of a country with a weak economy, which is cheap to buy and difficult to exchange for other currencies; **soft landing** = change in economic strategy to counteract inflation, which does not cause unemployment or a fall in the standard of living, and has only minor effects on the bulk of the population; **soft loan** = loan (from a company to an employee or from a government to another government) at very low or nil interest; **to take the soft option** = to decide to do something which involves least risk, effort or problems; **soft sell** = persuading people to buy by encouraging them, but not forcing them to do so

software ['sɒftweə] *noun* computer programs (as opposed to machines, which are 'hardware')

sole [səʊl] *adjective* only; **sole agency** = agreement to be the only person to represent a company or to sell a product in a certain area; *he has the sole agency for Ford cars*; **sole agent** = person who has the sole agency for a product in an area; **sole distributor** = retailer who is the only one in an area who is allowed to sell a certain product; **sole owner** *or* **sole proprietor** = person who owns a business on his own, with no partners, without forming a company; **sole trader** = person who runs a business by himself but has not registered it as a company

solemn ['sɒləm] *adjective* **solemn and binding agreement** = agreement which is not legally binding, but which all parties are supposed to obey

solicit [sə'lɪsɪt] *verb* **to solicit orders** = to ask for orders, to try to get people to order goods

solicitor [sə'lɪsɪtə] *noun GB (in England and Wales)* lawyer who has passed the examinations of the Law Society and has a valid certificate to practise and who gives advice to members of the public and acts for them in legal matters; **to instruct a solicitor** = to give orders to a solicitor to act on your behalf

solus (advertisement) ['səʊləs əd'vɜːtɪsmənt] *noun* advertisement which does not appear near other advertisements for similar products

solution [sə'luːʃən] *noun* answer to a problem; *to look for a solution to the company's financial problems; the programmer came up with a solution to the systems problem; we think we have found a solution to the problem of getting skilled staff*

solve [sɒlv] *verb* **to solve a problem** = to find an answer to a problem; *the loan will solve some of our short-term problems*

solvency ['sɒlvənsi] *noun* being able to pay all debts

solvent ['sɒlvənt] *adjective* having enough money to pay debts; *when he bought the company it was barely solvent*

sort [sɔːt] *verb* to put (a lot of things) in order; *she is sorting index cards into alphabetical order*

sort out ['sɔːt 'aʊt] *verb* to put into order; to settle (a problem); *did you sort out the accounts problem with the auditors?*

sound [saʊnd] *adjective* reasonable, which can be trusted; *the company's financial situation is very sound; he gave us some very sound advice*

soundness ['saʊndnəs] *noun* being reasonable

source [sɔːs] **1** *noun* place where something comes from; *what is the source of her income?; you must declare income from all sources to the tax office*; **income which is taxed at source** = where the tax is removed before the income is paid; **source and application of funds statement** = statement in a company's annual accounts, showing where new funds came from during the year, and how they were used **2** *verb* to get supplies from somewhere; *we source these spare parts in Germany*

sourcing ['sɔːsɪŋ] *noun* getting supplies from a certain place or supplier; *the sourcing of spare parts can be diversified to suppliers outside Europe*; *see also* OUTSOURCING

space [speɪs] *noun* empty place or empty area; **advertising space** = space in a newspaper set aside for advertisements; **to take advertising space in a newspaper** = to place a large advertisement in a newspaper; **floor space** = area of the floor in an office; **office space** = area available for offices or used by offices; *we are looking for extra office space for our new accounts department*

space bar ['speɪs 'bɑː] *noun* key on a typewriter or computer which makes a single space between letters

space out ['speɪs 'aʊt] *verb* to place things with spaces between them; *the company name is written in spaced-out letters; payments can be spaced out over a period of ten years*

spare [speə] *adjective* extra, not being used; *he has invested his spare capital in a computer shop*; **to use up spare capacity** = to make use of time or space which has not been fully used; **spare part** = small piece of machinery used to replace part of a machine which is broken; *the photocopier will not work - it needs a spare part*; **spare time** = time when you are not at work; *he built himself a car in his spare time*

spec [spek] *noun* **to buy something on spec** = to buy something as a speculation, without being sure of its value

special ['speʃəl] *adjective* different, not normal, referring to one particular thing; *he* *offered us special terms*; *the car is being offered at a special price*; **special delivery** = type of postal service for rapid delivery of letters and packets; **special deposits** = large sums of money which banks have to deposit with the Bank of England

---

airlines offer special stopover rates and hotel packages to attract customers to certain routes

Business Traveller

---

special drawing rights (SDRs)

['speʃəl 'drɔːɪŋ 'raɪts] *noun* unit of account used by the International Monetary Fund, allocated to each member country for use in loans and other international operations; their value is calculated daily on the weighted values of a group of currencies shown in dollars

specialist ['speʃəlɪst] *noun* person or company which deals with one particular type of product or one subject; *you should go to a specialist in computers or to a computer specialist for advice*

speciality *or* **specialty** [speʃɪ'æləti or 'speʃəlti] *noun* particular interest or special type of product which a company deals in; *their speciality is computer programs; US* **specialty store** = shop selling a limited range of items of good quality

specialization [speʃəlaɪ'zeɪʃən] *noun* study of one particular thing, dealing with one particular type of product; *the company's area of specialization is accounts packages for small businesses*

specialize ['speʃəlaɪz] *verb* to trade in one particular type of product or service; *the company specializes in electronic components*; *they have a specialized product line*; *he sells very specialized equipment for the electronics industry*

---

the group specializes in the sale, lease and rental of new and second-user hardware

Financial Times

---

special resolution ['speʃəl rezə'luːʃn]

noun resolution of the members of a company which is only valid if it is approved by 75% of the votes cast at a meeting (a resolution concerning an important matter, such as a change to the company's articles of association)

COMMENT: 21 days' notice must be given for a special resolution to be put to a meeting, as opposed to an 'extraordinary resolution' for which notice must be given, but no minimum period is specified by law, An extraordinary resolution could be a proposal to wind up a company voluntarily, but changes to the articles of association, such as a change of name, or of the objects of the company, or a reduction in share capital, need a special resolution

---

specie ['spiːʃiː] *plural noun* coins

specification [spesɪfɪ'keɪʃən] *noun* detailed information about what is needed or about a product to be supplied; *to detail the specifications of a computer system*; **job specification** = very detailed description of what is involved in a job; **to work to standard specifications** = to work to specifications which are acceptable anywhere in the industry; **the work is not up to specification** *or* **does not meet our specifications** = the product is not made in the way which was detailed

specify ['spesɪfaɪ] *verb* to state clearly what is needed; *to specify full details of the goods ordered*; *do not include VAT on the invoice unless specified*

specimen ['spesɪmən] *noun* thing which is given as a sample; **to give specimen signatures on a bank mandate** = to write the signatures of all people who can sign cheques for an account so that the bank can recognize them

specs [speks] *plural noun* = SPECIFICATIONS

speculate ['spekjuleɪt] *verb* to take a risk in business which you hope will bring you profits; **to speculate on the Stock Exchange** = to buy shares which you hope will rise in value

speculation [spekju'leɪʃən] *noun* risky deal which may produce a short-term profit; *he bought the company as a speculation*; *she lost all her money in Stock Exchange speculations*

speculative ['spekjulətɪv] *adjective* **speculative builder** = builder who builds houses in the hope that someone will want to buy them; **speculative share** = share which may go sharply up or down in value

> some thrifts came to grief on speculative property deals, some in the high-risk junk bond market, others simply by lending too much to too many people
>
> *Times*

speculator ['spekjʊleɪtə] *noun* person who buys goods, shares or foreign currency in the hope that they will rise in value; *a property speculator*; *a currency speculator*; *a speculator on the Stock Exchange or a Stock Exchange speculator*

speed [spiːd] *noun* rate at which something moves; **dictation speed** = number of words per minute which a secretary can write down in shorthand; **keyboarding speed** = number of words per minute which a keyboarder can enter

speed up ['spiːd 'ʌp] *verb* to make something go faster; *we are aiming to speed up our delivery times*

spend [spend] *verb* (a) to pay money; *they spent all their savings on buying the shop*; *the company spends thousands of pounds on research* (b) to use time; *the company spends hundreds of man-hours on meetings*; *the chairman spent yesterday afternoon with the auditors* (NOTE: **spending - spent**)

spending ['spendɪŋ] *noun* paying money; *both cash spending and credit card spending increase at Christmas*; **consumer spending** = spending by consumers; **spending money** = money for ordinary personal expenses; **spending power** = having money to spend on goods; amount of goods which can be bought for a certain sum of money; *the spending power of the pound has fallen over the last ten years*; *the spending power of the student market*

sphere [sfɪə] *noun* area; *sphere of activity*; *sphere of influence*

spin doctor ['spɪn 'dɒktə] *noun* (*informal*) person who explains news in a way that makes it flattering to the person or organization employing him; *government spin doctors have been having some*

difficulty in dealing with the news items about the rise in unemployment

spin off ['spɪn 'ɒf] *verb* **to spin off a subsidiary company** = to take a part of a large company and make a smaller subsidiary from it (NOTE: **spinning - spun**)

spinoff ['spɪnɒf] *noun* useful product developed as a secondary product from a main item; *one of the spinoffs of the research programme has been the development of the non-stick frying pan*

spiral ['spaɪərəl] **1** *noun* thing which twists round and round getting higher all the time; **the economy is in an inflationary spiral** *or* **wage-price spiral** = the economy is in a situation where price rises encourage higher wage demands which in turn make prices rise **2** *verb* to twist round and round, getting higher all the time; *a period of spiralling prices*; **spiralling inflation** = inflation where price rises make workers ask for higher wages which then increase prices again (NOTE: **spiralling - spiralled** but American spelling **spiraling - spiraled**)

split [splɪt] **1** *noun* (a) dividing up; **share split** = dividing of shares into smaller denominations; **the company is proposing a five for one split** = the company is proposing that each existing share should be divided into five smaller shares (b) lack of agreement; *a split in the family shareholders* **2** *verb* (a) **to split shares** = to divide shares into smaller denominations; **the shares were split five for one** = five new shares were given for each existing share held (b) **to split the difference** = to come to an agreement over a price by dividing the difference between the amount the seller is asking and amount the buyer wants to pay and agreeing on a price between the two (NOTE: **splitting - split**) **3** *adjective* which is divided into parts; **split commission** = commission which is divided between brokers or agents; **split payment** = payment which is divided into small units

> COMMENT: a company may decide to split its shares if the share price becomes too 'heavy' (i.e., each share is priced at such a high level that small investors may be put off, and trading in

the share is restricted); in the UK, a share price of £10.00 is considered 'heavy', though such prices are common on other stock markets

split-level investment trust

['splɪtlevl ɪn'vestmənt 'trʌst] *noun* investment trust with two categories of shares: 'income shares' which receive income from the investments, but do not benefit from the rise in their capital value; and 'capital shares', which increase in value as the value of the investments rises, but do not receive any income

spoil [spɔɪl] *verb* to ruin, to make something bad; *half the shipment was spoiled by water*; *the company's results were spoiled by a disastrous last quarter*

sponsor ['spɒnsə] **1** *noun* **(a)** person who pays money to help research, to pay for a business venture; company which pays to help a sport, in return for advertising rights **(b)** company which advertises on TV **2** *verb* to pay money to help research or business development; *to sponsor a television programme*; *the company has sponsored the football match*; *government-sponsored trade exhibition*

sponsorship ['spɒnsəʃɪp] *noun* act of sponsoring; *government sponsorship of overseas selling missions*

spot [spɒt] *noun* **(a)** buying something for immediate delivery; **spot cash** = cash paid for something bought immediately; **the spot market in oil** = the market for buying oil for immediate delivery; **spot price** *or* **spot rate** = price or rate for something which is delivered immediately **(b)** place; **to be on the spot** = to be at a certain place; *we have a man on the spot to deal with any problems which happen on the building site* **(c)** TV **spot** = short period on TV which is used for commercials; *we are running a series of TV spots over the next three weeks*

with most of the world's oil now traded on spot markets, Opec's official prices are much less significant than they once were
Economist

the average spot price of Nigerian light crude oil for the month of July was 27.21 dollars per barrel
Business Times (Lagos)

spread [spred] **1** *noun* **(a)** range; **he has a wide spread of investments** *or* **of interests** = he has shares in many different types of companies **(b)** *(on the Stock Exchange)* difference between buying and selling prices (i.e., between the 'bid' and 'offer' prices) **2** *verb* to space out over a period of time; *to spread payments over several months*; **to spread a risk** = to make the risk of insurance less great by asking other companies to help cover it (NOTE: **spreading - spread**)

dealers said markets were thin, with gaps between trades and wide spreads between bid and ask prices on the currencies
Wall Street Journal

to ensure an average return you should hold a spread of different shares covering a wide cross-section of the market
Investors Chronicle

spreadsheet ['spredʃiːt] *noun* computer printout showing a series of columns of figures

square [skweə] **1** *noun* **(a)** shape with four equal straight sides and four right angles; *graph paper is drawn with a series of small squares* **(b)** way of measuring area, by multiplying the length by the width; *the office is ten metres by twelve - its area is one hundred and twenty square metres*; **square measure** = area in square feet or metres (NOTE: written with figures as ^{2}: **10ft^2** = ten square feet; **6m^2** = six square metres) **2** *adjective* **(a)** with four right angles and four equal straight sides; **square cut file** = simple folded card file, with one side taller than the other, used for filing documents (the file is inserted into a suspension file) **(b)** *(informal)* settled, not owing anything; **now we're all square** = we do not owe each other anything **3** *verb* US **to square a bill** = to pay a bill; **to square away** = to put (papers) in order

squared paper ['skweəd 'peɪpə] *noun* paper printed with a series of small squares, like graph paper

Square Mile ['skweə 'maɪl] *noun* the City (of London), the British financial centre

squeeze [skwiːz] **1** *noun* government control carried out by reducing amounts available; **credit squeeze** = period when lending by the banks is restricted by the government; **profit squeeze** = control of the amount of profits which companies can pay out as dividend **2** *verb* to crush or to press; to make smaller; *to squeeze margins or profits or credit;* **our margins have been squeezed by the competition** = profits have been reduced because our margins have to be smaller for us to stay competitive

---

the real estate boom of the past three years has been based on the availability of easy credit. Today, money is tighter, so property should bear the brunt of the credit squeeze

Money Observer

SRO = SELF-REGULATORY ORGANIZATION

SSP = STATUTORY SICK PAY

St = STREET

stability [stə'bɪləti] *noun* being steady, not moving up or down; *price stability is essential; a period of economic stability; the stability of the currency markets; finance ministers are hoping to maintain currency stability*

stabilization [steɪbɪlaɪ'zeɪʃən] *noun* making stable, preventing sudden changes in prices, etc.; **stabilization of the economy** = keeping the economy stable by preventing inflation from rising, cutting high interest rates and excess money supply

stabilize ['steɪbɪlaɪz] *verb* to make steady; **prices have stabilized** = prices have stopped moving up or down; **to have a stabilizing effect on the economy** = to make the economy more stable

stable ['steɪbl] *adjective* steady, not moving up or down; *stable prices; stable*

exchange rate; stable currency; stable economy

stack [stæk] **1** *noun* pile, heap of things on top of each other; *there is a stack of replies to our advertisement* **2** *verb* to pile things on top of each other; *the boxes are stacked in the warehouse*

staff [stɑːf] **1** *noun* people who work for a company or for an organization; *the office staff have complained about the lack of heating;* **to be on the staff** *or* **a member of staff** *or* **a staff member** = to be employed permanently by a company; **staff agency** = agency which looks for office staff for companies; **staff appointment** = a job on the staff; **staff association** = society formed by members of staff of a company to represent them to the management and to organize entertainments; **accounts staff** = people who work in the accounts department; **clerical staff** *or* **office staff** = people who work in offices; **counter staff** = sales staff who work behind counters; **senior staff** = older members of staff; people in more important positions in a company; **junior staff** = younger members of staff; people in less important positions in a company (NOTE: **staff** refers to a group of people and so is often followed by a verb in the plural) **2** *verb* to employ workers; *to be staffed with skilled part-timers; to have difficulty in staffing the factory*

staffer ['stɑːfə] *noun US* member of the permanent staff

staffing ['stɑːfɪŋ] *noun* providing workers for a company; **staffing levels** = numbers of members of staff required in a department of a company for it to work efficiently; **the company's staffing policy** = the company's views on staff - how many are needed for each department, if they should be full-time or part-time, what the salaries should be, etc.

stag [stæg] **1** *noun* **(a)** person who buys new issues of shares and sells them immediately to make a profit **(b)** *US* dealer in stocks who is not a member of a Stock Exchange **2** *verb* **to stag an issue** = to buy a new issue of shares not as an investment, but to sell immediately at a profit (NOTE: **stagging - stagged**)

stage [steɪdʒ] **1** *noun* period, one of several points of development; *the different stages of the production process*; **the contract is still in the drafting stage** = the contract is still being drafted; **in stages** = in different steps; *the company has agreed to repay the loan in stages* **2** *verb* **(a)** to put on or to organize (a show); *the exhibition is being staged in the conference centre*; **to stage a recovery** = to recover; *the company has staged a strong recovery from a point of near bankruptcy* **(b) staged payments** = payments made in stages

stagflation [stæg'fleɪʃən] *noun* inflation and stagnation of an economy

stagger ['stægə] *verb* to arrange (holidays, working hours) so that they do not all begin and end at the same time; *staggered holidays help the tourist industry*; *we have to stagger the lunch hour so that there is always someone on the switchboard*; *we asked our supplier to stagger deliveries so that the warehouse can cope*

stagnant ['stægnənt] *adjective* not active, not increasing; *turnover was stagnant for the first half of the year*; *a stagnant economy is not a good sign*

stagnate [stæg'neɪt] *verb* not to increase, not to make progress; *the economy is stagnating*; *after six hours the talks were stagnating*

stagnation [stæg'neɪʃən] *noun* not increasing, not making any progress; *the country entered a period of stagnation*; **economic stagnation** = lack of expansion in the economy

stake [steɪk] **1** *noun* money invested; **to have a stake in a business** = to have money invested in a business; **to acquire a stake in a business** = to buy shares in a business; *he acquired a 25% stake in the business* **2** *verb* **to stake money on something** = to risk money on something

stakeholder ['steɪkhəʊldə] *noun* person who has a stake in a business, such as a shareholder, an employee, a supplier, etc.

stall [stɔːl] *noun* small moveable wooden booth, used for selling goods in a market

stallholder ['stɔːlhəʊldə] *noun* person who has a stall in a market and pays rent for the site it occupies

stamp [stæmp] **1** *noun* **(a)** device for making marks on documents; mark made in this way; *the invoice has the stamp 'Received with thanks' on it*; *the customs officer looked at the stamps in his passport*; **date stamp** = stamp with rubber figures which can be moved, used for marking the date on documents; **rubber stamp** = stamp made of hard rubber cut to form words; **stamp pad** = soft pad of cloth with ink on which a stamp is pressed, before marking the paper **(b) postage stamp** = small piece of gummed paper which you buy from a post office and stick on a letter or parcel to pay for the postage; *you'll need two £1 stamps for the parcel* **(c) stamp duty** = tax on legal documents (such as the conveyance of a property to a new owner) **2** *verb* **(a)** to mark a document with a stamp; *to stamp an invoice 'Paid'*; *the documents were stamped by the customs officials* **(b)** to put a postage stamp on (an envelope, etc.); **stamped addressed envelope (s.a.e.)** = envelope with your own address written on it and a stamp stuck on it to pay for the return postage; *send a stamped addressed envelope for further details and catalogue*

stand [stænd] **1** *noun* arrangement of shelves or tables, etc., at an exhibition for showing a company's products; **display stand** = special stand for displaying goods for sale; **exhibition stand** = separate section of an exhibition where a company exhibits its products or services; **news stand** = small wooden shop on a pavement, for selling newspapers **2** *verb* to be or to stay; **to stand liable for damages** = to be liable to pay damages; **the company's balance stands at £24,000** = the balance is £24,000 (NOTE: **standing - stood**)

standard ['stændəd] **1** *noun* normal quality or normal conditions which other things are judged against; **standard of living** *or* **living standards** = quality of personal home life (such as amount of food or clothes bought, size of family car, etc.); **production standards** = quality of production; **up to standard** = of acceptable quality; *this batch is not up to standard or does not meet our standards*; **gold standard** = linking of the value of a currency to value of a quantity of gold **2** *adjective* normal or usual; *a standard model car*; *we have a standard charge of £250 for a thirty-minute session*; **standard agreement** *or* **standard contract** = normal printed contract form; *US* **standard deduction** = amount that can be deducted from income on a federal income tax form, if deductions are not itemized; **standard letter** = letter which is sent without any change to various correspondents; **standard rate** = basic rate of income tax which is paid by most taxpayers

standardization [stændədaɪˈzeɪʃən] *noun* making sure that everything fits a standard or is produced in the same way; *standardization of design is necessary if we want to have a uniform company style*; *standardization of measurements throughout the EU*; **standardization of products** = reducing a large number of different products to a series which have the same measurements, design, packaging, etc.

standardize ['stændədaɪz] *verb* to make sure that everything fits a standard or is produced in the same way

standby ['stændbaɪ] *noun* **(a) standby ticket** = cheap air ticket which allows the passenger to wait until the last moment to see if there is an empty seat on the plane; **standby fare** = cheap fare for a standby ticket **(b) standby arrangements** = plans for what should be done if an emergency happens, especially money held in reserve in the International Monetary Fund for use by a country in financial difficulties; **standby credit** = credit which is available if a company needs it

stand down [stænd 'daʊn] *verb* to withdraw your name from an election; *at the last minute the two other candidates stood down, so she was elected chairman*

stand in for ['stænd 'ɪn fə] *verb* to take someone's place; *Mr Smith is standing in for the chairman, who is ill*

standing ['stændɪŋ] **1** *adjective* **standing order** = order written by a customer asking a bank to pay money regularly to an account; *I pay my subscription by standing order* **2** *noun* **(a) long-standing customer** *or* **customer of long standing** = person who has been a customer for many years **(b)** good reputation; *the financial standing of a company*; **company of good standing** = very reputable company

standstill ['stændstɪl] *noun* situation where work has stopped; *production is at a standstill*; *the strike brought the factory to a standstill*

staple ['steɪpl] **1** *adjective* **staple commodity** = basic food or raw material; **staple industry** = main industry in a country; **staple product** = main product **2** *noun* small piece of bent metal for attaching papers together; *he used a pair of scissors to take the staples out of the documents* **3** *verb* to **staple papers together** = to attach papers with staples; *he could not take away separate pages, because the documents were stapled together*

stapler ['steɪplə] *noun* small device used to attach papers together with staples

start [stɑːt] **1** *noun* beginning; **cold start** = beginning a new business or opening a new shop with no previous turnover to base it on; **house starts** *US* **housing starts** = number of new private houses or flats of which construction has been started during a year **2** *verb* **to start a business from cold** or **from scratch** = to begin a new business, with no previous turnover to base it on

starting ['stɑ:tɪŋ] *adjective* beginning; **starting date** = date on which something starts; **starting salary** = salary for an employee when he starts work with a company

start-up ['stɑ:tʌp] *noun* beginning of a new company or new product; *we went into the red for the first time because of the start-up costs of the new subsidiary in the USA*; **start-up financing** = the first stage in financing a new project, which is followed by several rounds of investment capital as the project gets under way (NOTE: plural is **start-ups**)

state [steɪt] **1** *noun* **(a)** independent country; semi-independent section of a federal country (such as the USA); *US* **state bank** = commercial bank licensed by the authorities of a state, and not necessarily a member of the Federal Reserve system (as opposed to a 'national bank') **(b)** government of a country; **state enterprise** = company run by the state; *the bosses of state industries are appointed by the government*; **state ownership** = situation where an industry is nationalized **2** *verb* to say clearly; *the document states that all revenue has to be declared to the tax office*

> the unions had argued that public sector pay rates had slipped behind rates applying in state and local government areas
>
> *Australian Financial Review*

state-controlled ['steɪtkən'trəʊld] *adjective* run by the state; *state-controlled television*

statement ['steɪtmənt] *noun* **(a)** saying something clearly; **to make a false statement** = to give wrong details; **statement of expenses** = detailed list of money spent **(b)** **financial statement** = document which shows the financial situation of a company; *the accounts*

department have prepared a financial statement for the shareholders; *see also* INCOME STATEMENT **(c)** **statement (of account)** = list of invoices and credits and debits sent by a supplier to a customer at the end of each month; **bank statement** = written document from a bank showing the balance of an account; **monthly** *or* **quarterly statement** = statement which is sent every month or every quarter by the bank

state-of-the-art ['steɪtəvðɪ'ɑ:t] *adjective* technically as advanced as possible

> each year American manufacturers increase their budget for state-of-the-art computer-based hardware and software
>
> *Duns Business Month*

state-owned ['steɪt'əʊnd] *adjective* owned by the state or by a state

> state-owned banks cut their prime rates a percentage point to 11%
>
> *Wall Street Journal*

static market ['stætɪk 'mɑ:kɪt] *noun* a market which does not increase or decrease significantly over a period of time

station ['steɪʃən] *noun* **(a)** place where trains stop for passengers to get on or off; *the train leaves the Central Station at 14.15* **(b)** **TV station** *or* **radio station** = building where TV or radio programmes are produced

stationery ['steɪʃənəri] *noun* **(a)** office supplies for writing, such as paper, carbons, pens, etc.; *we use the same stationery supplier for all our office stationery*; **continuous stationery** = paper made as a long sheet used in computer printers **(b)** in particular, letter paper, envelopes, etc., with the company's name and address printed on them; *the letter was typed on his office stationery*

statistical [stə'tɪstɪkəl] *adjective* based on figures; *they took two weeks to provide the statistical analysis of the opinion poll data*; **statistical discrepancy** = amount by which sets of figures differ

statistician [stætɪ'stɪʃən] *noun* person who analyzes statistics

statistics [stə'tɪstɪks] *plural noun* study of facts in the form of figures; *to examine the sales statistics for the previous six months*; *government trade statistics show an increase in imports*

status ['steɪtəs] *noun* (a) importance, position in society; **the chairman's car is a status symbol** = the size of the car shows how important the company is; **loss of status** = becoming less important in a group (b) **legal status** = legal position; **status inquiry** = checking on a customer's credit rating

status quo ['steɪtəs 'kwəʊ] *noun* state of things as they are now; *the contract does not alter the status quo*

statute ['stætjuːt] *noun* established written law, especially an Act of Parliament; **statute book** = all laws passed by Parliament which are still in force; **statute of limitations** = law which allows only a certain amount of time (usually six years) for someone to start legal proceedings to claim property or compensation for damage, etc.

statutory ['stætjʊtəri] *adjective* fixed by law; *there is a statutory period of probation of thirteen weeks*; **statutory holiday** = holiday which is fixed by law; **statutory regulations** = regulations covering financial dealings which are based on Acts of Parliament, such as the Financial Services Act (as opposed to the rules of self-regulatory organizations which are non-statutory); **statutory sick pay (SSP)** = payment made each week by an employer to an employee who is away from work because of sickness

stay [steɪ] **1** *noun* (a) length of time spent in one place; *the tourists were in town only for a short stay*; **short-stay guests** = customers who spend only a few nights at a hotel (b) **stay of execution** = temporary stopping of a legal order; *the court granted the company a two-week stay of execution* **2** *verb* to stop at a place; *the chairman is staying at the Hotel London*; *profits have stayed below 10% for two years*; *inflation has stayed high in spite of the government's efforts to bring it down*

steadily ['stedɪli] *adverb* in a regular or continuous way; *output increased steadily over the last two quarters*; *the company has steadily increased its market share*

steadiness ['stedɪnəs] *noun* being firm, not fluctuating; *the steadiness of the markets is due to the government's intervention*

steady ['stedi] **1** *adjective* continuing in a regular way; *the company can point to a steady increase in profits*; *the market stayed steady in spite of the collapse of the bank*; *there is a steady demand for computers* **2** *verb* to become firm, to stop fluctuating; *the markets steadied after last week's fluctuations*; *prices steadied on the commodity markets*; *the government's figures had a steadying influence on the exchange rate*

steal [stiːl] *verb* to take something which does not belong to you; *the rival company stole our best clients*; *one of our biggest problems is stealing in the wine department* (NOTE: **stealing - stole - has stolen**)

steep [stiːp] *adjective* very sharp, very high (price); *a steep increase in interest charges*; *a steep decline in overseas sales*

steeply ['stiːpli] *adverb* sharply, suddenly; *prices rose steeply after the budget*

> if oil prices should fall steeply it may lead to an equally steep fall in naira value if supply cannot meet demand. Then there might be political consequences if devaluation leads to inflation
>
> *Business in Africa*

stencil ['stensl] *noun* sheet of special paper which can be written or typed on, and used in a duplicating machine

stenographer [ste'nɒgrəfə] *noun* official person who can write in shorthand

step [step] *noun* (a) type of action; *the first step taken by the new MD was to analyse all the expenses*; **to take steps to prevent something happening** = to act to stop something happening (b) movement forward; *becoming assistant to the MD is a step up the promotion ladder*; **in step with** = moving at the same rate as; *the pound rose in step with the dollar*; **out of**

step with = not moving at the same rate as; *the pound was out of step with other European currencies*; *wages are out of step with the cost of living*

step down ['step 'daʊn] *verb* to retire from a position; *the chairman will be 70 this month and he is stepping down from his post to give way to his nephew* (NOTE: **stepping - stepped**)

the chairman of the investment bank is to step down after less than 12 months in the job

Times

step up ['step 'ʌp] *verb* to increase; *the union is stepping up its industrial action*; *the company has stepped up production of the latest models* (NOTE: **stepping - stepped**)

sterling ['stɜːlɪŋ] *noun* standard currency used in the United Kingdom; *to quote prices in sterling or to quote sterling prices*; **pound sterling** = official term for the British currency; **sterling area** = formerly, an area of the world where the pound sterling was the main trading currency; **sterling balances** = a country's trade balances expressed in pounds sterling; **sterling crisis** = fall in the exchange rate of the pound sterling

it is doubtful that British goods will price themselves back into world markets as long as sterling labour costs continue to rise faster than in competitor countries

Sunday Times

stevedore ['stiːvədɔː] *noun* person who works in a port, loading or unloading ships

steward ['stjuəd] *noun* (a) man who serves drinks or food on a ship or plane; *she called the steward and asked for a glass of water* (b) **shop steward** = elected trade union representative who reports workers' complaints to the management

stewardess [stjuə'des] *noun* woman who serves drinks or food on a ship or plane

stick [stɪk] *verb* (a) to attach with glue; *to stick a stamp on a letter*; *they stuck a poster on the door* (b) to stay still, not to move; *sales have stuck at £2m for the last two years* (NOTE: **sticking - stuck**)

sticker ['stɪkə] **1** *noun* small piece of gummed paper or plastic to be stuck on something as an advertisement or to indicate a price; **airmail sticker** = blue sticker with the words 'air mail', which can be stuck on an envelope or parcel to show that it is being sent by air **2** *verb* to put a price sticker on an article for sale; *we had to sticker all the stock*

sticky ['stɪki] *adjective* (label) which is already covered with glue and can be stuck on a surface without having to be licked (sticky labels are sold stuck to a sheet of backing paper, and can be peeled off easily and stuck to an envelope, etc.)

stiff [stɪf] *adjective* strong or difficult; *they are facing stiff competition from the American chain*; *he had to take a stiff test before he qualified*

stimulate ['stɪmjʊleɪt] *verb* to encourage, to make (something) become more active; *what can the government do to stimulate the economy?*; *the aim of the subsidies is to stimulate trade with the Middle East*

stimulus ['stɪmjʊləs] *noun* thing which encourages activity (NOTE: plural is **stimuli**)

stipulate ['stɪpjʊleɪt] *verb* to demand that a condition be put into a contract; *to stipulate that the contract should run for five years*; *they found it difficult to pay the stipulated charges*; *the company failed to pay on the date stipulated in the contract*; *the contract stipulates that the seller pays the buyer's legal costs*

stipulation [stɪpjʊ'leɪʃən] *noun* condition in a contract

stock [stɒk] **1** *noun* (a) quantity of raw materials; *we have large stocks of oil or coal*; *the country's stocks of butter or sugar* (b) quantity of goods for sale; **opening stock** = details of stock at the beginning of an accounting period; **closing stock** = details of stock at the end of an accounting period; **stock code** = number and letters which indicate an item of stock; **stock control** = making sure that enough stock is kept and that quantities and movements of stock are noted; **stock depreciation** = reduction in value of stock which is held in a warehouse for some time; **stock figures** = details of how many goods are in the warehouse, store, etc.; **stock in hand** = stock held in a shop or warehouse; **stock level** = quantity of goods kept in stock; *we try to keep stock levels low during the summer*; **stock turn** *or* **stock turnround** *or* **stock turnover** = total value of stock sold in a year divided by the average value of goods in stock; **stock valuation** = estimating the value of stock at the end of an accounting period; **to buy a shop with stock at valuation** = when buying a shop, to pay for the stock the same price as its value as estimated by the valuer; **to purchase stock at valuation** = to pay for stock the price it is valued at (NOTE: the word **inventory** is used in the USA where British English uses the word **stock**. So, the British **stock control** is **inventory control** in American English) **(c) in stock** = available in the warehouse or store; *to hold 2,000 lines in stock*; **out of stock** = not available in the warehouse or store; *the item went out of stock just before Christmas but came back into stock in the first week of January*; *we are out of stock of this item*; **to take stock** = to count the items in a warehouse **(d)** investments in a company, represented by shares or fixed interest securities; **stocks and shares** = shares in ordinary companies; **stock certificate** = document proving that someone owns stock in a company; *US* **common stock** = ordinary shares in a company giving the shareholders the right to vote at meetings and receive a dividend; **debenture stock** = capital borrowed by a company, using its fixed assets as security; **dollar stocks** = shares in American companies; **government stock** = government securities; **loan stock** = money lent to a company at a fixed rate of interest; **convertible loan stock** = money lent to a company which can be converted into shares at a later date (NOTE: in Britain, the term **stocks** is generally applied to government **stocks** and **shares** to shares of commercial companies. In the USA, shares in corporations are usually called **stocks** while government stocks are called **bonds**. In practice, **shares** and **stocks** are interchangeable terms, and this can lead to some confusion) **(e)** normal, usually kept in stock; *butter is a stock item for any good grocer*; **stock size** = normal

size; *we only carry stock sizes of shoes* **2** *verb* to hold goods for sale in a warehouse or store; *the average supermarket stocks more than 4500 lines*

US crude oil stocks fell last week by nearly 2.5m barrels
Financial Times

the stock rose to over $20 a share, higher than the $18 bid
Fortune

stockbroker ['stɒkbrəʊkə] *noun* person who buys or sells shares for clients; **stockbroker's commission** = payment to a broker for a deal carried out on behalf of a client

stockbroking ['stɒkbrəʊkɪŋ] *noun* trade of dealing in shares for clients; *a stockbroking firm*

stock controller ['stɒk kən'trəʊlə] *noun* person who notes movements of stock

Stock Exchange ['stɒk ɪks'tʃeɪndʒ] *noun* place where stocks and shares are bought and sold; *he works on the Stock Exchange*; *shares in the company are traded on the Stock Exchange*; **Stock Exchange listing** = official list of shares which can be bought or sold on the Stock Exchange (NOTE: capital letters are used when referring to a particular stock exchange: **the London Stock Exchange;** but **the Stock Exchange** is also generally used to refer to the local stock exchange of whichever country the speaker happens to be in)

the news was favourably received on the Sydney Stock Exchange, where the shares gained 40 cents to A$9.80
Financial Times

stockholder ['stɒkhəʊldə] *noun* person who holds shares in a company

stockholding ['stɒkhəʊldɪŋ] *noun* shares in a company held by someone

stock-in-trade ['stɒkɪn'treɪd] *noun* goods held by a business for sale

stockist ['stɒkɪst] *noun* person or shop which stocks a certain item

stock jobber ['stɒkdʒɒbə] *noun* *(formerly)* person who bought and sold shares from other traders on the Stock Exchange

stock jobbing ['stɒkdʒɒbɪŋ] *noun* (*formerly*) buying and selling shares from other traders on the Stock Exchange

stocklist ['stɒklɪst] *noun* list of items carried in stock

stock market ['stɒk 'mɔːkɪt] *noun* place where shares are bought and sold (i.e., a stock exchange); *stock market price or price on the stock market*; **stock market valuation** = value of a company based on the current market price of its shares

stockout ['stɒkaʊt] *noun* situation where an item is out of stock

stockpile ['stɒkpaɪl] **1** *noun* supplies kept by a country or a company in case of need; *a stockpile of raw materials* **2** *verb* to buy items and keep them in case of need; *to stockpile raw materials*

stockroom ['stɒkrʊm] *noun* room where stores are kept

stocktaking ['stɒkteɪkɪŋ] *noun* counting of goods in stock at the end of an accounting period; *the warehouse is closed for the annual stocktaking*; **stocktaking sale** = sale of goods cheaply to clear a warehouse before stocktaking

stock up ['stɒk 'ʌp] *verb* to buy supplies of something which you will need in the future; *they stocked up with computer paper*

stop [stɒp] **1** *noun* (**a**) end of an action; *work came to a stop when the company could not pay the workers' wages*; *the new finance director put a stop to the reps' expense claims* (**b**) not supplying; **account on stop** = account which is not supplied because it has not paid its latest invoices; *we put their account on stop and sued them for the money they owed*; **to put a stop on a cheque** = to tell the bank not to pay a cheque which you have written **2** *verb* (**a**) to make (something) not to move any more; *the shipment was stopped by customs*; *the government has stopped the import of luxury items* (**b**) not to do anything any more; *the work force stopped work when the company could not pay their wages*; *the office staff stop work at 5.30*; *we have stopped supplying Smith &*

Co. (**c**) **to stop an account** = not to supply an account any more on credit because bills have not been paid; **to stop a cheque** *US* **to stop payment on a check** = to ask a bank not to pay a cheque you have written; **to stop payments** = not to make any further payments (**d**) **to stop someone's wages** = to take money out of someone's wages; *we stopped £25 from his pay because he was late* (NOTE: **stopping - stopped**)

stop-loss order ['stɒp'lɒs 'ɔːdə] *noun* instruction to a stockbroker to sell a share if the price falls to a certain level (NOTE: the American equivalent is **stop order**)

stop over ['stɒp 'əʊvə] *verb* to stay for a short time in a place on a long journey; *we stopped over in Hong Kong on the way to Australia*

stopover ['stɒpəʊvə] *noun* staying for a short time in a place on a long journey; *the ticket allows you two stopovers between London and Tokyo*

stoppage ['stɒpɪdʒ] *noun* (**a**) act of stopping; *bad weather was responsible for the stoppage of deliveries*; *deliveries will be late because of stoppages on the production line* (**b**) money taken from a worker's wage packet for insurance, tax, etc.

the commission noted that in the early 1960s there was an average of 203 stoppages each year arising out of dismissals

Employment Gazette

storage ['stɔːrɪdʒ] *noun* (**a**) keeping in store or in a warehouse; *we put our furniture into storage*; **storage capacity** = space available for storage; **storage company** = company which keeps items for customers; **storage facilities** = equipment and buildings suitable for storage; **storage unit** = device attached to a computer for storing information on disk or tape; **cold storage** = keeping food, etc., in a cold store to prevent it going bad; **to put a plan into cold storage** = to postpone work on a plan, usually for a very long time (**b**) cost of keeping goods in store; *storage rose to 10% of value, so we scrapped the stock*

(c) facility for storing data in a computer; *disk with a storage capacity of 100Mb*

store [stɔː] **1** *noun* **(a)** place where goods are kept; **cold store** = warehouse or room where food can be kept cold **(b)** quantity of items or materials kept because they will be needed; *I always keep a store of envelopes ready in my desk* **(c)** large shop; *a furniture store; a big clothing store*; **chain store** = one store in a number of stores belonging to the same group; **department store** = large store with sections for different types of goods; **discount store** = shop which specializes in cheap goods sold at a high discount; **general stores** = small country shop which sells a wide range of products; **store card** = credit card issued by a large department store, which can only be used for purchases in that store **(d)** *US* any shop **2** *verb* **(a)** to keep in a warehouse; *to store goods for six months* **(b)** to keep for future use; *we store our pay records on computer*

storekeeper *or* **storeman** ['stɔːkiːpə *or* 'stɔːmən] *noun* person in charge of a storeroom

storeroom ['stɔːrʊm] *noun* room where stock can be kept; small warehouse attached to a factory

straight line depreciation ['streɪt 'laɪn dɪpriːʃɪ'eɪʃn] *noun* depreciation calculated by dividing the cost of an asset, less its residual value, by the number of years it is likely to be used

strategic [strə'tiːdʒɪk] *adjective* based on a plan of action; **strategic planning** = planning the future work of a company

strategy ['strætədʒi] *noun* plan of future action; *business strategy*; *company strategy*; *marketing strategy*; *financial strategy*

stream [striːm] *noun* mass of people or traffic, all going in the same direction; *we had a stream of customers on the first day of the sale*; **to come on stream** = to start production; *the new production unit is expected to come on stream next month*

streamer ['striːmə] *noun* device for attaching a tape storage unit to a computer

streamline ['striːmlaɪn] *verb* to make (something) more efficient or more simple;

to streamline the accounting system; *to streamline distribution services*

streamlined ['striːmlaɪnd] *adjective* efficient or rapid; *we need a more streamlined production system*; *the company introduced a streamlined system of distribution*

streamlining ['striːmlaɪnɪŋ] *noun* making efficient

street [striːt] *noun* road in a town; *their new address is 25 Broad Street*; **High Street** = main shopping street in a British town; **the High Street banks** = main British banks which accept deposits from individual customers; **street directory** = (i) list of people living in a street; (ii) map of a town with all the streets listed in alphabetical order in an index (NOTE: in addresses, **Street** is usually shortened to **St: 25 Broad St**)

strength [streŋθ] *noun* being strong, at a high level; *the company took advantage of the strength of the demand for mobile phones*; *the strength of the pound increases the possibility of high interest rates* (NOTE: the opposite is **weakness**)

stress [stres] *noun* nervous tension or worry; *people in positions of responsibility suffer from stress-related illnesses*; *the new work schedules caused too much stress on the shop floor*; **stress management** = way of coping with stress-related problems at work

> manual and clerical workers are more likely to suffer from stress-related diseases. Causes of stress include the introduction of new technology, job dissatisfaction, fear of job loss, poor working relations with the boss and colleagues, and bad working conditions
>
> *Personnel Management*

stressful ['stresfʊl] *adjective* (situation) which causes stress; *psychologists claim that repetitive work can be just as stressful as more demanding but varied work*

stretch [stretʃ] *verb* to pull out or to make longer; *the investment programme has stretched the company's resources*; *he is*

not fully stretched = his job does not make him work as hard as he could

strict [strɪkt] *adjective* exact; *the partners are listed in strict order of seniority*

strictly ['strɪktli] *adverb* exactly; *the company asks all staff to follow strictly the buying procedures*

strike [straɪk] **1** *noun* **(a)** stopping of work by the workers (because of lack of agreement with management or because of orders from a union); **all-out strike** = complete strike by all workers; **general strike** = strike of all the workers in a country; **official strike** = strike which has been approved by the main office of a union; **protest strike** = strike in protest at a particular grievance; **sit-down strike** = strike where workers stay in their place of work and refuse to work or leave; **sympathy strike** = strike to show that workers agree with another group of workers who are already on strike; **token strike** = short strike to show that workers have a grievance; **unofficial strike** = strike by local workers, which has not been approved by the main union; **wildcat strike** = strike organized suddenly by workers without the main union office knowing about it **(b) to take strike action** = to go on strike; **strike call** = demand by a union for a strike; **no-strike agreement** *or* **no-strike clause** = (clause in an) agreement where the workers say that they will never strike; **strike fund** = money collected by a trade union from its members, used to pay strike pay; **strike pay** = wages paid to striking workers by their trade union; **strike ballot** *or* **strike vote** = vote by workers to decide if a strike should be held **(c) to come out on strike** *or* **to go on strike** = to stop work; *the office workers are on strike for higher pay;* **to call the workforce out on strike** = to tell the workers to stop work; *the union called its members out on strike* **2** *verb* **(a)** to stop working because there is no agreement with management; *to strike for higher wages* *or* *for shorter working hours; to strike in protest against bad working conditions;* **to strike in sympathy with the postal workers** = to strike to show that you agree with the postal workers who are on strike **(b) to strike a bargain with**

someone = to come to an agreement; **a deal was struck at £25 a unit** = we agreed the price of £25 a unit; **striking price** = (i) price at which a new issue of shares is offered for sale; (ii) the lowest selling price when selling a new issue of shares by tender (applicants who tendered at a higher price will get shares; those who tendered at a lower price will not) (NOTE: **striking - struck)**

strikebound ['straɪkbaʊnd] *adjective* not able to work or to move because of a strike; *six ships are strikebound in the docks*

strikebreaker ['straɪkbreɪkə] *noun* worker who goes on working while everyone else is on strike

striker ['straɪkə] *noun* worker who is on strike; *strikers marched to the company headquarters*

stripper ['strɪpə] *noun* **asset stripper** = person who buys a company to sell its assets

stripping ['strɪpɪŋ] *noun* **asset stripping** = buying a company in order to sell its assets

strong [strɒŋ] *adjective* with a lot of force or strength; *this Christmas saw a strong demand for mobile phones; the company needs a strong chairman;* **strong currency** = currency which is high against other currencies (the opposite is a 'weak currency'); **strong pound** = pound which is high against other currencies

> everybody blames the strong dollar for US trade problems
>
> *Duns Business Month*

> in a world of floating exchange rates the dollar is strong because of capital inflows rather than weak because of the nation's trade deficit
>
> *Duns Business Month*

strongbox ['strɒŋbɒks] *noun* safe, heavy metal box which cannot be opened easily, in which valuable documents, money, etc., can be kept

strongroom ['strɒŋrʊm] *noun* special room (in a bank) where valuable documents, money, golds, etc., can be kept

structural ['strʌktʃərəl] *adjective* referring to a structure; *to make structural changes in a company*; **structural unemployment** = unemployment caused by the changing structure of an industry or of society

structure ['strʌktʃə] **1** *noun* way in which something is organized; *the paper gives a diagram of the company's organizational structure*; *the price structure in the small car market*; *the career structure within a corporation*; *the company is reorganizing its discount structure*; **capital structure of a company** = way in which a company's capital is set up; **the company's salary structure** = organization of salaries in a company with different rates of pay for different types of job **2** *verb* to arrange in a certain way; *to structure a meeting*

stub [stʌb] *noun* slip of paper left after writing a cheque, an invoice or a receipt, as a record of the deal which has taken place; **cheque stub** = piece of paper left in a cheque book after a cheque has been written and taken out

studio ['stjuːdɪəu] *noun* place where designers, film producers, artists, etc., work; **design studio** = independent firm which specializes in creating designs for companies

study ['stʌdi] **1** *noun* examining something carefully; *the company has asked the consultants to prepare a study of new production techniques*; *he has read the government study on sales opportunities*; **to carry out a feasibility study on a project** = to examine the costs and possible profits to see if the project should be started **2** *verb* to examine (something) carefully; *we are studying the possibility of setting up an office in New York*; *the government studied the committee's proposals for two months*; *you will need to study the market carefully before deciding on the design of the product*

stuff [stʌf] *verb* to put papers, etc., into envelopes; *we pay casual workers £6 an hour for stuffing envelopes or for envelope stuffing*

stuffer ['stʌfə] *noun* advertising paper to be put in an envelope for mailing

style [staɪl] *noun* way of doing or making something; *a new style of product*; *old-style management techniques*

sub [sʌb] *noun (informal)* **(a)** wages paid in advance **(b)** = SUBSCRIPTION

sub- [sʌb] *prefix* under, less important

sub-agency ['sʌb'eɪdʒənsi] *noun* small agency which is part of a large agency

sub-agent ['sʌb'eɪdʒənt] *noun* person who is in charge of a sub-agency

subcommittee ['sʌbkəmɪti] *noun* small committee which is part of or set up by a main committee; *the next item on the agenda is the report of the finance subcommittee*

subcontract 1 [sʌb'kɒntrækt] *noun* contract between the main contractor for a whole project and another firm who will do part of the work; *they have been awarded the subcontract for all the electrical work in the new building*; *we will put the electrical work out to subcontract* **2** [sʌbkən'trækt] *verb* to agree with a company that they will do part of the work for a project; *the electrical work has been subcontracted to Smith Ltd*

subcontractor [sʌbkən'træktə] *noun* company which has a contract to do work for a main contractor

subdivision ['sʌbdɪvɪʒən] *noun US* piece of empty land to be used for building new houses

subject to ['sʌbdʒɪkt tʊ] *adjective* **(a)** depending on; **the contract is subject to government approval** = the contract will be valid only if it is approved by the government; **agreement** *or* **sale subject to contract** = agreement or sale which is not legal until a proper contract has been signed; **offer subject to availability** = the offer is valid only if the goods are available **(b)** **these articles are subject to import tax** = import tax has to be paid on these articles

sub judice ['sʌb 'dʒuːdɪsi] *adverb* being considered by a court (and so not to be mentioned in the media); *the papers cannot report the case because it is still sub judice*

sublease 1 ['sʌbliːs] *noun* lease from a tenant to another tenant; *they signed a sublease for the property* **2** [sʌb'liːs] *verb* to lease a leased property from another tenant; *they subleased a small office in the centre of town*

sublessee [sʌble'siː] *noun* person or company which takes a property on a sublease

sublessor [sʌble'sɔː] *noun* tenant who leases a leased property to another tenant

sublet [sʌb'let] *verb* to let a leased property to another tenant; *we have sublet part of our office to a financial consultancy* (NOTE: **subletting - sublet**)

subliminal advertising [sʌb'lɪmɪnəl 'ædvətaɪzɪŋ] *noun* advertising that attempts to leave certain impressions on the mind of the person who sees it or hears it (without that person realising that this is being done)

submit [səb'mɪt] *verb* to put (something) forward to be examined; *the planners submitted the proposal to the committee*; *he submitted a claim to the insurers*; *the reps are asked to submit their expenses claims once a month* (NOTE: **submitting - submitted**)

subordinate [sə'bɔːdɪnət] **1** less important; **subordinate to** = governed by, which depends on **2** *noun* member of staff who is directed by someone; *his subordinates find him difficult to work with*

subpoena [səb'piːnə] **1** *noun* court order telling someone to appear as a witness (NOTE: an old term, now called a **witness summons**) **2** *verb* to order someone to appear in court; *the finance director was subpoenaed by the prosecution*

subscribe [səb'skraɪb] *verb* **(a) to subscribe to a magazine** = to pay for a series of issues of a magazine **(b) to subscribe for shares** = to apply for shares in a new company

the rights issue is to be a
one-for-four, at FFr 1,000 a
share; it will grant
shareholders free warrants to
subscribe to further new
shares

Financial Times

subscriber [səb'skraɪbə] *noun* **(a) subscriber to a magazine** *or* **magazine subscriber** = person who has paid in advance for a series of issues of a magazine; *the extra issue is sent free to subscribers* **(b) subscriber to a share issue** = person who has applied for shares in a new company **(c) telephone subscriber** = person who has a telephone

subscription [səb'skrɪpʃən] *noun* **(a)** money paid in advance for a series of issues of a magazine or for membership of a society; *did you remember to pay the subscription to the computer magazine?*; *he forgot to renew his club subscription*; **to take out a subscription to a magazine** = to start paying for a series of issues of a magazine; **to cancel a subscription to a magazine** = to stop paying for a magazine; **subscription rate** = amount of money to be paid for a series of issues of a magazine **(b) subscription to a new share issue** = offering shares in a new company for sale; **subscription list** = list of subscribers to a new share issue; **the subscription lists close at 10.00 on September 24th** = no new applicants will be allowed to subscribe for the share issue after that date

subsidiary [səb'sɪdjəri] **1** *adjective* (thing) which is less important; *they agreed to most of the conditions in the contract but queried one or two subsidiary items*; **subsidiary company** = company which is more than 50% owned by a holding company, and where the holding company controls the board of directors **2** *noun* company which is owned by a parent company; *most of the group profit was contributed by the subsidiaries in the Far East*

subsidize ['sʌbsɪdaɪz] *verb* to help by giving money; *the government has refused to subsidize the car industry*; **subsidized accommodation** = cheap accommodation which is partly paid for by an employer or a local authority, etc.

subsidy ['sʌbsɪdi] *noun* **(a)** money given to help something which is not profitable; *the industry exists on government subsidies*; *the government has increased its subsidy to the car industry* **(b)** money given by a government to make something cheaper; *the subsidy on butter or the butter subsidy*

subsistence [səb'sıstəns] *noun* minimum amount of food, money, housing, etc., which a person needs; **subsistence allowance** = money paid by a company to cover the cost of hotels, meals, etc., for a member of staff who is travelling on business; **to live at subsistence level** = to have only just enough money to live on

substantial [səb'stænʃəl] *adjective* large or important; **she was awarded substantial damages** = she received a large sum of money as damages; **to acquire a substantial interest in a company** = to buy a large number of shares in a company

substitute ['sʌbstɪtjuːt] **1** *noun* person or thing which takes the place of someone or something else **2** *verb* to take the place of something else

subtenancy [sʌb'tenənsi] *noun* agreement to sublet a property

subtenant [sʌb'tenənt] *noun* person or company to which a property has been sublet

subtotal ['sʌbtəʊtl] *noun* total of one section of a complete set of figures; *he added all the subtotals to make a grand total*

subtract [səb'trækt] *verb* to take away (something) from a total; *the credit note should be subtracted from the figure for total sales*; *if the profits from the Far Eastern operations are subtracted, you will see that the group has not been profitable in the European market*

subtraction [səb'trækʃn] *noun* taking one number away from another

subvention [səb'venʃn] *noun* subsidy

succeed [sək'siːd] *verb* **(a)** to do well, to be profitable; *the company has succeeded best in the overseas markets*; *his business has succeeded more than he had expected* **(b)** to do what was planned; *she succeeded in passing her shorthand test*; *they succeeded in putting their rivals out of business* **(c)** to follow (someone); *Mr Smith was succeeded as chairman by Mr Jones*

success [sək'ses] *noun* **(a)** doing something well; *the launch of the new model was a great success*; *the company has had great success in the Japanese market* **(b)** doing what was intended; *we had no success in trying to sell the lease*; *he has been looking for a job for six months, but with no success*

successful [sək'sesful] *adjective* which does well; *a successful businessman*; *a successful selling trip to Germany*

successfully [sək'sesfəli] *adverb* done well; *he successfully negotiated a new contract with the unions*; *the new model was successfully launched last month*

successor [sək'sesə] *noun* person who takes over from someone; *Mr Smith's successor as chairman will be Mr Jones*

sue [suː] *verb* to take someone to court, to start legal proceedings against someone to get money as compensation; *they are planning to sue the construction company for damages*; *he is suing the company for $50,000 compensation*

suffer ['sʌfə] *verb* to be in a bad situation, to do badly; *exports have suffered during the last six months*; **to suffer from something** = to do badly because of something; *the company's products suffer from bad design*; *the group suffers from bad management*

> the bank suffered losses to the extent that its capital has been wiped out
>
> *South China Morning Post*

> the holding company has seen its earnings suffer from big writedowns in conjunction with its agricultural loan portfolio
>
> *Duns Business Month*

sufficient [sə'fıʃənt] *adjective* enough; *the company has sufficient funds to pay for its expansion programme*

suggest [sə'dʒest] *verb* to put forward a proposal; *the chairman suggested (that) the next meeting should be held in October*; *we suggested Mr Smith for the post of treasurer*

suggestion [sə'dʒestʃən] *noun* proposal, idea which is put forward;

suggestion box = place in a company where members of staff can put forward their ideas for making the company more efficient and profitable

suitable ['su:təbl] *adjective* convenient, which fits; *Wednesday is the most suitable day for board meetings*; *we had to readvertise the job because there were no suitable candidates*

suitcase ['su:tkeɪs] *noun* box with a handle for carrying clothes and personal belongings when travelling; *the customs officer made him open his three suitcases*

sum [sʌm] *noun* **(a)** quantity of money; *a sum of money was stolen from the personnel office*; *he lost large sums on the Stock Exchange*; *she received the sum of £5000 in compensation*; **the sum insured** = the largest amount which an insurer will pay under the terms of an insurance; **lump sum** = money paid in one payment, not in several small payments **(b)** total of a series of figures added together; *the sum of the various subtotals is £18,752*

summary ['sʌməri] *noun* short account of what has happened or of what has been written; *the chairman gave a summary of his discussions with the German trade delegation*; *the sales department has given a summary of sales in Europe for the first six months*

summons ['sʌmənz] *noun* official order from a court requiring someone to appear in court to be tried for a criminal offence or to defend a civil action; *he threw away the summons and went on holiday to Spain*; **witness summons** = court order requiring someone to appear as a witness (NOTE: this term has now replaced **subpoena**)

Sunday trading laws ['sʌndi 'treɪdɪŋ 'lɔːz] *noun* regulations which govern business activities on Sundays (NOTE: the American equivalent is **Blue Laws**)

sundry ['sʌndri] *adjective & noun* various; **sundry items** *or* **sundries** = small items which are not listed in detail

sunrise industries ['sʌnraɪz 'ɪndʌstrɪz] *noun* companies in the fields of electronics and other high-tech areas

sunset industries ['sʌnset 'ɪndʌstrɪz] *noun* old-style industries which are being replaced by new technology

superannuation [su:pərænju'eɪʃn] *noun* pension paid to someone who is too old or ill to work any more; **superannuation plan** *or* **scheme** = pension plan or scheme

superintend [su:pərɪn'tend] *verb* to be in charge of work, to watch carefully, to see that work is well done; *he superintends the company's overseas sales*

superintendent [su:pərɪn'tendənt] *noun* title of an official in charge; **police superintendent** = senior police officer, above a chief inspector

superior [su:'pɪərɪə] **1** *adjective* better, of better quality; *our product is superior to all competing products*; *their sales are higher because of their superior distribution service* **2** *noun* more important person; *each manager is responsible to his superior for accurate reporting of sales*

supermarket ['su:pəmɑ:kɪt] *noun* large store, usually selling food, where customers serve themselves and pay at a checkout; *sales in supermarkets or supermarket sales account for half the company's turnover*; **supermarket trolley** = metal basket on wheels, used by shoppers to put their purchases in as they go round a supermarket (NOTE: American English for this is **shopping cart**)

superstore ['su:pəstɔ:] *noun* very large self-service store which sells a wide range of goods; *we bought the laptop at a computer superstore*

supertanker ['su:pətæŋkə] *noun* very large oil tanker

supervise ['su:pəvaɪz] *verb* to watch work carefully to see if it is well done; *the move to the new offices was supervised by the administrative manager*; *she supervises six girls in the accounts department*

supervision [su:pə'vɪʒən] *noun* being supervised; *new staff work under supervision for the first three months*; *she is very experienced and can be left to work without any supervision*; *the cash was* *counted under the supervision of the finance manager*

supervisor ['su:pəvaɪzə] *noun* person who supervises

supervisory [su:pə'vaɪzəri] *adjective* as a supervisor; *supervisory staff checked the trainees' work*; *he works in a supervisory capacity*

supplement ['sʌplɪmənt] **1** *noun* thing which is added; *the company gives him a supplement to his pension* **2** *verb* to add; *we will supplement the warehouse staff with six part-timers during the Christmas rush*

supplementary [sʌplɪ'mentəri] *adjective* in addition to; *GB* **supplementary benefit** = payments from the government to people with very low incomes; *US* **supplementary unemployment benefits** = payments made by a company to workers who have been laid off, in addition to regular unemployment insurance payments

supplier [sə'plaɪə] *noun* person or company which supplies or sells goods or services; *we use the same office equipment supplier for all our stationery purchases*; *they are major suppliers of spare parts to the car industry*

supply [sə'plaɪ] **1** *noun* **(a)** providing something which is needed; **money supply** = amount of money which exists in a country; **supply price** = price at which something is provided; **supply and demand** = amount of a product which is available and the amount which is wanted by customers; **the law of supply and demand** = general rule that the amount of a product which is available is related to the needs of the possible customer **(b) in short supply** = not available in large enough quantities to meet the demand; *spare parts are in short supply because of the strike* **(c)** stock of something which is needed; *the factory is running short of supplies of coal*; *supplies of coal to the factory have been hit by the rail strike*; **office supplies** = goods needed to run an office (such as paper, pens, typewriters) **2** *verb* to provide something which is needed; *to supply a factory with spare parts*; *the finance department supplied the committee with*

the figures; *details of staff addresses and phone numbers can be supplied by the personnel staff*

supply side economics [sə'plaɪ 'saɪd i:kə'nɒmɪks] *noun* economic theory, that governments should encourage producers and suppliers of goods by cutting taxes, rather than encourage demand by making more money available in the economy

support [sə'pɔːt] **1** *noun* **(a)** giving money to help; *the government has provided support to the car industry*; *we have no financial support from the banks* **(b)** agreement or encouragement; *the chairman has the support of the committee*; **support price** = price (in the EU) at which a government will buy agricultural produce to stop the price falling **2** *verb* **(a)** to give money to help; *the government is supporting the car industry to the tune of $2m per annum*; *we hope the banks will support us during the expansion period* **(b)** to encourage, to agree with; *she hopes the other members of the committee will support her*; *the market will not support another price increase*

surcharge ['sɜːtʃɑːdʒ] *noun* extra charge; **import surcharge** = extra duty charged on imported goods, to try to stop them from being imported and to encourage local manufacture

surety ['ʃuərəti] *noun* **(a)** person who guarantees that someone will do something; *to stand surety for someone* **(b)** deeds, share certificates, etc., deposited as security for a loan

surface ['sɜːfɪs] *noun* top part of the earth; **to send a package by surface mail** = to send it by land or sea, but not by air; **surface transport** = transport on land or sea

surplus ['sɜːpləs] *noun* extra stock, something which is more than is needed; *an auction of surplus government equipment*; *surplus butter is on sale in the shops*; *we are holding a sale of surplus stock*; *governments are trying to find ways of reducing the agricultural surpluses in the EU*; *we are trying to let surplus capacity in the warehouse*; **a budget surplus** = more revenue than was planned for in the budget; **these items are surplus to our requirements** = we do not need these items; **to absorb a surplus** = to take a surplus into a larger amount

---

Both imports and exports reached record levels in the latest year. This generated a $371 million trade surplus in June, the seventh consecutive monthly surplus and close to market expectations

Dominion (Wellington, New Zealand)

---

surrender [sə'rendə] **1** *noun* giving up of an insurance policy before the contracted date for maturity; **surrender value** = money which an insurer will pay if an insurance policy is given up **2** *verb* to **surrender a policy** = to give up an insurance policy before the date on which it matures

surtax ['sɜːtæks] *noun* extra tax on high income

survey 1 ['sɜːveɪ] *noun* **(a)** general report on a problem; *the government has published a survey of population trends*; *we have asked the sales department to produce a survey of competing products* **(b)** careful examination of something, such as a building, to see if it is in good enough condition; *we have asked for a survey of the house before buying it*; *the insurance company is carrying out a survey of the damage*; **damage survey** = report on the amount of damage done **(c)** measuring exactly; **quantity survey** = calculating the amount of materials and cost of labour needed for a construction project **2** [sə'veɪ] *verb* **(a)** to make a survey of a building; *a buildings surveyor was called in to survey the damage caused by the fire* **(b)** to measure land in order to produce a plan or map; *they're surveying the area where the new motorway will be built*

surveyor [sə'veɪə] *noun* person who examines buildings to see if they are in good condition; person who surveys land; *the surveyor's report was favourable*; **quantity surveyor** = person who calculates the amount of materials and cost of labour needed for a construction project

suspend [səs'pend] *verb* **(a)** to stop (something) for a time; *we have suspended*

payments while we are waiting for news from our agent; *sailings have been suspended until the weather gets better*; *work on the construction project has been suspended*; *the management decided to suspend negotiations* **(b)** to stop (someone) working for a time; *he was suspended on full pay while the police investigations were going on*

suspense account [səs'pens ə'kaʊnt] *noun* account into which payments are put temporarily when the accountant cannot be sure where they should be entered

suspension [səs'penʃən] *noun* **(a)** stopping something for a time; *there has been a temporary suspension of payments*; *we are trying to avoid a suspension of deliveries during the strike* **(b)** **suspension file** = stiff card file, with metal edges, which can be hooked inside the drawer of a filing cabinet so that it hangs loose

swap [swɒp] **1** *noun* exchange of one thing for another **2** *verb* to exchange one thing for another; *he swapped his old car for a new motorcycle*; *they swapped jobs* = each of them took the other's job (NOTE: **swapping - swapped**)

swatch [swɒtʃ] *noun* small sample; *the interior designer showed us swatches of the curtain fabric*; **colour swatch** = small sample of colour which the finished product must look like

sweated labour ['swetɪd 'leɪbə] *noun* **(a)** people who work hard for very little money; *of course the firm makes a profit - it employs sweated labour* **(b)** hard work which is very badly paid

sweatshop ['swetʃɒp] *noun* factory using sweated labour

swipe [swaɪp] *verb* to pass a credit card or charge card through a reader; *he swiped the card but it didn't register*

Swiss franc ['swɪs 'fræŋk] *noun* currency used in Switzerland (normally considered a very stable currency)

switch [swɪtʃ] *verb* to change from one thing to another; *to switch funds from one investment to another*; *the job was switched from our British factory to the States*

switchboard ['swɪtʃbɔːd] *noun* central point in a telephone system, where all lines meet; **switchboard operator** = person who works the central telephone system

switch over to ['swɪtʃ 'əuvə tu] *verb* to change to something quite different; *we have switched over to a French supplier*; *the factory has switched over to gas for heating*

swop [swɒp] = SWAP

SWOT analysis ['swɒt ə'næləsɪs] *noun* method of developing a marketing strategy based on an assessment of the Strengths and Weaknesses of the company and the Opportunities and Threats in the market

symbol ['sɪmbəl] *noun* sign, picture or object which represents something; *they use a bear as their advertising symbol*

sympathy ['sɪmpəθi] *noun* feeling sorry because someone else has problems; *the manager had no sympathy for his secretary who complained of being overworked*; **sympathy strike** = strike to show that workers agree with another group of workers who are already on strike; **to strike in sympathy** = to stop work to show that you agree with another group of workers who are on strike; *the postal workers went on strike and the telephone engineers came out in sympathy*

sympathetic [sɪmpə'θetɪk] *adjective* showing sympathy; **sympathetic strike** = sympathy strike

syndicate 1 ['sɪndɪkət] *noun* group of people or companies working together to make money; *a German finance syndicate*; **arbitrage syndicate** = group of people who together raise the capital to invest in arbitrage deals; **underwriting syndicate** = group of underwriters who insure a large risk **2** ['sɪndɪkeɪt] *verb* **(a)** to produce an article, drawing, etc., which is published in several newspapers or magazines **(b)** to arrange for a large loan to be underwritten by several international banks

over the past few weeks, companies raising new loans from international banks have been forced to pay more, and an unusually high number of attempts to syndicate loans among banks has failed

Financial Times

syndicated ['sɪndɪkeɪtɪd] *adjective* (article which is) published in several newspapers or magazines; *he writes a syndicated column on personal finance*

synergy ['sɪnədʒi] *noun* producing greater effects by joining forces than by acting separately; *there is considerable synergy between the two companies*

synthetic [sɪn'θetɪk] *adjective* artificial, made by man; **synthetic fibres** *or* **synthetic materials** = materials made as products of a chemical process

system ['sɪstəm] *noun* **(a)** arrangement or organization of things which work together; *our accounting system has worked well in spite of the large increase in orders*; **decimal system** = system of mathematics based on the number 10; **filing system** = way of putting documents in order for easy reference; **to operate a quota system** = to regulate supplies by fixing quantities which are allowed; *we arrange our distribution using a quota system - each agent is allowed only a certain number of units* **(b)** computer system = set of programs, commands, etc., which run a computer **(c)** systems analysis = using a computer to suggest how a company should work by analyzing the way in which it works at present; **systems analyst** = person who specializes in systems analysis

systematic [sɪstə'mætɪk] *adjective* in order, using method; *he ordered a systematic report on the distribution service*

Tt

tab [tæb] *noun* = TABULATOR

table ['teɪbl] **1** *noun* **(a)** piece of furniture with a flat top and legs; **typing table** = table for a typewriter **(b)** list of figures or facts set out in columns; **table of contents** = list of contents in a book; **actuarial tables** = lists showing how long people of certain ages are likely to live **2** *verb* **(a)** to put items of information on the table before a meeting; *the report of the finance committee was tabled*; **to table a motion** = to put forward a proposal for discussion by putting details of it on the table at a meeting **(b)** *US* **to table a proposal** = to remove a proposal from discussion; *the motion to hold a new election was tabled*

tabular ['tæbjʊlə] *adjective* **in tabular form** = arranged in a table

tabulate ['tæbjʊleɪt] *verb* to set out in a table

tabulation [tæbjʊ'leɪʃən] *noun* arrangement of figures in a table

tabulator ['tæbjʊleɪtə] *noun* part of a typewriter or computer which sets words or figures automatically in columns

tachograph ['tækəgrɑːf] *noun* device attached to the engine of a lorry, which records details of the distance travelled and the time of journeys

tacit ['tæsɪt] *adjective* agreed but not stated; *the committee gave the proposals their tacit approval*; *I think we have their tacit agreement to the proposal*

tactic ['tæktɪk] *noun* way of doing things so as to be at an advantage; *his usual tactic is to buy shares in a company, then mount a takeover bid, and sell out at a profit*; *the directors planned their tactics before going into the meeting with the union representatives*

tael [taɪl] *noun* measurement of the weight of gold, used in the Far East (= 1.20oz)

tag [tæg] *noun* label; *price tag*; *name tag*

tailor ['teɪlə] *verb* to design something for a specific purpose; *we mail out press releases tailored to the reader interests of each particular newspaper or periodical*

take [teɪk] **1** *noun* money received in a shop; *our weekly take is over £5,000* **2** *verb* **(a)** to receive, to get; **the shop takes £2,000 a week** = the shop receives £2,000 a week in cash sales; **he takes home £250 a week** = his salary, after deductions for tax, etc., is £250 a week **(b)** to do a certain action; **to take action** = to do something; *you must take immediate action if you want to stop thefts*; **to take a call** = to answer the telephone; **to take the chair** = to be chairman of a meeting; *in the absence of the chairman his deputy took the chair*; **to take dictation** = to write down what someone is saying; *the secretary was taking dictation from the managing director*; **to take stock** = to count the items in a warehouse; **to take stock of a situation** = to examine the state of things before deciding what to do **(c)** to need (a time or a quantity); *it took the factory six weeks or the factory took six weeks to clear the backlog of orders*; *it will take her all morning to do my letters*; *it took six men and a crane to get the computer into the building* (NOTE: **taking - took - has taken**)

take away ['teɪk ə'weɪ] *verb* **(a)** to remove one figure from a total; *if you take away the home sales, the total turnover is down* **(b)** to remove; *we had to take the work away from the supplier because the quality was so bad*; *the police took away piles of documents from the office*; *sales*

of food to take away = cooked food sold by a shop to be eaten at some other place

takeaway ['teɪkəweɪ] *noun* shop which sells food to be eaten at some other place; *there is no VAT on takeaway meals*; *there's a Chinese takeaway on the corner of the street*

take back ['teɪk 'bæk] *verb* **(a)** to return with something; *when the watch went wrong, he took it back to the shop*; *if you do not like the colour, you can take it back to change it* **(b) to take back dismissed workers** = to allow former workers to join the company again

take-home pay ['teɪkhəʊm 'peɪ] *noun* amount of money received in wages, after tax, etc., has been deducted; *after all the deductions, his take-home pay is only £300 a week*

take into ['teɪk 'ɪntʊ] *verb* to take inside; *to take items into stock or into the warehouse*

take off ['teɪk 'ɒf] *verb* **(a)** to remove, to deduct; *he took £25 off the price* **(b)** to start to rise fast; *sales took off after the TV commercials* **(c) she took the day off** = she decided not to work for the day

take on ['teɪk 'ɒn] *verb* **(a)** to agree to employ someone; *to take on more staff* **(b)** to agree to do something; *she took on the job of preparing the VAT returns*; *he has taken on a lot of extra work*

take out ['teɪk 'aʊt] *verb* to remove; **to take out a patent for an invention** = to apply for and receive a patent; **to take out insurance against theft** = to pay a premium to an insurance company, so that if a theft takes place the company will pay compensation

> capital gains are not taxed, but money taken out in profits and dividends is taxed
> *Toronto Star*

take over ['teɪk 'əʊvə] *verb* **(a)** to start to do something in place of someone else; *Miss Black took over from Mr Jones on May 1st*; *the new chairman takes over on July 1st*; **the take-over period is always difficult** = the period when one person is taking over work from another **(b) to take over a company** = to buy (a business) by

offering to buy most of its shares; *the buyer takes over the company's liabilities*; *the company was taken over by a large multinational*

takeover ['teɪkəʊvə] *noun* buying a controlling interest in a business by buying more than 50% of its shares; **takeover bid** = offer to buy all or most of the shares in a company so as to control it; **to make a takeover bid for a company** = to offer to buy most of the shares in a company; **to withdraw a takeover bid** = to say that you no longer offer to buy the shares in a company; **the company rejected the takeover bid** = the directors recommended that the shareholders should not accept the offer; *share prices rose sharply on the disclosure of the takeover bid*; **contested takeover** *or* **hostile takeover** = takeover where the board of the company being bought do not recommend it, and try to fight it; **Takeover Code** *or* **City Code on Takeovers and Mergers** = code of practice which regulates how takeovers should take place; it is enforced by the Takeover Panel; **Takeover Panel** *or* **Panel on Takeovers and Mergers** = non-statutory body which examines takeovers and applies the Takeover Code

> many takeovers result in the new managers/owners rationalizing the capital of the company through better asset management
> *Duns Business Month*

taker ['teɪkə] *noun* buyer, person who wants to buy; *there were no takers for the new shares*

take up ['teɪk 'ʌp] *verb* **to take up an option** = to accept an option which has been offered and put into action; **to take up a rights issue** = to agree to buy rights in shares which have been offered; *half the rights issue was not taken up by the shareholders*; **take up rate** = percentage of acceptances for a rights issue

takings ['teɪkɪŋz] *plural noun* money received in a shop or a business; *the week's takings were stolen from the cash desk*

tally ['tælɪ] **1** *noun* note of things counted or recorded; *to keep a tally of stock movements or of expenses*; **tally clerk** =

person whose job is to note quantities of cargo; **tally sheet** = sheet on which quantities are noted **2** *verb* to agree, to be the same; *the invoices do not tally*; *the accounts department tried to make the figures tally*

tangible ['tændʒəbl] *adjective* **tangible assets** *or* **property** = assets which are visible (such as machinery, buildings, furniture, jewellery, etc.); **tangible fixed assets** = assets such as land, buildings, plant and equipment, etc.

tanker ['tæŋkə] *noun* special ship or vehicle for carrying liquids (especially oil)

tap [tæp] *noun GB* issue of government stocks issued direct to the Bank of England

tape [teɪp] *noun* long, flat, narrow piece of plastic; **magnetic tape** = sensitive tape for recording information; **computer tape** = magnetic tape used in computers; **measuring tape** *or* **tape measure** = long tape with centimetres or inches marked on it for measuring how long something is

tap stock ['tæp 'stɒk] *noun* British government securities issued to the Bank of England

tare [teə] *noun* (allowance made for the) weight of a container and packing which is deducted from the total weight; (allowance made for the) weight of a vehicle in calculating transport costs; *to allow for tare*

target ['tɑːgɪt] **1** *noun* thing to aim for; **monetary targets** = figures such as the money supply, PSBR, etc., which are given as targets by the government when setting out its budget for the forthcoming year; **production targets** = amount of units a factory is expected to produce; **sales targets** = amount of sales a representative is expected to achieve; **takeover target** *or* **target company** = company which is the object of a takeover bid; **target market** = market in which a company is planning to sell its goods; **to set targets** = to fix amounts or quantities which workers have to produce or reach; **to meet a target** = to produce the quantity of goods or sales which are expected; **to miss a target** = not to produce the amount of goods or sales which are expected; *they missed the target figure of £2m turnover* **2** *verb* to aim to

sell; **to target a market** = to plan to sell goods in a certain market; *I'll follow up your idea of targeting our address list with a special mailing*

> in a normal leveraged buyout the acquirer raises money by borrowing against the assets of the target company
> *Fortune*

> the minister is persuading the oil, gas, electricity and coal industries to target their advertising towards energy efficiency
> *Times*

> he believes that increased competition could keep inflation below the 2.5 per cent target
> *Investors Chronicle*

tariff ['tærɪf] *noun* **(a) customs tariffs** = tax to be paid for importing or exporting goods; **tariff barriers** = customs duty intended to make imports more difficult; *to impose tariff barriers on* **or** *to lift tariff barriers from a product*; **differential tariffs** = different duties for different types of goods **(b)** rate of charging for electricity, hotel rooms, train tickets, etc.

task [tɑːsk] *noun* **(a)** work which has to be done; **to list task processes** = to make a list of various parts of a job which have to be done **(b) task force** = special group of workers or managers who are chosen to carry out a special job or to deal with a special problem; *he is heading the government task force on inner city poverty*

tax [tæks] **1** *noun* **(a)** money taken by the government or by an official body to pay for government services; **airport tax** = tax added to the price of an air ticket to cover the cost of running an airport; **capital gains tax (CGT)** = tax on capital gains; **capital transfer tax** = tax on gifts or bequests of money or property; **corporation tax** = tax on profits made by companies; **advance corporation tax (ACT)** = tax paid by a company in advance of its main corporation tax payments; it is paid when dividends are paid to shareholders and is deducted from the main tax payment when that falls due; it appears on the tax voucher attached to a dividend warrant; **mainstream corporation tax (MCT)** = total tax paid by a company on its profits (less any ACT which the company will already have paid); **excess profits tax** = tax on profits which are higher than what is thought to be normal; **income tax** = tax on salaries and wages and other forms of income; **land tax** = tax on the amount of land owned; **sales tax** = tax on the price of goods sold; **turnover tax** = tax on company turnover; **value added tax (VAT)** = tax on goods and services, added as a percentage to the invoiced sales price **(b)** **ad valorem tax** = tax calculated according to the value of the goods taxed; **back tax** = tax which is owed; **basic tax** = tax paid at the normal rate; **direct tax** = tax (such as income tax) paid directly to the government; **indirect tax** = tax (such as VAT) paid to someone who then pays it to the government; **to levy a tax** *or* **to impose a tax** = to make a tax payable; *the government has imposed a 15% tax on petrol*; **to lift a tax** = to remove a tax; *the tax on fuel charges has been lifted*; **exclusive of tax** = not including tax; **tax abatement** = reduction of tax; **tax adjustments** = changes made to tax; **tax adviser** *or* **tax consultant** = person who gives advice on tax problems; **tax allowance** *or* **allowances against tax** = part of the income which a person is allowed to earn and not pay tax on; **tax avoidance** = trying (legally) to minimize the amount of tax to be paid; **in the top tax bracket** = paying the highest level of tax; **tax code** = number given to indicate the amount of tax allowances a person has; **tax collector** = person who collects taxes which are owed; **tax concession** = allowing less tax to be paid; **tax credit** = part of a dividend on which the company has already paid advance corporation tax which is deducted from the shareholder's income tax charge; **tax deductions** = (i) money removed from a salary to pay tax; (ii) *US* business expenses which can be claimed against tax; **tax deducted at source** = tax which is removed from a salary or interest before the money is paid out; **tax evasion** = trying illegally not to pay tax; **tax exemption** = (i) being free

from payment of tax; (ii) *US* part of income which a person is allowed to earn and not pay tax on; **tax exile** = person who lives in a country where taxes are low in order to avoid paying tax at home; **tax form** = blank form to be filled in with details of income and allowances and sent to the tax office each year; **tax haven** = country where taxes are low, encouraging companies to set up their main offices there; **tax holiday** = period when a new company pays no tax; **tax inspector** *or* **inspector of taxes** = official of the Inland Revenue who examines tax returns and decides how much tax someone should pay; **tax incentive** = reduction of tax to encourage people to work harder and make more money; **tax loophole** = legal means of not paying tax; **tax loss** = loss made by a company during an accounting period, for which relief from tax is given; **tax relief** = allowing someone not to pay tax on certain parts of his income; **tax return** *or* **tax declaration** = completed tax form, with details of income and allowances; *GB* **tax schedules** = types of income as classified for tax; *see comment at* SCHEDULE; **tax shelter** = financial arrangement (such as a pension scheme) where investments can be made without tax; **tax threshold** = point at which another percentage of tax is payable; **tax year** = twelve month period on which taxes are calculated (in the UK, 6th April to 5th April of the following year) **2** *verb* to make someone pay a tax, to impose a tax on something; *businesses are taxed at 40%; income is taxed at 35%; luxury items are heavily taxed*

taxable ['tæksəbl] *adjective* which can be taxed; **taxable items** = items on which a tax has to be paid; **taxable income** = income on which a person has to pay tax

taxation [tæk'seɪʃən] *noun* act of taxing; **direct taxation** = taxes (such as income tax) which are paid direct to the government; **indirect taxation** = taxes (such as sales tax) which are not paid direct to the government; *the government raises more money by indirect taxation than by direct*; **double taxation** = taxing the same income twice; **double taxation agreement** = agreement between two countries that a person living in one country will not be taxed in both countries on the income earned in the other country; **graduated taxation** *or* **progressive taxation** = taxation system where tax levels increase as income rises; **regressive taxation** = system of taxation in which tax gets progressively less as income rises

tax-deductible ['tæksdɪ'dʌktəbl] *adjective* which can be deducted from an income before tax is calculated; **these expenses are not tax-deductible** = tax has to be paid on these expenses

tax-exempt ['tæksɪg'zempt] *adjective* not required to pay tax; (income or goods) which are not subject to tax

tax-free ['tæks'friː] *adjective* on which tax does not have to be paid; *people working for n international organization such as UN enjoy a tax-free income*

taxi ['tæksi] *noun* car which takes people from one place to another for money; *he took a taxi to the airport; taxi fares are very high in New York*

taxpayer ['tækspeɪə] *noun* person or company which has to pay tax; *basic taxpayer* or *taxpayer at the basic rate*; *corporate taxpayers are being targeted by the government*

tax point ['tæks 'pɔɪnt] *noun* date on which goods or services are supplied, which is the date when VAT becomes is due

team [tiːm] *noun* group of people who work together; **management team** = group of all the managers working in the same company; **sales team** = all representatives, salesmen and sales managers working in a company

teamster ['tiːmstə] *noun* US truck driver

teamwork ['tiːmwɜːk] *noun* being able to work together as a group without arguing

tear sheet ['teə 'ʃiːt] *noun* page taken from a published magazine or newspaper, sent to an advertiser as proof that his advertisement has been run

teaser ['tiːzə] *noun* advertisement that gives a little information about a product in order to attract customers by making them curious to know more

technical ['teknɪkəl] *adjective* **(a)** referring to a particular machine or process; *the document gives all the technical details on the new computer* **(b)** **technical correction** = situation where a share price or a currency moves up or down because it was previously too low or too high

> market analysts described the falls in the second half of last week as a technical correction
>
> *Australian Financial Review*

> at the end of the day, it was clear the Fed had not loosened the monetary reins, and Fed Funds forged ahead on the back of technical demand
>
> *Financial Times*

technician [tek'nɪʃən] *noun* person who is specialized in industrial work; *computer technicians worked to install the new system*; **laboratory technician** = person who deals with practical work in a laboratory

technique [tek'niːk] *noun* skilled way of doing a job; *the company has developed a new technique for processing steel; he has a special technique for answering complaints from customers*; **management techniques** = skill in managing a business; **marketing techniques** = skill in marketing a product

technological [teknə'lɒdʒɪkəl] *adjective* referring to technology; **the technological revolution** = changing of industry by introducing new technology

technology [tek'nɒlədʒi] *noun* applying scientific knowledge to industrial processes; **information technology** = working with data stored on computers; **the introduction of new technology** = putting new electronic equipment into a business or industry

tel = TELEPHONE

telecommunications [telɪkəmjuːnɪ'keɪʃənz] *plural noun* systems of passing messages over long distances (by cable, radio, etc.)

teleconference [telɪ'kɒnfərəns] *noun* discussion between several people in different places, using the telephone, microphones and loudspeakers

telegram ['telɪgræm] *noun* message sent to another country by telegraph; *to send a telegram to an agent in South Africa*

telegraph ['telɪgrɑːf] **1** *noun* system of sending messages along wires; *to send a message by telegraph*; **telegraph office** = office from which telegrams can be sent **2** *verb* to send a message by telegraph; *to telegraph an order*

telegraphic [telɪ'græfɪk] *adjective* referring to a telegraph system; **telegraphic address** = short address used for sending telegrams

telegraphic transfer ['telɪgræfɪk 'trɑːnsfə] *noun* transfer of money from one account to another by telegraph (often used for sending money abroad, it is quicker than sending a draft through the post)

telemarketing ['telɪmɑːkɪtɪŋ] *noun* selling a product or service by telephone

telemessage ['telɪmesɪdʒ] *noun GB* message sent by telephone, and delivered as a card (as for a birthday, wedding, etc.)

telephone ['telɪfəun] **1** *noun* machine used for speaking to someone over a long distance; *we had a new telephone system installed last week*; **to be on the telephone** = to be speaking to someone using the telephone; *the managing director is on the telephone to Hong Kong*; *she has been on the telephone all day*; **by telephone** = using the telephone; *to place an order by telephone*; *to reserve a room by telephone*; **house telephone** *or* **internal telephone** = telephone for calling from one room to another in an office or hotel; **telephone book** *or* **telephone directory** = book which lists all people and businesses in alphabetical order with their telephone numbers; *he looked up the number of the company in the telephone book*; **telephone call** = speaking to someone on the telephone; **to make a telephone call** = to speak to someone on the telephone; **to answer the telephone** *or* **to take a telephone call** = to speak in reply to a call on the telephone; **telephone exchange** = centre where the telephones of a whole district are linked; **telephone number** = set of figures for a particular telephone

subscriber; *can you give me your telephone number?*; **telephone operator** = person who operates a telephone switchboard; **telephone orders** = orders received by telephone; *since we mailed the catalogue we have received a large number of telephone orders*; **telephone selling** = making sales by phoning prospective customers and trying to persuade them to buy; **telephone subscriber** = person who has a telephone; **telephone switchboard** = central point in a telephone system where all internal and external lines meet **2** *verb* **to telephone a place** *or* **a person** = to call a place or someone by telephone; *his secretary telephoned to say he would be late*; **he telephoned the order through to the warehouse** = he telephoned the warehouse to place an order; **to telephone about something** = to make a telephone call to speak about something; *he telephoned about the January invoice*; **to telephone for something** = to make a telephone call to ask for something; *he telephoned for a taxi*

telephonist [tə'lefənɪst] *noun* person who works a telephone switchboard

teleprinter ['telɪprɪntə] *noun* machine like a typewriter, which can send messages by telegraph and print incoming messages; *teleprinter operator*

telesales ['telɪseɪlz] *plural noun* sales made by telephone

teletypewriter ['telɪ'taɪpraɪtə] *noun US* = TELEPRINTER

telex ['teleks] **1** *noun* **(a)** old system of sending messages by telephone lines to a special printer; *the order came by telex*; **telex line** = wire linking a telex machine to the telex system; *we cannot communicate with our Nigerian office because of the breakdown of the telex lines* **(b)** a **telex** = (i) a machine for sending and receiving telex messages; (ii) a message sent by telex; *he sent a telex to his head office*; *we received his telex this morning* **2** *verb* to send a message using the telex system; *can you telex the Canadian office before they open?*; *he telexed the details of the contract to New York*

teller ['telə] *noun* person who takes cash from or pays cash to customers at a bank

tem *see* PRO TEM

temp [temp] **1** *noun* temporary secretary; *we have had two temps working in the office this week to clear the backlog of letters*; **temp agency** = office which deals with finding temporary secretaries for offices **2** *verb* to work as a temporary secretary

temping ['tempɪŋ] *noun* working as a temporary secretary; *she can earn more money from temping than from a full-time job*

temporarily ['temprərəli] *adverb* lasting only for a short time

temporary ['temprəri] *adjective* which only lasts a short time; *he was granted a temporary export licence*; *to take temporary measures*; *she has a temporary post with a construction company*; *he has a temporary job as a filing clerk or he has a job as a temporary filing clerk*; **temporary employment** = full-time work which does not last for more than a few days or months; **temporary staff** = staff who are appointed for a short time

tenancy ['tenənsi] *noun* (i) agreement by which a tenant can occupy a property; (ii) period during which a tenant has an agreement to occupy a property

tenant ['tenənt] *noun* person or company which rents a house, flat or office to live or work in; *the tenant is liable for repairs*; **sitting tenant** = tenant who is occupying a building when the freehold or lease is sold

tend [tend] *verb* to be likely to do something; *he tends to appoint young girls to his staff*

tendency ['tendənsi] *noun* being likely to do something; *the market showed an upward tendency*; *there has been a downward tendency in the market for several days*; **the market showed a tendency to stagnate** = the market seemed to stagnate rather than advance

tender ['tendə] **1** *noun* **(a)** offer to do something for a certain price; *a successful tender or an unsuccessful tender*; **to put a project out to tender** *or* **to ask for** *or* **to invite tenders for a project** = to ask

contractors to give written estimates for a job; **to put in a tender** *or* **to submit a tender** = to make an estimate for a job; **to sell shares by tender** = to ask people to offer in writing a price for shares; **sealed tenders** = tenders sent in sealed envelopes which will all be opened together at a certain time **(b)** **legal tender** = coins or notes which can be legally used to pay a debt (small denominations cannot be used to pay large debts) **2** *verb* **(a)** **to tender for a contract** = to put forward an estimate of cost for work to be carried out under contract; *to tender for the construction of a hospital* **(b)** **to tender your resignation** = to resign, to give in your resignation **(c)** to offer money; *please tender the correct fare*

tenderer ['tendərə] *noun* person or company which tenders for work; *the company was the successful tenderer for the project*

tendering ['tendrɪŋ] *noun* act of putting forward an estimate of cost; *to be successful, you must follow the tendering procedure as laid out in the documents*

tentative ['tentətɪv] *adjective* not certain; *they reached a tentative agreement over the proposal*; *we suggested Wednesday May 10th as a tentative date for the next meeting*

tentatively ['tentətɪvli] *adverb* not sure; *we tentatively suggested Wednesday as the date for our next meeting*

tenure ['tenjə] *noun* **(a)** right to hold property or position; **security of tenure** = right to keep a job, rented accommodation provided certain conditions are met **(b)** time when a position is held; *during his tenure of the office of chairman*

term [tɜːm] *noun* **(a)** period of time when something is legally valid; *we have renewed the lease for a term of five years*; *the term of the loan is fifteen years*; *we have the loan for a term of fifteen years*; *during his term of office as chairman*; **term deposit** = money invested for a fixed period at a higher rate of interest; **term assurance** *or* **term insurance** = life assurance which covers a person's life for a period of time (at the end of the period, if the person is still alive he receives nothing from the insurance); *he took out a ten-year term insurance*; **term loan** = loan for a fixed period of time; **term shares** = type of building society deposit for a fixed period of time at a higher rate of interest **(b) short-term** = for a period of months; **long-term** = for a long period of time; **medium-term** = for a period of one or two years **(c) terms** = conditions or duties which have to be carried out as part of a contract, arrangements which have to be agreed before a contract is valid; *he refused to agree to some of the terms of the contract*; *by or under the terms of the contract, the company is responsible for all damage to the property*; *to negotiate for better terms*; **terms of payment** *or* **payment terms** = conditions for paying something; **terms of sale** = conditions attached to a sale; **cash terms** = lower terms which apply if the customer pays cash; **'terms: cash with order'** = terms of sale showing that payment has to be made in cash when the order is placed; **easy terms** = terms which are not difficult to accept, price which is easy to pay; *the shop is let on very easy terms*; *to pay for something on easy terms*; **on favourable terms** = on especially good terms; *the shop is let on very favourable terms*; **trade terms** = special discount for people in the same trade **(c)** part of a legal or university year **(d) terms of employment** = conditions set out in a contract of employment

---

companies have been improving communications, often as part of deals to cut down demarcation and to give everybody the same terms of employment

Economist

---

the Federal Reserve Board has eased interest rates in the past year, but they are still at historically high levels in real terms

Sunday Times

---

terminable ['tɜːmɪnəbl] *adjective* which can be terminated

terminal ['tɜːmɪnl] **1** *noun* **(a) computer terminal** = keyboard and screen, by which information can be put into a computer or

can be called up from a database; *computer system consisting of a microprocessor and six terminals* **(b) air terminal** = building in a town where passengers meet to be taken by bus to an airport outside the town; **airport terminal** *or* **terminal building** = main building at an airport where passengers arrive and leave; **container terminal** = area of a harbour where container ships are loaded or unloaded; **ocean terminal** = building at a port where passengers arrive and depart **2** *adjective* at the end; **terminal bonus** = bonus received when an insurance comes to an end

terminate ['tɜːmɪneɪt] *verb* to end (something), to bring (something) to an end; *to terminate an agreement*; *his employment was terminated*; *the offer terminates on July 31st*; *the flight from Paris terminates in New York*

termination [tɜːmɪ'neɪʃən] *noun* **(a)** bringing to an end; **termination clause** = clause which explains how and when a contract can be terminated **(b)** *US* leaving a job (resigning, retiring, or being fired or made redundant)

territorial waters [terɪ'tɔːriəl 'wɔːtəz] *noun* sea waters near the coast of a country, which are part of the country and governed by the laws of that country; **outside territorial waters** = in international waters, over which no single country has jurisdiction

territory ['terɪtri] *noun* area visited by a salesman; *we are adding two new reps and reducing all the reps' territories*; *his territory covers all the north of the country*

tertiary ['tɜːʃəri] *adjective* **tertiary industry** = service industry, industry which does not produce or manufacture anything but offers a service (such as banking, retailing or accountancy); **tertiary sector** = section of the economy containing the service industries

test [test] **1** *noun* **(a)** examination to see if something works well, or if it is possible; **test certificate** = certificate to show that something has passed a test; **driving test** = examination to see if someone is able to drive a car; **feasibility test** = test to see if something is possible; **market test** =

examination to see if a sample of a product will sell in a market **(b) test case** = legal action where the decision will fix a principle which other cases can follow **2** *verb* to examine something to see if it is working well; *we are still testing the new computer system*; **to test the market for a product** = to show samples of a product in a market to see if it will sell well; *we are testing the market for the toothpaste in Scotland*

testament ['testəmənt] *noun* **last will and testament** = will, a document by which a person says what he or she wants to happen to their property when they die

testamentary [testə'mentəri] *adjective* referring to a will; **testamentary disposition** = passing of property to people in a will

testate ['testeɪt] *adjective* having made a will; *did he die testate?*; *see also* INTESTATE

testator [te'steɪtə] *noun* man who has made a will

testatrix [te'steɪtrɪks] *noun* woman who has made a will

test-drive ['testdraɪv] *verb* **to test-drive a car** = to drive a car (before buying it) to see if it works well

testimonial [testɪ'məʊnjəl] *noun* written report about someone's character or ability; *she has asked me to write her a testimonial*; **unsolicited testimonial** = letter praising someone or a product, without the writer having been asked to write it

testing ['testɪŋ] *noun* examining something to see if it works well; *during the testing of the system several defects were corrected*

test-market ['test'mɑːkɪt] *verb* **to test-market a product** = to show samples of a product in a market to see if it will sell well; *we are test-marketing the toothpaste in Scotland*

text [tekst] *noun* written part of something; *he wrote notes at the side of the text of the agreement*; **text processing** = working with words, using a computer to produce, check and change documents, reports, letters, etc.

thank [θæŋk] *verb* to show someone that you are grateful for what has been done; *the committee thanked the retiring chairman for his work*; *'Thank you for your letter of June 25th'*

thanks [θæŋks] *plural noun* word showing that someone is grateful; *'many thanks for your letter of June 25th'*; **vote of thanks** = official vote at a meeting to show that the meeting is grateful for what someone has done; *the meeting passed a vote of thanks to the organizing committee for their work in setting up the international conference*

thanks to ['θæŋks tʊ] *adverb* because of; *the company was able to continue trading thanks to a loan from the bank*; **it was no thanks to the bank that we avoided making a loss** = we avoided making a loss in spite of what the bank did

theft [θeft] *noun* stealing; act of stealing something; *we have brought in security guards to protect the store against theft*; *more cases of theft or more thefts have occurred during the Christmas period*; *they are trying to cut their losses by theft*; *to take out insurance against theft*

theory ['θɪəri] *noun* statement of the general principle of how something should work; **in theory the plan should work** = the plan may work, but it has not been tried in practice

think tank ['θɪŋk 'tæŋk] *noun* group of experts who advise or put forward plans

third [θɜːd] *noun* one part of something which is divided into three; **to sell everything at one third off** = to sell everything at a discount of 33%; **the company has two thirds of the total market** = the company has 66% of the total market

third party ['θɜːd 'pɑːti] *noun* any person other than the two main parties involved in a contract (i.e., in an insurance contract, anyone who is not the insurance company nor the person who is insured); **third party insurance** *or* **third party policy** = insurance to cover damage to any person who is not one of the people named in the insurance contract (that is, not the insured person nor the insurance company); **the case is in the hands of a third party** = the case is being dealt with by someone who is not one of the main interested parties

third quarter ['θɜːd 'kwɔːtə] *noun* three months' period from July to September

Third World ['θɜːd 'wɜːld] *noun* countries of Africa, Asia and South America which do not all have highly developed industries; *we sell tractors into the Third World or to Third World countries*

three-part ['θriː'pɑːt] *adjective* paper (for computers or typewriters) with a top sheet for the original and a two sheets for copies; *three-part invoices; three-part stationery*

threshold ['θreʃəʊld] *noun* limit, the point at which something changes; **threshold agreement** = contract which says that if the cost of living goes up by more than a certain amount, pay will go up to match it; **threshold price** = in the EU, the lowest price at which farm produce imported into the EU can be sold; **pay threshold** *or* **wage threshold** = point at which pay increases because of a threshold agreement; **tax threshold** = point at which another percentage of tax is payable; *the government has raised the minimum tax threshold from £4,000 to £4,500*

thrift [θrɪft] *noun* (a) saving money by spending carefully (b) *US* private local bank, savings and loan association or credit union, which accepts and pays interest on deposits from small investors

the thrift, which had grown from $4.7 million in assets in 1980 to 1.5 billion this year, has ended in liquidation
Barrons

some thrifts came to grief on speculative property deals, some in the high-risk junk bond market, others simply by lending too much to too many people
Times

thrifty ['θrɪfti] *adjective* careful not to spend too much money

thrive [θraɪv] *verb* to grow well, to be profitable; *the country has a thriving economy based on oil; there is a thriving black market in car radios; the company is thriving in spite of the recession*

throughput ['θruːpʊt] *noun* amount of work done or of goods produced in a certain time; *we hope to increase our throughput by putting in two new machines; the invoice department has a throughput of 6,000 invoices a day*

throw out ['θrəʊ 'aʊt] *verb* (a) to reject, to refuse to accept; *the proposal was thrown out by the planning committee; the board threw out the draft contract submitted by the union* (b) to get rid of (something which is not wanted); *we threw out the old telephones and installed a computerized system; the AGM threw out the old board of directors* (NOTE: **throwing - threw - has thrown**)

thumbtack ['θʌmtæk] *noun* pin with a flat head for attaching a sheet of paper to something hard; *she used thumbtacks to pin the poster to the door* (NOTE: British English is **drawing pin**)

tick [tɪk] **1** *noun* (a) *(informal)* credit; *all the furniture in the house is bought on tick* (b) mark on paper to show that something is correct or that something is approved; *put a tick in the box marked 'R'* (NOTE: American English for this meaning is **check**) **2** *verb* to mark with a sign to show that something is correct; *tick the box marked 'R' if you require a receipt*

ticker ['tɪkə] *noun US* machine (operated by telegraph) which prints details of share prices and transactions rapidly on paper tape

ticket ['tɪkɪt] *noun* (a) piece of paper or card which allows you to do something; **entrance ticket** *or* **admission ticket** = ticket which allows you to go in; **theatre ticket** = ticket which allows you a seat in a theatre (b) piece of paper or card which allows you to travel; *train ticket or bus ticket or plane ticket;* **season ticket** = train or bus ticket which can be used for any number of journeys over a period (usually one, three, six or twelve months); **single ticket** *or* **one-way ticket** = ticket for one journey from one place to another; **return ticket** *or* **round-trip ticket** = ticket for a journey from one place to another and back again (c) **ticket agency** = shop which sells tickets to theatres; **ticket counter** = counter where tickets are sold (d) paper which shows something; **baggage ticket =** paper showing that you have left a piece of baggage with someone; **price ticket =** piece of paper showing a price

tie [taɪ] *verb* to attach or to fasten (with string, wire, etc.); *he tied the parcel with thick string*; *she tied two labels on to the parcel* (NOTE: **tying - tied**)

tie-in [ˈtaɪˈɪn] *noun* type of advertising which links one product to another; **tie-in promotion =** special display linking the product to a major advertising campaign, or to a TV programme

tie-on label [ˈtaɪˈɒn ˈleɪbl] *noun* label with a piece of string attached so that it can be tied to an item

tie up [ˈtaɪ ˈʌp] *verb* **(a)** to attach or to fasten tightly; *the parcel is tied up with string*; *the ship was tied up to the quay*; **he is rather tied up at the moment =** he is very busy **(b)** to invest money in one way, so that it cannot be used for other investments; *he has £100,000 tied up in long-dated gilts*; *the company has £250,000 tied up in stock which no one wants to buy*

> a lot of speculator money is said to be tied up in sterling because of the interest-rate differential between US and British rates
>
> *Australian Financial Review*

tie-up [ˈtaɪˈʌp] *noun* link or connection; *the company has a tie-up with a German distributor* (NOTE: plural is **tie-ups**)

tight [taɪt] *adjective* which is controlled, which does not allow any movement; *the manager has a very tight schedule today - he cannot fit in any more appointments*; *expenses are kept under tight control*; **tight money =** money which is borrowed at a high interest rate; **tight money policy =** government policy to restrict money supply

> mortgage money is becoming tighter
>
> *Times*

> a tight monetary policy by the central bank has pushed up interest rates and drawn discretionary funds into bank deposits
>
> *Far Eastern Economic Review*

> the UK economy is at the uncomfortable stage in the cycle where the two years of tight money are having the desired effect on demand
>
> *Sunday Times*

-tight [taɪt] *suffix* which prevents something getting in; *the computer is packed in a watertight case*; *send the films in an airtight container*

tighten [ˈtaɪtn] *verb* to make (something) tight, to control (something); *the accounts department is tightening its control over departmental budgets*

> the decision by the government to tighten monetary policy will push the annual inflation rate above the previous high
>
> *Financial Times*

tighten up on [ˈtaɪtn ˈʌp ɒn] *verb* to control (something) more; *the government is tightening up on tax evasion*; *we must tighten up on the reps' expenses*

till [tɪl] *noun* drawer for keeping cash in a shop; **cash till =** cash register, a machine which shows and adds prices of items bought, with a drawer for keeping the cash received; *there was not much money in the till at the end of the day*

time [taɪm] *noun* **(a)** period during which something takes place (such as one hour, two days, fifty minutes, etc.); **computer time =** time when a computer is being used (paid for at an hourly rate); **real time =** time when a computer is working on the processing of data while the problem to which the data refers is actually taking place; *the website allows you to check share prices in real time or gives real time information on share prices*; **time and motion study =** study in an office or factory of how long it takes to do certain jobs and the movements workers have to make to do them; **time and motion expert =** person who analyzes time and motion studies and suggests changes in the way work is done **(b)** hour of the day (such as 9.00, 12.15, ten o'clock at night, etc.); *the time of arrival or the arrival time is indicated on the screen*; *departure times are delayed by up to fifteen minutes* *because of the volume of traffic*; on **time** = at the right time; *the plane was on time*; *you will have to hurry if you want to get to the meeting on time or if you want to be on time for the meeting*; **opening time** *or* **closing time** = time when a shop or office starts or stops work **(c)** system of hours on the clock; **Summer Time** *or* **Daylight Saving Time** = system where clocks are set forward one hour in the summer to take advantage of the longer hours of daylight; **Standard Time** = normal time as in the winter months **(d)** hours worked; **he is paid time and a half on Sundays** = he is paid the normal rate plus 50% extra when he works on Sundays; **full-time** = working for the whole normal working day; **overtime** = hours worked more than the normal working time; **part-time** = not working for a whole working day **(e)** period before something happens; **time deposit** = deposit of money for a fixed period, during which it cannot be touched; **delivery time** = number of days before something will be delivered; **lead time** = time between placing an order and receiving the goods; **time limit** = period during which something should be done; **to keep within the time limits** *or* **within the time schedule** = to complete work by the time stated

time-card *or* time-clock card

['taɪmkɑːd or 'taɪm'klɒk kɑːd] *noun* card which is put into a timing machine when a worker clocks in or clocks out, and records the time when he starts and stops work

time clock ['taɪm 'klɒk] *noun* machine which records when a worker arrives for work and punches in his card

time-keeping ['taɪmkiːpɪŋ] *noun* being on time for work; *he was warned for bad time-keeping*

time rate ['taɪm 'reɪt] *noun* rate for work which is calculated as money per hour or per week, and not money for work completed

time-saving ['taɪm'seɪvɪŋ] **1** *adjective* which saves time; *a time-saving device* **2** *noun* trying to save time; *the management is keen on time-saving*

timescale ['taɪmskeɪl] *noun* time which will be taken to complete work; *our*

timescale is that all work should be completed by the end of August; he is working to a strict timescale

time share ['taɪm 'ʃeə] *noun* system where several people each own part of a property (such as a holiday flat), each being able to use it for a certain period each year

time-sharing ['taɪmʃeərɪŋ] *noun* **(a)** = TIME SHARE **(b)** sharing a computer system, with different users using different terminals

time sheet ['taɪm 'ʃiːt] *noun* paper showing when a worker starts work in the morning and leaves work in the evening, or one which shows how much time a worker spends on various jobs in different locations

timetable ['taɪmteɪbl] **1** *noun* **(a)** list showing times of arrivals and departures of buses, trains, planes, etc.; *according to the timetable, there should be a train to London at 10.22*; *the bus company has brought out its winter timetable* **(b)** list of appointments or events; *the manager has a very full timetable, so I doubt if he will be able to see you today*; **conference timetable** = list of speakers or events at a conference **2** *verb* to make a list of times

time work ['taɪm 'wɜːk] *noun* work which is paid for at a rate per hour or per day, not per piece of work completed

time zone ['taɪm 'zəun] *noun* one of 24 bands in the world in which the same standard time is used; *when you fly across the USA you cross several time zones*

time-zone differences are an attraction for Asian speculators. In Hongkong, it is 5 p.m. when the London exchange opens and 9.30 or 10 p.m. when New York starts trading

Far Eastern Economic Review

timing ['taɪmɪŋ] *noun* way in which something happens at a particular time; *the timing of the conference is very convenient, as it comes just before my summer holiday*; *his arrival ten minutes after the meeting finished was very bad timing*

tip [tɪp] **1** *noun* **(a)** money given to someone who has helped you; *I gave the taxi driver a 10 cent tip*; *the staff are not allowed to accept tips* **(b)** advice on something to buy or to do which could be profitable; *the newspaper gave several stock market tips*; *he gave me a tip about a share which was likely to rise because of a takeover bid*; **tip sheet** = newspaper which gives information about shares which should be bought or sold **2** *verb* **(a)** to give money to someone who has helped you; *he tipped the receptionist £5* **(b)** to say that something is likely to happen, that something might be profitable; *two shares were tipped in the business section of the paper*; *he is tipped to become the next chairman* (NOTE: **tipping - tipped**)

TIR   =   **TRANSPORTS INTERNATIONAUX ROUTIERS**

title [ˈtaɪtl] *noun* **(a)** right to own a property; *she has no title to the property*; *he has a good title to the property*; **title deeds** = document showing who is the owner of a property **(b)** name given to a person in a certain job; *he has the title 'Chief Executive'* **(c)** name of a book, film, etc.

token [ˈtəʊkən] *noun* **(a)** thing which acts as a sign or symbol; **token charge** = small charge which does not cover the real costs; *a token charge is made for heating*; **token payment** = small payment to show that a payment is being made; **token rent** = very low rent payment to show that some rent is being asked; **token strike** = short strike to show that workers have a grievance **(b)** **book token** *or* **flower token** = card bought in a shop which is given as a present and which must be exchanged for books or flowers; **gift token** = card bought in a shop which is given as a present and which must be exchanged in that shop for goods

toll [təʊl] *noun* payment for using a service (usually a bridge or a road); *we had to cross a toll bridge to get to the island*; *you have to pay a toll to cross the bridge*

toll call [ˈtəʊl ˈkɔːl] *noun* *US* long-distance telephone call

toll free [ˈtəʊl ˈfriː] *adverb* *US* without having to pay a charge for a long-distance

telephone call; *to call someone toll free*; *a toll-free number*

> COMMENT: toll-free numbers usually start with the digits 800

tombstone [ˈtuːmstəʊn] *noun (informal)* official announcement in a newspaper that a major loan has been subscribed

ton [tʌn] *noun* measure of weight; *GB* **long ton** = measure of weight (= 1016 kilos); *US* **short ton** = measure of weight (= 907 kilos); **metric ton** = 1,000 kilos

tone [təʊn] *noun* **dialling tone** = noise made by a telephone to show that it is ready for you to dial a number; **engaged tone** = sound made by a telephone when the line dialled is busy

toner [ˈtəʊnə] *noun* black powder, like dry ink, used in laser printers and photocopiers; *we need more toner - the message is showing 'TONER LOW'*; **toner cartridge** = sealed plastic box containing toner

tonnage [ˈtʌnɪdʒ] *noun* space for cargo in a ship, measured in tons; **gross tonnage** = amount of total space in a ship; **deadweight tonnage** = largest amount of cargo which a ship can carry safely

> in the dry cargo sector a total of 956 cargo vessels of 11.6m tonnes are laid up - 3% of world dry cargo tonnage
> *Lloyd's List*

tonne [tʌn] *noun* metric ton, 1,000 kilos

> Canada agreed to the new duty-free quota of 600,000 tonnes a year
> *Globe and Mail (Toronto)*

tool [tuːl] *noun* instrument used for doing manual work (such as a hammer, screwdriver); **machine tools** = tools worked by motors, used to work on wood or metal

tool up [ˈtuːl ˈʌp] *verb* to put machinery into a factory

top [tɒp] **1** *adjective & noun* **(a)** upper surface, upper part; *do not put coffee cups on top of the computer*; **top copy** = first sheet of a document which is typed with several carbon copies or photocopies **(b)** highest point, most important place; *the*

company is one of the top six exporters;
top-flight *or* **top-ranking** = in the most
important position; *top-flight managers
can earn very high salaries*; *he is the
top-ranking official in the delegation*;
top-grade = most important, of the best
quality; *the car only runs on top-grade
petrol*; **top management** = the main
directors of a company; **to give something
top priority** = to make something the most
important item, so that it is done very fast;
top quality = very best quality; *we
specialize in top quality imported goods* **2**
verb to go higher than; *sales topped £1m in
the first quarter* (NOTE: **topping - topped**)

---

gross wool receipts for the
selling season appear likely
to top $2 billion
Australian Financial Review

---

the base lending rate, or
prime rate, is the rate at
which banks lend to their top
corporate borrowers
Wall Street Journal

---

fill huge warehouses with
large quantities of
top-brand, first-quality
merchandise, sell the goods
at rock-bottom prices
Duns Business Month

---

top-hat pension ['tɒphæt 'penʃən]
noun special extra pension for senior
managers

top out ['tɒp 'aʊt] **1** *noun US* period of
peak demand for a product **2** *verb* to finish
the roof of a new building; **topping-out
ceremony** = ceremony when the roof of a
new building is finished

top-selling ['tɒp'selɪŋ] *adjective* which
sells better than all other products;
top-selling brands of toothpaste

top up ['tɒp 'ʌp] *verb* **(a)** to fill up
something which is not full; *to top up
stocks before the Christmas rush* **(b)** to
add to something to make it more
complete; *he topped up his pension
contributions to make sure he received the
maximum allowable pension when he
retired*

tort [tɔːt] *noun* harm done to someone or
property which can be the basis of a lawsuit

total ['təʊtl] **1** *adjective* complete, with
everything added together; *the total
amount owed is now £1000*; *the company
has total assets of over £1bn*; *the total cost
was much more than expected*; *total
expenditure on publicity is twice that of
last year*; *our total income from exports
rose last year*; *the factory's total output
was bought by a Germany supermarket*;
*her total revenue puts her into the highest
tax bracket*; **the cargo was written off as
a total loss** = the cargo was so badly
damaged that the insurers said it had no
value **2** *noun* amount which is complete,
with everything added up; *the total of the
charges comes to more than £1,000*;
grand total = final total made by adding
several subtotals **3** *verb* to add up to; *costs
totalling more than £25,000* (NOTE:
totalling - totalled but American English
totaling - totaled)

totally ['təʊtli] *adverb* completely; *the
factory was totally destroyed in the fire*;
the cargo was totally ruined by water

tour [tʊə] *noun* (holiday) journey to
various places, coming back in the end to
the place the journey started from; *the
group went on a tour of Italy*; *the minister
went on a fact-finding tour of the region*;
conducted tour = tour with a guide who
shows places to the tourists; **package tour**
= tour where the hotel, travel, and meals
are all arranged in advance and paid for in
one payment; **tour operator** = person or
company which organizes tours; **to carry
out a tour of inspection** = to visit various
places, offices or factories, etc., to inspect
them

tourism ['tʊərɪzm] *noun* business of
providing travel, hotel rooms, food,
entertainment, etc., for tourists

tourist ['tʊərɪst] *noun* person who goes
on holiday to visit places away from home;
tourist bureau *or* **tourist information
office** = office which gives information to
tourists about the place where it is situated;
tourist class = lower quality or less
expensive way of travelling; *he always
travels first class, because he says tourist
class is too uncomfortable*; **tourist visa** =
visa which allows a person to visit a
country for a short time on holiday

tout [taʊt] **1** *noun* person who sells tickets (to games or shows) for more than the price printed on them **2** *verb* **(a) to tout for custom** = to try to attract customers **(b)** *US* to make extravagant publicity for a product

trace [treɪs] **1** *noun* very small amount; *there was a trace of powder on his coat*; *she showed no trace of anger* **2** *verb* **(a)** to find where someone or something is; *we couldn't trace the order* **(b)** to copy a drawing, etc., by placing a sheet of transparent paper over it and drawing on it; *she traced the map*

tracing paper ['treɪsɪŋ 'peɪpə] *noun* transparent paper for copying drawings, etc.; *this is a copy I made on tracing paper*

track [træk] **1** *noun* **to keep track of** = to keep an account, to keep yourself informed about; *I like to keep track of new developments in computer technology*; **to lose track of someone or something** = not to know where someone or something is; *we lost track of our rep in Turkey* **2** *verb* to follow someone or something; to follow how something develops, such as one of the stock market indices; *this fund tracks the Footsie Index*

> tracking the stock market is a good way of providing for the long term, if you're prepared to ride the ups and downs
>
> *Investors Chronicle*

tracker fund ['trækə 'fʌnd] *noun* fund which tracks (i.e. follows closely) one of the stock market indices, such as the Footsie

track record ['træk 'rekɔːd] *noun* success or failure of a company or salesman in the past; *he has a good track record as a secondhand car salesman*; *the company has no track record in the computer market*

trade [treɪd] **1** *noun* **(a)** business of buying and selling; **export trade** *or* **import trade** = the business of selling to other countries or buying from other countries; **foreign trade** *or* **overseas trade** *or* **external trade** = trade with other countries; **home trade** = trade in the country where a company is based; **trade cycle** = period during which trade expands, then slows down, then expands again; **balance of trade** *or* **trade balance** = international trading position of a country, excluding invisible trade; **adverse balance of trade** = situation when a country imports more than it exports; *the country had an adverse balance of trade for the second month running*; **favourable balance of trade** = situation where a country's exports are larger than its imports; **trade deficit** *or* **trade gap** = difference in value between a country's low exports and higher imports; **trade figures** = government statistics showing the value of a country's trade with other countries; **trade surplus** = difference in value between a country's high exports and lower imports **(b) to do a good trade in a range of products** = to sell a large number of a range of products; **fair trade** = international business system where countries agree not to charge import duties on certain items imported from their trading partners; **free trade** = system where goods can go from one country to another without any restrictions; **free trade area** = group of countries practising free trade **(c) trade agreement** = international agreement between countries over general terms of trade; **trade bureau** = office which specializes in commercial enquiries; **to impose trade barriers on** = to restrict the import of certain goods by charging high duty; **trade creditors** = companies which are owed money by a company in the normal course of trading (the amount owed to trade creditors is shown in the annual accounts); **trade debtors** = debtors who owe money to a company in the normal course of that company's trading; **trade description** = description of a product to attract customers; *GB* **Trade Descriptions Act** = act which limits the way in which products can be described so as to protect customers from wrong descriptions made by manufacturers; **trade directory** = book which lists all the businesses and business people in a town; **trade mission** = visit to a country by a group of foreign businessmen to discuss trade **(d)** people or companies dealing in the same type of product; *he is in the secondhand car trade*; *she is very well known in the clothing trade*; **trade association** = group which links together companies in the same trade; **trade counter** = shop in a factory or warehouse where goods are sold to retailers; **trade discount** *or*

trade terms = reduction in price given to a customer in the same trade; **trade fair** = large exhibition and meeting for advertising and selling a certain type of product; *there were two trade fairs running in London at the same time*; *to organize or to run a trade fair*; **trade journal** *or* **trade magazine** *or* **trade paper** *or* **trade publication** = magazine or newspaper produced for people and companies in a certain trade; **trade press** = all magazines produced for people working in a certain trade; **trade price** = special wholesale price paid by a retailer to the manufacturer or wholesaler; **to ask a company to supply trade references** = to ask a company to give names of traders who can report on the company's financial situation and reputation; **trade secret** = information (especially about manufacturing) which a company has and will not give to other companies **2** *verb* to buy and sell, to carry on a business; *we trade with all the countries of the EU*; *he trades on the Stock Exchange*; *the company has stopped trading*; *the company trades under the name 'Eeziphitt'*

a sharp setback in foreign trade accounted for most of the winter slowdown. The trade balance sank $17 billion

Fortune

at its last traded price, the bank was capitalized around $1.05 billion

South China Morning Post

with most of the world's oil now traded on spot markets, Opec's official prices are much less significant than they once were

Economist

the London Stock Exchange said that the value of domestic UK equities traded during the year was £1.4066 trillion, more than the capitalization of the entire London market and an increase of 36 per cent compared with previous year's total of £1.037 trillion

Times

trade in ['treɪd 'ɪn] *verb* **(a)** to buy and sell certain items; *the company trades in imported goods*; *he trades in French wine* **(b)** to give in an old item as part of the payment for a new one; *the chairman traded in his old Rolls Royce for a new model*

trade-in ['treɪdɪn] *noun* old item (such as a car or washing machine) given as part of the payment for a new one; *she bought a new car and gave her old one as a trade-in*; **trade-in price** = amount allowed by the seller for an old item being traded in for a new one

trademark *or* **trade name** ['treɪdmɑːk or 'treɪd 'neɪm] *noun* particular name, design, etc., which has been registered by the manufacturer and which cannot be used by other manufacturers (it is an 'intangible asset'); *you cannot call your beds 'Soft'n'kumfi' - it is a registered trademark*

trade-off ['treɪdɒf] *noun* exchanging one thing for another as part of a business deal

trader ['treɪdə] *noun* person who does business; **commodity trader** = person whose business is buying and selling commodities; **free trader** = person who is in favour of free trade; **sole trader** = person who runs a business, usually by himself, but has not registered it as a company

tradesman ['treɪdzmən] *noun* **(a)** shopkeeper, person who runs a shop **(b)** *US* skilled craftsman (NOTE: plural is **tradesmen)**

tradespeople ['treɪdzpiːpl] *plural noun* shopkeepers

trade union *or* **trades union** ['treɪd 'juːnjən or 'treɪdz 'juːnjən] *noun* organization which represents workers who are its members in discussions with employers about wages and conditions of employment; *they are members of a trades union or they are trade union members*; *he has applied for trade union membership or he has applied to join a trades union*; **Trades Union Congress** = organization linking all British trade unions (NOTE: although **Trades Union Congress** is the official name for the organization, **trade union** is commoner than **trades union** in British English. American English is **labor union**)

trade unionist ['treɪd 'juːnjənɪst] *noun* member of a trade union

trade-weighted index ['treɪd'weɪtɪd 'ɪndeks] *noun* index of the value of a currency calculated against a basket of currencies

> the trade-weighted dollar chart shows there has been a massive devaluation of the dollar and the currency is at its all-time low. In terms of purchasing power, it is considerably undervalued
>
> *Financial Weekly*

trading ['treɪdɪŋ] *noun* business of buying and selling; **trading account** = account of a company's gross profit; **trading area** = group of countries which trade with each other; **trading bloc** = group of countries which trade with each other on special terms; **trading company** = company which specializes in buying and selling goods; **adverse trading conditions** = bad conditions for trade; **trading estate** = area of land near a town specially for building factories and warehouses; **trading floor** = *see* FLOOR; **trading loss** = situation where a company's receipts are less than its expenditure; **trading partner** = company or country which trades with another; **trading profit** = situation where a company's gross receipts are more than its gross expenditure; **trading stamp** = special stamp given away by a shop, which the customer can collect and exchange later for free goods; **fair trading** = way of doing business which is reasonable and does not harm the customer; *GB* **Office of Fair Trading** = government department which protects consumers against unfair or illegal business; **insider trading** = illegal buying or selling of shares by staff of a company who have secret information about the company's plans

traffic ['træfɪk] **1** *noun* **(a)** movement of cars, lorries, trains or planes; movement of people or goods in vehicles; *there is an increase in commuter traffic or goods traffic on the motorway; passenger traffic on the commuter lines has decreased during the summer*; **air traffic controller** = person who controls the landing and taking off of planes at an airport **(b)** illegal trade; *drugs traffic or traffic in drugs* **2** *verb* to deal illegally; *they are trafficking in drugs* (NOTE: **trafficking - trafficked**)

trafficker ['træfɪkə] *noun* **drug(s) trafficker** = person who deals illegally in drugs; *he was stopped at customs because they suspected he was a drug trafficker*

train [treɪn] **1** *noun* set of coaches or wagons pulled by an engine along railway lines; *a passenger train or a goods train; to take the 09.30 train to London; he caught his train or he missed his train; to ship goods by train*; **freight train** *or* **goods train** = train used for carrying goods **2** *verb* to teach (someone) to do something; to learn how to do something; *he trained as an accountant; the company has appointed a trained lawyer as its managing director*

trainee [treɪ'niː] *noun* person who is learning how to do something; *we employ a trainee accountant to help in the office at peak periods; graduate trainees come to work in the laboratory when they have finished their courses at university*; **management trainee** = young member of staff being trained to be a manager

traineeship [treɪ'niːʃɪp] *noun* post of trainee

training ['treɪnɪŋ] *noun* being taught how to do something; *there is a ten-week training period for new staff; the shop is closed for staff training*; **industrial training** = training of new workers to work in an industry; **management training** = training staff to be managers, by making them study problems and work out solutions to them; **on-the-job training** = training given to workers at their place of work; **off-the-job training** = training given to workers away from their place of work (such as at a college or school); **staff training** = teaching staff better and more profitable ways of working; **training levy** = tax to be paid by companies to fund the government's training schemes; **training officer** = person who deals with the training of staff; **training unit** = special group of teachers who organize training for companies

tranche [trɑːnʃ] *noun* one of series of instalments (used when referring to loans to companies, government securities which are issued over a period of time, or money withdrawn by a country from the IMF); *the second tranche of interest on the loan is now due for payment*

transact [trænˈzækt] *verb* to transact business = to carry out a piece of business

transaction [trænˈzækʃən] *noun* business transaction = piece of business, buying or selling; **cash transaction** = transaction paid for in cash; **a transaction on the Stock Exchange** = purchase or sale of shares on the Stock Exchange; *the paper publishes a daily list of Stock Exchange transactions*; **exchange transaction** = purchase or sale of foreign currency; **fraudulent transaction** = transaction which aims to cheat someone

the Japan Financial Intelligence Office will receive reports on suspected criminal transactions from financial institutions, determine where a probe should be launched and provide information to investigators
Nikkei Weekly

transfer 1 [ˈtrænsfə] *noun* (a) moving someone or something to a new place; *he applied for a transfer to our branch in Scotland*; **transfer of property** *or* **transfer of shares** = moving the ownership of property or shares from one person to another; **airmail transfer** = sending money from one bank to another by airmail; **bank transfer** = moving money from a bank account to an account in another country; **credit transfer** *or* **transfer of funds** = moving money from one account to another; **stock transfer form** = form to be signed by the person transferring shares (b) changing to another form of transport; **transfer passenger** = traveller who is changing from one aircraft or train or bus to another, or to another form of transport **2** [trænsˈfɜː] *verb* (a) to move someone or something to a new place; *the accountant was transferred to our Scottish branch*; *he transferred his shares to a family trust*; *she transferred*

her money to a deposit account; **transferred charge call** = phone call where the person receiving the call agrees to pay for it (b) to change from one type of travel to another; *when you get to London airport, you have to transfer onto an internal flight* (NOTE: **transferring - transferred**)

transferable [trænsˈfɜːrəbl] *adjective* which can be passed to someone else; **the season ticket is not transferable** = the ticket cannot be given or lent to someone else to use

tranship [trænˈʃɪp] *verb* to move cargo from one ship to another (NOTE: **transhipping - transhipped**)

transit [ˈtrænzɪt] *noun* (a) movement of passengers or goods on the way to a destination; *to pay compensation for damage suffered in transit or for loss in transit*; *some of the goods were damaged in transit*; **goods in transit** = goods being transported from warehouse to customer (b) **transit lounge** = room in an airport where passengers wait for connecting flights; **transit visa** *or* **transit permit** = document which allows someone to spend a short time in one country while travelling to another country

translate [trænsˈleɪt] *verb* to put something which is said or written in one language into another language; *he asked his secretary to translate the letter from the German agent*; *we have had the contract translated from French into Japanese*

translation [trænsˈleɪʃən] *noun* something which has been translated; *she passed the translation of the letter to the accounts department*; **translation bureau** = office which translates documents for companies

translator [trænsˈleɪtə] *noun* person who translates

transmission [trænzˈmɪʃən] *noun* sending; *transmission of a message*

transmit [trænzˈmɪt] *verb* to send (a message) (NOTE: **transmitting - transmitted**)

trans-national corporation [ˈtrænzˈnæʃnl kɔːpəˈreɪʃn] *noun* large company which operates in various countries

transport 1 ['trænspɔːt] *noun* moving of goods or people; *air transport or transport by air; rail transport or transport by rail; road transport or transport by road; passenger transport or the transport of passengers; the passenger transport services into London; what means of transport will you use to get to the factory?;* **the visitors will be using public transport** *or* **private transport** = the visitors will be coming by bus, train, etc., or in their own cars; **public transport system** = system of trains, buses, etc., used by the general public **2** [træns'pɔːt] *verb* to move goods or people from one place to another in a vehicle; *the company transports millions of tons of goods by rail each year; the visitors will be transported to the factory by air or by helicopter or by taxi*

transportable [træns'pɔːtəbl] *adjective* which can be moved

transportation [trænspə'teɪʃən] *noun* **(a)** moving goods or people from one place to another **(b)** vehicles used to move goods or people from one place to another; *the company will provide transportation to the airport;* **ground transportation** = buses, taxis, etc., available to take passengers from an airport to the town

transporter [træns'pɔːtə] *noun* company which transports goods

Transports Internationaux Routiers (TIR) ['trɔːnspɔːz ænte'næsjənəʊ 'ruːtieɪ] *noun* system of international documents which allows dutiable goods to cross several European countries by road without paying duty until they reach their final destination

travel ['trævl] **1** *noun* moving of people from one place to another or from one country to another; *business travel is a very important part of our overhead expenditure;* **travel agent** = person in charge of a travel agency; **travel agency** = office which arranges travel for customers; **travel allowance** = money which an employee is allowed to spend on travelling; **travel expenses** = money spent on travelling and hotels for business purposes;

travel magazine = magazine with articles on holidays and travel; **the travel trade** = all businesses which organize travel for people **2** *verb* **(a)** to move from one place to another or from one country to another; *he travels to the States on business twice a year; in her new job, she has to travel abroad at least ten times a year* **(b)** to go from one place to another, showing a company's goods to buyers and taking orders from them; *he travels in the north of the country for an insurance company* (NOTE: **travelling - travelled** but American spelling **traveling - traveled**)

traveller *US* **traveler** ['trævlə] *noun* **(a)** person who travels; **business traveller** = person who is travelling on business; **traveller's cheques** *US* **traveler's checks** = cheques taken by a traveller which can be cashed in a foreign country **(b)** **commercial traveller** = salesman who travels round an area visiting customers on behalf of his company

travelling expenses ['trævəlɪŋ ek'spensɪz] *noun* money spent on travelling and hotels for business purposes

tray [treɪ] *noun* **filing tray** = container kept on a desk for documents which have to be filed; **in tray** = basket on a desk for letters or memos which have been received and are waiting to be dealt with; **out tray** = basket on a desk for letters or memos which have been dealt with and are ready to be sent out; **pending tray** = basket on a desk for papers which cannot be dealt with immediately

treasurer ['treʒərə] *noun* **(a)** person who looks after the money or finances of a club or society, etc.; **honorary treasurer** = treasurer who does not receive any fee **(b)** *GB* company official responsible for finding new finance for the company and using its existing financial resources in the best possible way **(c)** *US* main financial officer of a company **(d)** *(Australia)* finance minister in the government

treasury ['treʒəri] *noun* **(a) the Treasury** = government department which deals with the country's finance (NOTE: the term is used in both the UK and the USA; in most other countries this department is called the **Ministry of Finance**); **treasury bill** = short-term financial instrument which does not give any interest and is sold by the government at a discount through the central bank (in the UK, their term varies from three to six months; in the USA, they are for 91 or 182 days, or for 52 weeks (NOTE: in American English they are also called **Treasuries** or **T-bills**); **treasury bonds** = long-term bonds issued by the British or American governments; **treasury notes** = medium-term bonds issued by the US government; **treasury stocks** = stocks issued by the British government (NOTE: also called **exchequer stocks**); *US* **Treasury Secretary** = member of the US government in charge of finance (NOTE: the equivalent of the **Finance Minister** in most countries, or of the **Chancellor of the Exchequer** in the UK); *GB* **Chief Secretary to the Treasury** = government minister responsible to the Chancellor of the Exchequer for the control of public expenditure (NOTE: in the USA, this is the responsibility of the **Director of the Budget**) **(b)** **treasury tag** = short piece of string with two metal pieces at the ends, which are put through holes in sheets of paper or cards to hold them together

treaty ['triːti] *noun* **(a)** agreement between countries; *the two countries signed a commercial treaty* **(b)** agreement between individual persons; **to sell a house by private treaty** = to sell a home to another person not by auction

treble ['trebl] *verb* to increase three times; *the company's borrowings have trebled*; *the acquisition of the chain of stores has trebled the group's turnover*

trend [trend] *noun* general way things are going; *there is a trend away from old-established food stores*; *a downward trend in investment*; *we notice a general trend to sell to the student market*; *the report points to inflationary trends in the economy*; *an upward trend in sales*; **economic trends** = way in which a country's economy is moving; **market trends** = gradual changes taking place in a market

the quality of building design and ease of accessibility will become increasingly important,

adding to the trend towards out-of-town office development
Lloyd's List

trial ['traɪəl] *noun* **(a)** court case to judge a person accused of a crime; *he is on trial or is standing trial for embezzlement* **(b)** test to see if something is good; **on trial** = being tested; *the product is on trial in our laboratories*; **trial period** = time when a customer can test a product before buying it; **trial sample** = small piece of a product used for testing; **free trial** = testing of a machine or product with no payment involved **(c)** **trial balance** = draft calculation of debits and credits to see if they balance

tribunal [traɪ'bjuːnl] *noun* official court which examines special problems and makes judgements; **adjudication tribunal** = group which adjudicates in industrial disputes; **industrial tribunal** = court which can decide in disputes about employment; **rent tribunal** = court which can decide if a rent is too high or low

trick [trik] *noun* clever act to make someone believe something which is not true; **confidence trick** = business where someone gains another person's confidence and then tricks him

trickster ['trikstə] *noun* **confidence trickster** = person who carries out a confidence trick on someone

trigger ['trigə] **1** *noun* thing which starts a process **2** *verb* to start a process; **trigger point** = point in acquiring shares in a company where the purchaser has to declare an interest or to take certain action

COMMENT: if an individual or a company buys 5% of a company's shares, this shareholding must be declared to the company. If 15% is acquired it is assumed that a takeover bid will be made, and no more shares can be acquired for seven days to give the target company time to respond. There is no obligation to make a bid at this stage, but if the holding is increased to 30%, then a takeover bid must be made for the remaining 70%. If 90% of shares are owned, then the owner can purchase all outstanding shares compulsorily. These trigger points are often not crossed, and it is common to see that a company has acquired 14.9% or 29.9% of another company's shares

```
the  recovery  is  led  by
significant  declines  in
short-term  interest  rates,
which  are  forecast  to  be
roughly  250  basis  points
below  their  previous  peak.
This should trigger a rebound
in  the  housing  markets  and
consumer spending on durables
```
Toronto Globe & Mail

trillion ['trɪljən] *number* one million millions (NOTE: British English now has the same meaning as American English; formerly in British English it meant one million million millions, and it is still sometimes used with this meaning; see also the note at BILLION)

```
if land is assessed at roughly
half  its  current  market
value, the new tax could yield
up to ¥10 trillion annually
```
Far Eastern Economic Review

```
behind the decline was a 6.1%
fall  in  exports  to  ¥47.55
trillion, the second year of
falls. Automobiles and steel
were among categories showing
particularly  conspicuous
drops
```
Nikkei Weekly

```
the  London  Stock  Exchange
said  that  the  value  of
domestic UK equities traded
during the year was £1.4066
trillion,  more  than  the
capitalization of the entire
London market and an increase
of 36 per cent compared with
previous  year's  total  of
£1.037 trillion
```
Times

trip [trɪp] *noun* journey; **business trip =** journey to discuss business matters with people who live a long way away or overseas

triple ['trɪpl] **1** *verb* to multiply three times; *the company's debts tripled in twelve months*; *the acquisition of the chain of stores has tripled the group's*

turnover 2 *adjective* three times as much; *the cost of airfreighting the goods is triple their manufacturing cost*

triplicate ['trɪplɪkət] *noun* **in triplicate =** with an original and two copies; *the invoices are printed in triplicate*; **invoicing in triplicate =** preparing three copies of invoices

trolley ['trɒli] *noun* device on wheels which can be used to carry things; **supermarket trolley =** metal basket on wheels, used by shoppers to put their purchases in as they go round a supermarket (NOTE: American English for this is **shopping cart**); **suspension file trolley =** trolley which carries rows of suspension files, and can easily be moved from place to place in an office

trouble ['trʌbl] *noun* problem, difficult situation; *we are having some computer trouble or some trouble with the computer*; *there was some trouble in the warehouse after the manager was fired*

troubleshooter ['trʌblʃuːtə] *noun* person whose job is to solve problems in a company; *they brought in a troubleshooter to try to sort out the management problems*

trough [trɒf] *noun* low point in the economic cycle

troy weight ['trɔɪ 'weɪt] *noun* system of measurement of weight used for gold and other metals, such as silver and platinum; **troy ounce =** measurement of weight (= 31.10 grammes) (NOTE: in writing, often shortened to **troy oz.** after figures: **25.2 troy oz.**)

COMMENT: troy weight is divided into grains, pennyweights (24 grains = 1 pennyweight), ounces (20 pennyweights = 1 ounce) and pounds (12 troy ounces = 1 pound). Troy weights are slightly less than their avoirdupois equivalents; the troy pound equals 0.37kg or 0.82lb avoirdupois; see also AVOIRDUPOIS

truck [trʌk] *noun* **(a)** large motor vehicle for carrying goods; **fork-lift truck =** type of small tractor with two metal arms in front, used for lifting and moving pallets **(b)** open railway wagon for carrying goods

trucker ['trʌkə] *noun* person who drives a truck

trucking ['trʌkɪŋ] *noun* carrying goods in trucks; *trucking firm*

truckload ['trʌkləud] *noun* quantity of goods that fills a truck

true [truː] *adjective* correct or accurate; **true copy** = exact copy; *I certify that this is a true copy*; *it is certified as a true copy*; **true and fair view** = correct statement of a company's financial position as shown in its accounts and confirmed by the auditors

truly ['truːli] *adverb* **Yours truly** *US* **Truly yours** = ending to a formal business letter where you do not know the person you are writing to

trust [trʌst] **1** *noun* **(a)** being confident that something is correct, will work, etc.; **we took his statement on trust** = we accepted his statement without examining it to see if it was correct **(b)** legal arrangement to pass goods, money or valuables to someone who will look after them well; *he left his property in trust for his grandchildren*; **he was guilty of a breach of trust** = he did not act correctly or honestly when people expected him to; **he has a position of trust** = his job shows that people believe he will act correctly and honestly **(c)** management of money or property for someone; *they set up a family trust for their grandchildren; US* **trust company** = organization which supervises the financial affairs of private trusts, executes wills, and acts as a bank to a limited number of customers; **trust deed** = document which sets out the details of a private trust; **trust fund** = assets (money, securities, property) held in trust for someone; **investment trust** = company whose shares can be bought on the Stock Exchange and whose business is to make money by buying and selling stocks and shares; **unit trust** = organization which takes money from investors and invests it in stocks and shares for them under a trust deed **(d)** *US* small group of companies which control the supply of a product **2** *verb* **to trust someone with something** = to give something to someone to look after; *can he be trusted with all that cash?*

trustbusting ['trʌstbʌstɪŋ] *noun US* breaking up monopolies to encourage competition

trustee [trʌs'tiː] *noun* person who has charge of money in trust, person who is responsible for a family trust; *the trustees of the pension fund*

trustworthy ['trʌstwɜːði] *adjective* (person) who can be trusted; *our cashiers are completely trustworthy*

Truth in Lending Act ['truːθ ɪn 'lendɪŋ 'ækt] US Act of 1969, which forces lenders to state the full terms of their interest rates to borrowers

TUC ['tiːjuː'siː] = TRADES UNION CONGRESS

tune [tjuːn] *noun* **the bank is backing him to the tune of £10,000** = the bank is helping him with a loan of £10,000

turkey ['tɜːki] *noun (informal)* bad investment, investment which has turned out to be worthless

turn [tɜːn] **1** *noun* **(a)** movement in a circle, change of direction **(b)** profit or commission; *he makes a turn on everything he sells* **(c)** **stock turn** = total value of stocks sold in a year divided by the average value of goods in stock; *the company has a stock turn of 6.7* **2** *verb* to change direction, to go round in a circle

turn down ['tɜːn 'daun] *verb* to refuse; *the board turned down their takeover bid*; *the bank turned down their request for a loan*; *the application for a licence was turned down*

turnkey operation ['tɜːnkiː ɒpə'reɪʃən] *noun* deal where a company takes all responsibility for constructing, fitting and staffing a building (such as a school, hospital or factory) so that it is completely ready for the purchaser to take over

turn out ['tɜːn 'aut] *verb* to produce; *the factory turns out fifty units per day*

turn over ['tɜːn 'əuvə] *verb* **(a)** to have a certain amount of sales; *we turn over £2,000 a week* **(b)** *US* to pass something to someone; *she turned over the documents to the lawyer* (NOTE: in this meaning, British English is usually **hand over**)

```
a  100,000  square  foot
warehouse  can  turn  its
```

inventory over 18 times a
year, more than triple a
discounter's turnover

Duns Business Month

---

he is turning over his CEO
title to one of his teammates,
but will remain chairman for a
year

Duns Business Month

turnover ['tɜːnəʊvə] *noun* **(a)** *GB* amount of sales of goods or services by a company; *the company's turnover has increased by 235%*; *we based our calculations on the forecast turnover* (NOTE: the American equivalent is **sales volume**); **gross turnover** = turnover including VAT and discounts; **net turnover** = turnover before VAT and after trade discounts have been deducted **(b)** changes in staff, when some leave and others join; *staff turnover or turnover of staff* **(c)** number of times something is used or sold in a period (usually one year), expressed as a percentage of a total; **stock turnover** = total value of stock sold in a year divided by the average value of goods held in stock

turn round ['tɜːn 'raʊnd] *verb* to make (a company) change from making a loss to become profitable; **he turned the company round in less than a year** = he made the company profitable in less than a year

turnround *US* turnaround

['tɜːnraʊnd *or* 'tɜːnəraʊnd] *noun* **(a)** value of goods sold during a year divided by the average value of goods held in stock **(b)** action of emptying a ship, plane, etc., and getting it ready for another commercial journey **(c)** making a company profitable again **(d)** processing orders and sending out the goods; **turnround time** = time taken from receiving an order and supplying the goods

---

the US now accounts for more
than half our world-wide
sales; it has made a huge
contribution to our earnings
turnround

Duns Business Month

24-hour banking ['twentifɔː'æʊə 'bæŋkɪŋ] banking service provided during the whole day (by cash dispensers in the street, online services, etc.); **24-hour trading** = trading in bonds, securities and currencies during the whole day

---

time-zone differences are an
attraction for Asian
speculators. In Hongkong, it
is 5 p.m. when the London
exchange opens and 9.30 or 10
p.m. when New York starts
trading

Far Eastern Economic Review

COMMENT: 24-hour trading is now possible because of instant communication to Stock Exchanges in different time zones; the Tokyo Stock Exchange closes about two hours before the London Stock Exchange opens; the New York Stock Exchange opens at the same time as the London one closes

---

two-bin system ['tuːbɪn 'sɪstəm] *noun* warehousing system, where the first bin contains the current working stock, and the second bin has the backup stock

two-part ['tuː'pɑːt] *adjective* paper (for computers or typewriters) with a top sheet for the original and a second sheet for a copy; *two-part invoices*; *two-part stationery*

two-way trade ['tuːweɪ 'treɪd] *noun* trade between two countries or partners

tycoon [taɪ'kuːn] *noun* important businessman

type [taɪp] **1** *noun* printed letters; *can you read the small type on the back of the contract?* **2** *verb* to write with a typewriter; *he can type quite fast*; *all his reports are typed on his portable typewriter*

typewriter ['taɪpraɪtə] *noun* machine which prints letters or figures on a piece of paper when keys are pressed; *portable typewriter*; *electronic typewriter*

typewritten ['taɪprɪtn] *adjective* written on a typewriter; *he sent in a typewritten job application*

typing ['taɪpɪŋ] *noun* writing letters with a typewriter; **typing error** = mistake made when using a typewriter; *the secretary must have made a typing error*; **typing pool** = group of typists, working together in a company, offering a secretarial service to several departments; **copy typing** = typing documents from handwritten originals, not from dictation

typist ['taɪpɪst] *noun* person whose job is to write letters using a typewriter; **copy** **typist** = person who types documents from handwritten originals not from dictation; **shorthand typist** = typist who takes dictation in shorthand and then types it

Uu

ultimate ['ʌltɪmət] *adjective* last or final; **ultimate consumer** = the person who actually uses the product

ultimately ['ʌltɪmətli] *adverb* in the end; *ultimately, the management had to agree to the demands of the union*

ultimatum [ʌltɪ'meɪtəm] *noun* statement to a someone that unless he does something within a period of time, action will be taken against him; *the union officials argued among themselves over the best way to deal with the ultimatum from the management* (NOTE: plural is **ultimatums** or **ultimata**)

umbrella organization [ʌm'brelə 'ɔːgənaɪzeɪʃn] *noun* large organization which includes several smaller ones

UN ['juː'en] = THE UNITED NATIONS

unable [ʌn'eɪbl] *adjective* not able; *the chairman was unable to come to the meeting*

unacceptable [ʌnək'septəbl] *adjective* which cannot be accepted; *the terms of the contract are quite unacceptable*

unaccounted for [ʌnə'kauntɪd fɔː] *adjective* lost, without any explanation; *several thousand units are unaccounted for in the stocktaking*

unanimous [juː'nænɪməs] *adjective* where everyone votes in the same way; *there was a unanimous vote against the proposal*; *they reached unanimous agreement*

unanimously [juː'nænɪməsli] *adverb* with everyone agreeing; *the proposals were adopted unanimously*

unaudited [ʌn'ɔːdɪtɪd] *adjective* which has not been audited; *unaudited accounts*

unauthorized [ʌn'ɔːθəraɪzd] *adjective* not permitted; *unauthorized access to the company's records*; *unauthorized expenditure*; *no unauthorized persons are allowed into the laboratory*

unavailability [ʌnəveɪlə'bɪləti] *noun* not being available; *the unavailability of any reliable sales data makes forecasting difficult*

unavailable [ʌnə'veɪləbl] *adjective* not available; *the following items on your order are temporarily unavailable*

unavoidable [ʌnə'vɔɪdəbl] *adjective* which cannot be avoided; *flights are subject to unavoidable delays*

unbalanced [ʌn'bælənst] *adjective* (budget) which does not balance or which is in deficit

unbanked [ʌn'bæŋkt] *adjective* (cheque) which has not been deposited in a bank account

uncalled [ʌn'kɔːld] *adjective* (capital) which a company is authorized to raise and has been issued but for which payment has not yet been requested

uncashed [ʌn'kæʃt] *adjective* which has not been cashed; *uncashed cheques*

unchanged [ʌn'tʃeɪndʒd] *adjective* which has not changed

> the dividend is unchanged at L90 per ordinary share
> *Financial Times*

unchecked [ʌn'tʃekt] *adjective* which has not been checked; *unchecked figures*

unclaimed [ʌn'kleɪmd] *adjective* which has not been claimed; **unclaimed baggage** = cases which have been left with someone and have not been claimed by their owners;

unclaimed property or unclaimed baggage will be sold by auction after six months

uncollected [ʌnkə'lektɪd] *adjective* which has not been collected; *uncollected subscriptions*; *uncollected taxes*

unconditional [ʌnkən'dɪʃənl] *adjective* with no conditions; *unconditional acceptance of the offer by the board*; **the offer went unconditional last Thursday** = the takeover bid was accepted by the majority of the shareholders and therefore the conditions attached to it no longer apply

COMMENT: a takeover bid will become unconditional if more than 50% of shareholders accept it

unconditionally [ʌnkən'dɪʃənli] *adverb* without imposing any conditions; *the offer was accepted unconditionally by the trade union*

unconfirmed [ʌnkən'fɜːmd] *adjective* which has not been confirmed; *there are unconfirmed reports that our agent has been arrested*

unconstitutional [ʌnkɒnstɪ'tjuːʃənl] *adjective* not allowed by the rules of an organization or by the laws of a country; *the chairman ruled that the meeting was unconstitutional*

uncontrollable [ʌnkən'trəʊləbl] *adjective* which cannot be controlled; *uncontrollable inflation*

uncrossed cheque ['ʌnkrɒst 'tʃek] *noun* cheque which does not have two lines across it, and can be cashed anywhere (NOTE: also called an **open cheque**: they are no longer used in the UK, but are still found in other countries)

undated [ʌn'deɪtɪd] *adjective* with no date written; *he tried to cash an undated cheque*; **undated bond** = bond with no maturity date

under ['ʌndə] *preposition* **(a)** lower than, less than; *the interest rate is under 10%*; *under half of the shareholders accepted the offer* **(b)** controlled by, according to; *under the terms of the agreement, the goods should be delivered in October*; *he is acting under rule 23 of the union constitution*

under- ['ʌndə] *prefix* less important than, lower than

underbid [ʌndə'bɪd] *verb* to bid less than someone (NOTE: **underbidding - underbid**)

underbidder [ʌndə'bɪdə] *noun* person who bids less than the person who buys at an auction

undercapitalized [ʌndə'kæpɪtəlaɪzd] *adjective* without enough capital; *the company is severely undercapitalized*

undercharge [ʌndə'tʃɑːdʒ] *verb* to ask for too little money; *he undercharged us by £25*

undercut [ʌndə'kʌt] *verb* to offer something at a lower price than someone else; *they increased their market share by undercutting their competitors*

underdeveloped [ʌndədɪ'veləpt] *adjective* which has not been developed; *Japan is an underdeveloped market for our products*; **underdeveloped countries** = countries which are not fully industrialized

underemployed [ʌndərɪm'plɔɪd] *adjective* with not enough work; *the staff is underemployed because of the cutback in production*; **underemployed capital** = capital which is not producing enough interest

underemployment [ʌndərɪm'plɔɪmənt] *noun* **(a)** situation where workers in a company do not have enough work to do **(b)** situation where there is not enough work for all the workers in a country

underequipped [ʌndərɪ'kwɪpt] *adjective* with not enough equipment

underestimate 1 [ʌndər'estɪmɪt] *noun* estimate which is less than the actual figure; *the figure of £50,000 in turnover was a considerable underestimate* **2** [ʌndər'estɪmeɪt] *verb* to think that something is smaller or not as bad as it really is; *they underestimated the effects of the strike on their sales*; *he underestimated the amount of time needed to finish the work*

underlease ['ʌndəliːs] *noun* lease from a tenant to another tenant

undermanned [ʌndə'mænd] *adjective* with not enough staff to do the work

undermanning [ˌʌndəˈmænɪŋ] *noun* having too few workers than are needed to do the company's work; *the company's production is affected by undermanning on the assembly line*

undermentioned [ˌʌndəˈmenʃənd] *adjective* mentioned lower down in a document; *see the undermentioned list of countries to which these terms apply*

underpaid [ˌʌndəˈpeɪd] *adjective* not paid enough; *our staff say that they are underpaid and overworked*

underperform [ˌʌndəpəˈfɔːm] *verb* **to underperform the market** = to perform worse than the rest of the market; *the hotel group has underperformed the sector this year*

underperformance [ˌʌndəpəˈfɔːməns] *noun* performing worse than others; *the underperformance of the shares has worried investors*

> Australia has been declining again. Because it has had such a long period of underperfomance, it is now not as vulnerable as other markets
>
> *Money Observer*

underrate [ˌʌndəˈreɪt] *verb* to value less highly than should be; *do not underrate the strength of the competition in the European market*; *the power of the yen is underrated*

undersell [ˌʌndəˈsel] *verb* to sell more cheaply than; *to undersell a competitor*; **the company is never undersold** = no other company sells goods as cheaply as this one (NOTE: **underselling - undersold**)

undersigned [ˌʌndəˈsaɪnd] *noun* person who has signed a letter; **we, the undersigned** = we, the people who have signed below (NOTE: can be followed by a plural verb)

underspend [ˌʌndəˈspend] *verb* to spend less; **he has underspent his budget** = he has spent less than was allowed in the budget (NOTE: **underspending - underspent**)

understaffed [ˌʌndəˈstɑːft] *adjective* with not enough staff to do the company's work

understand [ˌʌndəˈstænd] *verb* to know or to see what something means (NOTE: **understanding - understood**)

understanding [ˌʌndəˈstændɪŋ] *noun* private agreement; **to come to an understanding about the divisions of the market**; **on the understanding that** = on condition that, provided that; *we accept the terms of the contract, on the understanding that it has to be ratified by our main board*

understate [ˌʌndəˈsteɪt] *verb* to make something seem less than it really is; *the company accounts understate the real profit*

undersubscribed [ˌʌdəsʌbˈskraɪbd] *adjective* (share issue) where applications are not made for all the shares on offer, and part of the issue remains with the underwriters

undertake [ˌʌndəˈteɪk] *verb* to agree to do something; *we asked the research unit to undertake an investigation of the market*; *they have undertaken not to sell into our territory* (NOTE: **undertaking - undertook - has undertaken**)

undertaking [ˌʌndəˈteɪkɪŋ] *noun* **(a)** business; *he is the MD of a large commercial undertaking* **(b)** (legally binding) promise; *they have given us a written undertaking not to sell their products in competition with ours*

underutilized [ˌʌndəˈjuːtɪlaɪzd] *adjective* not used enough

undervaluation [ˌʌndəvæljuˈeɪʃən] *noun* being valued at a lower worth than should be

undervalued [ˌʌndəˈvæljuːd] *adjective* not valued highly enough; *the properties are undervalued on the balance sheet*; *the dollar is undervalued on the foreign exchanges*

> in terms of purchasing power, the dollar is considerably undervalued, while the US trade deficit is declining month by month
>
> *Financial Weekly*

underweight [ˌʌndəˈweɪt] *adjective* **the pack is twenty grams underweight** = the pack weighs twenty grams less than it should

underworked [ˌʌndəˈwɜːkt] *adjective* not given enough work to do; *the directors think our staff are overpaid and underworked*

underwrite [ˌʌndəˈraɪt] *verb* **(a)** to accept responsibility for; **to underwrite a share issue** = to guarantee that a share issue will be sold by agreeing to buy all shares which are not subscribed; *the issue was underwritten by three underwriting companies* **(b)** to insure, to cover (a risk); *to underwrite an insurance policy* **(c)** to agree to pay for costs; *the government has underwritten the development costs of the project* (NOTE: underwriting - underwrote - has underwritten)

under the new program, mortgage brokers are allowed to underwrite mortgages and get a much higher fee

Forbes Magazine

underwriter [ˈʌndəraɪtə] *noun* person who underwrites a share issue or an insurance; **Lloyd's underwriter** = member of an insurance group at Lloyd's who accepts to underwrite insurances; **marine underwriter** = person who insures ships and their cargoes

COMMENT: when a major company flotation or share issue or loan is prepared, a group of companies (such as merchant banks) will form a syndicate to underwrite the flotation: the syndicate will be organized by the 'lead underwriter', together with a group of main underwriters; these in turn will ask others ('sub-underwriters') to share in the underwriting

undischarged bankrupt [ˈʌndɪstʃɑːdʒd ˈbæŋkrʌpt] *noun* person who has been declared bankrupt and has not been released from that state

undistributed profit [ˌʌndɪsˈtrɪbjuːtɪd ˈprɒfɪt] *noun* profit which has not been distributed as dividends to shareholders

unearned income [ˈʌnɜːnd ˈɪnkʌm] *noun* income (such as interest and dividends) from investments, not from salary, wages or profits of your business

(also called 'investment income'); *compare* EARNED INCOME

uneconomic [ˌʌniːkəˈnɒmɪk] *adjective* which does not make a commercial profit; **it is an uneconomic proposition** = it will not be commercially profitable; **uneconomic rent** = rent which is not enough to cover costs

unemployed [ˌʌnɪmˈplɔɪd] *adjective* not employed, without any work; **unemployed office workers** = office workers with no jobs; **the unemployed** = the people without any jobs; **the long-term unemployed** = people who have been out of work for more than a year

unemployment [ˌʌnɪmˈplɔɪmənt] *noun* lack of work; **mass unemployment** = unemployment of large numbers of workers; **unemployment benefit** *US* **unemployment compensation** = payment made to someone who is unemployed; **seasonal unemployment** = unemployment which rises and falls according to the season

tax advantages directed toward small businesses will help create jobs and reduce the unemployment rate

Toronto Star

unfair [ʌnˈfeə] *adjective* **unfair competition** = trying to do better than another company by using techniques such as importing foreign goods at very low prices or by wrongly criticizing a competitor's products; **unfair dismissal** = removing someone from a job for reasons which are not fair

unfavourable *US* **unfavorable** [ʌnˈfeɪvərəbl] *adjective* not favourable; **unfavourable balance of trade** = situation where a country imports more than it exports; **unfavourable exchange rate** = exchange rate which gives an amount of foreign currency for the home currency which is not good for trade; *the unfavourable exchange rate hit the country's exports*

unfulfilled [ˌʌnfʊlˈfɪld] *adjective* (order) which has not yet been supplied

ungeared [ʌnˈgɪəd] *adjective* with no borrowings

unilateral [ˌjuːnɪˈlætərəl] *adjective* on one side only, done by one party only; *they took the unilateral decision to cancel the contract*

unilaterally [ˌjuːnɪˈlætərəli] *adverb* by one party only; *they cancelled the contract unilaterally*

uninsured [ˌʌnɪnˈʃuəd] *adjective* not insured; *his art collection is uninsured*; *she was charged with driving while uninsured*

union [ˈjuːnjən] *noun* (a) **trade union** *or* **trades union** *US* **labor union** = organization which represents workers who are its members in discussions with management about wages and conditions of work; **union agreement** = agreement between a management and a trade union over wages and conditions of work; **union dues** *or* **union subscription** = payment made by workers to belong to a union; **union officials** = paid organizers of a union; **union recognition** = act of agreeing that a union can act on behalf of staff in a company (b) **customs union** = agreement between several countries that goods can go between them without paying duty, while goods from other countries have special duties charged on them

the blue-collar unions are the people who stand to lose most in terms of employment growth

Sydney Morning Herald

unionist [ˈjuːnjənɪst] *noun* member of a trade union

unionized [ˈjuːnjənaɪzd] *adjective* (company) where the members of staff belong to a trade union

after three days of tough negotiations, the company reached agreement with its 1,200 unionized workers

Toronto Star

unique [juːˈniːk] *adjective* special, with nothing like it; **unique selling point** *or* **unique selling proposition (USP)** = special quality of a product which makes it different from other goods and therefore more attractive to customers

unissued capital [ʌnˈɪʃuːd ˈkæpɪtl] *noun* capital which a company is authorized to issue but has not issued as shares

unit [ˈjuːnɪt] *noun* (a) single product for sale; **unit cost** = the cost of one item (i.e total product costs divided by the number of units produced); **unit price** = the price of one item (b) separate piece of equipment or furniture; **display unit** = special stand for showing goods for sale; **visual display unit** = screen attached to a computer which shows the information stored in the computer (c) (factory) **unit** = single building on an industrial estate; *as production has increased, we have moved to a larger unit on the same estate* (d) **production unit** = separate small group of workers which produces a certain product; **research unit** = separate small group of research workers (e) **monetary unit** *or* **unit of currency** = main item of currency of a country (a dollar, pound, yen, etc.); **unit of account** = standard unit used in financial transactions among members of a group, such as SDRs in the IMF (f) single share in a unit trust; **accumulation units** = units in a unit trust, where the dividend is left to accumulate as new units; **income units** = units in a unit trust, where the investor receives dividends in the form of income; **unit-linked insurance** = insurance policy which is linked to the security of units in a unit trust or fund

unite [juːˈnaɪt] *verb* to join together; *the directors united with the managers to reject the takeover bid*; **United Nations** = organization which links almost all the countries of the world to promote good relations between them

unit trust [ˈjuːnɪt ˈtrʌst] *noun* organization which takes money from small investors and invests it in stocks and shares for them under a trust deed, the investment being in the form of shares (or units) in the trust

COMMENT: unit trusts have to be authorized by the Department of Trade and Industry before they can offer units for sale to the public, although unauthorized private unit trusts exist. The US equivalent is the 'mutual fund'

unladen [ʌn'leɪdn] *adjective* empty, without a cargo; *the ship was unladen when she arrived in port*

unlawful [ʌn'lɔːfʊl] *adjective* against the law, not legal

unlimited [ʌn'lɪmɪtɪd] *adjective* with no limits; *the bank offered him unlimited credit*; **unlimited liability** = situation where a sole trader or each partner is responsible for all the firm's debts with no limit at the amount each may have to pay

unlined paper ['ʌnlaɪnd 'peɪpə] *noun* paper with no lines printed on it

unlisted [ʌn'lɪstɪd] *adjective* **unlisted securities** = shares which are not listed on the Stock Exchange

unload [ʌn'ləʊd] *verb* **(a)** to take goods off (a ship, etc.); *the ship is unloading at Hamburg*; *we need a fork-lift truck to unload the lorry*; *we unloaded the spare parts at Lagos*; *there are no unloading facilities for container ships* **(b)** to sell (shares which do not seem attractive); *we tried to unload our shareholding as soon as the company published its accounts*

unobtainable [ʌnəb'teɪnəbl] *adjective* which cannot be obtained; *this spare part is currently unobtainable*

unofficial [ʌnə'fɪʃəl] *adjective* not official; **unofficial strike** = strike by local workers which has not been approved by the main union

unofficially [ʌnə'fɪʃəli] *adverb* not officially; *the tax office told the company unofficially that it would be prosecuted*

unpaid [ʌn'peɪd] *adjective* not paid; **unpaid holiday** = holiday where the worker does not receive any pay; **unpaid invoices** = invoices which have not been paid

unprofitable [ʌn'prɒfɪtəbl] *adjective* which is not profitable

---

the airline has already eliminated a number of unprofitable flights

Duns Business Month

---

unquoted shares ['ʌnkwəʊtɪd 'ʃeəz] *plural noun* shares which have no Stock Exchange quotation

unredeemed pledge [ʌnrɪ'diːmd 'pledʒ] *noun* pledge which the borrower has not claimed back because he has not paid back his loan

unregistered [ʌn'redʒɪstəd] *adjective* (company) which has not been registered

unreliable [ʌnrɪ'laɪəbl] *adjective* which cannot be relied on; *the postal service is very unreliable*

unsealed envelope ['ʌnsiːld 'envələʊp] *noun* envelope where the flap has been pushed into the back of the envelope, not stuck down

unsecured [ʌnsɪ'kjʊəd] *adjective* **unsecured creditor** = creditor who is owed money, but has no security from the debtor for it; **unsecured debt** = debt which is not guaranteed by assets; **unsecured loan** = loan made with no security

unseen [ʌn'siːn] *adverb* not seen; **to buy something sight unseen** = to buy something without having inspected it

unsettled [ʌn'setld] *adjective* which changes often, which is upset; *the market was unsettled by the news of the failure of the takeover bid*

unskilled [ʌn'skɪld] *adjective* without any particular skill; **unskilled labour** *or* **unskilled workforce** *or* **unskilled workers**

unsocial [ʌn'səʊʃəl] *adjective* **to work unsocial hours** = to work at times (i.e. in the evening, at night or during public holidays) when most people are not at work

unsold [ʌn'səʊld] *adjective* not sold; *unsold items will be scrapped*

unsolicited [ʌnsə'lɪsɪtɪd] *adjective* which has not been asked for; *an unsolicited gift*; **unsolicited testimonial** = letter praising someone or a product without the writer having been asked to write it

unstable [ʌn'steɪbl] *adjective* not stable, changing frequently; *unstable exchange rates*

unsubsidized [ʌn'sʌbsɪdaɪzd] *adjective* with no subsidy

unsuccessful [ʌnsək'sesfʊl] *adjective* not successful; *an unsuccessful businessman*; *the project was expensive and unsuccessful*

unsuccessfully [ʌnsək'sesfəli] *adverb* with no success; *the company unsuccessfully tried to break into the South American market*

untrue [ʌn'truː] *adjective* not true

unused [ʌn'juːzd] *adjective* which has not been used; *we are trying to sell off six unused typewriters*

unwaged [ʌn'weɪdʒd] *adjective* the **unwaged** = people with no jobs (NOTE: is followed by a plural verb)

unwritten agreement [ʌn'rɪtn ə'griːmənt] *noun* agreement which has been reached in speaking (such as in a telephone conversation) but has not been written down

up [ʌp] *adverb & preposition* in a higher position, to a higher position; *the inflation rate is going up steadily*; *shares were up slightly at the end of the day*

update 1 ['ʌpdeɪt] *noun* information added to something to make it up to date; *here is the latest update on sales* **2** [ʌp'deɪt] *verb* to revise something so that it is always up to date; *the figures are updated annually*

up front ['ʌp 'frʌnt] *adverb* in advance; **money up front** = payment in advance; *they are asking for £100,000 up front before they will consider the deal*; *he had to put money up front before he could clinch the deal*

upgrade [ʌp'greɪd] *verb* to increase the importance of someone or of a job; *his job has been upgraded to senior manager level*

upkeep ['ʌpkiːp] *noun* cost of keeping a building or machine in good order

uplift ['ʌplɪft] *noun* increase; *the contract provides for an annual uplift of charges*

up market ['ʌp 'mɑːkɪt] *adverb* more expensive, appealing to a wealthy section of the population; **the company has decided to move up market** = the company has decided to start to produce more luxury items (NOTE: the opposite is **down market**)

upset price ['ʌpset 'praɪs] *noun* lowest price which the seller will accept at an auction

upside ['ʌpsaɪd] *noun* **upside potential** = possibility for a share to increase in value (NOTE: the opposite is **downside**)

up to ['ʌp 'tʊ] *adverb* as far as, as high as; *we will buy at prices up to £25*

up to date ['ʌp tə 'deɪt] *adjective & adverb* current, recent or modern; *an up-to-date computer system*; **to bring something up to date** = to add the latest information or equipment to something; **to keep something up to date** = to keep adding information to something so that it always has the latest information in it; *we spend a lot of time keeping our mailing list up to date*

upturn ['ʌptɜːn] *noun* movement towards higher sales or profits; *an upturn in the economy*; *an upturn in the market*

upward ['ʌpwəd] *adjective* towards a higher position; *an upward movement*

upwards ['ʌpwədz] *adverb* towards a higher position; *the market moved upwards after the news of the budget* (NOTE: American English uses **upward** as both adjective and adverb)

urgent ['ɜːdʒənt] *adjective* which has to be done quickly; *this is an urgent delivery - it has to be in New York tomorrow afternoon*

urgently ['ɜːdʒəntli] *adverb* immediately

usage ['juːzɪdʒ] *noun* how something is used

usance ['juːzəns] *noun* the time between the date when a bill of exchange is presented and the date when it is paid

use 1 [juːs] *noun* way in which something can be used; **directions for use** = instructions on how to run a machine; **to make use of something** = to use something; **in use** = being worked; *the computer is in use twenty-four hours a day*; **items for personal use** = items which a person will use for himself, not on behalf of the company; **he has the use of a company car** = he has a company car which he uses privately; **land zoned for industrial use** = land where planning permission has been given to build factories **2** [juːz] *verb* to take a machine, a company, a process, etc., and work with it; *we use airmail for all our overseas* *correspondence*; *the photocopier is being used all the time*; *they use freelancers for most of their work*

useful ['juːsfʊl] *adjective* which can help

user ['juːzə] *noun* person who uses something; **end user** = person who actually uses a product; **user's guide** *or* **handbook** *or* **manual** = book showing someone how to use something

user-friendly ['juːzə'frendli] *adjective* which a user finds easy to work; *these programs are really user-friendly*

USP = UNIQUE SELLING POINT, UNIQUE SELLING PROPOSITION

usual ['juːʒʊəl] *adjective* normal or ordinary; *our usual terms or usual conditions are thirty days' credit*; *the usual practice is to have the contract signed by the MD*; *the usual hours of work are from 9.30 to 5.30*

usury ['juːʒəri] *noun* lending money at high interest

utility [juˈtɪləti] *noun* public service company, such as one that supplies water, gas or electricity or runs public transport; *shares in utility companies or utilities offer good dividends*

utilization [juːtɪlaɪˈzeɪʃən] *noun* making use of something; **capacity utilization** = using something as much as possible

```
control       permits       the
manufacturer   to   react   to
changing   conditions   on   the
plant floor and to keep people
and machines at a high level
of utilization
```
Duns Business Month

utilize ['juːtɪlaɪz] *verb* to use

Vv

vacancy ['veɪkənsi] *noun* **(a)** job which is not filled; *we advertised a vacancy in the local press*; *we have been unable to fill the vacancy for a skilled machinist*; *they have a vacancy for a secretary*; **job vacancies** = jobs which are empty and need people to do them **(b)** empty place, empty room; **vacancy rate** = (i) average number of rooms empty in a hotel over a period of time, shown as a percentage of the total number of rooms; (ii) average number of office buildings, shops, etc., which are not let at a particular time

vacant ['veɪkənt] *adjective* empty, not occupied; **vacant possession** = being able to occupy a property immediately after buying it because it is empty; *the house is for sale with vacant possession*; **situations vacant** *or* **appointments vacant** = list (in a newspaper) of jobs which are available

> the current vacancy rate in Tokyo stands at 7%. The supply of vacant office space, if new buildings are built at the current rate, is expected to take up to five years to absorb
>
> *Nikkei Weekly*

vacate [və'keɪt] *verb* **to vacate the premises** = to leave premises, so that they become empty

vacation [və'keɪʃən] *noun* **(a)** *GB* period when the law courts are closed **(b)** *US* holiday, period when people are not working; *the CEO is on vacation in Montana*

valid ['vælɪd] *adjective* **(a)** which is acceptable because it is true; *that is not a valid argument or excuse* **(b)** which can be used lawfully; *the contract is not valid if it has not been witnessed*; *ticket which is*

valid for three months; *he was carrying a valid passport*

validate ['vælɪdeɪt] *verb* **(a)** to check to see if something is correct; *the document was validated by the bank* **(b)** to make (something) valid

validation [vælɪ'deɪʃən] *noun* act of making something valid

validity [və'lɪdəti] *noun* being valid; **period of validity** = length of time for which a document is valid

valorem [və'lɔːrəm] *see* AD VALOREM

valuable ['væljʊbl] *adjective* which is worth a lot of money; **valuable property** *or* **valuables** = personal items which are worth a lot of money

valuation [vælju'eɪʃən] *noun* estimate of how much something is worth; *to ask for a valuation of a property before making an offer for it*; **stock valuation** = estimating the value of stock at the end of an accounting period; **to buy a shop with stock at valuation** = when buying a shop, to pay for the stock the same price as its value as estimated by the valuer; **stock market valuation** = value of a company based on the current market price of its shares

value ['væljuː] **1** *noun* amount of money which something is worth; *he imported goods to the value of £250*; *the fall in the value of sterling*; *the valuer put the value of the stock at £25,000*; **good value (for money)** = a bargain, something which is worth the price paid for it; *that restaurant gives value for money*; *buy that computer now - it is very good value*; *holidays in Italy are good value because of the exchange rate*; **to rise in value** *or* **to fall in value** = to be worth more or less; **added**

value *or* **value added** = amount added to the value of a product or service, being the difference between its cost and the amount received when it is sold (wages, taxes, etc., are deducted from the added value to give the profit); *see also* VALUE ADDED TAX; **asset value** = value of a company calculated by adding together all its assets; **book value** = value as recorded in the company's accounts; **'sample only - of no commercial value'** = not worth anything if sold; **declared value** = value of goods entered on a customs declaration form; **discounted value** = difference between the face value of a share and its lower market price; **face value** = value written on a coin, banknote or share; **market value** = value of an asset, of a product or of a company, if sold today; **par value** = value written on a share certificate; **scarcity value** = value of something which is worth a lot because it is rare and there is a large demand for it; **surrender value** = money which an insurer will pay if an insurance policy is given up before maturity date **2** *verb* to estimate how much money something is worth; *he valued the stock at £25,000; we are having the jewellery valued for insurance*

Value Added Tax ['vælju: 'ædɪd 'tæks] *noun* tax imposed as a percentage of the invoice value of goods and services; *see also* VAT

valuer ['væljʊə] *noun* person who estimates how much money something is worth

van [væn] *noun* small goods vehicle; **delivery van** = van for delivering goods to customers

variability [veərɪə'bɪləti] *noun* being variable

variable ['veərɪəbl] *adjective* which changes; **variable costs** = money paid to produce a product which increases with the quantity made (such as wages, raw materials)

variance ['veərɪəns] *noun* difference; **budget variance** = difference between the cost as estimated for the budget, and the actual cost; **at variance with** = which does not agree with; *the actual sales are at variance with the sales reported by the reps*

variation [veərɪ'eɪʃən] *noun* amount by which something changes; **seasonal variations** = changes which take place because of the seasons; *seasonal variations in buying patterns*

variety [və'raɪəti] *noun* different types of things; *the shop stocks a variety of goods; we had a variety of visitors at the office today;* US **variety store** = shop selling a wide range of usually cheap items

vary ['veəri] *verb* to change or to differ; *the gross margin varies from quarter to quarter; we try to prevent the flow of production from varying in the factory*

VAT ['vi:eɪ'ti: or væt] = VALUE ADDED TAX; *the invoice includes VAT at 17.5%; the government is proposing to increase VAT to 22%; some items (such as books) are zero-rated for VAT; he does not charge VAT because he asks for payment in cash;* **VAT declaration** = statement declaring VAT income to the VAT office; **VAT invoicing** = sending of an invoice including VAT; **VAT invoice** = invoice which shows VAT separately; **VAT inspector** = government official who examines VAT returns and checks that VAT is being paid; **VAT office** = government office dealing with the collection of VAT in an area

COMMENT: In the UK, VAT is organized by the Customs and Excise Department, and not by the Treasury. It is applied at each stage in the process of making or selling a product or service. Company 'A' charges VAT for their work, which is bought by Company 'B', and pays the VAT collected from 'B' to the Customs and Excise; Company 'B' can reclaim the VAT element in Company 'A''s invoice from the Customs and Excise, but will charge VAT on their work in their invoice to Company 'C'. Each company along the line charges VAT and pays it to the Customs and Excise, but claims back any VAT charged to them. The final consumer pays a price which includes VAT, and which is the final VAT revenue paid to the Customs and Excise. Any company or individual should register for VAT if their annual turnover or income is above a certain level

the directive means that the services of stockbrokers and managers of authorized unit trusts are now exempt from VAT; previously they were liable to VAT at the standard rate. Zero-rating for stockbrokers' services is still available as before, but only where the recipient of the service belongs outside the EC

Accountancy

VATman *or* **vatman** ['vætmæn] *noun* VAT inspector

VDU *or* **VDT** ['viːdiːˈjuː or 'viːdiːˈtiː] = VISUAL DISPLAY UNIT *or* VISUAL DISPLAY TERMINAL

vehicle ['viːɪkl] *noun* machine with wheels, used to carry goods or passengers on a road; **commercial vehicle** *or* **goods vehicle** = van or truck used for business purposes; **heavy goods vehicle** = very large lorry; *goods vehicles can park in the loading bay*

vending ['vendɪŋ] *noun* selling; **(automatic) vending machine** = machine which provides drinks, cigarettes, etc., when a coin is put in

vendor ['vendə] *noun* **(a)** person who sells (a property); *the solicitor acting on behalf of the vendor* **(b)** **street vendor** = person who sells food or small items in the street

venture ['ventʃə] **1** *noun* business or commercial deal which involves a risk; *he lost money on several import ventures*; *she has started a new venture - a computer shop*; **joint venture** = very large business project where two or more companies, often from different countries, join together, sometimes forming a joint company to manage the project; **venture capital** = capital for investment which may easily be lost in risky projects, but can also provide high returns **2** *verb* to risk (money)

the Securities and Exchange Board of India allowed new companies to enter the primary market provided venture capital funds took up 10 per cent of the equity. At present, new companies are allowed to make initial public offerings provided their projects have been appraised by banks or financial institutions which take up 10 per cent of the equity

The Hindu

along with the stock market boom of the 1980s, the venture capitalists piled more and more funds into the buyout business, backing bigger and bigger deals with ever more extravagant financing structures

Guardian

venue ['venjuː] *noun* place where a meeting is to be held; *we have changed the venue for the conference*; *what is the venue for the exhibition?*

verbal ['vɜːbəl] *adjective* using spoken words, not writing; **verbal agreement** = agreement which is spoken (such as over the telephone)

verbally ['vɜːbəli] *adverb* using spoken words, not writing; *they agreed to the terms verbally, and then started to draft the contract*

verification [verɪfɪˈkeɪʃən] *noun* checking if something is correct; *the shipment was allowed into the country after verification of the documents by customs*

verify ['verɪfaɪ] *verb* to check to see if something is correct

vertical ['vɜːtɪkəl] *adjective* upright, straight up or down; **vertical communication** = communication between senior managers via the middle management to the workers; **vertical integration** = joining two businesses together which deal with different stages in the production or sale of the same product

vessel ['vesl] *noun* ship; **merchant vessel** = commercial ship which carries a cargo

vested interest ['vestɪd 'ɪntrest] *noun* special interest in keeping an existing state of affairs; **she has a vested interest in keeping the business working** = she wants to keep the business working because she will make more money if it does

vet [vet] *verb* to examine something carefully; *all candidates have to be vetted by the managing director; the contract has been sent to the legal department for vetting* (NOTE: **vetting - vetted**)

via ['vaɪə] *preposition* using (a means or a route); *the shipment is going via the Suez Canal; we are sending the cheque via our office in New York; they sent the message via email*

viability [vaɪə'bɪləti] *noun* being viable; being able to make a profit

viable ['vaɪəbl] *adjective* which can work in practice; **not commercially viable** = not likely to make a profit

vice- [vaɪs] *prefix* deputy, second-in-command; *he is the vice-chairman of an industrial group; she was appointed to the vice-chairmanship of the committee*

vice-president ['vaɪs'prezɪdənt] *noun* US one of the executive directors of a company; **senior vice-president** = one of a few main executive directors of a company

view [vjuː] *noun* way of thinking about something; *we asked the sales manager for his views on the reorganization of the reps' territories; the chairman takes the view that credit should never be longer than thirty days;* **to take the long view** = to plan for a long period before your current investment will become profitable; **in view of** = because of; *in view of the falling exchange rate, we have redrafted our sales forecasts*

vigorous ['vɪgərəs] *adjective* energetic, very active; *we are planning a vigorous publicity campaign*

VIP ['viːaɪ'piː] = VERY IMPORTANT PERSON; **VIP lounge** = special room at an airport for important travellers; **we laid on VIP treatment for our visitors** *or* **we gave our visitors a VIP reception** = we

arranged for our visitors to be looked after and entertained well

virement ['vaɪəmənt] *noun* (*administration*) transfer of money from one account to another or from one section of a budget to another

visa ['viːzə] *noun* special document, special stamp in a passport which allows someone to enter a country; *you will need a visa before you go to the USA; he filled in his visa application form;* **entry visa** = visa allowing someone to enter a country; **multiple entry visa** = visa allowing someone to enter a country many times; **tourist visa** = visa which allows a person to visit a country for a short time on holiday; **transit visa** = visa which allows someone to spend a short time in one country while travelling to another country

visible ['vɪzəbl] *adjective* which can be seen; **visible imports** *or* **exports** = real products which are imported or exported (NOTE: the opposite is **invisible**)

visit ['vɪzɪt] **1** *noun* short stay in a place; *we are expecting a visit from our German agents; he is on a business visit to London; we had a visit from the VAT inspector* **2** *verb* to go to a place, to see someone for a short time; *he spent a week in Scotland, visiting clients in Edinburgh and Glasgow; the trade delegation visited the Ministry of Commerce*

visitor ['vɪzɪtə] *noun* **(a)** person who visits; *the chairman showed the Japanese visitors round the factory;* **visitors' bureau** = office which deals with visitors' questions **(b)** person who visits a website

> During the week to December 19, the number of visitors to consumer e-commerce sites jumped 37% compared with the same week last year
>
> *Times*

visual display terminal (VDT) *or* **visual display unit (VDU)** ['vɪzjʊəl dɪs'pleɪ 'tɜːmɪnəl *or* 'vɪzjʊəl dɪs'pleɪ 'juːnɪt] *noun* screen attached to a computer which shows the information stored in the computer

vivos *see* INTER VIVOS

vocation [vəˈkeɪʃən] *noun* type of job which you feel you want to do; wanting to be in a certain type of job; *he followed his vocation and became an architect*

vocational [vəˈkeɪʃənl] *adjective* referring to a choice of job; **vocational guidance** = helping young people to choose a suitable job; **vocational training** = training for a particular job

void [vɔɪd] **1** *adjective* not legally valid; **the contract was declared null and void** = the contract was said to be no longer valid **2** *verb* **to void a contract** = to make a contract invalid

volatile [ˈvɒlətaɪl] *adjective* (market or price) which is not stable, but which rises and falls sharply; *the share has been very volatile since it was launched*

> blue chip stocks are the least volatile while smaller stocks are the most volatile
>
> *The Times*

> the investment markets appear to have become ever more volatile, with interest rates moving at times to extreme levels, and the stock market veering wildly from boom to slump and back again
>
> *Financial Times Review*

> the FTSE 100 Index ended another volatile session a net 96.3 easier at 6027
>
> *Financial Times*

volatility [vɒləˈtɪlɪti] *noun* being volatile; *investors are recommended to keep their money in building society accounts because the increasing volatility of the stock market*

> while the technology sector has certainly captured the imagination of private investors, the enthusiasm it has aroused among them is likely to cause extreme share price volatility in the short term
>
> *Financial Times*

volume [ˈvɒljuːm] *noun* quantity of items; **volume business** = dealing in large quantities of items; **volume discount** = discount given to a customer who buys a

large quantity of goods; **volume of output** = number of items produced; **volume of sales** *or* **sales volume** = number of items sold; **low** *or* **high volume of sales** = small or large number of items sold; **volume of trade** *or* **volume of business** = number of items sold, number of shares sold on the Stock Exchange during a day's trading; *the company has maintained the same volume of business in spite of the recession*

voluntarily [ˈvɒləntərəli] *adverb* without being forced or paid

voluntary [ˈvɒləntəri] *adjective* (a) done without being forced; **voluntary liquidation** = situation where a company itself decides it must close and sell its assets; **voluntary redundancy** = situation where a worker asks to be made redundant (b) done without being paid; **voluntary organization** = organization which does not receive funding from the government, but relies on contributions from the public

vostro account [ˈvɒstrəʊ əˈkaʊnt] *noun* account held by a correspondent bank for a foreign bank; *see also* **NOSTRO ACCOUNT**

vote [vəʊt] **1** *noun* marking a paper, holding up your hand, etc., to show your opinion or to show who you want to be elected; **to take a vote on a proposal** *or* **to put a proposal to the vote** = to ask people present at a meeting to say if they do or do not agree with the proposal; **block vote** = casting of a large number of votes (such as of a trade union delegation) all together in the same way; **casting vote** = vote used by the chairman in the case where the votes for and against a proposal are equal; *the chairman has the casting vote*; *he used his casting vote to block the motion*; **postal vote** = election where the voters send in their voting papers by post **2** *verb* to show an opinion by marking a paper or by holding up your hand at a meeting; *the meeting voted to close the factory*; *52% of the members voted for Mr Smith as chairman*; **to vote for a proposal** *or* **to vote against a proposal** = to say that you agree or do not agree with a proposal; **two directors were voted off the board at the AGM** = the AGM voted to dismiss two directors; **she was voted on to the**

committee = she was elected a member of the committee

voter ['vəʊtə] *noun* person who votes

voting ['vəʊtɪŋ] *noun* act of making a vote; **voting paper** = paper on which the voter puts a cross to show for whom he wants to vote; **voting rights** = rights of shareholders to voting at company meetings; **voting shares** = shares which give the holder the right to vote at company meetings; **non-voting shares** = shares which do not allow the shareholder to vote at company meetings

voucher ['vaʊtʃə] *noun* (a) paper which is given instead of money; **cash voucher** = paper which can be exchanged for cash; *with every £20 of purchases, the customer gets a cash voucher to the value of £2*; **gift voucher** = card, bought in a store, which is given as a present and which must be exchanged in that store for goods; **luncheon voucher** = ticket, given by an employer to a worker, which can be exchanged in a restaurant for food (b) written document from an auditor to show that the accounts are correct or that money has really been paid

voyage ['vɔɪdʒ] *noun* long journey by ship

Ww

wage [weɪdʒ] *noun* money paid (usually in cash each week) to a worker for work done; *she is earning a good wage or good wages in the supermarket*; **basic wage** = normal pay without any extra payments; *the basic wage is £110 a week, but you can expect to earn more than that with overtime*; **hourly wage** *or* **wage per hour** = amount of money paid for an hour's work; **minimum wage** = lowest hourly wage which a company can legally pay its workers; **wage adjustments** = changes made to wages; **wage claim** = asking for an increase in wages; **wages clerk** = office worker who deals with the pay of other workers; **wage differentials** = differences in salary between workers in similar types of jobs; **wage freeze** *or* **freeze on wages** = period when wages are not allowed to increase; **wage levels** = rates of pay for different types of work; **wage negotiations** = discussions between management and workers about pay; **wage packet** = envelope containing money and pay slip; **wages policy** = government policy on what percentage increases should be paid to workers; **wage-price spiral** = situation where price rises encourage higher wage demands which in turn make prices rise; **wage scale** = list of wages, showing different rates of pay for different jobs in the same company (NOTE: the plural **wages** is more usual when referring to the money earned, but **wage** is used before other nouns)

> COMMENT: the term 'wages' refers to weekly or hourly pay for workers, usually paid in cash. For workers paid by a monthly cheque, the term used is 'salary'

real wages have been held down dramatically: they have risen at an annual rate of only 1% in the last two years

Sunday Times

European economies are being held back by rigid labor markets and wage structures

Duns Business Month

wage-earner [ˈweɪdʒˈɜːnə] *noun* person who earns money paid weekly in a job

wage-earning [ˈweɪdʒˈɜːnɪŋ] *adjective* **the wage-earning population** = people who have jobs and earn money

wagon [ˈwægən] *noun* goods truck used on the railway

waive [weɪv] *verb* to give up (a right); *he waived his claim to the estate*; **to waive a payment** = to say that payment is not necessary

waiver [ˈweɪvə] *noun* giving up (a right), removing the conditions (of a rule); *if you want to work without a permit, you will have to apply for a waiver*; **waiver clause** = clause in a contract giving the conditions under which the rights in the contract can be given up

walk [wɔːk] *verb* to go on foot; *he walks to the office every morning*; *the visitors walked round the factory*

walk off [ˈwɔːk ˈɒf] *verb* to go on strike, to stop working and leave an office or factory; *the builders walked off the site because they said it was too dangerous*

walk out [ˈwɔːk ˈaʊt] *verb* to go on strike, to stop working and leave an office or factory; *the whole workforce walked out in protest*

walk-out [ˈwɔːkaʊt] *noun* strike, stopping work; *production has been held up by the* *walk-out of the workers* (NOTE: plural is **walk-outs**)

wallet ['wɒlɪt] *noun* small leather case in which you can keep bank notes, credit cards, etc., in your pocket; **wallet envelope** = type of envelope with the flap along the longer side (an envelope with a flap at the end, on the shorter side, is called a 'pocket envelope'); **wallet file** = cardboard file, with a wide pocket on one side and a flap which folds down

Wall Street ['wɔːl 'striːt] *noun* street in New York where the Stock Exchange is situated; the American financial centre; *Wall Street analysts predict a rise in interest rates*; *she writes the Wall Street column in the newspaper*

want [wɒnt] *noun* thing which is needed; **want ads** = advertisements listed in a newspaper under special headings (such as 'property for sale', or 'jobs wanted'); **to draw up a wants list** = to make a list of things which you need

war [wɔː] *noun* fighting or argument between countries or companies; *consumers benefited from lower prices following the price war*

warehouse ['weəhaʊs] **1** *noun* large building where goods are stored; **bonded warehouse** = warehouse where goods are stored until excise duty has been paid; **warehouse capacity** = space available in a warehouse; **price ex warehouse** = price for a product which is to be collected from the manufacturer's or agent's warehouse and so does not include delivery **2** *verb* to store (goods) in a warehouse; *our offices are in London but our stock is warehoused in Scotland*

warehouseman ['weəhaʊsmən] *noun* person who works in a warehouse

warehousing ['weəhaʊzɪŋ] *noun* act of storing goods; *warehousing costs are rising rapidly*

warn [wɔːn] *verb* to say that there is a possible danger; *he warned the shareholders that the dividend might be cut*; *the government warned of possible import duties* (NOTE: you warn someone of something, or warn that something may happen)

warning ['wɔːnɪŋ] *noun* notice of possible danger; *warning notices were put up around the construction site*; **to issue a profits warning** = to state that profits will not be as good as last year, or much as predicted

warrant ['wɒrənt] **1** *noun* official document which allows someone to do something; **dividend warrant** = cheque which makes payment of a dividend; **share warrant** = document which says that someone has the right to a number of shares in a company **2** *verb* **(a)** to guarantee; *all the spare parts are warranted* **(b)** to show that something is reasonable; *the company's volume of trade with the USA does not warrant six trips a year to New York by the sales director*

the rights issue will grant shareholders free warrants to subscribe for further new shares

Financial Times

warrantee [wɒrən'tiː] *noun* person who is given a warranty

warrantor ['wɒrəntɔː] *noun* person who gives a warranty

warranty ['wɒrənti] *noun* **(a)** guarantee, a legal document which promises that a machine will work properly or that an item is of good quality; *the car is sold with a twelve-month warranty*; *the warranty covers spare parts but not labour costs* **(b)** promise in a contract; **breach of warranty** = supplying goods which do not meet the standards of the warranty applied to them **(c)** statement made by an insured person which declares that the facts stated by him are true

wastage ['weɪstɪdʒ] *noun* amount lost by being wasted; *allow 10% extra material for wastage*; **natural wastage** = losing workers because they resign or retire, not because they are made redundant or are sacked; *the company is hoping to avoid redundancies and reduce its staff by natural wastage*

waste [weɪst] **1** *noun* rubbish, things which are not used; *the company was fined for putting industrial waste into the river*; *it is a waste of time asking the chairman for a rise*; *that computer is a waste of* *money - there are plenty of cheaper models which would do the work just as well* **2** *adjective* not used; *waste materials are collected from the factory each week*; *cardboard is made from recycled waste paper*; **waste paper basket** *US* **wastebasket** = container near an office desk into which pieces of rubbish can be put **3** *verb* to use more than is needed; *to waste money or paper or electricity or time*; *the MD does not like people wasting his time with minor details*; *we turned off all the heating so as not to waste energy*

COMMENT: industrial waste has no value, as opposed to scrap which may be sold to a scrap dealer

---

wastebasket ['weistbɑːskɪt] *noun US* = WASTE PAPER BASKET

wasteful ['weistfʊl] *adjective* which wastes a lot of something; *this photocopier is very wasteful of paper*

wasting asset ['weistɪŋ 'æsɪt] *noun* asset which becomes gradually less valuable as time goes by (for example a short lease on a property)

waterproof ['wɔːtəpruːf] *adjective* which will not let water through; *the parts are sent in waterproof packing*

waybill ['weibɪl] *noun* list of goods carried, made out by the carrier

weak [wiːk] *adjective* not strong, not active; **weak market** = share market where prices tend to fall because there are no buyers; **share prices remained weak** = share prices did not rise

weaken ['wiːkən] *verb* to become weak; **the market weakened** = share prices fell

the Fed started to ease monetary policy months ago as the first stories appeared about weakening demand in manufacturing industry
Sunday Times

weakness ['wiːknəs] *noun* being weak

indications of weakness in the US economy were contained in figures from the Fed on industrial production
Financial Times

wealth [welθ] *noun* large quantity of money owned by a person; **wealth tax** = tax on money, property or investments owned by a person

wealthy ['welθi] *adjective* very rich; *the company is owned by a wealthy American businessman*

wear and tear ['weər ən 'teə] *noun* **fair wear and tear** = acceptable damage caused by normal use; *the insurance policy covers most damage but not fair wear and tear to the machine*

web [web] *noun* **the Web** = the World Wide Web, the thousands of web sites and web pages within the Internet, which users can visit; **web site** = position on the Web, which is created by a company, organization or individual, and which anyone can visit; *how many hits did we have on our web site last week?*; **web page** = single file of text and graphics, forming part of a web site

week [wiːk] *noun* period of seven days (from Monday to Sunday); **to be paid by the week** = to be paid a certain amount of money each week; *he earns £500 a week or per week*; *she works thirty-five hours per week or she works a thirty-five-hour week*

weekday ['wiːkdei] *noun* normal working day (not Saturday or Sunday)

weekly ['wiːkli] *adjective* done every week; *the weekly rate for the job is £250*; **a weekly magazine** *or* **a weekly** = magazine which is published each week

weigh [wei] *verb* **(a)** to measure how heavy something is; *he weighed the packet at the post office* **(b)** to have a certain weight; *the packet weighs twenty-five grams*

weighbridge ['weibridʒ] *noun* platform for weighing a lorry and its load

weighing machine ['weiiŋ mə'ʃiːn] *noun* machine which measures how heavy a thing or a person is

weight [weit] *noun* measurement of how heavy something is; **to sell fruit by weight** = the price is per pound or per kilo of the fruit; **false weight** = weight on a shop scales which is wrong and so cheats customers; **gross weight** = weight of both the container and its contents; **net weight** =

weight of goods after deducting the packing material and container; **to give short weight** = to give less than you should; **inspector of weights and measures** = government official who inspects goods sold in shops to see if the quantities and weights are correct

weighted ['weɪtɪd] *adjective* **weighted average** = average which is calculated taking several factors into account, giving some more value than others; **weighted index** = index where some important items are given more value than less important ones

weighting ['weɪtɪŋ] *noun* additional salary or wages paid to compensate for living in an expensive part of the country; *salary plus a London weighting*

welfare ['welfeə] *noun* **(a)** looking after people; *the chairman is interested in the welfare of the workers' families*; **welfare state** = country which looks after the health, education, etc., of the people **(b)** money paid by the government to people who need it

California become the latest state for enact a program forcing welfare recipients to work for their benefits
Fortune

well-known [wel'nəʊn] *adjective* known by many people

well-paid [wel'peɪd] *adjective* earning a high salary

wharf [wɔːf] *noun* place in a dock where a ship can tie up to load or unload (NOTE: plural is **wharfs** or **wharves**)

wharfage ['wɔːfɪdʒ] *noun* charge for tying up at a wharf

wharfinger ['wɔːfɪndʒə] *noun* person who works on a wharf

wheeler-dealer ['wiːlə'diːlə] *noun* person who lives on money from a series of profitable business deals

whereof [weər'ɒv] *adverb (formal)* in witness whereof I sign my hand = I sign as a witness that this is correct

white-collar ['waɪt'kɒlə] *adjective* referring to office workers; **white-collar crime** = crime (especially fraud) committed by office workers, such as

computer analysts; **white-collar union** = trade union formed of white-collar workers; **white-collar worker** = worker in an office, not in a factory

the share of white-collar occupations in total employment rose from 44 per cent to 49 per cent
Sydney Morning Herald

white goods ['waɪt 'gʊdz] *plural noun* **(a)** machines (such as refrigerators, washing machines) which are used in the kitchen **(b)** sheets, towels, etc.

white knight ['waɪt 'naɪt] *noun* person or company which rescues a firm in financial difficulties, especially one which saves a firm from being taken over by an unacceptable purchaser

White Paper ['waɪt 'peɪpə] *noun GB* report issued by the government as a statement of government policy on a particular problem; *compare* **GREEN PAPER**

white sale ['waɪt 'seɪl] *noun* sale of sheets, towels, etc.

whole-life insurance ['həʊllaɪf ɪn'ʃʊərəns] *noun* insurance where the insured person pays a fixed premium each year and the insurance company pays a sum when he or she dies (also called 'whole-of-life assurance')

wholesale ['həʊlseɪl] *adjective & adverb* buying goods from manufacturers and selling in large quantities to traders who then sell in smaller quantities to the general public; *I persuaded him to give us a wholesale discount*; **wholesale dealer** = person who buys in bulk from manufacturers and sells to retailers; **wholesale price index** = index showing the rises and falls of prices of manufactured goods as they leave the factory; **he buys wholesale and sells retail** = he buys goods in bulk at a wholesale discount and then sells in small quantities to the public

wholesaler ['həʊlseɪlə] *noun* person who buys goods in bulk from manufacturers and sells them to retailers

wholly-owned subsidiary ['həʊlɪaʊnd səb'sɪdjərɪ] *noun* company which is owned completely by another company

wildcat strike ['waɪldkæt 'straɪk] *noun* strike organized suddenly by workers without the main union office knowing about it

will [wɪl] *noun* legal document where someone says what should happen to his property when he dies; *he wrote his will in 1984*; *according to her will, all her property is left to her children*

> COMMENT: a will should best be drawn up by a solicitor; it can also be written on a form which can be bought from a stationery shop. To be valid, a will must be dated and witnessed by a third party (i.e., by someone who is not mentioned in the will)

win [wɪn] *verb* to be successful; **to win a contract** = to be successful in tendering for a contract; *the company announced that it had won a contract worth £25m to supply buses and trucks* (NOTE: **winning - won**)

windfall ['wɪnfɔːl] *noun* sudden winning of money, sudden profit which is not expected; **windfall profit** = sudden profit which is not expected; **windfall (profits) tax** = tax on sudden profits

winding up ['waɪndɪŋ 'ʌp] *noun* liquidation, closing of a company and selling its assets; **compulsory winding up** = liquidation which is ordered by a court; **a compulsory winding up order** = order from a court saying that a company must be wound up

window ['wɪndəʊ] *noun* (a) opening in a wall, with glass in it; **shop window** = large window in a shop front, where customers can see goods displayed; **window display** = display of goods in a shop window; **window envelope** = envelope with a hole in it covered with plastic like a window, so that the address on the letter inside can be seen; **window shopping** = looking at goods in shop windows, without buying anything (b) short period when something is available; **window of opportunity** = short period which allows an action to take place

window dressing ['wɪndəʊ 'dresɪŋ] *noun* (a) putting goods on display in a shop window, so that they attract customers (b) putting on a display to make a business seem better or more profitable or more efficient than it really is

wind up ['waɪnd 'ʌp] *verb* (a) to end (a meeting); *he wound up the meeting with a vote of thanks to the committee* (b) to **wind up a company** = to put a company into liquidation; *the court ordered the company to be wound up* (NOTE: **winding - wound**)

WIP = WORK IN PROGRESS

wire ['waɪə] **1** *noun* telegram; *to send someone a wire* **2** *verb* to send a telegram to (someone); *he wired the head office to say that the deal had been signed*

withdraw [wɪθ'drɔː] *verb* (a) to take (money) out of an account; *to withdraw money from the bank or from your account*; *you can withdraw up to £50 from any cash machine by using your card* (b) to take back (an offer); **one of the company's backers has withdrawn** = he stopped supporting the company financially; *we expect they will withdraw their takeover bid*; *the chairman asked him to withdraw the remarks he has made about the finance director* (NOTE: **withdrawing - withdrew - has withdrawn**)

withdrawal [wɪθ'drɔːəl] *noun* removing money from an account; *to give seven days' notice of withdrawal*; *withdrawals from bank accounts reached a peak in the week before Christmas*; **withdrawal without penalty at seven days' notice** = money can be taken out of a deposit account, without losing any interest, provided that seven days' notice has been given

withholding tax [wɪθ'həʊldɪŋ 'tæks] *noun* (i) tax which removes money from interest or dividends before they are paid to the investor (usually applied to non-resident investors); (ii) any amount deducted from a person's income which is an advance payment of tax owed (such as PAYE); (iii) *US* income tax deducted from the paycheck of a worker before he is paid

with profits ['wɪθ 'prɒfɪts] *adverb* (insurance policy) which guarantees the policyholder a share in the profits of the fund in which the premiums are invested

witness ['wɪtnəs] **1** *noun* person who sees something happen; **to act as a witness to a document** *or* **a signature** = to sign a document to show that you have watched the main signatory sign it; *the MD signed as a witness*; *the contract has to be signed in front of two witnesses* **2** *verb* to sign (a document) to show that you guarantee that the other signatures on it are genuine; *the two directors were asked to witness the agreement or the signature*

wobbler ['wɒblə] *noun* **shelf wobbler** = card placed on the shelf in a shop to promote a product

wording ['wɜːdɪŋ] *noun* series of words; *did you read the wording on the contract?*

word-processing ['wɜːd'prəʊsesɪŋ] *noun* working with words, using a computer to produce, check and change texts, reports, letters, etc.; *load the word-processing program before you start keyboarding*; **word-processing bureau** = office which specializes in word-processing for other companies

word-processor ['wɜːd'prəʊsesə] *noun* small computer (or typewriter with a computer in it), used for working with words to produce texts, reports, letters, etc.

work [wɜːk] **1** *noun* **(a)** things done using the hands or brain; **casual work** = work where the workers are hired for a short period; **clerical work** = work done in an office; **manual work** = heavy work done by hand; **work in progress (WIP)** = value of goods being manufactured which are not complete at the end of an accounting period **(b)** job, something done to earn money; *he goes to work by bus*; *she never gets home from work before 8 p.m.*; *his work involves a lot of travelling*; *he is still looking for work*; *she has been out of work for six months*; **work permit** = official document which allows someone who is not a citizen to work in a country **2** *verb* **(a)** to do things with your hands or brain, for money; *the factory is working hard to complete the order*; *she works better now that she has been promoted*; **to work a machine** = to make a machine function; **to work to rule** = to work strictly according to rules agreed between the company and the trade union, and therefore

work very slowly **(b)** to have a paid job; *she works in an office*; *he works at Smith's*; *he is working as a cashier in a supermarket*

> the control of materials from purchased parts through work in progress to finished goods provides manufacturers with an opportunity to reduce the amount of money tied up in materials
> *Duns Business Month*

> the quality of the work environment demanded by employers and employees alike
> *Lloyd's List*

workaholic [wɜːkə'hɒlɪk] *noun* person who works all the time, and is unhappy when not working

worker ['wɜːkə] *noun* **(a)** person who is employed; **blue-collar worker** = manual worker in a factory; **casual worker** = worker who can be hired for a short period; **clerical worker** = person who works in an office; **factory worker** = person who works in a factory; **manual worker** = worker who works with his hands; **white-collar worker** = office worker; **worker director** = director of a company who is a representative of the workforce; **worker representation on the board** = having a representative of the workers as a director of the company **(b)** person who works hard; *she's a real worker*

workforce ['wɜːkfɔːs] *noun* all the workers (in an office or factory)

working ['wɜːkɪŋ] *adjective* **(a)** (person) who works; *the new rules apply to the whole working population of the country*; **working partner** = partner who works in a partnership; **working party** = group of experts who study a problem; *the government has set up a working party to study the problems of industrial waste*; *Professor Smith is the chairman of the working party on computers in society* **(b)** referring to work; **working capital** = capital in cash and stocks needed for a company to be able to work; **working conditions** = general state of the place where people work (if it is hot, noisy, dark, dangerous, etc.); **the normal working**

week = the usual number of hours worked per week; *even though he is a freelance, he works a normal working week*

workload ['wɜːkləʊd] *noun* amount of work which a person has to do; *he has difficulty in coping with his heavy workload*

workman ['wɜːkmən] *noun* man who works with his hands (NOTE: plural is **workmen**)

workmanship ['wɜːkmənʃɪp] *noun* skill of a good workman; **bad** *or* **shoddy workmanship** = bad work done by a workman

work out ['wɜːk 'aʊt] *verb* (a) to calculate; *he worked out the costs on the back of an envelope*; *he worked out the discount at 15%*; *she worked out the discount on her calculator* (b) he is **working out his notice** = he is working during the time between resigning and actually leaving the company

workplace ['wɜːkpleɪs] *noun* place where you work

> every house and workplace in Britain is to be directly involved in an energy efficiency campaign
> *Times*

works [wɜːks] *noun* factory; *there is a small engineering works in the same street as our office*; *the steel works is expanding*; **works committee** *or* **works council** = committee of workers and management which discusses the organization of work in a factory; **price ex works** = price not including transport from the manufacturer's factory; **the works manager** = person in charge of a works (NOTE: not plural, and takes a singular verb)

work-sharing ['wɜːk'ʃeərɪŋ] *noun* system where two part-timers share one job

workshop ['wɜːkʃɒp] *noun* small factory

workspace ['wɜːkspeɪs] *noun* memory, the space available on a computer for temporary work

workstation ['wɜːksteɪʃn] *noun* desk with a computer terminal, printer, telephone, etc., where a word-processing operator works

work-to-rule ['wɜːktə'ruːl] *noun* working strictly according to the rules agreed between the union and management and therefore very slowly, as a protest

workweek ['wɜːkwiːk] *noun* US the usual number of hours worked per week; *she works a normal 35-hour workweek*

world [wɜːld] *noun* (a) the earth; **the world market for steel** = the possible sales of steel in the whole world; **he has world rights to a product** = he has the right to sell the product anywhere in the world (b) people in a particular business, people with a special interest; *the world of big business*; *the world of publishing or the publishing world*; *the world of lawyers or the legal world*

> the EU pays farmers 27 cents a pound for sugar and sells it on the world market for 5 cents
> *Duns Business Month*

> manufactures and services were the fastest growing sectors of world trade
> *Australian Financial Review*

World Bank ['wɜːld 'bæŋk] *noun* central bank, controlled by the United Nations, whose funds come from the member states of the UN and which lends money to member states (its official title is the International Bank for Reconstruction and Development)

World Trade Organization (WTO) ['wɜːld 'treɪd ɔːgənaɪ'zeɪʃn] international organization set up with the aim of reducing restrictions in trade between countries

worldwide ['wɜːldwaɪd] *adjective & adverb* everywhere in the world; *the company has a worldwide network of distributors*; *worldwide sales or sales worldwide have topped two million units*; *this make of computer is available worldwide*

worth [wɜːθ] **1** *adjective* having a value or a price; *don't get it repaired - it's worth only £25*; *the car is worth £6,000 on the secondhand market*; *he is worth £10m* = his property, investments, etc., would sell for £10m; **what are ten pounds worth in dollars?** = what is the equivalent of £10 in

dollars? (NOTE: always follows the verb **to be**)
2 noun value; **give me ten pounds' worth
of petrol** = give me as much petrol as £10
will buy

worthless ['wɜːθləs] adjective having no
value; **the cheque is worthless if it is not
signed**

wrap (up) ['ræp 'ʌp] verb to cover
something all over (in paper); **he wrapped
(up) the parcel in green paper**; **to
gift-wrap a present** = to wrap a present in
special coloured paper; **shrink-wrapped** =
covered in tight plastic protective cover
(NOTE: **wrapping - wrapped**)

wrapper ['ræpə] noun material which
wraps something; **the biscuits are packed
in plastic wrappers**

wrapping ['ræpɪŋ] noun **wrapping
paper** = special coloured paper for
wrapping presents; **gift-wrapping** = (i)
service in a store for wrapping presents for
customers; (ii) coloured paper for
wrapping presents; **shrink-wrapping** = act
of covering (a book, fruit, record, etc.) in a
tight plastic film

wreck [rek] **1** noun **(a)** ship which has
sunk, which has been badly damaged and
cannot float; **they saved the cargo from the
wreck**; **oil poured out of the wreck of the
tanker** **(b)** company which has collapsed;
**he managed to save some of his
investment from the wreck of the
company**; **investors lost thousands of
pounds in the wreck of the investment
trust** **2** verb to damage badly, to ruin; **they
are trying to salvage the wrecked tanker**;
**the negotiations were wrecked by the
unions**

writ [rɪt] noun legal document which
begins an action in the High Court; **the
court issued a writ to prevent the trade
union from going on strike**; **to serve
someone with a writ** or **to serve a writ on
someone** = to give someone a writ
officially, so that he has to defend it

write [raɪt] verb to put words or figures on
to paper; **she wrote a letter of complaint to
the manager**; **the telephone number is
written at the bottom of the notepaper**
(NOTE: **writing - wrote - has written**)

write back ['raɪt 'bæk] verb to give value
to an asset which has been written down or

written off (as when a bad debt is finally
paid)

write down ['raɪt 'daʊn] verb to note an
asset at a lower value than previously;
written down value; **the car is written
down in the company's books**

writedown ['raɪtdaʊn] noun noting of an
asset at a lower value

the holding company has seen
its earnings suffer from big
writedowns in conjunction
with its $1 billion loan
portfolio

Duns Business Month

write off ['raɪt 'ɒf] verb to cancel (a debt),
to remove an asset from the accounts as
having no value; **we had to write off
£20,000 in bad debts**; **two cars were
written off after the accident** = the
insurance company considered that both
cars were a total loss; **the cargo was
written off as a total loss** = the cargo was
so badly damaged that the insurers said it
had no value

$30 million from usual
company borrowings will
either be amortized or
written off in one sum

Australian Financial Review

write-off ['raɪtɒf] noun total loss or
cancellation of a bad debt, removal of an
asset's value in a company's accounts; **the
car was a write-off**; **to allow for write-offs
in the yearly accounts**

write out ['raɪt 'aʊt] verb to write in full;
**she wrote out the minutes of the meeting
from her notes**; **to write out a cheque** = to
write the words and figures on a cheque
and then sign it

writing ['raɪtɪŋ] noun something which
has been written; **to put the agreement in
writing**; **he has difficulty in reading my
writing**

wrong [rɒŋ] adjective not right or not
correct; **the total in the last column is
wrong**; **the sales director reported the
wrong figures to the meeting**; **I tried to
phone, but I got the wrong number**

wrongful ['rɒŋfʊl] adjective unlawful;
wrongful dismissal = removing someone
from a job for reasons which are wrong

wrongly ['rɒŋli] *adverb* not correctly, badly; *he wrongly invoiced Smith Ltd for £250, when he should have credited them with the same amount*

WTO = WORLD TRADE ORGANIZATION

Xx Yy Zz

X = EXTENSION

brand X ['brænd 'eks] *noun* the anonymous brand used in TV commercials to compare with the brand being advertised

Xerox ['zɪərɒks] **1** *noun* **(a)** trade mark for a type of photocopier; *to make a xerox copy of a letter*; *we must order some more xerox paper for the copier*; *we are having a new xerox machine installed tomorrow* **(b)** photocopy made with a Xerox machine; *to send the other party a xerox of the contract*; *we have sent xeroxes to each of the agents* **2** *verb* to make a photocopy with a Xerox machine; *to xerox a document*; *she xeroxed all the file*

yard [jɑːd] *noun* **(a)** measure of length (= 0.91 metres) (NOTE: can be written **yd** after figures: **10yd.** Note also that the yard is now no longer officially used in the UK) **(b)** factory which builds ships; *this yard builds mainly fishing boats*

yd = YARD

year [jɜː] *noun* period of twelve months; **calendar year** = year from January 1st to December 31st; **financial year** = the twelve month period for a firm's accounts (it does not need to be the same as a calendar year); **fiscal year** = twelve month period on which taxes are calculated (in the UK it is April 6th to April 5th of the following year); **year end** = the end of the financial year, when a company's accounts are prepared; *the accounts department has started work on the year-end accounts*; **year planner** = large wall planner covering all the days of a whole year

yearbook ['jɜːbʊk] *noun* reference book which is published each year with updated or new information

yearly ['jɜːli] *adjective* happening once a year; *we make a yearly payment of £1000*; *his yearly insurance premium has risen to £250*

yellow pages ['jeləʊ 'peɪdʒɪz] *plural noun* section of a telephone directory (printed on yellow paper) which lists businesses under various headings (such as computer shops or newsagents, etc.)

yen [jen] *noun* currency used in Japan (NOTE: usually written as ¥ before a figure: ¥2,700 (say 'two thousand seven hundred yen')

yield [jiːld] **1** *noun* money produced as a return on an investment; **current yield** = dividend calculated as a percentage of the price paid per share; *share with a current yield of 5%*; **dividend yield** = dividend expressed as a percentage of the price of a share; **earnings yield** = money earned in dividends per share as a percentage of the market price of the share; **effective yield** = actual yield shown as a percentage of the price paid; **fixed yield** = fixed percentage return which does not change; **gross yield** = profit from investments before tax is deducted; **maturity yield** *US* **yield to maturity** = calculation of the yield on a fixed-interest investment, assuming it is bought at a certain price and held to maturity **2** *verb* to produce (as interest or dividend, etc.); *government stocks which yield a small interest*; *shares which yield 10%*

> COMMENT: to work out the yield on an investment, take the gross dividend per annum, multiply it by 100 and divide by the price you paid for it (in pence): an investment paying a dividend of 20p per share and costing £3.00, is yielding 6.66%

if you wish to cut your risks
you should go for shares with
yields higher than average

Investors Chronicle

zero ['zɪərəʊ] *noun* nought, the number 0; *the code for international calls is zero zero (00)* **zero inflation** = inflation at 0%

zero-coupon bond ['zɪərəʊkuːpɒn 'bɒnd] *noun* bond which carries no interest, but which is issued at a discount and so provides a capital gain when it is redeemed at face value

zero-rated ['zɪərəʊ'reɪtɪd] *adjective* (item) which has a VAT rate of 0%

zero-rating ['zɪərəʊ'reɪtɪŋ] *noun* rating of an item at 0% VAT

ZIP code ['zɪp 'kəʊd] *noun US* numbers used to indicate a postal delivery area in an address on an envelope (NOTE: the British equivalent for this is the **postcode)**

zipper clause ['zɪpə 'klɔːz] *noun US* clause in a contract of employment which prevents any discussion of employment conditions during the term of the contract

zone [zəʊn] **1** *noun* area of a town or country (for administrative purposes); **development zone** *or* **enterprise zone** = area which has been given special help from the government to encourage businesses and factories to set up there; **free trade zone** = area where there are no customs duties **2** *verb* to divide (a town) into different areas for planning purposes; **land zoned for light industrial use** = land where planning permission has been given to build small factories for light industry; **zoning regulations** *US* **zoning ordinances** = local bylaws which regulate the types of building and land use in a town

SUPPLEMENT

International Telephone Codes

Albania	355	Greece	30
Algeria	213	Guatemala	502
Andorra	33 628	Guinea	224
Angola	244	Guyana	592
Argentina	54	Haiti	509
Australia	61	Honduras	504
Austria	43	Hungary	36
Bahamas	1 809	Iceland	354
Bahrain	973	India	91
Bangladesh	880	Indonesia	62
Barbados	1 809	Iran	98
Belgium	32	Iraq	964
Benin	229	Ireland	353
Bolivia	591	Italy	39
Brazil	55	Ivory Coast	225
Bulgaria	359	Jamaica	1 809
Burma	95	Japan	81
Burundi	257	Jordan	962
Cameroon	237	Kenya	254
Canada	1	Korea	82
Central African		Kuwait	965
Republic	236	Lebanon	961
Chad	235	Liberia	231
Chile	56	Libya	218
China	86	Liechtenstein	41 75
Colombia	57	Luxembourg	352
Congo	242	Madagascar	261
Costa Rica	506	Malawi	265
Croatia	38	Malaysia	60
Cuba	53	Mali	223
Cyprus	357	Malta	356
Czech		Mauritius	230
Republic	42	Mexico	52
Denmark	45	Monaco	33 93
Dominican		Morocco	212
Republic	1 809	Mozambique	258
Ecuador	593	Namibia	264
Egypt	20	Nepal	977
El Salvador	503	Netherlands	31
Ethiopia	251	New Zealand	64
Falkland Is	500	Nicaragua	505
Finland	358	Niger	227
France	33	Nigeria	234
French Guiana	594	Norway	47
Gabon	241	Oman	968
Gambia	220	Pakistan	92
Germany	49	Panama	507
Ghana	233	Paraguay	595
Gibraltar	350	Peru	51
Great Britain	44	Philippines	63

International Telephone Codes *continued.*

Poland	48	Syria	963
Portugal	351	Tanzania	255
Puerto Rico	1 809	Thailand	66
Romania	40	Togo	228
Russia	7	Trinidad & Tobago	1 809
Rwanda	250	Tunisia	216
Saudi Arabia	966	Turkey	90
Senegal	221	Uganda	256
Sierra Leone	232	Ukraine	7
Singapore	65	United Arab	
Slovakia	42	Emirates	971
Slovenia	38	United Kingdom	44
Somalia	252	U.S.A.	1
South Africa	27	Uruguay	598
Spain	34	Venezuela	58
Sri Lanka	94	Vietnam	84
Sweden	46	Zaire	243
Switzerland	41	Zambia	260

Local times around the world

London time	*1200*	*London time*	*1200*
Adelaide	2100	Kuwait	1500
Algiers	1300	Lagos	1300
Amsterdam	1300	Lima	0700
Ankara	1500	Luxembourg	1300
Athens	1400	Madeira	1200
Beijing	2000	Madrid	1300
Beirut	1400	Malta	1300
Berlin	1300	Mexico	0600
Bern(e)	1300	Montreal	0700
Bombay	1730	Moscow	1500
Brasilia	0900	Nairobi	1500
Brussels	1300	New York	0700
Bucharest	1400	Oslo	1300
Budapest	1300	Ottawa	0700
Buenos Aires	0900	Panama	0700
Cairo	1400	Paris	1300
Calcutta	1730	Perth	2000
Cape Town	1400	Prague	1300
Chicago	0600	Quebec	0700
Copenhagen	1300	Rangoon	1830
Delhi	1730	Rio de Janeiro	0900
Dublin	1200	Riyadh	1500
Gibraltar	1300	San Francisco	0400
Helsinki	1400	Santiago	0800
Hong Kong	2000	Singapore	2000
Istanbul	1500	Stockholm	1300
Jerusalem	1400	Sydney	2200

Local times around the world *continued.*

London time	*1200*	*London time*	*1200*
Tehran	1530	Tunis	1300
Tokyo	2100	Vienna	1300
Toronto	0700	Warsaw	1300

You say

Numbers

one, two, three, four	1, 2, 3, 4
five, six, seven, eight	5, 6, 7, 8
nine, ten, eleven, twelve	9, 10, 11, 12
thirteen, fourteen	13, 14
fifteen, sixteen	15, 16
seventeen, eighteen	17, 18
nineteen, twenty	19, 20
twenty-one, twenty-two, twenty-three	21, 22, 23
thirty, thirty-one, thirty-two	30, 31, 32
forty, fifty, sixty	40, 50, 60
seventy, eighty, ninety	70, 80, 90
one hundred, a hundred and one	100, 101
two hundred, three hundred	200, 300
four hundred, five hundred	400, 500
six hundred, seven hundred	600, 700
eight hundred, nine hundred	800, 900
one thousand	1,000
ten thousand	10,000
one million	1,000,000
one billion	1,000,000,000
one trillion	1,000,000,000,000

Decimals

0.5	zero point five
0.23	zero point two three
2.5	two point five

Money

£1	one pound
30p	thirty pence *or* thirty pee
£1.25	one pound twenty-five *or* one twenty-five
£27.36	twenty-seven pounds thirty-six (pee)
$1	one dollar
10¢	ten cents *or* a dime
25¢	twenty-five cents *or* a quarter
30¢	thirty cents
$1.25	one dollar twenty-five *or* one twenty-five

Telephone numbers

020 7222 1155	oh-two-oh, seven-two-two-two, one-one-five-five

Year

2002	two thousand and two
2000	the year two thousand
1905	nineteen five *or* nineteen hundred and five *or* nineteen oh five

Weights and Measures - Metric Measures

Length
1 millimetre (mm)		= 0.0394 in
1 centimetre (cm)	= 10 mm	= 0.3937 in
1 metre (m)	= 100 cm	= 1.0936 yds
1 kilometre (km)	= 1000 m	= 0.6214 mile

Weight
1 milligramme (mg)		= 0.0154 grain
1 gramme (g)	= 1000 mg	= 0.0353 oz
1 kilogramme (kg)	= 1000 g	= 2.2046 lb
1 tonne (t)	= 1000 kg	= 0.9842 ton

Area
1cm^2	= 100 mm^2	= 0.1550 sq.in.
1m^2	= 10,000 cm^2	= 1.1960 sq.yds
1 are (a)	= 100 m^2	= 119.60 sq.yds
1 hectare (ha)	= 100 ares	= 2.4711 acres
1km^2	= 100 hectares	= 0.3861 sq. mile

Capacity
1 cm^3	= 0.0610 cu. in	
1 dm^3	= 1000 cm^3	= 0.0351 cu. ft
1 m^3	= 1000 dm^3	= 1.3080 cu. yds
1 litre	= 1 dm^3	= 0.2200 gallon
1 hectolitre	= 100 litres	= 2.7497 bushels

Imperial Measures

Length
1 inch		= 2.54 cm
1 foot	= 12 inches	= 0.3048 m
1 yard	= 3 feet	= 0.9144 m
1 rod	= 5.5 yards	= 4.0292 m
1 chain	= 22 yards	= 20.117 m
1 furlong	= 220 yards	= 201.17 m
1 mile	= 1760 yards	= 1.6093 km

Weight
1 ounce	= 437.6 grains	= 28.350 g
1 pound	= 16 ounces	= 0.4536 kg
1 stone	= 14 pounds	= 6.3503 kg
1 hundredweight	= 112 pounds	= 50.802 kg
1 ton	= 20 cwt	= 1.0161 tonnes

Area
1 sq.inch		= 6.4516 cm^2
1 sq.foot	= 144 sq.ins	= 0.0929 m^2
1 sq. yard	= 9 sq.ft	= 0.8361 m^2
1 acre	= 4840 sq.yds	= 4046.9 m^2
1 sq.mile	= 640 acres	= 259.0 hectares

Capacity
1 cu.inch		= 16.387 cm^3
1 cu.foot	= 1728 cu.ins	= 0.0283 m^3
1 cu.yard	= 27 cu.ft	= 0.7646 m^3
1 pint	= 4 gills	= 0.5683 litre
1 quart	= 2 pints	= 1.1365 litres
1 gallon	= 8 pints	= 4.5461 litres
1 bushel	= 8 gallons	= 36.369 litres
1 fluid ounce	= 8 fl.drachms	= 28.413 cm^3
1 pint	= 20 fl.oz	= 568.26 cm^3

JOB APPLICATION

Personnel Department
James Brown & Co. Ltd
12 Chapel Street
Liverpool
L25 7AX

26th August 2001

Dear Sirs,

re: PM2/08/01 Purchasing Manager

I have seen your advertisement in the `Liverpool Echo' and would like to apply for the post. I am enclosing my CV.

From the CV you will see that I am currently employed in the purchasing department of Well & Goode Ltd, where my responsibilities cover purchasing of all stationery supplies for departments in the firm. I feel that the experience I have had in my current job would qualify me for a more responsible post such as the one which you are advertising.

I am also attaching a sheet with names of three people who are willing to give references about my character and work experience.

If selected for interview, I can come on any day of the week in the afternoon. However, I am planning to go on holiday from 7th to 21st September so if an interview can be arranged before those dates, this would be most convenient.

Yours faithfully,

Jonathan R. Porter

CURRICULUM VITAE

Name: **Peter Smith**

Address: 12 Oxford St
                       RUGBY RG1 0XB

Telephone: Home: (032) 123 4567
                       Office: (032) 987 6543

Date of Birth: 15th June 1965

Nationality: British

Family: Married, two children

Education: "A" Levels
                          (English, French, German 1973;
                           Computer Studies 1978)
                       BA (Com) University of Rugby 1986

Work Experience:
1986-1990   Assistant Sales Manager
                       J. Brown Construction Ltd.
                       123 Cambridge Road
                       OXFORD OX1 2XY

1990- present   Sales Manager (Export)
                       Bell & Jones plc
                       45 London Road
                       RUGBY RG2 3QY

Other
qualifications: Diploma in IBM word-processing
                       Clean driving licence

Languages: French (good)
                       German (basic)

BUSINESS LETTERS

Smith & Bell Ltd
123 St James Street
BIRMINGHAM
B1 2HE

15th April 2001

Dear Sirs,

We should be grateful if you could send us a copy of your current catalogue and price list.

Yours faithfully,

....
P. Williams
Purchasing Manager

BUSINESS LETTERS

Mr P. Williams
Purchasing Manager
Black & White Ltd
12 Waterloo Street
Norwich NH2 4QX

Our ref: 1234   25th April 2001

Dear Sir,

Thank you for your letter of 15th April. Please find enclosed this year's catalogue and our current price list. Please let me know if there is any further information you need.

Yours faithfully,

....
Smith & Bell Ltd

Encl.

BUSINESS LETTERS

Smith & Bell Ltd
123 St James Street
BIRMINGHAM
B1 2HE

20th May 2001

Dear Sirs,

Order Number: PW/5678/5/01

From your current catalogue, please supply the following items:
    20 x 8765/WB
    10 x 6543/QA
    2 x 3210/ZP
Please deliver with invoice in triplicate to the following address:
    Black & White Ltd
    The Works
    24 Blenheim Street
    Norwich NH25 2PZ

Yours faithfully

....
P. Williams
Purchasing Manager

BUSINESS LETTERS

Mr P. Williams
Purchasing Manager
Black & White Ltd
12 Waterloo Street
Norwich NH2 4QX

Our ref: 2456

27th May 2001

Dear Sir,

Order Number: PW/5678/5/01

Thank you for your order. We are able to supply all the items listed
immediately, with the exception of 6543/QA which is currently out of stock. We
expect new stock to be delivered within the next two weeks, and that part of
your order will be supplied as soon as stock is in our warehouse.

Yours faithfully,

....
Smith & Bell Ltd

BUSINESS LETTERS

Smith & Bell Ltd
123 St James Street
BIRMINGHAM
B1 2HE

20th June 2001

Dear Sirs,

Invoice SB/1097

Our Order Number: PW/5678/5/01

We have received the items ordered, but one box of 8765/WB was damaged
when delivered and some of the contents are unusable. We should be grateful if
you could replace it.

Yours faithfully

....
P. Williams
Purchasing Manager

BUSINESS LETTERS

Black & White Ltd
12 Waterloo Street
Norwich NH2 4QX

Attn: Mr P. Williams
          Purchasing Manager

1st September 2001

Dear Sir,

Invoice SB/1097

We note that this invoice has not been paid and would be grateful if you could
settle it within seven days.

Yours faithfully,

....
Accounts Dept
Smith & Bell Ltd

Money

In the list of world currencies that follows, words marked (*) usually have no plural: e.g. 1 kyat (one kyat), 200 kyat (two hundred kyat), etc.

Country	Currency	Divided into	Abbreviation
Afghanistan	Afghani*	puli	Af *or* Afs
Albania	Lek*	qindars	Lk
Algeria	Algerian dinar	centimes	DA
Andorra	French franc, Spanish peseta	centimes	
Angola	Kwanza*	lwei	Kzrl
Antigua	East Caribbean dollar	cents	Ecar$ *or* EC$
Argentina	Argentinian peso	australes	
Australia	Australian dollar	cents	A$
Austria	Schilling *or* euro	groschen	Sch *or* ASch
Bahamas	Bahamian dollar	cents	B$
Bahrain	Bahraini dinar	fils	BD
Bangladesh	Taka*	poisha	Tk
Barbados	Barbados dollar	cents	Bd$ *or* BD$
Belarus	Rouble	kopeks	
Belgium	Belgian franc *or* euro	centimes	Bfr *or* Bf *or* FB
Belize	Belize dollar	cents	BZ$
Benin	CFA franc	centimes	CFA Fr
Bermuda	Bermuda dollar	cents	Bda$
Bhutan	Ngultrum*	chetrum	N
Bolivia	Boliviano *or* Bolivian peso	centavos	$b
Bosnia	Marka	para	
Botswana	Pula	thebe	P
Brazil	Real	centavos	R$
Brunei	Brunei dollar	sen	B$
Bulgaria	Lev*	stotinki	Lv
Burkina Faso	CFA franc	centimes	CFA Fr
Burma (*see* Myanmar)			
Burundi	Burundi franc	centimes	Bur Fr *or* FrBr
Cambodia	Riel*	sen	RI
Cameroon	CFA franc	centimes	CFA Fr
Canada	Canadian dollar	cents	Can$ *or* C$
Cape Verde Islands	Escudo Caboverdiano	centavos	CV esc
Cayman Islands	Cayman Island dollar	cents	CayI$
Central African Republic	CFA franc	centimes	CFA Fr
Chad	CFA franc	centimes	CFA Fr
Chile	Chilean peso	centavos	Ch$
China	Yuan* *or* renminbi*	fen	Y
Colombia	Colombian peso	centavos	Col$
Comoros	CFA franc	centimes	CFA Fr
Congo (Republic of)	CFA franc	centimes	CFA Fr
Congo (Democratic Republic of)	Congolese franc	centimes	
Costa Rica	Colón*	centimos	₡

Money *continued.*

Country	Currency	Divided into	Abbreviation
Croatia	Kuna	lipas	
Cuba	Cuban peso	centavos	Cub$
Cyprus	Cyprus pound	cents	£C or C£
Czech Republic	Koruna	haleru	K¢
Dahomey (*see* Benin)			
Denmark	Krone	öre	DKr or DKK
Djibouti	Djibouti franc	centimes	Dj Fr
Dominica	East Caribbean dollar	cents	EC$
Dominican Republic	Dominican peso	centavos	DR$
Ecuador	Sucre*	centavos	Su
Egypt	Egyptian pound	piastres	£E or E£
Eire (*see* Irish Republic)			
El Salvador	Colón*	centavos	ES¢
Equatorial Guinea	CFA franc	centimes	CFA Fr
Estonia	Kroon	sents	
Ethiopia	Birr* or Ethiopian dollar	cents	EB
Fiji	Fiji dollar	cents	$F or F$
Finland	Marka or Markka or euro	pennia	MK
France	French franc or euro	centimes	Fr or F or FF
French Guiana	French franc	centimes	Fr or F or FF
Gabon	CFA franc	centimes	CFA Fr
Gambia, The	Dalasi*	butut	Di
Germany	Mark or euro	pfennig	DM
Ghana	Cedi*	pesewas	¢
Georgia	Lari	tetri	
Great Britain (*see* United Kingdom)			
Greece	Drachma or euro	lepta	Dr
Grenada	East Caribbean dollar	cents	Ecar$ or EC$
Guatemala	Quetzal	centavos	Q
Guinea	Guinea franc	centimes	
Guinea-Bissau	CFA franc	centimes	CFA Fr
Guyana	Guyana dollar	cents	G$ or Guy$
Haiti	Gourde*	centimes	Gde
Holland (*see* Netherlands)			
Honduras	Lempira*	centavos	La
Hong Kong	Hong Kong dollar	cents	HK$
Hungary	Forint	filler	Ft
Iceland	Króna	aurar	Ikr
India	Rupee	paisa	R or Re or R$
Indonesia	Rupiah*	sen	Rp
Iran	Rial*	dinars	RI
Iraq	Iraqi dinar	fils	ID
Irish Republic	punt or Irish Pound or euro	pence	IR£
Israel	Shekel	agora	IS
Italy	Lira or euro	centesimi	L
Ivory Coast	CFA franc	centimes	CFA Fr

Money *continued.*

Country	Currency	Divided into	Abbreviation
Jamaica	Jamaican dollar	cents	J$
Japan	Yen*	sen	Y *or* ¥
Jordan	Jordanian dinar	fils	JD
Kazakhstan	Tenge		
Kenya	Kenya shilling	cents	KSh *or* Sh
Korea (North)	North Korean won*	chon	NK W
Korea (South)	South Korean won*	jeon	SK W
Kuwait	Kuwaiti dinar	fils	KD
Kyrgystan	Som	tyin	
Laos	Kip*	at	K *or* Kp
Latvia	Lat	santims	
Lebanon	Lebanese pound	piastres	£Leb *or* L£
Lesotho	Loti*	lisente	L
Liberia	Liberian dollar	cents	L$
Libya	Libyan dinar	dirhams	LD
Liechtenstein	Swiss franc	centimes	SFr *or* FS
Lithuania	Lita		
Luxembourg	Luxembourg franc *or* euro	centimes	LFr
Macedonia	Dinar	paras	
Macau	Pataca*	avos	P *or* $
Madeira	Portuguese escudo	centavos	Esc
Malagasy Republic	Malagasy franc	centimes	FMG *or* Mal Fr
Malawi	Kwacha*	tambala	K *or* MK
Malaysia	Ringgit *or* Malaysian Dollar	sen	M$
Maldives	Rufiyaa	laaris	MvRe
Mali	CFA franc	cents	CFA Fr
Malta	Maltese pound *or* lira	cents	£M *or* M£
Mauritania	Ouguiya*	khoums	U
Mauritius	Mauritius rupee	cents	Mau Rs *or* R
Mexico	Peso	centavos	Mex$
Moldova	Leu		
Monaco	French franc	centimes	Fr *or* F *or* FF
Mongolian Republic	Tugrik*	möngö	Tug
Montserrat	East Caribbean dollar	cents	Ecar$ *or* EC$
Morocco	Dirham	centimes	DH
Mozambique	Metical*	centavos	M
Myanmar	Kyat*	pyas	Kt
Namibia	Namibian dollar	cents	
Nauru	Australian dollar	cents	A$
Nepal	Nepalese rupee	paise	NR *or* Nre
Netherlands	Guilder *or* Gulden *or* Gld *or* Florin *or* euro	cents	HFl *or* DFl *or* Fl
New Hebrides (*see* Vanuatu)			
New Zealand	New Zealand dollar	cents	NZ$
Nicaragua	Córdoba	centavos	C$ *or* C
Niger	CFA franc	centimes	CFA Fr
Nigeria	Naira*	kobo	N *or* ₦

Money *continued.*

Country	Currency	Divided into	Abbreviation
Norway	Krone	øre	NKr
Oman	Rial Omani	baizas	RO
Pakistan	Pakistan rupee	paise	R *or* Pak Re
Panama	Balboa	centesimos	Ba
Papua New Guinea	Kina*	toea	Ka *or* K
Paraguay	Guarani*	centimos	G
Peru	Sol	cents	S
Philippines	Philippine peso	centavos	P *or* PP
Poland	Zloty	groszy	Zl
Portugal	Escudo *or* euro	centavos	Esc
Puerto Rico	US dollar	cents	$ *or* US$
Qatar	Qatar Riyal	dirhams	QR
Reunion	CFA franc	centimes	CFA Fr
Romania	Leu*	bani	L *or* l
Russia	Rouble	kopeks	Rub
Rwanda	Rwanda franc	centimes	Rw Fr
St Lucia	East Caribbean dollar	cents	Ecar$ *or* EC$
St Vincent	East Caribbean dollar	cents	Ecar$ *or* EC$
Samoa	Tala	sene	
Saudi Arabia	Saudi riyal *or* rial	halala	SA R
Senegal	CFA franc	centimes	CFA Fr
Seychelles	Seychelles rupee	cents	Sre *or* R
Sierra Leone	Leone	cents	Le
Singapore	Singapore dollar	cents	S$ *or* Sing$
Slovakia	Koruna	haliers	Sk
Slovenia	Tolar	stotin	SIT
Solomon Islands	Solomon Island dollar	cents	SI$
Somalia	Somali shilling	cents	Som Sh *or* So Sh
South Africa	Rand*	cents	R
Spain	Peseta *or* euro	centimos	Pta
Sri Lanka	Sri Lankan rupee	cents	SC Re
Sudan	Sudanese dinar	pounds	SD
Suriname	Suriname guilder	cents	S Gld
Swaziland	Lilangeni*	cents	Li *or* E
Sweden	Krona	örer	SKr
Syria	Syrian pound	piastres	S£
Taiwan	New Taiwan dollar	cents	T$ *or* NT$
Tanzania	Tanzanian shilling	cents	TSh
Thailand	Baht*	satang	Bt
Togo	CFA franc	centimes	CFA Fr
Tonga	Pa'anga	seniti	
Trinidad & Tobago	Trainidad & Tobago dollar	cents	TT$
Tunisia	Tunisian dinar	millimes	TD
Turkey	Turkish lira	kurus	TL
Turkmenistan	Manat	tenesi	
Tuvalu	Australian dollar	cents	$A
Uganda	Uganda Shilling	cents	Ush
Ukraine	Hryvna	kopiykas	
United Arab Emirates	UAE dirham	fils	UAE Dh *or* UD

Money *continued.*

Country	*Currency*	*Divided into*	*Abbreviation*
United Kingdom	Pound sterling	pence	£ *or* £Stg
United States of America	Dollar	cents	$ *or* US$
Uruguay	Uruguayan peso	centesimos	N$
Uzbekistan	Sum	tiyin	
Vanuatu	Vatu	centimes	
Venezuela	Bolívar	centimos	BS
Vietnam	Dong*	xu	D
Virgin Islands	US dollar	cents	US$
Yemen	Riyal	fils	YR
Yugoslavia	Dinar	paras	DN
Zambia	Kwacha*	ngwee	K
Zimbabwe	Zimbabwe dollar	cents	Z$

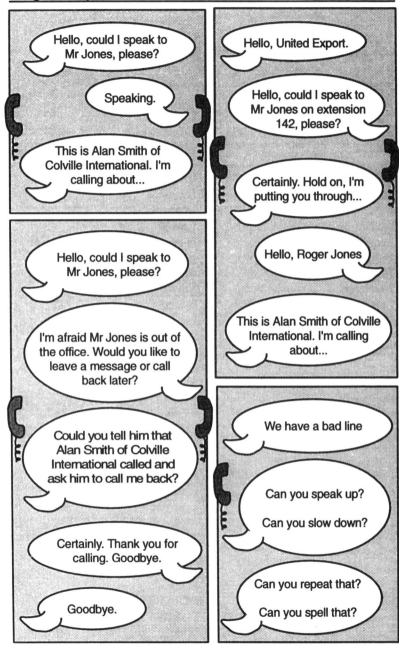